FOURTH EDITION

Java Cookbook
Problems and Solutions for Java Developers

Ian F. Darwin

Beijing · Boston · Farnham · Sebastopol · Tokyo

Java Cookbook

by Ian F. Darwin

Copyright © 2020 RejmiNet Group, Inc. All rights reserved.

Printed in the United States of America.

Published by O'Reilly Media, Inc., 1005 Gravenstein Highway North, Sebastopol, CA 95472.

O'Reilly books may be purchased for educational, business, or sales promotional use. Online editions are also available for most titles (*http://oreilly.com*). For more information, contact our corporate/institutional sales department: 800-998-9938 or *corporate@oreilly.com*.

Acquisition Editor: Zan McQuade	**Indexer:** Potomac Indexing, LLC
Development Editor: Corbin Collins	**Interior Designer:** David Futato
Production Editor: Beth Kelly	**Cover Designer:** Karen Montgomery
Copyeditor: Amanda Kersey	**Illustrator:** Rebecca Demarest
Proofreader: Charles Roumeliotis	

June 2001:	First Edition
June 2004:	Second Edition
July 2014:	Third Edition
March 2020:	Fourth Edition

Revision History for the Fourth Edition
2020-03-17: First Release

See *http://oreilly.com/catalog/errata.csp?isbn=9781492072584* for release details.

The O'Reilly logo is a registered trademark of O'Reilly Media, Inc. *Java Cookbook*, the cover image, and related trade dress are trademarks of O'Reilly Media, Inc.

The views expressed in this work are those of the author, and do not represent the publisher's views. While the publisher and the author have used good faith efforts to ensure that the information and instructions contained in this work are accurate, the publisher and the author disclaim all responsibility for errors or omissions, including without limitation responsibility for damages resulting from the use of or reliance on this work. Use of the information and instructions contained in this work is at your own risk. If any code samples or other technology this work contains or describes is subject to open source licenses or the intellectual property rights of others, it is your responsibility to ensure that your use thereof complies with such licenses and/or rights.

978-1-492-07258-4

[LSI]

In Memoriam
Andrej Cerar Darwin 1989-2014
Son, friend, fellow writer, and craftsman.

Table of Contents

Preface

Like any of the most-used programming languages, Java has its share of detractors, advocates, issues, quirks,[1] and a learning curve. The *Java Cookbook* aims to help the Java developer get up to speed on some of the most important parts of Java development. I focus on the standard APIs and some third-party APIs, but I don't hesitate to cover language issues as well.

This is the fourth edition of this book, and it has been shaped by many people and by the myriad changes that Java has undergone over its first two decades of popularity. Readers interested in Java's history can refer to Appendix A.

Java 11 is the current long-term supported version, but Java 12 and 13 are out. Java 14 is in early access and scheduled for final release the very same day as this book's fourth edition. The new cadence of releases every six months may be great for the Java SE development team at Oracle and for click-driven, Java-related news sites, but it "may cause some extra work" for Java book authors, since books typically have a longer revision cycle than Java now does! Java 9, which came out after the previous edition of this book, was a breaking release, the first release in a very long time to break backwards compatibility, primarily the Java module system. Everything in the book is assumed to work on any JVM that is still being used to develop code. Nobody should be using Java 7 (or anything before it!) for anything, and nobody should be doing new development in Java 8. If you are, it's time to move on!

The goal of this revision is to keep the book up to date with all this change. While cutting out a lot of older material, I've added information on new features such as Modules and the interactive JShell, and I've updated a lot of other information along the way.

---

1 For the quirks, see the *Java Puzzlers* books (*http://javapuzzlers.com*) by Joshua Bloch and Neal Gafter (Addison-Wesley).

Who This Book Is For

I'm going to assume that you know the basics of Java. I won't tell you how to println a string, nor how to write a class that extends another and/or implements an interface. I presume you've taken a Java course such as Learning Tree's Introduction (*https://learningtree.com/471*) or that you've studied an introductory book such as *Head First Java* (*http://shop.oreilly.com/product/9780596009205.do*), *Learning Java* (*http://shop.oreilly.com/product/0636920023463.do*), or *Java in a Nutshell* (*http://shop.oreilly.com/product/9780596007737.do*) (O'Reilly). However, Chapter 1 covers some techniques that you might not know very well and that are necessary to understand some of the later material. Feel free to skip around! Both the printed version of the book and the electronic copy are heavily cross-referenced.

What's in This Book?

Java has seemed better suited to "development in the large," or enterprise application development, than to the one-line, one-off script in Perl, Awk, or Python. That's because it is a compiled, object-oriented language. However, this suitability has changed somewhat with the appearance of JShell (see Recipe 1.4). I illustrate many techniques with shorter Java class examples and even code fragments; some of the simpler ones will be shown using JShell. All of the code examples (other than some one- or two-liners) are in one of my public GitHub repositories, so you can rest assured that every fragment of code you see here has been compiled, and most have been run recently.

Some of the longer examples in this book are tools that I originally wrote to automate some mundane task or another. For example, a tool called MkIndex (in the *javasrc* repository) reads the top-level directory of the place where I keep my Java example source code, and it builds a browser-friendly *index.html* file for that directory. Another example is XmlForm, which was used to convert parts of the manuscript from XML into the form needed by another publishing software. XmlForm also handled— by use of another program, GetMark—full and partial code insertions from the *javasrc* directory into the book manuscript. XmlForm is included in the Github repository I mentioned, as is a later version of GetMark, though neither of these was used in building the fourth edition. These days, O'Reilly's Atlas publishing software uses Asciidoctor (*https://asciidoctor.org*), which provides the mechanism we use for inserting files and parts of files into the book.

Organization of This Book

Let's go over the organization of this book. Each chapter consists of a handful of recipes, short sections that describe a problem and its solution, along with a code example. The code in each recipe is intended to be largely self-contained; feel free to borrow bits and pieces of any of it for use in your own projects. The code is distributed with a Berkeley-style copyright, just to discourage wholesale reproduction.

I start off Chapter 1, *Getting Started: Compiling and Running Java*, by describing some methods of compiling your program on different platforms, running them in different environments (browser, command line, windowed desktop), and debugging.

Chapter 2, *Interacting with the Environment*, moves from compiling and running your program to getting it to adapt to the surrounding countryside—the other programs that live in your computer.

The next few chapters deal with basic APIs. Chapter 3, *Strings and Things*, concentrates on one of the most basic but powerful data types in Java, showing you how to assemble, dissect, compare, and rearrange what you might otherwise think of as ordinary text. This chapter also covers the topic of internationalization/localization so that your programs can work as well in Akbar, Afghanistan, Algiers, Amsterdam, and Angleterre as they do in Alberta, Arkansas, and Alabama.

Chapter 4, *Pattern Matching with Regular Expressions*, teaches you how to use the powerful regular expressions technology from Unix in many string-matching and pattern-matching problem domains. Regex processing has been standard in Java for years, but if you don't know how to use it, you may be reinventing the flat tire.

Chapter 5, *Numbers*, deals both with built-in numeric types such as int and double, as well as the corresponding API classes (Integer, Double, etc.) and the conversion and testing facilities they offer. There is also brief mention of the "big number" classes. Because Java programmers often need to deal in dates and times, both locally and internationally, Chapter 6, *Dates and Times*, covers this important topic.

The next few chapters cover data processing. As in most languages, arrays in Java are linear, indexed collections of similar objects, as discussed in Chapter 7, *Structuring Data with Java*. This chapter goes on to deal with the many Collections classes: powerful ways of storing quantities of objects in the java.util package, including use of Java Generics.

Despite some syntactic resemblance to procedural languages such as C, Java is at heart an Object-Oriented Programming (OOP) language, with some important Functional Programming (FP) constructs skilfully blended in. Chapter 8, *Object-Oriented Techniques*, discusses some of the key notions of OOP as it applies to Java, including the commonly overridden methods of java.lang.Object and the important issue of design patterns. Java is not, and never will be, a pure FP language. However, it is possible to use some aspects of FP, increasingly so with Java 8 and its support of lambda expressions (a.k.a. closures). This is discussed in Chapter 9, *Functional Programming Techniques: Functional Interfaces, Streams, and Parallel Collections*.

The next chapter deals with aspects of traditional input and output. Chapter 10, *Input and Output: Reading, Writing, and Directory Tricks*, details the rules for reading and writing files (don't skip this if you think files are boring; you'll need some of this information in later chapters). The chapter also shows you everything else about files—such as finding their size and last-modified time—and about reading and modifying directories, creating temporary files, and renaming files on disk.

Big data and data science have become a thing, and Java is right in there. Apache Hadoop, Apache Spark, and much more of the big data infrastructure is written in, and extensible with, Java, as described in Chapter 11, *Data Science and R*. The R programming language is popular with data scientists, statsticians, and other scientists. There are at least two reimplementations of R coded in Java, and Java can also be interfaced directly with the standard R implementation in both directions, so this chapter covers R as well.

Because Java was originally promulgated as the programming language for the internet, it's only fair to spend some time on networking in Java. Chapter 12, *Network Clients*, covers the basics of network programming from the client side, focusing on sockets. Today so many applications need to access a web service, primarily RESTful web services, that this seemed to be necessary. I'll then move to the server side in Chapter 13, *Server-Side Java*, wherein you'll learn some server-side programming techniques.

One simple text-based representation for data interchange is JSON, the JavaScript object notation. Chapter 14, *Processing JSON Data*, describes the format and some of the many APIs that have emerged to deal with it.

Chapter 15, *Packages and Packaging*, shows how to create packages of classes that work together. This chapter also talks about deploying (a.k.a. distributing and installing) your software.

Chapter 16, *Threaded Java*, tells you how to write classes that appear to do more than one thing at a time and let you take advantage of powerful multiprocessor hardware.

Chapter 17, *Reflection, or "A Class Named Class"*, lets you in on such secrets as how to write API cross-reference documents mechanically and how web servers are able to load any old Servlet—never having seen that particular class before—and run it.

Sometimes you already have code written and working in another language that can do part of your work for you, or you want to use Java as part of a larger package. Chapter 18, *Using Java with Other Languages*, shows you how to run an external program (compiled or script) and also interact directly with native code in C/C++ or other languages.

There isn't room in a book this size for everything I'd like to tell you about Java. The Afterword presents some closing thoughts and a link to my online summary of Java APIs that every Java developer should know about.

Finally, Appendix A, *Java Then and Now*, gives the storied history of Java in a release-by-release timeline, so whatever version of Java you learned, you can jump in here and get up to date quickly.

So many topics, and so few pages! Many topics do not recieve 100% coverage; I've tried to include the most important or most useful parts of each API. To go beyond, check the official *javadoc* pages for each package; many of these pages have some brief tutorial information on how the package is to be used.

Besides the parts of Java covered in this book, two other platform editions, Java ME and Java EE, have been standardized. Java Micro Edition (Java ME) is concerned with small devices such as handhelds, cell phones, and fax machines. At the other end of the size scale—large server machines—there's Eclipse Jakarta EE (*https://projects.eclipse.org/projects/ee4j.jakartaee-platform*), replacing the former Java EE, which in the last century was known as J2EE. Jakarta EE is concerned with building large, scalable, distributed applications. APIs that are part of Jakarta EE include Servlets, JavaServer Pages, JavaServer Faces, JavaMail, Enterprise JavaBeans (EJBs), Container and Dependency Injection (CDI), and Transactions. Jakarta EE packages normally begin with "javax" because they are not core packages. This book mentions but a few of these; there is also a *Java EE 8 Cookbook* (*https://www.oreilly.com/library/view/java-ee-8/9781788293037*) by Elder Moraes (O'Reilly) that covers some of the Jakarta EE APIs, as well as an older *Java Servlet & JSP Cookbook* (*http://shop.oreilly.com/product/9780596005726.do*) by Bruce Perry (O'Reilly).

This book doesn't cover Java Micro Edition, Java ME. At all. But speaking of cell phones and mobile devices, you probably know that Android uses Java as its language. What should be comforting to Java developers is that Android also uses most of the core Java API, except for Swing and AWT, for which it provides Android-specific replacements. The Java developer who wants to learn Android may consider looking at my *Android Cookbook* (*http://shop.oreilly.com/product/0636920038092.do*) (O'Reilly), or the book's website (*http://androidcookbook.com*).

Java Books

A lot of useful information is packed into this book. However, due to the breadth of topics, it is not possible to give book-length treatment to any one topic. Because of this, the book contains references to many websites and other books. In pointing out these references, I'm hoping to serve my target audience: the person who wants to learn more about Java.

O'Reilly publishes, in my opinion, the best selection of Java books on the market. As the API continues to expand, so does the coverage. Check out the complete list of O'Reilly's collection of Java books (*https://ssearch.oreilly.com/?i=1;m_Sort=search Date;q=java+o%27reilly;q1=Books;x1=t1&act=sort*); you can buy them at most bookstores, both physical and virtual. You can also read them online through the O'Reilly Online Learning Platform (*http://oreilly.com*), a paid subscription service. And, of course, most are now available in ebook format; O'Reilly ebooks are DRM free, so you don't have to worry about their copy-protection scheme locking you into a particular device or system, as you do with certain other publishers.

Though many books are mentioned at appropriate spots in the book, a few deserve special mention here.

First and foremost, David Flanagan and Benjamin Evan's *Java in a Nutshell* (*http://shop.oreilly.com/product/9780596007737.do*) (O'Reilly) offers a brief overview of the language and API and a detailed reference to the most essential packages. This is handy to keep beside your computer. *Head First Java* (*http://shop.oreilly.com/product/9780596009205.do*) by Bert Bates and Kathy Sierra offers a much more whimsical introduction to the language and is recommended for the less experienced developer.

Java 8 Lambdas (*http://shop.oreilly.com/product/0636920030713.do*) (Warburton, O'Reilly) covers the Lambda syntax introduced in Java 8 in support of functional programming and more concise code in general.

Java 9 Modularity: Patterns and Practices for Developing Maintainable Applications (*http://shop.oreilly.com/product/0636920049494.do*) by Sander Mak and Paul Bakker (O'Reilly) covers the important changes made in the language in Java 9 for the Java module system.

Java Virtual Machine (*http://shop.oreilly.com/product/9781565921948.do*) by Jon Meyer and Troy Downing (O'Reilly) will intrigue the person who wants to know more about what's under the hood. This book is out of print but can be found used and in libraries.

A definitive (and monumental) description of programming the Swing GUI is *Java Swing* (*http://shop.oreilly.com/product/9780596004088.do*) by Robert Eckstein et al. (O'Reilly).

Java Network Programming (*http://shop.oreilly.com/product/0636920028420.do*) and *Java I/O* (*http://shop.oreilly.com/product/9780596527501.do*), both by Elliotte Harold (O'Reilly), are also useful references.

For Java Database work, *Database Programming with JDBC & Java* (*http://shop.oreilly.com/product/9781565926165.do*) by George Reese (O'Reilly) and *Pro JPA 2: Mastering the Java Persistence API* by Mike Keith and Merrick Schincariol (Apress) are recommended. Or my forthcoming overview of Java Database (*https://darwin sys.com/db_in_java*).

Although the book you're now reading doesn't have much coverage of the Java EE, I'd like to mention two books on that topic:

- Arun Gupta covers the Enterprise Edition in *Java EE 7 Essentials* (*http://shop.oreilly.com/product/0636920030614.do*) (O'Reilly).
- Adam Bien's *Real World Java EE Patterns: Rethinking Best Practices* (*http://real worldpatterns.com*) offers useful insights in designing and implementing an Enterprise application.

You can find more at the O'Reilly website (*https://shop.oreilly.com*).

Finally, although it's not a book, Oracle has a great deal of Java information (*https://docs.oracle.com/en/java/javase/13/docs*) on the web. This web page used to feature a large diagram showing all the components of Java in a "conceptual diagram." An early version of this is shown in Figure P-1; each colored box is a clickable link to details on that particular technology.

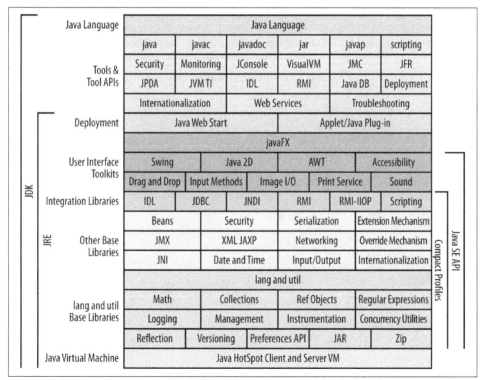

Figure P-1. Java conceptual diagram from Oracle documentation

For better or for worse, newer versions of Java have replaced this with a text page; for Java 13 the page is at *https://docs.oracle.com/en/java/javase/13*.

General Programming Books

Donald E. Knuth's *The Art of Computer Programming* (*https://en.wikipedia.org/wiki/ The_Art_of_Computer_Programming*) (Addison-Wesley) has been a source of inspiration to generations of computing students since its first publication in 1968. Volume 1 covers *Fundamental Algorithms*, Volume 2 is *Seminumerical Algorithms*, Volume 3 is *Sorting and Searching*, and Volume 4A is *Combinatorial Algorithms, Part 1*. The remaining volumes in the projected series are not completed. Although his examples are far from Java (he invented the hypothetical assembly language MIX for his examples), many of his discussions of algorithms—of how computers ought to be used to solve real problems—are as relevant today as they were years ago.[2]

Though its code examples are quite dated now, the book *The Elements of Programming Style* by Brian Kernighan and P. J. Plauger (McGraw-Hill) set the style (literally) for a generation of programmers with examples from various structured programming languages. Kernighan and Plauger also wrote a pair of books, *Software Tools* (Addison-Wesley) and *Software Tools in Pascal* (Addison-Wesley), which demonstrated so much good advice on programming that I used to advise all programmers to read them. However, these three books are dated now; many times I wanted to write a follow-on book in a more modern language. Instead I now defer to *The Practice of Programming*, Kernighan's follow-on—cowritten with Rob Pike (Addison-Wesley)—to the *Software Tools* series. This book continues the Bell Labs tradition of excellence in software textbooks. In previous editions of this book, I had even adapted one bit of code from their book, their CSV parser. Finally, Kernighan recently published *UNIX: A History and a Memoir*, his take on the story of Unix.

See also *The Pragmatic Programmer* by Andrew Hunt and David Thomas (Addison-Wesley).

Design Books

Peter Coad's *Java Design* (PTR-PH/Yourdon Press) discusses the issues of object-oriented analysis and design specifically for Java. Coad is somewhat critical of Java's implementation of the observable-observer paradigm and offers his own replacement for it.

One of the most famous books on object-oriented design in recent years is *Design Patterns* by Erich Gamma, Richard Helm, Ralph Johnson, and John Vlissides

---

2 With possible exceptions for algorithm decisions that are less relevant today given the massive changes in computing power now available.

(Addison-Wesley). These authors are often collectively called the "Gang of Four," resulting in their book sometimes being referred to as the GoF book. One of my colleagues called it "the best book on object-oriented design ever," and I agree; at the very least, it's among the best.

Refactoring by Martin Fowler (Addison-Wesley) covers a lot of "coding cleanups" that can be applied to code to improve readability and maintainability. Just as the GoF book introduced new terminology that helps developers and others communicate about how code is to be designed, Fowler's book provided a vocabulary for discussing how it is to be improved. But this book may be less useful than others; many of the refactorings now appear in the Refactoring Menu of the Eclipse IDE (see Recipe 1.3).

Two important streams of methodology theories are currently in circulation. The first is collectively known as Agile methods, and its best-known members are Scrum (*https://en.wikipedia.org/wiki/Scrum_(software_development)*) and Extreme Programming (XP). XP (the methodology, not that really old flavor of Microsoft's OS) is presented in a series of small, short, readable texts led by its designer, Kent Beck. The first book in the XP series is *Extreme Programming Explained* (Addison-Wesley). A good overview of all the Agile methods is Jim Highsmith's *Agile Software Development Ecosystems* (Addison-Wesley).

Another group of important books on methodology, covering the more traditional object-oriented design, is the UML series led by "the Three Amigos" (Booch, Jacobson, and Rumbaugh). Their major works are the *UML User Guide*, *UML Process*, and others. A smaller and more approachable book in the same series is Martin Fowler's *UML Distilled*.

Conventions Used in This Book

This book uses the following conventions.

Programming Conventions

I use the following terminology in this book. A program means any unit of code that can be run: from a five-line main program, to a servlet or web tier component, an EJB, or a full-blown GUI application. Applets were Java programs for use in a web browser; these were popular for a while but barely exist today. A servlet is a Java component built using Jakarta EE APIs for use in a web server, normally via HTTP. EJBs are business-tier components built using Jakarta APIs. An application is any other type of program. A desktop application (a.k.a. client) interacts with the user. A server program deals with a client indirectly, usually via a network connection (usually HTTP/HTTPS these days).

The examples shown are in two varieties. Those that begin with zero or more import statements, a javadoc comment, and a `public class` statement are complete examples. Those that begin with a declaration or executable statement, of course, are excerpts. However, the full versions of these excerpts have been compiled and run, and the online source includes the full versions.

Recipes are numbered by chapter and number, so, for example, Recipe 8.1 refers to the first recipe in Chapter 8.

Typesetting Conventions

The following typographic conventions are used in this book:

Italic

Used for commands, filenames, and example URLs. It is also used for emphasis and to define new terms when they first appear in the text.

`Constant width`

Used in code examples to show partial or complete Java source code program listings. It is also used for class names, method names, variable names, and other fragments of Java code.

`Constant width bold`

Used for user input, such as commands that you type on the command line.

`Constant width italic`

Shows text that should be replaced with user-supplied values or by values determined by context.

 This element signifies a tip or suggestion.

 This element signifies a general note.

 This icon indicates a warning or caution.

Code Examples

The code samples for this book are on the author's GitHub. Most are in the repository *javasrc* (*https://github.com/IanDarwin/javasrc*), but a few are pulled in from one other repository, *darwinsys-api* (*https://github.com/IanDarwin/darwinsys-api*). Details on downloading these are in Recipe 1.6.

Many programs are accompanied by an example showing them in action, run from the command line. These will usually show a prompt ending in either $ for Unix or > for Windows, depending on which computer I was using the day I wrote that example. If there is text before this prompt character, it can be ignored. It may be a path-name or a hostname, again, depending on the system.

These examples will usually also show the full package name of the class because Java requires this when starting a program from the command line. And because that will remind you which subdirectory of the source repository to find the source code in, I won't be pointing it out explicitly very often.

We appreciate, but generally do not require, attribution. An attribution usually includes the title, author, publisher, and ISBN. For example: "*Java Cookbook* by Ian F. Darwin (O'Reilly). Copyright 2020 RejmiNet Group, Inc., 978-1-492-07258-4."

If you feel your use of code examples falls outside fair use or the permission given above, feel free to contact us at *permissions@oreilly.com*.

O'Reilly Online Learning

 For more than 40 years, *O'Reilly Media* has provided technology and business training, knowledge, and insight to help companies succeed.

Our unique network of experts and innovators share their knowledge and expertise through books, articles, conferences, and our online learning platform. O'Reilly's online learning platform gives you on-demand access to live training courses, in-depth learning paths, interactive coding environments, and a vast collection of text and video from O'Reilly and 200+ other publishers. For more information, please visit *http://oreilly.com*.

Comments and Questions

As mentioned earlier, I've tested all the code on at least one of the reference platforms, and most on several. Still, there may be platform dependencies, or even bugs, in my code or in some important Java implementation. Please report any errors you find, as well as your suggestions for future editions, by writing to:

O'Reilly Media, Inc.
1005 Gravenstein Highway North
Sebastopol, CA 95472
800-998-9938 (in the United States or Canada)
707-829-0515 (international or local)
707-829-0104 (fax)

There is a web page for this book where we list errata, examples, and any additional information. It can be accessed at *http://shop.oreilly.com/product/0636920304371.do.*

Email *bookquestions@oreilly.com* to comment or ask technical questions about this book.

For more information about our books, courses, conferences, and news, see our website at *http://www.oreilly.com.*

Find us on Facebook: *http://facebook.com/oreilly*

Follow us on Twitter: *http://twitter.com/oreillymedia*

Watch us on YouTube: *http://www.youtube.com/oreillymedia*

The O'Reilly site lists errata. You'll also find the source code for all the Java code examples to download; *please* don't waste your time typing them again! For specific instructions, see Recipe 1.6.

Acknowledgments

I wrote in the Afterword to the first edition that "writing this book has been a humbling experience." I should add that maintaining it has been humbling, too. While many have been lavish with their praise—one very kind reviewer called it "arguably the best book ever written on the Java programming language"—I have been humbled by the number of errors and omissions in earlier editions. I have endeavored to correct these.

My life has been touched many times by the flow of the fates bringing me into contact with the right person to show me the right thing at the right time. Steve Munro (*https://en.wikipedia.org/wiki/Steve_Munro*), with whom I've long since lost touch, introduced me to computers when we were in the same class in high school—in particular an IBM 360/30 at the Toronto Board of Education that was bigger than a living room, had 32 or 64*K* (not *M* or *G*!) of memory, and had perhaps the power of a PC/XT. The late Herb Kugel took me under his wing at the University of Toronto while I was learning about the larger IBM mainframes that came later. Terry Wood and Dennis Smith at the University of Toronto introduced me to mini- and microcomputers before there was an IBM PC. On evenings and weekends, the Toronto Business Club of Toastmasters International (*http://www.toastmasters.org*) and Al

Lambert's Canada SCUBA School allowed me to develop my public speaking and teaching abilities. Several people at the University of Toronto, but especially Geoffrey Collyer (*https://en.wikipedia.org/wiki/Geoff_Collyer*), taught me the features and benefits of the Unix operating system at a time when I was ready to learn it.

Thanks to the many Learning Tree (*https://www.learningtree.com*) instructors and students who showed me ways of improving my presentations. I still teach for "The Tree" and recommend their courses for the busy developer who wants to zero in on one topic in detail over four days.

Closer to this project, Tim O'Reilly believed in my "little Lint book" when it was just a sample chapter from a proposed longer work, enabling my early entry into the rarefied circle of O'Reilly authors. Years later, Mike Loukides encouraged me to keep trying to find a Java book idea that both he and I could work with. And he stuck by me when I kept falling behind the deadlines. Mike also read the entire manuscript and made many sensible comments, some of which brought flights of fancy down to earth. Jessamyn Read turned many faxed and emailed scratchings of dubious legibility into the quality illustrations you see in this book. And many, many other talented people at O'Reilly helped put this book into the form in which you now see it.

The code examples are now dynamically included (so updates get done faster) rather than pasted in. My son (and functional programming developer) Benjamin Darwin helped meet the deadline by converting almost the entire code base to O'Reilly's newest "include" mechanism and by resolving a couple of other non-Java presentation issues. He also helped make Chapter 9 clearer and more functional.

At O'Reilly

For this fourth edition of the book, Suzanne McQuade was the editorial overseer, and Corbin Collins the principal editor. Corbin was especially meticulous in checking the manuscript. Meghan Blanchette, Sarah Schneider, Adam Witwer, Melanie Yarbrough, and the many production people listed on the Copyright page all played a part in getting the third edition ready for you to read. Thanks to Mike Loukides, Deb Cameron, and Marlowe Shaeffer for editorial and production work on the second edition.

Technical Reviewers

For the fourth edition I was blessed to have two very thorough technical reviewers, Sander Mak and Daniel Hinojosa. Many issues that I hadn't considered during the main revision were called out by these two, leading to extensive rewrites and changes in the last few weeks before the O'Reilly production team took over. Thanks so much to both of you!

My reviewer for the third edition, Alex Stangl, read the third edition manuscript and went far above the call of duty, making innumerable helpful suggestions, even finding typos that had been present in previous editions! Helpful suggestions on particular sections were made by Benjamin Darwin, Mark Finkov, and Igor Savin. For anyone I've forgotten to mention, I thank you all!

Bil Lewis and Mike Slinn made helpful comments on multiple drafts of the first edition. Ron Hitchens and Marc Loy carefully read the entire final draft of the first edition. I am grateful to Mike Loukides for his encouragement and support throughout the process. Editor Sue Miller helped shepherd the manuscript through the somewhat energetic final phases of production. Sarah Slocombe read the XML chapter in its entirety and made many lucid suggestions; unfortunately, time did not permit me to include all of them in the first edition.

Jonathan Knudsen, Andy Oram, and David Flanagan commented on book's outline when it was little more than a list of chapters and recipes, and they were able to see the kind of book it could become and suggest ways to make it better.

Each of these people made this book better in many ways, particularly by suggesting additional recipes or revising existing ones. Thanks to one and all! The faults that remain are my own.

Readers

My sincere thanks to all the readers who found errata and suggested improvements. Every new edition is better for the efforts of folks like you who take the time and trouble to report that which needs reporting!

Special mention must be made of one of the book's German translators,[3] Gisbert Selke, who read the first edition cover to cover during its translation and clarified my English. Gisbert did it all over again for the second edition and provided many code refactorings, which have made this a far better book than it would be otherwise. Going beyond the call of duty, Gisbert even contributed one recipe (Recipe 18.5) and revised some of the other recipes in the same chapter. Thank you, Gisbert!

The second edition also benefited from comments by Jim Burgess, who read large parts of the book. Comments on individual chapters were received from Jonathan Fuerth, the late Kim Fowler, Marc Loy, and Mike McCloskey. My wife, Betty, and my then-teenaged children each proofread several chapters as well.

The following people contributed significant bug reports or suggested improvements: Rex Bosma, Rod Buchanan, John Chamberlain, Keith Goldman, Gilles-Philippe Gre-

---

3 Earlier editions are or have been available in English, German, French, Polish, Russian, Korean, Traditional Chinese, and Simplified Chinese. My thanks to all the translators for their efforts in making the book available to a wider audience.

goire, B. S. Hughes, Jeff Johnston, Rob Konigsberg, Tom Murtagh, Jonathan O'Connor, Mark Petrovic, Steve Reisman, Bruce X. Smith, and Patrick Wohlwend.

Etc.

My dear wife, Betty Cerar, still knows more about the caffeinated beverage that I drink while programming than the programming language I use, but her passion for clear expression and correct grammar has benefited so much of my writing during our life together.

No book on Java would be complete without a note of thanks to James Gosling for inventing Java (he also invented the first Unix Emacs, the *sc* spreadsheet, and the NeWS window system). Thanks also to his employer Sun Microsystems (before they were taken over by Oracle) for releasing not only the Java language but an incredible array of Java tools and API libraries freely available over the internet.

Willi Powell of Apple Canada provided macOS access for the first edition, back in the early days of macOS.

To each and every one of you, my sincere thanks.

Book Production Software

I used a variety of tools and operating systems in preparing, compiling, and testing this book. The developers of OpenBSD (*http://www.openbsd.org*), "the proactively secure Unix-like system," deserve thanks for making a stable and secure Unix clone that is also closer to traditional Unix than other freeware systems. I used the *vi* editor (*vi* on OpenBSD and *vim* on Windows) while inputting the original manuscript in XML, and I used Adobe FrameMaker (a wonderful GUI-based documentation tool that Adobe bought and subsequently destroyed) to format the documents. I do not know if I can ever forgive Adobe for destroying what was arguably the world's best documentation system and for making the internet such a dangerous place by keeping the bug-infested Flash alive long past its best-before century. I do know I will never use a documentation system from Adobe for anything.

Because of this, the crowd-sourced *Android Cookbook* that I edited was not prepared with FrameMaker, but instead XML DocBook (generated from wiki markup on a Java-powered website that I wrote for the purpose) and a number of custom tools provided by O'Reilly's tools group.

The third and fourth editions of this *Java Cookbook* were formatted in Asciidoctor (*http://asciidoctor.org*) and brought to life on the publishing toolchain of O'Reilly's Atlas (*http://atlas.oreilly.com*).

## CHAPTER 1

Getting Started: Compiling and Running Java

1.0 Introduction

This chapter covers some entry-level tasks that you need to know how to do before you can go on. It is said you must crawl before you can walk, and walk before you can ride a bicycle. Before you can try out anything in this book, you need to be able to compile and run your Java code, so I start there, showing several ways to do that: the JDK way, the Integrated Development Environment (IDE) way, and the build tools (Ant, Maven, etc.) way. Another issue people run into is setting CLASSPATH correctly, so that's dealt with next. Deprecation warnings follow after that, because you're likely to encounter them in maintaining old Java code. The chapter ends with some general information about conditional compilation, unit testing, assertions, and debugging.

If you don't already have Java installed, you'll need to download it. Be aware that there are several different downloads. The JRE (Java Runtime Environment) was, up until Java 8, a smaller download for end users. Since there is far less desktop Java than there once was, the JRE was eliminated in favor of jlink to make a custom download (see Recipe 15.8). The JDK or Java SDK download is the full development environment, which you'll want if you're going to be developing Java software.

Standard downloads for the current release of Java are available at Oracle's website (*http://www.oracle.com/technetwork/java/javase/downloads/index.html*).

You can sometimes find prerelease builds of the next major Java version on *http://jdk.java.net*. The entire JDK is maintained as an open source project, and the OpenJDK source tree is used (with changes and additions) to build the commercial and supported Oracle JDKs.

If you're already happy with your IDE, you may wish to skip some or all of this material. It's here to ensure that everybody can compile and debug their programs before we move on.

1.1 Compiling and Running Java: Standard JDK

Problem

You need to compile and run your Java program.

Solution

This is one of the few areas where your computer's operating system impinges on Java's portability, so let's get these issues out of the way first.

JDK

Using the command-line Java Development Kit (JDK) may be the best way to keep up with the very latest improvements in Java. Assuming you have the standard JDK installed in the standard location and/or have set its location in your PATH, you should be able to run the command-line JDK tools. Use the commands *javac* to compile and *java* to run your program (and, on Windows only, *javaw* to run a program without a console window), like this:

```
C:\javasrc>javac HelloWorld.java

C:\javasrc>java HelloWorld
Hello, World

C:\javasrc>
```

If the program refers to other classes for which the source is available (in the same directory) and a compiled *.class* file is not, *javac* will automatically compile it for you. Effective with Java 11, for simple programs that don't need any such co-compilation, you can combine the two operations by simply passing the Java source file to the *java* command:

```
$ java HelloWorld.java
Hello, Java
$
```

As you can see from the compiler's (lack of) output, both *javac* and *java* compilation works on the Unix "no news is good news" philosophy: if a program was able to do what you asked it to, it shouldn't bother nattering at you to say that it did so.

There is an optional setting called CLASSPATH, discussed in Recipe 1.5, that controls where Java looks for classes. CLASSPATH, if set, is used by both *javac* and *java*. In older versions of Java, you had to set your CLASSPATH to include "." even to run a simple program from the current directory; this is no longer true on current Java implementations.

Sun/Oracle's *javac* compiler is the official reference implementation. There were several alternative open source command-line compilers, including Jikes (*http://source forge.net/projects/jikes*) and Kaffe (*http://github.com/kaffe/kaffe*), but they are, for the most part, no longer actively maintained.

There have also been some Java runtime clones, including Apache Harmony (*http:// harmony.apache.org*), Japhar (*http://www.hungry.com/old-hungry/products/japhar*), the IBM Jikes Runtime (from the same site as Jikes), and even JNode (*http:// www.jnode.org*), a complete, standalone operating system written in Java; but since the Sun/Oracle JVM has been open sourced (GPL), most of these projects have stopped being maintained. Harmony was retired by Apache in November 2011.

macOS

The JDK is pure command line. At the other end of the spectrum in terms of keyboard-versus-visual, we have the Apple Macintosh. Books have been written about how great the Mac user interface is, and I won't step into that debate. macOS (Release 10.x of the OS) is built upon a BSD Unix (and "Mach") base. As such, it has a regular command line (the Terminal application, hidden away under */Applications/ Utilities*), as well as both the traditional Unix command-line tools and the graphical Mac tools. If you're using macOS, you can use the command-line JDK tools or any of the modern build tools. Compiled classes can be packaged into clickable applications using the Jar Packager discussed in Recipe 15.6. Mac fans can use one of the many full IDE tools discussed in Recipe 1.3. Apple provides XCode as its IDE, but out of the box it isn't very Java-friendly.

1.2 Compiling and Running Java: GraalVM for Better Performance

Problem

You've heard that Graal is a JVM from Oracle that's faster than the standard JDK, and you want to try it out. Graal promises to offer better performance, and it offers the ability to mix and match programming languages and pre-compile your Java code into executable form for a given platform.

Solution

Download and install GraalVM.

Discussion

GraalVM bills itself as "a universal virtual machine for running applications written in JavaScript, Python, Ruby, R, JVM-based languages like Java, Scala, Clojure, Kotlin, and LLVM-based languages such as C and C++."

Note that Graal is undergoing rapid change. While this recipe reflects the latest information at press time (late 2019), there may be newer versions and changed functionality by the time you are ready to install.

As we go to press, GraalVM is based on OpenJDK 11, which means you can use Modules and other Java 9, 10, and 11 features, but it doesn't have support for Java 12, 13 or 14 features. You can build your own Graal on later releases, since the complete source is on GitHub (*https://github.com/oracle/graal*).

See the GraalVM website (*https://www.graalvm.org*) for more information on GraalVM. See also this presentation (*https://www.infoq.com/presentations/graal-jvm-jit*) by Chris Thalinger, who has worked on JVMs for a decade and a half.

Start at the downloads page (*https://www.graalvm.org/downloads*). You will have to choose between the Community Edition and the Enterprise Edition. To avoid any licensing issues, this recipe starts with the Community Edition. You can download a tarball for Linux, macOS, and Windows. There is no formal installer at this point. To install it, open a terminal window and try the following (the directory chosen is for macOS):

```
$ cd /Library/Java/JavaVirtualMachines
$ tar xzvf ~/Downloads/graalvm-ce-NNN-VVV.tar.gz # replace with actual version
$ cd
$ /usr/libexec/java_home -V # macOS only
11.0.2, x86_64:     "OpenJDK 11.0.2"
    /Library/Java/JavaVirtualMachines/jdk-11.0.2.jdk/Contents/Home
1.8.0_221, x86_64:     "GraalVM CE 19.2.0.1"
    /Library/Java/JavaVirtualMachines/graalvm-ce-19.2.0.1/Contents/Home
$
```

On other systems, do the install in a sensible place. On most versions of Linux, after installing a JDK, you can use the standard Linux *alternatives* command (*https:// access.redhat.com/documentation/en-US/JBoss_Communications_Platform/5.1/html/ Platform_Installation_Guide/sect-Setting_the_Default_JDK.html*) to make this your default. On MacOS, the *java_home* command output confirms that you have installed GraalVM, but it's not your default JVM yet. To do that, you have to set your PATH:

```
export JAVA_HOME=<where you installed GraalVM>/Contents/Home
export PATH=$JAVA_HOME/bin:$PATH
```

Be very sure to include the :$PATH at the end of the line—no space—or all your standard command-line tools will appear to disappear (if you made this mistake, just log out and log back in to restore your path). I suggest you don't update your login scripts until you are sure the settings you have are correct.

Now you should be running the Graal version of Java. This is what you should see:

```
$ java -version
openjdk version "1.8.0_222"
OpenJDK Runtime Environment (build
  1.8.0_222-20190711112007.graal.jdk8u-src-tar-gz-b08)
OpenJDK 64-Bit GraalVM CE 19.2.0.1 (build 25.222-b08-jvmci-19.2-b02, mixed mode)
```

Your output may differ, but as long as it says "GraalVM" you should be good.

Graal includes a number of useful tools, including *native-image*, which can in some cases translate a class file into a binary executable for the platform it's running on, optimizing startup speed and also reducing the download size needed to run a single application. The *native-image* tool must be downloaded separately using `gu install native-image`.

We'll explore running some of the other non-Java languages in Recipe 18.4.

1.3 Compiling, Running, and Testing with an IDE

Problem

It is cumbersome to use several tools for the various development tasks.

Solution

Use an Integrated Development Environment (IDE), which combines editing, testing, compiling, running, debugging, and package management.

Discussion

Many programmers find that using a handful of separate tools—a text editor, a compiler, and a runner program, not to mention a debugger—is too many. An IDE *integrates* all of these into a single toolset with a graphical user interface. Many IDEs are available, and the better ones are fully integrated tools with their own compilers and virtual machines. Class browsers and other features of IDEs round out the ease-of-use feature sets of these tools. Today most developers use an IDE because of the productivity gains. Although I started as a command-line junkie, I do find that IDE features like the following make me more productive:

Code completion:: *Ian's Rule* here is that I never type more than three characters of any name that is known to the IDE; let the computer do the typing! Incremental compiling features:: Note and report compilation errors as you type, instead of waiting until you are finished typing. Refactoring:: The ability to make far-reaching yet behavior-preserving changes to a code base without having to manually edit dozens of individual files.

Beyond that, I don't plan to debate the merits of IDE versus the command-line process; I use both modes at different times and on different projects. I'm just going to show a few examples of using a couple of the Java-based IDEs.

The three most popular Java IDEs, which run on all mainstream computing platforms and quite a few niche ones, are *Eclipse*, *NetBeans*, and *IntelliJ IDEA*. Eclipse is the most widely used, but the others each have a special place in the hearts and minds of some developers. If you develop for Android, the ADT has traditionally been developed for Eclipse, but it has now transitioned to IntelliJ as the basis for Android Studio, which is the standard IDE for Android, and for Google's other mobile platform, Flutter (*https://flutter.io*). All three IDEs are plug-in based and offer a wide selection of optional and third-party plug-ins to enhance the IDE, such as supporting other programming languages, frameworks, and file types. While the following paragraph shows creating and running a program with Eclipse, the IntelliJ IDEA and NetBeans IDEs all offer similar capabilities.

One of the most popular cross-platform, open source IDEs for Java is Eclipse, originally from IBM and now shepherded by the Eclipse Foundation (*http://eclipse.org*), the home of many software projects including Jakarta (*https://projects.eclipse.org/projects/ee4j.jakartaee-platform*), the follow-on to the Java Enterprise Edition. The Eclipse Platform is also used as the basis of other tools such as SpringSource Tool Suite (STS) and IBM's Rational Application Developer (RAD). All IDEs do basically the same thing for you when getting started. The example in Figure 1-1 shows starting a new project.

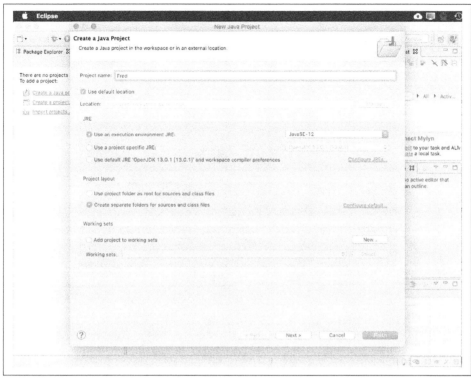

Figure 1-1. Starting a new project with the Eclipse New Java Class Wizard

The Eclipse New Java Class Wizard shown in Figure 1-2 shows creating a new class.

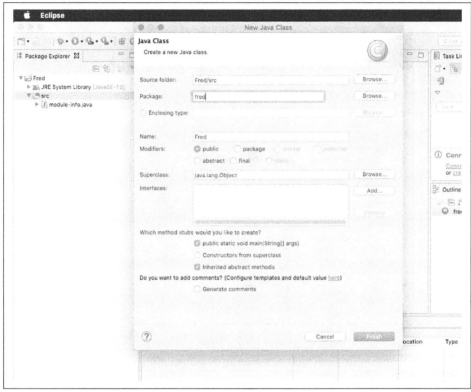

Figure 1-2. Creating a new class with the Eclipse New Java Class Wizard

Eclipse, like all modern IDEs, features a number of refactoring capabilities, shown in Figure 1-3.

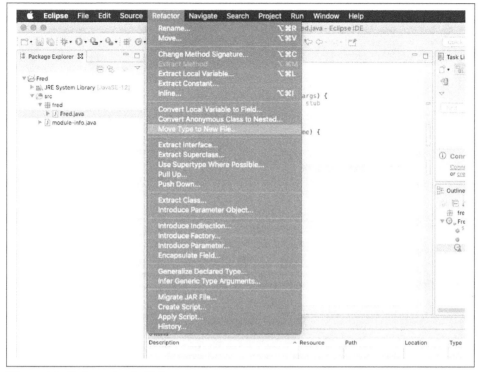

Figure 1-3. Refactoring in Eclipse

And, of course, all the IDEs allow you to run and/or debug your application. Figure 1-4 shows running an application; for variety and neutrality, this is shown using IntelliJ IDEA.

macOS includes Apple's Developer Tools. The main IDE is Xcode. Unfortunately, current versions of Xcode do not really support Java development, so I can't recommend it for our purposes; it is primarily for those building nonportable (iOS-only or OS X–only) applications in the Swift or Objective-C programming languages. So even if you are on OS X, to do Java development you should use one of the three Java IDEs.

Microsoft VSCode (formerly part of Visual Studio) has been getting some attention in Java circles lately, but it's not a Java-specific IDE. Give it a try if you like.

How do you choose an IDE? Perhaps it will be dictated by your organization or chosen by majority vote of your fellow developers. Given that all three major IDEs (Eclipse, NetBeans, and IntelliJ) can be downloaded free and are 100% open source, why not try them all and see which one best fits the kind of development you do? Regardless of what platform you use to develop Java, if you have a Java runtime, you should have plenty of IDEs from which to choose.

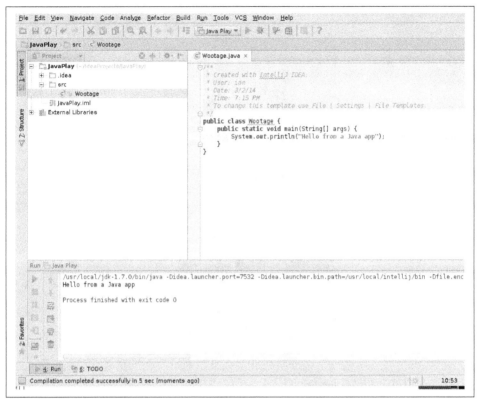

Figure 1-4. IntelliJ program output

See Also

Each IDE's website maintains an up-to-date list of resources, including books. See Table 1-1 for the website for each.

Table 1-1. The three major Java IDEs and their websites

Product name	Project URL	Note
Eclipse	*https://eclipse.org/*	Basis of STS, RAD
IntelliJ Idea	*https://jetbrains.com/idea/*	Basis of Android Studio
Netbeans	*https://netbeans.apache.org*	Run anywhere JavaSE does

These major IDEs are extensible; see their documentation for a list of the many, many plug-ins available. Most of them allow you to find and install plug-ins from within the IDE. For Eclipse, use the Eclipse Marketplace, near the bottom of the Help menu. As a last resort, if you need/want to write a plug-in that extends the functionality of your IDE, you can do that too, and in Java.

For Eclipse, I have some useful information at *https://darwinsys.com/java*. The site includes a list of shortcuts to aid developer productivity.

1.4 Exploring Java with JShell

Problem

You want to try out Java expressions and APIs quickly, without having to create a file with `public class X { public static void main(String[] args) { … }` every time.

Solution

Use JShell, Java's REPL (Read-Evaluate-Print-Loop) interpreter.

Discussion

Starting with Java 11, `JShell` is included as a standard part of Java. It allows you to enter Java statements and have them evaluated without the bother of creating a class and a main program. You can use it for quick calculations, to try out an API to see how it works, or for almost any purpose; if you find an expression you like, you can copy it into a regular Java source file and make it permanent. JShell can also be used as a scripting language over Java, but the overhead of starting the JVM means that it won't be as fast as awk, Perl, or Python for quick scripting.

REPL programs are very convenient, and they are hardly a new idea (LISP languages from the 1950s included them). You can think of Command-Line Interpreters (CLIs) such as the Bash or Ksh shells on UNIX/Linux, or Command.com and PowerShell on Microsoft Windows, as REPLs for the system as a whole. Many interpreted languages like Ruby and Python can also be used as REPLs. Java finally has its own REPL, *JShell*. Here's an example of using it:

```
$ jshell
|  Welcome to JShell -- Version 11.0.2
|  For an introduction type: /help intro

jshell> "Hello"
$1 ==> "Hello"

jshell> System.out.println("Hello");
Hello

jshell> System.out.println($1)
Hello

jshell> "Hello" + sqrt(57)
|  Error:
```

```
|  cannot find symbol
|    symbol:   method sqrt(int)
|  "Hello" + sqrt(57)
|              ^--^

jshell> "Hello" + Math.sqrt(57)
$2 ==> "Hello7.54983443527075"

jshell> String.format("Hello %6.3f", Math.sqrt(57)
   ...> )
$3 ==> "Hello  7.550"

jshell> String x = Math.sqrt(22/7) + " " + Math.PI +
   ...> " and the end."
x ==> "1.7320508075688772 3.141592653589793 and the end."

jshell>
```

You can see some obvious features and benefits here:

- The value of an expression is printed without needing to call `Sys
  tem.out.println` every time, but you can call it if you like.
- Values that are not assigned to a variable get assigned synthetic identifiers, like
  `$1`, that can be used in subsequent statements.
- The semicolon at the end of a statment is optional (unless you type more than
  one statement on a line).
- If you make a mistake, you get a helpful message immediately.
- You can get completion with a single tab, as in shell filename completion.
- You can get the relevant portion of the Javadoc documentation on known classes
  or methods with just a double tab.
- If you omit a close quote, parenthesis, or other punctuation, JShell will just wait
  for you, giving a continuation prompt (...).
- If you do make a mistake, you can use "shell history" (i.e., up arrow) to recall the
  statement so you can repair it.

JShell is also useful in prototyping Java code. For example, I wanted one of those
health-themed timers that reminds you to get up and move around a bit every half
hour:

```
$ jshell
|  Welcome to JShell -- Version 11.0.2
|  For an introduction type: /help intro

jshell> while (true) { sleep (30*60); JOptionPane.showMessageDialog(null,
   "Move it"); }
|  Error:
```

```
|  cannot find symbol
|    symbol:   method sleep(int)
|  while (true) { sleep (30*60); JOptionPane.showMessageDialog(null, "Move
it");}
|                    ^---^
|  Error:
|  cannot find symbol
|    symbol:   variable JOptionPane
|  while (true) { sleep (30*60); JOptionPane.showMessageDialog(null, "Move
it");}
|                                ^---------^

jshell> import javax.swing.*;

jshell> while (true) { Thread.sleep (30*60); JOptionPane.showMessageDialog(null,
"Move it"); }

jshell> while (true) { Thread.sleep (30*60 * 1000);
  JOptionPane.showMessageDialog(null, "Move it"); }

jshell> ^D
```

I then put the final working version into a Java file called *MoveTimer.java*, put a class statement and a main() method around the main line, told the IDE to reformat the whole thing, and saved it into my *darwinsys-api* repository.

So go ahead and experiment with JShell. Read the built-in introductory tutorial for more details! When you get something you like, either use /save, or copy and paste it into a Java program and save it.

Read more about JShell at the OpenJDK JShell Tutorial (*https://cr.openjdk.java.net/ ~rfield/tutorial/JShellTutorial.html*).

1.5 Using CLASSPATH Effectively

Problem

You need to keep your class files in a common directory, or you're wrestling with CLASSPATH.

Solution

Set CLASSPATH to the list of directories and/or JAR files that contain the classes you want.

Discussion

CLASSPATH is a list of class files in any of a number of directories, JAR files, or ZIP files. Just like the PATH your system uses for finding programs, the CLASSPATH is used by the Java runtime to find classes. Even when you type something as simple as *java HelloWorld*, the Java interpreter looks in each of the places named in your CLASSPATH until it finds a match. Let's work through an example.

The CLASSPATH can be set as an environment variable the same way you set other environment variables, such as your PATH environment variable. However, it's usually preferable to specify the CLASSPATH for a given command on the command line:

```
C:\> java -classpath c:\ian\classes MyProg
```

Suppose your CLASSPATH were set to *C:\classes;.* on Windows or *~/classes:.* on Unix or Mac. Suppose you had just compiled a source file named *HelloWorld.java* (with no package statement) into *HelloWorld.class* in the default directory (which is your current directory) and tried to run it. On Unix, if you run one of the kernel tracing tools (trace, strace, truss, or ktrace), you would probably see the Java program open or stat or access the following files:

- Some file(s) in the JDK directory
- Then *~/classes/HelloWorld.class*, which it probably wouldn't find
- Finally, *./HelloWorld.class*, which it would find, open, and read into memory

The vague "some file(s) in the JDK directory" is release dependent. You should not mess with the JDK files, but if you're curious, you can find them in the System Properties (see Recipe 2.2). There used to be a variable named sun.boot.class.path, but that is not found anymore. Let's look for any property with boot in its name:

```
jshell> System.getProperties().forEach((k,v) -> {
...  if (((String)k).contains("boot")) System.out.println(k + "->" +v);})
sun.boot.library.path->/usr/local/jdk-11/lib
```

The reason I and others suggest *not* setting CLASSPATH as an environment variable is that we don't like surprises. It's easy to add a JAR to your CLASSPATH and then forget that you've done so; a program might then work for you but not for your colleagues, due to their being unaware of your hidden dependency. And if you add a new version to CLASSPATH without removing the old version, you may run into conflicts.

Note also that providing the -classpath argument causes the CLASSPATH environment variable to be ignored.

If you still want to set CLASSPATH as an environment variable, you can. Suppose you had also installed the JAR file containing the supporting classes for programs from this book, *darwinsys-api.jar* (the actual filename if you download it may have a version number as part of the filename). You might then set your CLASSPATH to *C:\classes;C:\classes\darwinsys-api.jar;.* on Windows or *~/classes:~/classes/darwinsys-api.jar:.* on Unix.

Notice that you *do* need to list the full name of the JAR file explicitly. Unlike a single class file, placing a JAR file into a directory listed in your CLASSPATH does not make it available.

Certain specialized programs (such as a web server running a Servlet container) might not use either bootpath or CLASSPATH exactly as shown; these application servers typically provide their own ClassLoader (see Recipe 17.5 for information on class loaders). EE Web containers, for example, set your web app CLASSPATH to include the directory *WEB-INF/classes* and all the JAR files found under *WEB-INF/lib*.

How can you easily generate class files into a directory in your CLASSPATH? The *javac* command has a -d dir option, which specifies where the compiler output should go. For example, using -d to put the *HelloWorld* class file into my *$HOME/classes* directory, I just type the following (note that from here on I will be using the package name in addition to the class name, like a good kid):

```
javac -d $HOME/classes HelloWorld.java
java -cp $HOME/classes starting.HelloWorld
Hello, world!
```

As long as this directory remains in my CLASSPATH, I can access the class file regardless of my current directory. That's one of the key benefits of using CLASSPATH.

While these examples show explicit use of java with -classpath, it is generally more convenient (and reproducible) to use a build tool such as Maven (Recipe 1.7) or Gradle, which automatically provide the CLASSPATH for both compilation and execution.

Note that Java 9 and later also have a module path (environment variable MODULEPATH, command-line argument --module-path entry[:,…]) with the same syntax as the class path. The module path contains code that has been modularized; the Java Module System is discussed in Recipe 2.5 and Recipe 15.9.

1.6 Downloading and Using the Code Examples

Problem

You want to try out my example code and/or use my utility classes.

Solution

Download the latest archive of the book source files, unpack it, and run Maven (see Recipe 1.7) to compile the files.

Discussion

The source code used as examples in this book is included in a couple of source code repositories that have been in continuous development since 1995. These are listed in Table 1-2.

Table 1-2. The main source repositories

Repository name	GitHub URL	Package description	Approx. size
javasrc	http://github.com/IanDarwin/javasrc	Java code examples/demos	1,400 classes
darwinsys-api	http://github.com/Iandarwin/darwinsys-api	A published API	200 classes

You can download these repositories from the GitHub URLs shown in Table 1-2. GitHub allows you to download a ZIP file of the entire repository's current state, as well as view individual files on the web interface. Downloading with *git clone* instead of as an archive is preferred because you can then update at any time with a simple *git pull* command. And with the amount of updating this code base has undergone for the current release of Java, you are sure to find changes after the book is published.

If you are not familiar with Git, see "CVS, Subversion, Git, Oh My!" on page 20.

javasrc

This is the largest repo and consists primarily of code written to show a particular feature or API. The files are organized into subdirectories by topic, many of which correspond more or less to book chapters—for example, a directory for *strings* examples (Chapter 3), *regex* for regular expressions (Chapter 4), *numbers* (Chapter 5), and so on. The archive also contains the index by name and index by chapter files from the download site, so you can easily find the files you need.

The *javasrc* library is further broken down into a dozen Maven modules (shown in Table 1-3) so that you don't need all the dependencies for everything on your CLASS PATH all the time.

Table 1-3. JavaSrc Maven modules

Directory/module name	Description
pom.xml	Maven *parent pom*
Rdemo-web	R demo using a web framework
desktop	AWT and Swing stuff (no longer covered in the *Java Cookbook*)
ee	Enterprise stuff (no longer covered in the *Java Cookbook*)
graal	GraalVM demos
jlink	JLink demos
json	JSON processing
main	Contains the majority of the files, i.e., those not required to be in one of the other modules due to CLASSPATH or other issues
restdemo	REST service demo
spark	Apache Spark demo
testing	Code for testing
unsafe	Demo of Unsafe class
xml	XML stuff (no longer covered in the *Java Cookbook*)

darwinsys-api

I have built up a collection of useful stuff partly by moving some reusable classes from *javasrc* into my own API, which I use in my own Java projects. I use example code from it in this book, and I import classes from it into many of the other examples. So, if you're going to be downloading and compiling the examples *individually*, you should first download the file *darwinsys-api-1.x.jar* (for the latest value of *x*) and include it in your CLASSPATH. Note that if you are going to build the *javasrc* code with Eclipse or Maven, you can skip this download because the top-level Maven script starts off by including the JAR file for this API.

A compiled JAR file of *darwinsys-api* is available in Maven Central (*http://search.maven.org*); find it by searching for *darwinsys*. This is the current Maven artifact:

```
<dependency>
    <groupId>com.darwinsys</groupId>
    <artifactId>darwinsys-api</artifactId>
    <version>1.1.3</version>
</dependency>
```

This API consists of about two dozen com.darwinsys packages, listed in Table 1-4. The structure vaguely parallels the standard Java API; this is intentional. These packages now include around 200 classes and interfaces. Most of them have javadoc documentation that can be viewed with the source download.

Table 1-4. The com.darwinsys packages

Package name	Package description
com.darwinsys.csv	Classes for comma-separated values files
com.darwinsys.database	Classes for dealing with databases in a general way
com.darwinsys.diff	Comparison utilities
com.darwinsys.genericui	Generic GUI stuff
com.darwinsys.geo	Classes relating to country codes, provinces/states, and so on
com.darwinsys.graphics	Graphics
com.darwinsys.html	Classes (only one so far) for dealing with HTML
com.darwinsys.io	Classes for input and output operations, using Java's underlying I/O classes
com.darwinsys.jsptags	Java EE JSP tags
com.darwinsys.lang	Classes for dealing with standard features of Java
com.darwinsys.locks	Pessimistic locking API
com.darwinsys.mail	Classes for dealing with email, mainly a convenience class for sending mail
com.darwinsys.model	Sample data models
com.darwinsys.net	Networking
com.darwinsys.preso	Presentations
com.darwinsys.reflection	Reflection
com.darwinsys.regex	Regular expression stuff: an REDemo program, a Grep variant
com.darwinsys.security	Security
com.darwinsys.servlet	Servlet API helpers
com.darwinsys.sql	Classes for dealing with SQL databases
com.darwinsys.swingui	Classes for helping construct and use Swing GUIs
com.darwinsys.swingui.layout	A few interesting LayoutManager implementations
com.darwinsys.testdata	Test data generators
com.darwinsys.testing	Testing tools
com.darwinsys.unix	Unix helpers
com.darwinsys.util	A few miscellaneous utility classes
com.darwinsys.xml	XML utilities

Many of these classes are used as examples in this book; just look for files whose first line begins with the following:

```
package com.darwinsys;
```

You'll also find that many of the other examples have imports from the com.darwin sys packages.

General notes

Your best bet is to use *git clone* to download a copy of both the Git projects and then do a *git pull* every few months to get updates. Alternatively, you can download from this book's catalog page (*http://shop.oreilly.com/product/0636920026518.do*) a single intersection subset of both libraries that is made up almost exclusively of files actually used in the book. This archive is made from the sources that are dynamically included into the book at formatting time, so it should reflect exactly the examples you see in the book. But it will not include as many examples as the three individual archives, nor is it guaranteed that everything will compile because of missing dependencies, nor will it get updated often. But if all you want is to copy pieces into a project you're working on, this may be the one to get. You can find links to all of these files from my own website for this book (*http://javacook.darwinsys.com*); just follow the Downloads link.

The two separate repositories contain multiple self-contained projects with support for building both with Eclipse (Recipe 1.3) and with Maven (Recipe 1.7). Note that Maven will automatically fetch a vast array of prerequisite libraries when first invoked on a given project, so be sure you're online on a high-speed internet link. Maven will thus ensure that all prerequisites are installed before building. If you choose to build pieces individually, look in the file *pom.xml* for the list of dependencies. Unfortunately, I will not be able to help you if you are using tooling other than Eclipse or Maven with the control files included in the download.

If you have a version of Java older than Java 12, a few files will not compile. You can make up exclusion elements for the files that are known not to compile.

All my code in the two projects is released under the least-restrictive credit-only license, the two-clause BSD license. If you find it useful, incorporate it into your own software. There is no need to write to ask me for permission; just use it, with credit. If you get rich off it, send me some money.

 Most of the command-line examples refer to source files, assuming you are in *src/main/java*, and runnable classes, assuming you are in (or have added to your CLASSPATH) the build directory (e.g., usually *target/classes*). This will not be mentioned with each example, as doing so would waste a lot of paper.

Caveat lector

The repos have been in development since 1995. This means that you will find some code that is not up to date or that no longer reflects best practices. This is not surprising: any body of code will grow old if any part of it is not actively maintained. (Thus, at this point, I invoke Culture Club's song "Do You Really Want to Hurt Me": "Give me time to realize my crime.") Where advice in the book disagrees with some code you found in the repo, keep this in mind. One of the practices of Extreme Programming is Continuous Refactoring, the ability to improve any part of the code base at any time. Don't be surprised if the code in the online source directory differs from what appears in the book; it is a rare month that I don't make some improvement to the code, and the results are committed and pushed quite often. So if there are differences between what's printed in the book and what you get from GitHub, be glad, not sad, for you'll have received the benefit of hindsight. Also, people can contribute easily on GitHub via pull requests; that's what makes it interesting. If you find a bug or an improvement, do send me a pull request! The consolidated archive on the page for this book (*http://shop.oreilly.com/product/0636920304371.do*) will not be updated as frequently.

CVS, Subversion, Git, Oh My!

Many distributed version control systems or source code management systems are available. These are the ones that have been widely used in open source over the years:

- Concurrent Versions System (CVS) (*http://en.wikipedia.org/wiki/Concurrent_Versions_System*)
- Apache Subversion (*http://subversion.apache.org*)
- Git (*http://git-scm.com*)
- As well as others that are used in particular niches (e.g., Bazaar, Mercurial)

Although each has its advantages and disadvantages, the use of Git in the Linux build process (and projects based on Linux, such as the Android mobile environment), as well as the availability of sites like *github.com* and *gitorious.org*, give Git a massive momentum over the others. I don't have statistics, but I suspect the number of projects in Git repositories probably exceeds the others combined. Several well-known organizations using Git are listed on the Git home page.

For this reason, I have moved my public projects to GitHub; see *http://github.com/IanDarwin*. To download the projects and be able to get updates applied automatically, use Git to download them. Options include the following:

- The command-line Git client (*http://git-scm.com*). If you are on any modern Unix or Linux system, Git is either included or available in your ports or packaging or developer tools, but it can also be downloaded for MS Windows, Mac, Linux, and Solaris from the home page under Downloads.
- All modern IDEs have Git support built in (though IntelliJ doesn't include Git itself; it relies on the command-line Git client, possibly because the main Java implementation `jgit` is owned by Eclipse).
- Numerous standalone GUI clients (*http://git-scm.com/downloads/guis*).

- Even Continuous Integration servers such as Jenkins/Hudson (see Recipe 1.11) have plug-ins available for updating a project with Git (and other popular SCMs) before building them.

You will want to have one or more of these Git clients at your disposal to download my code examples. You could instead download the code examples as ZIP archive files, but then you won't get updates! You can also view or download individual files from the GitHub page via a web browser.

Make Versus Java Build Tools

Make is the original build tool from the 1970s, used in Unix and C/C++ development. Make and the Java-based tools each have advantages; I'll try to compare them without too much bias.

The Java build tools work the same on all platforms, as much as possible. Make is rather platform-dependent; there is GNU Make, BSD Make, Xcode Make, Visual Studio Make, and several others, each with slightly different syntax.

That said, there are many Java build tools to choose from, including these:

- Apache Ant
- Apache Maven
- Gradle
- Apache Buildr

Makefiles and Gradle build files are the shortest. Make just lets you list the commands you want run and their dependencies. Buildr and Gradle each have their own language (based on Ruby and Groovy, respectively). Maven uses XML, which is generally more verbose but with a lot of sensible defaults and a standard, default workflow. Ant also uses XML but makes you specify each task you want performed.

Make runs faster for single tasks; most implementations are written in C. However, the Java tools can run many Java tasks in a single JVM, such as the built-in Java compiler or *.jar/.war/.tar/.zip* files—to the extent that it may be more efficient to run several Java compilations in one JVM process than to run the same compilations using Make. In other words, once the JVM that is running Ant/Maven/Gradle itself is up and running, it doesn't take long at all to run the Java compiler and run the compiled class. This is Java as it was meant to be!

Java build tool files can do more for you. These tools automatically find all the **.java* files in and under *src/main/java*. With *make*, you have to spell such things out.

The Java tools have special knowledge of CLASSPATH, making it easy to set a CLASS PATH in various ways for compile time. Maven offers a scope of tests for classes and other files that will be on your CLASSPATH only when running tests, for example. You may have to duplicate this in other ways—shell scripts or batch files—for using Make or for manually running or testing your application.

Maven and Gradle also handle dependency management. You simply list the API and version that you want, and the tool finds it, downloads it over the internet, saves it in a cache folder for future use, and adds it to your CLASSPATH at the right time—all without writing any rules.

Gradle goes further yet and allows scripting logic in its configuration file. (Strictly speaking, Ant and Maven do as well, but Gradle's is much easier to use.)

Make is simpler to extend but harder to do so portably. You can write a one-line Make rule for getting a CVS archive from a remote site, but you may run into incompatibilities between GNU Make, BSD Make, Microsoft Make, and so on. There is a built-in Ant task for getting an archive from CVS using Ant; it was written as a Java source file instead of just a series of command-line commands.

Make has been around much longer. There are probably millions (literally) more makefiles than Ant files. Non-Java developers have typically not heard of Ant; they almost all use Make. Most non-Java open source projects use Make, except for programming languages that provide their own build tool (e.g., Ruby provides Rake and Thor, and Haskell provides Cabal).

The advantages of the Java tools make more sense on larger projects. Primarily, Make has been used on the really large non-Java projects. For example, Make is used for telephone switch source code, which consists of hundreds of thousands of source files totaling tens or hundreds of millions of lines of source code. By contrast, Tomcat is about 500,000 lines of code, and the JBoss Java EE server WildFly is about 800,000 lines. Use of the Java tools is growing steadily, particularly now that most of the widely used Java IDEs (IntelliJ, Eclipse, NetBeans, etc.) have interfaces to Ant, Maven, and/or Gradle. Effectively all Java open source projects use Maven; some still use Ant, or the newest kid on that block, Gradle.

Make is included with most Unix and Unix-like systems and shipped with many Windows IDEs. Ant and Maven and gradle are not included with any operating system distribution that I know of, but they can be installed as packages on almost all systems, and both are available direct from Apache. Gradle installs from *http:// gradle.org*, and Buildr from the Apache website (*http://buildr.apache.org*).

To sum up, although Make and the Java tools are good, new Java projects should use one of the newer Java-based tools such as Maven or Gradle.

1.7 Automating Dependencies, Compilation, Testing, and Deployment with Apache Maven

Problem

You want a tool that does it all automatically: downloads your dependencies, compiles your code, compiles and runs your tests, packages the app, and installs or deploys it.

Solution

Use Apache Maven.

Discussion

Maven is a Java-centric build tool that includes a sophisticated, distributed dependency management system that also gives it rules for building application packages such as JAR, WAR, and EAR files and deploying them to an array of different targets. Whereas older build tools focus on the *how*, Maven files focus on the *what*, specifying what you want done.

Maven is controlled by a file called *pom.xml* (for Project Object Model). A sample *pom.xml* might look like this:

```
<project xmlns="http://maven.apache.org/POM/4.0.0"
    xmlns:xsi="http://www.w3.org/2001/XMLSchema-instance"
    xsi:schemaLocation="http://maven.apache.org/POM/4.0.0
                        http://maven.apache.org/xsd/maven-4.0.0.xsd">
    <modelVersion>4.0.0</modelVersion>

    <groupId>com.example</groupId>
    <artifactId>my-se-project</artifactId>
    <version>1.0-SNAPSHOT</version>
    <packaging>jar</packaging>

    <name>my-se-project</name>
    <url>http://com.example/</url>

    <properties>
      <project.build.sourceEncoding>UTF-8</project.build.sourceEncoding>
    </properties>

    <dependencies>
      <dependency>
        <groupId>junit</groupId>
        <artifactId>junit</artifactId>
        <version>4.8.1</version>
        <scope>test</scope>
```

```
            </dependency>
        </dependencies>
    </project>
```

This specifies a project called *my-se-project* (my standard-edition project) that will be
packaged into a JAR file; it depends on the JUnit 4.x framework for unit testing (see
Recipe 1.10) but only needs it for compiling and running tests. If I type *mvn install* in
the directory with this POM, Maven will ensure that it has a copy of the given version
of JUnit (and anything that JUnit depends on). Then it will compile everything (setting CLASSPATH and other options for the compiler), run any and all unit tests, and
if they all pass, generate a JAR file for the program. It will then install it in my
personal Maven repo (under *~/.m2/repository*) so that other Maven projects can
depend on my new project JAR file. Note that I haven't had to tell Maven where the
source files live, nor how to compile them—this is all handled by sensible defaults,
based on a well-defined project structure. The program source is expected to be
found in *src/main/java*, and the tests in *src/test/java*; if it's a web application, the web
root is expected to be in *src/main/webapp* by default. Of course, you can override
these settings.

Note that even the preceding config file does not have to be, and was not, written by
hand; Maven's archetype generation rules let it build the starting version of any of
several hundred types of projects. Here is how the file was created:

```
$ mvn archetype:generate \
    -DarchetypeGroupId=org.apache.maven.archetypes \
    -DarchetypeArtifactId=maven-archetype-quickstart \
    -DgroupId=com.example -DartifactId=my-se-project

[INFO] Scanning for projects...
Downloading: http://repo1.maven.org/maven2/org/apache/maven/plugins/
    maven-deploy-plugin/2.5/maven-deploy-plugin-2.5.pom
[several dozen or hundred lines of downloading POM files and Jar files...]
[INFO] Generating project in Interactive mode
[INFO] Archetype [org.apache.maven.archetypes:maven-archetype-quickstart:1.1]
    found in catalog remote
[INFO] Using property: groupId = com.example
[INFO] Using property: artifactId = my-se-project
Define value for property 'version':  1.0-SNAPSHOT: :
[INFO] Using property: package = com.example
Confirm properties configuration:
groupId: com.example
artifactId: my-se-project
version: 1.0-SNAPSHOT
package: com.example
 Y: : y
[INFO] ------------------------------------------------------------------------
[INFO] Using following parameters for creating project from Old (1.x) Archetype:
    maven-archetype-quickstart:1.1
[INFO] ------------------------------------------------------------------------
[INFO] Parameter: groupId, Value: com.example
```

```
[INFO] Parameter: packageName, Value: com.example
[INFO] Parameter: package, Value: com.example
[INFO] Parameter: artifactId, Value: my-se-project
[INFO] Parameter: basedir, Value: /private/tmp
[INFO] Parameter: version, Value: 1.0-SNAPSHOT
[INFO] project created from Old (1.x) Archetype in dir: /private/tmp/
    my-se-project
[INFO] ------------------------------------------------------------------
[INFO] BUILD SUCCESS
[INFO] ------------------------------------------------------------------
[INFO] Total time: 6:38.051s
[INFO] Finished at: Sun Jan 06 19:19:18 EST 2013
[INFO] Final Memory: 7M/81M
[INFO] ------------------------------------------------------------------
```

Alternately, you can do *mvn archetype:generate* and select the default from a rather long list of choices. The default is a quickstart Java archetype, which makes it easy to get started.

The IDEs (see Recipe 1.3) have support for Maven. For example, if you use Eclipse, M2Eclipse (m2e) is an Eclipse plug-in that will build your Eclipse project dependencies from your POM file; this plug-in ships by default with current Java Developer builds of Eclipse. It is also available for some older releases; see the Eclipse website (*http://eclipse.org/m2e*) for plug-in details.

A POM file can redefine any of the standard goals. Common Maven goals (predefined by default to do something sensible) include the following:

clean
> Removes all generated artifacts

compile
> Compiles all source files

test
> Compiles and runs all unit tests

package
> Builds the package

install
> Installs *pom.xml* and the package into your local Maven repository for use by your other projects

deploy
> Tries to install the package (e.g., on an application server)

Most of the steps implicitly invoke the previous ones. For example, package will compile any missing *.class* files and run the tests if that hasn't already been done in this run.

There is an optional `distributionManagement` element in the POM file or a `-DaltDeploymentRepository` on the command line to specify an alternate deployment location. There are application-server–specific targets provided by the app server vendors; as a single example, with the WildFly Application Server (known as JBoss AS a decade or more ago), you would install some additional plug-in(s) as per their documentation and then deploy to the app server using

```
mvn wildfly:deploy
```

instead of the regular deploy. Since I use this Maven incantation frequently, I have a shell alias or batch file `mwd` to automate even that.

Maven pros and cons

Maven can handle complex projects and is very configurable. I build the *darwinsys-api* and *javasrc* projects with Maven and let it handle finding dependencies, making the download of the project source code smaller (actually, moving the download overhead to the servers of the projects themselves). The only real downsides to Maven are that it takes a while to get fully up to speed with it, and it can be hard to diagnose when things go wrong. A good web search engine is your friend when things fail.

One issue I fear is that a hacker could gain access to a project's site and modify, or install a new version of, a POM. Maven automatically fetches updated POM versions. However, it does use hash signatures to verify that files have not been tampered with during the download process, and all files to be uploaded must be signed with PGP/GPG, so an attacker would have to compromise both the upload account and the signing keys. I am not aware of this ever having happened though.

See Also

Start at *http://maven.apache.org*.

Maven Central: Mapping the World of Java Software

There is an immense collection of software freely available to Maven users just for adding a <dependency> element or "Maven Artifact" into your *pom.xml*. You can search this repository at *http://search.maven.org* or *https://repository.sonatype.org/index.html*.

Figure 1-5 shows a search for my *darwinsys-api* project and the information it reveals. Note that the *dependency* information listed there is all you need to have the library added to your Maven project; just copy the Dependency Information section and paste it into the <dependencies> of your POM, and you're done! Because Maven Central has become the definitive place to look for software, many other Java build tools piggyback on Maven Central. To accommodate these users, in turn, Maven

---

Central offers to serve up the dependency information in a form that half a dozen other build tools can directly use in the same copy-and-paste fashion.

When you get to the stage of having a useful open source project that others can build upon, you may, in turn, want to share it on Maven Central. The process is longer than building for yourself but not onerous. Refer to this Maven guide (*http://maven.apache.org/guides/mini/guide-central-repository-upload.html*) or the Sonatype OSS Maven Repository Usage Guide (*https://help.sonatype.com/repomanager3/formats/maven-repositories*).

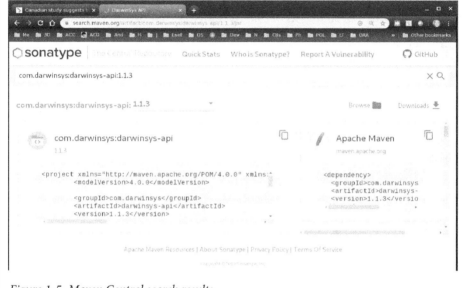

Figure 1-5. Maven Central search results

1.8 Automating Dependencies, Compilation, Testing, and Deployment with Gradle

Problem

You want a build tool that doesn't make you use a lot of XML in your configuration file.

Solution

Use Gradle's simple build file format with configuration by convention for shorter build files and fast builds.

Discussion

Gradle is the latest in the succession of build tools (Make, Ant, and Maven). Gradle bills itself as "the enterprise automation tool" and has integration with the other build tools and IDEs.

Unlike the other Java-based tools, Gradle doesn't use XML as its scripting language, but rather a Domain-Specific Language (DSL) based on the JVM-based and Java-based scripting language Groovy (*http://groovy.codehaus.org*).

You can install Gradle by downloading from the Gradle website (*http://gradle.org*), unpacking the ZIP, and adding its *bin* subdirectory to your path.

Then you can begin to use Gradle. Assuming you use the standard source directory (*src/main/java*, *src/main/test*) that is shared by Maven and Gradle, among other tools, the example *build.gradle* file in Example 1-1 will build your app and run your unit tests.

Example 1-1. Example build.gradle file

```
# Simple Gradle Build for the Java-based DataVis project
apply plugin: 'java'
# Set up mappings for Eclipse project too
apply plugin: 'eclipse'

# The version of Java to use
sourceCompatibility = 11
# The version of my project
version = '1.0.3'
# Configure JAR file packaging
jar {
    manifest {
        attributes 'Main-class': 'com.somedomainnamehere.data.DataVis',
        'Implementation-Version': version
    }
}

# optional feature: like -Dtesting=true but only when running tests ("test task")
test {
    systemProperties 'testing': 'true'
}
```

You can bootstrap the industry's vast investment in Maven infrastructure by adding lines like these into your *build.gradle*:

```
# Tell Gradle to look in Maven Central
repositories {
    mavenCentral()
}
```

```
# We need darwinsys-api for compiling as well as JUnit for testing
dependencies {
    compile group: 'com.darwinsys', name: 'darwinsys-api', version: '1.0.3+'
    testCompile group: 'junit', name: 'junit', version: '4.+'
}
```

See Also

There is much more functionality in Gradle. Start at Gradle's website (*http://www.gradle.org*), and see the documentation (*http://www.gradle.org/docs*).

1.9 Dealing with Deprecation Warnings

Problem

Your code used to compile cleanly, but now it gives deprecation warnings.

Solution

You must have blinked. Either live—dangerously—with the warnings or revise your code to eliminate them.

Discussion

Each new release of Java includes a lot of powerful new functionality, but at a price: during the evolution of this new stuff, Java's maintainers find some old stuff that wasn't done right and shouldn't be used anymore because they can't really fix it. In the first major revision, for example, they realized that the `java.util.Date` class had some serious limitations with regard to internationalization. Accordingly, many of the `Date` class methods and constructors are marked "deprecated." According to the *American Heritage Dictionary*, to deprecate something means to "express disapproval of; deplore." Java's developers are therefore disapproving of the old way of doing things. Try compiling this code:

```
import java.util.Date;

/** Demonstrate deprecation warning */
public class Deprec {

    public static void main(String[] av) {

        // Create a Date object for May 5, 1986
        @SuppressWarnings("deprecation")
        // EXPECT DEPRECATION WARNING without @SuppressWarnings
        Date d = new Date(86, 04, 05);
        System.out.println("Date is " + d);
```

```
        }
    }
```

What happened? When I compiled it (prior to adding the @SuppressWarnings()
annotation), I got this warning:

```
C:\javasrc>javac Deprec.java
Note: Deprec.java uses or overrides a deprecated API.  Recompile with
"-deprecation" for details.
1 warning
C:\javasrc>
```

So, we follow orders. For details, recompile with -deprecation to see the additional
details:

```
C:\javasrc>javac -deprecation Deprec.java
Deprec.java:10: warning: constructor Date(int,int,int) in class java.util.Date
has been deprecated
                Date d = new Date(86, 04, 05);         // May 5, 1986
                         ^

1 warning

C:\javasrc>
```

The warning is simple: the Date constructor that takes three integer arguments has
been deprecated. How do you fix it? The answer is, as in most questions of usage, to
refer to the javadoc documentation for the class. The introduction to the Date page
says, in part:

> The class Date represents a specific instant in time, with millisecond precision.
>
> Prior to JDK 1.1, the class Date had two additional functions. It allowed the interpreta-
> tion of dates as year, month, day, hour, minute, and second values. It also allowed the
> formatting and parsing of date strings. Unfortunately, the API for these functions was
> not amenable to internationalization. As of JDK 1.1, the Calendar class should be used
> to convert between dates and time fields and the DateFormat class should be used to
> format and parse date strings. The corresponding methods in Date are deprecated.

And more specifically, in the description of the three-integer constructor, the Date
javadoc says:

> Date(int year, int month, int date)
>
> Deprecated. As of JDK version 1.1, replaced by Calendar.set(year + 1900, month,
> date) or GregorianCalendar(year + 1900, month, date).

Of course, the older Date class is replaced by LocalDate and LocalDateTime (see
Chapter 6), so you'd only see that particular example in legacy code, but the principles
of dealing with deprecation warnings matter, because many new releases of Java add
deprecation warnings to parts of the API that were previously "OK" to use.

As a general rule, when something has been deprecated, you should not use it in any
new code; and, when maintaining code, strive to eliminate the deprecation warnings.

In addition to `Date` (Java 8 includes a whole new date/time API; see Chapter 6), the main areas of deprecation warnings in the standard API are the really ancient event handling and some methods (a few of them important) in the `Thread` class.

You can also deprecate your own code, when you come up with a better way of doing things. Put an `@Deprecated` annotation immediately before the class or method you wish to deprecate and/or use a `@deprecated` tag in a javadoc comment (see Recipe 15.2). The javadoc comment allows you to explain the deprecation, whereas the annotation is easier for some tools to recognize because it is present at runtime (so you can use Reflection; see Chapter 17).

See Also

Numerous other tools perform extra checking on your Java code. See my Checking Java Programs (*https://cjp.darwinsys.com/*) website.

1.10 Maintaining Code Correctness with Unit Testing: JUnit

Problem

You don't want to have to debug your code.

Solution

Use unit testing to validate each class as you develop it.

Discussion

Stopping to use a debugger is time-consuming, and finding a bug in released code is much worse! It's better to *test* beforehand. The methodology of unit testing has been around for a long time; it is a tried-and-true means of getting your code tested in small blocks. Typically, in an OO language like Java, unit testing is applied to individual classes, in contrast to system or integration testing where a complete slice or even the entire application is tested.

I have long been an advocate of this very basic testing methodology. Indeed, developers of the software methodology known as Extreme Programming (*http://www.extremeprogramming.org*) (XP for short) advocate *Test-Driven Development* (TDD): writing the unit tests *before* you write the code. They also advocate running your tests almost every time you build your application. And they ask one good question: *If you don't have a test, how do you know your code (still) works?* This group of unit-testing advocates has some well-known leaders, including Erich Gamma of

Design Patterns book fame and Kent Beck of *eXtreme Programming* book fame (both Addison-Wesley). I definitely go along with their advocacy of unit testing.

Indeed, many of my classes used to come with a "built-in" unit test. Classes that are not main programs in their own right would often include a main method that just tests out or at least exercises the functionality of the class. What surprised me is that, before encountering XP, I used to think I did this often, but an actual inspection of two projects indicated that only about a third of my classes had test cases, either internally or externally. Clearly what is needed is a uniform methodology. That is provided by JUnit.

JUnit is a Java-centric methodology for providing test cases, and can be downloaded for free (*http://www.junit.org*). It is a very simple but useful testing tool. It is easy to use—you just write a test class that has a series of methods and annotate them with @Test (the older JUnit 3.8 required you to have test methods' names begin with test). JUnit uses introspection (see Chapter 17) to find all these methods and then runs them for you. Extensions to JUnit handle tasks as diverse as load testing and testing enterprise components; the JUnit website provides links to these extensions. All modern IDEs provide built-in support for generating and running JUnit tests.

How do you get started using JUnit? All that's necessary is to write a test. Here I have written a simple test of my Person class and placed it into a class called PersonTest (note the obvious naming pattern):

```java
public class PersonTest {

    @Test
    public void testNameConcat() {
        Person p = new Person("Ian", "Darwin");
        String f = p.getFullName();
        assertEquals("Name concatenation", "Ian Darwin", f);
    }
}
```

JUnit 4 has been around for ages and works well. JUnit 5 is only a few years old and has some improvements. A simple test like this PersonTest class will be the same in JUnit 4 or 5 (but with different imports). Using additional features, like setup methods to be run before each test, requires different annotations between JUnit 4 and 5.

To show you running PersonTest manually, I compile the test and invoke the command-line test harness TestRunner:

```
$ javac PersonTest.java
$ java -classpath .:junit4.x.x.jar junit.textui.TestRunner testing.PersonTest
.
Time: 0.188

OK (1 tests)

$
```

In practice, running tests that way is incredibly tedious, so I just put my tests in the standard directory structure (i.e., *src/test/java/*) with the same package as the code being tested and run Maven (see Recipe 1.7), which will automatically compile and run all the unit tests and will halt the build if any test fails, *every time you try to build, package, or deploy your application.* Gradle will do so too.

All modern IDEs provide built-in support for running JUnit tests; in Eclipse, you can right-click a project in the Package Explorer and select Run As→Unit Test to have it find and run all the JUnit tests in the entire project. The MoreUnit plugin (free in the Eclipse Marketplace) aims to simplify creation and running of tests.

The *Hamcrest matchers* allow you to write more expressive tests at the cost of an additional download. Support for them is built into JUnit 4 with the assertThat static method, but you need to download the matchers from Hamcrest (*http://hamcrest.org*) or via the Maven artifact.

Here's an example of using the Hamcrest matchers:

```
public class HamcrestDemo {

    @Test
    public void testNameConcat() {
        Person p = new Person("Ian", "Darwin");
        String f = p.getFullName();
        assertThat(f, containsString("Ian"));
        assertThat(f, equalTo("Ian Darwin"));
        assertThat(f, not(containsString("/"))); // contrived, to show syntax
    }
}
```

See Also

JUnit offers considerable documentation of its own; download it from the website listed earlier.

An alternative unit test framework for Java is *TestNG*; it got some early traction by adopting features such as Java annotations before JUnit did; but since JUnit got with the annotations program, it has remained the dominant package for Java unit testing.

Another package of interest is AssertJ (*https://assertj.github.io/doc*), which appears to offer similar power to the combination of JUnit with Hamcrest.

Finally, one often needs to create substitute objects for use by the class being tested (the dependencies of the class under test). While you can code these by hand, in general I encourage use of packages such as Mockito (*https://site.mockito.org*), which can generate *mock objects* dynamically, have these mocks provide fixed return values, verify that the dependencies were called correctly, and so on.

Remember: *test early and often!*

1.11 Maintaining Your Code with Continuous Integration

Problem

You want to be sure that your entire code base compiles and passes its tests periodically.

Solution

Use a Continuous Integration server such as Jenkins/Hudson.

Discussion

If you haven't previously used Continuous Integration, you are going to wonder how you got along without it. CI is simply the practice of having all developers on a project periodically *integrate* (e.g., commit) their changes into a single master copy of the project's source and then building and testing the project to make sure it still works and passes its tests. This might be a few times a day, or every few days, but should not be more than that or else the integration will likely run into larger hurdles where multiple developers have modified the same file.

But it's not just big projects that benefit from CI. Even on a one-person project, it's great to have a single button you can click that will check out the latest version of everything, compile it, link or package it, run all the automated tests, and give a red or green pass/fail indicator. Better yet, it can do this automatically every day or even on every commit to the master branch.

It's not just code-based projects that benefit from CI. If you have a number of small websites, putting them all under CI control is one of several important steps toward developing an automated, DevOps culture around website deployment and management.

If you are new to the idea of CI, I can do no better than to plead with you to read Martin Fowler's insightful (as ever) paper on the topic (*http://martinfowler.com/arti cles/continuousIntegration.html*). One of the key points is to automate both the *management* of the code *and* all the other artifacts needed to build your project, and to automate the actual process of *building* it, possibly using one of the build tools discussed earlier in this chapter.[1]

There are many CI servers, both free and commercial. In the open source world, CruiseControl (*http://cruisecontrol.sourceforge.net*) and Jenkins/Hudson[2] are among the best known CI servers that you deploy yourself. There are also hosted solutions such as Travis CI (*https://travis-ci.com*), TeamCity (*https://www.jetbrains.com/teamcity*), or CircleCI (*https://circleci.com*). These hosted ones eliminate the need for setting up and running your own CI server. They also tend to have their configuration right in your repo (*travis.yml* etc.) so deployment to them is simplified.

Jenkins runs as a web application, either inside a Jakarta EE server or in its own standalone web server. Once it's started, you can use any standard web browser as its user interface. Installing and starting Jenkins can be as simple as unpacking a distribution and invoking it as follows:

```
java -jar jenkins.war
```

This will start up its own tiny web server. If you do that, be sure to configure security if your machine is reachable from the internet!

Many people find it more secure to run Jenkins in a full-function Java EE or Java web server; anything from Tomcat to JBoss to WebSphere or Weblogic will do the job and let you impose additional security constraints.

Once Jenkins is up and running and you have enabled security and are logged in on an account with sufficient privilege, you can create *jobs*. A job usually corresponds to one project, both in terms of origin (one source code checkout) and in terms of results (one *.war* file, one executable, one library, one whatever). Setting up a project is as simple as clicking the New Job button at the top left of the dashboard, as shown in Figure 1-6.

You can fill in the first few pieces of information: the project's name and a brief description. Note that each and every input field has a question mark icon beside it, which will give you hints as you go along. Don't be afraid to peek at these hints! Figure 1-7 shows the first few steps of setting up a new job.

In the next few sections of the form, Jenkins uses dynamic HTML to make entry fields appear based on what you've checked. My demo project "TooSmallToFail" starts

---

1 If the deployment or build includes a step like "Get Smith to process file X on his desktop and copy to the server," you probably don't quite get the notion of automated testing.

2 Jenkins (*http://jenkins-ci.org*) and Hudson (*https://www.eclipse.org/hudson*) began as Hudson, largely written by Kohsuke Kawaguchi while working for Sun Microsystems. There was later a cultural spat that resulted in Jenkins splitting off from Hudson, creating a new fork of the project. Kohsuke works on the half now known as Jenkins. I'll just use the name Jenkins, because that's the one I use, and because it takes too long to say "Jenkins/Hudson" all the time. But almost everything here applies to Hudson as well.

off with no Source Code Management (SCM) repository, but your real project is probably already in Git, Subversion, or ome other SCM. Don't worry if yours is not listed; there are hundreds of plug-ins to handle almost any SCM. Once you've chosen your SCM, you will enter the parameters to fetch the project's source from that SCM repository, using text fields that ask for the specifics needed for that SCM: a URL for Git, a CVSROOT for CVS, and so on.

Figure 1-6. The dashboard in Jenkins

Figure 1-7. Creating a new job in Jenkins

You also have to tell Jenkins *when* and *how* to build (and package, test, deploy…) your project. For the *when*, you have several choices such as building it after another Jenkins project, building it every so often based on a cron-like schedule, or based on polling the SCM to see if anything has changed (using the same cron-like scheduler). If your project is at GitHub (not just a local Git server), or some other SCMs, you can have the project built whenever somebody pushes changes up to the repository. It's all a matter of finding the right plug-ins and following the documentation for them.

Then we have the *how*, or the build process. Again, a few build types are included with Jenkins, and many more are available as plug-ins: I've used Apache Maven, Gradle, the traditional Unix make tool, and even shell or command lines. As before, text fields specific to your chosen tool will appear once you select the tool. In the toy example, TooSmallToFail, I just use the shell command */bin/false* (which should be present on any Unix or Linux system) to ensure that the project does, in fact, fail to build, just so you can see what that looks like.

You can have zero or more build steps; just keep clicking the Add button and add additional ones, as shown in Figure 1-8.

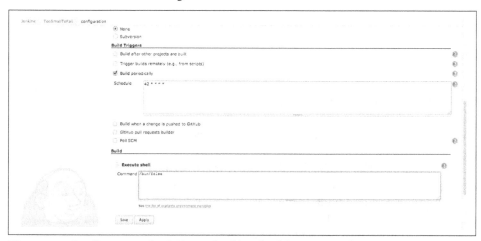

Figure 1-8. Configuration for SCM and adding build steps in Jenkins

Once you think you've entered all the necessary information, click the Save button at the bottom of the page, and you'll go back to the project's main page. Here you can click the funny little Build Now icon at the far left to initiate a build right away. Or if you have set up build triggers, you could wait until they kick in; but then again, wouldn't you rather know right away whether you've got it just right? Figure 1-9 shows the build starting.

Should a job fail to build, you get a red ball instead of a green one. Actually, a successful build shows a blue ball by default (the *go* bulb in Japanese traffic lights, where Kohsuke lives, is blue rather than green), but most people outside Japan prefer green for success, so the optional Green Balls plug-in is often one of the first to be added to a new installation.

Beside the red or green ball, you will see a weather report ranging from sunny (the last several builds have succeeded) to cloudy, rainy, or stormy (no recent builds have succeeded).

Click the link to the project that failed, and then the link to Console Output, and figure out what went wrong. The usual workflow is then to make changes to the project, commit/push them to the source code repository, and run the Jenkins build again.

Figure 1-9. After a new job is added in Jenkins

There are *hundreds* of optional plug-ins for Jenkins. To make your life easier, almost all of them can be installed by clicking the Manage Jenkins link and then going to Manage Plug-ins. The Available tab lists all the ones that are available from Jenkins.org; you just need to click the checkbox beside the ones you want, and click Apply. You can also find updates there. If your plug-in addtion or upgrade requires a restart, you'll see a yellow ball and words to that effect; otherwise you should see a green (or blue) ball indicating plug-in success. You can also see the list of plug-ins directly on the web (*https://wiki.jenkins-ci.org/display/JENKINS/Plugins*).

I mentioned that Jenkins began life under the name Hudson. The Hudson project still exists and is hosted at the Eclipse website. Last I checked, both projects had maintained plug-in compatibility, so many or most plug-ins from one can be used with the other. In fact, the most popular plug-ins appear in the Available tab of both, and most of what's said in this recipe about Jenkins applies equally to Hudson. If you use a different CI system, you'll need to check that system's documentation, but the concepts and the benefits will be similar.

1.12 Getting Readable Stack Traces

Problem

You're getting an exception stack trace at runtime, but most of the important parts don't have line numbers.

Solution

Be sure you have compiled with debugging enabled.

Discussion

When a Java program throws an exception, the exception propagates up the call stack until there is a catch clause that matches it. If none is found, the Java interpreter program that invoked your main() method catches the exception and prints a stack traceback showing all the method calls that got from the top of the program to the place where the exception was thrown. You can print this traceback yourself in any catch clause: the Throwable class has several overloads of the method called print StackTrace().

The traceback includes line numbers only if they were compiled in. When using *javac*, this is the default. If you add the -g option, *javac* will also include local variable names and other information in the compiled code, which will make for better debugging information in the event of a crash.

1.13 Finding More Java Source Code

Problem

You want to build a large application and need to minimize coding, avoiding the "Not Invented Here" syndrome.

Solution

Use the Source, Luke. There are thousands of Java apps, frameworks, and libraries available in open source.

Discussion

Java source code is everywhere. As mentioned earlier, all the code examples from this book can be downloaded: see Recipe 1.6.

Another valuable resource is the source code for the Java API. You may not have realized it, but the source code for all the public parts of the Java API are included with each release of the Java Development Kit. Want to know how java.util.ArrayList actually works? You have the source code. Got a problem making a JTable behave? The standard JDK includes the source for all the public classes! Look for a file called *src.zip* or *src.jar*; some versions unzip this and some do not.

If that's not enough, you can get the source for the whole JDK for free over the internet, either via the Mercurial source code librarian at *openjdk.java.net* (*http://*

hg.openjdk.java.net/jdk/jdk) or from the Git mirror at AdoptOpenJDK at *github.com* (*https://github.com/AdoptOpenJDK/openjdk-jdk*). This includes the source for the public and nonpublic parts of the API, as well as the compiler (written in Java) and a large body of code written in C/C++ (the runtime itself and the interfaces to the native library). For example, `java.io.Reader` has a method called `read()`, which reads bytes of data from a file or network connection. There is a version of this written in C for each operating system because it calls down to the `read()` system call for Unix, Windows, macOS, or whatever. The JDK source kit includes the source for all this stuff.

1.14 Finding Runnable Java Libraries

Problem

You want to reuse a published library rather than reinventing a well-known solution to your problem at hand.

Solution

Use the internet to find reusable software.

Discussion

Although most of this book is about writing Java code, this recipe is about *not* writing code, but about using code written by others. There are hundreds of good frameworks to add to your Java application—why reinvent the flat tire when you can buy a perfectly round one? Many of these frameworks have been around for years and have become well rounded by feedback from users.

What, though, is the difference between a library and a framework? It's sometimes a bit vague, but in general, a framework is a program with holes that you fill in, whereas a library is code you call. It is roughly the difference between building a car by buying a car almost complete but with no engine and building a car by buying all the pieces and bolting them together yourself.

When considering using a third-party framework, there are many choices and issues to consider. One is cost, which gets into the issue of open source versus closed source. Most open source tools can be downloaded for free and used, either without any conditions or with conditions that you must comply with. There is not the space here to discuss these licensing issues, so I will refer you to *Understanding Open Source and Free Software Licensing* (O'Reilly).

Much open source software is available in compiled library form on Maven Central, as discussed in "Maven Central: Mapping the World of Java Software" on page 26.

Some well-known collections of open source frameworks and libraries for Java are listed in Table 1-5. Most of the projects on these sites are curated—that is, judged and found worthy—by some sort of community process.

Table 1-5. Reputable open source Java collections

Organization	URL	Notes
Apache Software Foundation	*http://projects.apache.org*	Not just a web server!
Eclipse Software Foundation	*https://eclipse.org/projects*	Home of IDE and of Jakarta EE
Spring Framework	*http://spring.io/projects*	Home to a dozen frameworks: Spring IOC (DI factory), Spring MVC (web), more
JBoss community	*https://redhatofficial.github.io/*	Lists half a dozen of their projects, plus a long list of current open source projects they use and/or support.
Codehaus	—	See footnote[a]

[a] Codehaus itself went offline a few years ago. As of 2019, the domain is owned by the Apache Software Foundation but does not respond to browser requests. There is also a Codehaus account on github (*https://github.com/codehaus*) holding some of the projects that were previously on Codehaus, some active and some not. See this article (*https://www.javaworld.com/article/2892227/codehaus-the-once-great-house-of-code-has-fallen.html*) for more on the history of Codehaus.

There are also a variety of open source code repositories, which are not curated—anybody who signs up can create a project there, regardless of the existing community size (if any). Sites like this that are successful accumulate too many projects to have a single page listing them—you have to search. Most are not specific to Java. Table 1-6 shows some of the open source code repos.

Table 1-6. Open source code repositories

Name	URL	Notes
Sourceforge.net	*https://sourceforge.net/*	One of the oldest
GitHub	*http://github.com/*	"Social Coding"; probably most heavily used, now owned by Microsoft
Bitbucket	*https://bitbucket.org/*	Public and private repos; free and paid plans
GitLab	*https://gitlab.org/*	Public and private repos; free and paid plans
Maven Central	*https://search.maven.org/*	Has compiled jar, source jar and javadoc jar for each project

I'm not trying to disparage these repositories—indeed, the collection of demo programs for this book is hosted on GitHub. I'm only saying that you have to know what you're looking for and exercise a bit of care before deciding on a framework. Is there a community around it, or is it a dead end?

I maintain a small Java site (*https://darwinsys.com/java*) that may be of value. It includes a listing of Java resources and material related to this book.

For the Java enterprise or web tier, there are two main frameworks that also provide dependency injection: the first is JavaServer Faces (JSF) and CDI, and the second is the Spring Framework SpringMVC package. JSF and the built-in CDI (Contexts and Dependency Injection) provides DI as well as some additional contexts, such as a very useful Web Conversation context that holds objects across multiple web page interactions. The Spring Framework provides dependency injection and the SpringMVC web-tier helper classes. Table 1-7 shows some web tier resources. Spring MVC and JSF are far from the only web frameworks; the list in Table 1-7 includes many others, which may be a better fit for your application. You have to decide!

Table 1-7. Web tier resources

Name	URL	Notes
Ian's List of 100 Java Web Frameworks	*http://darwinsys.com/jwf/*	
JSF	*http://www.oracle.com/technetwork/java/javaee/overview/*	Java EE standard technology for web pages

Because JSF is a component-based framework, there are many add-on components that will make your JSF-based website much more capable (and better looking) than the default JSF components. Table 1-8 shows some of the JSF add-on libraries.

Table 1-8. JSF add-on libraries

Name	URL	Notes
BootsFaces	*https://bootsfaces.net/*	Combines BootStrap with JSF
ButterFaces	*http://butterfaces.org/*	Rich components library
ICEfaces	*http://icefaces.org/*	Rich components library
OpenFaces	*http://openfaces.org/*	Rich components library
PrimeFaces	*http://primefaces.org/*	Rich components library
RichFaces	*http://richfaces.org/*	Rich components; no longer maintained
Apache DeltaSpike	*http://deltaspike.apache.org/*	Numerous code add-ons for JSF
JSFUnit	*http://www.jboss.org/jsfunit/*	JUnit Testing for JSF
OmniFaces	*http://omnifaces.org/*	JSF Utilities add-on

There are frameworks and libraries for almost everything these days. If my lists don't lead you to what you need, a web search probably will. Try not to reinvent the flat tire!

As with all free software, be sure that you understand the ramifications of the various licensing schemes. Code covered by the GPL, for example, automatically transfers the GPL to any code that uses even a small part of it. Consult a lawyer. Your mileage may vary. Despite these caveats, the source code is an invaluable resource to the person who wants to learn more Java.

## CHAPTER 2

Interacting with the Environment

2.0 Introduction

This chapter describes how your Java program can deal with its immediate surroundings with what we call the runtime environment. In one sense, everything you do in a Java program using almost any Java API involves the environment. Here we focus more narrowly on things that directly surround your program. Along the way we'll be introduced to the System class, which knows a lot about your particular system.

Two other runtime classes deserve brief mention. The first, java.lang.Runtime, lies behind many of the methods in the System class. System.exit(), for example, just calls Runtime.exit(). Runtime is technically part of the environment, but the only time we use it directly is to run other programs, which is covered in Recipe 18.1.

2.1 Getting Environment Variables

Problem

You want to get the value of environment variables from within your Java program.

Solution

Use System.getenv().

Discussion

The seventh edition of Unix, released in 1979, had a new feature known as environment variables. Environment variables are in all modern Unix systems (including macOS) and in most later command-line systems, such as the DOS or Command

Prompt in Windows, but they are not in some older platforms or other Java runtimes. Environment variables are commonly used for customizing an individual computer user's runtime environment, hence the name. To take one familiar example, on Unix or DOS the environment variable PATH determines where the system looks for executable programs. So, of course people want to know how they access environment variables from their Java program.

The answer is that you can do this in all modern versions of Java, but you should exercise caution in depending on being able to specify environment variables because some rare operating systems may not provide them. That said, it's unlikely you'll run into such a system because all "standard" desktop systems provide them at present.

In some ancient versions of Java, System.getenv() was deprecated and/or just didn't work. Nowadays the getenv() method is no longer deprecated, though it still carries the warning that system properties (see Recipe 2.2) should be used instead. Even among systems that support environment variables, their names are case sensitive on some platforms and case insensitive on others. The code in Example 2-1 is a short program that uses the getenv() method.

Example 2-1. main/src/main/java/environ/GetEnv.java

```
public class GetEnv {
    public static void main(String[] argv) {
        System.out.println("System.getenv(\"PATH\") = " + System.getenv("PATH"));
    }
}
```

Running this code will produce output similar to the following:

```
C:\javasrc>java environ.GetEnv
System.getenv("PATH") = C:\windows\bin;c:\jdk1.8\bin;c:\documents
    and settings\ian\bin
C:\javasrc>
```

The no-argument form of the method System.getenv() returns *all* the environment variables in the form of an immutable String Map. You can iterate through this map and access all the user's settings or retrieve multiple environment settings.

Both forms of getenv() require you to have permissions to access the environment, so they typically do not work in restricted environments such as applets.

2.2 Getting Information from System Properties

Problem

You need to get information from the system properties.

Solution

Use `System.getProperty()` or `System.getProperties()`.

Discussion

What is a *property* anyway? A property is just a name and value pair stored in a `java.util.Properties` object, which we discuss more fully in Recipe 7.10.

The `System.Properties` object controls and describes the Java runtime. The `System` class has a static `Properties` member whose content is the merger of operating system specifics (`os.name`, for example), system and user tailoring (`java.class.path`), and properties defined on the command line (as we'll see in a moment). Note that the use of periods in these names (like `os.arch`, `os.version`, `java.class.path`, and `java.lang.version`) makes it look as though there is a hierarchical relationship similar to that for package/class names. The `Properties` class, however, imposes no such relationships: each key is just a string, and dots are not special.

To view all the defined system properties, you can iterate through the output of calling `System.getProperties()` as in Example 2-2.

Example 2-2. jshell System.getProperties()

```
jshell> System.getProperties().forEach((k,v) -> System.out.println(k + "->" +v))
awt.toolkit->sun.awt.X11.XToolkit
java.specification.version->11
sun.cpu.isalist->
sun.jnu.encoding->UTF-8
java.class.path->.
java.vm.vendor->Oracle Corporation
sun.arch.data.model->64
java.vendor.url->http://java.oracle.com/
user.timezone->
os.name->OpenBSD
java.vm.specification.version->11
... many more ...
jshell>
```

Remember that properties whose names begin with "sun" are unsupported and subject to change.

To retrieve one system-provided property, use `System.getProperty(propName)`. If I just wanted to find out if the `System Properties` had a property named `"pencil_color"`, I could say:

```
String sysColor = System.getProperty("pencil_color");
```

But what does that return? Surely Java isn't clever enough to know about everybody's favorite pencil color? Right you are! But we can easily tell Java about our pencil color (or anything else we want to tell it) using the -D argument.

When starting a Java runtime, you can define a value in the system properties object using a -D option. Its argument must have a name, an equals sign, and a value, which are parsed the same way as in a properties file (see Recipe 7.10). You can have more than one -D definition between the java command and your class name on the command line. At the Unix or Windows command line, type:

```
java -D"pencil_color=Deep Sea Green" environ.SysPropDemo
```

When running this under an IDE, put the variable's name and value in the appropriate dialog box, for example, in Eclipse's Run Configuration dialog under Program Arguments. You can also set environment variables and system properties using the build tools (Maven, Gradle, etc.).

The SysPropDemo program has code to extract just one or a few properties, so you can run it like this:

```
$ java environ.SysPropDemo os.arch
os.arch = x86
```

If you invoke the SysPropDemo program with no arguments, it outputs the same information as the jshell fragment in Example 2-2.

Which reminds me—this is a good time to mention system-dependent code. Recipe 2.3 talks about OS-dependent code and release-dependent code.

See Also

Recipe 7.10 lists more details on using and naming your own Properties files. The javadoc page for java.util.Properties lists the exact rules used in the load() method, as well as other details.

2.3 Dealing with Code That Depends on the Java Version or the Operating System

Problem

You need to write code that adapts to the underlying operating system.

Solution

You can use `System.Properties` to find out the Java version and the operating system, various features in the `File` class to find out some platform-dependent features, and `java.awt.TaskBar` to see if you can use the system-dependent Taskbar or Dock.

Discussion

Some things depend on the version of Java you are running. Use `System.getProperty()` with an argument of `java.specification.version`.

Alternatively, and with greater generality, you may want to test for the presence or absence of particular classes. One way to do this is with `Class.forName("class")` (see Chapter 17), which throws an exception if the class cannot be loaded—a good indication that it's not present in the runtime's library. Example 2-3 shows code for this, from an application wanting to find out whether the common Swing UI components are available. The javadoc for the standard classes reports the version of the JDK in which this class first appeared, under the heading "Since." If there is no such heading, it normally means that the class has been present since the beginnings of Java:

Example 2-3. main/src/main/java/starting/CheckForSwing.java

```java
public class CheckForSwing {
    public static void main(String[] args) {
        try {
            Class.forName("javax.swing.JButton");
        } catch (ClassNotFoundException e) {
            String failure =
                "Sorry, but this version of MyApp needs \n" +
                "a Java Runtime with JFC/Swing components\n" +
                "having the final names (javax.swing.*)";
            // Better to make something appear in the GUI. Either a
            // JOptionPane, or: myPanel.add(new Label(failure));
            System.err.println(failure);
        }
        // No need to print anything here - the GUI should work...
    }
}
```

It's important to distinguish between testing this code at compile time and at runtime. In both cases, it must be compiled on a system that includes the classes you are testing for: JDK >= 1.1 and Swing, respectively. These tests are only attempts to help the poor backwater Java runtime user trying to run your up-to-date application. The goal is to provide this user with a message more meaningful than the simple "class not found" error that the runtime gives. It's also important to note that this test becomes unreachable if you write it inside any code that depends on the code you are testing.

Put the test early in the main flow of your application, before any GUI objects are constructed. Otherwise the code just sits there wasting space on newer runtimes and never gets run on Java systems that don't include Swing. Obviously this is a very early example, but you can use the same technique to test for any runtime feature added at any stage of Java's evolution (see Appendix A for an outline of the features added in each release of Java). You can also use this technique to determine whether a needed third-party library has been successfully added to your CLASSPATH.

Also, although Java is designed to be portable, some things aren't. These include such variables as the filename separator. Everybody on Unix knows that the filename separator is a slash character (/) and that a backward slash, or backslash (\), is an escape character. Back in the late 1970s, a group at Microsoft was actually working on Unix —their version was called Xenix, later taken over by SCO—and the people working on DOS saw and liked the Unix filesystem model. The earliest versions of MS-DOS didn't have directories; it just had user numbers like the system it was a clone of, Digital Research CP/M (itself a clone of various other systems). So the Microsoft developers set out to clone the Unix filesystem organization. Unfortunately, MS-DOS had already committed the slash character for use as an option delimiter, for which Unix had used a dash (-); and the PATH separator (:) was also used as a drive letter delimiter, as in C: or A:. So we now have commands like those shown in Table 2-1.

Table 2-1. Directory listing commands

System	Directory list command	Meaning	Example PATH setting
Unix	*ls -R /*	Recursive listing of /, the top-level directory	*PATH=/bin:/usr/bin*
DOS	*dir/s *	Directory with subdirectories option (i.e., recursive) of \, the top-level directory (but only of the current drive)	*PATH=C:\windows;D:\mybin*

Where does this get us? If we are going to generate filenames in Java, we may need to know whether to put a / or a \ or some other character. Java has two solutions to this. First, when moving between Unix and Microsoft systems, at least, it is *permissive*: either / or \ can be used,[1] and the code that deals with the operating system sorts it out. Second, and more generally, Java makes the platform-specific information available in a platform-independent way. For the file separator (and also the PATH separator), the `java.io.File` class makes available some static variables containing this information. Because the `File` class manages platform-dependent information, it makes sense to anchor this information here. The variables are shown in Table 2-2.

---

[1] When compiling strings for use on Windows, remember to double them because \ is an escape character in most places other than the MS-DOS command line: `String rootDir = "C:\\";`.

Table 2-2. Table 2-2. File properties

Name	Type	Meaning
separator	static String	The system-dependent filename separator character (e.g., / or \)
separatorChar	static char	The system-dependent filename separator character (e.g., / or \)
pathSeparator	static String	The system-dependent path separator character, represented as a string for convenience
pathSeparatorChar	static char	The system-dependent path separator character

Both filename and path separators are normally characters, but they are also available in String form for convenience.

A second, more general, mechanism is the System Properties object mentioned in Recipe 2.2. You can use this to determine the operating system you are running on. Here is code that simply lists the system properties; it can be informative to run this on several different implementations:

```
public class SysPropDemo {
    public static void main(String[] argv) throws IOException {
        if (argv.length == 0) {
            // tag::sysprops[]
            System.getProperties().list(System.out);
            // end::sysprops[]
        } else {
            for (String s : argv) {
                System.out.println(s + " = " +
                    System.getProperty(s));
            }
        }
    }
}
```

Some OSes, for example, provide a mechanism called the null device that can be used to discard output (typically used for timing purposes). Here is code that asks the system properties for the os.name and uses it to make up a name that can be used for discarding data (if no null device is known for the given platform, we return the name jnk, which means that on such platforms, we'll occasionally create, well, junk files; I just remove these files when I stumble across them):

```
package com.darwinsys.lang;

import java.io.File;

/** Some things that are system-dependent.
 * All methods are static.
 * @author Ian Darwin
 */
public class SysDep {
```

```
final static String UNIX_NULL_DEV = "/dev/null";
final static String WINDOWS_NULL_DEV = "NUL:";
final static String FAKE_NULL_DEV = "jnk";

/** Return the name of the null device on platforms which support it,
 * or "jnk" (to create an obviously well-named temp file) otherwise.
 * @return The name to use for output.
 */
public static String getDevNull() {

    if (new File(UNIX_NULL_DEV).exists()) {          ❶
        return UNIX_NULL_DEV;
    }

    String sys = System.getProperty("os.name");      ❷
    if (sys==null) {                                 ❸
        return FAKE_NULL_DEV;
    }
    if (sys.startsWith("Windows")) {                 ❹
        return WINDOWS_NULL_DEV;
    }
    return FAKE_NULL_DEV;                             ❺
  }
}
```

❶ If /dev/null exists, use it.

❷ If not, ask System properties if it knows the OS name.

❸ Nope, so give up, return jnk.

❹ We know it's Microsoft Windows, so use NUL:.

❺ All else fails, go with jnk.

Although Java's Swing GUI aims to be portable, Apple's implementation for macOS does not automatically do the right thing for everyone. For example, a JMenuBar menu container appears by default at the top of the application window. This is the norm on Windows and on most Unix platforms, but Mac users expect the menu bar for the active application to appear at the top of the screen. To enable normal behavior, you have to set the System property apple.laf.useScreenMenuBar to the value true before the Swing GUI starts up. You might want to set some other properties too, such as a short name for your application to appear in the menu bar (the default is the full class name of your main application class).

There is an example of this in the book's source code, at *src/main/java/gui/MacOsUi-Hints.java*.

There is probably no point in setting these properties unless you are, in fact, being run under macOS. How do you tell? Apple's recommended way is to check for the system property `mrj.runtime` and, if so, assume you are on macOS:

```
boolean isMacOS = System.getProperty("mrj.version") != null;
if (isMacOS) {
  System.setProperty("apple.laf.useScreenMenuBar", "true");
  System.setProperty("com.apple.mrj.application.apple.menu.about.name",
  "My Super App");
}
```

On the other hand, these properties are likely harmless on non-Mac systems, so you could just skip the test and set the two properties unconditionally.

Finally, the Mac's Dock or the Taskbar on most other systems can be accessed using the `java.awt.Taskbar` class that was added in Java 9. This is not discussed here, but there is an example `TaskbarDemo` in the `main/gui` subdirectory.

2.4 Using Extensions or Other Packaged APIs

Problem

You have a JAR file of classes you want to use.

Solution

Simply add the JAR file to your CLASSPATH.

Discussion

As you build more sophisticated applications, you will need to use more and more third-party libraries. You can add these to your CLASSPATH.

It used to be recommended that you drop these JAR files into the Java Extensions mechanism directory, typically something like *jdk1.x**jre**lib**ext*., instead of listing each JAR file in your CLASSPATH variable. However, this is no longer generally recommended and is no longer available in the latest JDKs. Instead, you may wish to use build tools like Maven (see Recipe 1.7) or Gradle, as well as IDEs, to automate the addition of JAR files to your CLASSPATH.

One reason I've never been fond of using the extensions directory is that it requires modifying the installed JDK or JRE, which can lead to maintenance issues and problems when a new JDK or JRE is installed.

Java 9 introduced a major change to Java, the Java 9 Modules system for program modularization, which we discuss in Recipe 2.5.

2.5 Using the Java Modules System

Problem

You are using Java 9 or later, and need to deal with the Modules mechanism.

Solution

Read on.

Discussion

Java's Modules system, formerly known as Project Jigsaw, was designed to handle the need to build large applications out of many small pieces. To an extent this problem had been solved by tools like Maven and Gradle, but the Modules system solves a slightly different problem than those tools. Maven or Gradle will find dependencies, download them, install them on your development and test runtimes, and package them into runnable JAR files. The Modules system is more concerned with the visbility of classes from one chunk of application code to another, typically provided by different developers who may not know or trust each other. As such, it is an admission that Java's original set of access modifiers—such as `public`, `private`, `protected`, and default visibility—was not sufficient for building large-scale applications.

What follows is a brief discussion of using JPMS, the Java Platform Module System, to import modules into your application. There is an introduction to creating your own modules in Chapter 15. For a more detailed presentation, you should refer to a book-length treatment such as *Java 9 Modularity: Patterns and Practices for Developing Maintainable Applications* (*http://shop.oreilly.com/product/0636920049494.do*) by Sander Mak and Paul Bakker (O'Reilly).

Java has always been a language for large-scale development. Object orientation is one of the keys: classes and objects group methods, and access modifiers can be applied so that public and private methods are clearly separated. When developing large applications, having just a single flat namespace of classes is still not enough. Enter packages: they gather classes into logical groups within their own namespace. Access control can be applied at the package level as well so that some classes are only accessible inside a package. Modules are the next logical step up. A module groups some number of related packages, has a distinct name, and can restrict access to some packages while exposing other packages to different modules as public API.

One thing to understand at the outset: JPMS is not a replacement for your existing build tool. Whether you use Maven, Gradle, Ant, or just dump all needed JAR files into a lib directory, you still need to do that. Also, don't confuse Maven's modules with JPMS modules; the former is the physical structuring of a project into subprojects, and the latter is something the Java platform (compiler, runtime) understands.

Usually when working with Java modules, each Java module will equate to a single Maven module.

When you're dealing with a tiny, self-contained program, you don't need to be concerned with modules. Just put all the necessary JAR files on your CLASSPATH at compile time and runtime, and all will be well. Probably.

You may see warning messages like this along the way:

```
Illegal reflective access by com.foo.Bar
    (file:/Users/ian/.m2/repository/com/foo/1.3.1/foo-1.3.1.jar)
    to field java.util.Properties.defaults
Please consider reporting this to the maintainers of com.foo.Bar
Use --illegal-access=warn to enable warnings of further
 illegal reflective access operations
All illegal access operations will be denied in a future release
```

The warning message comes about as a result of JPMS doing its job, checking that no types are accessed in encapsulated packages within a module. Such messages will go away over time as all public Java libraries and all apps being developed get modularized.

Why will all be well only "probably"? If you are using certain classes that were deprecated over the last few releases, things won't compile. For that, you must make the requisite modules available. In the *unsafe* subdirectory (also a Maven module) under javasrc, there is a class called LoadAverage. The load average is a feature of Unix/Linux systems that gives a rough measure of system load or busyness, by reporting the number of processes that are waiting to be run. There are almost always more processes running than CPU cores to run them on, so some always have to wait. Higher numbers mean a busier system with slower response.

Sun's unsupported Unsafe class has a method for obtaining the load average, on systems that support it. The code has to use the Reflection API (see Chapter 17) to obtain the Unsafe object; if you try to instantiate Unsafe directly you will get a SecurityException (this was the case before the Modules system). Once the instance is obtained and casted to Unsafe, you can invoke methods such as loadAverage() (Example 2-4).

Example 2-4. unsafe/src/main/java/unsafe/LoadAverage.java (use of Unsafe.java)

```java
public class LoadAverage {
    public static void main(String[] args) throws Exception {
        Field f = Unsafe.class.getDeclaredField("theUnsafe");
        f.setAccessible(true);
        Unsafe unsafe = (Unsafe) f.get(null);
        int nelem = 3;
        double loadAvg[] = new double[nelem];
        unsafe.getLoadAverage(loadAvg, nelem);
```

```
        for (double d : loadAvg) {
            System.out.printf("%4.2f ", d);
        }
        System.out.println();
    }
}
```

This code, which used to compile, gives warnings. If we are using Java Modules, we must modify our *module-info.java* file to tell the compiler and VM that we require use of the module with the semi-obvious name jdk.unsupported.

```
module javasrc.unsafe {
    requires jdk.unsupported;
        // others...
}
```

We'll say more about the module file format in Recipe 15.9.

Now that we have the code in place and the module file in the top level of the source folder, we can build the project, run the program, and compare its output against the system-level tool for displaying the load average, uptime. We'll still get the "internal proprietary API" warnings, but it works:

```
$ java -version
openjdk version "14-ea" 2020-03-17
OpenJDK Runtime Environment (build 14-ea+27-1339)
OpenJDK 64-Bit Server VM (build 14-ea+27-1339, mixed mode, sharing)
$ mvn clean package
[INFO] Scanning for projects...
[INFO]
[INFO] --------------------< com.darwinsys:javasrc-unsafe >--------------------
[INFO] Building javasrc - Unsafe 1.0.0-SNAPSHOT
[INFO] --------------------------------[ jar ]---------------------------------
[INFO]
[INFO] --- maven-clean-plugin:2.5:clean (default-clean) @ javasrc-unsafe ---
[INFO] Deleting /Users/ian/workspace/javasrc/unsafe/target
[INFO]
[INFO] --- maven-resources-plugin:2.6:resources (default-resources) @ javasrc-
unsafe ---
[INFO] Using 'UTF-8' encoding to copy filtered resources.
[INFO] skip non existing resourceDirectory /Users/ian/workspace/javasrc/
unsafe/src/main/resources
[INFO]
[INFO] --- maven-compiler-plugin:3.1:compile (default-compile) @ javasrc-unsafe
---
[INFO] Changes detected - recompiling the module!
[INFO] Compiling 2 source files to /Users/ian/workspace/javasrc/unsafe/target/
classes
[WARNING] /Users/ian/workspace/javasrc/unsafe/src/main/java/unsafe/LoadAver
age.java:[3,16] sun.misc.Unsafe is internal proprietary API and may be removed
in a future release
[WARNING] /Users/ian/workspace/javasrc/unsafe/src/main/java/unsafe/LoadAver
```

```
age.java:[12,27] sun.misc.Unsafe is internal proprietary API and may be removed
in a future release
[WARNING] /Users/ian/workspace/javasrc/unsafe/src/main/java/unsafe/LoadAver
age.java:[14,17] sun.misc.Unsafe is internal proprietary API and may be removed
in a future release
[WARNING] /Users/ian/workspace/javasrc/unsafe/src/main/java/unsafe/LoadAver
age.java:[14,34] sun.misc.Unsafe is internal proprietary API and may be removed
in a future release
[INFO]
[INFO] --- maven-resources-plugin:2.6:testResources (default-testResources) @
javasrc-unsafe ---
[INFO] Using 'UTF-8' encoding to copy filtered resources.
[INFO] skip non existing resourceDirectory /Users/ian/workspace/javasrc/
unsafe/src/test/resources
[INFO]
[INFO] --- maven-compiler-plugin:3.1:testCompile (default-testCompile) @
javasrc-unsafe ---
[INFO] No sources to compile
[INFO]
[INFO] --- maven-surefire-plugin:2.12.4:test (default-test) @ javasrc-unsafe ---
[INFO] No tests to run.
[INFO]
[INFO] --- maven-jar-plugin:2.4:jar (default-jar) @ javasrc-unsafe ---
[INFO] Building jar: /Users/ian/workspace/javasrc/unsafe/target/javasrc-
unsafe-1.0.0-SNAPSHOT.jar
[INFO] ------------------------------------------------------------------------
[INFO] BUILD SUCCESS
[INFO] ------------------------------------------------------------------------
[INFO] Total time:  4.668 s
[INFO] Finished at: 2020-01-05T14:53:55-05:00
[INFO] ------------------------------------------------------------------------
$
$ java -cp target/classes unsafe/LoadAverage
3.54 1.94 1.62
$ uptime
14:54  up 1 day, 21:50, 5 users, load averages: 3.54 1.94 1.62
$
```

Thankfully, it works and gives the same numbers as the standard Unix *uptime* command. At least, it works on Java 11. As the warnings imply, it *may* (i.e., probably will) be removed in a later release.

If you are building a more complex app, you will probably need to put together a more complete *module-info.java* file. But at this stage it's primarily a matter of requiring the modules you need. The standard Java API is divided into several modules, which you can list using the *java* command:

```
$ java --list-modules
java.base
java.compiler
java.datatransfer
java.desktop
```

```
java.instrument
java.logging
java.management
java.management.rmi
java.naming
java.net.http
java.prefs
java.rmi
java.scripting
java.se
java.security.jgss
java.security.sasl
java.smartcardio
java.sql
java.sql.rowset
java.transaction.xa
java.xml
java.xml.crypto
... plus a bunch of JDK modules ...
```

Of these, `java.base` is always available and doesn't need to be listed in your module file, `java.desktop` adds AWT and Swing for graphics, and `java.se` includes basically all of what used to be public API in the Java SDK. If our load average program wanted to display the result in a Swing window, for example, it would need to add this into its module file:

```
requires java.desktop;
```

When your application is big enough to be divided into tiers or layers, you will probably want to describe these modules using JPMS. Since that topic comes under the heading of packaging, it is described in Recipe 15.9.

## CHAPTER 3

Strings and Things

3.0 Introduction

Character strings are an inevitable part of just about any programming task. We use them for printing messages for the user; for referring to files on disk or other external media; and for people's names, addresses, and affiliations. The uses of strings are many, almost without number (actually, if you need numbers, we'll get to them in Chapter 5).

If you're coming from a programming language like C, you'll need to remember that String is a defined type (class) in Java—that is, a string is an object and therefore has methods. It is not an array of characters (though it contains one) and should not be thought of as an array. Operations like fileName.endsWith(".gif") and extension.equals(".gif") (and the equivalent ".gif".equals(extension)) are commonplace.[1]

Java old-timers should note that Java 11 and 12 added several new String methods, including indent(int n), stripLeading() and stripTrailing(), Stream<T> lines(), isBlank(), and transform(). Most of these provide obvious functionality; the last one allows applying an instance of a functional interface (see Recipe 9.0) to a string and returning the result of that operation.

Although we haven't discussed the details of the java.io package yet (we will, in Chapter 10), you need to be able to read text files for some of these programs. Even if you're not familiar with java.io, you can probably see from the examples of reading

---

1 The two .equals() calls are equivalent with the exception that the first can throw a NullPointerException while the second cannot.

text files that a `BufferedReader` allows you to read chunks of data and that this class has a very convenient `readLine()` method.

Going the other way, `System.out.println()` is normally used to print strings or other values to the terminal or standard output. String concatenation is commonly used here, like this:

```
System.out.println("The answer is " + result);
```

One caveat with string concatenation is that if you are appending a bunch of things, and a number and a character are concatenated at the front, they are added before concatenation due to Java's precedence rules. So don't do as I did in this contrived example:

```
int result = ...;
System.out.println(result + '=' + " the answer.");
```

Given that `result` is an integer, then `result + '='` (`result added to the equals sign, which is of the numeric type +char`) is a valid *numeric* expression, which will result in a single value of type `int`. If the variable `result` has the value 42, and given that the character = in a Unicode (or ASCII) code chart has the value 61, the two-line fragment would print:

```
103 the answer.
```

The wrong value and no equals sign! Safer approaches include using parentheses, double quotes around the equals sign, a `StringBuilder` (see Recipe 3.2), or `String.format()` (see Recipe 10.4). Of course in this simple example you could just move the = to be part of the string literal, but the example was chosen to illustrate the problem of arithmetic on `char` values being confused with string contatenation. I won't show you how to sort an array of strings here; the more general notion of sorting a collection of objects will be taken up in Recipe 7.11.

Java 14 enables text blocks, also known as multiline text strings. These are delimited with a set of three double quotes, the opening of which *must* have a newline after the quotes (which doesn't become part of the string; the following newlines do):

```
String long = """
This is a long
text String."""
```

Timeless, Immutable, and Unchangeable

Notice that a given `String` object, once constructed, is immutable. In other words, once I have said `String s = "Hello" + yourName;`, the contents of the particular object that reference variable s refers to can never be changed. You can assign s to refer to a different string, even one derived from the original, as in `s = s.trim()`. And you can retrieve characters from the original string using `charAt()`, but it isn't

---

called getCharAt() because there is not, and never will be, a setCharAt() method. Even methods like toUpperCase() don't change the String; they return a new String object containing the translated characters. If you need to change characters within a String, you should instead create a StringBuilder (possibly initialized to the starting value of the String), manipulate the StringBuilder to your heart's content, and then convert that to String at the end, using the ubiquitous toString() method.[2]

How can I be so sure they won't add a setCharAt() method in the next release? Because the immutability of strings is one of the fundamentals of the Java Virtual Machine. Immutable objects are generally good for software reliability (some languages do not even allow mutable objects). Immutability avoids conflicts, particularly where multiple threads are involved, or where software from multiple organizations has to work together; for example, you can safely pass immutable objects to a third-party library and expect that the objects will not be modifed.

It may be possible to tinker with the String's internal data structures using the Reflection API, as shown in Recipe 17.3, but then all bets are off. Secured environments do not permit access to the Reflection API, and the Java Modules system from Java 9 tightens reflective access to such internals even further.

Remember also that the String is a fundamental type in Java. Unlike most of the other classes in the core API, the behavior of strings is not changeable; the class is marked final so it cannot be subclassed. So you can't declare your own String subclass. Think if you could—you could masquerade as a String but provide a setCh arAt() method! Again, they thought of that. If you don't believe me, try it out:

```java
public class WolfInStringsClothing
    extends java.lang.String {//EXPECT COMPILE ERROR

    public void setCharAt(int index, char newChar) {
        // The implementation of this method
        // would be left as an exercise for the reader.
        // Hint: compile this code exactly as is before bothering!
    }
}
```

Got it? They thought of that!

Of course you do need to be able to modify strings. Some methods extract part of a String; these are covered in the first few recipes in this chapter. And StringBuilder is an important set of classes that deals in characters and strings and has many methods for changing the contents, including, of course, a toString() method. Reformed C programmers should note that Java strings are not arrays of chars as in C. Therefore you must use methods for such operations as processing a string one character at

---

2 StringBuilder was added in Java 5. It is functionally equivalent to the older StringBuffer. We will delve into the details in Recipe 3.2.

a time; see Recipe 3.3. Figure 3-1 shows an overview of String, StringBuilder, and C-language strings.

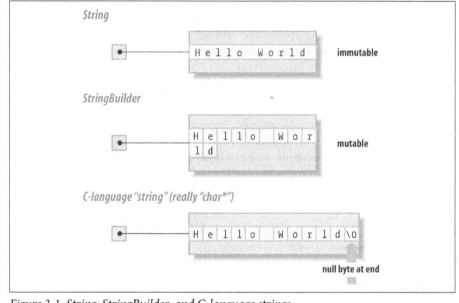

Figure 3-1. String, StringBuilder, and C-language strings

3.1 Taking Strings Apart with Substrings or Tokenizing

Problem

You want to break a string apart, either by indexing positions or by using fixed token characters (e.g., break on spaces to get words).

Solution

For substrings, use the String object's substring() method. For tokenizing, construct a StringTokenizer around your string and call its methods hasMoreTokens() and nextToken().

Or, use regular expressions (see Chapter 4).

Discussion

We'll look first at substrings, and then discuss tokenizing.

Substrings

The `substring()` method constructs a new `String` object made up of a run of characters contained somewhere in the original string, the one whose `substring()` you called. The `substring` method is overloaded: both forms require a starting index (which is always *zero-based*). The one-argument form returns from `startIndex` to the end. The two-argument form takes an ending index (not a length, as in some languages) so that an index can be generated by the `String` methods `indexOf()` or `last IndexOf()`:

```
public class SubStringDemo {
    public static void main(String[] av) {
        String a = "Java is great.";
        System.out.println(a);
        String b = a.substring(5);      // b is the String "is great."
        System.out.println(b);
        String c = a.substring(5,7);// c is the String "is"
        System.out.println(c);
        String d = a.substring(5,a.length());// d is "is great."
        System.out.println(d);
    }
}
```

When run, this prints the following:

```
C:> java strings.SubStringDemo
Java is great.
is great.
is
is great.
C:>
```

 Note that the end index is one beyond the last character! Java adopts this policy of having a half-open interval (or inclusive start, exclusive end) fairly consistently; there are good practical reasons for adopting this approach, and some other languages do so too.

Tokenizing

The easiest way is to use a regular expression. We'll discuss regular expressions in Chapter 4, but for now, a string containing a space is a valid regular expression to match space characters, so you can most easily split a string into words like this:

```
for (String word : some_input_string.split(" ")) {
    System.out.println(word);
}
```

If you need to match multiple spaces, or spaces and tabs, use the string `"\s+"`.

If you want to split a file, you can try the string "," or use one of several third-party libraries for CSV files.

Another method is to use `StringTokenizer`. The `StringTokenizer` methods implement the `Iterator` interface and design pattern (see Recipe 7.6):

main/src/main/java/strings/StrTokDemo.java

```
StringTokenizer st = new StringTokenizer("Hello World of Java");

while (st.hasMoreTokens( ))
    System.out.println("Token: " + st.nextToken( ));
```

`StringTokenizer` also implements the `Enumeration` interface (see Recipe 7.6), but if you use the methods thereof, you need to cast the results to `String`.

A `StringTokenizer` normally breaks the `String` into tokens at what we would think of as word boundaries in European languages. Sometimes you want to break at some other character. No problem. When you construct your `StringTokenizer`, in addition to passing in the string to be tokenized, pass in a second string that lists the break characters, like this:

main/src/main/java/strings/StrTokDemo2.java

```
StringTokenizer st = new StringTokenizer("Hello, World|of|Java", ", |");

while (st.hasMoreElements( ))
    System.out.println("Token: " + st.nextElement( ));
```

It outputs the four words, each on a line by itself, with no punctuation.

But wait, there's more! What if you are reading lines like

```
FirstName|LastName|Company|PhoneNumber
```

and your dear old Aunt Begonia hasn't been employed for the last 38 years? Her Company field will in all probability be blank.[3] If you look very closely at the previous code example, you'll see that it has two delimiters together (the comma and the space); but if you run it, there are no "extra" tokens—that is, the `StringTokenizer` normally discards adjacent consecutive delimiters. For cases like the phone list, where you need to preserve null fields, there is good news and bad news. The good news is that you can do it: you simply add a second argument of `true` when constructing the `StringTokenizer`, meaning that you wish to see the delimiters as tokens. The bad news is that you now get to see the delimiters as tokens, so you have to do the arithmetic yourself. Want to see it? Run this program:

main/src/main/java/strings/StrTokDemo3.java

---

3 Unless, perhaps, you're as slow at updating personal records as I am.

```
StringTokenizer st =
    new StringTokenizer("Hello, World|of|Java", ", |", true);

while (st.hasMoreElements( ))
    System.out.println("Token: " + st.nextElement( ));
```

You will get this output:

```
C:\>java strings.StrTokDemo3
Token: Hello
Token: ,
Token:
Token: World
Token: |
Token: of
Token: |
Token: Java
C:\>
```

This isn't how you'd like StringTokenizer to behave, ideally, but it is serviceable enough most of the time. Example 3-1 processes and ignores consecutive tokens, returning the results as an array of Strings.

Example 3-1. main/src/main/java/strings/StrTokDemo4.java (StringTokenizer)

```java
public class StrTokDemo4 {
    public final static int MAXFIELDS = 5;
    public final static String DELIM = "|";

    /** Processes one String, returns it as an array of Strings */
    public static String[] process(String line) {
        String[] results = new String[MAXFIELDS];

        // Unless you ask StringTokenizer to give you the tokens,
        // it silently discards multiple null tokens.
        StringTokenizer st = new StringTokenizer(line, DELIM, true);

        int i = 0;
        // Stuff each token into the current slot in the array.
        while (st.hasMoreTokens()) {
            String s = st.nextToken();
            if (s.equals(DELIM)) {
                if (i++>=MAXFIELDS)
                    // This is messy: See StrTokDemo4b which uses
                    // a List to allow any number of fields.
                    throw new IllegalArgumentException("Input line " +
                        line + " has too many fields");
                continue;
            }
            results[i] = s;
        }
        return results;
```

```
    }

    public static void printResults(String input, String[] outputs) {
        System.out.println("Input: " + input);
        for (String s : outputs)
            System.out.println("Output " + s + " was: " + s);
    }

    public static void main(String[] a) {
        printResults("A|B|C|D", process("A|B|C|D"));
        printResults("A||C|D", process("A||C|D"));
        printResults("A|||D|E", process("A|||D|E"));
    }
}
```

When you run this, you will see that A is always in Field 1, B (if present) is in Field 2, and so on. In other words, the null fields are being handled properly:

```
Input: A|B|C|D
Output 0 was: A
Output 1 was: B
Output 2 was: C
Output 3 was: D
Output 4 was: null
Input: A||C|D
Output 0 was: A
Output 1 was: null
Output 2 was: C
Output 3 was: D
Output 4 was: null
Input: A|||D|E
Output 0 was: A
Output 1 was: null
Output 2 was: null
Output 3 was: D
Output 4 was: E
```

See Also

Many occurrences of StringTokenizer may be replaced with regular expressions (see Chapter 4) with considerably more flexibility. For example, to extract all the numbers from a String, you can use this code:

```
Matcher tokenizer = Pattern.compile("\\d+").matcher(inputString);
while (tokenizer.find( )) {
        String courseString = tokenizer.group(0);
        int courseNumber = Integer.parseInt(courseString);
        ...
```

This allows user input to be more flexible than you could easily handle with a String Tokenizer. Assuming that the numbers represent course numbers at some educa-

---

tional institution, the inputs "471,472,570" or "Courses 471 and 472, 570" or just "471 472 570" should all give the same results.

3.2 Putting Strings Together with StringBuilder

Problem

You need to put some String pieces (back) together.

Solution

Use string concatenation: the + operator. The compiler implicitly constructs a StringBuilder for you and uses its append() methods (unless all the string parts are known at compile time).

Better yet, construct and use a StringBuilder yourself.

Discussion

An object of one of the StringBuilder classes basically represents a collection of characters. It is similar to a String object.[4] However, as mentioned, Strings are immutable; StringBuilders are mutable and designed for, well, building Strings. You typically construct a StringBuilder, invoke the methods needed to get the character sequence just the way you want it, and then call toString() to generate a String representing the same character sequence for use in most of the Java API, which deals in Strings.

StringBuffer is historical—it's been around since the beginning of time. Some of its methods are synchronized (see Recipe 16.5), which involves unneeded overhead in a single-threaded context. In Java 5, this class was split into StringBuffer (which is synchronized) and StringBuilder (which is not synchronized); thus, it is faster and preferable for single-threaded use. Another new class, AbstractStringBuilder, is the parent of both. In the following discussion, I'll use "the StringBuilder classes" to refer to all three because they mostly have the same methods.

The book's example code provides a StringBuilderDemo and a StringBufferDemo. Except for the fact that StringBuilder is not thread-safe, these API classes are identical and can be used interchangeably, so my two demo programs are almost identical except that each one uses the appropriate builder class.

---

4 String and StringBuilder have several methods that are forced to be identical by their implementation of the CharSequence interface.

The StringBuilder classes have a variety of methods for inserting, replacing, and otherwise modifying a given StringBuilder. Conveniently, the append() methods return a reference to the StringBuilder itself, so stacked statements like .append(…).append(…) are fairly common. This style of coding is referred to as a *fluent API* because it reads smoothly, like prose from a native speaker of a human language. You might even see this style of coding in a toString() method, for example. Example 3-2 shows three ways of concatenating strings.

Example 3-2. main/src/main/java/strings/StringBuilderDemo.java

```java
public class StringBuilderDemo {

    public static void main(String[] argv) {

        String s1 = "Hello" + ", " + "World";
        System.out.println(s1);

        // Build a StringBuilder, and append some things to it.
        StringBuilder sb2 = new StringBuilder();
        sb2.append("Hello");
        sb2.append(',');
        sb2.append(' ');
        sb2.append("World");

        // Get the StringBuilder's value as a String, and print it.
        String s2 = sb2.toString();
        System.out.println(s2);

        // Now do the above all over again, but in a more
        // concise (and typical "real-world" Java) fashion.

        System.out.println(
          new StringBuilder()
            .append("Hello")
            .append(',')
            .append(' ')
            .append("World"));
    }
}
```

In fact, all the methods that modify more than one character of a StringBuilder's contents (i.e., append(), delete(), deleteCharAt(), insert(), replace(), and reverse()) return a reference to the builder object to facilitate this fluent API style of coding.

As another example of using a StringBuilder, consider the need to convert a list of items into a comma-separated list while avoiding getting an extra comma after the last element of the list. This can be done using a StringBuilder, although in Java 8+

there is a static `String` method to do the same. Code for these are shown in Example 3-3.

Example 3-3. main/src/main/java/strings/StringBuilderCommaList.java

```
System.out.println(
    "Split using String.split; joined using 1.8 String join");
System.out.println(String.join(", ", SAMPLE_STRING.split(" ")));

System.out.println(
    "Split using String.split; joined using StringBuilder");
StringBuilder sb1 = new StringBuilder();
for (String word : SAMPLE_STRING.split(" ")) {
    if (sb1.length() > 0) {
        sb1.append(", ");
    }
    sb1.append(word);
}
System.out.println(sb1);

System.out.println(
    "Split using StringTokenizer; joined using StringBuilder");
StringTokenizer st = new StringTokenizer(SAMPLE_STRING);
StringBuilder sb2 = new StringBuilder();
while (st.hasMoreElements()) {
    sb2.append(st.nextToken());
    if (st.hasMoreElements()) {
        sb2.append(", ");
    }
}
System.out.println(sb2);
```

The first method is clearly the most compact; the static `String.join()` makes short work of this task. The next method uses the `StringBuilder.length()` method, so it will only work correctly when you are starting with an empty `StringBuilder`. The second method relies on calling the informational method `hasMoreElements()` in the `Enumeration` (or `hasNext()` in an `Iterator`, as discussed in Recipe 7.6) more than once on each element. An alternative method, particularly when you aren't starting with an empty builder, would be to use a `boolean` flag variable to track whether you're at the beginning of the list.

3.3 Processing a String One Character at a Time

Problem

You want to process the contents of a string, one character at a time.

Solution

Use a for loop and the String's charAt() or codePointAt() method. Or use a "for each" loop and the String's toCharArray method.

Discussion

A string's charAt() method retrieves a given character by index number (starting at zero) from within the String object. Since Unicode has had to expand beyond 16 bits, not all Unicode characters can fit into a Java char variable. There is thus an analogous codePointAt() method, whose return type is int. To process all the characters in a String, one after another, use a for loop ranging from zero to String.length()-1. Here we process all the characters in a String:

main/src/main/java/strings/strings/StrCharAt.java

```
public class StrCharAt {
    public static void main(String[] av) {
        String a = "A quick bronze fox";
        for (int i=0; i < a.length(); i++) { // no forEach, need the index
            String message = String.format(
                "charAt is '%c', codePointAt is %3d, casted it's '%c'",
                    a.charAt(i),
                    a.codePointAt(i),
                    (char)a.codePointAt(i));
            System.out.println(message);
        }
    }
}
```

Given that the "for each" loop has been in the language for ages, you might be excused for expecting to be able to write something like for (char ch : myString) {…}. Unfortunately, this does not work. But you can use myString.toCharArray() as in the following:

```
public class ForEachChar {
    public static void main(String[] args) {
        String mesg = "Hello world";

        // Does not compile, Strings are not iterable
        // for (char ch : mesg) {
        //      System.out.println(ch);
        // }

        System.out.println("Using toCharArray:");
        for (char ch : mesg.toCharArray()) {
            System.out.println(ch);
        }

        System.out.println("Using Streams:");
```

```
    mesg.chars().forEach(c -> System.out.println((char)c));
    }
}
```

A *checksum* is a numeric quantity representing and confirming the contents of a file. If you transmit the checksum of a file separately from the contents, a recipient can checksum the file—assuming the algorithm is known—and verify that the file was received intact. Example 3-4 shows the simplest possible checksum, computed just by adding the numeric values of each character. Note that on files, it does not include the values of the newline characters; in order to fix this, retrieve `System.get Property("line.separator");` and add its character value(s) into the sum at the end of each line. Or give up on line mode and read the file a character at a time.

Example 3-4. main/src/main/java/strings/CheckSum.java

```
/** CheckSum one text file, given an open BufferedReader.
 * Checksum does not include line endings, so will give the
 * same value for given text on any platform. Do not use
 * on binary files!
 */
public static int process(BufferedReader is) {
    int sum = 0;
    try {
        String inputLine;

        while ((inputLine = is.readLine()) != null) {
            for (char c : inputLine.toCharArray()) {
                sum += c;
            }
        }
    } catch (IOException e) {
        throw new RuntimeException("IOException: " + e);
    }
    return sum;
}
```

3.4 Aligning, Indenting, and Unindenting Strings

Problem

You want to align strings to the left, right, or center.

Solution

Do the math yourself, and use `substring` (see Recipe 3.1) and a `StringBuilder` (see Recipe 3.2). Or, use my `StringAlign` class, which is based on the `java.text.Format` class. For left or right alignment, use `String.format()`.

Discussion

Centering and aligning text comes up fairly often. Suppose you want to print a simple report with centered page numbers. There doesn't seem to be anything in the standard API that will do the job fully for you. But I have written a class called `String Align` that will. Here's how you might use it:

```
public class StringAlignSimple {

    public static void main(String[] args) {
        // Construct a "formatter" to center strings.
        StringAlign formatter = new StringAlign(70, StringAlign.Justify.CENTER);
        // Try it out, for page "i"
        System.out.println(formatter.format("- i -"));
        // Try it out, for page 4. Since this formatter is
        // optimized for Strings, not specifically for page numbers,
        // we have to convert the number to a String
        System.out.println(formatter.format(Integer.toString(4)));
    }
}
```

If you compile and run this class, it prints the two demonstration line numbers centered, as shown:

```
> javac -d . StringAlignSimple.java
> java strings.StringAlignSimple
                              - i -
                               4

>
```

Example 3-5 is the code for the `StringAlign` class. Note that this class extends the class `Format` in the package `java.text`. There is a series of `Format` classes that all have at least one method called `format()`. It is thus in a family with numerous other formatters, such as `DateFormat` and `NumberFormat`, that we'll take a look at in upcoming chapters.

Example 3-5. main/src/main/java/strings/StringAlign.java

```
public class StringAlign extends Format {

    private static final long serialVersionUID = 1L;

    public enum Justify {
        /* Constant for left justification. */
        LEFT,
        /* Constant for centering. */
        CENTER,
        /** Constant for right-justified Strings. */
        RIGHT,
    }
```

```
/** Current justification */
private Justify just;
/** Current max length */
private int maxChars;

/** Construct a StringAlign formatter; length and alignment are
 * passed to the Constructor instead of each format() call as the
 * expected common use is in repetitive formatting e.g., page numbers.
 * @param maxChars - the maximum length of the output
 * @param just - one of the enum values LEFT, CENTER or RIGHT
 */
public StringAlign(int maxChars, Justify just) {
    switch(just) {
    case LEFT:
    case CENTER:
    case RIGHT:
        this.just = just;
        break;
    default:
        throw new IllegalArgumentException("invalid justification arg.");
    }
    if (maxChars < 0) {
        throw new IllegalArgumentException("maxChars must be positive.");
    }
    this.maxChars = maxChars;
}

/** Format a String.
 * @param input - the string to be aligned.
 * @parm where - the StringBuilder to append it to.
 * @param ignore - a FieldPosition (may be null, not used but
 * specified by the general contract of Format).
 */
@Override
public StringBuffer format(
    Object input, StringBuffer where, FieldPosition ignore) {

    String s = input.toString();
    String wanted = s.substring(0, Math.min(s.length(), maxChars));

    // Get the spaces in the right place.
    switch (just) {
        case RIGHT:
            pad(where, maxChars - wanted.length());
            where.append(wanted);
            break;
        case CENTER:
            int toAdd = maxChars - wanted.length();
            pad(where, toAdd/2);
            where.append(wanted);
            pad(where, toAdd - toAdd/2);
```

```
                break;
            case LEFT:
                where.append(wanted);
                pad(where, maxChars - wanted.length());
                break;
        }
        return where;
    }

    protected final void pad(StringBuffer to, int howMany) {
        for (int i=0; i<howMany; i++)
            to.append(' ');
    }

    /** Convenience Routine */
    String format(String s) {
        return format(s, new StringBuffer(), null).toString();
    }

    /** ParseObject is required, but not useful here. */
    public Object parseObject (String source, ParsePosition pos)  {
        return source;
    }
}
```

Java 12 introduced a new method public String indent(int n) that prepends *n* spaces to the string, which is treated as a sequence of lines with line separators. This works well in conjunction with the Java 11 Stream<String> lines() method. For example, for the case where a series of lines, already stored in a single string, needs the same indent (Streams, and the "::" notation, are explained in Recipe 9.0):

```
jshell> "abc\ndef".indent(30).lines().forEach(System.out::println);
                              abc
                              def

jshell> "abc\ndef".indent(30).indent(-10).lines().forEach(System.out::println);
                    abc
                    def

jshell>
```

See Also

The alignment of numeric columns is considered in Chapter 5.

3.5 Converting Between Unicode Characters and Strings

Problem

You want to convert between Unicode characters and `String`s.

Solution

Use Java `char` or `String` data types to deal with characters; these intrinsically support Unicode. Print characters as integers to display their *raw* value if needed.

Discussion

Unicode is an international standard that aims to represent all known characters used by people in their various languages. Though the original ASCII character set is a subset, Unicode is huge. At the time Java was created, Unicode was a 16-bit character set, so it seemed natural to make Java `char` values be 16 bits in width, and for years a `char` could hold any Unicode character. However, over time, Unicode has grown, to the point that it now includes over a million code points, or characters, more than the 65,525 that could be represented in 16 bits.[5] Not all possible 16-bit values were defined as characters in UCS-2, the 16-bit version of Unicode originally used in Java. A few were reserved as escape characters, which allows for multicharacter-length mappings to less common characters. Fortunately, there is a go-between standard, called UTF-16 (16-bit Unicode Transformation Format). As the `String` class documentation puts it:

> A `String` represents a string in the UTF-16 format in which *supplementary characters* are represented by *surrogate pairs* (see the section Unicode Character Representations in the `Character` class for more information). Index values refer to char code units, so a supplementary character uses two positions in a `String`.

> The `String` class provides methods for dealing with Unicode code points (i.e., characters), in addition to those for dealing with Unicode code units (i.e., char `values`).

The `charAt()` method of `String` returns the char value for the character at the specified offset. The `StringBuilder append()` method has a form that accepts a `char`. Because char is an integer type, you can even do arithmetic on chars, though this is not needed as frequently as in, say, C. Nor is it often recommended, because the `Char acter` class provides the methods for which these operations were normally used in

---

5 Indeed, there are so many characters in Unicode that a fad has emerged of displaying your name upside down using characters that approximate upside-down versions of the Latin alphabet. Do a web search for "upside-down Unicode."

languages such as C. Here is a program that uses arithmetic on chars to control a loop and that also appends the characters into a StringBuilder (see Recipe 3.2):

```
// UnicodeChars.java
StringBuilder b = new StringBuilder();
for (char c = 'a'; c<'d'; c++) {
    b.append(c);
}
b.append('\u00a5');      // Japanese Yen symbol
b.append('\u01FC');      // Roman AE with acute accent
b.append('\u0391');      // GREEK Capital Alpha
b.append('\u03A9');      // GREEK Capital Omega

for (int i=0; i<b.length(); i++) {
    System.out.printf(
        "Character #%d (%04x) is %c%n",
        i, (int)b.charAt(i), b.charAt(i));
}
System.out.println("Accumulated characters are " + b);
```

When you run it, the expected results are printed for the ASCII characters. On Unix and characters in Mac systems, the default fonts don't include all the additional characters, so they are either omitted or mapped to irregular characters:

```
$ java -cp target/classes strings.UnicodeChars
Character #0 (0061) is a
Character #1 (0062) is b
Character #2 (0063) is c
Character #3 (00a5) is ¥
Character #4 (01fc) is Ǽ
Character #5 (0391) is Α
Character #6 (03a9) is Ω
Accumulated characters are abc¥ǼΑΩ
$
```

The Windows system used to try this doesn't have most of those characters either, but at least it prints as question marks the ones it knows are lacking (Windows system fonts are more homogenous than those of the various Unix systems, so it is easier to know what won't work). On the other hand, it tries to print the yen sign as an N with a tilde:

```
Character #0 is a
Character #1 is b
Character #2 is c
Character #3 is ¥
Character #4 is ?
Character #5 is ?
Character #6 is ?
Accumulated characters are abc¥___
```

The "_" characters are unprintable characters.

See Also

The `Unicode` program in this book's online source displays any 256-character section of the Unicode character set. You can download documentation listing every character in the Unicode character set from the Unicode Consortium (*http://www.unicode.org*).

3.6 Reversing a String by Word or by Character

Problem

You wish to reverse a string, a character at a time or a word at a time.

Solution

You can reverse a string by character easily, using a `StringBuilder`. There are several ways to reverse a string a word at a time. One natural way is to use a `StringToken izer` and a stack. `Stack` is a class (defined in `java.util`; see Recipe 7.16) that implements an easy-to-use last-in, first-out (LIFO) stack of objects.

Discussion

To reverse the characters in a string, use the `StringBuilder reverse()` method:

main/src/main/java/strings/StringRevChar.java

```
String sh = "FCGDAEB";
System.out.println(sh + " -> " + new StringBuilder(sh).reverse());
```

The letters in this example list the order of the sharps in the key signatures of Western music; in reverse, it lists the order of flats. Alternatively, of course, you could reverse the characters yourself, using character-at-a-time mode (see Recipe 3.3).

A popular mnemonic, or memory aid, to help music students remember the order of sharps and flats consists of one word for each sharp instead of just one letter. Let's reverse this *one word at a time*. Example 3-6 adds each one to a `Stack` (see Recipe 7.16), then processes the whole lot in LIFO order, which reverses the order.

Example 3-6. main/src/main/java/strings/StringReverse.java

```
String s = "Father Charles Goes Down And Ends Battle";

// Put it in the stack frontwards
Stack<String> myStack = new Stack<>();
StringTokenizer st = new StringTokenizer(s);
while (st.hasMoreTokens()) {
    myStack.push(st.nextToken());
```

```
    }

    // Print the stack backwards
    System.out.print('"' + s + '"' + " backwards by word is:\n\t\"");
    while (!myStack.empty()) {
        System.out.print(myStack.pop());
        System.out.print(' ');      // inter-word spacing
    }
    System.out.println('"');
```

3.7 Expanding and Compressing Tabs

Problem

You need to convert space characters to tab characters in a file, or vice versa. You might want to replace spaces with tabs to save space on disk or go the other way to deal with a device or program that can't handle tabs.

Solution

Use my Tabs class or its subclass EnTab.

Discussion

Because programs that deal with tabbed text or data expect tab stops to be at fixed positions, you cannot use a typical text editor to replace tabs with spaces or vice versa. Example 3-7 is a listing of EnTab, complete with a sample main program. The program works a line at a time. For each character on the line, if the character is a space, we see if we can coalesce it with previous spaces to output a single tab character. This program depends on the Tabs class, which we'll come to shortly. The Tabs class is used to decide which column positions represent tab stops and which do not.

Example 3-7. main/src/main/java/strings/Entab.java

```java
public class EnTab {

    private static Logger logger = Logger.getLogger(EnTab.class.getSimpleName());

    /** The Tabs (tab logic handler) */
    protected Tabs tabs;

    /**
     * Delegate tab spacing information to tabs.
     */
    public int getTabSpacing() {
        return tabs.getTabSpacing();
    }
```

```
/**
 * Main program: just create an EnTab object, and pass the standard input
 * or the named file(s) through it.
 */
public static void main(String[] argv) throws IOException {
    EnTab et = new EnTab(8);
    if (argv.length == 0) // do standard input
        et.entab(
            new BufferedReader(new InputStreamReader(System.in)),
            System.out);
    else
        for (String fileName : argv) { // do each file
            et.entab(
                new BufferedReader(new FileReader(fileName)),
                System.out);
        }
}

/**
 * Constructor: just save the tab values.
 * @param n The number of spaces each tab is to replace.
 */
public EnTab(int n) {
    tabs = new Tabs(n);
}

public EnTab() {
    tabs = new Tabs();
}

/**
 * entab: process one file, replacing blanks with tabs.
 * @param is A BufferedReader opened to the file to be read.
 * @param out a PrintWriter to send the output to.
 */
public void entab(BufferedReader is, PrintWriter out) throws IOException {

    // main loop: process entire file one line at a time.
    is.lines().forEach(line -> {
        out.println(entabLine(line));
    });
}

/**
 * entab: process one file, replacing blanks with tabs.
 *
 * @param is A BufferedReader opened to the file to be read.
 * @param out A PrintStream to write the output to.
 */
public void entab(BufferedReader is, PrintStream out) throws IOException {
    entab(is, new PrintWriter(out));
```

```java
    }

    /**
     * entabLine: process one line, replacing blanks with tabs.
     * @param line the string to be processed
     */
    public String entabLine(String line) {
        int N = line.length(), outCol = 0;
        StringBuilder sb = new StringBuilder();
        char ch;
        int consumedSpaces = 0;

        for (int inCol = 0; inCol < N; inCol++) { // Cannot use foreach here
            ch = line.charAt(inCol);
            // If we get a space, consume it, don't output it.
            // If this takes us to a tab stop, output a tab character.
            if (ch == ' ') {
                logger.info("Got space at " + inCol);
                if (tabs.isTabStop(inCol)) {
                    logger.info("Got a Tab Stop " + inCol);
                    sb.append('\t');
                    outCol += consumedSpaces;
                    consumedSpaces = 0;
                } else {
                    consumedSpaces++;
                }
                continue;
            }

            // We're at a non-space; if we're just past a tab stop, we need
            // to put the "leftover" spaces back out, since we consumed
            // them above.
            while (inCol-1 > outCol) {
                logger.info("Padding space at " + inCol);
                sb.append(' ');
                outCol++;
            }

            // Now we have a plain character to output.
            sb.append(ch);
            outCol++;

        }
        // If line ended with trailing (or only!) spaces, preserve them.
        for (int i = 0; i < consumedSpaces; i++) {
            logger.info("Padding space at end # " + i);
            sb.append(' ');
        }
        return sb.toString();
    }
}
```

This code was patterned after a program in Kernighan and Plauger's classic work *Software Tools*. While their version was in a language called RatFor (Rational Fortran), my version has since been through several translations. Their version actually worked one character at a time, and for a long time I tried to preserve this overall structure. Eventually, I rewrote it to be a line-at-a-time program.

The program that goes in the opposite direction—putting tabs in rather than taking them out—is the `DeTab` class shown in Example 3-8; only the core methods are shown.

Example 3-8. main/src/main/java/strings/DeTab.java

```java
public class DeTab {
    Tabs ts;

    public static void main(String[] argv) throws IOException {
        DeTab dt = new DeTab(8);
        dt.detab(new BufferedReader(new InputStreamReader(System.in)),
                new PrintWriter(System.out));
    }

    public DeTab(int n) {
        ts = new Tabs(n);
    }
    public DeTab() {
        ts = new Tabs();
    }

    /** detab one file (replace tabs with spaces)
     * @param is - the file to be processed
     * @param out - the updated file
     */
    public void detab(BufferedReader is, PrintWriter out) throws IOException {
        is.lines().forEach(line -> {
            out.println(detabLine(line));
        });
    }

    /** detab one line (replace tabs with spaces)
     * @param line - the line to be processed
     * @return the updated line
     */
    public String detabLine(String line) {
        char c;
        int col;
        StringBuilder sb = new StringBuilder();
        col = 0;
        for (int i = 0; i < line.length(); i++) {
            // Either ordinary character or tab.
            if ((c = line.charAt(i)) != '\t') {
```

```
            sb.append(c); // Ordinary
            ++col;
            continue;
        }
        do { // Tab, expand it, must put >=1 space
            sb.append(' ');
        } while (!ts.isTabStop(++col));
    }
    return sb.toString();
    }
}
```

The Tabs class provides two methods: settabpos() and istabstop(). Example 3-9 is the source for the Tabs class.

Example 3-9. main/src/main/java/strings/Tabs.java

```java
public class Tabs {
    /** tabs every so often */
    public final static int DEFTABSPACE =    8;
    /** the current tab stop setting. */
    protected int tabSpace = DEFTABSPACE;
    /** the longest line that we initially set tabs for */
    public final static int MAXLINE  = 255;

    /** Construct a Tabs object with a given tab stop settings */
    public Tabs(int n) {
        if (n <= 0) {
            n = 1;
        }
        tabSpace = n;
    }

    /** Construct a Tabs object with a default tab stop settings */
    public Tabs() {
        this(DEFTABSPACE);
    }

    /**
     * @return Returns the tabSpace.
     */
    public int getTabSpacing() {
        return tabSpace;
    }

    /** isTabStop - returns true if given column is a tab stop.
     * @param col - the current column number
     */
    public boolean isTabStop(int col) {
        if (col <= 0)
            return false;
```

```
        return (col+1) % tabSpace == 0;
    }
}
```

3.8 Controlling Case

Problem

You need to either convert strings to uppercase or lowercase or compare strings without regard for case.

Solution

The String class has a number of methods for dealing with documents in a particular case. toUpperCase() and toLowerCase() each return a new string that is a copy of the current string but converted, as the name implies. Each can be called either with no arguments or with a Locale argument specifying the conversion rules; this is necessary because of internationalization. Java's API provides significant internationalization and localization features, as covered in "Ian's Basic Steps: Internationalization and Localization" on page 85. Whereas the equals() method tells you if another string is exactly the same, equalsIgnoreCase() tells you if all characters are the same regardless of case. Here, you can't specify an alternative locale; the system's default locale is used:

```
String name = "Java Cookbook";
System.out.println("Normal:\t" + name);
System.out.println("Upper:\t" + name.toUpperCase());
System.out.println("Lower:\t" + name.toLowerCase());
String javaName = "java cookBook"; // If it were Java identifiers :-)
if (!name.equals(javaName))
    System.err.println("equals() correctly reports false");
else
    System.err.println("equals() incorrectly reports true");
if (name.equalsIgnoreCase(javaName))
    System.err.println("equalsIgnoreCase() correctly reports true");
else
    System.err.println("equalsIgnoreCase() incorrectly reports false");
```

If you run this, it prints the first name changed to uppercase and lowercase, then it reports that both methods work as expected:

```
C:\javasrc\strings>java strings.Case
Normal: Java Cookbook
Upper:  JAVA COOKBOOK
Lower:  java cookbook
equals( ) correctly reports false
equalsIgnoreCase( ) correctly reports true
```

See Also

Regular expressions make it simpler to ignore case in string searching (as we see in Chapter 4).

3.9 Entering Nonprintable Characters

Problem

You need to put nonprintable characters into strings.

Solution

Use the backslash character and one of the Java string escapes.

Discussion

The Java string escapes are listed in Table 3-1.

Table 3-1. String escapes

To get	Use	Notes
Tab	\t	
Linefeed (Unix newline)	\n	The call System.getProperty("line.separator") will give you the platform's line end.
Carriage return	\r	
Form feed	\f	
Backspace	\b	
Single quote	\'	
Double quote	\"	
Unicode character	\u *NNNN*	Four hexadecimal digits (no \x as in C/C++). See *http://www.unicode.org* for codes.
Octal(!) character	+\+*NNN*	Who uses octal (base 8) these days?
Backslash	\\	

Here is a code example that shows most of these in action:

```
public class StringEscapes {
    public static void main(String[] argv) {
        System.out.println("Java Strings in action:");
        // System.out.println("An alarm or alert: \a");     // not supported
        System.out.println("An alarm entered in Octal: \007");
        System.out.println("A tab key: \t(what comes after)");
        System.out.println("A newline: \n(what comes after)");
        System.out.println("A UniCode character: \u0207");
        System.out.println("A backslash character: \\");
```

```
        }
    }
```

If you have a lot of non-ASCII characters to enter, you may wish to consider using Java's input methods, discussed briefly in the online documentation (*https:// docs.oracle.com/javase/8/docs/technotes/guides/imf/index.html*).

3.10 Trimming Blanks from the End of a String

Problem

You need to work on a string without regard for extra leading or trailing spaces a user may have typed.

Solution

Use the `String` class `strip()` or `trim()` methods.

Discussion

There are four methods in the `String` class for this:

`strip()`
  Returns a string with all leading and trailing whitespace removed

`stripLeading()`
  Returns a string whose value is this string, with all leading white space removed

`stripTrailing()`
  Returns the string with all trailing whitespace removed

`String trim()`
  Returns the string with all leading and trailing spaces removed

For the `strip()` methods, whitespace is as defined by `Character.isSpace()`. For the `trim()` method, space includes any character whose numeric value is less than or equal to 32, or *U+0020* (the space character).

Example 3-10 uses `trim()` to strip an arbitrary number of leading spaces and/or tabs from lines of Java source code in order to look for the characters `//+` and `//-`. These strings are special Java comments I previously used to mark the parts of the programs in this book that I wanted to include in the printed copy.

Example 3-10. main/src/main/java/strings/GetMark.java (trimming and comparing strings)

```java
public class GetMark {
    /** the default starting mark */
    public final String START_MARK = "//+";
    /** the default ending mark */
    public final String END_MARK = "//-";
    /** Set this to TRUE for running in "exclude" mode (e.g., for
     * building exercises from solutions) and to FALSE for running
     * in "extract" mode (e.g., writing a book and omitting the
     * imports and "public class" stuff).
     */
    public final static boolean START = true;
    /** True if we are currently inside marks */
    protected boolean printing = START;
    /** True if you want line numbers */
    protected final boolean number = false;

    /** Get Marked parts of one file, given an open LineNumberReader.
     * This is the main operation of this class, and can be used
     * inside other programs or from the main() wrapper.
     */
    public void process(String fileName,
        LineNumberReader is,
        PrintStream out) {
        int nLines = 0;
        try {
            String inputLine;

            while ((inputLine = is.readLine()) != null) {
                if (inputLine.trim().equals(START_MARK)) {
                    if (printing)
                        // These go to stderr, so you can redirect the output
                        System.err.println("ERROR: START INSIDE START, " +
                            fileName + ':' + is.getLineNumber());
                    printing = true;
                } else if (inputLine.trim().equals(END_MARK)) {
                    if (!printing)
                        System.err.println("ERROR: STOP WHILE STOPPED, " +
                            fileName + ':' + is.getLineNumber());
                    printing = false;
                } else if (printing) {
                    if (number) {
                        out.print(nLines);
                        out.print(": ");
                    }
                    out.println(inputLine);
                    ++nLines;
                }
            }
            is.close();
```

```
        out.flush(); // Must not close - caller may still need it.
        if (nLines == 0)
            System.err.println("ERROR: No marks in " + fileName +
                "; no output generated!");
    } catch (IOException e) {
        System.out.println("IOException: " + e);
    }
}
```

Ian's Basic Steps: Internationalization and Localization

Internationalization and localization consist of the following:

Sensitivity training (Internationalization, or I18N)
    Making your software sensitive to these issues

Language lessons (Localization, or L10N)
    Writing configuration files for each language

Culture lessons (optional)
    Customizing the presentation of numbers, fractions, dates, and message formatting

For more information, see *Java Internationalization* by Andy Deitsch and David Czarnecki (O'Reilly).

3.11 Creating a Message with I18N Resources

Problem

You want your program to take sensitivity training so that it can communicate well internationally.

Solution

Your program must obtain all control and message strings via the internationalization software. Here's how:

1. Get a ResourceBundle:

    ```
    ResourceBundle rb = ResourceBundle.getBundle("Menus");
    ```

    I'll talk about ResourceBundle in Recipe 3.13, but briefly, a ResourceBundle represents a collection of name-value pairs (resources). The names are names you assign to each GUI control or other user interface text, and the values are the text to assign to each control in a given language.

2. Use this ResourceBundle to fetch the localized version of each control name.

Old way:

```
String label = "Exit";
// Create the control, e.g., new JButton(label);
```

New way:

```
try { label = rb.getString("exit.label"); }
catch (MissingResourceException e) { label="Exit"; } // fallback
// Create the control, e.g., new JButton(label);
```

This may seem quite a bit of code for one control, but you can write a convenience routine to simplify it, like this:

```
JButton exitButton = I18NUtil.getButton("exit.label", "Exit");
```

The file *I18NUtil.java* is included in the book's code distribution.

While the example is a Swing `JButton`, the same approach goes with other UIs, such as the web tier. In JSF, for example, you might place your strings in a properties file called *resources.properties* and store it in *src/main/resources*. You would load this in *faces-config.xml*:

```
<application>
  <locale-config>
      <default-locale>en</default-locale>
      <supported-locale>en</supported-locale>
      <supported-locale>es</supported-locale>
      <supported-locale>fr</supported-locale>
  </locale-config>
  <resource-bundle>
      <base-name>resources</base-name>
      <var>msg</var>
  </resource-bundle>
</application>
```

Then in each web page that needs these strings, refer to the resource using the `msg` variable in an expression:

```
// In signup.xhtml:
<h:outputText value="#{msg.prompt_firstname}"/>
<h:inputText required="true" id="firstName" value="#{person.firstName}" />
```

What happens at runtime?

The default locale is used, because we didn't specify one. The default locale is platform dependent:

Unix/POSIX
  LANG environment variable (per user)

Windows
  Control Panel→Regional Settings

macOS

System Preferences→Language & Text

Others

See platform documentation

`ResourceBundle.getBundle()` locates a file with the named resource bundle name (`Menus`, in the previous example), plus an underscore and the locale name (if a non-default locale is set), plus another underscore and the locale variation (if any variation is set), plus the extension *.properties*. If a variation is set but the file can't be found, it falls back to just the country code. If that can't be found, it falls back to the original default. Table 3-2 shows some examples for various locales.

Note that Android apps—usually written in Java or Kotlin—use a similar mechanism but with the files in XML format instead of Java Properties and with some small changes in the name of the file in which the properties files are found.

Table 3-2. Property filenames for different locales

Locale	Filename
Default locale	*Menus.Properties*
Swedish	*Menus_sv.properties*
Spanish	*Menus_es.properties*
French	*Menus_fr.properties*
French-Canadian	*Menus_fr_CA.properties*

Locale names are two-letter ISO-639 language codes (lowercase), and they normally abbreviate the country's *endonym* (the name its language speakers refer to it by); thus, Sweden is *sv* for *Sverige*, Spain is *es* for *Espanol*, etc. Locale variations are two-letter ISO country codes (uppercase); for example, e.g., CA for Canada, US for the United States, SV for Sweden, ES for Spain, etc.

Setting the locale

On Windows, go into Regional Settings in the Control Panel. Changing this setting may entail a reboot, so exit any editor windows.

On Unix, set your `LANG` environment variable. For example, a Korn shell user in Mexico might have this line in her *.profile*:

```
export LANG=es_MX
```

On either system, for testing a different locale, you need only define the locale in the System Properties at runtime using the command-line option -D, as in:

```
java -Duser.language=es i18n.Browser
```

This runs the Java program named Browser in package i18n in the Spanish locale.

You can get a list of the available locales with a call to Locale.getAvailable Locales().

3.12 Using a Particular Locale

Problem

You want to use a locale other than the default in a particular operation.

Solution

Obtain a Locale by using a predefined instance or the Locale constructor. Optionally make it global to your application by using Locale.setDefault(newLocale).

Discussion

Classes that provide formatting services, such as DateTimeFormatter and NumberFor mat, provide overloads so they can be called either with or without a Locale-related argument.

To obtain a Locale object, you can employ one of the predefined locale variables provided by the Locale class, or you can construct your own Locale object giving a language code and a country code:

```
Locale locale1 = Locale.FRANCE;    // predefined
Locale locale2 = new Locale("en", "UK");    // English, UK version
```

These can then be used in the various formatting operations:

```
DateFormat frDateFormatter = DateFormat.getDateInstance(
            DateFormat.MEDIUM, frLocale);
DateFormat ukDateFormatter = DateFormat.getDateInstance(
            DateFormat.MEDIUM, ukLocale);
```

Either of these can be used to format a date or a number, as shown in class Use Locales:

```
package i18n;

import java.time.LocalDateTime;
import java.time.format.DateTimeFormatter;
import java.time.format.FormatStyle;
import java.util.Locale;

/** Use some locales; based on user's OS "settings"
 * choices or -Duser.lang= or -Duser.region=.
 */
```

```
public class UseLocales {
    public static void main(String[] args) {

        Locale frLocale = Locale.FRANCE;     // predefined
        Locale ukLocale = new Locale("en", "UK");    // English, UK version

        DateTimeFormatter defaultDateFormatter =
            DateTimeFormatter.ofLocalizedDateTime(
                FormatStyle.MEDIUM);
        DateTimeFormatter frDateFormatter =
            DateTimeFormatter.ofLocalizedDateTime(
                FormatStyle.MEDIUM).localizedBy(frLocale);
        DateTimeFormatter ukDateFormatter =
            DateTimeFormatter.ofLocalizedDateTime(
                FormatStyle.MEDIUM).localizedBy(ukLocale);

        LocalDateTime now = LocalDateTime.now();
        System.out.println("Default: " + ' ' +
            now.format(defaultDateFormatter));
        System.out.println(frLocale.getDisplayName() + ' ' +
            now.format(frDateFormatter));
        System.out.println(ukLocale.getDisplayName() + ' ' +
            now.format(ukDateFormatter));
    }
}
```

The program prints the locale name and formats the date in each of the locales:

```
$ java i18n.UseLocales
Default:  Oct 16, 2019, 4:41:45 PM
French (France) 16 oct. 2019 à 16:41:45
English (UK) Oct 16, 2019, 4:41:45 PM$
```

3.13 Creating a Resource Bundle

Problem

You need to create a resource bundle for use with I18N.

Solution

A resource bundle is simply a collection of names and values. You could write a
java.util.ResourceBundle subclass, but it is easier to create textual Properties files
(see Recipe 7.10) that you then load with ResourceBundle.getBundle(). The files
can be created using any plain text editor. Leaving it in a text file format also allows
user customization in desktop applications; a user whose language is not provided
for, or who wishes to change the wording somewhat due to local variations in dialect,
should be able to edit the file.

Note that the resource bundle text file should not have the same name as any of your Java classes. The reason is that the `ResourceBundle` constructs a class dynamically with the same name as the resource files.

Discussion

Here is a sample properties file for a few menu items:

```
# Default Menu properties
# The File Menu
file.label=File Menu
file.new.label=New File
file.new.key=N
file.save.label=Save
file.new.key=S
```

Creating the default properties file is usually not a problem, but creating properties files for other languages might be. Unless you are a large multinational corporation, you will probably not have the resources (pardon the pun) to create resource files inhouse. If you are shipping commercial software or using the web for global reach, you need to identify your target markets and understand which of these are most sensitive to wanting menus and the like in their own languages. Then, hire a professional translation service that has expertise in the required languages to prepare the files. Test them well before you ship, as you would any other part of your software.

If you need special characters, multiline text, or other complex entry, remember that a `ResourceBundle` is also a `Properties` file, so see the documentation for `java.util.Properties`.

3.14 Program: A Simple Text Formatter

This program is a primitive text formatter, representative of what people used on most computing platforms before the rise of standalone graphics-based word processors, laser printers, and, eventually, desktop publishing and office suites. It simply reads words from a file, previously created with a text editor, and outputs them until it reaches the right margin, when it calls `println()` to append a line ending. For example, here is an input file:

```
It's a nice
day, isn't it, Mr. Mxyzzptllxy?
I think we should
go for a walk.
```

Given that file as the input, the `Fmt` program prints the lines formatted neatly:

```
It's a nice day, isn't it, Mr. Mxyzzptllxy? I think we should go for a
walk.
```

As you can see, it fits the text we gave it to the margin and discards all the line breaks present in the original. Here's the code:

```java
public class Fmt {
    /** The maximum column width */
    public static final int COLWIDTH=72;
    /** The file that we read and format */
    final BufferedReader in;
    /** Where the output goes */
    PrintWriter out;

    /** If files present, format each one, else format the standard input. */
    public static void main(String[] av) throws IOException {
        if (av.length == 0)
            new Fmt(System.in).format();
        else for (String name : av) {
            new Fmt(name).format();
        }
    }

    public Fmt(BufferedReader inFile, PrintWriter outFile) {
        this.in = inFile;
        this.out = outFile;
    }

    public Fmt(PrintWriter out) {
        this(new BufferedReader(new InputStreamReader(System.in)), out);
    }

    /** Construct a Formatter given an open Reader */
    public Fmt(BufferedReader file) throws IOException {
        this(file, new PrintWriter(System.out));
    }

    /** Construct a Formatter given a filename */
    public Fmt(String fname) throws IOException {
        this(new BufferedReader(new FileReader(fname)));
    }

    /** Construct a Formatter given an open Stream */
    public Fmt(InputStream file) throws IOException {
        this(new BufferedReader(new InputStreamReader(file)));
    }

    /** Format the File contained in a constructed Fmt object */
    public void format() throws IOException {
        format(in.lines(), out);
    }

    /** Format a Stream of lines, e.g., bufReader.lines() */
    public static void format(Stream<String> s, PrintWriter out) {
        StringBuilder outBuf = new StringBuilder();
```

```
        s.forEachOrdered((line -> {
            if (line.length() == 0) {     // null line
                out.println(outBuf);      // end current line
                out.println();     // output blank line
                outBuf.setLength(0);
            } else {
                // otherwise it's text, so format it.
                StringTokenizer st = new StringTokenizer(line);
                while (st.hasMoreTokens()) {
                    String word = st.nextToken();

                    // If this word would go past the margin,
                    // first dump out anything previous.
                    if (outBuf.length() + word.length() > COLWIDTH) {
                        out.println(outBuf);
                        outBuf.setLength(0);
                    }
                    outBuf.append(word).append(' ');
                }
            }
        }));
        if (outBuf.length() > 0) {
            out.println(outBuf);
        } else {
            out.println();
        }
    }
}
```

A slightly fancier version of this program, Fmt2, is in the online source for this book. It uses *dot commands*—lines beginning with periods—to give limited control over the formatting. A family of dot-command formatters includes Unix's *roff, nroff, troff,* and *groff,* which are in the same family with programs called *runoff* on Digital Equipment systems. The original for this is J. Saltzer's *runoff,* which first appeared on Multics and from there made its way into various OSes. To save trees, I did not include Fmt2 here; it subclasses Fmt and overrides the format() method to include additional functionality (the source code is in the full *javasrc* repository for the book).

3.15 Program: Soundex Name Comparisons

The difficulties in comparing American-style names inspired the US Census Bureau to develop the Soundex algorithm in the early 1900s. Each of a given set of consonants maps to a particular number, the effect being to map similar-sounding names together, on the grounds that in those days many people were illiterate and could not spell their family names consistently. But it is still useful today, for example, in a company-wide telephone book application. The names Darwin and Derwin map to

D650, and Darwent maps to D653, which puts it adjacent to D650. All of these are believed to be historical variants of the same name. Suppose we needed to sort lines containing these names together: if we could output the Soundex numbers at the beginning of each line, this would be easy. Here is a simple demonstration of the Soundex class:

```java
public class SoundexSimple {

    /** main */
    public static void main(String[] args) {
        String[] names = {
            "Darwin, Ian",
            "Davidson, Greg",
            "Darwent, William",
            "Derwin, Daemon"
        };
        for (String name : names) {
            System.out.println(Soundex.soundex(name) + ' ' + name);
        }
    }
}
```

Let's run it:

```
> javac -d . SoundexSimple.java
> java strings.SoundexSimple | sort
D132 Davidson, Greg
D650 Darwin, Ian
D650 Derwin, Daemon
D653 Darwent, William
>
```

As you can see, the Darwin-variant names (including Daemon Derwin[6]) all sort together and are distinct from the Davidson (and Davis, Davies, etc.) names that normally appear between Darwin and Derwin when using a simple alphabetic sort. The Soundex algorithm has done its work.

Here is the Soundex class itself—it uses Strings and StringBuilders to convert names into Soundex codes:

main/src/main/java/strings/Soundex.java

```java
public class Soundex {

    static boolean debug = false;
```

---

6 In Unix terminology, a daemon is a server. The old English word has nothing to do with satanic demons but refers to a helper or assistant. Derwin Daemon was actually a character in Susannah Coleman's *Source Wars* online comic strip, which long ago was online at a now-departed site called *darby.daemonnews.org*.

```java
/* Implements the mapping
 * from: AEHIOUWYBFPVCGJKQSXZDTLMNR
 * to:   00000000011111222222222334556
 */
public static final char[] MAP = {
    //A   B   C   D   E   F   G   H   I   J   K   L   M
    '0','1','2','3','0','1','2','0','0','2','2','4','5',
    //N   O   P   W   R   S   T   U   V   W   X   Y   Z
    '5','0','1','2','6','2','3','0','1','0','2','0','2'
};

/** Convert the given String to its Soundex code.
 * @return null If the given string can't be mapped to Soundex.
 */
public static String soundex(String s) {

    // Algorithm works on uppercase (mainframe era).
    String t = s.toUpperCase();

    StringBuilder res = new StringBuilder();
    char c, prev = '?', prevOutput = '?';

    // Main loop: find up to 4 chars that map.
    for (int i=0; i<t.length() && res.length() < 4 &&
        (c = t.charAt(i)) != ','; i++) {

        // Check to see if the given character is alphabetic.
        // Text is already converted to uppercase. Algorithm
        // only handles ASCII letters, do NOT use Character.isLetter()!
        // Also, skip double letters.
        if (c>='A' && c<='Z' && c != prev) {
            prev = c;

            // First char is installed unchanged, for sorting.
            if (i==0) {
                res.append(c);
            } else {
                char m = MAP[c-'A'];
                if (debug) {
                    System.out.println(c + " --> " + m);
                }
                if (m != '0' && m != prevOutput) {
                    res.append(m);
                    prevOutput = m;
                }
            }
        }
    }
    if (res.length() == 0)
        return null;
    for (int i=res.length(); i<4; i++)
        res.append('0');
```

```
        return res.toString();
    }
```

There are apparently some nuances of the full Soundex algorithm that are not implemented by this application. A more complete test using JUnit (see Recipe 1.10) is also online as *SoundexTest.java*, in the *src/tests/java/strings* directory. The dedicated reader may use this to provoke failures of such nuances and send a pull request with updated versions of the test and the code.

See Also

The Levenshtein string edit distance algorithm can be used for doing approximate string comparisons in a different fashion. You can find this in Apache Commons StringUtils (*http://commons.apache.org/proper/commons-lang*). I show a non-Java (Perl) implementation of this algorithm in Recipe 18.5.

## CHAPTER 4

Pattern Matching with Regular Expressions

4.0 Introduction

Suppose you have been on the internet for a few years and have been faithful about saving all your correspondence, just in case you (or your lawyers, or the prosecution) need a copy. The result is that you have a 5 GB disk partition dedicated to saved mail. Let's further suppose that you remember that somewhere in there is an email message from someone named Angie or Anjie. Or was it Angy? But you don't remember what you called it or where you stored it. Obviously, you have to look for it.

But while some of you go and try to open up all 15,000,000 documents in a word processor, I'll just find it with one simple command. Any system that provides regular expression support allows me to search for the pattern in several ways. The simplest to understand is:

```
Angie|Anjie|Angy
```

which you can probably guess means just to search for any of the variations. A more concise form (more thinking, less typing) is:

```
An[^ dn]
```

The syntax will become clear as we go through this chapter. Briefly, the "A" and the "n" match themselves, in effect finding words that begin with "An", while the cryptic [^ dn] requires the "An" to be followed by a character other than (^ means *not* in this context) a space (to eliminate the very common English word "an" at the start of a sentence) or "d" (to eliminate the common word "and") or "n" (to eliminate "Anne," "Announcing," etc.). Has your word processor gotten past its splash screen yet? Well, it doesn't matter, because I've already found the missing file. To find the answer, I just typed this command:

```
grep 'An[^ dn]' *
```

Regular expressions, or *regexes* for short, provide a concise and precise specification of patterns to be matched in text. One good way to think of regular expressions is as a little language for matching patterns of characters in text contained in strings. A regular expression API is an interpreter (*https://en.wikipedia.org/wiki/Inter preter_(computing)*) for matching regular expressions.

As another example of the power of regular expressions, consider the problem of bulk-updating hundreds of files. When I started with Java, the syntax for declaring array references was `baseType arrayVariableName[]`. For example, a method with an array argument, such as every program's main method, was commonly written like this:

```
public static void main(String args[]) {
```

But as time went by, it became clear to the stewards of the Java language that it would be better to write it as `baseType[] arrayVariableName`, like this:

```
public static void main(String[] args) {
```

This is better Java style because it associates the "array-ness" of the type with the type itself, rather than with the local argument name, and the compiler still accepts both modes. I wanted to change all occurrences of `main` written the old way to the new way. I used the pattern *main(String [a-z]* with the *grep* utility described earlier to find the names of all the files containing old-style main declarations (i.e., `main(String` followed by a space and a name character rather than an open square bracket). I then used another regex-based Unix tool, the stream editor *sed*, in a little shell script to change all occurrences in those files from *main(String *([a-z][a-z]*)[]* to *main(String[] $1* (the regex syntax used here is discussed later in this chapter). Again, the regex-based approach was orders of magnitude faster than doing it interactively, even using a reasonably powerful editor such as `vi` or `emacs`, let alone trying to use a graphical word processor.

Historically, the syntax of regexes has changed as they get incorporated into more tools and more languages, so the exact syntax in the previous examples is not exactly what you'd use in Java, but it does convey the conciseness and power of the regex mechanism.[6]

As a third example, consider parsing an Apache web server logfile, where some fields are delimited with quotes, others with square brackets, and others with spaces.

---

6 Non-Unix fans fear not, for you can use tools like *grep* on Windows systems using one of several packages. One is an open source package alternately called CygWin (after Cygnus Software) or GnuWin32 (*http://sour ces.redhat.com/cygwin*). Another is Microsoft's *findstr* command for Windows. Or you can use my *Grep* program in Recipe 4.6 if you don't have *grep* on your system. Incidentally, the name *grep* comes from an ancient Unix line editor command *g/RE/p*, the command to find the regex globally in all lines in the edit buffer and print the lines that match—just what the *grep* program does to lines in files.

Writing ad hoc code to parse this is messy in any language, but a well-crafted regex can break the line into all its constituent fields in one operation (this example is developed in Recipe 4.10).

These same time gains can be had by Java developers. Regular expression support has been in the standard Java runtime for ages and is well integrated (e.g., there are regex methods in the standard class `java.lang.String` and in the new I/O package). There are a few other regex packages for Java, and you may occasionally encounter code using them, but pretty well all code from this century can be expected to use the built-in package. The syntax of Java regexes themselves is discussed in Recipe 4.1, and the syntax of the Java API for using regexes is described in Recipe 4.2. The remaining recipes show some applications of regex technology in Java.

See Also

Mastering Regular Expressions by Jeffrey Friedl (O'Reilly) is the definitive guide to all the details of regular expressions. Most introductory books on Unix and Perl include some discussion of regexes; *Unix Power Tools* by Mike Loukides, Tim O'Reilly, Jerry Peek, and Shelley Powers (O'Reilly) devotes a chapter to them.

4.1 Regular Expression Syntax

Problem

You need to learn the syntax of Java regular expressions.

Solution

Consult Table 4-1 for a list of the regular expression characters.

Discussion

These pattern characters let you specify regexes of considerable power. In building patterns, you can use any combination of ordinary text and the *metacharacters*, or special characters, in Table 4-1. These can all be used in any combination that makes sense. For example, `a+` means any number of occurrences of the letter `a`, from one up to a million or a gazillion. The pattern `Mrs?\.` matches `Mr.` or `Mrs.` And `.*` indicates any character, any number of times, and is similar in meaning to most command-line interpreters' meaning of the `\*` alone. The pattern `\d+` means any number of numeric digits. `\d{2,3}` means a two- or three-digit number.

Table 4-1. Regular expression metacharacter syntax

Subexpression	Matches	Notes
General		
\^	Start of line/string	
$	End of line/string	
\b	Word boundary	
\B	Not a word boundary	
\A	Beginning of entire string	
\z	End of entire string	
\Z	End of entire string (except allowable final line terminator)	See Recipe 4.9
.	Any one character (except line terminator)	
[...]	"Character class"; any one character from those listed	
[\^...]	Any one character not from those listed	See Recipe 4.2
Alternation and grouping		
(...)	Grouping (capture groups)	See Recipe 4.3
|	Alternation	
(?:_re_)	Noncapturing parenthesis	
\G	End of the previous match	
+\+*n*	Back-reference to capture group number *n*	
Normal (greedy) quantifiers		
{ *m,n* }	Quantifier for from *m* to *n* repetitions	See Recipe 4.4
{ *m* ,}	Quantifier for *m* or more repetitions	
{ *m* }	Quantifier for exactly *m* repetitions	See Recipe 4.10
{,*n* }	Quantifier for 0 up to *n* repetitions	
*	Quantifier for 0 or more repetitions	Short for {0,}
+	Quantifier for 1 or more repetitions	Short for {1,}; see Recipe 4.2
?	Quantifier for 0 or 1 repetitions (i.e., present exactly once, or not at all)	Short for {0,1}
Reluctant (nongreedy) quantifiers		
{ *m,n* }?	Reluctant quantifier for from *m* to *n* repetitions	
{ *m* ,}?	Reluctant quantifier for *m* or more repetitions	
{,*n* }?	Reluctant quantifier for 0 up to *n* repetitions	
*?	Reluctant quantifier: 0 or more	
+?	Reluctant quantifier: 1 or more	See Recipe 4.10
??	Reluctant quantifier: 0 or 1 times	

Subexpression	Matches	Notes
Possessive (very greedy) quantifiers		
{ *m,n* }+	Possessive quantifier for from *m* to *n* repetitions	
{ *m* ,}+	Possessive quantifier for *m* or more repetitions	
{,*n* }+	Possessive quantifier for 0 up to *n* repetitions	
*+	Possessive quantifier: 0 or more	
++	Possessive quantifier: 1 or more	
?+	Possessive quantifier: 0 or 1 times	
Escapes and shorthands		
\	Escape (quote) character: turns most metacharacters off; turns subsequent alphabetic into metacharacters	
\Q	Escape (quote) all characters up to \E	
\E	Ends quoting begun with \Q	
\t	Tab character	
\r	Return (carriage return) character	
\n	Newline character	See Recipe 4.9
\f	Form feed	
\w	Character in a word	Use \w+ for a word; see Recipe 4.10
\W	A nonword character	
\d	Numeric digit	Use \d+ for an integer; see Recipe 4.2
\D	A nondigit character	
\s	Whitespace	Space, tab, etc., as determined by `java.lang.Character.isWhitespace()`
\S	A nonwhitespace character	See Recipe 4.10
Unicode blocks (representative samples)		
\p{InGreek}	A character in the Greek block	(Simple block)
\P{InGreek}	Any character not in the Greek block	
\p{Lu}	An uppercase letter	(Simple category)
\p{Sc}	A currency symbol	
POSIX-style character classes (defined only for US-ASCII)		
\p{Alnum}	Alphanumeric characters	`[A-Za-z0-9]`
\p{Alpha}	Alphabetic characters	`[A-Za-z]`
\p{ASCII}	Any ASCII character	`[\x00-\x7F]`

Subexpression	Matches	Notes
\p{Blank}	Space and tab characters	
\p{Space}	Space characters	[\t\n\x0B\f\r]
\p{Cntrl}	Control characters	[\x00-\x1F\x7F]
\p{Digit}	Numeric digit characters	[0-9]
\p{Graph}	Printable and visible characters (not spaces or control characters)	
\p{Print}	Printable characters	Same as \p{Graph}
\p{Punct}	Punctuation characters	One of !"#$%&'()* +,-./:;<=>?@[]\^_`{|} \~
\p{Lower}	Lowercase characters	[a-z]
\p{Upper}	Uppercase characters	[A-Z]
\p{XDigit}	Hexadecimal digit characters	[0-9a-fA-F]

Regexes match any place possible in the string. Patterns followed by greedy quantifiers (the only type that existed in traditional Unix regexes) consume (match) as much as possible without compromising any subexpressions that follow. Patterns followed by possessive quantifiers match as much as possible without regard to following subexpressions. Patterns followed by reluctant quantifiers consume as few characters as possible to still get a match.

Also, unlike regex packages in some other languages, the Java regex package was designed to handle Unicode characters from the beginning. The standard Java escape sequence \u+nnnn is used to specify a Unicode character in the pattern. We use methods of java.lang.Character to determine Unicode character properties, such as whether a given character is a space. Again, note that the backslash must be doubled if this is in a Java string that is being compiled because the compiler would otherwise parse this as "backslash-u" followed by some numbers.

To help you learn how regexes work, I provide a little program called REDemo.[6] The code for REDemo is too long to include in the book; in the online directory *regex* of the *darwinsys-api* repo, you will find *REDemo.java*, which you can run to explore how regexes work.

In the uppermost text box (see Figure 4-1), type the regex pattern you want to test. Note that as you type each character, the regex is checked for syntax; if the syntax is OK, you see a checkmark beside it. You can then select Match, Find, or Find All. Match means that the entire string must match the regex, and Find means the regex

---

6 REDemo was inspired by (but does not use any code from) a similar program provided with the now-retired Apache Jakarta Regular Expressions package.

must be found somewhere in the string (Find All counts the number of occurrences that are found). Below that, you type a string that the regex is to match against. Experiment to your heart's content. When you have the regex the way you want it, you can paste it into your Java program. You'll need to escape (backslash) any characters that are treated specially by both the Java compiler and the Java regex package, such as the backslash itself, double quotes, and others. Once you get a regex the way you want it, there is a Copy button (not shown in these screenshots) to export the regex to the clipboard, with or without backslash doubling, depending on how you want to use it.

 Remember that because a regex is entered as a string that will be compiled by a Java compiler, you usually need two levels of escaping for any special characters, including backslash and double quotes. For example, the regex (which includes the double quotes):

```
"You said it\."
```

has to be typed like this to be a valid compile-time Java language String:

```
String pattern = "\"You said it\\.\""
```

In Java 14+ you could also use a text block to avoid escaping the quotes:

```
String pattern = """
        "You said it\\."""""
```

I can't tell you how many times I've made the mistake of forgetting the extra backslash in \d+, \w+, and their kin!

In Figure 4-1, I typed qu into the REDemo program's Pattern box, which is a syntactically valid regex pattern: any ordinary characters stand as regexes for themselves, so this looks for the letter q followed by u. In the top version, I typed only a q into the string, which is not matched. In the second, I have typed quack and the q of a second quack. Because I have selected Find All, the count shows one match. As soon as I type the second u, the count is updated to two, as shown in the third version.

Regexes can do far more than just character matching. For example, the two-character regex ^T would match beginning of line (^) immediately followed by a capital T—that is, any line beginning with a capital T. It doesn't matter whether the line begins with "Tiny trumpets," "Titanic tubas," or "Triumphant twisted trombones," as long as the capital T is present in the first position.

But here we're not very far ahead. Have we really invested all this effort in regex technology just to be able to do what we could already do with the java.lang.String method startsWith()? Hmmm, I can hear some of you getting a bit restless. Stay in your seats! What if you wanted to match not only a letter T in the first position, but also a vowel immediately after it, followed by any number of letters in a word, followed by an exclamation point? Surely you could do this in Java by checking `starts With("T")` and `charAt(1) == 'a' || charAt(1) == 'e'`, and so on? Yes, but by the time you did that, you'd have written a lot of very highly specialized code that you couldn't use in any other application. With regular expressions, you can just give the pattern `^T[aeiou]\w*!`. That is, `^` and `T` as before, followed by a character class listing the vowels, followed by any number of word characters (`\w*`), followed by the exclamation point.

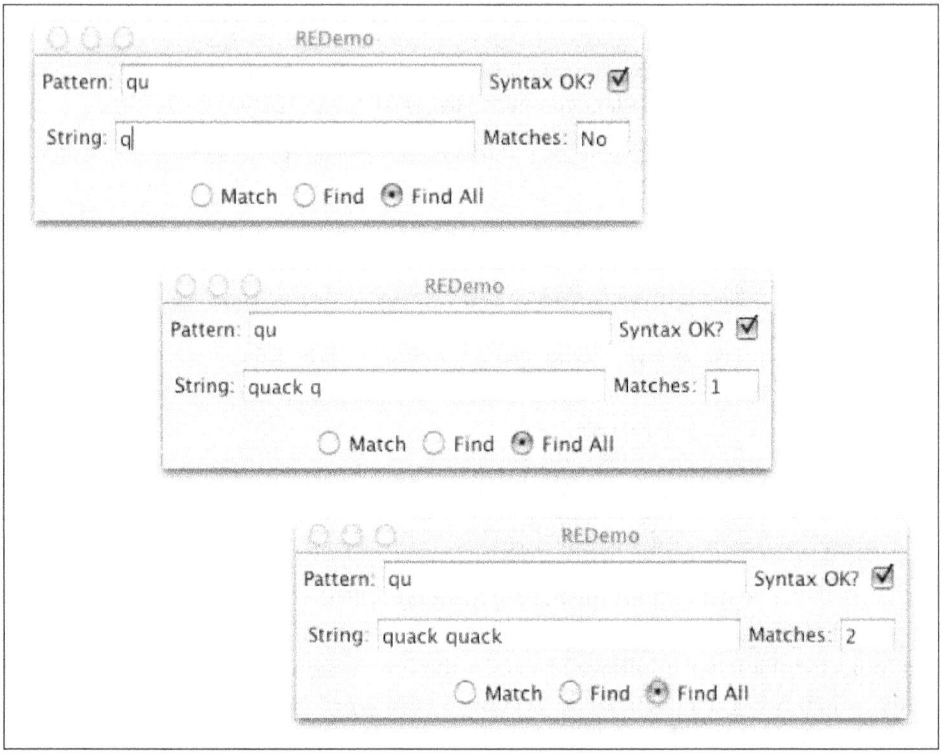

Figure 4-1. REDemo with simple examples

"But wait, there's more!" as my late, great boss Yuri Rubinsky (*https://en.wikipedia.org/wiki/Yuri_Rubinsky*) used to say. What if you want to be able to change the pattern you're looking for *at runtime*? Remember all that Java code you just wrote to match `T` in column 1, plus a vowel, some word characters, and an exclamation point? Well, it's time to throw it out. Because this morning we need to match `Q`, followed by a letter other than u, followed by a number of digits, followed by a period. While some of you start writing a new function to do that, the rest of us will just saunter over to the RegEx Bar & Grille, order a `^Q[^u]\d+\.` from the bartender, and be on our way.

OK, if you want an explanation: the [^u] means match any one character that is not the character u. The \d+ means one or more numeric digits. The + is a quantifier meaning one or more occurrences of what it follows, and \d is any one numeric digit. So \d+ means a number with one, two, or more digits. Finally, the \.? Well, . by itself is a metacharacter. Most single metacharacters are switched off by preceding them with an escape character. Not the Esc key on your keyboard, of course. The regex escape character is the backslash. Preceding a metacharacter like . with this escape turns off its special meaning, so we look for a literal period rather than any character. Preceding a few selected alphabetic characters (e.g., n, r, t, s, w) with escape turns them into metacharacters. Figure 4-2 shows the ^Q[^u]\d+\.. regex in action. In the first frame, I have typed part of the regex as ^Q[^u. Because there is an unclosed square bracket, the Syntax OK flag is turned off; when I complete the regex, it will be turned back on. In the second frame, I have finished typing the regex, and I've typed the data string as QA577 (which you should expect to match the $$^Q[^u]\d+$$ but not the period since I haven't typed it). In the third frame, I've typed the period so the Matches flag is set to Yes.

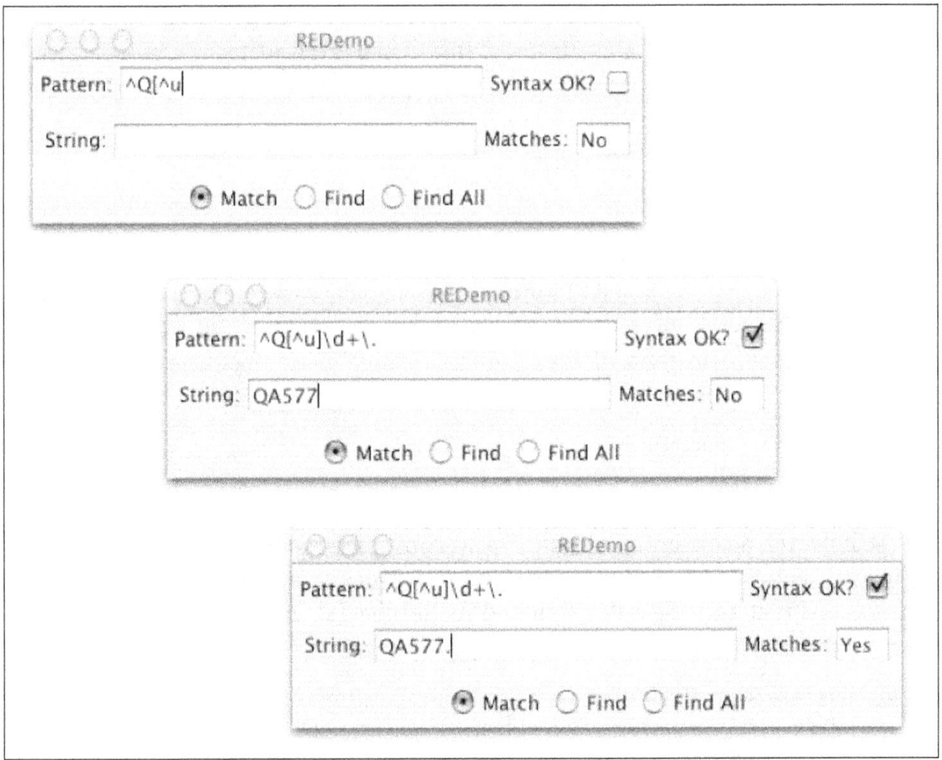

Figure 4-2. REDemo with "Q not followed by u" example

Because backslashes need to be escaped when pasting the regex into Java code, the current version of REDemo has both a Copy Pattern button, which copies the regex verbatim for use in documentation and in Unix commands, and a Copy Pattern Backslashed button, which copies the regex to the clipboard with backslashes doubled, for pasting into Java strings.

By now you should have at least a basic grasp of how regexes work in practice. The rest of this chapter gives more examples and explains some of the more powerful topics, such as capture groups. As for how regexes work in theory—and there are a lot of theoretical details and differences among regex flavors—the interested reader is referred to *Mastering Regular Expressions*. Meanwhile, let's start learning how to write Java programs that use regular expressions.

4.2 Using Regexes in Java: Test for a Pattern

Problem

You're ready to get started using regular expression processing to beef up your Java code by testing to see if a given pattern can match in a given string.

Solution

Use the Java Regular Expressions Package, `java.util.regex`.

Discussion

The good news is that the Java API for regexes is actually easy to use. If all you need is to find out whether a given regex matches a string, you can use the convenient `boolean matches()` method of the `String` class, which accepts a regex pattern in `String` form as its argument:

```
if (inputString.matches(stringRegexPattern)) {
    // it matched... do something with it...
}
```

This is, however, a convenience routine, and convenience always comes at a price. If the regex is going to be used more than once or twice in a program, it is more efficient to construct and use a `Pattern` and its `Matcher`(s). A complete program constructing a `Pattern` and using it to `match` is shown here:

```
public class RESimple {
    public static void main(String[] argv) {
        String pattern = "^Q[^u]\\d+\\.";
        String[] input = {
            "QA777. is the next flight. It is on time.",
            "Quack, Quack, Quack!"
        };
```

```
        Pattern p = Pattern.compile(pattern);

        for (String in : input) {
            boolean found = p.matcher(in).lookingAt();

            System.out.println("'" + pattern + "'" +
            (found ? " matches '" : " doesn't match '") + in + "'");
        }
    }
}
```

The `java.util.regex` package contains two classes, `Pattern` and `Matcher`, which provide the public API shown in Example 4-1.

Example 4-1. Regex public API

```
/**
 * The main public API of the java.util.regex package.
 */

package java.util.regex;

public final class Pattern {
    // Flags values ('or' together)
    public static final int
        UNIX_LINES, CASE_INSENSITIVE, COMMENTS, MULTILINE,
        DOTALL, UNICODE_CASE, CANON_EQ;
    // No public constructors; use these Factory methods
    public static Pattern compile(String patt);
    public static Pattern compile(String patt, int flags);
    // Method to get a Matcher for this Pattern
    public Matcher matcher(CharSequence input);
    // Information methods
    public String pattern();
    public int flags();
    // Convenience methods
    public static boolean matches(String pattern, CharSequence input);
    public String[] split(CharSequence input);
    public String[] split(CharSequence input, int max);
}

public final class Matcher {
    // Action: find or match methods
    public boolean matches();
    public boolean find();
    public boolean find(int start);
    public boolean lookingAt();
    // "Information about the previous match" methods
    public int start();
    public int start(int whichGroup);
    public int end();
```

```
        public int end(int whichGroup);
        public int groupCount();
        public String group();
        public String group(int whichGroup);
        // Reset methods
        public Matcher reset();
        public Matcher reset(CharSequence newInput);
        // Replacement methods
        public Matcher appendReplacement(StringBuffer where, String newText);
        public StringBuffer appendTail(StringBuffer where);
        public String replaceAll(String newText);
        public String replaceFirst(String newText);
        // information methods
        public Pattern pattern();
}

/* String, showing only the RE-related methods */
public final class String {
        public boolean matches(String regex);
        public String replaceFirst(String regex, String newStr);
        public String replaceAll(String regex, String newStr);
        public String[] split(String regex);
        public String[] split(String regex, int max);
}
```

This API is large enough to require some explanation. These are the normal steps for
regex matching in a production program:

1. Create a `Pattern` by calling the static method `Pattern.compile()`.

2. Request a `Matcher` from the pattern by calling `pattern.matcher(CharSequence)`
   for each `String` (or other `CharSequence`) you wish to look through.

3. Call (once or more) one of the finder methods (discussed later in this section) in
   the resulting `Matcher`.

The `java.lang.CharSequence` interface provides simple read-only access to objects
containing a collection of characters. The standard implementations are `String` and
`StringBuffer/StringBuilder` (described in Chapter 3), and the new I/O class
`java.nio.CharBuffer`.

Of course, you can perform regex matching in other ways, such as using the convenience methods in `Pattern` or even in `java.lang.String`, like this:

```
public class StringConvenience {
    public static void main(String[] argv) {

        String pattern = ".*Q[^u]\\d+\\..*";
        String line = "Order QT300. Now!";
        if (line.matches(pattern)) {
            System.out.println(line + " matches \"" + pattern + "\"");
```

```
        } else {
            System.out.println("NO MATCH");
        }
    }
}
```

But the three-step list is the standard pattern for matching. You'd likely use the String convenience routine in a program that only used the regex once; if the regex were being used more than once, it is worth taking the time to compile it because the compiled version runs faster.

In addition, the Matcher has several finder methods, which provide more flexibility than the String convenience routine match(). These are the Matcher methods:

match()

Used to compare the entire string against the pattern; this is the same as the routine in java.lang.String. Because it matches the entire String, I had to put .* before and after the pattern.

lookingAt()

Used to match the pattern only at the beginning of the string.

find()

Used to match the pattern in the string (not necessarily at the first character of the string), starting at the beginning of the string or, if the method was previously called and succeeded, at the first character not matched by the previous match.

Each of these methods returns boolean, with true meaning a match and false meaning no match. To check whether a given string matches a given pattern, you need only type something like the following:

```
Matcher m = Pattern.compile(patt).matcher(line);
if (m.find( )) {
    System.out.println(line + " matches " + patt)
}
```

But you may also want to extract the text that matched, which is the subject of the next recipe.

The following recipes cover uses of the Matcher API. Initially, the examples just use arguments of type String as the input source. Use of other CharSequence types is covered in Recipe 4.5.

4.3 Finding the Matching Text

Problem

You need to find the text that the regex matched.

Solution

Sometimes you need to know more than just whether a regex matched a string. In editors and many other tools, you want to know exactly what characters were matched. Remember that with quantifiers such as *, the length of the text that was matched may have no relationship to the length of the pattern that matched it. Do not underestimate the mighty .*, which happily matches thousands or millions of characters if allowed to. As you saw in the previous recipe, you can find out whether a given match succeeds just by using find() or matches(). But in other applications, you will want to get the characters that the pattern matched.

After a successful call to one of the preceding methods, you can use these information methods on the Matcher to get information on the match:

start(), end()
    Returns the character position in the string of the starting and ending characters that matched.

groupCount()
    Returns the number of parenthesized capture groups, if any; returns 0 if no groups were used.

group(int i)
    Returns the characters matched by group *i* of the current match, if *i* is greater than or equal to zero and less than or equal to the return value of groupCount(). Group 0 is the entire match, so group(0) (or just group()) returns the entire portion of the input that matched.

The notion of parentheses, or capture groups, is central to regex processing. Regexes may be nested to any level of complexity. The group(int) method lets you retrieve the characters that matched a given parenthesis group. If you haven't used any explicit parens, you can just treat whatever matched as level zero. Example 4-2 shows part of *REMatch.java*.

Example 4-2. Part of main/src/main/java/regex/REMatch.java

```java
public class REmatch {
    public static void main(String[] argv) {

        String patt = "Q[^u]\\d+\\.";
        Pattern r = Pattern.compile(patt);
        String line = "Order QT300. Now!";
        Matcher m = r.matcher(line);
        if (m.find()) {
            System.out.println(patt + " matches \"" +
                m.group(0) +
                "\" in \"" + line + "\"");
```

```
        } else {
            System.out.println("NO MATCH");
        }
    }
}
```

When run, this prints:

```
Q[\^u]\d+\. matches "QT300." in "Order QT300. Now!"
```

With the Match button checked, REDemo provides a display of all the capture groups in a given regex; one example is shown in Figure 4-3.

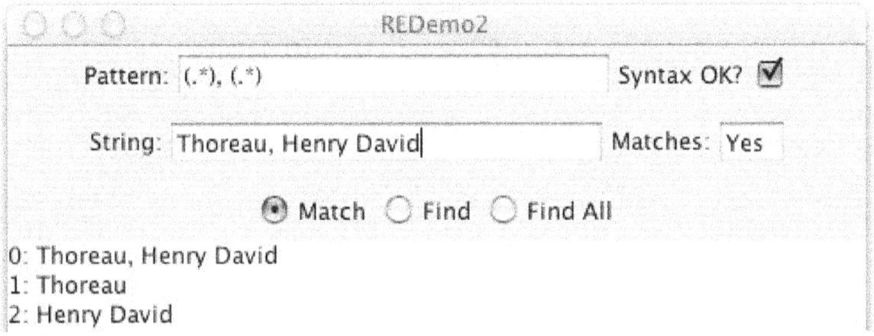

Figure 4-3. REDemo in action

It is also possible to get the starting and ending indices and the length of the text that the pattern matched (remember that terms with quantifiers, such as the \d+ in this example, can match an arbitrary number of characters in the string). You can use these in conjunction with the String.substring() methods as follows:

```
String patt = "Q[^u]\\d+\\.";
Pattern r = Pattern.compile(patt);
String line = "Order QT300. Now!";
Matcher m = r.matcher(line);
if (m.find()) {
    System.out.println(patt + " matches \"" +
        line.substring(m.start(0), m.end(0)) +
        "\" in \"" + line + "\"");
} else {
    System.out.println("NO MATCH");
}
```

Suppose you need to extract several items from a string. If the input is

```
Smith, John
Adams, John Quincy
```

and you want to get out

```
John Smith
John Quincy Adams
```

just use the following:

```
public class REmatchTwoFields {
    public static void main(String[] args) {
        String inputLine = "Adams, John Quincy";
        // Construct an RE with parens to "grab" both field1 and field2
        Pattern r = Pattern.compile("(.*), (.*)");
        Matcher m = r.matcher(inputLine);
        if (!m.matches())
            throw new IllegalArgumentException("Bad input");
        System.out.println(m.group(2) + ' ' + m.group(1));
    }
}
```

4.4 Replacing the Matched Text

Problem

Having found some text using a Pattern, you want to replace the text with different text, without disturbing the rest of the string.

Solution

As we saw in the previous recipe, regex patterns involving quantifiers can match a lot of characters with very few metacharacters. We need a way to replace the text that the regex matched without changing other text before or after it. We could do this manually using the String method substring(). However, because it's such a common requirement, the Java Regular Expression API provides some substitution methods.

Discussion

The Matcher class provides several methods for replacing just the text that matched the pattern. In all these methods, you pass in the replacement text, or "righthand side," of the substitution (this term is historical: in a command-line text editor's substitute command, the lefthand side is the pattern and the righthand side is the replacement text). These are the replacement methods:

replaceAll(newString)
: Replaces all occurrences that matched with the new string

replaceFirst(newString)
: As above but only the first occurence

appendReplacement(StringBuffer, newString)
: Copies up to before the first match, plus the given newString

```
appendTail(StringBuffer)
```
Appends text after the last match (normally used after `appendReplacement`)

Despite their names, the `replace*` methods behave in accord with the immutability of `Strings` (see "Timeless, Immutable, and Unchangeable" on page 58): they create a new `String` object with the replacement performed; they do not (indeed, could not) modify the string referred to in the `Matcher` object.

Example 4-3 shows use of these three methods.

Example 4-3. main/src/main/java/regex/ReplaceDemo.java

```
/**
 * Quick demo of RE substitution: correct U.S. 'favor'
 * to Canadian/British 'favour', but not in "favorite"
 * @author Ian F. Darwin, http://www.darwinsys.com/
 */
public class ReplaceDemo {
    public static void main(String[] argv) {

        // Make an RE pattern to match as a word only (\b=word boundary)
        String patt = "\\bfavor\\b";

        // A test input
        String input = "Do me a favor? Fetch my favorite.";
        System.out.println("Input: " + input);

        // Run it from a RE instance and see that it works
        Pattern r = Pattern.compile(patt);
        Matcher m = r.matcher(input);
        System.out.println("ReplaceAll: " + m.replaceAll("favour"));

        // Show the appendReplacement method
        m.reset();
        StringBuffer sb = new StringBuffer();
        System.out.print("Append methods: ");
        while (m.find()) {
            // Copy to before first match,
            // plus the word "favor"
            m.appendReplacement(sb, "favour");
        }
        m.appendTail(sb);        // copy remainder
        System.out.println(sb.toString());
    }
}
```

Sure enough, when you run it, it does what we expect:

```
Input: Do me a favor? Fetch my favorite.
ReplaceAll: Do me a favour? Fetch my favorite.
Append methods: Do me a favour? Fetch my favorite.
```

The replaceAll() method handles the case of making the same change all through a string. If you want to change each matching occurrence to a different value, you can use replaceFirst() in a loop, as in Example 4-4. Here we make a pass through an entire string, turning each occurrence of either cat or dog into feline or canine. This is simplified from a real example that looked for *bit.ly* URLs and replaced them with the actual URL; the computeReplacement method there used the network client code from Recipe 12.1.

Example 4-4. main/src/main/java/regex/ReplaceMulti.java

```java
/**
 * To perform multiple distinct substitutions in the same String,
 * you need a loop, and must call reset() on the matcher.
 */
public class ReplaceMulti {
    public static void main(String[] args) {

        Pattern patt = Pattern.compile("cat|dog");
        String line = "The cat and the dog never got along well.";
        System.out.println("Input: " + line);
        Matcher matcher = patt.matcher(line);
        while (matcher.find()) {
            String found = matcher.group(0);
            String replacement = computeReplacement(found);
            line = matcher.replaceFirst(replacement);
            matcher.reset(line);
        }
        System.out.println("Final: " + line);
    }

    static String computeReplacement(String in) {
        switch(in) {
        case "cat": return "feline";
        case "dog": return "canine";
        default: return "animal";
        }
    }
}
```

If you need to refer to portions of the occurrence that matched the regex, you can mark them with extra parentheses in the pattern and refer to the matching portion with $1, $2, and so on in the replacement string. Example 4-5 uses this to interchange two fields, in this case, turn names in the form Firstname Lastname into Lastname, FirstName.

Example 4-5. main/src/main/java/regex/ReplaceDemo2.java

```java
public class ReplaceDemo2 {
    public static void main(String[] argv) {

        // Make an RE pattern
        String patt = "(\\w+)\\s+(\\w+)";

        // A test input
        String input = "Ian Darwin";
        System.out.println("Input: " + input);

        // Run it from a RE instance and see that it works
        Pattern r = Pattern.compile(patt);
        Matcher m = r.matcher(input);
        m.find();
        System.out.println("Replaced: " + m.replaceFirst("$2, $1"));

        // The short inline version:
        // System.out.println(input.replaceFirst("(\\w+)\\s+(\\w+)", "$2, $1"));
    }
}
```

4.5 Printing All Occurrences of a Pattern

Problem

You need to find all the strings that match a given regex in one or more files or other sources.

Solution

This example reads through a file one line at a time. Whenever a match is found, I extract it from the line and print it.

This code takes the group() methods from Recipe 4.3, the substring method from the CharacterIterator interface, and the match() method from the regex and simply puts them all together. I coded it to extract all the names from a given file; in running the program through itself, it prints the words import, java, until, regex, and so on, each on its own line:

```
C:\> java ReaderIter.java ReaderIter.java
import
java
util
regex
import
java
io
```

```
Print
all
the
strings
that
match
given
pattern
from
file
public
...
C:\\>
```

I interrupted it here to save paper. This can be written two ways: a line-at-a-time pattern shown in Example 4-6 and a more compact form using new I/O shown in Example 4-7 (the new I/O package used in both examples is described in Chapter 10).

Example 4-6. main/src/main/java/regex/ReaderIter.java

```java
public class ReaderIter {
    public static void main(String[] args) throws IOException {
        // The RE pattern
        Pattern patt = Pattern.compile("[A-Za-z][a-z]+");
        // See the I/O chapter
        // For each line of input, try matching in it.
        Files.lines(Path.of(args[0])).forEach(line -> {
            // For each match in the line, extract and print it.
            Matcher m = patt.matcher(line);
            while (m.find()) {
                // Simplest method:
                // System.out.println(m.group(0));

                // Get the starting position of the text
                int start = m.start(0);
                // Get ending position
                int end = m.end(0);
                // Print whatever matched.
                // Use CharacterIterator.substring(offset, end);
                System.out.println(line.substring(start, end));
            }
        });
    }
}
```

Example 4-7. main/src/main/java/regex/GrepNIO.java

```java
public class GrepNIO {
    public static void main(String[] args) throws IOException {

        if (args.length < 2) {
```

```
        System.err.println("Usage: GrepNIO patt file [...]");
        System.exit(1);
    }

    Pattern p=Pattern.compile(args[0]);
    for (int i=1; i<args.length; i++)
        process(p, args[i]);
}

static void process(Pattern pattern, String fileName) throws IOException {

    // Get a FileChannel from the given file
    FileInputStream fis = new FileInputStream(fileName);
    FileChannel fc = fis.getChannel();

    // Map the file's content
    ByteBuffer buf = fc.map(FileChannel.MapMode.READ_ONLY, 0, fc.size());

    // Decode ByteBuffer into CharBuffer
    CharBuffer cbuf =
        Charset.forName("ISO-8859-1").newDecoder().decode(buf);

    Matcher m = pattern.matcher(cbuf);
    while (m.find()) {
        System.out.println(m.group(0));
    }
    fis.close();
}
}
```

The non-blocking I/O (NIO) version shown in Example 4-7 relies on the fact that an NIO Buffer can be used as a CharSequence. This program is more general in that the pattern argument is taken from the command-line argument. It prints the same output as the previous example if invoked with the pattern argument from the previous program on the command line:

```
java regex.GrepNIO "[A-Za-z][a-z]+"  ReaderIter.java
```

You might think of using \w+ as the pattern; the only difference is that my pattern looks for well-formed capitalized words, whereas \w+ would include Java-centric oddities like theVariableName, which have capitals in nonstandard positions.

Also note that the NIO version will probably be more efficient because it doesn't reset the Matcher to a new input source on each line of input as ReaderIter does.

4.6 Printing Lines Containing a Pattern

Problem

You need to look for lines matching a given regex in one or more files.

Solution

Write a simple *grep*-like program.

Discussion

As I've mentioned, once you have a regex package, you can write a *grep*-like program. I gave an example of the Unix *grep* program earlier. *grep* is called with some optional arguments, followed by one required regular expression pattern, followed by an arbitrary number of filenames. It prints any line that contains the pattern, differing from Recipe 4.5, which prints only the matching text itself. Here's an example:

```
grep "[dD]arwin" *.txt
```

The code searches for lines containing either darwin or Darwin in every line of every file whose name ends in *.txt*.[6] Example 4-8 is the source for the first version of a program to do this, called *Grep0*. It reads lines from the standard input and doesn't take any optional arguments, but it handles the full set of regular expressions that the Pattern class implements (it is, therefore, not identical to the Unix programs of the same name). We haven't covered the java.io package for input and output yet (see Chapter 10), but our use of it here is simple enough that you can probably intuit it. The online source includes *Grep1*, which does the same thing but is better structured (and therefore longer). Later in this chapter, Recipe 4.11 presents a *JGrep* program that parses a set of command-line options.

Example 4-8. main/src/main/java/regex/Grep0.java

```java
public class Grep0 {
    public static void main(String[] args) throws IOException {
        BufferedReader is =
            new BufferedReader(new InputStreamReader(System.in));
        if (args.length != 1) {
            System.err.println("Usage: MatchLines pattern");
            System.exit(1);
        }
```

---

6 On Unix, the shell or command-line interpreter expands *.txt to all the matching filenames before running the program, but the normal Java interpreter does this for you on systems where the shell isn't energetic or bright enough to do it.

```
    Pattern patt = Pattern.compile(args[0]);
    Matcher matcher = patt.matcher("");
    String line = null;
    while ((line = is.readLine()) != null) {
        matcher.reset(line);
        if (matcher.find()) {
            System.out.println("MATCH: " + line);
        }
    }
  }
}
```

4.7 Controlling Case in Regular Expressions

Problem

You want to find text regardless of case.

Solution

Compile the `Pattern` passing in the `flags` argument `Pattern.CASE_INSENSITIVE` to indicate that matching should be case-independent (i.e., that it should fold, ignore differences in case). If your code might run in different locales (see Recipe 3.12), then you should add `Pattern.UNICODE_CASE`. Without these flags, the default is normal, case-sensitive matching behavior. This flag (and others) are passed to the `Pattern.compile()` method, like this:

```
// regex/CaseMatch.java
Pattern  reCaseInsens = Pattern.compile(pattern, Pattern.CASE_INSENSITIVE |
    Pattern.UNICODE_CASE);
reCaseInsens.matches(input);          // will match case-insensitively
```

This flag must be passed when you create the `Pattern`; because `Pattern` objects are immutable, they cannot be changed once constructed.

The full source code for this example is online as *CaseMatch.java*.

Pattern.compile() Flags

Half a dozen flags can be passed as the second argument to `Pattern.compile()`. If more than one value is needed, they can be or'd together using the bitwise or operator `|`. In alphabetical order, these are the flags:

CANON_EQ
    Enables so-called canonical equivalence. In other words, characters are matched by their base character so that the character e followed by the combining charac-

---

ter mark for the acute accent (´) can be matched either by the composite charac-ter é or the letter e followed by the character mark for the accent (see Recipe 4.8).

CASE_INSENSITIVE
Turns on case-insensitive matching (see Recipe 4.7).

COMMENTS
Causes whitespace and comments (from # to end-of-line) to be ignored in the pattern. See *CommentedRegEx.java* in the *regex* source directory.

DOTALL
Allows dot (.) to match any regular character or the newline, not just any regular character other than newline (see Recipe 4.9).

MULTILINE
Specifies multiline mode (see Recipe 4.9).

UNICODE_CASE
Enables Unicode-aware case folding (see Recipe 4.7).

UNIX_LINES
Makes \n the only valid newline sequence for MULTILINE mode (see Recipe 4.9).

4.8 Matching Accented, or Composite, Characters

Problem

You want characters to match regardless of the form in which they are entered.

Solution

Compile the Pattern with the flags argument Pattern.CANON_EQ for canonical equality.

Discussion

Composite characters can be entered in various forms. Consider, as a single example, the letter e with an acute accent. This character may be found in various forms in Unicode text, such as the single character é (Unicode character \u00e9) or the two-character sequence e´ (e followed by the Unicode combining acute accent, \u0301). To allow you to match such characters regardless of which of possibly multiple fully decomposed forms are used to enter them, the regex package has an option for *can-onical matching*, which treats any of the forms as equivalent. This option is enabled by passing CANON_EQ as (one of) the flags in the second argument to Pattern.com pile(). This program shows CANON_EQ being used to match several forms:

```
public class CanonEqDemo {
    public static void main(String[] args) {
        String pattStr = "\u00e9gal"; // egal
        String[] input = {
                "\u00e9gal", // egal - this one had better match :-)
                "e\u0301gal", // e + "Combining acute accent"
                "e\u02cagal", // e + "modifier letter acute accent"
                "e'gal", // e + single quote
                "e\u00b4gal", // e + Latin-1 "acute"
        };
        Pattern pattern = Pattern.compile(pattStr, Pattern.CANON_EQ);
        for (int i = 0; i < input.length; i++) {
            if (pattern.matcher(input[i]).matches()) {
                System.out.println(
                    pattStr + " matches input " + input[i]);
            } else {
                System.out.println(
                    pattStr + " does not match input " + input[i]);
            }
        }
    }
}
```

This program correctly matches the combining accent and rejects the other characters, some of which, unfortunately, look like the accent on a printer, but are not considered combining accent characters:

```
égal matches input égal
égal matches input e?gal
égal does not match input e?gal
égal does not match input e'gal
égal does not match input e´gal
```

For more details, see the character charts (*http://www.unicode.org*).

4.9 Matching Newlines in Text

Problem

You need to match newlines in text.

Solution

Use \n or \r in your regex pattern. See also the flags constant `Pattern.MULTILINE`, which makes newlines match as beginning-of-line and end-of-line (\^ and $).

Discussion

Though line-oriented tools from Unix such as *sed* and *grep* match regular expressions one line at a time, not all tools do. The *sam* text editor from Bell Laboratories was the first interactive tool I know of to allow multiline regular expressions; the Perl scripting language followed shortly after. In the Java API, the newline character by default has no special significance. The `BufferedReader` method `readLine()` normally strips out whichever newline characters it finds. If you read in gobs of characters using some method other than `readLine()`, you may have some number of \n, \r, or \r\n sequences in your text string.[6] Normally all of these are treated as equivalent to \n. If you want only \n to match, use the UNIX_LINES flag to the `Pattern.compile()` method.

In Unix, ^ and $ are commonly used to match the beginning or end of a line, respectively. In this API, the regex metacharacters \^ and $ ignore line terminators and only match at the beginning and the end, respectively, of the entire string. However, if you pass the MULTILINE flag into `Pattern.compile()`, these expressions match just after or just before, respectively, a line terminator; $ also matches the very end of the string. Because the line ending is just an ordinary character, you can match it with . or similar expressions; and, if you want to know exactly where it is, \n or \r in the pattern match it as well. In other words, to this API, a newline character is just another character with no special significance. See the sidebar "Pattern.compile() Flags" on page 119. An example of newline matching is shown in Example 4-9.

Example 4-9. main/src/main/java/regex/NLMatch.java

```java
public class NLMatch {
    public static void main(String[] argv) {

        String input = "I dream of engines\nmore engines, all day long";
        System.out.println("INPUT: " + input);
        System.out.println();

        String[] patt = {
            "engines.more engines",
            "ines\nmore",
            "engines$"
        };

        for (int i = 0; i < patt.length; i++) {
            System.out.println("PATTERN " + patt[i]);

            boolean found;
            Pattern p1l = Pattern.compile(patt[i]);
            found = p1l.matcher(input).find();
            System.out.println("DEFAULT match " + found);
```

---

6 Or a few related Unicode characters, including the next-line (\u0085), line-separator (\u2028), and paragraph-separator (\u2029) characters.

```
        Pattern pml = Pattern.compile(patt[i],
            Pattern.DOTALL|Pattern.MULTILINE);
        found = pml.matcher(input).find();
        System.out.println("MultiLine match " + found);
        System.out.println();
        }
    }
}
```

If you run this code, the first pattern (with the wildcard character .) always matches, whereas the second pattern (with $) matches only when MATCH_MULTILINE is set:

```
> java regex.NLMatch
INPUT: I dream of engines
more engines, all day long

PATTERN engines
more engines
DEFAULT match true
MULTILINE match: true

PATTERN engines$
DEFAULT match false
MULTILINE match: true
```

4.10 Program: Apache Logfile Parsing

The Apache web server is the world's leading web server and has been for most of the web's history. It is one of the world's best-known open source projects, and it's the first of many fostered by the Apache Foundation. The name Apache is often claimed to be a pun on the origins of the server; its developers began with the free NCSA server and kept hacking at it, or patching, it until it did what they wanted. When it was sufficiently different from the original, a new name was needed. Because it was now a patchy server, the name Apache was chosen. Officialdom denies the story, but it's cute anyway. One place actual patchiness does show through is in the logfile format. Consider Example 4-10.

Example 4-10. Apache log file excerpt

```
123.45.67.89 - - [27/Oct/2000:09:27:09 -0400] "GET /java/javaResources.html
HTTP/1.0" 200 10450 "-" "Mozilla/4.6 [en] (X11; U; OpenBSD 2.8 i386; Nav)"
```

The file format was obviously designed for human inspection but not for easy parsing. The problem is that different delimiters are used: square brackets for the date, quotes for the request line, and spaces sprinkled all through. Consider trying to use a StringTokenizer; you might be able to get it working, but you'd spend a lot of time fiddling with it. Actually, no, you wouldn't get it working. However, this somewhat contorted regular expression[6] makes it easy to parse (this is one single Moby-sized regex; we had to break it over two lines to make it fit the book's margins):

```
\^([\d.]+) (\S+) (\S+) \[(([\w:/]+\s[+\-]\d{4})\] "(.+?)" (\d{3}) (\d+)
   "([\^"]+)" "([\^"]+)"
```

You may find it informative to refer back to Table 4-1 and review the full syntax used here. Note in particular the use of the nongreedy quantifier +? in \"(.+?)\" to match a quoted string; you can't just use .+ because that would match too much (up to the quote at the end of the line). Code to extract the various fields such as IP address, request, referrer URL, and browser version is shown in Example 4-11.

Example 4-11. main/src/main/java/regex/LogRegExp.java

```java
public class LogRegExp {

    final static String logEntryPattern =
            "^([\\d.]+) (\\S+) (\\S+) \\[(([\\w:/]+\\s[+-]\\d{4})\\] " +
            "\"(.+?)\" (\\d{3}) (\\d+) \"([^\"]+)\" \"([^\"]+)\"";

    public static void main(String argv[]) {

        System.out.println("RE Pattern:");
        System.out.println(logEntryPattern);

        System.out.println("Input line is:");
        String logEntryLine = LogParseInfo.LOG_ENTRY_LINE;
        System.out.println(logEntryLine);

        Pattern p = Pattern.compile(logEntryPattern);
        Matcher matcher = p.matcher(logEntryLine);
        if (!matcher.matches() ||
            LogParseInfo.MIN_FIELDS > matcher.groupCount()) {
            System.err.println("Bad log entry (or problem with regex):");
            System.err.println(logEntryLine);
            return;
        }
        System.out.println("IP Address: " + matcher.group(1));
        System.out.println("UserName: " + matcher.group(3));
        System.out.println("Date/Time: " + matcher.group(4));
        System.out.println("Request: " + matcher.group(5));
        System.out.println("Response: " + matcher.group(6));
        System.out.println("Bytes Sent: " + matcher.group(7));
        if (!matcher.group(8).equals("-"))
            System.out.println("Referer: " + matcher.group(8));
        System.out.println("User-Agent: " + matcher.group(9));
```

---

6 You might think this would hold some kind of world record for complexity in regex competitions, but I'm sure it's been outdone many times.

```
        }
    }
```

The `implements` clause is for an interface that just defines the input string; it was used in a demonstration to compare the regular expression mode with the use of a `String Tokenizer`. The source for both versions is in the online source for this chapter. Running the program against the sample input from Example 4-10 gives this output:

```
Using regex Pattern:
\^([\d.]+) (\S+) (\S+) \[(([\w:/]+\s[+\-]\d{4})\] "(.+?)" (\d{3}) (\d+) "([\^"]
+)"
"([\^"]+)"
Input line is:
123.45.67.89 - - [27/Oct/2000:09:27:09 -0400] "GET /java/javaResources.html
HTTP/1.0" 200 10450 "-" "Mozilla/4.6 [en] (X11; U; OpenBSD 2.8 i386; Nav)"
IP Address: 123.45.67.89
Date&Time: 27/Oct/2000:09:27:09 -0400
Request: GET /java/javaResources.html HTTP/1.0
Response: 200
Bytes Sent: 10450
Browser: Mozilla/4.6 [en] (X11; U; OpenBSD 2.8 i386; Nav)
```

The program successfully parsed the entire logfile format entry with one call to `matcher.matches()`.

4.11 Program: Full Grep

Now that we've seen how the regular expressions package works, it's time to write JGrep, a full-blown version of the line-matching program with option parsing. Table 4-2 lists some typical command-line options that a Unix implementation of *grep* might include. For those not familiar with *grep*, it is a command-line tool that searches for regular expressions in text files. There are three or four programs in the standard *grep* family, and a newer replacement *ripgrep*, or *rg*. This program is my addition to this family of programs.

Table 4-2. Grep command-line options

Option	Meaning
-c	Count only; don't print lines, just count them
-C	Context; print some lines above and below each line that matches (not implemented in this version; left as an exercise for the reader)
-f pattern	Take pattern from file named after -f instead of from command line
-h	Suppress printing filename ahead of lines
-i	Ignore case
-l	List filenames only: don't print lines, just the names they're found in
-n	Print line numbers before matching lines

Option	Meaning
-s	Suppress printing certain error messages
-v	Invert: print only lines that do NOT match the pattern

The Unix world features several *getopt* library routines for parsing command-line arguments, so I have a reimplementation of this in Java. As usual, because main() runs in a static context but our application main line does not, we could wind up passing a lot of information into the constructor. To save space, this version just uses global variables to track the settings from the command line. Unlike the Unix *grep* tool, this one does not yet handle combined options, so -l -r -i is OK, but -lri will fail, due to a limitation in the GetOpt parser used.

The program basically just reads lines, matches the pattern in them, and, if a match is found (or not found, with -v), prints the line (and optionally some other stuff, too). Having said all that, the code is shown in Example 4-12.

Example 4-12. darwinsys-api/src/main/java/regex/JGrep.java

```java
/** A command-line grep-like program. Accepts some command-line options,
 * and takes a pattern and a list of text files.
 * N.B. The current implementation of GetOpt does not allow combining short
 * arguments, so put spaces e.g., "JGrep -l -r -i pattern file..." is OK, but
 * "JGrep -lri pattern file..." will fail. Getopt will hopefully be fixed soon.
 */
public class JGrep {
    private static final String USAGE =
        "Usage: JGrep pattern [-chilrsnv][-f pattfile][filename...]";
    /** The pattern we're looking for */
    protected Pattern pattern;
    /** The matcher for this pattern */
    protected Matcher matcher;
    private boolean debug;
    /** Are we to only count lines, instead of printing? */
    protected static boolean countOnly = false;
    /** Are we to ignore case? */
    protected static boolean ignoreCase = false;
    /** Are we to suppress printing of filenames? */
    protected static boolean dontPrintFileName = false;
    /** Are we to only list names of files that match? */
    protected static boolean listOnly = false;
    /** Are we to print line numbers? */
    protected static boolean numbered = false;
    /** Are we to be silent about errors? */
    protected static boolean silent = false;
    /** Are we to print only lines that DONT match? */
    protected static boolean inVert = false;
    /** Are we to process arguments recursively if directories? */
    protected static boolean recursive = false;
```

```
/** Construct a Grep object for the pattern, and run it
 * on all input files listed in args.
 * Be aware that a few of the command-line options are not
 * acted upon in this version - left as an exercise for the reader!
 * @param args args
 */
public static void main(String[] args) {

    if (args.length < 1) {
        System.err.println(USAGE);
        System.exit(1);
    }
    String patt = null;

    GetOpt go = new GetOpt("cf:hilnrRsv");

    char c;
    while ((c = go.getopt(args)) != 0) {
        switch(c) {
            case 'c':
                countOnly = true;
                break;
            case 'f':    /* External file contains the pattern */
                try (BufferedReader b =
                    new BufferedReader(new FileReader(go.optarg()))) {
                    patt = b.readLine();
                } catch (IOException e) {
                    System.err.println(
                        "Can't read pattern file " + go.optarg());
                    System.exit(1);
                }
                break;
            case 'h':
                dontPrintFileName = true;
                break;
            case 'i':
                ignoreCase = true;
                break;
            case 'l':
                listOnly = true;
                break;
            case 'n':
                numbered = true;
                break;
            case 'r':
            case 'R':
                recursive = true;
                break;
            case 's':
                silent = true;
                break;
```

```java
                case 'v':
                    inVert = true;
                    break;
                case '?':
                    System.err.println("Getopts was not happy!");
                    System.err.println(USAGE);
                    break;
            }
        }

        int ix = go.getOptInd();

        if (patt == null)
            patt = args[ix++];

        JGrep prog = null;
        try {
            prog = new JGrep(patt);
        } catch (PatternSyntaxException ex) {
            System.err.println("RE Syntax error in " + patt);
            return;
        }

        if (args.length == ix) {
            dontPrintFileName = true; // Don't print filenames if stdin
            if (recursive) {
                System.err.println("Warning: recursive search of stdin!");
            }
            prog.process(new InputStreamReader(System.in), null);
        } else {
            if (!dontPrintFileName)
                dontPrintFileName = ix == args.length - 1; // Nor if only one file
            if (recursive)
                dontPrintFileName = false;                 // unless a directory!

            for (int i=ix; i<args.length; i++) { // note starting index
                try {
                    prog.process(new File(args[i]));
                } catch(Exception e) {
                    System.err.println(e);
                }
            }
        }
    }

    /**
     * Construct a JGrep object.
     * @param patt The regex to look for
     * @throws PatternSyntaxException if pattern is not a valid regex
     */
    public JGrep(String patt) throws PatternSyntaxException {
        if (debug) {
```

```
                System.err.printf("JGrep.JGrep(%s)%n", patt);
        }
        // compile the regular expression
        int caseMode = ignoreCase ?
            Pattern.UNICODE_CASE | Pattern.CASE_INSENSITIVE :
            0;
        pattern = Pattern.compile(patt, caseMode);
        matcher = pattern.matcher("");
    }

    /** Process one command line argument (file or directory)
     * @param file The input File
     * @throws FileNotFoundException If the file doesn't exist
     */
    public void process(File file) throws FileNotFoundException {
        if (!file.exists() || !file.canRead()) {
            throw new FileNotFoundException(
                "Can't read file " + file.getAbsolutePath());
        }
        if (file.isFile()) {
            process(new BufferedReader(new FileReader(file)),
                file.getAbsolutePath());
            return;
        }
        if (file.isDirectory()) {
            if (!recursive) {
                System.err.println(
                    "ERROR: -r not specified but directory given " +
                    file.getAbsolutePath());
                return;
            }
            for (File nf : file.listFiles()) {
                process(nf);    // "Recursion, n.: See Recursion."
            }
            return;
        }
        System.err.println(
            "WEIRDNESS: neither file nor directory: " + file.getAbsolutePath());
    }

    /** Do the work of scanning one file
     * @param     ifile     Reader     Reader object already open
     * @param     fileName String     Name of the input file
     */
    public void process(Reader ifile, String fileName) {

        String inputLine;
        int matches = 0;

        try (BufferedReader reader = new BufferedReader(ifile)) {

            while ((inputLine = reader.readLine()) != null) {
```

```java
                    matcher.reset(inputLine);
                    if (matcher.find()) {
                        if (listOnly) {
                            // -l, print filename on first match, and we're done
                            System.out.println(fileName);
                            return;
                        }
                        if (countOnly) {
                            matches++;
                        } else {
                            if (!dontPrintFileName) {
                                System.out.print(fileName + ": ");
                            }
                            System.out.println(inputLine);
                        }
                    } else if (inVert) {
                        System.out.println(inputLine);
                    }
                }
                if (countOnly)
                    System.out.println(matches + " matches in " + fileName);
            } catch (IOException e) {
                System.err.println(e);
            }
        }
    }
}
```

## CHAPTER 5

Numbers

5.0 Introduction

Numbers are basic to just about any computation. They're used for array indices, temperatures, salaries, ratings, and an infinite variety of things. Yet they're not as simple as they seem. With floating-point numbers, how accurate is accurate? With random numbers, how random is random? With strings that should contain a number, what actually constitutes a number?

Java has several built-in, or *primitive*, types that can be used to represent numbers, summarized in Table 5-1 with their *wrapper* (object) types, as well as some numeric types that do not represent primitive types. Note that unlike languages such as C or Perl, which don't specify the size or precision of numeric types, Java—with its goal of portability—specifies these exactly and states that they are the same on all platforms.

Table 5-1. Numeric types

Built-in type	Object wrapper	Size of built-in (bits)	Contents
byte	Byte	8	Signed integer
short	Short	16	Signed integer
int	Integer	32	Signed integer
long	Long	64	Signed integer
float	Float	32	IEEE-754 floating point
double	Double	64	IEEE-754 floating point
char	Character	16	Unsigned Unicode character
n/a	BigInteger	unlimited	Arbitrary-size immutable integer value
n/a	BigDecimal	unlimited	Arbitrary-size-and-precision immutable floating-point value

As you can see, Java provides a numeric type for just about any purpose. There are four sizes of signed integers for representing various sizes of whole numbers. There are two sizes of floating-point numbers to approximate real numbers. There is also a type specifically designed to represent and allow operations on Unicode characters. The primitive numeric types are discussed here. The "Big" value types are described in Recipe 5.12.

When you read a string representing a number from user input or a text file, you need to convert it to the appropriate type. The object wrapper classes in the second column have several functions, one of which is to provide this basic conversion functionality—replacing the C programmer's *atoi/atof* family of functions and the numeric arguments to *scanf*.

Going the other way, you can convert any number (indeed, anything at all in Java) to a string just by using string concatenation. If you want a little bit of control over numeric formatting, Recipe 5.5 shows you how to use some of the object wrappers' conversion routines. And if you want full control, that recipe also shows the use of NumberFormat and its related classes to provide full control of formatting.

As the name *object wrapper* implies, these classes are also used to wrap a number in a Java object, as many parts of the standard API are defined in terms of objects. Later on, "Solution" on page 394 shows using an Integer object to save an int's value to a file using object serialization and retrieving the value later.

But I haven't yet mentioned the issues of floating point. Real numbers, you may recall, are numbers with a fractional part. There is an infinite number of real numbers. A floating-point number—what a computer uses to approximate a real number—is not the same as a real number. The number of floating-point numbers is finite, with only 2^{32} different bit patterns for floats, and 2^{64} for doubles. Thus, most real values have only an approximate correspondence to floating point. The result of printing the real number 0.3 works correctly, like this:

```
// numbers/RealValues.java
System.out.println("The real value 0.3 is " + 0.3);
```

That code results in this printout:

```
The real value 0.3 is 0.3
```

But the difference between a real value and its floating-point approximation can accumulate if the value is used in a computation; this is often called a *rounding error*. Continuing the previous example, the real 0.3 multiplied by 3 yields:

```
The real 0.3 times 3 is 0.89999999999999991
```

Surprised? Not only is it off by a bit from what you might expect, but you will of course get the same output on any conforming Java implementation. I ran it on machines as disparate as an AMD/Intel PC with OpenBSD, a PC with Windows and the standard JDK, and on macOS. Always the same answer.

And what about random numbers? How random are they? You have probably heard the term *Pseudorandom Number Generator*, or PRNG. All conventional random number generators, whether written in Fortran, C, or Java, generate pseudorandom numbers. That is, they're not truly random! True randomness comes only from specially built hardware: an analog source of Brownian noise connected to an analog-to-digital converter, for example.[6] Your average PC of today may have some good sources of entropy, or even hardware-based sources of randomness (which have not been widely used or tested yet). However, pseudorandom number generators are good enough for most purposes, so we use them. Java provides one random generator in the base library `java.lang.Math`, and several others; we'll examine these in Recipe 5.9.

The class `java.lang.Math` contains an entire math library in one class, including trigonometry, conversions (including degrees to radians and back), rounding, truncating, square root, minimum, and maximum. It's all there. Check the javadoc for `java.lang.Math`.

The package `java.math` contains support for *big numbers*—those larger than the normal built-in long integers, for example. See Recipe 5.12.

Java works hard to ensure that your programs are reliable. The usual ways you'd notice this are in the common requirement to catch potential exceptions—all through the Java API—and in the need to *cast*, or convert, when storing a value that might or might not fit into the variable you're trying to store it in. I'll show examples of these.

Overall, Java's handling of numeric data fits well with the ideals of portability, reliability, and ease of programming.

See Also

The Java Language Specification (*https://docs.oracle.com/javase/specs*), and the javadoc page for `java.lang.Math`.

---

6 For a low-cost source of randomness, check out the now-defunct Lavarand (*http://en.wikipedia.org/wiki/Lavarand*). The process used digitized video of 1970s lava lamps to provide "hardware-based" randomness. Fun!

5.1 Checking Whether a String Is a Valid Number

Problem

You need to check whether a given string contains a valid number, and, if so, convert it to binary (internal) form.

Solution

To accomplish this, use the appropriate wrapper class's conversion routine and catch the NumberFormatException. This code converts a string to a double:

```
public static void main(String[] argv) {
    String aNumber = argv[0];    // not argv[1]
    double result;
    try {
        result = Double.parseDouble(aNumber);
        System.out.println("Number is " + result);
    } catch(NumberFormatException exc) {
        System.out.println("Invalid number " + aNumber);
        return;
    }
}
```

Discussion

This code lets you validate only numbers in the format that the designers of the wrapper classes expected. If you need to accept a different definition of numbers, you could use regular expressions (see Chapter 4) to make the determination.

There may also be times when you want to tell if a given number is an integer number or a floating-point number. One way is to check for the characters ., d, e, or f in the input; if one of these characters is present, convert the number as a double. Otherwise, convert it as an int:

```
/*
 * Process one String, returning it as a Number subclass
 */
public static Number process(String s) {
    if (s.matches("[+-]*\\d*\\.\\d+[dDeEfF]*")) {
        try {
            double dValue = Double.parseDouble(s);
            System.out.println("It's a double: " + dValue);
            return Double.valueOf(dValue);
        } catch (NumberFormatException e) {
            System.out.println("Invalid double: " + s);
            return Double.NaN;
        }
    } else // did not contain . d e or f, so try as int.
```

```
        try {
            int iValue = Integer.parseInt(s);
            System.out.println("It's an int: " + iValue);
            return Integer.valueOf(iValue);
        } catch (NumberFormatException e2) {
            System.out.println("Not a number: " + s);
            return Double.NaN;
        }
    }
```

See Also

A more involved form of parsing is offered by the DecimalFormat class, discussed in Recipe 5.5.

There is also the Scanner class; see Recipe 10.6.

5.2 Converting Numbers to Objects and Vice Versa

Problem

You need to convert numbers to objects and objects to numbers.

Solution

Use the object wrapper classes listed in Table 5-1 at the beginning of this chapter.

Discussion

Often you have a primitive number and you need to pass it into a method where an Object is required, or vice versa. Long ago you had to invoke the conversion routines that are part of the wrapper classes, but now you can generally use automatic conversion (called *auto-boxing/auto-unboxing*). See Example 5-1 for examples of both.

Example 5-1. main/src/main/java/structure/AutoboxDemo.java

```
public class AutoboxDemo {

    /** Shows auto-boxing (in the call to foo(i), i is wrapped automatically)
     * and auto-unboxing (the return value is automatically unwrapped).
     */
    public static void main(String[] args) {
        int i = 42;
        int result = foo(i);              ❶
        System.out.println(result);
    }

    public static Integer foo(Integer i) {
```

```
        System.out.println("Object = " + i);
        return Integer.valueOf(123);        ❷
    }
}
```

❶ Auto-boxing: int 42 is converted to Integer(42). Also auto-unboxing: the Integer returned from foo() is auto-unboxed to assign to int result.

❷ No auto-boxing: valueOf() returns Integer. If the line said return Inte ger.intValueOf(123), then it would be a second example of auto-boxing because the method return value is Integer.

To explicitly convert between an int and an Integer object, or vice versa, you can use the wrapper class methods:

```
public class IntObject {
    public static void main(String[] args) {
        // int to Integer
        Integer i1 = Integer.valueOf(42);
        System.out.println(i1.toString());        // or just i1

        // Integer to int
        int i2 = i1.intValue();
        System.out.println(i2);
    }
}
```

5.3 Taking a Fraction of an Integer Without Using Floating Point

Problem

You want to multiply an integer by a fraction without converting the fraction to a floating-point number.

Solution

Multiply the integer by the numerator and divide by the denominator.

This technique should be used only when efficiency is more important than clarity because it tends to detract from the readability—and therefore the maintainability—of your code.

Discussion

Because integers and floating-point numbers are stored differently, it may sometimes be desirable and feasible, for efficiency purposes, to multiply an integer by a fractional value without converting the values to floating point and back, and without requiring a cast:

```java
public class FractMult {
    public static void main(String[] u) {

        double d1 = 0.666 * 5;   // fast but obscure and inaccurate: convert
        System.out.println(d1); // 2/3 to 0.666 in programmer's head

        double d2 = 2/3 * 5;     // wrong answer - 2/3 == 0, 0*5 = 0
        System.out.println(d2);

        double d3 = 2d/3d * 5;   // "normal"
        System.out.println(d3);

        double d4 = (2*5)/3d;    // one step done as integers, almost same answer
        System.out.println(d4);

        int i5 = 2*5/3;          // fast, approximate integer answer
        System.out.println(i5);
    }
}
```

Running the code looks like this:

```
$ java numbers.FractMult
3.33
0.0
3.333333333333333
3.3333333333333335
3
$
```

You should beware of the possibility of numeric overflow and avoid this optimization if you cannot guarantee that the multiplication by the numerator will not overflow.

5.4 Working with Floating-Point Numbers

Problem

You want to be able to compare and round floating-point numbers.

Solution

Compare with the INFINITY constants, and use isNaN() to check for NaN (not a number).

Compare floating values with an epsilon value.

Round floating point values with Math.round() or custom code.

Discussion

Comparisons can be a bit tricky: fixed-point operations that can do things like divide by zero result in Java notifying you abruptly by throwing an exception. This is because integer division by zero is considered a *logic error*.

Floating-point operations, however, do not throw an exception because they are defined over an (almost) infinite range of values. Instead, they signal errors by producing the constant POSITIVE_INFINITY if you divide a positive floating-point number by zero, the constant NEGATIVE_INFINITY if you divide a negative floating-point value by zero, and NaN if you otherwise generate an invalid result. Values for these three public constants are defined in both the Float and the Double wrapper classes. The value NaN has the unusual property that it is not equal to itself (i.e., NaN != NaN). Thus, it would hardly make sense to compare a (possibly suspect) number against NaN, because the following expression can never be true:

```
x == NaN
```

Instead, the methods Float.isNaN(float) and Double.isNaN(double) must be used:

```
public static void main(String[] argv) {
    double d = 123;
    double e = 0;
    if (d/e == Double.POSITIVE_INFINITY)
        System.out.println("Check for POSITIVE_INFINITY works");
    double s = Math.sqrt(-1);
    if (s == Double.NaN)
        System.out.println("Comparison with NaN incorrectly returns true");
    if (Double.isNaN(s))
        System.out.println("Double.isNaN() correctly returns true");
}
```

Note that this, by itself, is not sufficient to ensure that floating-point calculations have been done with adequate accuracy. For example, the following program demonstrates a contrived calculation—Heron's formula for the area of a triangle—both in float and in double. The double values are correct, but the floating-point value comes out as zero due to rounding errors. This happens because, in Java, operations involving only float values are performed as 32-bit calculations. Related languages such as C automatically promote these to double during the computation, which can eliminate some loss of accuracy. Let's take a look:

```
public class Heron {
    public static void main(String[] args) {
        // Sides for triangle in float
        float af, bf, cf;
        float sf, areaf;

        // Ditto in double
```

```
        double ad, bd, cd;
        double sd, aread;

        // Area of triangle in float
        af = 12345679.0f;
        bf = 12345678.0f;
        cf = 1.01233995f;

        sf = (af+bf+cf)/2.0f;
        areaf = (float)Math.sqrt(sf * (sf - af) * (sf - bf) * (sf - cf));
        System.out.println("Single precision: " + areaf);

        // Area of triangle in double
        ad = 12345679.0;
        bd = 12345678.0;
        cd = 1.01233995;

        sd = (ad+bd+cd)/2.0d;
        aread = Math.sqrt(sd * (sd - ad) * (sd - bd) * (sd - cd));
        System.out.println("Double precision: " + aread);
    }
}
```

Now let's run it:

```
$ java numbers.Heron
Single precision: 0.0
Double precision: 972730.0557076167
```

If in doubt, use double!

To ensure consistency of very large-magnitude double computations on different Java implementations, Java provides the keyword strictfp, which can apply to classes, interfaces, or methods within a class.[6] If a computation is Strict-FP, then it must always, for example, return the value INFINITY if a calculation would overflow the value of Double.MAX_VALUE (or underflow the value Double.MIN_VALUE). Non-Strict-FP calculations—the default—are allowed to perform calculations on a greater range and can return a valid final result that is in range even if the interim product was out of range. This is pretty esoteric and affects only computations that approach the bounds of what fits into a double.

Comparing floating-point values

Based on what we've just discussed, you probably won't just go comparing two floats or doubles for equality. You might expect the floating-point wrapper classes, Float and Double, to override the equals() method, which they do. The equals() method

---

6 Note that an expression consisting entirely of compile-time constants, like Math.PI * 2.1e17, is also considered to be Strict-FP.

returns true if the two values are the same bit for bit (i.e., if and only if the numbers are the same or are both NaN). It returns false otherwise, including if the argument passed in is null, or if one object is +0.0 and the other is –0.0.

I said earlier that NaN != Nan, but if you compare with equals(), the result is true:

```
jshell> Float f1 = Float.valueOf(Float.NaN)
f1 ==> NaN

jshell> Float f2 = Float.valueOf(Float.NaN)
f2 ==> NaN

jshell> f1 == f2 # Comparing object identities
$4 ==> false

jshell> f1.equals(f1) # bitwise comparison of values
$5 ==> true
```

If this sounds weird, remember that the complexity comes partly from the nature of doing real number computations in the less-precise floating-point hardware. It also comes partly from the details of the IEEE Standard 754, which specifies the floating-point functionality that Java tries to adhere to so that underlying floating-point processor hardware can be used even when Java programs are being interpreted.

To actually compare floating-point numbers for equality, it is generally desirable to compare them within some tiny range of allowable differences; this range is often regarded as a tolerance or as *epsilon*. Example 5-2 shows an equals() method you can use to do this comparison, as well as comparisons on values of NaN. When run, it prints that the first two numbers are equal within epsilon:

```
$ java numbers.FloatCmp
True within epsilon 1.0E-7
$
```

Example 5-2. main/src/main/java/numbers/FloatCmp.java

```java
public class FloatCmp {

    final static double EPSILON = 0.0000001;

    public static void main(String[] argv) {
        double da = 3 * .3333333333;
        double db = 0.99999992857;

        // Compare two numbers that are expected to be close.
        if (da == db) {
            System.out.println("Java considers " + da + "==" + db);
        // else compare with our own equals overload
        } else if (equals(da, db, 0.0000001)) {
            System.out.println("Equal within epsilon " + EPSILON);
```

```
    } else {
        System.out.println(da + " != " + db);
    }

    System.out.println("NaN prints as " + Double.NaN);

    // Show that comparing two NaNs is not a good idea:
    double nan1 = Double.NaN;
    double nan2 = Double.NaN;
    if (nan1 == nan2)
        System.out.println("Comparing two NaNs incorrectly returns true.");
    else
        System.out.println("Comparing two NaNs correctly reports false.");

    if (Double.valueOf(nan1).equals(Double.valueOf(nan2)))
        System.out.println("Double(NaN).equals(NaN) correctly returns true.");
    else
        System.out.println(
            "Double(NaN).equals(NaN) incorrectly returns false.");
}

/** Compare two doubles within a given epsilon */
public static boolean equals(double a, double b, double eps) {
    if (a==b) return true;
    // If the difference is less than epsilon, treat as equal.
    return Math.abs(a - b) < eps;
}

/** Compare two doubles, using default epsilon */
public static boolean equals(double a, double b) {
    return equals(a, b, EPSILON);
}
}
```

Note that neither of the `System.err` messages about incorrect returns prints. The point of this example with NaNs is that you should always make sure values are not NaN before entrusting them to `Double.equals()`.

Rounding

If you simply cast a floating value to an integer value, Java truncates the value. A value like 3.999999 cast to an `int` or `long` becomes 3, not 4. To round floating-point numbers properly, use `Math.round()`. It has two overloads: if you give it a `double`, you get a `long` result; if you give it a `float`, you get an `int`.

What if you don't like the rounding rules used by `round`? If, for some bizarre reason, you wanted to round numbers greater than 0.54 instead of the normal 0.5, you could write your own version of `round()`:

```
public class Round {
    /** We round a number up if its fraction exceeds this threshold. */
    public static final double THRESHOLD = 0.54;

    /*
     * Round floating values to integers.
     * @return the closest int to the argument.
     * @param d A non-negative values to be rounded.
     */
    public static int round(double d) {
        return (int)Math.floor(d + 1.0 - THRESHOLD);
    }

    public static void main(String[] argv) {
        for (double d = 0.1; d<=1.0; d+=0.05) {
            System.out.println("My way:   " + d + "-> " + round(d));
            System.out.println("Math way:" + d + "-> " + Math.round(d));
        }
    }
}
```

If, on the other hand, you simply want to display a number with less precision than it normally gets, you probably want to use a DecimalFormat object or a Formatter object, which we look at in Recipe 5.5.

5.5 Formatting Numbers

Problem

You need to format numbers.

Solution

Use a NumberFormat subclass.

Java did not originally provide C-style printf/scanf functions because they tend to mix together formatting and input/output in a very inflexible way. Programs using printf/scanf can be hard to internationalize, for example. Of course, by popular demand, Java did eventually introduce printf(), which along with String.format() is now standard in Java; see Recipe 10.4.

Java has an entire package, java.text, full of formatting routines as general and flexible as anything you might imagine. As with printf, it has an involved formatting language, described in the javadoc page. Consider the presentation of long numbers. In North America, the number one thousand twenty-four and a quarter is written 1,024.25; in most of Europe it is 1 024,25; and in some other part of the world it might be written 1.024,25. Not to mention how currencies and percentages are formatted! Trying to keep track of this yourself would drive the average small software shop around the bend rather quickly.

Fortunately, the java.text package includes a Locale class; and, furthermore, the Java runtime automatically sets a default Locale object based on the user's environment (on the Macintosh and Windows, the user's preferences, and on Unix, the user's environment variables). To provide a nondefault locale in code, see Recipe 3.12. To provide formatters customized for numbers, currencies, and percentages, the Number Format class has static *factory methods* that normally return a DecimalFormat with the correct pattern already instantiated. A DecimalFormat object appropriate to the user's locale can be obtained from the factory method NumberFormat.getInstance() and manipulated using set methods. Surprisingly, the method setMinimumIntegerDigits() turns out to be the easy way to generate a number format with leading zeros. Here is an example:

```
public class NumFormat2 {
    /** A number to format */
    public static final double data[] = {
        0, 1, 22d/7, 100.2345678
    };

    /** The main (and only) method in this class. */
    public static void main(String[] av) {
        // Get a format instance
        NumberFormat form = NumberFormat.getInstance();

        // Set it to look like 999.99[99]
        form.setMinimumIntegerDigits(3);
        form.setMinimumFractionDigits(2);
        form.setMaximumFractionDigits(4);

        // Now print using it
        for (int i=0; i<data.length; i++)
            System.out.println(data[i] + "\tformats as " +
                form.format(data[i]));
    }
}
```

This prints the contents of the array using the NumberFormat instance form:

```
$ java numbers.NumFormat2
0.0      formats as 000.00
1.0      formats as 001.00
3.142857142857143       formats as 003.1429
100.2345678      formats as 100.2346
$
```

You can also construct a `DecimalFormat` with a particular pattern or change the pattern dynamically using `applyPattern()`. Some of the more common pattern characters are shown in Table 5-2.

Table 5-2. DecimalFormat pattern characters

Character	Meaning
#	Numeric digit (leading zeros suppressed)
0	Numeric digit (leading zeros provided)
.	Locale-specific decimal separator (decimal point)
,	Locale-specific grouping separator (comma in English)
-	Locale-specific negative indicator (minus sign)
%	Shows the value as a percentage
;	Separates two formats: the first for positive and the second for negative values
'	Escapes one of the above characters so it appears
Anything else	Appears as itself

The `NumFormatDemo` program uses one `DecimalFormat` to print a number with only two decimal places and a second to format the number according to the default locale:

```
/** A number to format */
public static final double intlNumber = 1024.25;
/** Another number to format */
public static final double ourNumber = 100.2345678;
    NumberFormat defForm = NumberFormat.getInstance();
    NumberFormat ourForm = new DecimalFormat("##0.##");
    // toPattern() will reveal the combination of #0., etc
    // that this particular Locale uses to format with!
    System.out.println("defForm's pattern is " +
        ((DecimalFormat)defForm).toPattern());
    System.out.println(intlNumber + " formats as " +
        defForm.format(intlNumber));
    System.out.println(ourNumber + " formats as " +
        ourForm.format(ourNumber));
    System.out.println(ourNumber + " formats as " +
        defForm.format(ourNumber) + " using the default format");
```

This program prints the given pattern and then formats the same number using several formats:

```
$ java numbers.NumFormatDemo
defForm's pattern is #,##0.###
1024.25 formats as 1,024.25
100.2345678 formats as 100.23
```

```
100.2345678 formats as 100.235 using the default format
$
```

Human-readable number formatting

To print a number in what Linux/Unix calls "human readable format" (many display commands accept a -h argument for this format), use the Java 12 CompactNumberFormat, as shown in Example 5-3.

Example 5-3. nmain/src/main/java/numbers/CompactFormatDemo.java

```java
public class CompactFormatDemo {

    static final Number[] nums = {
        0, 1, 1.25, 1234, 12345, 123456.78, 123456789012L
    };
    static final String[] strs = {
        "1", "1.25", "1234", "12.345K", "1234556.78", "123456789012L"
    };

    public static void main(String[] args) throws ParseException {
        NumberFormat cnf = NumberFormat.getCompactNumberInstance();
        System.out.println("Formatting:");
        for (Number n : nums) {
            cnf.setParseIntegerOnly(false);
            cnf.setMinimumFractionDigits(2);
            System.out.println(n + ": " + cnf.format(n));
        }
        System.out.println("Parsing:");
        for (String s : strs) {
            System.out.println(s + ": " + cnf.parse(s));
        }
    }

}
```

Roman numeral formatting

To work with roman numerals, use my RomanNumberFormat class, as in this demo:

```java
RomanNumberFormat nf = new RomanNumberFormat();
int year = LocalDate.now().getYear();
System.out.println(year + " -> " + nf.format(year));
```

Running RomanNumberSimple in 2020 produces this output:

```
2020->MMXX
```

The source of the RomanNumberFormat class is in *src/main/java/numbers/RomanNumberFormat.java*. Several of the public methods are required because I wanted it to be a subclass of Format, which is abstract. This accounts for some of the complexity, like having three different format methods.

Note that the RomanNumberFormat.parseObject( ) method is also required, but the code doesn't implement parsing in this version.

See Also

Java I/O by Elliotte Harold (O'Reilly) includes an entire chapter on NumberFormat and develops the subclass ExponentialNumberFormat.

5.6 Converting Among Binary, Octal, Decimal, and Hexadecimal

Problem

You want to display an integer as a series of bits—for example, when interacting with certain hardware devices—or in some alternative number base (binary is base 2, octal is base 8, decimal is 10, hexadecimal is 16). You want to convert a binary number or a hexadecimal value into an integer.

Solution

The class java.lang.Integer provides the solutions. Most of the time you can use Integer.parseInt(String input, int radix) to convert from any type of number to an Integer, and Integer.toString(int input, int radix) to go the other way. Example 5-4 shows some examples of using the Integer class.

Example 5-4. main/src/main/java/numbers/IntegerBinOctHexEtc.java

```
String input = "101010";
for (int radix : new int[] { 2, 8, 10, 16, 36 }) {
    System.out.print(input + " in base " + radix + " is "
            + Integer.valueOf(input, radix) + "; ");
    int i = 42;
    System.out.println(i + " formatted in base " + radix + " is "
            + Integer.toString(i, radix));
}
```

This program prints the binary string as an integer in various bases, and the integer 42 in those same number bases:

```
$ java numbers.IntegerBinOctHexEtc
101010 in base 2 is 42; 42 formatted in base 2 is 101010
101010 in base 8 is 33288; 42 formatted in base 8 is 52
101010 in base 10 is 101010; 42 formatted in base 10 is 42
```

```
101010 in base 16 is 1052688; 42 formatted in base 16 is 2a
101010 in base 36 is 60512868; 42 formatted in base 36 is 16
$
```

Discussion

There are also specialized versions of toString(int) that don't require you to specify the radix, for example, toBinaryString() to convert an integer to binary, toHex String() for hexadecimal, toOctalString(), and so on. The javadoc page for the Integer class is your friend here.

The String class itself includes a series of static methods—valueOf(int), value Of(double), and so on—that also provide default formatting. That is, they return the given numeric value formatted as a string.

5.7 Operating on a Series of Integers

Problem

You need to work on a range of integers.

Solution

For a contiguous set, use IntStream::range and rangeClosed, or the older for loop.

For discontinuous ranges of numbers, use a java.util.BitSet.

Discussion

To process a contiguous set of integers, Java provides both range() / rangeClosed() methods in the IntStream and LongStream classes. These take a starting and ending number; range() excludes the ending number while rangeClosed() closes on, or includes, the ending number. You can also iterate over a range of numbers using the traditional for loop. Loop control for the for loop is in three parts: initialize, test, and change. If the test part is initially false, the loop will never be executed, not even once. You can iterate over the elements of an array or collection (see Chapter 7) using a for-each loop.

The program in Example 5-5 demonstrates these techniques.

Example 5-5. main/src/main/java/numbers/NumSeries.java

```java
public class NumSeries {
    public static void main(String[] args) {

        // For ordinal list of numbers n to m, use rangeClosed(start, endInclusive)
        IntStream.rangeClosed(1, 12).forEach(
            i -> System.out.println("Month # " + i));

        // Or, use a for loop starting at 1.
        for (int i = 1; i <= months.length; i++)
            System.out.println("Month # " + i);

        // Or a foreach loop
        for (String month : months) {
            System.out.println(month);
        }

        // When you want a set of array indices, use range(start, endExclusive)
        IntStream.range(0, months.length).forEach(
            i -> System.out.println("Month " + months[i]));

        // Or, use a for loop starting at 0.
        for (int i = 0; i < months.length; i++)
            System.out.println("Month " + months[i]);

        // For e.g., counting by 3 from 11 to 27, use a for loop
        for (int i = 11; i <= 27; i += 3) {
            System.out.println("i = " + i);
        }

        // A discontiguous set of integers, using a BitSet

        // Create a BitSet and turn on a couple of bits.
        BitSet b = new BitSet();
        b.set(0);    // January
        b.set(3);    // April
        b.set(8);    // September

        // Presumably this would be somewhere else in the code.
        for (int i = 0; i<months.length; i++) {
            if (b.get(i))
                System.out.println("Month " + months[i]);
        }

        // Same example but shorter:
        // a discontiguous set of integers, using an array
        int[] numbers = {0, 3, 8};

        // Presumably somewhere else in the code... Also a foreach loop
        for (int n : numbers) {
            System.out.println("Month: " + months[n]);
```

```
        }
    }
    /** Names of months. See Dates/Times chapter for a better way to get these */
    protected static String months[] = {
        "January", "February", "March", "April",
        "May", "June", "July", "August",
        "September", "October", "November", "December"
    };
}
```

5.8 Formatting with Correct Plurals

Problem

You're printing something like "We used " + n + " items", but in English, "We used 1 items" is ungrammatical. You want "We used 1 item."

Solution

Use a `ChoiceFormat` or a conditional statement.

Use Java's ternary operator (cond ? `trueval` : `falseval`) in a string concatenation. Both zero and plurals get an "s" appended to the noun in English ("no books, one book, two books"), so we test for n==1:

```
public class FormatPlurals {
    public static void main(String[] argv) {
        report(0);
        report(1);
        report(2);
    }

    /** report -- using conditional operator */
    public static void report(int n) {
        System.out.println("We used " + n + " item" + (n==1?"":"s"));
    }
}
```

Does it work?

```
$ java numbers.FormatPlurals
We used 0 items
We used 1 item
We used 2 items
$
```

The final `println` statement is effectively equivalent to the following:

```
if (n==1)
    System.out.println("We used " + n + " item");
```

```
else
    System.out.println("We used " + n + " items");
```

This is a lot longer, so the ternary conditional operator is worth learning.

The ChoiceFormat is ideal for this. It is actually capable of much more, but here I'll show only this simplest use. I specify the values 0, 1, and 2 (or more), and the string values to print corresponding to each number. The numbers are then formatted according to the range they fall into:

```
public class FormatPluralsChoice extends FormatPlurals {

    // ChoiceFormat to just give pluralized word
    static double[] limits = { 0, 1, 2 };
    static String[] formats = { "reviews", "review", "reviews"};
    static ChoiceFormat pluralizedFormat = new ChoiceFormat(limits, formats);

    // ChoiceFormat to give English text version, quantified
    static ChoiceFormat quantizedFormat = new ChoiceFormat(
        "0#no reviews|1#one review|1<many reviews");

    // Test data
    static int[] data = { -1, 0, 1, 2, 3 };

    public static void main(String[] argv) {
        System.out.println("Pluralized Format");
        for (int i : data) {
            System.out.println("Found " + i + " " + pluralizedFormat.format(i));
        }

        System.out.println("Quantized Format");
        for (int i : data) {
            System.out.println("Found " + quantizedFormat.format(i));
        }
    }
}
```

This generates the same output as the basic version. It is slightly longer, but more general, and lends itself better to internationalization.

See Also

In addition to ChoiceFormat, the same result can be achieved with a MessageFormat. The online source in file *main/src/main/java/i18n/MessageFormatDemo.java* has an example.

5.9 Generating Random Numbers

Problem

You need to generate pseudorandom numbers in a hurry.

Solution

Use `java.lang.Math.random()` to generate random numbers. There is no claim that the random values it returns are very *good* random numbers, however. Like most software-only implementations, these are *Pseudorandom Number Generators* (PRNGs), meaning that the numbers are not totally random, but devised from an algorithm. That said, they are adequate for casual use. This code exercises the ran dom() method:

```
// numbers/Random1.java
// java.lang.Math.random( ) is static, don't need any constructor calls
System.out.println("A random from java.lang.Math is " + Math.random( ));
```

Note that this method only generates double values. If you need integers, construct a `java.util.Random` object and call its `nextInt()` method; if you pass it an integer value, this will become the upper bound. Here I generate integers from 1 to 10:

```
public class RandomInt {
    public static void main(String[] a) {
        Random r = new Random();
        for (int i=0; i<1000; i++)
            // nextInt(10) goes from 0-9; add 1 for 1-10;
            System.out.println(1+r.nextInt(10));
    }
}
```

To see if my RandomInt demo was really working well, I used the Unix tools *sort* and *uniq*, which together give a count of how many times each value was chosen. For 1,000 integers, each of 10 values should be chosen about 100 times. I ran it twice to get a better idea of the distribution:

```
$ java numbers.RandomInt | sort | uniq -c | sort -k 2 -n
  96 1
 107 2
 102 3
 122 4
  99 5
 105 6
  97 7
  96 8
  79 9
  97 10
$ java -cp build numbers.RandomInt | sort | uniq -c | sort -k 2 -n
  86 1
```

```
 88 2
110 3
 97 4
 99 5
109 6
 82 7
116 8
 99 9
114 10
$
```

The next step is to run these through a statistical program to see how really random they are; we'll return to this in a minute.

In general, to generate random numbers, you need to construct a `java.util.Random` object (not just any old random object) and call its `next*()` methods. These methods include `nextBoolean()`, `nextBytes()` (which fills the given array of bytes with random values), `nextDouble()`, `nextFloat()`, `nextInt()`, and `nextLong()`. Don't be confused by the capitalization of `Float`, `Double`, etc. They return the primitive types `boolean`, `float`, `double`, etc., not the capitalized wrapper objects. Clear enough? Maybe an example will help:

```
// java.util.Random methods are non-static, so need to construct
Random r = new Random();
for (int i=0; i<10; i++)
System.out.println("A double from java.util.Random is " + r.nextDouble());
for (int i=0; i<10; i++)
System.out.println("An integer from java.util.Random is " + r.nextInt());
```

A fixed value (*starting seed*) can be provided to generate repeatable values, as for testing. You can also use the `java.util.Random nextGaussian()` method, as shown next. The `nextDouble()` methods try to give a flat distribution between 0 and 1.0, in which each value has an equal chance of being selected. A Gaussian or normal distribution is a bell curve of values from negative infinity to positive infinity, with the majority of the values around zero (0.0).

```
// numbers/Random3.java
Random r = new Random();
for (int i = 0; i < 10; i++)
System.out.println("A gaussian random double is " + r.nextGaussian());
```

To illustrate the different distributions, I generated 10,000 numbers using `nextRandom()` first and then using `nextGaussian()`. The code for this is in *Random4.java* (not shown here) and is a combination of the previous programs with code to print the results into files. I then plotted histograms using the R statistics package (see Chapter 11 and *http://www.r-project.org*). The R script used to generate the graph, *randomnesshistograms.r*, is in *javasrc* under *main/src/main/resources*. The results are shown in Figure 5-1.

Looks like both PRNGs do their job!

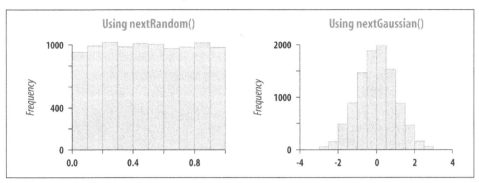

Figure 5-1. Flat (left) and Gaussian (right) distributions

See Also

The javadoc documentation for `java.util.Random`, and the warning in Recipe 5.0 about pseudorandomness versus real randomness.

For cryptographic use, see class `java.security.SecureRandom`, which provides cryptographically strong pseudorandom number generators.

5.10 Multiplying Matrices

Problem

You need to multiply a pair of two-dimensional arrays, as is common in mathematical and engineering applications.

Solution

Use the following code as a model.

Discussion

It is straightforward to multiply an array of a numeric type. In real life you would probably use a full-blown package such as the Efficient Java Matrix Library (EJML) (*http://ejml.org/wiki/index.php?title=Main_Page*) or DeepLearning4Java's ND4J package (*https://deeplearning4j.org/docs/latest/nd4j-overview*). However a simple implementation can serve to show the concepts involved; the code in Example 5-6 implements matrix multiplication.

Example 5-6. Matrix.java

```java
public class Matrix {

    /* Matrix-multiply two arrays together.
     * The arrays MUST be rectangular.
     * @author Adapted from Tom Christiansen & Nathan Torkington's
     * implementation in their Perl Cookbook.
     */
    public static int[][] multiply(int[][] m1, int[][] m2) {
        int m1rows = m1.length;
        int m1cols = m1[0].length;
        int m2rows = m2.length;
        int m2cols = m2[0].length;
        if (m1cols != m2rows)
            throw new IllegalArgumentException(
                "matrices don't match: " + m1cols + " != " + m2rows);
        int[][] result = new int[m1rows][m2cols];

        // multiply
        for (int i=0; i<m1rows; i++) {
            for (int j=0; j<m2cols; j++) {
                for (int k=0; k<m1cols; k++) {
                    result[i][j] += m1[i][k] * m2[k][j];
                }
            }
        }

        return result;
    }

    /** Matrix print.
     */
    public static void mprint(int[][] a) {
        int rows = a.length;
        int cols = a[0].length;
        System.out.println("array["+rows+"]["+cols+"] = {");
        for (int i=0; i<rows; i++) {
            System.out.print("{");
            for (int j=0; j<cols; j++)
                System.out.print(" " + a[i][j] + ",");
            System.out.println("},");
        }
        System.out.println("};");
    }
}
```

Here is a program that uses the `Matrix` class to multiply two arrays of `int`s:

```java
int x[][] = {
    { 3, 2, 3 },
    { 5, 9, 8 },
};
```

```
int y[][] = {
    { 4, 7 },
    { 9, 3 },
    { 8, 1 },
};
int z[][] = Matrix.multiply(x, y);
Matrix.mprint(x);
Matrix.mprint(y);
Matrix.mprint(z);
```

See Also

Consult a book on numerical methods for more things to do with matrices; one of our reviewers recommends the series of *Numerical Recipes* books, available from *http://nrbook.com*. (Note that this site has a link to their new web presence, *https://numerical.recipes* however, that site requires Adobe Flash, which most browsers no longer support due to security concerns.) There are several translations of the book's code into various languages, including Java (*http://numerical.recipes/aboutJava.html*). Pricing varies by package.

Commercial software packages can do some of these calculations for you; for one example, see the numeric libraries available from Rogue Wave Software (*http://www.roguewave.com*).

5.11 Using Complex Numbers

Problem

You need to manipulate complex numbers, as is common in mathematical, scientific, or engineering applications.

Solution

Java does not provide any explicit support for dealing with complex numbers. You could keep track of the real and imaginary parts and do the computations yourself, but that is not a very well-structured solution.

A better solution, of course, is to use a class that implements complex numbers. I once wrote just such a class, but now I recommend using the Apache Commons Math library for this. The build coordinates for this are `org.apache.commons:commons-math3:3.6.1` (or later). First, an example of using Apache's library:

```
public class ComplexDemoACM {

    public static void main(String[] args) {
        Complex c = new Complex(3,  5);
```

```
        Complex d = new Complex(2, -2);
        System.out.println(c);
        System.out.println(c + ".getReal() = " + c.getReal());
        System.out.println(c + " + " + d + " = " + c.add(d));
        System.out.println(c + " + " + d + " = " + c.add(d));
        System.out.println(c + " * " + d + " = " + c.multiply(d));
        System.out.println(c.divide(d));
    }
}
```

Running this demo program produces the following output:

```
(3.0, 5.0)
(3.0, 5.0).getReal() = 3.0
(3.0, 5.0) + (2.0, -2.0) = (5.0, 3.0)
(3.0, 5.0) + (2.0, -2.0) = (5.0, 3.0)
(3.0, 5.0) * (2.0, -2.0) = (16.0, 4.0)
(-0.5, 2.0)
```

Example 5-7 is the source for my version of the Complex class and shouldn't require much explanation. The Apache one is admittedly more sophisticated, but I leave mine here just to demystify the basic operation of complex numbers.

To keep the API general, I provide—for each of add, subtract, and multiply—both a static method that works on two complex objects and a nonstatic method that applies the operation to the given object and one other object.

Example 5-7. main/src/main/java/numbers/Complex.java

```java
public class Complex {
    /** The real part */
    private double r;
    /** The imaginary part */
    private double i;

    /** Construct a Complex */
    Complex(double rr, double ii) {
        r = rr;
        i = ii;
    }

    /** Display the current Complex as a String, for use in
     * println() and elsewhere.
     */
    public String toString() {
        StringBuilder sb = new StringBuilder().append(r);
        if (i>0)
            sb.append('+');     // else append(i) appends - sign
        return sb.append(i).append('i').toString();
    }

    /** Return just the Real part */
```

```java
public double getReal() {
    return r;
}
/** Return just the Real part */
public double getImaginary() {
    return i;
}
/** Return the magnitude of a complex number */
public double magnitude() {
    return Math.sqrt(r*r + i*i);
}

/** Add another Complex to this one
 */
public Complex add(Complex other) {
    return add(this, other);
}

/** Add two Complexes
 */
public static Complex add(Complex c1, Complex c2) {
    return new Complex(c1.r+c2.r, c1.i+c2.i);
}

/** Subtract another Complex from this one
 */
public Complex subtract(Complex other) {
    return subtract(this, other);
}

/** Subtract two Complexes
 */
public static Complex subtract(Complex c1, Complex c2) {
    return new Complex(c1.r-c2.r, c1.i-c2.i);
}

/** Multiply this Complex times another one
 */
public Complex multiply(Complex other) {
    return multiply(this, other);
}

/** Multiply two Complexes
 */
public static Complex multiply(Complex c1, Complex c2) {
    return new Complex(c1.r*c2.r - c1.i*c2.i, c1.r*c2.i + c1.i*c2.r);
}

/** Divide c1 by c2.
 * @author Gisbert Selke.
 */
public static Complex divide(Complex c1, Complex c2) {
```

```
        return new Complex(
            (c1.r*c2.r+c1.i*c2.i)/(c2.r*c2.r+c2.i*c2.i),
            (c1.i*c2.r-c1.r*c2.i)/(c2.r*c2.r+c2.i*c2.i));
    }

    /* Compare this Complex number with another
     */
    public boolean equals(Object o) {
        if (o.getClass() != Complex.class) {
            throw new IllegalArgumentException(
                    "Complex.equals argument must be a Complex");
        }
        Complex other = (Complex)o;
        return r == other.r && i == other.i;
    }

    /* Generate a hashCode; not sure how well distributed these are.
     */
    public int hashCode() {
        return (int)(r) |  (int)i;
    }
}
```

5.12 Handling Very Large Numbers

Problem

You need to handle integer numbers larger than Long.MAX_VALUE or floating-point values larger than Double.MAX_VALUE.

Solution

Use the BigInteger or BigDecimal values in package java.math, as shown in Example 5-8.

Example 5-8. main/src/main/java/numbers/BigNums.java

```
System.out.println("Here's Long.MAX_VALUE: " + Long.MAX_VALUE);
BigInteger bInt = new BigInteger("341922922337203685477580807");
System.out.println("Here's a bigger number: " + bInt);
System.out.println("Here it is as a double: " + bInt.doubleValue());
```

Note that the constructor takes the number as a string. Obviously you couldn't just type the numeric digits because, by definition, these classes are designed to represent numbers larger than will fit in a Java long.

Discussion

Both `BigInteger` and `BigDecimal` objects are immutable; that is, once constructed, they always represent a given number. That said, a number of methods return new objects that are mutations of the original, such as `negate()`, which returns the negative of the given `BigInteger` or `BigDecimal`. There are also methods corresponding to most of the Java language built-in operators defined on the base types `int`/`long` and `float`/`double`. The division method makes you specify the rounding method; consult a book on numerical analysis for details. Example 5-9 is a simple stack-based calculator using `BigDecimal` as its numeric data type.

Example 5-9. main/src/main/java/numbers/BigNumCalc.java

```java
public class BigNumCalc {

    /** an array of Objects, simulating user input */
    public static Object[] testInput = {
        new BigDecimal("3419229223372036854775807.23343"),
        new BigDecimal("2.0"),
        "*",
    };

    public static void main(String[] args) {
        BigNumCalc calc = new BigNumCalc();
        System.out.println(calc.calculate(testInput));
    }

    /**
     * Stack of numbers being used in the calculator.
     */
    Stack<BigDecimal> stack = new Stack<>();

    /**
     * Calculate a set of operands; the input is an Object array containing
     * either BigDecimal objects (which may be pushed onto the Stack) and
     * operators (which are operated on immediately).
     * @param input
     * @return
     */
    public BigDecimal calculate(Object[] input) {
        BigDecimal tmp;
        for (int i = 0; i < input.length; i++) {
            Object o = input[i];
            if (o instanceof BigDecimal) {
                stack.push((BigDecimal) o);
            } else if (o instanceof String) {
                switch (((String)o).charAt(0)) {
                // + and * are commutative, order doesn't matter
                case '+':
                    stack.push((stack.pop()).add(stack.pop()));
```

```
            break;
        case '*':
            stack.push((stack.pop()).multiply(stack.pop()));
            break;
        // - and /, order *does* matter
        case '-':
            tmp = (BigDecimal)stack.pop();
            stack.push((stack.pop()).subtract(tmp));
            break;
        case '/':
            tmp = stack.pop();
            stack.push((stack.pop()).divide(tmp,
                BigDecimal.ROUND_HALF_UP));
            break;
        default:
            throw new IllegalStateException("Unknown OPERATOR popped");
        }
    } else {
        throw new IllegalArgumentException("Syntax error in input");
    }
    }
    return stack.pop();
}
}
```

Running this produces the expected (very large) value:

```
> javac -d . numbers/BigNumCalc.java
> java numbers.BigNumCalc
6838458446744073709551614.466860
>
```

The current version has its inputs hardcoded, as does the JUnit test program, but in real life you can use regular expressions to extract words or operators from an input stream (as in Recipe 4.5), or you can use the StreamTokenizer approach of the simple calculator (see Recipe 10.5). The stack of numbers is maintained using a java.util.Stack (see Recipe 7.16).

BigInteger is mainly useful in cryptographic and security applications. Its method isProbablyPrime() can create prime pairs for public key cryptography. BigDecimal might also be useful in computing the size of the universe.

5.13 Program: TempConverter

The program shown in Example 5-10 prints a table of Fahrenheit temperatures (still used in daily weather reporting in the US and its territories, Liberia, and some countries in the Caribbean) and the corresponding Celsius temperatures (used in science everywhere and in daily life in the rest of the world).

Example 5-10. main/src/main/java/numbers/TempConverter.java

```java
public class TempConverter {

    public static void main(String[] args) {
        TempConverter t = new TempConverter();
        t.start();
        t.data();
        t.end();
    }

    protected void start() {
    }

    protected void data() {
        for (int i=-40; i<=120; i+=10) {
            double c = fToC(i);
            print(i, c);
        }
    }

    public static double cToF(double deg) {
        return ( deg * 9 / 5) + 32;
    }

    public static double fToC(double deg) {
        return ( deg - 32 ) * ( 5d / 9 );
    }

    protected void print(double f, double c) {
        System.out.println(f + " " + c);
    }

    protected void end() {
    }
}
```

This works, but these numbers print with about 15 digits of (useless) decimal fractions! The second version of this program subclasses the first and uses `printf` (see Recipe 10.4) to control the formatting of the converted temperatures (see Example 5-11). It will now look right, assuming you're printing in a monospaced font.

Example 5-11. main/src/main/java/numbers/TempConverter2.java

```java
public class TempConverter2 extends TempConverter {

    public static void main(String[] args) {
        TempConverter t = new TempConverter2();
        t.start();
        t.data();
        t.end();
```

```
    }

    @Override
    protected void print(double f, double c) {
        System.out.printf("%6.2f %6.2f%n", f, c);
    }

    @Override
    protected void start() {
        System.out.println("Fahr    Centigrade");
    }

    @Override
    protected void end() {
        System.out.println("------------------");
    }
}

C:\javasrc\numbers>java numbers.TempConverter2
Fahr    Centigrade
-40.00 -40.00
-30.00 -34.44
-20.00 -28.89
-10.00 -23.33
  0.00 -17.78
 10.00 -12.22
 20.00  -6.67
 30.00  -1.11
 40.00   4.44
 50.00  10.00
 60.00  15.56
 70.00  21.11
 80.00  26.67
 90.00  32.22
100.00  37.78
110.00  43.33
120.00  48.89
```

5.14 Program: Number Palindromes

My wife, Betty, recently reminded me of a theorem that I must have studied in high school but whose name I have long since forgotten: that any positive integer number can be used to generate a palindrome by adding to it the number comprised of its digits in reverse order. Palindromes are sequences that read the same in either direction, such as the name "Anna" or the phrase "Madam, I'm Adam" (ignoring spaces and punctuation). We normally think of palindromes as composed of text, but the concept can be applied to numbers: 13,531 is a palindrome. Start with the number 72, for example, and add to it the number 27. The results of this addition is 99, which is a (short) palindrome. Starting with 142, add 241, and you get 383. Some numbers take more than one try to generate a palindrome. 1,951 + 1,591 yields 3,542, which is not palindromic. The second round, however, 3,542 + 2,453, yields 5,995, which is. The number 17,892, which my son Benjamin picked out of the air, requires 12 rounds to generate a palindrome, but it does terminate:

```
C:\javasrc\numbers>java  numbers.Palindrome 72 142 1951 17892
Trying 72
72->99
Trying 142
142->383
Trying 1951
Trying 3542
1951->5995
Trying 17892
Trying 47763
Trying 84537
Trying 158085
Trying 738936
Trying 1378773
Trying 5157504
Trying 9215019
Trying 18320148
Trying 102422529
Trying 1027646730
Trying 1404113931
17892->2797227972

C:\javasrc\numbers>
```

If this sounds to you like a natural candidate for recursion, you are correct. *Recursion* involves dividing a problem into simple and identical steps that can be implemented by a function that calls itself and provides a way of termination. Our basic approach, as shown in method findPalindrome, is this:

```
long findPalindrome(long num) {
    if (isPalindrome(num))
        return num;
    return findPalindrome(num + reverseNumber(num));
}
```

That is, if the starting number is already a palindromic number, return it; otherwise, add it to its reverse, and try again. The version of the code shown here handles simple cases directly (single digits are always palindromic, for example). We won't think about negative numbers because these have a character at the front that loses its meaning if placed at the end, and hence are not strictly palindromic. Further, palindromic forms of certain numbers are too long to fit in Java's 64-bit long integer.

These cause underflow, which is trapped. As a result, an error message like "too big" is reported.[6] Having said all that, Example 5-12 shows the code.

Example 5-12. main/src/main/java/numbers/Palindrome.java

```java
public class Palindrome {

    public static boolean verbose = true;

    public static void main(String[] argv) {
        for (String num : argv) {
            try {
                long l = Long.parseLong(num);
                if (l < 0) {
                    System.err.println(num + " -> TOO SMALL");
                    continue;
                }
                System.out.println(num + "->" + findPalindrome(l));
            } catch (NumberFormatException e) {
                System.err.println(num + "-> INVALID");
            } catch (IllegalStateException e) {
                System.err.println(num + "-> " + e);
            }
        }
    }

    /** find a palindromic number given a starting point, by
     * recursing until we get a number that is palindromic.
     */
    static long findPalindrome(long num) {
        if (num < 0)
            throw new IllegalStateException("negative");
        if (isPalindrome(num))
            return num;
        if (verbose)
            System.out.println("Trying " + num);
        return findPalindrome(num + reverseNumber(num));
    }

    /** The number of digits in Long.MAX_VALUE */
    protected static final int MAX_DIGITS = 19;

    // digits array is shared by isPalindrome and reverseNumber,
    // which cannot both be running at the same time.

    /* Statically allocated array to avoid new-ing each time. */
    static long[] digits = new long[MAX_DIGITS];
```

---

6 Certain values do not work; for example, Ashish Batia reported that this version gets an exception on the value 8,989 (which it does).

```
/** Check if a number is palindromic. */
static boolean isPalindrome(long num) {
    // Consider any single digit to be as palindromic as can be
    if (num >= 0 && num <= 9)
        return true;

    int nDigits = 0;
    while (num > 0) {
        digits[nDigits++] = num % 10;
        num /= 10;
    }
    for (int i=0; i<nDigits/2; i++)
        if (digits[i] != digits[nDigits - i - 1])
            return false;
    return true;
}

static long reverseNumber(long num) {
    int nDigits = 0;
    while (num > 0) {
        digits[nDigits++] = num % 10;
        num /= 10;
    }
    long ret = 0;
    for (int i=0; i<nDigits; i++) {
        ret *= 10;
        ret += digits[i];
    }
    return ret;
}
}
```

While it's not strictly a numerical solution, Daniel Hinojosa noted that you can use StringBuilder to do the reversal portion, resulting in shorter, more elegant code that is only fractionally slower:

```
static boolean isPalindrome(long num) {
    long result = reverseNumber(num);
    return num == result;
}

private static long reverseNumber(long num) {
    StringBuilder stringBuilder = new StringBuilder();
    stringBuilder.append(num);
    return Long.parseLong(stringBuilder.reverse().toString());
}
```

A full version of his code is in the file *PalindromeViaStringBuilder.java*.

See Also

People using Java in scientific or large-scale numeric computing may wish to check out the value types forthcoming from "Project Valhalla" in Java (*https:// wiki.openjdk.java.net/display/valhalla/Main*). See also a 2019 presentation titled "Vectors and Numerics on the JVM" (*https://www.youtube.com/watch?v=UlnoCj4B8pU*).

## CHAPTER 6

Dates and Times

6.0 Introduction

Developers suffered for a decade and a half under the inconsistencies and ambiguities of the `Date` class from Java 1.0 and its replacement wannabe, the `Calendar` class from Java 1.1. Several alternative `Date` replacement packages emerged, including the simple and sensible Date4J (*http://date4j.net*) and the more comprehensive Joda-Time package (*http://www.joda.org/joda-time*). Java 8 introduced a new, consistent, and well-thought-out package for date and time handling under the aegis of the Java Community Process, JSR-310, shepherded by developer Stephen Colebourne, based on his earlier package Joda-Time, but with several important design changes.[6] This package is biased toward ISO 8601 dates; the default format is, for example, 2015-10-23T10:22:45. But it can, of course, work with other calendar schemes.

One of the key benefits of the new API is that it provides *useful operations* such as adding/subtracting dates/times. Much time was wasted by developers reimplementing these useful operations again and again. With the new APIs, one can use the built-in functionality. That said, millions of lines of code are based on the old APIs, so we'll review them briefly, and consider interfacing the new API to legacy code in the final recipe of this chapter, Recipe 6.9.

Another advantage of the new API is that almost all objects are immutable and thus thread-safe. This can be of considerable benefit as we move headlong into the massively parallel era.

---

6 For those with an interest in historical arcana, the differences are documented on his blog (*http:// blog.joda.org/2009/11/why-jsr-310-isn-joda-time_4941.html*).

Because there are no `set` methods, and thus the getter method paradigm doesn't always make sense, the API provides a series of new methods to replace such methods, listed in Table 6-1.

Table 6-1. New date/time API: common methods

Name	Description
at	Combines with another object
format	Use provided formatter to produce a formatted string
from	Factory: convert input parameters to instance of target
get	Retrieve one field from the instance
is	Examine the state of the given object
minus	Return a copy with the given amount subtracted
now	BuilderFactory: get the current time, date, etc.
of	Factory: create new method by parsing inputs
parse	Factory: parse single input string to produce instance of target
plus	Return a copy with the given amount added
to	Convert this object to another type
with	Return a copy with the given field changed; replaces `set` methods

The JSR 310 API specifies a dozen or so main classes. Those representing times are either continuous time or human time. *Continuous time* is based on Unix time, a deeper truth from the dawn of (computer) time, and is represented as a single monotonically increasing number. The time value of 0 in Unix represented the first second of January 1, 1970 UTC—about the time Unix was invented. Each unit of increment there represented one second of time. This has been used as a time base in most operating systems developed since. However, a 32-bit integer representing the number of seconds since 1970 runs out fairly soon—in the year 2038 AD. Most Unix systems have, in the aftermath of the Y2K frenzy, quietly and well in advance headed off a possible Y2038 frenzy by converting the time value from a 32-bit quantity to a 64-bit quantity. Java also used this time base, but used 64 bits, and stored its time in milliseconds, because a 64-bit time in milliseconds since 1970 will not overflow until quite a few years into the future (keep this date open in your calendar—August 17, 292,278,994 CE). Here is a calculation that shows how I got that date:

```
Date endOfTime = new Date(Long.MAX_VALUE);
System.out.println("Java time overflows on " + endOfTime);
```

The new API is in five packages, as shown in Table 6-2; as usual, the top-level one contains the most commonly used pieces.

Table 6-2. New date/time API: packages

Name	Description
java.time	Common classes for dates, times, instants, and durations
java.time.chrono	API for non-ISO calendar systems
java.time.format	Formatting classes (see Recipe 6.2)
java.time.temporal	Date and time access using fields, units, and adjusters
java.time.zone	Support for time zones and their rules

The basic `java.time` package contains a dozen or so classes, as well as a couple of enums and one general-purpose exception (shown in Tables 6-3, 6-4, and 6-5).

Table 6-3. New date/time API: basics

Class	Description
Clock	Replaceable factory for getting current time
Instant	A point in time since January 1, 1970, expressed in nanoseconds
Duration	A length of time, also expressed in nanoseconds

Human time represents times and dates as we use them in our everyday life. These classes are listed in Table 6-4.

Table 6-4. New date/time API: human time

Class	Description
Calendrical	Connects to the low-level API
DateTimeFields	Stores a map of field-value pairs, which are not required to be consistent
DayOfWeek	A day of the week (e.g., Tuesday)
LocalDate	A bare date (day, month, and year) with no adjustments
LocalTime	A bare time (hour, minute, seconds) with no adjustments
LocalDateTime	The combination of the above
MonthDay	Month and day
OffsetTime	A time of day with a time zone offset like −04:00, with no date or zone
OffsetDateTime	A date and time with a time zone offset like −04:00, with no time zone
Period	A descriptive amount of time, such as "2 months and 3 days"
ZonedDateTime	The date and time with a time zone and an offset
Year	A year by itself
YearMonth	A year and month

Almost all the top-level classes directly extend `java.lang.Object` and are held to consistency by a variety of interfaces, which are declared in the subpackages. The date and time classes mostly implement `Comparable`, which makes sense.

Table 6-5 shows the two time-zone-specific classes used with `ZonedDateTime`, `Offset DateTime`, and `OffsetTime`.

Table 6-5. New date/time API: support

Class	Description
`ZoneOffset`	A time offset from UTC (hours, minutes, seconds)
`ZoneId`	Defines a time zone such as *Canada/Eastern* and its conversion rules

The new API is a *fluent API*, in which most operations return the object they have operated upon, so that you can chain multiple calls without the need for tedious and annoying temporary variables:

```
LocalTime time = LocalTime.now().minusHours(5); // the time 5 hours ago
```

This results in a more natural and convenient coding style, in my opinion. You can always write code with lots of temporary variables if you want; you're the one who will have to read through it later.

6.1 Finding Today's Date

Problem

You want to find today's date and/or time.

Solution

Invoke the appropriate builder to obtain a `LocalDate`, `LocalTime`, or `LocalDateTime` object and call its `toString()` method.

Discussion

These classes do not provide public constructors, so you will need to call one of its factory methods to get an instance. They all provide a `now()` method, which does what its name implies. The `CurrentDateTime` demo program shows simple use of all three:

```
public class CurrentDateTime {
    public static void main(String[] args) {
        LocalDate dNow = LocalDate.now();
        System.out.println(dNow);
        LocalTime tNow = LocalTime.now();
```

```
            System.out.println(tNow);
            LocalDateTime now = LocalDateTime.now();
            System.out.println(now);
        }
    }
```

Running it produces this output:

```
2013-10-28
22:23:55.641
2013-10-28T22:23:55.642
```

The formatting is nothing spectacular, but it's adequate. We'll deal with fancier formatting in Recipe 6.2.

While this works, in full-scale applications, it's recommended to pass a Clock instance into all the now() methods. Clock is a factory object that is used internally to find the current time. In testing, you often want to have a known date or time used so you can compare against known output. The Clock class makes this easy. Example 6-1 uses a Clock and allows replacing the default Clock by calling a setter. Alternately you could use a dependency injection framework like CDI or Spring to provide the correct version of the Clock class.

Example 6-1. main/src/main/java/datetime/TestableDateTime

```java
package datetime;

import java.time.Clock;
import java.time.LocalDateTime;

/**
 * TestableDateTime allows test code to plug in a Fixed clock
 */
public class TestableDateTime {
    private static Clock clock = Clock.systemDefaultZone();
    public static void main(String[] args) {
        System.out.println("It is now " + LocalDateTime.now(clock));
    }
    public static void setClock(Clock clock) {
        TestableDateTime.clock = clock;
    }
}
```

In normal operation this would get the current date and time. In testing you would call the setClock() method with a Clock instance obtained from the static method Clock.fixed(Instant fixedInstant, ZoneId zone), passing in the time that your testing code expects. The fixed clock does not tick, so don't worry about the milliseconds between setting the clock to fixed and the invocation of your tests.

6.2 Formatting Dates and Times

Problem

You want to provide better formatting for date and time objects.

Solution

Use `java.time.format.DateTimeFormatter`.

Discussion

The `DateTimeFormatter` class provides an amazing number of possible formatting styles. If you don't want to use one of the provided 20 or so predefined formats, you can define your own using `DateTimeFormatter.ofPattern(String pattern)`. The `pattern` string can contain any characters, but almost every letter of the alphabet has been defined to mean something, in addition to the obvious *Y*, *M*, *D*, *h*, *m*, and *s*. In addition, the quote character and square bracket characters are defined, and the sharp sign (#) and curly braces are reserved for future use.

As is common with date formatting languages, the number of repetitions of a letter in the pattern gives a clue to its intended length of detail. Thus, for example, "MMM" gives "Jan," whereas "MMMM" gives "January."

Table 6-6 is an attempt at a complete list of the formatting characters, adapted from the javadoc for JSR-310.

Table 6-6. DateFormatter format characters

Symbol	Meaning	Presentation	Examples
G	Era	Text	AD; Anno Domini
y	Year of era	Year	2004; 04
u	Year of era	Year	See note.
D	Day of year	Number	189
M/L	Month of year	Number/text	7; 07; Jul; July; J
d	Day of month	Number	10
Q/q	Quarter of year	Number/text	3; 03; Q3; 3rd quarter
Y	Week based year	Year	1996; 96
w	Week of week based year	Number	27
W	Week of month	Number	4
e/c	Localized day of week	Number/text	2; 02; Tue; Tuesday; T
E	Day of week	Text	Tue; Tuesday; T
F	Week of month	Number	3

Symbol	Meaning	Presentation	Examples
a	am pm of day	Text	PM
h	Clock hour of am pm (1-12)	Number	12
K	Hour of am pm (0-11)	Number	0
k	Clock hour of am pm (1-24)	Number	0
H	Hour of day (0-23)	Number	0
m	Minute of hour	Number	30
s	Second of minute	Number	55
S	Fraction of second	Fraction	978
A	Millisecond of day	Number	1234
n	Nanosecond of second	Number	987654321
N	Nanosecond of day	Number	1234000000
V	Time zone ID	Zone-id	America/Los_Angeles; Z; −08:30
z	Time zone name	Zone-name	Pacific Standard Time; PST
X	Zone offset Z for zero	Offset-X	Z; −08; −0830; −08:30; −083015; −08:30:15;
x	Zone offset	Offset-x	+0000; −08; −0830; −08:30; −083015; −08:30:15;
Z	Zone offset	Offset-Z	+0000; −0800; −08:00;
O	Localized zone offset	Offset-O	GMT+8; GMT+08:00; UTC−08:00;
p	Pad next	Pad modifier	1

y and *u* work the same for AD years; however, for a year of 3 BC, the *y* pattern returns 3, whereas the *u* pattern returns −2 (a.k.a. proleptic year).

Example 6-2 contains some examples of converting in both directions between strings and dates.

Example 6-2. main/src/main/java/datetime/DateFormatter.java (example date formatting and parsing)

```java
public class DateFormatter {
    public static void main(String[] args) {

        // Format a date ISO8601-like but with slashes instead of dashes
        DateTimeFormatter df = DateTimeFormatter.ofPattern("yyyy/LL/dd");
        System.out.println(df.format(LocalDate.now()));

        // Parse a String to a date using the same formatter
        System.out.println(LocalDate.parse("2014/04/01", df));

        // Format a Date and Time without timezone information
```

```
DateTimeFormatter nTZ =
    DateTimeFormatter.ofPattern("d MMMM, yyyy h:mm a");
System.out.println(ZonedDateTime.now().format(nTZ));
    }
}
```

6.3 Converting Among Dates/Times, YMDHMS, and Epoch Seconds

Problem

You need to convert among dates/times, YMDHMS, epoch seconds, or some other numeric value.

Solution

Use the appropriate date/time factory or retrieval methods.

Discussion

The epoch is the beginning of time as far as modern operating systems go. Unix time, and some versions of Windows time, count off inexorably the seconds since the epoch. When Ken Thompson and Dennis Ritchie came up with this format in 1970, seconds seemed like a fine measure, and 32 bits' worth of seconds seemed nearly infinite. On operating systems that store the epoch in a 32-bit integer, however, time is running out. Older versions of most operating systems stored this as a 32-bit signed integer, which unfortunately will overflow in the year 2038.

When Java first came out, it featured a method called System.currentTimeMillis(), presenting epoch seconds with millisecond accuracy. The new Java API uses epoch nanoseconds that are still on the same time base and can be obtained with a call to System.nanoTime().

Any of these epoch-related numbers can be converted into, or obtained from, a local date/time. Other numbers can also be used, such as integer years, months, and days. As usual, there are factory methods that create new objects where a change is requested. Here is a program that shows some of these conversions in action:

main/src/main/java/datetime/DateConversions.java

```
// Convert a number of seconds since the epoch to a local date/time
Instant epochSec = Instant.ofEpochSecond(1000000000L);
ZoneId zId = ZoneId.systemDefault();
ZonedDateTime then = ZonedDateTime.ofInstant(epochSec, zId);
System.out.println("The epoch was a billion seconds old on " + then);

// Convert a date/time to epoch seconds
```

```
long epochSecond = ZonedDateTime.now().toInstant().getEpochSecond();
System.out.println("Current epoch seconds = " + epochSecond);

LocalDateTime now = LocalDateTime.now();
ZonedDateTime there = now.atZone(ZoneId.of("Canada/Pacific"));
System.out.printf("When it's %s here, it's %s in Vancouver%n",
    now, there);
```

6.4 Parsing Strings into Dates

Problem

You need to convert user input into `java.time` objects.

Solution

Use a `parse()` method.

Discussion

Many of the date/time classes have a `parse()` factory method, which tries to parse a string into an object of that class. For example, `LocalDate.parse(String)` returns a `LocalDate` object for the date given in the input `String`:

```
public class DateParse {
    public static void main(String[] args) {

        String armisticeDate = "1914-11-11";
        LocalDate aLD = LocalDate.parse(armisticeDate);
        System.out.println("Date: " + aLD);

        String armisticeDateTime = "1914-11-11T11:11";
        LocalDateTime aLDT = LocalDateTime.parse(armisticeDateTime);
        System.out.println("Date/Time: " + aLDT);
```

As you probably expect by now, the default format is the ISO8601 date format. However, we often have to deal with dates in other formats. For this, the `DateTimeFormat` ter allows you to specify a particular pattern. For example, "dd MMM uuuu" represents the day of the month (two digits), three letters of the name of the month (Jan, Feb, Mar, …), and a four-digit year:

```
DateTimeFormatter df = DateTimeFormatter.ofPattern("dd MMM uuuu");
String anotherDate = "27 Jan 2011";
LocalDate random = LocalDate.parse(anotherDate, df);
System.out.println(anotherDate + " parses as " + random);
```

The `DateTimeFormatter` object is bidirectional; it can both parse input and format output. We could add this line to the `DateParse` example:

```
System.out.println(aLD + " formats as " + df.format(aLD));
```

When we run the program, we see the output as follows:

```
Date: 1914-11-11
Date/Time: 1914-11-11T11:11
27 Jan 2011 parses as 2011-01-27
1914-11-11 formats as 11 Nov 1914
```

The DateTimeFormatter is also localized (see Recipe 3.12), and can be configured by calling withLocale() after calling ofPattern().

6.5 Difference Between Two Dates

Problem

You need to compute the difference between two dates.

Solution

Use the static method Period.between() to find the difference between two Local Dates.

Discussion

Given two LocalDate objects, you can find the difference between them, as a Period, simply using the static Period.between() method. You can toString() the Period or, if its default format isn't good enough, format the result yourself:

```
import java.time.LocalDate;
import java.time.Period;

/**
 * Tutorial/Example of LocalDate date difference subtraction
 */
public class DateDiff {

    public static void main(String[] args) {
        /** The date at the end of the last century */
        LocalDate endof20thCentury = LocalDate.of(2000, 12, 31);
        LocalDate now = LocalDate.now();
        if (now.getYear() > 2100) {
            System.out.println("The 21st century is over!");
            return;
        }

        Period diff = Period.between(endof20thCentury, now);

        System.out.printf("The 21st century (up to %s) is %s old%n", now, diff);
        System.out.printf(
```

```
                    "The 21st century is %d years, %d months and %d days old",
                    diff.getYears(), diff.getMonths(), diff.getDays());
    }
}
```

I wrote this recipe at the end of October 2013; the 20th century AD ended at the end of 2000, so the value should be about $12\,{}^{10}/_{12}$ years, and it is:

```
$ java datetime.DateDiff
The 21st century (up to 2013-10-28) is P12Y9M28D old
The 21st century is 12 years, 9 months and 28 days old
```

Because of the APIs regularity, you can use the same technique with LocalTime or LocalDateTime.

There is also ChronoUnit, which has numerous range values such as DAYS, HOURS, MINUTES, etc. (actually ranging from NANOS for nanoseconds up to MILLENIA, ERAS, and even FOREVER). If you want difference information in a certain unit:

```
jshell> import java.time.temporal.*;

jshell> ChronoUnit.DAYS.between(LocalDate.now(), LocalDate.parse("2022-02-22"))
$6 ==> 786

jshell> ChronoUnit.DECADES.between(LocalDate.of(1970,01,01),
    LocalDate.of(2020,01,01));
$7 ==> 5
```

Unix is on its fifth decade!

See Also

A higher-level way of formatting date/time values is discussed in Recipe 6.2.

6.6 Adding to or Subtracting from a Date

Problem

You need to add or subtract a fixed period to or from a date.

Solution

Create a past or future date by using a locution such as LocalDate.plus (Period.ofDays(N));.

Discussion

java.time offers a Period class to represent a length of time, such as a number of days or hours and minutes. LocalDate and friends offer plus() and minus()

methods to add or subtract a `Period` or other time-related object. `Period` offers factory methods such as `ofDays()`. The following code computes what the date will be 700 days from now:

```
import java.time.LocalDate;
import java.time.Period;

/** DateAdd -- compute the difference between two dates
 * (e.g., today and 700 days from now).
 */
public class DateAdd {
    public static void main(String[] av) {
        /** Today's date */
        LocalDate now = LocalDate.now();

        Period p = Period.ofDays(700);
        LocalDate then = now.plus(p);

        System.out.printf("Seven hundred days from %s is %s%n", now, then);
    }
}
```

Running this program reports the current date and time and what the date and time will be 700 days from now:

```
Seven hundred days from 2013-11-09 is 2015-10-10
```

6.7 Handling Recurring Events

Problem

You need to deal with recurring dates, for example, the third Wednesday of every month.

Solution

Use the `TemporalAdjusters` class.

Discussion

The `TemporalAdjuster` interface and the `TemporalAdjusters` factory class provide most of what you need for recurring events. There are many interesting and powerful adjusters available, shown in Table 6-7, and you can, of course, develop your own.

Table 6-7. New date/time API: TemporalAdjusters factory methods

Method signature
public static TemporalAdjuster firstDayOfMonth();
public static TemporalAdjuster lastDayOfMonth();
public static TemporalAdjuster firstDayOfNextMonth();
public static TemporalAdjuster firstDayOfYear();
public static TemporalAdjuster lastDayOfYear();
public static TemporalAdjuster firstDayOfNextYear();
public static TemporalAdjuster firstInMonth(java.time.DayOfWeek);
public static TemporalAdjuster lastInMonth(java.time.DayOfWeek);
public static TemporalAdjuster dayOfWeekInMonth(int, java.time.DayOfWeek);
public static TemporalAdjuster next(java.time.DayOfWeek);
public static TemporalAdjuster nextOrSame(java.time.DayOfWeek);
public static TemporalAdjuster previous(java.time.DayOfWeek);
public static TemporalAdjuster previousOrSame(java.time.DayOfWeek);
public static TemporalAdjuster ofDateAdjuster(java.util.function.UnaryOperator<java.time.LocalDate>);

The names of most of these tell you directly what they do. The last one will make sense after reading about functional interfaces such as UnaryOperator in Chapter 9.

These are used with the with() method of a date/time object. For example, the GTABUG group (*http://gtabug.org*) meets on the third Wednesday of every month. I have a RecurringEventDatePicker class in the darwinsys-api library; the core of it started as the method getMeetingDateInMonth(LocalDate dateContaining Month), which in our case picks the third Wednesday of a given month (given that *dayOfWeek* and *weekOfMonth* are both set in the constructor). We take the month (dateContainingMonth), adjust it to the first Wednesday in the month using the firstInMonth() factory method to get a temporal adjuster, then add the number of weeks to get the Wednesday in the correct week:

```
// Variant versions from older version of RecurringDatePicker.java
// First version, not for production use!
private LocalDate getMeetingForMonth(LocalDate dateContainingMonth) {
    return
        dateContainingMonth.with(TemporalAdjusters.firstInMonth(dayOfWeek))
            .plusWeeks(Math.max(0, weekOfMonth - 1));
}
```

The second version simplified it to better use the existing API:

```
private LocalDate getMeetingForMonth(LocalDate dateContainingMonth) {
    return dateWithMonth.with(
        TemporalAdjusters.dayOfWeekInMonth(weekOfMonth,dayOfWeek)
}
```

Since this version was only one statement and is only used twice, we inlined it into the getNextMeeting(int howManyMonthsAway) method, which returns a LocalDate for the correct day of the given month. Its only complexity is that, for the current month, the meeting might be before or after today's date, so we adjust accordingly:

```
public LocalDate getEventLocalDate(int meetingsAway) {
    LocalDate thisMeeting = now.with(
        TemporalAdjusters.dayOfWeekInMonth(weekOfMonth,dayOfWeek));
    // Has the meeting already happened this month?
    if (thisMeeting.isBefore(now)) {
        // start from next month
        meetingsAway++;
    }
    if (meetingsAway > 0) {
        thisMeeting = thisMeeting.plusMonths(meetingsAway).
            with(TemporalAdjusters.dayOfWeekInMonth(weekOfMonth,dayOfWeek));
    }
    return thisMeeting;
}
```

This in turn is called within a JavaServer Page (JSP) web view (somewhat simplified; the real code has the complexities of an Add To Calendar API done in JavaScript). If you've not used JSPs, plain HTML code is *outputted* directly, the contents of <% %> tags are *executed*, and the contents of <%= %> tags are *evaluated and printed* into the HTML page, like this:

```
Upcoming Meetings:
<ul>
    <%
    RecurringEventDatePicker mp =
      new RecurringEventDatePicker(3, DayOfWeek.WEDNESDAY);
    DateTimeFormatter dfm = DateTimeFormatter.ofPattern("MMMM dd, yyyy");
    for (int i = 0; i <= 2; i++) {
        LocalDateTime dt = mp.getEventLocalDateTime(i);
    %>
    <li>
        <%= dt.format(dfm) %>
    </li>
    <%
    }
    %>
</ul>
```

When visiting this site in June or July of 2015, you would have seen something like this:

```
Upcoming Meetings:

* July 15, 2015
* August 19, 2015
* September 16, 2015
```

6.8 Computing Dates Involving Time Zones

Problem

Imagine a problem like "Your kids are traveling on a trans-Atlantic flight from Toronto to London that takes 5 hours 10 minutes from the actual time of departure from YYZ. Your in-laws need one hour to get to LHR and find parking. What time should you phone them to leave for the airport?"

Solution

The solution needs to take account of time zone differences. It can be solved using the ZonedDateTime class and methods such as plus() and minus() from that class.

Discussion

The basic steps are shown in Example 6-3.

Example 6-3. main/src/main/java/datetime/FlightArrivalTimeCalc.java

```java
public class FlightArrivalTimeCalc {

    static Duration driveTime = Duration.ofHours(1);

    public static void main(String[] args) {
        LocalDateTime when = null;
        if (args.length == 0) {
            when = LocalDateTime.now();                                      ❶
        } else {
            String time = args[0];
            LocalTime localTime = LocalTime.parse(time);
            when = LocalDateTime.of(LocalDate.now(), localTime);             ❶
        }
        calulateArrivalTime(when);
    }

    public static ZonedDateTime calulateArrivalTime(LocalDateTime takeOffTime) {
        ZoneId torontoZone = ZoneId.of("America/Toronto"),
                londonZone = ZoneId.of("Europe/London");
        ZonedDateTime takeOffTimeZoned =
            ZonedDateTime.of(takeOffTime, torontoZone);                     ❷
        Duration flightTime =
            Duration.ofHours(5).plus(10, ChronoUnit.MINUTES);               ❸
        ZonedDateTime arrivalTimeUnZoned = takeOffTimeZoned.plus(flightTime); ❹
        ZonedDateTime arrivalTimeZoned =
            arrivalTimeUnZoned.toInstant().atZone(londonZone);              ❺
        ZonedDateTime phoneTimeHere = arrivalTimeUnZoned.minus(driveTime);  ❻

        System.out.println("Flight departure time " + takeOffTimeZoned);
```

```
        System.out.println("Flight expected length: " + flightTime);
        System.out.println(
            "Flight arrives there at " + arrivalTimeZoned + " London time.");
        System.out.println("You should phone at " + phoneTimeHere + " Toronto
time");
        return arrivalTimeZoned;
    }
}
```

❶ Get the departure time as a LocalDateTime (defaulting to now() if no arguments
    passed into main(), on the assumption that we run the app when the flight takes
    off).

❷ Convert departure time to ZonedDateTime.

❸ Convert flight time to a Duration.

❹ Get the arrival time by adding the departure time to the flight duration.

❺ Convert the arrival time to London time with atZone().

❻ Since the family takes an hour to get to the airport, subtract that from the arrival
    time. This yields the time when you should phone them.

6.9 Interfacing with Legacy Date and Calendar Classes

Problem

You need to deal with the old Date and Calendar classes.

Solution

Assuming you have code using the original java.util.Date and java.util.Calen
dar, you can convert values as needed using conversion methods.

Discussion

All the classes and interfaces in the new API were chosen to avoid conflicting with the
traditional API. It is thus possible, and will be common for a while, to have imports
from both packages into the same code.

To keep the new API clean, most of the necessary conversion routines were added *to
the old API*. Table 6-8 summarizes these conversion routines; note that the methods
are static if they are shown being invoked with a capitalized class name, otherwise
they are instance methods.

Table 6-8. Legacy date/time interchange

Legacy class	Convert to legacy	Convert to modern
`java.util.Date`	`date.from(Instant)`	`Date.toInstant()`
`java.util.Calendar`	`calendar.toInstant()`	-
`java.util.GregorianCalendar`	`GregorianCalendar.from(ZonedDateTime)`	`calendar.toZonedDateTime()`
`java.util.TimeZone`	-	`timeZone.toZoneId()`
`java.time.DateTimeFormatter`	-	`dateTimeFormatter.toFormat()`

Example 6-4 shows some of these APIs in action.

Example 6-4. main/src/main/java/datetime/LegacyDates.java

```
public class LegacyDates {
    public static void main(String[] args) {

        // There and back again, via Date
        Date legacyDate = new Date();
        System.out.println(legacyDate);

        LocalDateTime newDate =
            LocalDateTime.ofInstant(legacyDate.toInstant(),
            ZoneId.systemDefault());
        System.out.println(newDate);

        Date backAgain =
            Date.from(newDate.atZone(ZoneId.systemDefault()).toInstant());
        System.out.println("Converted back as " + backAgain);

        // And via Calendar
        Calendar c = Calendar.getInstance();
        System.out.println(c);
        LocalDateTime newCal =
            LocalDateTime.ofInstant(c.toInstant(),
            ZoneId.systemDefault());
        System.out.println(newCal);
    }
}
```

Of course you do not have to use these legacy converters; you are free to write your own. The file *LegacyDatesDIY.java* in the *javasrc* repository explores this option in the unlikely event you wish to pursue it.

Given the amount of code written before Java 8, it is likely that the legacy `Date` and `Calendar` will be around until the end of Java time.

The new date/time API has many capabilities that we have not explored. Almost enough for a small book on the subject, in fact. Meanwhile, you can study the API details at Oracle (*https://docs.oracle.com/en/java/javase/13/docs/api/java.base/java/time/package-summary.html*).

## CHAPTER 7

Structuring Data with Java

7.0 Introduction

Almost every application beyond "Hello, World" needs to keep track of some structured data. A simple numeric problem might work with three or four numbers only, but most applications have groups of similar data items. A GUI-based application may need to keep track of a number of dialog windows. A personal information manager, or PIM, needs to keep track of a number of, well, persons. An operating system needs to keep track of who is allowed to log in, who is currently logged in, and what those users are doing. A library needs to keep track of who has books checked out and when they're due. A network server may need to keep track of its active clients. A pattern emerges here, and it revolves around variations of what has traditionally been called *data structuring*.

There are data structures in the memory of a running program; there is structure in the data in a file on disk, and there is structure in the information stored in a database. In this chapter, we concentrate on the first aspect: in-memory data. We'll cover the second aspect in Chapter 10; the third is out of scope for this book.

If you had to think about in-memory data, you might want to compare it to a collection of index cards in a filing box or to a treasure hunt where each clue leads to the next. Or you might think of it like my desk—apparently scattered, but actually a very powerful collection filled with meaningful information. Each of these is a good analogy for a type of data structuring that Java provides. An array is a fixed-length linear collection of data items, like the card filing box: it can only hold so much, then it overflows. The treasure hunt is like a data structure called a *linked list*. The first release of Java had no standard linked list class, but you could write your own traditional data structure classes (and still can; you see a DIY linked list implementation in Recipe 7.8). The complex collection represents Java's `Collection` classes. A document entitled *Collections Framework Overview*, distributed with the Java Development Kit documentation (and stored therein as file *.../docs/guide/collections/overview.html* online (*http://docs.oracle.com/javase/8/docs/technotes/guides/collections/index.html*)), provides a detailed discussion of the Collections Framework. The framework aspects of Java collections are summarized in Recipe 7.3.

Beware of typographic issues. The word `Arrays` (in constant width font) refers to the class `java.util.Arrays`; but in the normal typeface, the word "arrays" is simply the plural of "array" (and will be found capitalized at the beginning of a sentence). Also, note that `HashMap` and `HashSet` follow the rule of having a midcapital at each word boundary, whereas the older `Hashtable` does not (the *t* is not capitalized).

The `java.util` package has become something of a catch-all over the years. Besides the legacy date/time API covered in Recipe 6.9, several other classes from `java.util` are not covered in this chapter. All the classes whose names begin with `Abstract` are, in fact, abstract, and we'll discuss their nonabstract subclasses. The `StringTokenizer` class is covered in Recipe 3.1. `BitSet` is used less frequently than some of the classes discussed here and is simple enough to learn on your own. `BitSet` stores the bits very compactly in memory, but because it predates the Collection API and wasn't retrofitted, it doesn't implement any of the standard collection interfaces. Also not covered here are `EnumSet` and `EnumMap`, specialized for efficient storage/retrieval of enums. These are newer than `BitSet` and *do* implement the modern collection interfaces.

We start our discussion of data structuring techniques with one of the oldest structures, the array. We'll discuss the overall structure of `java.util`'s Collections Framework. Then we'll go through a variety of structuring techniques using classes from `java.util`.

7.1 Using Arrays for Data Structuring

Problem

You need to keep track of a fixed amount of information and retrieve it (usually) sequentially.

Solution

Use an array.

Discussion

Arrays can be used to hold any linear collection of data. The items in an array must all be of the same type. You can make an array of any primitive type or any object type. For *arrays of primitive types*, such as `ints` and `booleans`, the data is stored in the array. For *arrays of objects*, a reference is stored in the array, so the normal rules of reference variables and casting apply. Note in particular that if the array is declared as Object[], object references of any type can be stored in it without casting, although a valid cast is required to take an Object reference out and use it as its original type. I'll say a bit more on two-dimensional arrays in Recipe 7.17; otherwise, you should treat this as a review example:

main/src/main/java/lang/Array1.java

```
public class Array1 {
    @SuppressWarnings("unused")
    public static void main(String[] argv) {
        int[] monthLen1;                // declare a reference
        monthLen1 = new int[12];        // construct it
        int[] monthLen2 = new int[12];  // short form
        // even shorter is this initializer form:
        int[] monthLen3 = {
                31, 28, 31, 30,
                31, 30, 31, 31,
                30, 31, 30, 31,
        };

        final int MAX = 10;
        LocalDate[] days = new LocalDate[MAX];
        for (int i=0; i<MAX; i++) {
            days[i] = LocalDate.of(2022, 02, i + 1);
        }

        // Two-Dimensional Arrays
        // Want a 10-by-24 array
        int[][] me = new int[10][];
        for (int i=0; i<10; i++)
            me[i] = new int[24];

        // Remember that an array has a ".length" attribute
        System.out.println(me.length);
        System.out.println(me[0].length);

    }
}
```

Arrays in Java work nicely. The type checking provides reasonable integrity, and array bounds are always checked by the runtime system, further contributing to reliability.

The only problem with arrays is: what if the array fills up and you still have data coming in? See Recipe 7.2.

7.2 Resizing an Array

Problem

The array filled up, and you got an ArrayIndexOutOfBoundsException.

Solution

Make the array bigger. Or, use an ArrayList.

Discussion

One approach is to allocate the array at a reasonable size to begin with; but if you find yourself with more data than will fit, reallocate a new, bigger array and copy the elements into it.[6] Here is code that does so:

main/src/main/java/lang/Array2.java

```
public class Array2  {
    public final static int INITIAL = 10,     ❶
        GROW_FACTOR = 2;                        ❷

    public static void main(String[] argv) {
        int nDates = 0;
        LocalDateTime[] dates = new LocalDateTime[INITIAL];
        StructureDemo source = new StructureDemo(21);
        LocalDateTime c;
        while ((c=source.getDate()) != null) {

            // if (nDates >= dates.length) {
            //     throw new RuntimeException(
            //         "Too Many Dates! Simplify your life!!");
            // }

            // better: reallocate, making data structure dynamic
            if (nDates >= dates.length) {
                LocalDateTime[] tmp =
                    new LocalDateTime[dates.length * GROW_FACTOR];
                System.arraycopy(dates, 0, tmp, 0, dates.length);
                dates = tmp;    // copies the array reference
                // old array will be garbage collected soon...
            }
            dates[nDates++] = c;
        }
        System.out.println("Final array size = " + dates.length);
```

---

6 You could copy it yourself using a for loop if you wish, but System.arrayCopy() is likely to be faster because it's implemented in native code.

```
        }
    }
```

❶ A good guess is necessary; know your data!

❷ The growth factor is arbitary; 2 is a good value here but will continue to double exponentially. You might want to use a factor like 1.5, which would mean more allocations at the low end but less explosive growth. You need to manage this somehow!

This technique works reasonably well for simple or relatively small linear collections of data. For data with a more variable structure, you probably want to use a more dynamic approach, as in Recipe 7.4.

7.3 The Collections Framework

Problem

You're having trouble keeping track of all these lists, sets, and iterators.

Solution

There's a pattern to it. See Figure 7-1 and Table 7-1.

Discussion

List, Set, Map, and Queue are the four fundamental data structures of the Collections Framework. List and Set are both sequences, with the difference that List preserves order and allows duplicate entries, whereas Set, true to the mathematical concept behind it, does not. Map is a key/value store, also known as a hash, a dictionary, or an associative store. Queues are, as the same suggests, structures that you can push into at one end and pull out from the other.

Table 7-1 shows some of the important collection-based classes from package java.util. It is intentionally not 100% complete due to space limitations.

See Also

The javadoc documentation on Collections, Arrays, List, Set, and the classes that implement them provides more details than there's room for here. Table 7-1 may further help you to absorb the regularity of the Collections Framework.

Table 7-1. Java collections

Interfaces	Implementations			
	Resizable array	Hashed table	Linked list	Balanced tree
List	ArrayList, Vector		LinkedList	
Set		HashSet		TreeSet
Map		HashMap, HashTable		TreeMap
Queue	Deques, BlockingQueues, etc.			

Figure 7-1 shows the relationships among several of these types.

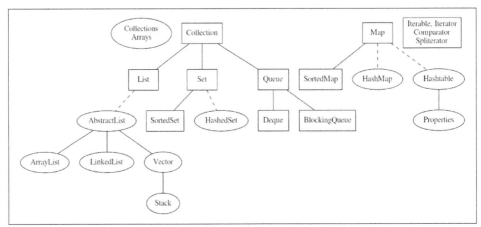

Figure 7-1. The Collections Framework: Rectangles are interfaces; ovals classes; Solid lines are inheritance; dashed lines represent implements

Queue and its subtypes are treated in Chapter 16.

7.4 Like an Array, but More Dynamic

Problem

You don't want to worry about storage reallocation (often because you don't know how big the incoming dataset is going to be); you want a standard class to handle it for you. You want to store your data in any of the Collection classes defined in Chapter 7 with type safety and without having to write downcasts when retrieving data from the collection.

Solution

Use a List implementation or one of the other Collections classes, along with Java's Generic Types mechanism, declaring the Collection with a *type parameter* identifying the type of your data. The type parameter name appears in angle brackets after the declaration and instantiation.

Discussion

The first of the `Collections` classes we will discuss, `ArrayList`, is a standard class from `java.util` that encapsulates the functionality of an array but allows it to expand automatically. You can just keep on adding things to it, and each addition behaves the same. If you watch *really* closely, you might notice a brief extra pause once in a while when adding objects as the `ArrayList` reallocates and copies. But you don't have to think about it.

However, because `ArrayList` is a class and isn't part of the syntax of Java, you can't use Java's array syntax; you must use methods to access the `ArrayList`'s data. It has methods to add objects, retrieve objects, find objects, and tell you how big the `List` is and how big it can become without having to reallocate (note that the `ArrayList` class is but one implementation of the `List` interface; more on that later). Like the other collection classes in `java.util`, `ArrayList`'s storing and retrieval methods were originally defined to have parameters and return values of `java.lang.Object`. Because `Object` is the ancestor of every defined type, you can store objects of any type in a `List` (or any collection) and cast it when retrieving it. If you need to store a small number of built-ins (like `int` and `float`) into a collection containing other data, use the appropriate wrapper class (see the introduction to Chapter 5). To store `boolean`s, either store them directly in a `java.util.BitSet` (see the online documentation) or store them in a `List` using the `Boolean` wrapper class.

Because `Object` is usually too general for accurate work, all modern versions of Java provide the *generic types* mechanism. Nowadays, you declare an `ArrayList` (or other collection) with a type parameter in angle brackets, and the parameters and returns are treated as being of that type by the compiler, ensuring that objects of the wrong type don't make it into your collections, and avoiding the need to write casts when retrieving objects. For example, this is how you declare an `ArrayList` for holding `String` object references:

```
List<String> myList = new ArrayList<>();
```

It is a good practice to *declare* the variable as the interface type `List`, even though you are *defining* it (constructing it) as an `ArrayList`. This makes it easier to change from one `List` implementation to another, and it avoids accidentally depending on an implementation-specific method not in the `List` interface (which would also make it harder to change the implementation).

The <> in the definition part is a vestige of legacy Java versions, in which you had to repeat the type definition, so you'd write new ArrayList<String>() in that example. Nowadays just use <> (as in the example) to indicate that you want the type copied from the declaration. The <> is called the *diamond operator*.

As of Java 13, you can simplify by using the new var keyword (for local variables only):

```
var myList = new ArrayList<String>();
```

Table 7-2 shows some of the most important methods of the List interface, which is implemented by ArrayList and other List implementations. This means that the exact same methods can be used with the older Vector class and several other implementing classes. You'd just have to change the name used in the constructor call.

Table 7-2. Common List<T> methods

Method signature	Usage
add(T o)	Add the given element at the end
add(int i, T o)	Insert the given element at the specified position
clear()	Remove all element references from the Collection
contains(T o)	True if the List contains the given object
forEach(lambda)	Perform the lambda for each element
get(int i)	Return the object reference at the specified position
indexOf(T o)	Return the index where the given object is found, or −1
of(T t, …)	Create a list from multiple objects
remove(T o), remove(int i)	Remove an object by reference or by position
toArray()	Return an array containing the objects in the Collection

ArrayListDemo stores data in an ArrayList and retrieves it for processing:

```
public class ArrayListDemo {
    public static void main(String[] argv) {
        List<LocalDate> editions = new ArrayList<>();

        // Add lots of elements to the ArrayList...
        editions.add(LocalDate.of(2001, 06, 01));
        editions.add(LocalDate.of(2004, 06, 01));
        editions.add(LocalDate.of(2014, 06, 20));

        // Use old-style 'for' loop to get index number.
        System.out.println("Retrieving by index:");
        for (int i = 0; i<editions.size(); i++) {
            System.out.printf("Edition %d was %s\n", i + 1, editions.get(i));
        }
        // Use normal 'for' loop for simpler access
```

```
        System.out.println("Retrieving by Iterable:");
        for (LocalDate dt : editions) {
            System.out.println("Edition " + dt);
        }

    }
}
```

The older `Vector` and `Hashtable` classes predate the Collections Framework, so they offer additional methods with different names: `Vector` provides `addElement()` and `elementAt()`. You may still run across these in legacy code, but you should use the `Collection` methods `add()` and `get()` instead. Another difference is that the methods of `Vector` are synchronized, meaning that they can be accessed safely from multiple threads (see Recipe 16.5). This does mean more overhead, though, so for single-threaded access it is faster to use an `ArrayList` (see timing results in Recipe 7.19).

There are various conversion methods. Table 7-2 mentions `toArray()`, which will expose the contents of a `List` as an array. The `List` interface in Java 9+ features a static `of()` method, which converts in the other direction, from an array into a `List`. In conjunction with the variable arguments feature of modern Java, you can create and populate a list in one call to `List.of()`, like this:

```
List<String> firstNames = List.of("Robin", "Jaime", "Joey");
```

In legacy code that you will find in older apps and in web searches, `Arrays.asList()` provided this functionality, so you will come across code like this:

```
List<String> lastNames = Arrays.asList("Smith", "Jones", "MacKenzie");
// or even
List<String> lastNames =
    Arrays.asList(new String[]{"Smith", "Jones", "MacKenzie"});
```

Java does indeed get less verbose as time goes by!

You can still instantiate classes such as `ArrayList` without using a specific type. In this case, you will get a compiler warning, and the class will behave as in the old days; that is, the objects returned from a `Collection` or `Iterator` will be of type `java.lang.Object` and must be downcast before you can call any class-specific methods or use them in any application-specific method calls.

As a further example, consider the `Map` interface mentioned in Chapter 7. A `Map` requires a key and a value in its `put()` method. A `Map`, therefore, has two parameterized types. To set up a `Map` whose keys are `Person` objects and whose values are `Address` objects (assuming these two classes exist in your application), you could define it like this:

```
Map<Person, Address> addressMap = new HashMap<>();
```

This `Map` expects a `Person` as its key and an `Address` as its value in the `put()` method. The `get()` method returns an `Address` object, the `keySet()` method returns `Set<Person>` (i.e., a `Set` specialized for `Person` objects). There are also convenience routines for when you want to create a `Map` from existing objects. The most useful is several overloads of before existing `Map.of(key,value,key,value…)` similar to `List.of()` (but limited to 10 pairs), and so on.

See Also

Although the generics avoid your having to write downcasts, the casts still occur at runtime; they are just provided by the compiler. The compiler techniques used in compiling these new constructs in a backward-compatible way include *erasure* and *bridging*, topics discussed in *Java Generics and Collections* (*http://shop.oreilly.com/prod uct/9780596527754.do*) by Maurice Naftalin and Philip Wadler.

7.5 Using Generic Types in Your Own Class

Problem

You wish to define your own container classes using the generic type mechanism to avoid needless casting.

Solution

Define a class using < *TypeName* > where the container type is declared and *TypeName* where it is used.

Discussion

Consider the very simple `Stack` class in Example 7-1. (We discuss the nature and uses of stack classes in Recipe 7.16.)

This version has been parameterized to take a type whose local name is `T`. This type `T` will be the type of the argument of the `push()` method, the return type of the `pop()` method, and so on. Because of this return type—more specific than the `Object` return type of the original Collections—the return value from `pop()` does not need to be downcasted. All containers in the Collections Framework (`java.util`) are parameterized similarly.

Example 7-1. main/src/main/java/structure/MyStack.java

```
public class MyStack<T> implements SimpleStack<T> {

    private int depth = 0;
```

```java
public static final int DEFAULT_INITIAL = 10;
private T[] stack;

public MyStack() {
    this(DEFAULT_INITIAL);
}

public MyStack(int howBig) {
    if (howBig <= 0) {
        throw new IllegalArgumentException(
        howBig + " must be positive, but was " + howBig);
    }
    stack = (T[])new Object[howBig];
}

@Override
public boolean empty() {
    return depth == 0;
}

/** push - add an element onto the stack */
@Override
public void push(T obj) {
    // Could check capacity and expand
    stack[depth++] = obj;
}

/* pop - return and remove the top element */
@Override
public T pop() {
    --depth;
    T tmp = stack[depth];
    stack[depth] = null;
    return tmp;
}

/** peek - return the top element but don't remove it */
@Override
public T peek() {
    if (depth == 0) {
        return null;
    }
    return stack[depth-1];
}

public boolean hasNext() {
    return depth > 0;
}

public boolean hasRoom() {
    return depth < stack.length;
}
```

```
    public int getStackDepth() {
        return depth;
    }
}
```

The association of a particular type is done at the time the class is instantiated. For example, to instantiate a `MyStack` specialized for holding `BankAccount` objects, you would need to code only the following:

```
MyStack<BankAccount> theAccounts = new MyStack<>( );
```

If you don't provide a type parameter T, this collection, like the ones in `java.util`, will behave as they did in the days before generic collections—accepting input arguments of any type, returning `java.lang.Object` from getter methods, and requiring downcasting—as their default, backward-compatible behavior. Example 7-2 shows a program that creates two instances of `MyStack`, one specialized for `Strings` and one left general. The general one, called `ms2`, is loaded up with the same two `String` objects as `ms1` but also includes a `Date` object. The printing code is now broken, because it will throw a `ClassCastException`: a `Date` is not a `String`. I handle this case specially for pedantic purposes: it is illustrative of the kinds of errors you can get into when using nonparameterized container classes.

Example 7-2. main/src/main/java/structure/MyStackDemo.java

```
public class MyStackDemo {

    @SuppressWarnings({"rawtypes","unchecked"})
    public static void main(String[] args) {
        MyStack<String> ms1 = new MyStack<>();
        ms1.push("billg");
        ms1.push("scottm");

        while (ms1.hasNext()) {
            String name = ms1.pop();
            System.out.println(name);
        }

        // Old way of using Collections: not type safe.
        // DO NOT GENERICIZE THIS
        MyStack ms2 = new MyStack();
        ms2.push("billg");                  // EXPECT WARNING
        ms2.push("scottm");                 // EXPECT WARNING
        ms2.push(new java.util.Date());     // EXPECT WARNING

        // Show that it is broken
        try {
            String bad = (String)ms2.pop();
            System.err.println("Didn't get expected exception, popped " + bad);
```

```
        } catch (ClassCastException ex) {
            System.out.println("Did get expected exception.");
        }

        // Removed the brokenness, print rest of it.
        while (ms2.hasNext()) {
            String name = (String)ms2.pop();
            System.out.println(name);
        }
    }
}
```

Because of this potential for error, the compiler warns that you have unchecked raw types. Like the deprecation warnings discussed in Recipe 1.9, by default, these warnings are not printed in detail by the *javac* compiler (they will appear in most IDEs). You ask for them with the rather lengthy option -Xlint:unchecked:

```
C:> javac -source 1.5 structure/MyStackDemo.java
Note: MyStackDemo.java uses unchecked or unsafe operations.
Note: Recompile with -Xlint:unchecked for details.
C:> javac -source 1.5 -Xlint:unchecked structure/MyStackDemo.java
MyStackDemo.java:14: warning: unchecked call to push(T) as a member of the raw
type MyStack
                ms2.push("billg");
                   ^
MyStackDemo.java:15: warning: unchecked call to push(T) as a member of the raw
type MyStack
                ms2.push("scottm");
                   ^
MyStackDemo.java:16: warning: unchecked call to push(T) as a member of the raw
type MyStack
                ms2.push(new java.util.Date( ));
                   ^

3 warnings
C:>
```

I say more about the development and evolution of MyStack in Recipe 7.16.

7.6 How Shall I Iterate Thee? Let Me Enumerate the Ways

Problem

You need to iterate over some structured data.

Solution

Java provides many ways to iterate over collections of data. Here they are, in newest-first order:

- `Stream.forEach()` method (Java 8)
- `Iterable.forEach()` method (Java 8)
- Java "foreach" loop (Java 5)
- `java.util.Iterator` (Java 2)
- Three-part `for` loop
- `while` loop * Enumeration

Pick one and use it. Or learn them all and save!

Discussion

A few words on each of the iteration methods are given here. Note that the first few are the most common.

Stream.forEach method (Java 8)

The `Stream` mechanism introduced as part of Java's functional programming provides one of the two most-recent ways of iterating, `Stream.forEach()`, and is discussed in Recipe 9.3. For now, here's a quick example, using the `BufferedReader` method `lines()` that returns a `Stream`:

```
$ jshell
jshell> import java.io.*;
jshell> BufferedReader is =
  new BufferedReader(new FileReader("/home/ian/.profile"));
is ==> java.io.BufferedReader@58651fd0
jshell> is.lines().forEach(System.out::println)
... prints the lines of the file ...
```

Iterable.forEach method (Java 8)

The other recent iteration technique is the `Iterable.forEach()` method, added in Java 8. This method can be called on any `Iterable` (unfortunately, the array class does not yet implement `Iterable`) and takes one argument implementing the *functional interface* `java.util.function.Consumer`. Functional interfaces are discussed in Chapter 9, but here is one example:

```
public class IterableForEach {

    public static void main(String[] args) {
        Collection<String> c =             ❶
                List.of("One", "Two", "Three");  ❷
        c.forEach(s -> System.out.println(s));   ❸
    }
}
```

① Declare a `Collection` (a `Collection` is an `Iterable`).

② Populate it with `Arrays.of()` with an array or sequence of objects (see Recipe 7.4 for how this arbitrary argument list becomes an array).

③ Invoke the collection's `forEach()` method, passing a lambda expression (see Chapter 9 for a discussion of how s→`System.out.println(s)` gets mapped to a `Consumer` interface implementation without your even having to import this interface).

This style of iteration—sometimes called *internal iteration*—inverts the control from the traditional `for` loop; the collection is in charge of when and how the iteration works.

 Both `Stream.forEach` and `Iterable.forEach()` take one argument, of type `java.util.function.Consumer`, so they work largely the same way, at least syntactically. This is intentional.

Java "foreach" loop (Java 5)

This is the for-each loop syntax:

```
for (Type var : Iterable<Type>) {
        // do something with "var"
}
```

The for-each loop is probably the most common style of loop in modern Java code. The `Iterable` can be an array or anything that implements `Iterable` (the `Collection` implementations included).

This style is used throughout the book. In addition, many third-party frameworks/ libraries provide their own types that implement `Iterable` for use with the `for` loop.

java.util.Iterator (Java 2)

The older `Iterator` interface has three methods:

```
public interface java.util.Iterator<E> {
  public abstract boolean hasNext();
  public abstract E next();
  public default void remove();
}
```

It was once common to write code like this, which you'll still find occasionally in older code:

```
Iterator it = ...; // legacy code; might not even have type parameter
while (it.hasNext()) {
        (MyDataType) c = it.next();
        // Do something with c
}
```

The remove() method throws an UnsupportedOperationException if called on a read-only collection. In conjunction with Streams and default methods, there is now a fourth method:

```
public default void forEachRemaining(java.util.function.Consumer<? super E>);
```

Three-part for loop

This is the traditional for loop invented by Dennis Ritchie in the early 1970s for the C language:

```
for (init; test; change) {
        // do something
}
```

Its most common form is with an int "index variable" or "loop variable":

```
MyDataType[] data = ...
for (int i = 0; i < data.length; i++)
        MyDataType d = data[i];
        // do something with it
}
```

while loop

A while loop executes its loop body as long as (while) the test condition is true. It's commonly used in conjunction with an Enumeration or Iterator, like this:

```
Iterator<MyData> iterator = ...
while (iterator.hasNext()) {
        MyData md = iterator.next();
        //
}
```

Enumeration

An Enumeration is like an Iterator (shown earlier), but it lacks the remove() method, and the control methods have longer names—for example, hasMore Elements() and nextElement(). For new code, there is little to recommend implementing Enumeration.

7.7 Eschewing Duplicates with a Set

Problem

You want a structure that will avoid storing duplicates.

Solution

Use a `Set` implementation instead of a `List` (e.g., `Set<String> myNames = new Hash Set<>()`).

Discussion

The `Set` interface is similar to the `List` interface,[6] with methods like `add()`, `remove()`, `contains()`, `size()`, and `isEmpty()`. The difference is that it doesn't preserve order; instead, it enforces uniqueness—if you add the same item (as considered by its `equals()` method) twice or more, it will only be present once in the set. For this reason, the index-based methods such as `add(int, Object)` and `get(int)` are missing from the `Set` implementation: you might know that you've added seven objects but only five of those were unique, so calling `get()` to retrieve the sixth one would have to throw an `ArrayIndexOutOfBoundsException`! It's better not to think of a `Set` as being indexed.

 As the Java 7 Set document states: "Note: Great care must be exercised if mutable objects are used as set elements. The behavior of a set is not specified if the value of an object is changed in a manner that affects equals comparisons while the object is an element in the set. A special case of this prohibition is that it is not permissible for a set to contain itself as an element."

This code shows a duplicate entry being made to a `Set`, which will contain only one copy of the string `"One"`:

```
Set<String> hashSet = new HashSet<>();
hashSet.add("One");
hashSet.add("Two");
hashSet.add("One"); // DUPLICATE
hashSet.add("Three");
hashSet.forEach(s -> System.out.println(s));
```

Not surprisingly, only the three distinct values are printed.

---

6 Both `List` and `Set` extend `Collection`.

If you need a sorted Set, there is in fact a SortedSet interface, of which the most common implementation is a TreeSet; see a TreeSet example in Recipe 7.12.

As with Lists, the Set interface offers the of method as of Java 9:

```
Set<Double> nums = Set.of(Math.PI, 22D/7, Math.E);
Set<String> firstNames = Set.of("Robin", "Jaime", "Joey");
```

7.8 Structuring Data in a Linked List

Problem

Your data isn't suitable for use in an array.

Solution

Use a linked list; Java's LinkedList class is quite suitable.

Discussion

Anybody who's taken Computer Science 101 (or any computer science course) should be familiar with data structuring, such as linked lists and binary trees. A linked list is commonly used when you have an unpredictably large number of data items, you wish to allocate just the right amount of storage, and you want to access them in the same order that you created them. Figure 7-2 is a diagram showing the normal arrangement.

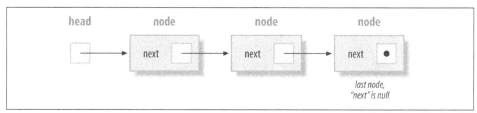

Figure 7-2. Linked list structure

Of course, the Collections API provides a LinkedList class; here is a simple program that uses it:

```
public class LinkedListDemo {
    public static void main(String[] argv) {
        System.out.println("Here is a demo of Java's LinkedList class");
        LinkedList<String> l = new LinkedList<>();
        l.add(new Object().toString());
        l.add("Hello");
        l.add("end of the list");

        System.out.println("Here is a list of all the elements");
```

```
        l.forEach(o ->
            System.out.println("Next element: " + o));

        if (l.indexOf("Hello") < 0)
            System.err.println("Lookup does not work");
        else
            System.err.println("Lookup works");

        // Now, for added fun, let's walk the linked list backwards.
        ListIterator<String> li = l.listIterator();
        while (li.hasPrevious()) {
            System.out.println("Back to: " + li.previous());
        }
    }
}
```

The ListIterator used here is a subinterface of Iterator, which was discussed in Recipe 7.6.

Just to show how this kind of list works, here is code that shows part of the implementation of a simple linked list:

```
public class LinkList<T> implements List<T> {

    /* A TNode stores one node or item in a Linked List */
    private static class TNode<T> {
        private TNode<T> next;
        private T data;
        TNode(T o, TNode<T> next) {
            data = o;
            this.next = next;
        }
        @Override
        public String toString() {
            return String.format("TNode: data='%s', next='%d'", data,
                    next == null ? 0 : next.hashCode());
        }
    }

    private boolean DIAGNOSTIC = false;

    /** The root or first TNode in the list; is a dummy pointer,
     * so its data will always be null. Simpler this way.
     */
    protected TNode<T> first;
    /**
     * For certain optimizations: A second ref to the last TNode in the list;
     * initially == first; always valid (never null), always has next == null.
     */
    protected TNode<T> last;

    /** Construct a LinkList: initialize the first and last nodes */
    public LinkList() {
```

```java
        clear();
    }

    /** Construct a LinkList given another Collection.
     * This method is recommended by the general contract of List.
     */
    public LinkList(Collection<T> c) {
        this();
        addAll(c);
    }

    /** Set the List (back) to its initial state.
     * Any references held will be discarded.
     */
    @Override
    public void clear() {
        first = new TNode<T>(null, null);
        last = first;
    }

    /** Add one object to the end of the list. Update the "next"
     * reference in the previous end, to refer to the new node.
     * Update "last" to refer to the new node.
     */
    @Override
    public boolean add(T o) {
        last.next = new TNode<T>(o, null);
        last = last.next;
        return true;
    }

    @Override
    public void add(int where, T o) {
        TNode<T> t = first;
        for (int i=0; i<=where; i++) {
            t = t.next;
            if (t == null) {
                throw new IndexOutOfBoundsException(
                    "'add(n,T) went off end of list");
            }
            if (DIAGNOSTIC) {
                System.out.printf("in add(int,T): i = %d, t = %s%n", i, t);
            }
        }
        if (DIAGNOSTIC) {
            System.out.printf("in add(int,T): to insert before %s\n", t);
        }
        final TNode<T> nn = new TNode<>(o, t.next);
        t.next = nn;
        if (DIAGNOSTIC) {
            System.out.printf("add(%d,%s)\n", where, o);
            dump("add(int,T)");
```

```java
        }
    }

    @Override
    public boolean addAll(Collection<? extends T> c) {
        c.forEach(o -> add((T) o));
        return false;
    }

    @Override
    public boolean addAll(int i, Collection<? extends T> c) {
        AtomicInteger j = new AtomicInteger(i);
        c.forEach(o -> { add(j.getAndIncrement(), o); });
        return true;
    }

    @Override
    public boolean contains(Object o) {
        TNode<T> t = first;
        while ((t = t.next) != null) {
            if (t.data.equals(o)) {
                return true;
            }
        }
        return false;
    }

    @Override
    public T get(int where) {
        TNode<T> t = first;
        int i=0;
        // If we get to the end of list before 'where', error out
        while (i++<=where) {
            if (t.next == null) {
                throw new IndexOutOfBoundsException();
            }
            t = t.next;
        }
        return t.data;
    }

    @Override
    public boolean isEmpty() {
        return first == last;
    }

    public Iterator<T> iterator() {
        return new Iterator<T>() {
            final int size = size();
            int n = 0;
            TNode<T> t = first;
            /**
```

```
     * Two cases in which next == null:
     * 1) The list is empty, we are at first
     * 2) The list is not empty, we are at last.
     */
    public boolean hasNext() {
        return n < size;
    }

    public T next() {
        if (t == first) {
            t = t.next;
        }
        TNode<T> result = t;
        t = t.next;
        ++n;
        return result.data;
    }
    public void remove() {
        throw new UnsupportedOperationException("remove");
    }
    };
}

@Override
public boolean remove(Object o) {
    TNode<T> p = first, prev = null;
    while (p != null) {
        if (p.data == o) {
            prev.next = p.next;
            return true;
        }
        prev = p; p = p.next;
    }
    return false;
}

@Override
public T set(int i, T o) {
    TNode<T> tmp = find(i);
    tmp.data = o;
    return o;
}

@Override
public int size() {
    TNode<T> t = first;
    int i;
    for (i=0; ; i++) {
        if (t == null)
            break;
        t = t.next;
    }
```

```
        return i - 1;     // subtract one for mandatory head node
    }

    @SuppressWarnings("unchecked")
    public T[] toArray(Object[] data) {
        // First is an empty anchor, start at its next
        TNode<T> p = first.next;
        for (int i = 0; p != null && i < data.length; i++) {
            data[i] = p.data;
            p = p.next;
        }
        return (T[]) data;
    }

    public Object[] toArray() {
        Object[] data = new Object[size()];
        return toArray(data);
    }
```

This is just to show how the implementation of a linked list might work. Do not use the simple LinkList class shown here; use the real one, java.util.LinkedList, shown in action in the first example.

7.9 Mapping with Hashtable and HashMap

Problem

You need a one-way mapping from one data item to another.

Solution

Use a HashMap.

Discussion

HashMap provides a one-way mapping from one set of object references to another. They are completely general purpose. I've used them to map from Swing push buttons to the URL that is to be opened when the button is pushed, to map names to addresses, and to implement a simple in-memory cache in a web server. You can map from anything to anything. In the following example, we map from company names to addresses; the addresses here are String objects, but in real life they'd probably be Address objects:

```
public class HashMapDemo {

    public static void main(String[] argv) {
```

```
// Construct and load the hash. This simulates loading a
// database or reading from a file, or wherever the data is.

Map<String,String> map = new HashMap<String,String>();

// The hash maps from company name to address.
// In real life this might map to an Address object...
map.put("Adobe", "Mountain View, CA");
map.put("IBM", "White Plains, NY");
map.put("Learning Tree", "Los Angeles, CA");
map.put("Microsoft", "Redmond, WA");
map.put("Netscape", "Mountain View, CA");
map.put("O'Reilly", "Sebastopol, CA");
map.put("Sun", "Mountain View, CA");

// Two versions of the "retrieval" phase.
// Version 1: get one pair's value given its key
// (presumably the key would really come from user input):
String queryString = "O'Reilly";
System.out.println("You asked about " + queryString + ".");
String resultString = map.get(queryString);
System.out.println("They are located in: " + resultString);
System.out.println();

// Version 2: get ALL the keys and values
// (maybe to print a report, or to save to disk)
for( String key : map.keySet()) {
    System.out.println("Key " + key +
        "; Value " + map.get(key));
}

// Version 3: Same but using a Map.Entry lambda
map.entrySet().forEach(mE ->
    System.out.println("Key + " + mE.getKey()+
        "; Value " +mE.getValue()));
    }
}
```

For this version we used both a for loop and a forEach() loop; the latter uses the
return from entrySet(), a set of Map.Entry, each of which contains one key and one
value (this may be faster on large maps because it avoids going back into the map to
get the value each time through the loop). If you are modifying the list as you are
going through it (e.g., removing elements), either inside the loop or in another
thread, then these forms will fail with a ConcurrentModificationException. You
then need to use the Iterator explicitly to control the loop:

```
// Version 2: get ALL the keys and values
// with concurrent modification
Iterator<String> it = map.keySet().iterator();
while (it.hasNext()) {
```

```
    String key = it.next();
    if (key.equals("Sun") || key.equals("Netscape")) {
        it.remove();
        continue;
    }
    System.out.println("Company " + key + "; " +
        "Address " + map.get(key));
}
```

A more functional (see Chapter 9) way of writing the removal, not involving explicit looping, would be this:

```
// Alternate to just do the removals, without explicit looping
map.keySet().removeIf(key -> Set.of("Netscape", "Sun").contains(key));
// or
map .entrySet()
    .removeIf(entry -> Set.of("Netscape", "Sun")
    .contains(entry.getKey()));
map.entrySet().forEach(System.out::println);
```

HashMap methods are not synchronized. The older and similar Hashtable methods are synchronized, for use with multiple threads.

7.10 Storing Strings in Properties and Preferences

Problem

You need to store keys and values that are both strings, possibly with persistence across runs of a program—for example, program customization.

Solution

Use a java.util.prefs.Preferences object or a java.util.Properties object.

Discussion

Here are three approaches to customization based on the user's environment. Java offers Preferences and Properties for cross-platform customizations.

Preferences

The Preferences class java.util.prefs.Preferences provides an easy-to-use mechanism for storing user customizations in a system-dependent way (which might mean dot files on Unix, a preferences file on the Mac, or the registry on Windows systems). This class provides a hierarchical set of nodes representing a user's preferences. Data is stored in the system-dependent storage format but can also be exported to or imported from an XML format. Here is a simple demonstration of Preferences:

```java
public class PrefsDemo {

    public static void main(String[] args) throws Exception {

        // Set up the Preferences for this application, by class.
        Preferences prefs = Preferences.userNodeForPackage(PrefsDemo.class);

        // Retrieve some preferences previously stored, with defaults in case
        // this is the first run.
        String text    = prefs.get("textFontName", "lucida-bright");
        String display = prefs.get("displayFontName", "lucida-blackletter");
        System.out.println(text);
        System.out.println(display);

        // Assume the user chose new preference values: Store them back.
        prefs.put("textFontName", "times-roman");
        prefs.put("displayFontName", "helvetica");

        // Toss in a couple more values for the curious who want to look
        // at how Preferences values are actually stored.
        Preferences child = prefs.node("a/b");
        child.putInt("meaning", 42);
        child.putDouble("pi", Math.PI);

        // And dump the subtree from our first node on down, in XML.
        prefs.exportSubtree(System.out);
    }
}
```

When you run the PrefsDemo program the first time, of course, it doesn't find any settings, so the calls to preferences.get() return the default values:

```
$ java -cp target/classes structure.PrefsDemo
lucida-bright
lucida-blackletter
<?xml version="1.0" encoding="UTF-8" standalone="no"?>
<!DOCTYPE preferences SYSTEM "http://java.sun.com/dtd/preferences.dtd">
<preferences EXTERNAL_XML_VERSION="1.0">
  <root type="user">
    <map/>
    <node name="structure">
      <map>
        <entry key="displayFontName" value="helvetica"/>
        <entry key="textFontName" value="times-roman"/>
      </map>
      <node name="a">
        <map/>
        <node name="b">
```

```
        <map>
            <entry key="meaning" value="42"/>
            <entry key="pi" value="3.141592653589793"/>
        </map>
      </node>
    </node>
  </node>
 </root>
</preferences>
```

On subsequent runs, it finds and returns the user-provided settings (I've elided the XML output from the second run because most of the XML output is the same):

```
> java structure.PrefsDemo
times-roman
helvetica
...
>
```

Properties

The `Properties` class is similar to a `HashMap` or `Hashtable` (it extends the latter) but with methods defined specifically for string storage and retrieval and for loading/saving. `Properties` objects are used throughout Java, for everything from setting the platform font names to customizing user applications into different `Locale` settings as part of internationalization and localization. When stored on disk, a `Properties` object looks just like a series of `name=value` assignments, with optional comments. Comments are added when you edit a `Properties` file by hand, ignored when the `Properties` object reads itself, and lost when you ask the `Properties` object to save itself to disk. Here is an example of a `Properties` file that could be used to internationalize the menus in a GUI-based program:

```
# Default properties for MenuIntl
program.title=Demonstrate I18N (MenuIntl)
program.message=Welcome to an English-localized Java Program
#
# The File Menu
#
file.label=File Menu
file.new.label=New File
file.new.key=N
file.open.label=Open...
file.open.key=O
file.save.label=Save
file.save.key=S
file.exit.label=Exit
file.exit.key=Q
```

Here is another example, showing some personalization properties:

```
name=Ian Darwin
favorite_popsicle=cherry
favorite_rock group=Fleetwood Mac
favorite_programming_language=Java
pencil_color=green
```

A `Properties` object can be loaded from a file. The rules are flexible: either =, :, or spaces can be used after a key name and its values. Spaces after a nonspace character are ignored in the key. A backslash can be used to continue lines or to escape other characters. Comment lines may begin with either # or !. Thus, a `Properties` file containing the previous items, if prepared by hand, could look like this:

```
# Here is a list of properties
! first, my name
name Ian Darwin
favorite_popsicle = cherry
favorite_rock\ group \
 Fleetwood Mac
favorite_programming_language=Java
pencil_color green
```

Fortunately, when a `Properties` object writes itself to a file, it uses the following simple format:

```
key=value
```

Here is an example of a program that creates a `Properties` object and adds into it the list of companies and their locations from Recipe 7.9. It then loads additional properties from disk. To simplify the I/O processing, the program assumes that the `Proper ties` file to be loaded is contained in the standard input, as would be done using a command-line redirection on either Unix or DOS:

```java
public class PropsCompanies {

    public static void main(String[] argv) throws java.io.IOException {

        Properties props = new Properties();

        // Get my data
        props.put("Adobe", "Mountain View, CA");
        props.put("IBM", "White Plains, NY");
        props.put("Learning Tree", "Los Angeles, CA");
        props.put("Microsoft", "Redmond, WA");
        props.put("Netscape", "Mountain View, CA");
        props.put("O'Reilly", "Sebastopol, CA");
        props.put("Sun", "Mountain View, CA");

        // Now load additional properties
        props.load(System.in);

        // List merged properties, using System.out
        props.list(System.out);
```

```
        }
    }
```

Running it as

```
java structure.PropsCompanies < PropsDemo.out
```

produces the following output in the file *PropsDemo.out*:

```
-- listing properties --
Sony=Japan
Sun=Mountain View, CA
IBM=White Plains, NY
Netscape=Mountain View, CA
Nippon_Kogaku=Japan
Acorn=United Kingdom
Adobe=Mountain View, CA
Ericsson=Sweden
O'Reilly & Associates=Sebastopol, CA
Learning Tree=Los Angeles, CA
```

In case you didn't notice in either the HashMap or the Properties examples, the order in which the outputs appear in these examples is neither sorted nor in the order we put them in. The hashing classes and the Properties subclass make no claim about the order in which objects are retrieved. If you need them sorted, see Recipe 7.11.

As a convenient shortcut, my FileProperties class includes a constructor that takes a filename:

```
import com.darwinsys.util.FileProperties;
...
Properties p = new FileProperties("PropsDemo.out");
```

Note that constructing a FileProperties object causes it to be loaded, and therefore the constructor may throw a checked exception of class IOException.

7.11 Sorting a Collection

Problem

You put your data into a collection in random order or used a Properties object that doesn't preserve the order, and now you want it sorted.

Solution

Use the static method Arrays.sort() or Collections.sort(), optionally providing a Comparator.

Discussion

If your data is in an array, then you can sort it using the static sort() method of the Arrays utility class. If it is in a Collection, you can use the static sort() method of the Collections class. Here is a set of strings being sorted in place in an Array:

```
public class SortArray {
    public static void main(String[] unused) {
        String[] strings = {
            "painful",
            "mainly",
            "gaining",
            "raindrops"
        };
        Arrays.sort(strings);
        for (int i=0; i<strings.length; i++) {
            System.out.println(strings[i]);
        }
    }
}
```

What if the default sort order isn't what you want? Well, you can create an object that implements the Comparator<T> interface and pass that as the second argument to sort. Fortunately, for the most common ordering next to the default, you don't have to: a public constant String.CASE_INSENSITIVE_ORDER can be passed as this second argument. The String class defines it as a Comparator<String> that orders String objects as by compareToIgnoreCase. But if you need something fancier, you probably need to write a Comparator<T>. In some cases you may be able to use the Comparator.comparing() method and other static methods on Comparator to create a custom comparator without having to create a class. Suppose that, for some strange reason, you need to sort strings using all but the first character of the string. One way to do this would be to write this Comparator<String>:

```
/** Comparator for comparing strings ignoring first character.
 */
public class SubstringComparator implements Comparator<String> {
    @Override
    public int compare(String s1, String s2) {
        s1 = s1.substring(1);
        s2 = s2.substring(1);
        return s1.compareTo(s2);
        // or, more concisely:
        // return s1.substring(1).compareTo(s2.substring(1));
    }
}
```

Using it is just a matter of passing it as the Comparator argument to the correct form of sort(), as shown here:

```
public class SubstringComparatorDemo {
    public static void main(String[] unused) {
        String[] strings = {
            "painful",
            "mainly",
            "gaining",
            "raindrops"
        };
        Arrays.sort(strings);
        dump(strings, "Using Default Sort");
        Arrays.sort(strings, new SubstringComparator());
        dump(strings, "Using SubstringComparator");

        // tag::functional[]
        System.out.println("Functional approach:");
        Arrays.stream(strings)
            .sorted(Comparator.comparing(s->s.substring(1)))
            .forEach(System.out::println);
        // end::functional[]
    }

    static void dump(String[] args, String title) {
        System.out.println(title);
        for (String s : args)
            System.out.println(s);
    }
}
```

Again, a more functional (see Chapter 9) way of writing this might be the following:

```
System.out.println("Functional approach:");
Arrays.stream(strings)
    .sorted(Comparator.comparing(s->s.substring(1)))
    .forEach(System.out::println);
```

Here is the output of running it:

```
$ java structure.SubstrCompDemo
Using Default Sort
gaining
mainly
painful
raindrops
Using SubstringComparator
raindrops
painful
gaining
mainly
```

And this is all as it should be.

On the other hand, you may be writing a class and want to build in the comparison functionality so that you don't always have to remember to pass the Comparator with it. In this case, you can directly implement the `java.lang.Comparable` interface, as is done by many classes in the standard API. These include `String` class; the wrapper classes `Byte`, `Character`, `Double`, `Float`, `Long`, `Short`, and `Integer`; `BigInteger` and `BigDecimal` from `java.math`; most objects in the date/time API in `java.time`; and `java.text.CollationKey`. Arrays or `Collections` of these types can be sorted without providing a `Comparator`. Classes that implement `Comparable` are said to have a natural ordering. The documentation strongly recommends that a class's natural ordering be consistent with its `equals()` method. It is consistent with `equals()` if and only if `e1.compareTo((Object)e2)` has the same Boolean value as `e1.equals((Object)e2)` for every instance e1 and e2 of the given class. This means that if you implement `Comparable`, you should also implement `equals()`, and the logic of `equals()` should be consistent with the logic of the `compareTo()` method. If you implement `equals()`, incidentally, you also should implement `hashCode()` (as discussed in "hashCode() and equals()" on page 241). Here, for example, is part of the appointment class `Appt` from a hypothetical scheduling program. The class has a `LocalDate` date variable and a `LocalTime` time variable; the latter may be null (e.g., an all-day appointment or a to-do item); this complicates the `compareTo()` function a little.

```
// public class Appt implements Comparable {
    // Much code and variables omitted - see online version
    //------------------------------------------------------------------
    //     METHODS - COMPARISON
    //------------------------------------------------------------------
    /** compareTo method, from Comparable interface.
     * Compare this Appointment against another, for purposes of sorting.
     * <P>Only date and time, then text, participate, not repetition!
     * (Repetition has to do with recurring events, e.g.,
     *   "Meeting every Tuesday at 9").
     * This methods is consistent with equals().
     * @return -1 if this<a2, +1 if this>a2, else 0.
     */
    @Override
    public int compareTo(Appt a2) {
        // If dates not same, trigger on their comparison
        int dateComp = date.compareTo(a2.date);
        if (dateComp != 0)
            return dateComp;
        // Same date. If times not same, trigger on their comparison
        if (time != null && a2.time != null) {
            // Neither time is null
            int timeComp = time.compareTo(a2.time);
            if (timeComp != 0)
                return timeComp;
        } else /* At least one time is null */ {
            if (time == null && a2.time != null) {
                return -1; // All-day appts sort low to appear first
            } else if (time != null && a2.time == null)
```

```
                    return +1;
                    // else both have no time set, so carry on
            }
        // Same date & time, trigger on text
        return text.compareTo(a2.text);
    }

    @Override
    public int hashCode() {
        final int prime = 31;
        int result = 1;
        result = prime * result + ((date == null) ? 0 : date.hashCode());
        result = prime * result + ((text == null) ? 0 : text.hashCode());
        result = prime * result + ((time == null) ? 0 : time.hashCode());
        return result;
    }

    @Override
    public boolean equals(Object o2) {
        if (this == o2)
            return true;
        if (o2.getClass() != Appt.class)
            return false;
        Appt a2 = (Appt) o2;
        if (!date.equals(a2.date))
            return false;
        if (time != null && !time.equals(a2.time))
            return false;
        return text.equals(a2.text);
    }

    /** Return a String representation of this Appt.
     * Output is intended for debugging, not presentation!
     */
    @Override
    public String toString() {
        var sb = new StringBuilder();
        sb.append(date).append(' ');
        if (time != null) {
            sb.append(time.getHour())
            .append(':')
            .append(time.getMinute())
            .append(' ');
        } else {
            sb.append("(All day)").append(' ');
        }
        sb.append(text).toString();
        return sb.toString();
    }
```

If you're still confused between Comparable and Comparator, you're probably not alone. Table 7-3 summarizes the two comparison interfaces.

Table 7-3. Comparable compared with Comparator

Interface name	Description	Method(s)
java.lang.Comparable<T>	Provides a natural ordering to objects. Written in the class whose objects are being sorted.	int compareTo(T o);
java.util.Comparator<T>	Provides total control over sorting objects of another class. Standalone strategy object; pass to sort() method or Collection constructor.	int compare(T o1, T o2); boolean equals(T c2)

7.12 Avoiding the Urge to Sort

Problem

Your data needs to be sorted, but you don't want to stop and sort it periodically.

Solution

Not everything that requires order requires an explicit *sort* operation. Just keep the data sorted at all times.

Discussion

You can avoid the overhead and elapsed time of an explicit sorting operation by ensuring that the data is in the correct order at all times, though this may or may not be faster overall, depending on your data and how you choose to keep it sorted. You can keep it sorted either manually or by using a TreeSet or a TreeMap. First, here is some code from a call tracking program that I first wrote on the very first public release of Java (the code has been modernized slightly!) to keep track of people I had extended contact with. Far less functional than a Rolodex, my CallTrack program maintained a list of people sorted by last name and first name. It also had the city, phone number, and email address of each person. Here is a very small portion of the code surrounding the event handling for the New User push button:

```
public class CallTrack {

    /** The list of Person objects. */
    protected List<Person> usrList = new ArrayList<>();

    /** The scrolling list */
    protected java.awt.List visList = new java.awt.List();

    /** Add one (new) Person to the list, keeping the list sorted. */
    protected void add(Person p) {
        String lastName = p.getLastName();
        int i;
        // Find in "i" the position in the list where to insert this person
        for (i=0; i<usrList.size(); i++)
```

```
            if (lastName.compareTo((usrList.get(i)).getLastName()) <= 0)
                break; // If we don't break, OK, will insert at end of list.
        usrList.add(i, p);

        // Now insert them in the scrolling list, in the same position.
        visList.add(p.getFullName(), i);
        visList.select(i);        // ensure current
    }

}
```

This code uses the `String` class `compareTo(String)` routine.

This code uses a linear search, which was fine for the original application but could get very slow on large lists (it is $O(n)$). You'd need
to use hashing or a binary search to find where to put the values on
large lists.

If I were writing this code today, I might well use a `TreeSet` (which keeps objects in
order) or a `TreeMap` (which keeps the keys in order and maps from keys to values; the
keys would be the name and the values would be the `Person` objects). Both insert the
objects into a tree in the correct order, so an `Iterator` that traverses the tree always
returns the objects in sorted order. In addition, they have methods such as `headSet()`
and `headMap()`, which give a new `Set` or `Map` of objects of the same class, containing
the objects lexically before a given value. The `tailSet()` and `tailMap()` methods,
similarly, return objects greater than a given value, and `subSet()` and `subMap()`
return a range. The `first()` and `last()` methods retrieve the obvious components
from the collection. The following program uses a `TreeSet` to sort some names:

```
        // A TreeSet keeps objects in sorted order. Use a Comparator
        // published by String for case-insensitive sorting order.
        TreeSet<String> theSet = new TreeSet<>(String.CASE_INSENSITIVE_ORDER);
        theSet.add("Gosling");
        theSet.add("da Vinci");
        theSet.add("van Gogh");
        theSet.add("Java To Go");
        theSet.add("Vanguard");
        theSet.add("Darwin");
        theSet.add("Darwin");     // TreeSet is Set, ignores duplicates.

        System.out.printf("Our set contains %d elements", theSet.size());

        // Since it is sorted we can easily get various subsets
        System.out.println("Lowest (alphabetically) is " + theSet.first());

        // Print how many elements are greater than "k"
        // Should be 2 - "van Gogh" and "Vanguard"
        System.out.println(theSet.tailSet("k").toArray().length +
```

```
                  " elements higher than \"k\"");

             // Print the whole list in sorted order
             System.out.println("Sorted list:");
             theSet.forEach(name -> System.out.println(name));
```

One last point to note is that if you have a `Hashtable` or `HashMap`, you can convert it to a `TreeMap`, and therefore get it sorted, just by passing it to the `TreeMap` constructor:

```
        TreeMap sorted = new TreeMap(unsortedHashMap);
```

7.13 Finding an Object in a Collection

Problem

You need to see whether a given collection contains a particular value.

Solution

Ask the collection if it contains an object of the given value.

Discussion

If you have created the contents of a collection, you probably know what is in it and what is not. But if the collection is prepared by another part of a large application, or even if you've just been putting objects into it and now need to find out if a given value was found, this recipe's for you. There is quite a variety of methods, depending on which collection class you have. The methods in Table 7-4 can be used.

Table 7-4. Finding objects in a collection

Method(s)	Meaning	Implementing classes
`binarySearch()`	Fairly fast search	`Arrays`, `Collections`
`contains()`	Search	`ArrayList`, `HashSet`, `Hashtable`, `Link List`, `Properties`, `Vector`
`containsKey()`, `containsValue()`	Checks if the collection contains the object as a Key or as a Value	`HashMap`, `Hashtable`, `Properties`, `TreeMap`
`indexOf()`	Returns location where object is found	`ArrayList`, `LinkedList`, `List`, `Stack`, `Vector`
`search()`	Search	`Stack`

The methods whose names start with `contains` will use a linear search if the collection is a collection (`List`, `Set`) but will be quite fast if the collection is hashed (`Hash Set`, `HashMap`). So you do have to know what implementation is being used in order to think about performance, particularly when the collection is (or is likely to grow) large.

The next example plays a little game of find the hidden number (or needle in a haystack): the numbers to look through are stored in an array. As games go, it's fairly pathetic: the computer plays against itself, so you probably know who's going to win. I wrote it that way so I would know that the data array contains valid numbers. The interesting part is not the generation of the random numbers (discussed in Recipe 5.9). The array to be used with `Arrays.binarySearch()` must be in sorted order, but because we just filled it with random numbers, it isn't initially sorted. Hence, we call `Arrays.sort()` on the array. Then we are in a position to call `Arrays.binary Search()`, passing in the array and the value to look for. If you run the program with a number, it runs that many games and reports on how it fared overall. If you don't bother, it plays only one game:

```java
public class ArrayHunt  {
    /** the maximum (and actual) number of random ints to allocate */
    protected final static int MAX     = 4000;
    /** the value to look for */
    protected final static int NEEDLE = 1999;
    int[] haystack;
    Random r;

    public static void main(String[] argv) {
        ArrayHunt h = new ArrayHunt();
        if (argv.length == 0)
            h.play();
        else {
            int won = 0;
            int games = Integer.parseInt(argv[0]);
            for (int i=0; i<games; i++)
                if (h.play())
                    ++won;
            System.out.println("Computer won " + won +
                " out of " + games + ".");
        }
    }

    /** Construct the hunting ground */
    public ArrayHunt() {
        haystack = new int[MAX];
        r = new Random();
    }

    /** Play one game. */
    public boolean play() {
        int i;

        // Fill the array with random data (hay?)
        for (i=0; i<MAX; i++) {
```

```
            haystack[i] = (int)(r.nextFloat() * MAX);
        }

        // Precondition for binary search is that data be sorted!
        Arrays.sort(haystack);

        // Look for needle in haystack
        i = Arrays.binarySearch(haystack, NEEDLE);

        if (i >= 0) {          // Found it, we win.
            System.out.println("Value " + NEEDLE +
                " occurs at haystack[" + i + "]");
            return true;
        } else {          // Not found, we lose.
            System.out.println("Value " + NEEDLE +
                " does not occur in haystack; nearest value is " +
                haystack[-(i+2)] + " (found at " + -(i+2) + ")");
            return false;
        }
    }
}
```

`Collections.binarySearch()` works almost exactly the same way, except it looks in a `Collection`, which must be sorted (presumably using `Collections.sort`, as discussed in Recipe 7.11).

7.14 Converting a Collection to an Array

Problem

You have a `Collection` but you need a Java language array.

Solution

Use the `Collection` method `toArray()`.

Discussion

If you have an `ArrayList` or other `Collection` and you need an array, you can get it just by calling the `Collection`'s `toArray()` method. With no arguments, you get an array whose type is `Object[]`. You can optionally provide an array argument, which is used for two purposes:

- The type of the array argument determines the type of array returned.
- If the array is big enough (and you can ensure that it is by allocating the array based on the `Collection`'s `size()` method), then this array is filled and returned. If the array is not big enough, a new array is allocated instead. If you provide an

array and objects in the `Collection` cannot be cast to this type, then you will get an `ArrayStoreException`.

Example 7-3 shows code for converting an `ArrayList` to an array of type `Object`.

Example 7-3. main/src/main/java/structure/ToArray.java

```java
List<String> list = new ArrayList<>();
list.add("Blobbo");
list.add("Cracked");
list.add("Dumbo");

// Convert a collection to Object[], which can store objects
// of any type.
Object[] ol = list.toArray();
System.out.println("Array of Object has length " + ol.length);

String[] sl = (String[]) list.toArray(new String[0]);
System.out.println("Array of String has length " + sl.length);
```

7.15 Making Your Data Iterable

Problem

You have written your own data structure, and you want to publish the data to be iterable so it can be used in the for-each loop.

Solution

Make your data class `Iterable`: this interace has only one method, `iterator()`. Write your own `Iterator`. Just implement (or provide an inner class that implements) the `Iterator` interface.

Discussion

To be usable in the modern Java for-each loop, your data class must implement `Iterable`, a simple interface with one method, `Iterator<T> iterator()`. Whether you use this interface or want to use the older `Iterator` interface directly, the way to make data from one part of your program available in a storage-independent way to other parts of the code is to generate an `Iterator`. Here is a short program that constructs, upon request, an `Iterator` for some data that it is storing—in this case, in an array. The `Iterator` interface has only three methods—`hasNext()`, `next()`, and `remove()`—demonstrated in Example 7-4.

Example 7-4. main/src/main/java/structure//IterableDemo

```java
public class IterableDemo {

    /** Demo implements Iterable, meaning it must provide an Iterator,
     * and that it can be used in a foreach loop.
     */
    static class Demo implements Iterable<String> {

        // Simple demo: use array instead of inventing new data structure
        String[] data = { "One", "Two", "Three"};

        /** This is the Iterator that makes it all happen */
        class DemoIterator implements Iterator<String> {
            int i = 0;

            /**
             * Tell if there are any more elements.
             * @return true if next() will succeed, false otherwise
             */
            public boolean hasNext() {
                return i < data.length;
            }

            /** @return the next element from the data */
            public String next() {
                return data[i++];
            }

            /** Remove the object that next() just returned.
             * An Iterator is not required to support this interface, and we don't.
             * @throws UnsupportedOperationException unconditionally
             */
            public void remove() {
                throw new UnsupportedOperationException("remove");
            }
        }

        /** Method by which the Demo class makes its iterator available */
        public Iterator<String> iterator() {
            return new DemoIterator();
        }
    }

    public static void main(String[] args) {
        Demo demo = new Demo();
        for (String s : demo) {
            System.out.println(s);
        }
    }
}
```

The comments on the remove() method remind me of an interesting point. This interface introduces java.util's attempt at something Java doesn't really have, the optional method. Because there is no syntax for this, and they didn't want to introduce any new syntax, the developers of the Collections Framework decided on an implementation using existing syntax. Optional methods that are not implemented are required to throw an UnsupportedOperationException if they ever get called. My remove() method does just that. Note that UnsupportedOperationException is subclassed from RuntimeException, so it is not required to be declared or caught.

This code is simplistic, but it does show the syntax and demonstrates how the Iterator interface works. In real code, the Iterator and the data are usually separate objects (the Iterator might be an inner class from the data store class). Also, you don't even need to write this code for an array; you can just construct an ArrayList object, copy the array elements into it, and ask it to provide the Iterator. However, I believe it's worth showing this simple example of the internals of an Iterator so that you can understand both how it works and how you could provide one for a more sophisticated data structure, should the need arise.

The Iterable interface has only one nondefault method, iterator(), which must provide an Iterator for objects of the given type. Because the ArrayIterator class implements this as well, we can use an object of type ArrayIterator in a "foreach" loop, as in Example 7-5.

Example 7-5. main/src/main/java/structure/ArrayIteratorDemo.java

```java
package structure;

import com.darwinsys.util.ArrayIterator;

public class ArrayIteratorDemo {

    private final static String[] names = {
        "rose", "petunia", "tulip"
    };

    public static void main(String[] args) {
        ArrayIterator<String> arrayIterator = new ArrayIterator<>(names);

        System.out.println("Java 5, 6 way");
        for (String s : arrayIterator) {
            System.out.println(s);
        }

        System.out.println("Java 5, 6 ways");
        arrayIterator.forEach(s->System.out.println(s));
        arrayIterator.forEach(System.out::println);
```

```
        }
}
```

Java 8 Iterable.foreach

Java 8 adds foreach to the Iterator interface, a *default method* (discussed in Recipe 9.0) that you don't have to write. Thus, without changing the ArrayIterator, after moving to Java 8 we can use the newest-style loop, Iterator.foreach(Consumer), with a lambda expression (see Chapter 9) to print each element (see Example 7-5).

7.16 Using a Stack of Objects

Problem

You need to process data in the order of last in, first out (LIFO) or most recently added.

Solution

Write your own code for creating a stack; it's easy. Or, use a java.util.Stack.

Discussion

You need to put things into a holding area quickly and retrieve them in last-in, first-out order. This is a common data structuring operation and is often used to reverse the order of objects. The basic operations of any stack are push() (add to stack), pop() (remove from stack), and peek() (examine top element without removing). ToyStack in Example 7-6 is a simple class for stacking values of the primitive type int. I'll expand it in a page or two to allow stacking of user-defined objects.

Example 7-6. main/src/main/java/structure/ToyStack.java

```java
public class ToyStack {

    /** The maximum stack depth */
    protected int MAX_DEPTH = 10;
    /** The current stack depth */
    protected int depth = 0;
    /* The actual stack */
    protected int[] stack = new int[MAX_DEPTH];

    /** push - add an element onto the stack */
    protected void push(int n) {
        stack[depth++] = n;
    }
    /** pop - return and remove the top element */
    protected int pop() {
```

```
        return stack[--depth];
    }
    /** peek - return the top element but don't remove it */
    protected int peek() {
        return stack[depth-1];
    }
}
```

If you are not familiar with the basic idea of a stack, you should work through the code here; if you are familiar with it, you can skip ahead. While looking at it, of course, think about what happens if pop() or peek() is called when push() has never been called or if push() is called to stack more data than will fit.

While working on ToyStack2 (not shown but in the online source), I extracted its interface into SimpleStack, which just lists the operations. At the same time I added the empty() method for some compatibility with the standard java.util.Stack class. And importantly, I made it a generic type, so it can be used with values of any type. This is shown in SimpleStack:

```
public interface SimpleStack<T> {

    /** empty - return true if the stack is empty */
    abstract boolean empty();

    /** push - add an element onto the stack */
    abstract void push(T n);

    /** pop - return and remove the top element */
    abstract T pop();

    /** peek - return the top element but don't remove it */
    abstract T peek();
}
```

I then made another demo stack class, MyStack, to implement the new interface:

```
public class MyStack<T> implements SimpleStack<T> {

    private int depth = 0;
    public static final int DEFAULT_INITIAL = 10;
    private T[] stack;

    public MyStack() {
        this(DEFAULT_INITIAL);
    }

    public MyStack(int howBig) {
        if (howBig <= 0) {
            throw new IllegalArgumentException(
            howBig + " must be positive, but was " + howBig);
        }
```

```java
        stack = (T[])new Object[howBig];
    }

    @Override
    public boolean empty() {
        return depth == 0;
    }

    /** push - add an element onto the stack */
    @Override
    public void push(T obj) {
        // Could check capacity and expand
        stack[depth++] = obj;
    }

    /* pop - return and remove the top element */
    @Override
    public T pop() {
        --depth;
        T tmp = stack[depth];
        stack[depth] = null;
        return tmp;
    }

    /** peek - return the top element but don't remove it */
    @Override
    public T peek() {
        if (depth == 0) {
            return null;
        }
        return stack[depth-1];
    }

    public boolean hasNext() {
        return depth > 0;
    }

    public boolean hasRoom() {
        return depth < stack.length;
    }

    public int getStackDepth() {
        return depth;
    }
}
```

This version has a lot more error checking (and a unit test, in the *src/test/java/structure* folder), as well as some additional methods not in the original. One example is hasRoom(). Unlike the full-blown java.util.Stack, MyStack does not expand beyond its original size, so we need a way to see if it is full without throwing an exception.

Now that you see how a stack works, I recommend using the provided `java.util.Stack` instead of my demo versions; it is more fully fleshed out, more fully tested, and widely used. Unlike the major Collections API components `List`, `Set`, and `Map`, `java.util.Stack` does not have an interface and implementation class(es); it is based on `Vector`, which is a `List` implementation. The real `java.util.Stack` works in a similar manner to mine but has more methods and more flexibility. To see that in operation, Recipe 5.12 provides a simple stack-based numeric calculator.

7.17 Multidimensional Structures

Problem

You need a multidimensional array or `ArrayList`.

Solution

No problem. Java supports this.

Discussion

As mentioned back in Recipe 7.1, Java arrays can hold any reference type. Because an array is a reference type, it follows that you can have arrays of arrays or, in other terminology, *multidimensional* arrays. Further, because each array has its own length attribute, the columns of a two-dimensional array, for example, do not all have to be the same length (see Figure 7-3).

Here is code to allocate a couple of two-dimensional arrays, one using a loop and the other using an initializer. Both are selectively printed:

```
public class ArrayTwoDObjects {

    /** Return list of subscript names (unrealistic; just for demo). */
    public static String[][] getArrayInfo() {
        String info[][];
        info = new String[10][10];
        for (int i=0; i < info.length; i++) {
            for (int j = 0; j < info[i].length; j++) {
                info[i][j] = "String[" + i + "," + j + "]";
            }
        }
        return info;
    }

    /** Run the initialization method and print part of the results */
    public static void main(String[] args) {
        print("from getArrayInfo", getArrayInfo());
```

```
        }

        /** Print selected elements from the 2D array */
        public static void print(String tag, String[][] array) {
            System.out.println("Array " + tag + " is " + array.length + " x " +
                array[0].length);
            System.out.println("Array[0][0] = " + array[0][0]);
            System.out.println("Array[0][1] = " + array[0][1]);
            System.out.println("Array[1][0] = " + array[1][0]);
            System.out.println("Array[0][0] = " + array[0][0]);
            System.out.println("Array[1][1] = " + array[1][1]);
        }
    }
```

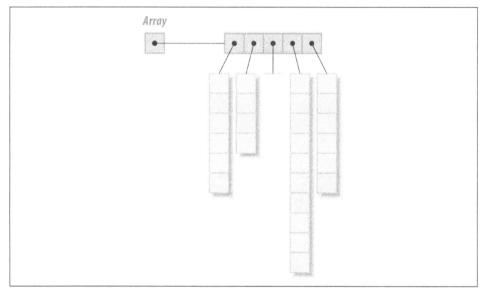

Figure 7-3. Multidimensional arrays

Running it produces this output:

```
> java structure.ArrayTwoDObjects
Array from getArrayInfo is 10 x 10
Array[0][0] = String[0,0]
Array[0][1] = String[0,1]
Array[1][0] = String[1,0]
Array[0][0] = String[0,0]
Array[1][1] = String[1,1]
Array from getParameterInfo is 2 x 3
Array[0][0] = fontsize
Array[0][1] = 9-18
Array[1][0] = URL
Array[0][0] = fontsize
Array[1][1] = -
>
```

The same kind of logic can be applied to any of the Collections. You could have an ArrayList of ArrayLists, or a Vector of linked lists, or whatever your little heart desires.

As Figure 7-3 shows, it is not necessary for the array to be regular (i.e., it's possible for each column of the 2D array to have a different height). That is why I used array[0].length for the length of the first column in the code example.

7.18 Simplifying Data Objects with Lombok or Record

Problem

You waste time writing data classes that are Plain Old Java Objects (POJO), with boilerplate code such as setters and getters, equals(), and toString().

Solution

Use Lombok to autogenerate boilerplate methods. In Java 14+, use the new record data type, which generates the boilerplate methods for you.

Discussion

When Java was new, before there were good IDEs, developers had to write getters and setters by hand, or by copy-paste-change. Back then I did a study of one existing large code base and found about a 1/2% failure rate. The setter stored the value in the wrong place or the getter retrieved the wrong value. Assuming random distribution, this meant that one getter call in a hundred gave the wrong answer! The application still worked, so I must assume those wrong answers didn't matter.

Now we have IDEs that can generate all the boilerplate methods such as setters/getters, equals, toString(), and so on. But you still have to remember to invoke these generators.

Lombok

Project Lombok provides one solution. It reads your *.class* files looking for its own annotations and, when it finds them, rewrites the class files to have the chosen methods.

To use Lombok, you need to add the dependency org.projectlombok:lombok:1.18.4 (or newer) to your build script. Or, if you are using an IDE, download the Lombok JAR file from *https://projectlombok.org* and install it as per the instructions there. Then you can annotate your class with annotations like these:

```
@Setters @Getters
```

Presto! No more forgetting to generate these methods; Lombok will do the work for you.

Other annotations include the following:

```
@ToString
@EqualsAndHashCode
@AllArgsConstructor
```

For data classes, there is even `@Data`, which is a shortcut for `@ToString`, `@EqualsAnd HashCode`, `@Getter` on all fields, `@Setter` on all nonfinal fields, and `@RequiredArgs Constructor`!

Java 14 record (preview)

The new `record` type provides another solution. A `record` is a class-like construct for data classes, a restricted form of class like enums and annotations. You need only write the name of a data object and its fields, and the compiler will provide a constructor, getters, `hashCode()` and `equals()`, and `toString()`:

```
public record Person(String name, String emailAddress) { }
```

The provided constructor has the same signature as the record declaration. All fields are implicitly final, and the `record` provides getters but not setters. The getters have the name of the field; they do not follow the JavaBeans *getName()* pattern. Immutable objects are important for reliable code (see Recipe 9.0). You can provide other members such as extra constructors, static fields, and static or instance methods. Records cannot be abstract and cannot declare additional instance fields. All in keeping with the fact that the state of the object is as declared in the `record` header. Here I create a Person record and make an instance of it, all in JShell:

```
$ jshell --enable-preview
|  Welcome to JShell -- Version 14-ea
|  For an introduction type: /help intro

jshell> record Person(String name, String email) {}

jshell> var p = new Person("Covington Roderick Smythe", "roddy@smythe.tld")
p ==> Person[name=Covington Roderick Smythe, email=roddy@smythe.tld]

jshell> p.name()
$3 ==> "Covington Roderick Smythe"

jshell>
```

One-line record definitions typically don't need to be in a source file all their own. To show a complete example, I baked the `Person` record into a new demo program `Per sonRecordDemo`. We can save this into a file, compile it with *javac*, and then use *javap* to view the class's structure:

```
$ javac --enable-preview -source 14 PersonRecordDemo.java
Note: PersonRecordDemo.java uses preview language features.
Note: Recompile with -Xlint:preview for details.
$ javap PersonRecordDemo'$'Person
Compiled from "PersonRecordDemo.java"
public final class PersonRecordDemo$Person extends java.lang.Record {
  public PersonRecordDemo$Person(java.lang.String, java.lang.String);
  public java.lang.String toString();
  public final int hashCode();
  public final boolean equals(java.lang.Object);
  public java.lang.String name();
  public java.lang.String email();
}
```

The $ in the filename has to be escaped from the Unix shell. We see that the compiler has generated the constructor, toString(), hashCode() and equals(), and read-only accessors name() and email().

 As of Java 14 the record mechanism is a preview, so it may change from what is described here or might even (however unlikely) not appear in the final Java 14 or in a future Java release (though we hope it will appear as is, nonpreview, in Java 15). If you are using Java 14 you need the --enable-preview option on commands like *javap*, *javac*, and *jshell*, as well as --source 14 on commands that read the source file.

See Also

The original description of and rationale for the record mechanism is in Java Enhancement Proposal JEP-359 (*https://openjdk.java.net/jeps/359*) at OpenJDK.net.

7.19 Program: Timing Comparisons

New developers sometimes worry about the overhead of these collections and think they should use arrays instead of data structures. To investigate, I wrote a program that creates and accesses 250,000 objects, once through a Java array and again through an ArrayList. This is a lot more objects than most programs use. First the code for the Array version:

```
public class Array {
    public static final int MAX = 250000;
    public static void main(String[] args) {
        System.out.println(new Array().run());
    }
    public int run() {
        MutableInteger list[] = new MutableInteger[MAX];
        for (int i=0; i<list.length; i++) {
            list[i] = new MutableInteger(i);
```

```
        }
        int sum = 0;
        for (int i=0; i<list.length; i++) {
            sum += list[i].getValue();
        }
        return sum;
    }
}
```

And here's the code for the `ArrayList` version:

```
public class ArrayLst {
    public static final int MAX = 250000;
    public static void main(String[] args) {
        System.out.println(new ArrayLst().run());
    }
    public int run() {
        ArrayList<MutableInteger> list = new ArrayList<>();
        for (int i=0; i<MAX; i++) {
            list.add(new MutableInteger(i));
        }
        int sum = 0;
        for (int i=0; i<MAX; i++) {
            sum += ((MutableInteger)list.get(i)).getValue();
        }
        return sum;
    }
}
```

The `Vector`-based version, `ArrayVec`, is sufficiently similar that I don't feel the need to kill a tree reprinting its code—it's online.

How can we time this? As covered in Recipe 17.7, you can either use the operating system's *time* command, if available, or just use a bit of Java that times a run of your main program. To be portable, I chose to use the latter on an older, slower machine. Its exact speed doesn't matter because the important thing is to compare only versions of this program running on the same machine.

Finally (drum roll, please), the results:

```
$ java performance.Time Array
Starting class class Array
1185103928
runTime=4.310
$ java performance.Time ArrayLst
Starting class class ArrayLst
1185103928
runTime=5.626
$ java performance.Time ArrayVec
Starting class class ArrayVec
1185103928
runTime=6.699
$
```

Notice that I have ignored one oft-quoted bit of advice that recommends giving a good initial estimate on the size of the `ArrayList`. I did time it that way as well; in this example, it made a difference of less than 4% in the total runtime.

The bottom line is that the efficiency of `ArrayList` is not totally awful compared to arrays. Obviously there is more overhead in calling a "get" method than in retrieving an element from an array. The overhead of objects whose methods actually do some computation probably outweighs the overhead of fetching and storing objects in an `ArrayList` rather than in an `Array`. Unless you are dealing with large numbers of objects, you may not need to worry about it. `Vector` is slightly slower but still only about two-thirds the speed of the original array version. If you are concerned about the time, once the finished size of the `ArrayList` is known, you can convert the `Array List` to an array (see Recipe 7.14).

## CHAPTER 8

Object-Oriented Techniques

8.0 Introduction

Java is an Object-Oriented (OO) language in the tradition of Simula-67, SmallTalk, and C++. It borrows syntax from C++ and ideas from SmallTalk. The Java API has been designed and built on the OO model. Design patterns (see the book of the same name), such as Factory and Delegate, are used throughout; an understanding of these patterns will help you better understand the use of the API and improve the design of your own classes.

Advice, or Mantras

There are any number of short bits of advice that I could give. A few recurring themes arise when learning the basics of Java, and I suggest reviewing them when learning more Java.

Use the API

I can't say this often enough. A lot of the things you need to do have already been done by the good folks who develop the standard Java library (and third-party libraries). And this grows with every release. Learning the API well is a good grounds for avoiding that deadly "reinventing the flat tire" syndrome—coming up with a second-rate equivalent of a first-rate product that was available to you the whole time. In fact, part of this book's mission is to prevent you from reinventing what's already there. One example of this is the Collections API in `java.util`, discussed in Chapter 7. The Collections API has a high degree of generality and regularity, so there is often no need to invent your own data structuring code.

Exceptions to the rule

There is one exception to the rule of using the API: the `clone()` method in `java.lang.Object` should generally *not* be used. If you need to copy an object, just write a copy method, or a *copy constructor*. Joshua Bloch's arguments against the `clone()` method in the book *Effective Java* (Addison-Wesley) are persuasive and should be read by any dedicated Java programmer. While you're at it, read that whole book.

Another exception is the `finalize()` method in `java.lang.Object()`. Don't use it. It has been deprecated since Java 9 because it isn't guaranteed to be invoked; but because it might get invoked, it will cause your dead objects not to be garbage collected, resulting in a memory leak. If you need some kind of cleanup, you must take responsibility for defining a method and invoking it before you let any object of that class go out of reference. You might call such a method `cleanUp()`. For application-level cleanup, see *https://darwinsys.com/java/shutdownhook.html*.

Generalize

There is a trade-off between generality (and the resulting reusability), which is emphasized here, and the convenience of application specificity. If you're writing one small part of a very large application designed according to OO design techniques, you'll have in mind a specific set of use cases. On the other hand, if you're writing toolkit-style code, you should write classes with few assumptions about how they'll be used. Making code easy to use from a variety of programs is the route to writing reusable code.

Read and write javadoc

You've no doubt looked at the Java online documentation in a browser, in part because I just told you to learn the API well. Do you think Sun/Oracle hired millions of tech writers to produce all that documentation? No. That documentation exists because the developers of the API took the time to write javadoc comments, those funny `/**` comments you've seen in code. So, one more bit of advice: use javadoc. The standard JDK provides a good, standard mechanism for API documentation. And use it as you write the code—don't think you'll come back and write it in later. That kind of tomorrow never comes.

See Recipe 15.2 for details on using javadoc.

Use subclassing and delegation

Use subclassing. But don't overuse subclassing. It is one of the best ways not only for avoiding code duplication, but for developing software that works. See any number of good books on the topic of object-oriented design and programming for more details.

There are several alternatives. One alternative to subclassing is delegation. Think about "is a" versus "has a." For example, instead of subclassing NameAndAddress to make BusinessPartner and Customer, make BusinessPartner and Customer have instances of NameAndAddress. That is a clearer structure; having BusinessPartner *be a* NameAndAddress just because the partner *has a* name and address would not make sense. And delegation also makes it easier for a Customer to have both a billing address and a shipping address. Another alternative is Aspect-Oriented Programming (AOP), which allows you to bolt on extra functionality from the outside of your classes. AOP is provided by the Java EE using EJB Interception and by the Spring Framework AOP mechanism.

Use design patterns

In the Preface, I mentioned *Design Patterns* as one of the Very Important Books on object-oriented programming. Often called the "Gang of Four" (GoF) book for its four authors, it provides a powerful catalog of things that programmers often reinvent. Some people find the GoF book to be somewhat academic in tone; a less-formal presentation on patterns is *Head First Design Patterns* by Bert Bates et al. (O'Reilly); this covers the same two dozen patterns as the GoF book. A design pattern provides a statement of a problem and its solution(s), rather like the present book, but generally at a higher level of abstraction. It is as important for giving a standard vocabulary of design as it is for its clear explanations of how the basic patterns work and how they can be implemented.

Table 8-1 shows some example uses of design patterns in the standard API.

Table 8-1. Design patterns in the JavaSE API

Pattern name	Meaning	Examples in Java API
Command	Encapsulate requests, allowing queues of requests, undoable operations, etc.	`javax.swing.Action;` `javax.swing.undo.UndoableEdit`
Decorator	One class decorates another	Swing Borders
Factory Method	One class makes up instances for you, controlled by subclasses	`getInstance` (in Calendar, Format, Locale...); `SocketFactory;` RMI InitialContext
Iterator	Loop over all elements in a collection, visiting each exactly once	`Iterator;` older Enumeration; `java.sql.Result Set`
Model-View-Controller	Model represents data; View is what the user sees; Controller responds to user requests	`ActionListener` and friends; Observer/Observable; used internally by all visible Swing components
Proxy	One object stands in for another	RMI, AOP, Dynamic Proxy
Singleton	Only one instance may exist	`java.lang.Runtime`, `java.awt.Toolkit`

I have written articles on the State (*https://blogs.oracle.com/javamagazine/the-state-pattern*), Proxy (*https://blogs.oracle.com/javamagazine/the-proxy-pattern*), Command *(https://blogs.oracle.com/javamagazine/the-command-pattern-in-depth)*, Decorator *(https://blogs.oracle.com/javamagazine/the-decorator-pattern-in-depth)*, and Visitor *(https://blogs.oracle.com/javamagazine/the-visitor-design-pattern-in-depth)* patterns for *Oracle Java Magazine*.

8.1 Object Methods: Formatting Objects with toString(), Comparing with Equals

Problem

You want your objects to have a useful default format and to behave themselves when placed in Collections classes.

Solution

There are four overridable methods inherited from java.lang.Object; of these, toString() provides default formatting, while equals() and hashCode() provide equality testing and efficient usage in Map implementations. The fourth, clone(), is not recommended for general use.

Discussion

toString()

Whenever you pass an object to System.out.println() or any equivalent method or involve it in string concatenation, Java automatically calls its toString() method. Java knows that every object has a toString() method because java.lang.Object has one and all classes are ultimately subclasses of Object. The default implementation, in java.lang.Object, is neither pretty nor interesting: it just prints the class name, an @ sign, and the object's hashCode() value. For example, if you run the code

```
public class ToStringWithout {
    int x, y;

    /** Simple constructor */
    public ToStringWithout(int anX, int aY) {
        x = anX; y = aY;
    }

    /** Main just creates and prints an object */
    public static void main(String[] args) {
        System.out.println(new ToStringWithout(42, 86));
    }
}
```

you might see this uninformative output:

```
ToStringWithout@990c747b
```

To make it print better, you should provide an implementation of toString() that prints the class name and some of the important states in all but the most trivial classes. This gives you formatting control in println(), in debuggers, and anywhere your objects get referred to in a String context. Here is the previous program rewritten with a toString() method:

```java
public class ToStringWith {
    int x, y;

    /** Simple constructor */
    public ToStringWith(int anX, int aY) {
        x = anX; y = aY;
    }

    @Override
    public String toString() {
        return "ToStringWith[" + x + "," + y + "]";
    }

    /** Main just creates and prints an object */
    public static void main(String[] args) {
        System.out.println(new ToStringWith(42, 86));
    }
}
```

This version produces the more useful output:

```
ToStringWith[42,86]
```

This example uses String concatenation, but you may also want to use String.format() or StringBuilder; see Chapter 3.

hashCode() and equals()

To ensure your classes work correctly when any client code calls equals() or when these objects are stored in Map or other Collection classes, outfit your class with equals() and hashCode() methods.

How do you determine equality? For arithmetic or Boolean operands, the answer is simple: you test with the equals operator (==). For object references, though, Java provides both == and the equals() method inherited from java.lang.Object. The equals operator can be confusing because it simply compares two object references to see if they refer to the same object. This is not the same as comparing the values of the objects themselves.

The inherited `equals()` method is also not as useful as you might imagine. Some people seem to start their lives as Java developers thinking that the default `equals()` magically does some kind of detailed, field-by-field or even binary comparison of objects. But it does *not* compare fields! It just does the simplest possible thing: it returns the value of an == comparison on the two objects involved! So, for any *value classes* you write, you probably have to write an `equals` method.[6] Note that both the `equals` and `hashCode` methods are used by `Map`s or hashes (such as `HashMap`; see Recipe 7.9). So if you think somebody using your class might want to create instances and put them into a `Map`, or even compare your objects, you owe it to them (and to yourself!) to implement both `equals()` and `hashCode()` and to implement them properly.

Most IDEs know how to generate correct `equals()` and `hashCode()` methods, but it's worth your while to understand what these are doing, for the occasional case where you need to tweak the generated code. The Eclipse IDE (see Recipe 1.3), for example, offers a `Source` menu item `Generate hashCode() and equals()`; it will only do both at the same time, not let you generate `equals()` without `hashCode()` nor vice versa.

Here are the rules for a correct `equals()` method:

It is reflexive
> `x.equals(x)` must be true.

It is symmetrical
> `x.equals(y)` must be true if and only if `y.equals(x)` is also true.

It is transitive
> If `x.equals(y)` is true and `y.equals(z)` is true, then `x.equals(z)` must also be true.

It is idempotent (repeatable)
> Multiple calls on `x.equals(y)` return the same value (unless state values used in the comparison are changed, as by calling a set method).

It is cautious
> `x.equals(null)` must return false rather than accidentally throwing a `NullPoin terException`.

In addition, beware of one common mistake: the argument to `equals()` must be declared as `java.lang.Object`, not the class it is in; this is so that polymorphism will work correctly (some classes may not have an `equals()` method of their own). To

---

6 A value class is one used mainly to hold state, rather than logic: a `Person` is a value class, whereas `java.lang.Math` is not. Many classes are somewhere in between.

prevent this mistake, the @Override annotation is usually added to the equals() override, as mentioned in Recipe 15.3.

Here is a class that endeavors to implement these rules:

```java
public class EqualsDemo {
    private int int1;
    private SomeClass obj1;

    /** Constructor */
    public EqualsDemo(int i, SomeClass o) {
        int1 = i;
        if (o == null) {
            throw new IllegalArgumentException("Data Object may not be null");
        }
        obj1 = o;
    }

    /** Default Constructor */
    public EqualsDemo() {
        this(0, new SomeClass());
    }

    /** Demonstration "equals" method */
    @Override
    public boolean equals(Object o) {
        if (o == this)                          ❶
            return true;

        if (o == null)                          ❷
            return false;

        // Of the correct class?
        if (o.getClass() != EqualsDemo.class)   ❸
            return false;

        EqualsDemo other = (EqualsDemo)o; // OK, cast to this class

        // compare field-by-field              ❹
        if (int1 != other.int1)            // compare primitives directly
            return false;
        if (!obj1.equals(other.obj1))      // compare objects using their equals
            return false;
        return true;
    }

    // ...
```

❶ Optimization: if same object, true by definition.

❷ If other object null, false by definition.

❸ Compare class descriptors using !=; see following paragraph.

❹ Optimization: compare primitives first. May or may not be worthwhile; may be better to order by those most likely to differ—depends on the data and the usage.

Another common mistake to avoid: note the use of class descriptor equality (i.e., o.getClass() != EqualsDemo.class) to ensure the correct class, rather than via instanceof, as is sometimes erroneously done. The reflexive requirement of the equals() method contract pretty much makes it impossible to compare a subclass with a superclass correctly, so we now use class equality (see Chapter 17, *Reflection, or "A Class Named Class"* for details on the class descriptor).

Here is a basic JUnit test (see Recipe 1.10) for the EqualsDemo class:

```java
/** Some JUnit test cases for EqualsDemo.
 * Writing a full set is left as "an exercise for the reader".
 */
public class EqualsDemoTest {

    /** an object being tested */
    EqualsDemo d1;
    /** another object being tested */
    EqualsDemo d2;

    /** Method to be invoked before each test method */
    @Before
    public void setUp() {
        d1 = new EqualsDemo();
        d2 = new EqualsDemo();
    }

    @Test
    public void testSymmetry() {
        assertTrue(d1.equals(d1));
    }

    @Test
    public void testSymmetric() {
        assertTrue(d1.equals(d2) && d2.equals(d1));
    }

    @Test
    public void testCaution() {
        assertFalse(d1.equals(null));
    }
}
```

With all that testing, what could go wrong? Well, some things still need care. What if the object is a *subclass* of EqualsDemo? We should test that it returns false in this case.

What else could go wrong? Well, what if either `obj1` or `other.obj1` is null? You might have just earned a nice shiny new `NullPointerException`. So you also need to test for any possible null values. Good constructors can avoid these `NullPointerExceptions`, as I've tried to do in `EqualsDemo`, or else test for them explicitly.

Finally, you should never override `equals()` without also overriding `hashCode()`, and the same fields must take part in both computations.

hashCode()

The `hashCode()` method is supposed to return an `int` that should uniquely identify any set of values in objects of its class.

A properly written `hashCode()` method will follow these rules:

It is repeatable
> `hashCode(x)` must return the same `int` when called repeatedly, unless set methods have been called.

It is consistent with equality
> If `x.equals(y)`, then `x.hashCode()` must `== y.hashCode()`.

Distinct objects should produce distinct hashCodes
> If `!x.equals(y)`, it is not required that `x.hashCode() != y.hashCode()`, but doing so may improve performance of hash tables (i.e., hashes may call `hash Code()` before `equals()`).

The default `hashCode()` on the standard JDK returns a machine address, which conforms to the first rule. Conformance to the second and third rules depends, in part, on your `equals()` method. Here is a program that prints the hashcodes of a small handful of objects:

```
public class PrintHashCodes {

    /** Some objects to hashCode() on */
    protected static Object[] data = {
        new PrintHashCodes(),
        new java.awt.Color(0x44, 0x88, 0xcc),
        new SomeClass()
    };

    public static void main(String[] args) {
        System.out.println("About to hashCode " + data.length + " objects.");
        for (int i=0; i<data.length; i++) {
            System.out.println(data[i].toString() + " --> " +
                data[i].hashCode());
        }
        System.out.println("All done.");
```

```
        }
    }
```

What does it print?

```
> javac -d . oo/PrintHashCodes.java
> java oo.PrintHashCodes
About to hashCode 3 objects.
PrintHashCodes@982741a0 --> -1742257760
java.awt.Color[r=68,g=136,b=204] --> -12285748
SomeClass@860b41ad --> -2046082643
All done.
>
```

The hashcode value for the Color object is interesting. It is actually computed as something like this:

```
alpha<<24 + r<<16 + g<<8 + b
```

In this formula, r, g, and b are the red, green, and blue components, respectively, and alpha is the transparency. Each of these quantities is stored in 8 bits of a 32-bit integer. If the alpha value is greater than 128, the high bit in this word—having been set by shifting into the sign bit of the word—causes the integer value to appear negative when printed as a signed integer. Hashcode values are of type int, so they are allowed to be negative.

Difficulties and Alternatives to Clone

The java.util.Observable class (designed to implement the Model-View-Controller pattern with AWT or Swing applications) contains a private Vector but no clone method to deep-clone it. Thus, Observable objects cannot safely be cloned, ever!

This and several other issues around clone()—such as the uncertainty of whether a given clone() implementation is deep or shallow—suggest that clone() was not as well thought out as might be. An alternative is simply to provide a copy constructor or similar method:

```java
public class CopyConstructorDemo {
    public static void main(String[] args) {
        CopyConstructorDemo object1 = new CopyConstructorDemo(123, "Hello");
        CopyConstructorDemo object2 = new CopyConstructorDemo(object1);
        if (!object1.equals(object2)) {
            System.out.println("Something is terribly wrong...");
        }
        System.out.println("All done.");
    }

    private int number;
    private String name;
```

```
/** Default constructor */
public CopyConstructorDemo() {
}

/** Normal constructor */
public CopyConstructorDemo(int number, String name) {
    this.number = number;
    this.name = name;
}

/** Copy constructor */
public CopyConstructorDemo(CopyConstructorDemo other) {
    this.number = other.number;
    this.name = other.name;
}
// hashCode() and equals() not shown
```

8.2 Using Inner Classes

Problem

You need to write a private class, or a class to be used in one other class at most.

Solution

Use a nonpublic class or an inner class.

Discussion

A nonpublic class can be written as part of another class's source file, but not inside that class. An inner class is Java terminology for a class defined inside another class. Inner classes were first popularized with early Java for use as event handlers for GUI applications, but they have a much wider application.

Inner classes can, in fact, be constructed in several contexts. An inner class defined as a member of a class can be instantiated anywhere in that class. An inner class defined inside a method can be referred to later only in the same method. Inner classes can also be named or anonymous. A named inner class has a full name that is compiler dependent; the standard JVM uses a name like MainClass$InnerClass for the resulting file. An anonymous inner class, similarly, has a compiler-dependent name; the JVM uses MainClass$1, MainClass$2, and so on.

These classes cannot be instantiated in any other context; any explicit attempt to refer to, say, OtherMainClass$InnerClass, is caught at compile time:

main/src/main/java/oo/AllClasses.java

```
public class AllClasses {
    public class Data {        ❶
        int x;
        int y;
    }
    public void getResults() {
        JButton b = new JButton("Press me");
        b.addActionListener(new ActionListener() { ❷
            public void actionPerformed(ActionEvent evt) {
                Data loc = new Data();
                loc.x = ((Component)evt.getSource()).getX();
                loc.x = ((Component)evt.getSource()).getY();
                System.out.println("Thanks for pressing me");
            }
        });
    }
}

/** Class contained in same file as AllClasses, but can be used
 * (with a warning) in other contexts.
 */
class AnotherClass {                           ❸
    // methods and fields here...
    AnotherClass() {
        // Inner class from above cannot be used here, of course
        // Data d = new Data();    // EXPECT COMPILE ERROR
    }
}
```

❶ This is an inner class, which can be used anywhere in class AllClasses.

❷ This shows the anonymous inner class syntax, which uses new with a type followed by (){, a class body, and }. The compiler will assign a name; the class will extend or implement the given type, as appropriate.

❸ This is a nonpublic class; it can be used in the main class and (with warning) in other classes.

One issue is that the inner class retains a reference to the outer class. If you want to avoid memory leaks if the inner class will be held for a longer time than the outer, you can make the inner class static.

Inner classes implementing a single-method interface can be written in a much more concise fashion as lambda expressions (see Chapter 9).

> ## Interface Changes in Java: default and static
>
> Java 8 added two new capabilities to interfaces, default methods and static methods.
>
> Default methods are implicitly added to any implementing class. They cannot directly access fields in the class. They are useful in functional programming (see Chapter 9). They are also useful in adding functionality to an existing, widely used interface without breaking all the implementing classes. For example, in Java 8 the List interface gained a forEach() instance method for a measure of compatibility with Streams. It was important that all the List implementations both in java.util and in applications be able to provide this method without changing all the code, which is why the mechanism was implemented as it was.
>
> Java also now allows static methods in interfaces. These allow addition of methods, again without breaking existing implementations. They become static methods in every implementing class. For example, the List interface gained a static of method that allows you to write code such as this:
>
> ```
> List<String> list = List.of("Hello", "World", "of", "Java");
> ```
>
> These two additions could not have been made without the addition of these two keywords to the syntax of interfaces. A trivial subset of List, called MyList in the *structure* directory, demonstrates how these two sample methods—the instance forEach() and the static of()—could be implemented.

8.3 Providing Callbacks via Interfaces

Problem

You want to provide callbacks—that is, have unrelated classes call back into your code.

Solution

One way is to use a Java interface.

Discussion

An interface is a class-like entity that can contain only abstract methods and final fields. As we've seen, interfaces are used a lot in Java! In the standard API, the following are a few of the commonly used interfaces:

- Runnable, Comparable, and Cloneable (in java.lang).

- List, Set, Map, and Enumeration/Iterator (in the Collections API; as you'll see in Chapter 7).

- ActionListener, WindowListener, and others in the GUI layer.

- Driver, Connection, Statement, and ResultSet in JDBC; see *https://darwin sys.com/javadatabase*.

- The *remote interface*—the contact between the client and the server—is specified as an Interface (in RMI, CORBA, and EJB).

Subclass, Abstract Class, or Interface?

There is usually more than one way to solve a problem. Some problems can be solved by subclassing, by use of abstract classes, or by interfaces. The following general guidelines may help:

- A class can only extend one other class, but it can implement any number of interfaces; keep this in mind when deciding to use abstract classes or interface.

- *Use an abstract class* when you want to provide a template for a series of subclasses, all of which may inherit some of their functionality from the parent class but are required to implement some of it themselves. (Any subclass of a geometric Shapes class might have to provide a computeArea() method; because the top-level Shapes class cannot do this, it would be abstract. This is implemented in Recipe 8.4.)

- *Use an interface with default methods* for many of the same things you'd have used an abstract class for prior to Java 8, which introduced default methods. Default methods can be added to an interface without breaking existing code, such as forEach and of methods being added to the Collection interface so that every List instance has a forEach method built in.

Subclass when you need to extend a class and add some functionality to it, whether the parent class is abstract or not. See the standard Java APIs and the examples in Recipe 1.10, Recipe 8.10, and Recipe 10.10.

- *Subclass* when you are required to extend a given class. Some APIs such as *servlets* use subclassing to ensure base functionality in classes that are dynamically loaded (see Recipe 17.4).

- *Define an interface* when there is no common parent class with the desired functionality and when you want only certain unrelated classes to have that functionality (see the PowerSwitchable interface in Recipe 8.2). You should also choose this option if you know that you'll need (or think there is a chance you might later need) to be able to pass in unrelated classes for testing purposes. Using mock objects is a very common strategy in unit testing. Some say that interfaces should be your first choice at least as often as subclassing.

- *Use interfaces as markers* to indicate something about a class. Marker interfaces commonly have no abstract methods. The standard API, for example, uses `Seri alizable` as a marker interface to indicate permission to serialize objects of the implementing class. See "Solution" on page 394 for information on serialization.

Suppose we are generating a building management system. To be energy efficient, we want to be able to remotely turn off (at night and on weekends) such things as room lights and computer monitors, which use a lot of energy. Assume we have some kind of remote control technology. It could be a commercial version of BSR's house-light control technology X10, it could be Bluetooth or 802.11—it doesn't matter. What matters is that we have to be very careful what we turn off. It would cause great ire if we turned off computer processors automatically—people often leave things running overnight. It would be a matter of public safety if we ever turned off the building emergency lighting.[6]

So we've come up with the design shown in Figure 8-1.

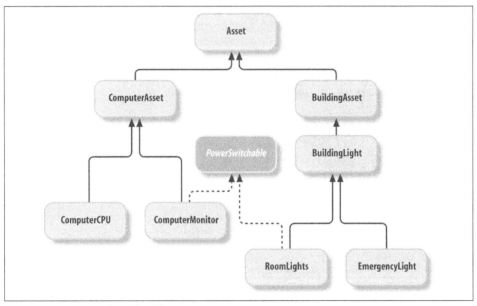

Figure 8-1. Classes for a building management system

---

6 Of course these lights wouldn't have remote power-off. But the computers might, for maintenance purposes.

The code for these data classes is not shown (it's pretty trivial), but it's in the *oo/interfaces* directory of the online source. The top-level classes (i.e., `BuildingLight` and `Asset`) are abstract classes. You can't instantiate them, because they don't have any specific functionality. To ensure—both at compile time and at runtime—that we can never switch off the emergency lighting, we need only ensure that the class representing it, `EmergencyLight`, does not implement the `PowerSwitchable` interface.

Note that we can't very well use direct inheritance here. No common ancestor class includes both `ComputerMonitor` and `RoomLights` that doesn't also include `Computer CPU` and `EmergencyLight`. Use interfaces to define functionality in unrelated classes.

How we use these is demonstrated by the `BuildingManagement` class; this class is not part of the hierarchy shown in Figure 8-1, but it *uses* a collection of `Asset` objects from that hierarchy.

Items that can't be switched must nonetheless be in the database, for various purposes (auditing, insurance, etc.). In the method that turns things off, the code is careful to check whether each object in the database is an instance of the `PowerSwitchable` interface. If so, the object is casted to `PowerSwitchable` so that its `powerDown()` method can be called. If not, the object is skipped, thus preventing any possibility of turning out the emergency lights or shutting off a machine that is busy running SETI@Home, downloading a big MP3 playlist, or performing system backups. The following code shows this set of classes in action:

```
public class BuildingManagement {

    List<Asset> things = new ArrayList<>();

    /** Scenario: goodNight() is called from a timer Thread at 2200, or when
     * we get the "shutdown" command from the security guard.
     */
    public void goodNight() {
        things.forEach(obj -> {
            if (obj instanceof PowerSwitchable)
                ((PowerSwitchable)obj).powerDown();
            });
    }

    // tag::functional[]
    public void goodNightFunctional() {
        things.stream().filter(obj -> obj instanceof PowerSwitchable)
            .forEach(obj -> ((PowerSwitchable)obj).powerDown());
    }
    // end::functional[]

    // goodMorning() would be similar, but call each one's powerUp().

    /** Add a Asset to this building */
    public void add(Asset thing) {
```

```
                System.out.println("Adding " + thing);
                things.add(thing);
        }

        /** The main program */
        public static void main(String[] av) {
                BuildingManagement b1 = new BuildingManagement();
                b1.add(new RoomLights(101));      // control lights in room 101
                b1.add(new EmergencyLight(101));      // and emerg. lights.
                // add the computer on desk#4 in room 101
                b1.add(new ComputerCPU(10104));
                // and its monitor
                b1.add(new ComputerMonitor(10104));

                // time passes, and the sun sets...
                b1.goodNight();
        }
}
```

When you run this program, it shows all the items being added but only the Power Switchable ones being switched off:

```
> java oo.interfaces.BuildingManagement
Adding RoomLights@2dc77f32
Adding EmergencyLight@2e3b7f32
Adding ComputerCPU@2e637f32
Adding ComputerMonitor@2f1f7f32
Dousing lights in room 101
Dousing monitor at desk 10104
>
```

8.4 Polymorphism/Abstract Methods

Problem

You want each of a number of subclasses to provide its own version of one or more methods.

Solution

Make the method abstract in the parent class; this makes the compiler ensure that each subclass implements it.

Discussion

A hypothetical drawing program uses a Shape subclass for anything that is drawn. Shape has an abstract method called computeArea() that computes the exact area of the given shape:

```
public abstract class Shape {
    protected int x, y;
    public abstract double computeArea( );
}
```

A `Rectangle` subclass, for example, has a `computeArea()` that multiplies width times height and returns the result:

```
public class Rectangle extends Shape {
    double width, height;
    public double computeArea( ) {
        return width * height;
    }
}
```

A `Circle` subclass returns πr^2:

```
public class Circle extends Shape {
    double radius;
    public double computeArea( ) {
        return Math.PI * radius * radius;
    }
}
```

This system has a high degree of generality. In the main program, we can iterate over a collection of `Shape` objects and—here's the real beauty—call `computeArea()` on any `Shape` subclass object without having to worry about what kind of shape it is. Java's polymorphic methods automatically call the correct `computeArea()` method in the class of which the object was originally constructed:

main/src/main/java/oo//shapes/ShapeDriver.java

```
/** Part of a main program using Shape objects */
public class ShapeDriver {

    Collection<Shape> allShapes;     // created in a Constructor, not shown

    /** Iterate over all the Shapes, getting their areas;
     * this cannot use the Java 8 Collection.forEach because the
     * variable total would have to be final, which would defeat the purpose :-)
     */
    public double totalAreas() {
        double total = 0.0;
        for (Shape s : allShapes) {
            total += s.computeArea();
        }
        return total;
    }
```

Polymorphism is a great boon for software maintenance: if a new subclass is added, the code in the main program does not change. Further, all the code that is specific to, say, polygon handling, is all in one place: in the source file for the `Polygon` class. This is a big improvement over older languages, where type fields in a structure were used with case or switch statements scattered all across the software. Java makes software more reliable and maintainable with the use of polymorphism.

8.5 Using Typesafe Enumerations

Problem

You need to manage a small list of discrete values within a program.

Solution

Use the Java enum mechanism.

Discussion

To enumerate means to list all the values. You often know that a small list of possible values is all that's wanted in a variable, such as the months of the year, the suits or ranks in a deck of cards, or the primary and secondary colors. The C programming language provided an enum keyword:

```
enum  { BLACK, RED, ORANGE} color;
```

Java was criticized in its early years for its lack of enumerations, which many developers have wished for. Many have had to develop custom classes to implement the *typesafe enumeration pattern*.

But C enumerations are not typesafe; they simply define constants that can be used in any integer context. For example, this code compiles without warning, even on *gcc* 3 with -Wall (all warnings), whereas a C++ compiler catches the error:[6]

```
enum { BLACK, RED, ORANGE} color;
enum { READ, UNREAD } state;

/*ARGSUSED*/
int main(int argc, char *argv[]) {
        color = RED;
        color = READ; // In C this will compile, give bad results
        return 0;
}
```

To replicate this mistake in Java, one needs only to define a series of final int values; it will still not be typesafe. By typesafe I mean that you cannot accidentally use values other than those defined for the given enumeration. The definitive statement

---

6 For Java folks not that familiar with C/C++, C is the older, non-OO language; C++ is an OO derivative of C; and Java is in part a portable, more strongly typesafe derivative of C++.

on the typesafe enumeration pattern is probably the version defined in item 21 of Joshua Bloch's book *Effective Java* (Addison-Wesley). All modern Java versions include enumerations in the language; it is no longer necessary to use the code from Bloch's book. Bloch was one of the authors of the Typesafe Enumeration specification (enum keyword), so you can be sure that Java now does a good job of implementing his pattern. These enums are implemented as classes, subclassed (transparently, by the compiler) from the class java.lang.Enum. Unlike C, and unlike a series of final ints, Java typesafe enumerations have the following qualities:

- They are printable (they print as the name, not as an underlying int implementation).

- They are almost as fast as int constants, but the code is more readable.

- They can be easily iterated over.

- They use a separate namespace for each enum type, which means you don't have to prefix each with some sort of constant name, like ACCOUNT_SAVINGS, ACCOUNT_CHECKING, etc.

Enum constants are not compiled into clients, giving you the freedom to reorder the constants within your enum without recompiling the client classes. That does not mean you should, however; think about the case where objects that use them have been persisted, and the person designing the database mapping used the numeric values of the enums. Bad idea to reorder then!

Additionally, an enum type is a class, so it can, for example, implement arbitrary interfaces; and you can add constructors, fields, and methods to an enum class.

Compared to Bloch's Typesafe Enum pattern in the book:

- Java enums are simpler to use and more readable (those in the book require a lot of methods, making them cumbersome to write).

- Enums can be used in switch statements.

So there are many benefits and few pitfalls.

The enum keyword is at the same level as the keyword class in declarations. That is, an enum may be declared in its own file with public or default access. It may also be declared inside classes, much like nested or inner classes (see Recipe 8.2). *Media.java*, shown in Example 8-1, is a code sample showing the definition of a typesafe enum.

Example 8-1. structure/Media.java

```java
public enum Media {
    BOOK, MUSIC_CD, MUSIC_VINYL, MOVIE_VHS, MOVIE_DVD;
}
```

Notice that an enum class *is* a class; see what *javap* thinks of the Media class:

```
C:> javap Media
Compiled from "Media.java"
public class Media extends java.lang.Enum{
    public static final Media BOOK;
    public static final Media MUSIC_CD;
    public static final Media MUSIC_VINYL;
    public static final Media MOVIE_VHS;
    public static final Media MOVIE_DVD;
    public static final Media[] values( );
    public static Media valueOf(java.lang.String);
    public Media(java.lang.String, int);
    public int compareTo(java.lang.Enum);
    public int compareTo(java.lang.Object);
    static {};
}
C:>
```

Product.java, shown in Example 8-2, is a code sample that uses the Media enum.

Example 8-2. main/src/main/java/structure/Product.java

```java
public class Product {
    String title;
    String artist;
    Media  media;

    public Product(String artist, String title, Media media) {
        this.title = title;
        this.artist = artist;
        this.media = media;
    }

    @Override
    public String toString() {
        switch (media) {
        case BOOK:
            return title + " is a book";
        case MUSIC_CD:
            return title + " is a CD";
        case MUSIC_VINYL:
            return title + " is a relic of the age of vinyl";
        case MOVIE_VHS:
            return title + " is on old video tape";
        case MOVIE_DVD:
```

```
        return title + " is on DVD";
    default:
        return title + ": Unknown media " + media;
    }
    }
}
```

In Example 8-3, MediaFancy shows how operations (methods) can be added to enumerations; the toString() method is overridden for the Book value of this enum.

Example 8-3. main/src/main/java/structure/MediaFancy.java

```
/** An example of an enum with method overriding */
public enum MediaFancy {
    /** The enum constant for a book, with a method override */
    BOOK {
        public String toString() { return "Book"; }
    },
    /** The enum constant for a Music CD */
    MUSIC_CD,
    /** ... */
    MUSIC_VINYL,
    MOVIE_VHS,
    MOVIE_DVD;

    /** It is generally disparaged to have a main() in an enum;
     * please forgive this tiny demo class for doing so.
     */
    public static void main(String[] args) {
        MediaFancy[] data = { BOOK, MOVIE_DVD, MUSIC_VINYL };
        for (MediaFancy mf : data) {
            System.out.println(mf);
        }
    }
}
```

Running the MediaFancy program produces this output:

```
Book
MOVIE_DVD
MUSIC_VINYL
```

That is, the Book values print in a user-friendly way compared to the default way the other values print. In real life you'd want to extend this to all the values in the enum.

Finally, EnumList, in Example 8-4, shows how to list all the possible values that a given enum can take on; simply iterate over the array returned by the enumeration class's inherited values() method.

Example 8-4. structure/EnumList.java

```java
public class EnumList {
    enum State {
        ON, OFF, UNKNOWN
    }
    public static void main(String[] args) {
        for (State i : State.values()) {
            System.out.println(i);
        }
    }
}
```

The output of the EnumList program is this, of course:

```
ON
OFF
UNKNOWN
```

8.6 Avoiding NPEs with Optional

Problem

You worry about null references causing a NullPointerException (NPE) in your code.

Solution

Use java.util.Optional.

Discusssion

The developer who invented the notion of null pointers, and a key early contributor to our discipline, has described the null reference as "my billion-dollar mistake" (*https://en.wikipedia.org/wiki/Tony_Hoare*). However, use of null is not going away anytime soon.

What we can do is make clear that we worry about null pointers in certain contexts. For this purpose, Java 8 introduced the class java.util.Optional. The Optional is an object wrapper around a possibly-null object reference. The Optional wrapper has a long history; a similar construct is found in LLVM's ADT, where its Optional describes itself in turn as "in the spirit of OCaml's *opt* variant."

Optionals can be created with one of the creational methods:

Optional.empty()
    Returns an empty optional

```
Optional.of(T obj)
```
Returns a nonempty optional containing the given value

```
Optional.ofNullable(T obj)
```
Returns either an empty optional or one containing the given value

The basic operation of this class is to behave in one of two ways, depending on whether it is full or empty. Optional objects are immutable, so they cannot transition from one state to the other.

The simplest use is to invoke isEmpty() or its opposite isPresent() and use program logic to behave differently. This is not much different from using an if statement to check for null, but it puts the choice in front of you, making it less likely that you'll forget to check:

```
jshell> Optional<String> opt = Optional.of("What a day!");
opt ==> Optional[What a day!]

jshell> if (opt.isPresent()) {
   ...>      System.out.println("Value is " + opt.get());
   ...> } else {
   ...>      System.out.println("Value is not present.");
   ...> }
Value is What a day!
```

A better form would use the orElse method:

```
jshell> System.out.println("Value is " + opt.orElse("not present"));
Value is What a day!
```

A useful use case is that of passing values into methods. The object can be wrapped in an Optional either before it is passed to a method or after; the latter is useful when migrating from code that didn't use Optional from the start. The Item demo in Example 8-5 might represent part of a shipments tracking program, a lending library manager, or anything else that has time-related data which might be missing.

Example 8-5. main/src/main/java/oo/OptionalDemo.java

```
    List.of(
        new Item("Item 1", LocalDate.now().plusDays(7)),
        new Item("Item 2")).
            forEach(System.out::println);
static class Item {
    String name;
    Optional<LocalDate> dueDate;
    Item(String name) {
        this(name, null);
    }
    Item(String name, LocalDate dueDate) {
        this.name = name;
```

```
            this.dueDate = Optional.ofNullable(dueDate);
    }

    public String toString() {
        return String.format("%s %s", name,
            dueDate.isPresent() ?
                "Item is due on " + dueDate.get() :
                "Sorry, do not know when item is due");
    }
}
```

There are methods that throw exceptions, that return null, and so on. There are also methods for interacting with the Streams mechanism (see Recipe 9.3). A full list of Optional's methods is at the start of the javadoc page (*https://docs.oracle.com/en/java/javase/13/docs/api/java.base/java/util/Optional.html*).

8.7 Enforcing the Singleton Pattern

Problem

You want to be sure there is only one instance of your class in a given Java Virtual Machine, or at least within your application.

Solution

There are several methods of making your class enforce the Singleton pattern:

- Enum implementation
- Having only a private constructor (or multiple) and a getInstance() method
- Use a framework such as Spring or CDI (Recipe 8.9) configured to give Singleton-style instantiation of plain classes

Discussion

It is often useful to ensure that only one instance of a class gets created, usually to funnel all requests for some resource through a single point. An example of a Singleton from the standard API is java.lang.Runtime: you cannot create instances of Runtime; you simply ask for a reference by calling the static method Runtime.getRuntime(). Singleton is also an example of a design pattern that can be easily implemented. In all forms, the point of the Singleton implementation is to provide an instance in which certain methods can run, typically to control access to some resource.

The easiest implementation uses a Java enum to provide Singleton-ness. The enum mechanism already guarantees that only one instance of each enum constant will exist in a given JVM context, so this technique piggy-backs on that, as shown in Example 8-6.

Example 8-6. main/src/main/java/oo/EnumSingleton.java

```
public enum EnumSingleton {

    INSTANCE;

    // instance methods protected by singleton-ness would be here...

    /** A simple demo method */
    public String demoMethod() {
        return "demo";
    }
}
```

Using it is simple:

```
        // Demonstrate the enum method:
        EnumSingleton.INSTANCE.demoMethod();
```

The next easiest implementation consists of a private constructor and a field to hold its result, as well as a static accessor method with a name like getInstance().

The private field can be assigned from within a static initializer block or, more simply, by using an initializer. The getInstance() method (which must be public) then simply returns this instance:

```
    public class Singleton {

        /**
         * Static Initializer is run before class is available to code, avoiding
         * broken anti-pattern of lazy initialization in instance method.
         * For more complicated construction, could use static block initializer.
         */
        private static Singleton instance = new Singleton();

        /** A private Constructor prevents any other class from instantiating. */
        private Singleton() {
            // nothing to do this time
        }

        /** Static 'instance' method */
        public static Singleton getInstance() {
            return instance;
        }

        // other methods protected by singleton-ness would be here...
```

```
/** A simple demo method */
public String demoMethod() {
    return "demo";
}
```
}

Note that the method of using *lazy evaluation* in the getInstance() method (as in *Design Patterns*) is not necessary in Java because Java already uses *lazy loading*. Your Singleton class will probably not get loaded until its getInstance() is called, so there is no point in trying to defer the Singleton construction until it's needed by having getInstance() test the singleton variable for null and creating the singleton there.

Using this class is equally simple: simply get the instance reference, and invoke methods on it:

```
// Demonstrate the codeBased method:
Singleton.getInstance().demoMethod();
```

Some commentators believe that a code-based Singleton should also provide a public final clone() method that just throws an exception, in order to avoid subclasses that cheat and clone() the Singleton. However, it is clear that a class with only a private constructor cannot be subclassed, so this paranoia does not appear to be necessary.

See Also

The Collections class in java.util has methods singletonList(), singleton Map(), and singletonSet(), which give out an immutable List, Map, or Set, respectively, containing only the one object that is passed to the method. This does not, of course, convert the object into a Singleton in the sense of preventing that object from being cloned or other instances from being constructed.

See page 127 of the original *Design Patterns* book.

8.8 Roll Your Own Exceptions

Problem

You'd like to use an application-specific exception class or two.

Solution

Go ahead and subclass Exception or RuntimeException.

Discussion

In theory, you could subclass Throwable directly, but that's considered rude. You normally subclass Exception (if you want a checked exception) or RuntimeException (if you want an unchecked exception). Checked exceptions are those that an application developer is required to catch or throw upward by listing them in the throws clause of the invoking method.

When subclassing either of these, it is customary to provide at least these constructors:

- A no-argument constructor
- A one-string argument constructor
- A two-argument constructor—a string message and a Throwable cause

The cause will appear if the code receiving the exception performs a stack trace operation on it, with the prefix "Root Cause is" or similar. Example 8-7 shows these three constructors for an application-defined exception, ChessMoveException.

Example 8-7. main/src/main/java/oo/ChessMoveException.java

```java
/** A ChessMoveException is thrown  when the user makes an illegal move. */
public class ChessMoveException extends Exception {

    private static final long serialVersionUID = 8029117369881790079L;

    public ChessMoveException () {
        super();
    }

    public ChessMoveException (String msg) {
        super(msg);
    }

    public ChessMoveException(String msg, Exception cause) {
        super(msg, cause);
    }
}
```

See Also

The javadoc documentation for Exception lists a large number of subclasses; you might look there first to see if there is one you can use.

8.9 Using Dependency Injection

Problem

You want to avoid excessive coupling between classes, and you want to avoid excessive code dedicated to object creation/lookup.

Solution

Use a dependency injection framework.

Discussion

A dependency injection framework allows you to have objects passed in to your code instead of making you either create them explicitly (which ties your code to the implementing class name, since you're calling the constructor) or looking for them (which requires use of a possibly cumbersome lookup API, such as JNDI, the Java Naming and Directory Interface).

Three of the best-known dependency injection frameworks are the Spring Framework (*http://springframework.org*), the Java Enterprise Edition's Context and Dependency Injection (CDI) (*http://docs.oracle.com/javaee/6/tutorial/doc/giwhl.html*), and Google Guice (*http://code.google.com/p/google-guice*). Suppose we have three classes, a Model, a View, and a Controller, implementing the traditional MVC pattern. Given that we may want to have different versions of some of these, especially the View, we'll define Java interfaces for simple versions of the Model (in Example 8-8) and View (in Example 8-9).

Example 8-8. MVC Model interface

```
public interface Model {
        String getMessage();
}
```

Example 8-9. main/src/main/java/di/View.java (MVC View interface)

```
public interface View {

    void displayMessage();

}
```

The implementations of these are not shown, because they're so trivial, but they are online. The Controller in this example is a main program, no interface needed. First, let's see a version of the main program *not* using dependency injection. Obviously the View requires the Model, to get the data to display:

main/src/main/java/di/ControllerTightlyCoupled.java

```java
public class ControllerTightlyCoupled {

    public static void main(String[] args) {
        Model m = new SimpleModel();
        ConsoleViewer v = new ConsoleViewer();
        v.setModel(m);
        v.displayMessage();
    }
}
```

Here we have four tasks to undertake:

1. Create the Model.

2. Create the View.

3. Tie the Model into the View.

4. Ask the View to display some data.

Now a version using dependency injection:

main/src/main/java/di/spring/MainAndController.java - Spring Controller

```java
public class MainAndController {

    public static void main(String[] args) {
        ApplicationContext ctx =
            new AnnotationConfigApplicationContext("di.spring");
        View v = ctx.getBean("myView", View.class);
        v.displayMessage();
        ((AbstractApplicationContext) ctx).close();
    }
}
```

In this version, we have only three tasks:

1. Set up the Spring context, which provides the dependency injection framework.

2. Get the View from the context; it already has the Model set into it!

3. Ask the View to display some data.

Furthermore, we don't depend on particular implementations of the interface.

How does Spring know to inject, or provide, a Model to the View? And how does it know what code to use for the View? There might be multiple implementations of the View interface. Of course we have to tell it these things, which we'll do here with annotations:

```java
@Named("myView")
public class ConsoleViewer implements View {
```

```
    Model messageProvider;

    @Override
    public void displayMessage() {
        System.out.println(messageProvider.getMessage());
    }

    @Resource(name="myModel")
    public void setModel(Model messageProvider) {
        this.messageProvider = messageProvider;
    }

}
```

While Spring has provided its own annotations, it will also accept the Java standard `@javax.annotation.Resource` annotation for injection and `@java.inject.Named` to specify the injectee.

Due to the persistence of information on the web, if you do a web search for Spring Injection, you will probably find zillions of articles that refer to the older Spring 2.x way of doing things, which is to use an XML configuration file. You can still use this, but modern Spring practice is generally to use Java annotations to configure the dependencies.

Annotations are also used in the Java Enterprise Edition Contexts and Dependency Injection (CDI). Although this is most widely used in web applications, we'll reuse the same example, using the open source Weld implementation of CDI. CDI is quite a bit more powerful than Spring's DI; because in CDI we don't even need to know the class from which a resource is being injected, we don't even need the interfaces from the Spring example! First, the Controller, or main program, which requires a Weld-specific import or two because CDI was originally designed for use in enterprise applications:

```
public class MainAndController {
    public static void main(String[] args) {
        final Instance<Object> weldInstance = new Weld().initial
ize().instance();
        weldInstance.select(ConsoleViewer.class).get().displayMessage();
    }
}
```

The `View` interface is shared between both implementations. The `ConsoleViewer` implementation is similar too, except it isn't coupled to the Model; it just asks to have a `String` injected. In this simple example there is only one `String` in the application; in a larger app you would need one additional annotation to specify which string to inject. Here is the CDI `ConsoleViewer`:

```
public class ConsoleViewer implements View {
    @Inject @MyModel
```

```
    private String message;

    @Override
    public void displayMessage() {
        System.out.println(message);
    }
}
```

Where does the injected `String` come from? From the Model, as before:

main/src/main/java/di/cdi/ModelImpl.java

```
public class ModelImpl {

    public @Produces @MyModel String getMessage(InjectionPoint ip)
        throws IOException {

        ResourceBundle props = ResourceBundle.getBundle("messages");
        return props.getString(
            ip.getMember().getDeclaringClass().getSimpleName() + "." +
            ip.getMember().getName());
    }
}
```

See Also

Spring DI, Java EE CDI, and Guice all provide powerful *dependency injection*. Spring's is more widely used; Java EE's has the same power and is built into every EE container. All three can be used standalone or in a web application, with minor variations. In the EE, Spring provides special support for web apps, and in EE containers, CDI is already set up so that the first statement in the `CDIMain` example is not needed in an EE app. There are many books on Spring. One book specifically treats Weld: *JBoss Weld CDI for Java Platform* by Ken Finnegan (O'Reilly).

8.10 Program: Plotter

Not because it is very sophisticated, but because it is simple, this program serves as an example of some of the things we've covered in this chapter, and also, in its subclasses, provides a springboard for other discussions. This class describes a series of old-fashioned (i.e., common in the 1970s and 1980s) pen plotters. A pen plotter, in case you've never seen one, is a device that moves a pen around a piece of paper and draws things. It can lift the pen off the paper or lower it, and it can draw lines, letters, and so on. Before the rise of laser printers and ink-jet printers, pen plotters were the dominant means of preparing charts of all sorts, as well as presentation slides (this was, ah, well before the rise of programs like Harvard Presents and Microsoft PowerPoint). Today, few, if any, companies still manufacture pen plotters, but I use them here because they are simple enough to be well understood from this brief description.

Today's 3D printers may be thought of as representing a resurgence of the pen plotter with just one additional axis of motion. And a fancier pen.

I'll present a high-level class that abstracts the key characteristics of a series of such plotters made by different vendors. It would be used, for example, in an analytical or data-exploration program to draw colorful charts showing the relationships found in data. But I don't want my main program to worry about the gory details of any particular brand of plotter, so I'll abstract into a `Plotter` class, whose source is as follows:

main/src/main/java/plotter/Plotter.java

```
/**
 * Plotter abstract class. Must be subclassed
 * for X, DOS, Penman, HP plotter, etc.
 *
 * Coordinate space: X = 0 at left, increases to right.
 *          Y = 0 at top, increases downward (same as AWT).
 *
 * @author    Ian F. Darwin
 */
public abstract class Plotter {
    public final int MAXX = 800;
    public final int MAXY = 600;
    /** Current X co-ordinate (same reference frame as AWT!) */
    protected int curx;
    /** Current Y co-ordinate (same reference frame as AWT!) */
    protected int cury;
    /** The current state: up or down */
    protected boolean penUp;
    /** The current color */
    protected int penColor;

    Plotter() {
        penUp = true;
        curx = 0; cury = 0;
    }
    abstract void rmoveTo(int incrx, int incry);
    abstract void moveTo(int absx, int absy);
    abstract void penUp();
    abstract void penDown();
    abstract void penColor(int c);

    abstract void setFont(String fName, int fSize);
    abstract void drawString(String s);

    /* Concrete methods */

    /** Draw a box of width w and height h */
    public void drawBox(int w, int h) {
        penDown();
        rmoveTo(w, 0);
        rmoveTo(0, h);
```

```
        rmoveTo(-w, 0);
        rmoveTo(0, -h);
        penUp();
    }

    /** Draw a box given an AWT Dimension for its size */
    public void drawBox(java.awt.Dimension d) {
        drawBox(d.width, d.height);
    }

    /** Draw a box given an AWT Rectangle for its location and size */
    public void drawBox(java.awt.Rectangle r) {
        moveTo(r.x, r.y);
        drawBox(r.width, r.height);
    }

    /** Show the current location; useful for
     * testing, if nothing else.
     */
    public Point getLocation() {
        return new Point(curx, cury);
    }
}
```

Note the variety of abstract methods. Those related to motion, pen control, or draw-ing are left abstract, due to the number of different ways of implementing motion on radically different devices. However, the method for drawing a rectangle (drawBox) has a default implementation, which simply puts the currently selected pen onto the paper at the last-moved-to location, draws the four sides, and raises the pen. Sub-classes for smarter plotters will likely override this method, but subclasses for less-evolved plotters will probably use the default version. This method also has two over-loaded convenience methods for cases where the client has an AWT Dimension for the size or an AWT Rectangle for the location and size.

To demonstrate one of the subclasses of this program, consider the following simple driver program. This is intended to simulate a larger graphics application such as gnuplot. The Class.forName() near the beginning of main is discussed in Recipe 17.2; for now, you can take my word that it simply creates an instance of the given subclass, which we store in a Plotter reference named r and use to draw the plot:

main/src/main/java/plotter/PlotDriver.java

```
    public class PlotDriver {

        /** Construct a Plotter driver, and try it out. */
        public static void main(String[] argv) {
            Plotter r ;
            if (argv.length != 1) {
                System.err.println("Usage: PlotDriver driverclass");
                return;
```

```
        }
        try {
            Class<?> c = Class.forName(argv[0]);
            Object o = c.newInstance();
            if (!(o instanceof Plotter))
                throw new ClassNotFoundException("Not instanceof Plotter");
            r = (Plotter)o;
        } catch (ClassNotFoundException e) {
            System.err.println("Sorry, class " + argv[0] +
                    " not a plotter class");
            return;
        } catch (Exception e) {
            e.printStackTrace();
            return;
        }
        r.penDown();
        r.penColor(1);
        r.moveTo(200, 200);
        r.penColor(2);
        r.drawBox(123, 200);
        r.rmoveTo(10, 20);
        r.penColor(3);
        r.drawBox(123, 200);
        r.penUp();
        r.moveTo(300, 100);
        r.penDown();
        r.setFont("Helvetica", 14);
        r.drawString("Hello World");
        r.penColor(4);
        r.drawBox(10, 10);
    }
}
```

We don't show any actual subclasses of this Plotter class in upcoming chapters, however there is a PlotterAWT proof-of-concept in the same source folder, and one could implement this for PostScript, PDF, or other output technologies.

## CHAPTER 9

Functional Programming Techniques: Functional Interfaces, Streams, and Parallel Collections

9.0 Introduction

Java is an Object-Oriented (OO) language. You know what that is. Functional Programming (FP) has been attracting attention lately. There may not be quite as many definitions of FP as there are FP languages, but it's close. Wikipedia's definition of functional programming is as follows (from *https://en.wikipedia.org/wiki/Functional_programming*, viewed December 2013):

> a programming paradigm, a style of building the structure and elements of computer programs, that treats computation as the evaluation of mathematical functions and avoids state and mutable data. Functional programming emphasizes functions that produce results that depend only on their inputs and not on the program state—i.e. pure mathematical functions. It is a declarative programming paradigm, which means programming is done with expressions. In functional code, the output value of a function depends only on the arguments that are input to the function, so calling a function f twice with the same value for an argument x will produce the same result f(x) both times. Eliminating side effects, i.e. changes in state that don't depend on the function inputs, can make it much easier to understand and predict the behavior of a program, which is one of the key motivations for the development of functional programming.

How can we benefit from the FP paradigm? One way would be to switch to using an FP language; some of the leading ones are Haskell,[6] Idris, Ocaml, Erlang, Julia, and

---

[6] Haskell was used to write a fairly complete Twitter clone in a few hundred lines; see *https://github.com/Gabriel439/simple-twitter*.

the LISP family. But most of those would require walking away from the Java ecosystem. You could consider using Scala (*http://www.scala-lang.org*) or Clojure (*http:// clojure.org*), JVM-based languages that provide functional programming support in the context of an OO language. And there is Kotlin (*https://kotlinlang.org*), the latest Java-like language for the JVM.

But this is the *Java Cookbook*, so you can imagine we're going to try to get as many benefits of functional programming as we can while remaining in the Java language. Some features of FP include the following:

- Pure functions having no side effects and whose results depend only on their inputs and not on mutable state elsewhere in the program
- First-class functions (e.g., functions as data)
- Immutable data
- Extensive use of recursion and lazy evaluation

Pure functions are completely self-contained; their operation depends only on the input parameters and internal logic, not on any variable state in other parts of the program—indeed, there are no global variables, only global *constants*. Although this can be hard to accept for those schooled in imperative languages like Java, it does make it much easier to test and ensure program correctness! It means that, no matter what else is going on in the program (even with multiple threads), a method call like computeValue(27) will always, unconditionally, return the same value every time (with exceptions, of course, for things like the current time, random seeds, etc., which are global state).

We'll use the terms *function* and *method* interchangeably in this chapter, although it's not strictly correct. FP people use the term *function* in the mathematical function sense, whereas in Java *methods* just means some code you can call (a Java method call is also referred to as a *message* being *sent* to an object, in the OO view of things).

Functions as data means that you can create *an object that is a function*, pass it into another function, write a function that returns another function, and so on—with no special syntax, because, well, functions *are* data.

One of Java's approaches to FP is the definition of functional interfaces. A *functional interface* in Java is one that has only one abstract method, such as the widely used Runnable, whose only method is run( ), or the common Swing action handler Action Listener, whose only method is actionPerformed(ActionEvent). Actually, also new in Java 8, interfaces can have methods annotated with the new-in-this-context default keyword. A default method in an interface becomes available for use in any class that implements the interface. Such methods cannot depend on instance state in a particular class because they would have no way of referring to it at compile time.

So a functional interface is more precisely defined as one that has a single nondefault method. You can do functional-style programming in Java if you use functional interfaces and if you restrict code in your methods to not depending on any nonfinal instance or class fields; using default methods is one way of achieving this. The first few recipes in this chapter discuss functional interfaces.

Another Java approach to functional-ness is lambda expressions. A lambda is an expression of a functional interface, and it can be used as data (i.e., assigned, returned, etc.). Just to give a couple of short examples for now:

```
ActionListener x = e -> System.out.println("You activated " + e.getSource());

public class RunnableLambda {

    public static void main(String[] args) {
        threadPool.submit(() -> System.out.println("Hello from a thread"));
```

Immutable data is easy in theory: just have a class with only read accessors ("get" methods). The standard String class, for example, is immutable: methods like sub string() or toUpperCase() don't change the original string, but make up new string objects with the requested change. Yet strings are universally used, and useful. Enums are also implicitly immutable. There is a proposal to add a new kind of class-like object called a record in Java 14 or 15. records are implicitly immutable; the compiler generates "get" methods for the fields (along with a constructor and the three common Object methods), but not "set" methods.

Also new in Java 8 is the notion of Stream classes. A Stream is like a pipeline that you can feed into, fan out, collect down—like a cross between the Unix notion of pipelines and Google's distributed programming concept of MapReduce, as exemplified in Hadoop (*http://hadoop.apache.org*), but running in a single VM, a single program. Streams can be sequential or parallel; the latter are designed to take advantage of the massive parallelism that is happening in hardware design (particularly servers, where 12- and 16-core processors are popular). We discuss Streams in several recipes in this chapter.

If you're familiar with Unix pipes and filters, this equivalence will make sense to you; if not, you can skip it for now. The Unix command is this:

```
cat lines.txt | sort | uniq | wc -l
```

The Java Streams equivalent is this:

```
jshell> long numberLines =
    new BufferedReader(
    new FileReader("lines.txt")).lines().sorted().distinct().count();
numberLines ==> 5
```

These commands are written out in more idiomatic Java in Example 9-1. Both approaches give the same answer. For small inputs, the Unix pipeline is faster; but for larger volumes, the Java one should be faster, especially when parallelized.

Example 9-1. main/src/main/java/functional/UnixPipesFiltersReplacement.java

```
long numberLines = Files.lines(Path.of(("lines.txt")))
    .sorted()
    .distinct()
    .count();
System.out.printf("lines.txt contains " + numberLines + " unique lines.");
```

Tied in with `Streams` is the notion of a `Spliterator`, a derivative (logically, not by inheritance) of the familiar `Iterator` but designed for use in parallel processing. Most users will not be expected to develop their own `Spliterator` and will likely not even call its methods directly very often, so we do not discuss them in detail.

See Also

For general information on functional programming, see the book *Functional Thinking* by Neal Ford (O'Reilly).

There is an entire book dedicated to lambda expressions and related tools, Richard Warburton's *Java 8 Lambdas* (O'Reilly).

9.1 Using Lambdas/Closures Instead of Inner Classes

Problem

You want to avoid all the typing that even the anonymous style of inner class requires.

Solution

Use Java's lambda expressions.

Discussion

The symbol lambda (λ) is the 11th letter of the Greek alphabet and thus as old as Western society. The Lambda calculus (*http://en.wikipedia.org/wiki/Lambda_calculus*) is about as old as our notions of computing. In this context, Lambda expressions are small units of calculation that can be referred to. They are functions as data. In that sense, they are a lot like anonymous inner classes, though it's probably better to think of them as *anonymous methods*. They are essentially used to replace inner classes for a *functional interface*—that is, an interface with one abstract method (function) in it. A very common example is the AWT `ActionListener` interface, widely used in GUI code, whose only method is this one:

```
public void actionPerformed(ActionEvent);
```

Using lambdas is now the preferred method of writing for GUI action listeners. Here's a single example:

```
quitButton.addActionListener(e -> shutDownApplication(0));
```

Because not everybody writes Swing GUI applications these days, let's start with an example that doesn't require GUI programming. Suppose we have a collection of camera model descriptor objects that has already been loaded from a database into memory, and we want to write a general-purpose API for searching them, for use by other parts of our application.

The first thought might be along the following lines:

```
public interface CameraInfo {
    public List<Camera> findByMake();
    public List<Camera> findByModel();
    ...
}
```

Perhaps you can already see the problem. You will also need to write `findByPrice()`, `findByMakeAndModel()`, `findByYearIntroduced()`, and so on as your application grows in complexity.

You could consider implementing a query by example method, where you pass in a `Camera` object and all its nonnull fields are used in the comparison. But then how would you implement finding cameras with interchangeable lenses *under $500*?[6]

So a better approach is probably to use a callback function to do the comparison. Then you can provide an anonymous inner class to do any kind of searching you need. You'd want to be able to write callback methods like this:

```
public boolean choose(Camera c) {
    return c.isIlc() && c.getPrice() < 500;
}
```

---

6 If you ever have to do this kind of thing where the data is stored in a relational database using the Java Persistence API (JPA), you should check out the Spring Data (*https://spring.io/projects/spring-data*) or Apache DeltaSpike (*http://deltaspike.apache.org*) frameworks. These allow you to define an `interface` with method names like `findCameraByInterchangeableTrueAndPriceLessThan(double price)` and have the framework implement these methods for you.

Accordingly, we'll build that into an interface:[6]

```
/** An Acceptor accepts some elements from a Collection */
public interface CameraAcceptor {
    boolean choose(Camera c);
}
```

Now the search application provides a method:

```
public List<Camera> search(CameraAcceptor acc);
```

which we can call with code like this:

```
results = searchApp.search(new CameraAcceptor() {
    public boolean choose(Camera c) {
        return c.isIlc() && c.getPrice() < 500;
    }
}
```

Or, if you were not comfortable with anonymous inner classes, you might have to type this:

```
class MyIlcPriceAcceptor implements CameraAcceptor {
    public boolean choose(Camera c) {
        return c.isIlc() && c.getPrice() < 500;
    }
}
CameraAcceptor myIlcPriceAcceptor = nwq MyIlcPriceAcceptor();
results = searchApp.search(myIlcPriceAcceptor);
```

That's really a great deal of typing just to get one method packaged up for sending into the search engine. Java's support for lambda expressions or closures was argued about for many years (literally) before the experts agreed on how to do it. And the result is staggeringly simple. One way to think of Java lambda expressions is that each one is just a method that implements a functional interface. With lambda expressions, you can rewrite the preceding code as just:

```
results = searchApp.search(c -> c.isIlc() && c.getPrice() < 500);
```

The arrow notation -> indicates the code to execute. If it's a simple expression as here, you can just write it as shown. If there is conditional logic or other statements, you have to use a block, as is usual in Java.

Here I just rewrite the search example to show it as a block:

```
results = searchApp.search(c -> {
    if (c.isIlc() && c.getPrice() < 500)
```

---

6 If you're just not that into cameras, the description "Interchangeable Lens Camera (ILC)" includes two categories of what you might find in a camera store: traditional DSLR (Digital Single Lens Reflex) cameras, and the newer category of "Compact System Cameras" like the Nikon 1 and Z series, Sony ILCE (formerly known as NEX), and the Canon EOS-M, all of which are smaller and lighter than the older DSLRs.

```
        return true;
    else
        return false;
});
```

The first `c` inside the parenthesis corresponds to `Camera` `c` in the explicitly implemented `choose()` method: you can omit the type because the compiler knows it! If
there is more than one argument to the method, you must parenthesize them. Suppose we had a compare method that takes two cameras and returns a quantitative
value (oh, and good luck trying to get two photographers to agree on *that*
algorithm!):

```
double goodness = searchApp.compare((c1, c2) -> {
    // write some amazing code here
});
```

This notion of *lambdas* seems pretty potent, and it is! You will see much more of this
in Java as Java 8 moves into the mainstream of computing.

Up to here, we still have to write an interface for each type of method that we want to
be able to lambda-ize. The next recipe shows some predefined interfaces that you can
use to further simplify (or at least shorten) your code.

And, of course, there are many existing interfaces that are functional, such as the
`ActionListener` interface from GUI applications. Interestingly, the IntelliJ IDE (see
Recipe 1.3) automatically recognizes inner class definitions that are replaceable by
lambdas and, when using *code folding* (the IDE feature of representing an entire
method definition with a single line), replaces the inner class with the corresponding
lambda! Figures 9-1 and 9-2 show a before-and-after picture of this code folding.

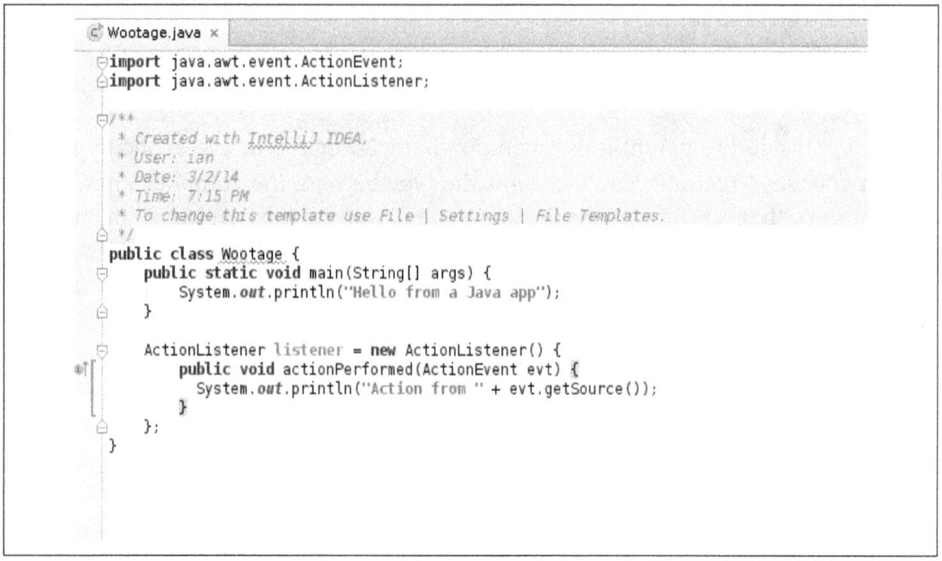

Figure 9-1. IntelliJ code unfolded

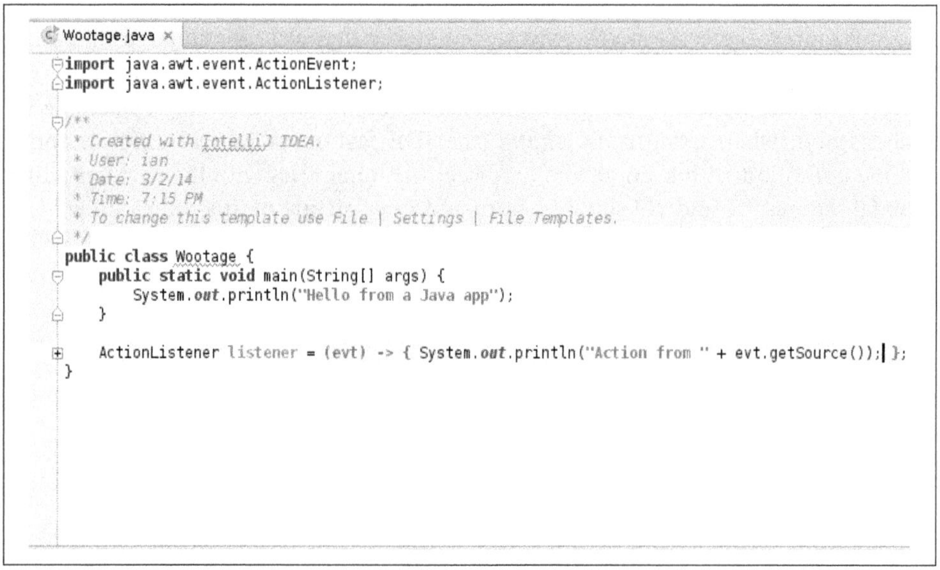

Figure 9-2. IntelliJ code folded

9.2 Using Lambda Predefined Interfaces Instead of Your Own

Problem

You want to use existing interfaces, instead of defining your own, for use with Lambdas.

Solution

Use the Java 8 lambda functional interfaces from `java.util.function`.

Discussion

In Recipe 9.1, we used the interface method `acceptCamera()` defined in the interface `CameraAcceptor`. Acceptor-type methods are quite common, so the package `java.util.function` includes the `Predicate<T>` interface, which we can use instead of `CameraAcceptor`. This interface has only one method—`boolean test(T t)`:

```
interface Predicate<T> {
    boolean test(T t);
}
```

This package includes about 50 of the most commonly needed functional interfaces, such as `IntUnaryOperator`, which takes one `int` argument and returns an `int` value; `LongPredicate`, which takes one `long` and returns `boolean`; and so on.

To use the `Predicate` interface, as with any generic type, we provide an actual type for the parameter `Camera`, giving us (in this case) the parameterized type `Predicate<Camera>`, which is the following (although we don't have to write this out):

```
interface Predicate<Camera> {
    boolean test(Camera c);
}
```

So now our search application will be changed to offer us the following search method:

```
public List<Camera> search(Predicate p);
```

Conveniently, this has the same signature as our own `CameraAcceptor` from the point of view of the anonymous methods that lambdas implement, so the rest of our code doesn't have to change! This is still a valid call to the `search()` method:

```
results = searchApp.search(c -> c.isIlc() && c.getPrice() < 500);
```

Here is the implementation of the `search` method:

main/src/main/java/functional/CameraSearchPredicate.java

```
public List<Camera> search(Predicate<Camera> tester) {
    List<Camera> results = new ArrayList<>();
    privateListOfCameras.forEach(c -> {
        if (tester.test(c))
            results.add(c);
    });
    return results;
}
```

Suppose we only need the list to do one operation on each element, and then we'll discard it. Upon reflection, we don't actually need to get the list back; we merely need to get our hooks on each element that matches our Predicate in turn.

Roll Your Own Functional Interface

While the JDK provides a good set of functional interfaces, there may be cases where you'd want to create your own. This is a simple example of a functional interface:

```
interface MyFunctionalInterface {
    int compute(int x);
}
```

The @FunctionalInterface annotation tells the compiler to ensure that a given interface is and remains functional. Its use is analogous to @Override (both annotations are in java.lang). It is always optional.

MyFunctionalInterface could be used to process an array of integers, like this:

```
public class ProcessIntsUsingFunctional {
    static int[] integers = {1, 2, 3};

    public static void main(String[] args) {
        int total = 0;
        for (int i : integers)
            total += process(i, x ->  x * x + 1);
        System.out.println("The total is " + total);
    }

    private static int process(int i, MyFunctionalInterface o) {
        return o.compute(i);
    }
}
```

If compute were a nonfunctional interface—having multiple abstract methods—you would not be able to use it in this fashion.

Sometimes, of course, you really do need an interface to have more than one method. In that case, the illusion (or the effect) of functionality can sometimes be preserved by denoting all but one of the methods with the default keyword—the nondefault method will still be usable in lambdas. A default method has a method body:

```
public interface ThisIsStillFunctional {
    default int compute(int ix) { return ix * ix + 1 };
    int anotherMethod(int y);
}
```

Only default methods may contain executable statements, and there may only be one nondefault method per functional interface.

By the way, the `MyFunctionalInterface` given earlier can be totally replaced by `java.util.function.IntUnaryOperator`, changing the method name `apply()` to `applyAsInt()`. There is a version of the `ProcessInts` program under the name `ProcessIntsIntUnaryOperator` in the *javasrc* repository.

Default methods in interfaces can be used to produce *mixins*, as described in Recipe 9.7.

9.3 Simplifying Processing with Streams

Problem

You want to process some data through a pipeline-like mechanism.

Solution

Use a `Stream` class and its operations.

Discussion

Streams are a new mechanism introduced with Java 8 to allow a collection to send its values out one at a time through a pipeline-like mechanism where they can be processed in various ways, with varying degrees of parallelism. There are three types of methods involved with `Streams`:

- Stream-producing methods (see Recipe 7.3).
- Stream-passing methods, which operate on a Stream and return a reference to it, in order to allow for *fluent programming* (chained methods calls); examples include `distinct()`, `filter()`, `limit()`, `map()`, `peek()`, `sorted()`, and `unsorted()`.
- Stream-terminating methods, which conclude a streaming operation; examples include `collect()`, `count()`, `findFirst()`, `max()`, `min()`, `reduce()`, and `sum()`.

In Example 9-2, we have a list of `Hero` objects representing superheroes through the ages. We use the `Stream` mechanism to filter just the adult heroes and then sum their ages. We use it again to sort the heroes' names alphabetically.

In both operations we start with a stream generator (`Arrays.stream()`); we run it through several steps, one of which involves a mapping operation (don't confuse with `java.util.Map`!) that causes a different value to be sent along the pipeline. The stream is wrapped up by a terminal operation. The map and filter operations almost invariably are controlled by a lambda expression (inner classes would be too tedious to use in this style of programming!).

Example 9-2. main/src/main/java/functional/SimpleStreamDemo.java

```java
static Hero[] heroes = {
    new Hero("Grelber", 21),
    new Hero("Roderick", 12),
    new Hero("Francisco", 35),
    new Hero("Superman", 65),
    new Hero("Jumbletron", 22),
    new Hero("Mavericks", 1),
    new Hero("Palladin", 50),
    new Hero("Athena", 50) };

public static void main(String[] args) {

    long adultYearsExperience = Arrays.stream(heroes)
            .filter(b -> b.age >= 18)
            .mapToInt(b -> b.age).sum();
    System.out.println("We're in good hands! The adult superheros have " +
            adultYearsExperience + " years of experience");

    List<Object> sorted = Arrays.stream(heroes)
            .sorted((h1, h2) -> h1.name.compareTo(h2.name))
            .map(h -> h.name)
            .collect(Collectors.toList());
    System.out.println("Heroes by name: " + sorted);
}
```

And let's run it to be sure it works:

```
We're in good hands! The adult superheroes have 243 years of experience
Heroes by name: [Athena, Francisco, Grelber, Jumbletron, Mavericks, Palladin,
                 Roderick, Superman]
```

See the javadoc for the `java.util.stream.Stream` interface for a complete list of the operations.

9.4 Simplifying Streams with Collectors

Problem

You construct Streams but they are complicated or inefficient.

Solution

Use `Collectors`.

Discussion

Example 9-2 ended the first half with a call to `collect()`. The argument to `collect()` is of type `Collector`, which this recipe considers in more detail. `Collectors` are a form of what classical FP languages call *folds* (*https://en.wikipedia.org/wiki/Fold_(higher-order_function)*). Folds are also called reduce, accumulate, aggregate, compress, or inject operations. A *fold* in functional programming is a terminal operation, analogous to collapsing a whole string of tickets into a flat pile (see Figure 9-3). The string of tickets represents the `Stream`, the folding operation is represented by a function, and the final result is, well, the final result, all folded up. It will often include a combining operation, analogous to counting the tickets as they are folded.

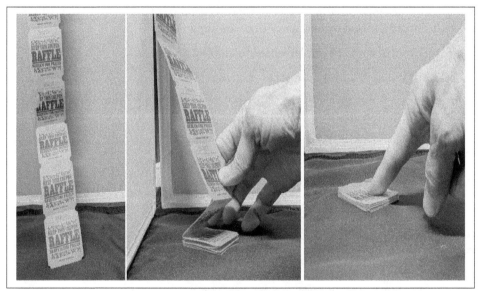

Figure 9-3. Stream of tickets before folding, during folding, and after folding: a terminal operation

Note that in the first panel of Figure 9-3 we don't know how long the `Stream` is, but we expect that it will terminate eventually.

Collector as used in Java refers to a terminal function that analyses/summarizes the content of a `Stream`. Technically, `Collector` is an interface whose implementation is specified by three (or four) functions that work together to accumulate entries into a Collection or Map or other mutable result container, and optionally a final transform on the result. The functions are as follows:

- Creating a new result container (the `supplier()`)
- Adding a new data element into the result container (the `accumulator()`)
- Combining two result *containers* into one (the `combiner()`)
- Performing a final transform on the container (the `finisher()`, which is optional)

While you can easily compose your own `Collector` implementation, it is often expedient to use one of the many useful ones predefined in the `Collectors` class. Here are a couple of simple examples:

```
int howMany = cameraList.stream().collect(Collectors.counting());
double howMuch = cameraList.filter(desiredFilter).
        collect(Collectors.summingDouble(Camera::getPrice);
```

In Example 9-3 I implement the classic *word frequency count* algorithm: take a text file, break it into individual words, count the occurrence of each word, and list the *n* most-used words, sorted by frequency in descending order.

In Unix terms this could be implemented (assuming *n* = 20) as:

```
prep $file | sort | uniq -c | sort -nr | head -20
```

where `prep` is a script that uses the Unix tool `tr` to break lines into words and turn the words into lowercase.

Example 9-3. main/src/main/java/functional/WordFreq.java

```
package functional;

import java.io.*;
import java.nio.file.*;
import java.util.*;
import java.util.stream.*;

/**
 * Implement word frequency count, in two statements
 */
public class WordFreq {
    public static void main(String[] args) throws IOException {

        // 1) Collect words with a mutable reduction into Map<String,Long>.
        Map<String,Long> map = Files.lines(Path.of(args[0]))
            .flatMap(s -> Stream.of(s.split(" +")))
            .collect(Collectors.groupingBy(
                String::toLowerCase, Collectors.counting()));

        // 2) Print results sorted numerically descending, limit 20
        map.entrySet().stream()
            .sorted(Map.Entry.<String,Long>comparingByValue() .reversed())
```

```
            .limit(20)
            .map(entry -> String.format("%4d %s", entry.getValue(), entry.getKey()))
            .forEach(System.out::println);
    }
}
```

There are two steps. First, create a map of the words and their frequencies. Second, sort these in reverse order, stop at number 20, and format them neatly and print.

The first part uses `Files.lines()` from Chapter 10 to get a `Stream` of `Strings`, which is broken into individual words using the `Stream` method `flatMap()` combined with the `String` method `split()` to break on one or more spaces. The result of that is collected into a map using a `Collector`. I had initially used a homemade collector:

```
.collect(HashMap::new, (m,s)->m.put(s, m.getOrDefault(s,0)+1), HashMap::putAll);
```

This form of `collect()` takes three arguments:

- A `Supplier<R>` or factory method to create an empty container; here I'm just using the `HashMap` constructor.

- An accumulator of type `BiConsumer<R,? super T>` to add each element into the map, adding one each time the same word is found.

- A Combiner of type `BiConsumer<R,R> combiner)` to combine all the collections used.

In the case of parallel streams (see Recipe 9.5), the `Supplier` may be called multiple times to create multiple containers, and each part of the Stream's content will be handled by one Accumulator into one of the containers. The `Combiner` will merge all the containers into one at the end of processing.

However, Sander Mak pointed out that it's easier to use the existing `Collectors` class's predefined Collector `groupingBy`, combining the `toLowerCase()` call and the `collect()` call with this:

```
.collect(Collectors.groupingBy(String::toLowerCase, Collectors.counting()));
```

To further simplify the code, you could combine the two statements into one, by doing the following:

- Removing the return value and assignment `Map<String,Long>` =

- Removing the semicolon from the end of the `collect` call

- Removing the `.map()` from the `entrySet()` call

Then you can say you've implemented something useful in a single Java statement!

9.5 Improving Throughput with Parallel Streams and Collections

Problem

You want to combine `Streams` with parallelism and still be able to use the non-thread-safe Collections API.

Solution

Use a parallel stream.

Discussion

The standard Collections classes, such as most `List`, `Set`, and `Map` implementations, are not thread-safe for update; if you add or remove objects from one in one thread while another thread is accessing the objects stored in the collection, failure will result. Multiple threads reading from the same collection with no modification is OK. We discuss multithreading in Chapter 16.

The Collections Framework does provide *synchronized wrappers*, which provide automatic synchronization but at the cost of adding thread contention, which reduces parallelism. To enable efficient operations, *parallel streams* let you use the non-thread-safe collections safely, as long as you do not modify the collection while you are operating on it.

To use a parallel stream, you just ask the collection for it, using `parallelStream()` instead of the `stream()` method we used in Recipe 9.3.

For example, suppose that our camera business takes off, and we need to find cameras by type and price range *quickly* (and with less code than we used before):

```
public static void main(String[] args) {
    System.out.println("Search Results using For Loop");
    for (Object camera : privateListOfCameras.parallelStream().   ❶
            filter(c -> c.isIlc() && c.getPrice() < 500).           ❷
            toArray()) {                                            ❸
        System.out.println(camera);                                ❹
    }

    System.out.println(
        "Search Results from shorter, more functional approach");
    privateListOfCameras.parallelStream().                         ❺
            filter(c -> c.isIlc() && c.getPrice() < 500).
            forEach(System.out::println);
}
```

❶ Create a parallel stream from the List of Camera objects. The end result of the stream will be iterated over by the foreach loop.

❷ Filter the cameras on price, using the same Predicate lambda that we used in Recipe 9.1.

❸ Terminate the Stream by converting it to an array.

❹ The body of the foreach loop: print one Camera from the Stream.

❺ A more concise way of writing the search.

 This is reliable as long as no thread is modifying the data at the same time as the searching is going on. See the thread interlocking mechanisms in Chapter 16 to see how to ensure this.

9.6 Using Existing Code as Functional with Method References

Problem

You have existing code that matches a functional interface and want to use it without renaming methods to match the interface name.

Solution

Use function references such as MyClass::myFunc or someObj::someFunc.

Discussion

The word *reference* is almost as overloaded in Java as the word *Session*. Consider the following:

- Ordinary objects are usually accessed with references.

- Reference types such as WeakReference have defined semantics for garbage collection.

- And now, for something completely different, Java 8 lets you reference an individual method.

- You can even reference what Oracle documentation calls "an Instance Method of an Arbitrary Object of a Particular Type."

The new syntax consists of an object or class name, two colons, and the name of a method that can be invoked in the context of the object or class name (as per the usual rules of Java, a class name can refer to static methods and an instance can refer to an instance method). To refer to a constructor as the method, you can use new—for example, MyClass::new. The reference creates a lambda that can be invoked, stored in a variable of a functional interface type, and so on.

In Example 9-4, we create a Runnable reference that holds, not the usual run method, but a method with the same type and arguments but with the name walk. Note the use of this as the object part of the method reference. We then pass this Runnable into a Thread constructor and start the thread, with the result that walk is invoked where run would normally be.

Example 9-4. main/src/main/java/functional/ReferencesDemo.java

```java
/** "Walk, don't run" */
public class ReferencesDemo {

    // Assume this is an existing method we don't want to rename
    public void walk() {
        System.out.println("ReferencesDemo.walk(): Stand-in run method called");
    }

    // This is our main processing method; it runs "walk" in a Thread
    public void doIt() {
        Runnable r = this::walk;
        new Thread(r).start();
    }

    // The usual simple main method to start things off
    public static void main(String[] args) {
        new ReferencesDemo().doIt();
    }
}
```

The output is as follows:

```
ReferencesDemo.walk(): Stand-in run method called
```

Example 9-5 creates an AutoCloseable for use in a try-with-resource. The normal AutoCloseable method is close(), but ours is named cloz(). The AutoCloseable reference variable autoCloseable is created inside the try statement, so its close-like method will be called when the body completes. In this example, we are in a static main method wherein we have a reference rnd2 to an instance of the class, so we use this in referring to the AutoCloseable-compatible method.

Example 9-5. main/src/main/java/functional/ReferencesDemo2.java

```java
public class ReferencesDemo2 {
    void cloz() {
        System.out.println("Stand-in close() method called");
    }

    public static void main(String[] args) throws Exception {
        ReferencesDemo2 rd2 = new ReferencesDemo2();

        // Use a method reference to assign the AutoCloseable interface
        // variable "ac" to the matching method signature "c" (obviously
        // short for close, but just to show the method name isn't what matters).
        try (AutoCloseable autoCloseable = rd2::cloz) {
            System.out.println("Some action happening here.");
        }
    }
}
```

The output is as follows:

```
Some action happening here.
Stand-in close() method called
```

It is, of course, possible to use this with your own functional interfaces, defined as in "Roll Your Own Functional Interface" on page 282. You're also probably at least vaguely aware that any normal Java object reference can be passed to Sys tem.out.println() and you'll get some description of the referenced object. Example 9-6 explores these two themes. We define a functional interface imaginatively known as FunInterface with a method with a bunch of arguments (merely to avoid it being mistaken for any existing functional interface). The method name is process, but as you now know the name is not important; our implementation method goes by the name work. The work method is static, so we could not state that the class implements FunInterface (even if the method names were the same; a static method may not hide an inherited instance method), but we can nonetheless create a lambda reference to the work method. We then print this out to show that it has a valid structure as a Java object.

Example 9-6. main/src/main/java/functional/ReferencesDemo3.java

```java
public class ReferencesDemo3 {

    interface FunInterface {
        void process(int i, String j, char c, double d);
    }

    public static void work(int i, String j, char c, double d){
        System.out.println("Moo");
    }
```

```
    public static void main(String[] args) {
        FunInterface sample = ReferencesDemo3::work;
        System.out.println("My process method is " + sample);
    }
}
```

This generates the following output:

```
My process method is functional.ReferencesDemo3$$Lambda$1/713338599@4a574795
```

The Lambda$1 in the name is structurally similar to the "$1" used in anonymous inner classes.

The fourth way, "an Instance Method of an Arbitrary Object of a Particular Type," may be the most esoteric thing in all of Java 8. It allows you to declare a reference to an instance method but without specifying which instance. Because there is no particular instance in mind, you again use the class name. This means you can use it with any instance of the given class! In Example 9-7, we have an array of Strings to sort. Because the names in this array can begin with a lowercase letter, we want to sort them using the String method compareToIgnoreCase( ), which nicely ignores case differences for us.

Because I want to show the sorting several different ways, I set up two array references, the original, unsorted one, and a working one that is re-created, sorted, and printed using a simple dump routine, which isn't shown (it's just a for loop printing the strings from the passed array).

Example 9-7. main/src/main/java/functional/ReferencesDemo4.java

```
import java.util.Arrays;
import java.util.Comparator;

public class ReferencesDemo4 {

    static final String[] unsortedNames = {
        "Gosling", "de Raadt", "Torvalds", "Ritchie", "Hopper"
    };

    public static void main(String[] args) {
        String[] names;

        // Sort using
        // "an Instance Method of an Arbitrary Object of a Particular Type"
        names = unsortedNames.clone();
        Arrays.sort(names, String::compareToIgnoreCase);              ❶
        dump(names);

        // Equivalent Lambda:
        names = unsortedNames.clone();
```

```
        Arrays.sort(names, (str1, str2) -> str1.compareToIgnoreCase(str2));  ❷
        dump(names);

        // Equivalent old way:
        names = unsortedNames.clone();
        Arrays.sort(names, new Comparator<String>() {                        ❸
            @Override
            public int compare(String str1, String str2) {
                return str1.compareToIgnoreCase(str2);
            }
        });
        dump(names);

        // Simpest way, using existing comparator
        names = unsortedNames.clone();
        Arrays.sort(names, String.CASE_INSENSITIVE_ORDER);                   ❹
        dump(names);
    }
```

❶ Using "an Instance Method of an Arbitrary Object of a Particular Type," declares a reference to the `compareToIgnoreCase` method of any `String` used in the invocation.

❷ Shows the equivalent lambda expression.

❸ Shows "Your grandparents' Java" way of doing things.

❹ Using the exported `Comparator` directly, just to show that there is always more than one way to do things.

Just to be safe, I ran the demo, and got the expected output:

```
Amdahl, de Raadt, Gosling, Hopper, Ritchie, Turing
Amdahl, de Raadt, Gosling, Hopper, Ritchie, Turing
Amdahl, de Raadt, Gosling, Hopper, Ritchie, Turing
Amdahl, de Raadt, Gosling, Hopper, Ritchie, Turing
```

9.7 Java Mixins: Mixing in Methods

Problem

You've heard about mixins and want to apply them in Java.

Solution

Use static imports. Or, declare one or more functional interfaces with a default method containing the code to execute, and simply implement it.

Discussion

Developers from other languages sometimes deride Java for its inability to handle mixins, the ability to mix in bits of code from other classes.

One way to implement mixins is with the *static import* feature, which has been in the language for a decade. This is often done in unit testing (see Recipe 1.10). A limitation of this approach is that, as the name implies, the methods must be static methods, not instance methods.

A newer mechanism depends on an interesting bit of fallout from the Java 8 language changes in support of lambdas: you can now mix in code from unrelated places into one class. Has Java finally abandoned its staunch opposition to multiple inheritance? It may seem that way when you first hear it, but relax: you can only pull methods from multiple interfaces, not from multiple classes. If you didn't know that you could have methods defined (rather than merely declared) in interfaces, see "Subclass, Abstract Class, or Interface?" on page 250. Consider the following example:

main/src/main/java/lang/MixinsDemo.java

```java
interface Bar {
    default String filter(String s) {
        return "Filtered " + s;
    }
}

interface Foo {
    default String convolve(String s) {
        return "Convolved " + s;
    }
}

public class MixinsDemo implements Foo, Bar{

    public static void main(String[] args) {
        String input = args.length > 0 ? args[0] : "Hello";
        String output = new MixinsDemo().process(input);
        System.out.println(output);
    }

    private String process(String s) {
        return filter(convolve(s)); // methods mixed in!
    }
}
```

If we run this, we see the expected results:

```
C:\javasrc>javac -d build lang/MixinsDemo.java
C:\javasrc>java -cp build lang.MixinsDemo
Filtered Convolved Hello
```

```
C:\javasrc>
```

Presto—Java now supports mixins!

Does this mean you should go crazy trying to build interfaces with code in them? No. Remember this mechanism was designed to do the following:

- Provide the notion of functional interfaces for use in lambda calculations.
- Give the ability to retrofit interfaces with new methods, without having to change *old* implementations. As with many changes made in Java over the years, backward compatibility was a huge driver.

Used sparingly, functional interfaces can provide the ability to mix in code to build up applications in another way than direct inheritance, aggregation, or AOP. Overused, it can make your code heavy, drive pre–Java 8 developers crazy, and lead to chaos.

## CHAPTER 10

Input and Output: Reading, Writing, and Directory Tricks

10.0 Introduction

Most programs need to interact with the outside world, and one common way of doing so is by reading and writing files. Files are normally on some persistent medium such as a disk drive; and, for the most part, we shall happily ignore the differences between files on a hard disk (and all the operating system–dependent filesystem types), a USB drive or SD card, a DVD-ROM, and other memory devices. For now, they're just files. And, like most other languages and OSes, Java extends the reading-and-writing model to network (socket) communications, which we'll touch on in Chapters 12 and 13.

Java provides many classes for input and output; they are summarized in Figure 10-1. This chapter covers all the normal input/output operations such as opening/closing and reading/writing files. Files are assumed to reside on some kind of file store or permanent storage. Distributed filesystems such as Apache Hadoop HDFS, Sun's Network File System (NFS, common on Unix and available for Windows), SMB (the Windows network filesystem, available for Unix via the open source Samba program), and FUSE (Filesystem in User SpacE, implementations for most Unix/Linux systems) are assumed to work just like disk filesystems, except where noted.

The support for reading and writing is in two major parts:

- The `InputStream/OutputStream/Reader/Writer` classes, which are the traditional ways of reading/writing files, have been largely unchanged since the days of Java 1.0 and 1.1. In modern Java, a new class, `java.nio.file.Files`, is provided.

- All modern operating systems provide the means to organize groups of files into directories, or folders. This chapter covers directories: how to create them, how to navigate them. Files provides most of the support for processing directories, but it also introduces a number of convenience routines for easily reading, writing, and copying files that are covered in this chapter. These are generally more convenient than using the traditional I/O classes. We cover both in this chapter.

 There are two different uses of the term *stream*. The first is for a stream of bytes to be read or written, and is unrelated to the second use, which is used in modern Java to refer to a connection among cooperating methods. I'll try to keep these meanings straight by only using InputStream and/or OutputStream for the former, and Stream for the latter.

To give you control over the format of data that you read and write, the Formatter and Scanner classes provide formatting and scanning operations. Formatter allows many formatting tasks to be performed either into a String or to almost any output destination. Scanner parses many kinds of objects, again either from a String or from almost any input source. These are fairly powerful; each is given its own recipe in this chapter.

The second part of the chapter is largely devoted to the Files and Path classes in java.nio.file. These two classes provide the ability to list directories, obtain file status, rename and delete files on disk, create directories, and perform other filesystem operations. They also provide the ability to read a file line by line into a Stream<String>. These two classes together largely supplant the older java.io.File class. They were introduced in Java 7, so very little new code should be using the older File class.

Note that many of the methods of this class attempt to modify the permanent file store, or disk filesystem, of the computer you run them on. Naturally, you might not have permission to change certain files in certain ways. This can be detected by the Java Virtual Machine's SecurityManager, which will throw the unchecked exception SecurityException if you don't have permission to do the attempted operation. But failure can also be detected by the underlying operating system: if the security manager approves it, but the user running your program lacks permissions on the directory, for example, you will either get back an indication (such as false) or an instance of the checked exception IOException. This must be caught (or declared in the throws clause) in any code that calls any method that tries to change the filesystem.

10.1 About InputStreams/OutputStreams and Readers/Writers

Java provides two sets of classes for reading and writing. The InputStream/Output Stream section of package java.io (see Figure 10-1) is for reading or writing bytes of data. Older languages tended to assume that a byte (which is a machine-specific collection of bits, usually eight bits on modern computers) is exactly the same thing as a character—a letter, digit, or other linguistic element. However, Java is designed to be used internationally, and eight bits is simply not enough to handle the many different character sets used around the world. Script-based languages, and pictographic languages like Chinese and Japanese, each have many more than 256 characters, the maximum that can be represented in an eight-bit byte. The unification of these many character code sets is called, not surprisingly, Unicode. Both Java and XML use Unicode as their character sets, allowing you to read and write text in any of these human languages. But you should use Readers and Writers, not Streams, for textual data.

Unicode itself doesn't solve the entire problem. Many of these human languages were used on computers long before Unicode was invented, and they didn't all pick the same representation as Unicode. And they all have zillions of files encoded in a particular representation that isn't Unicode. So routines are needed when reading and writing to convert between Unicode String objects used inside the Java machine and the particular external representation in which a user's files are written. These converters are packaged inside a powerful set of classes called Readers and Writers. Readers and Writers should always be used instead of InputStreams and Output Streams when you want to deal with characters instead of bytes. We'll see more on this conversion, and how to specify which conversion, a little later in this chapter.

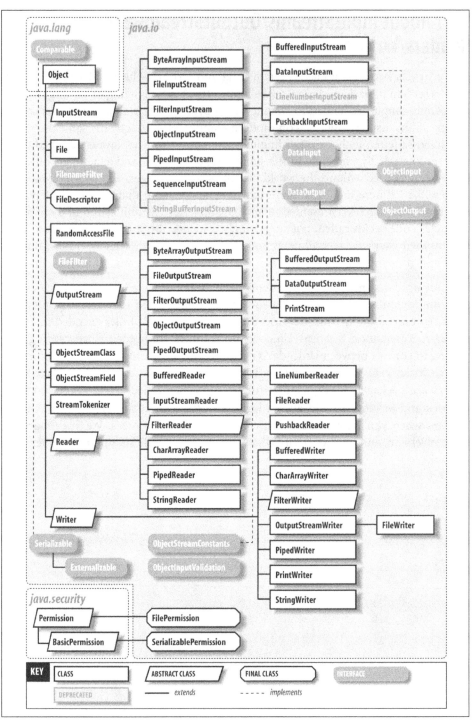

Figure 10-1. java.io classes

See Also

One topic *not* addressed in depth here is the reading/writing capabilities of Channels classes in the Java "new I/O" package.[6] This part of NIO is more complex to use than either Files or the input/output streams, and the benefits accrue primarily in large-scale server-side processing. Recipe 4.5 provides one example of using NIO. The NIO package is given full coverage in the book *Java NIO* by Ron Hitchens (O'Reilly).

Another topic not covered here is that of having the read or write occur concurrently with other program activity. This requires the use of threads, or multiple flows of control within a single program. Threaded I/O is a necessity in many programs: those reading from slow devices such as tape drives, those reading from or writing to network connections, and those with a GUI. For this reason, the topic is given considerable attention, in the context of multithreaded applications, in Chapter 16.

For traditional I/O topics, Elliotte Rusty Harold's *Java I/O*, although somewhat dated, should be considered the antepenultimate documentation. The penultimate reference is the javadoc documentation, while the ultimate reference is, if you really need it, the source code for the Java API. Due in part to the quality of the javadoc documentation, I have not needed to refer to the source code in writing this chapter.

10.2 Reading a Text File

Problem

The Java documentation doesn't have methods for opening files. How do I open and read a text file and then either process it a line at a time, or get a collection of all the lines?

Solution

Use the Files::lines() method, which returns a Stream of Strings. Or, use Files.newBufferedReader(), Files.newBufferedWriter(), Files.newInput Stream(), and Files.newOutputStream(). Or, construct a FileReader or a FileIn putStream. Once you have that, construct a BufferedReader, and use the older $ $while ((line == readLine()) != null)$$ pattern.

---

6 A poor choice of name: it was new in Java SE 1.4. But newer than InputStream/OutputStream (Java 1.0) and Readers/Writers (1.1).

Discussion

There is no explicit open operation,[6] perhaps as a kind of rhetorical flourish of the Java API's object-oriented design.

The quickest way to process a text file a line at a time is to use `Files.lines()`, which takes a `Path` argument and returns a functional `Stream<String>` into which it feeds the lines from the file:

```
Files.lines(Path.of("myFile.txt")).forEach(System.out::println);
```

The `Files` class has several other static methods which open a file and read some or all of it:

`List<String> Files.readAllLines(Path)`
    Reads the whole file into a `List<String>`.

`byte[] Files.readAllBytes`
    Reads the whole file into an array of bytes.

There is a series of methods with names like `newReader()`, `newBufferedWriter()`, etc., each of which takes a `Path` argument and return the appropriate `Reader`/`Writer` or `InputStream`/`OutputStream`. A `Path` is a descriptor for an abstract path (filename) that may or may not exist. The explicit constructors for a `FileReader`, `FileWriter`, `FileInputStream`, or `FileOutputStream` take a filename or an instance of the older `File` class containing the path. These operations correspond to the "open" operation in most other languages' I/O packages.

Historically, Java used to require use of the code pattern `while ((line == read Line()) != null` to read lines from a `BufferedReader`. This still works, of course, and will continue to work until the last JavaBean sets in the west, in the far future.

Example 10-1 shows the code for each of these ways of reading lines from a file.

Example 10-1. main/src/main/java/io/ReadLines.java (reading lines from a file)

```
System.out.println("Using Path.lines()");
Files.lines(Path.of(fileName)).forEach(System.out::println);

System.out.println("Using Path.readAllLines()");
List<String> lines = Files.readAllLines(Path.of(fileName));
lines.forEach(System.out::println);

System.out.println("Using BufferedReader.lines().forEach()");
new BufferedReader(new FileReader(fileName)).lines().forEach(s -> {
```

---

6 Not strictly true; there is, but only in the `java.nio.FileChannel` class, which we're not covering.

```
            System.out.println(s);
    });

    System.out.println("The old-fashioned way");
    BufferedReader is = new BufferedReader(new FileReader(fileName));
    String line;
    while ((line = is.readLine()) != null) {
        System.out.println(line);
    }
```

Most of these methods can throw the checked exception IOException, so you must have a throws clause or a try/catch around these invocations.

If you create an InputStream, OutputStream, Reader, or Writer, you should close it when finished. This avoids memory leaks and, in the case of writing, ensures that all buffered data is actually written to disk. One way to ensure this is not forgotten is to use the try-with-resources syntax. This puts the declaration and definition of a Close able resource into the try statement:

```
static void oldWayShorter() throws IOException {
    try (BufferedReader is =
        new BufferedReader(new FileReader(INPUT_FILE_NAME));
        BufferedOutputStream bytesOut = new BufferedOutputStream(
          new FileOutputStream(OUTPUT_FILE_NAME.replace("\\.", "-1.")));) {

        // Read from is, write to bytesOut
        String line;
        while ((line = is.readLine()) != null) {
            line = doSomeProcessingOn(line);
            bytesOut.write(line.getBytes("UTF-8"));
            bytesOut.write('\n');
        }

    }
}
```

The lines() and read-related methods in Files obviate the need for closing the resource, but not the need for handling IOException; the compiler or IDE will remind you if you forget those.

There are options that can be passed to the Files methods that open a file; these are discussed in the sidebar "Understanding I/O Options: StandardOpenOptions, FileAttribute, PosixFileAttribute, and More" on page 321.

To read the entire contents of a file into single string, in Java 8+, use Files.read String():

```
String input = Files.readString(Path.of(INPUT_FILE_NAME)));
```

In older Java versions, use my `FileIO.readerToString()` method. This will read the entire named file into one long string, with embedded newline (\n) characters between each line. To read a binary file, use `Files.readAllBytes()` instead.

See Also

There is formal documentation online for `Files` (*https://docs.oracle.com/javase/8/ docs/api/java/nio/file/Files.html*) and `Path` (*https://docs.oracle.com/javase/8/docs/api/ java/nio/file/Path.html*).

10.3 Reading from the Standard Input or from the Console/Controlling Terminal

Problem

You want to read from the program's standard input or directly from the program's controlling terminal or console terminal.

Solution

For the standard input, read bytes by wrapping a `BufferedInputStream()` around `System.in`. For reading text, use an `InputStreamReader` and a `BufferedReader`. For the console or controlling terminal, use Java's `System.console()` method to obtain a `Console` object, and use its methods.

Discussion

Sometimes you really do need to read from the standard input, or console. One reason is that simple test programs are often console-driven. Another is that some programs naturally require a lot of interaction with the user and you want something faster than a GUI (consider an interactive mathematics or statistical exploration program). Yet another is piping the output of one program directly to the input of another, a very common operation among Unix users and quite valuable on other platforms, such as Windows, that support this operation.

Standard input

Most desktop platforms support the notion of *standard input* (a keyboard, a file, or the output from another program) and *standard output* (a terminal window, a printer, a file on disk, or the input to yet another program). Most such systems also support a standard error output so that error messages can be seen by the user even if the standard output is being redirected. When programs on these platforms start up, the three streams are preassigned to particular platform-dependent handles, or *file descriptors.* The net result is that ordinary programs on these operating systems can read the standard input or write to the standard output or standard error stream without having to open any files or make any other special arrangements.

Java continues this tradition and enshrines it in the System class. The static variables System.in, System.out, and System.err are connected to the three operating system streams before your program begins execution (an application is free to reassign these; see Recipe 10.10). So, to read the standard input, you need only refer to the variable System.in and call its methods. For example, to read one byte from the standard input, you call the read method of System.in, which returns the byte in an int variable:

```
int b = System.in.read( );
```

But is that enough? No, because the read() method can throw an IOException. So you must either declare that your program throws an IOException:

```
public static void main(String args[]) throws IOException {
...
}
```

Or you can put a try/catch block around the read() method:

```
int b = 0;
try {
    b = System.in.read();
    System.out.println("Read this data: " + (char)b);
} catch (Exception e) {
    System.out.println("Caught " + e);
}
```

In this case, it makes sense to print the results inside the try block because there's no point in trying to print the value you read, if the read() threw an IOException.

That code works and gives you the ability to read a byte at a time from the standard input. But most applications are designed in terms of larger units, such as integers, or a line of text. To read a value of a known type, such as int, from the standard input, you can use the Scanner class (covered in more detail in Recipe 10.6):

```
Scanner sc = Scanner.create(System.in);
int i = sc.nextInt();
```

For reading characters of text with an input character converter so that your program will work with multiple input encodings around the world, use a Reader class. The particular subclass that allows you to read lines of characters is a BufferedReader. But there's a hitch. Remember I mentioned those two categories of input classes, Streams and Readers? But I also said that System.in is a Stream, and you want a Reader. How do you get from a Stream to a Reader? A crossover class called Input StreamReader is tailor-made for this purpose. Just pass your Stream (like System.in) to the `InputStreamReader` constructor and you get back a `Reader`, which you in turn pass to the `BufferedReader` constructor. The usual idiom for writing this in Java is to nest the constructor calls:

```
BufferedReader is = new BufferedReader(new InputStreamReader(System.in));
```

You can then read lines of text using the `readLine()` method. This method takes no argument and returns a `String` that is made up for you by `readLine()` containing the characters (converted to Unicode) from the next line of text in the file. When there are no more lines of text, the literal value `null` is returned:

```
public class CatStdin {

    public static void main(String[] av) {
        try (BufferedReader is =
                new BufferedReader(new InputStreamReader(System.in))) {
            String inputLine;

            while ((inputLine = is.readLine()) != null) {
                System.out.println(inputLine);
            }
        } catch (IOException e) {
            System.out.println("IOException: " + e);
        }
    }
}
```

To read a single `Integer` from the standard input, read a line and parse it using `Integer.parseInt()`. To read a series of integers, one per line, you could combine these with a functional style, since the `BufferedReader` has a `lines()` method that produces a `Stream<String>`:

```
public class ReadStdinIntsFunctional {
    private static Stream<Integer> parseIntSafe(String s) {
        try {
            return Stream.of(Integer.parseInt(s));
        } catch (NumberFormatException e) {
            return Stream.empty();
        }
    }

    public static void main(String[] args) throws IOException {
        try (BufferedReader is =
                new BufferedReader(new InputStreamReader(System.in));) {
            is.lines()
                .flatMap(ReadStdinIntsFunctional::parseIntSafe)
                .forEach(System.out::println);
        }
    }
}
```

The Console (Controlling Terminal)

The `Console` class is intended for reading directly from a program's controlling terminal. When you run an application from a *terminal window* or *command prompt window* on most systems, its console and its standard input are both connected to the terminal, by default. However, the standard input can be changed by piping or redirection on most OSes. If you really want to read from wherever the user is sitting, bypassing any indirections, then the `Console` class is usually your friend.

You cannot instantiate `Console` yourself; you must get an instance from the `System` class's `console()` method. You can then call methods such as `readLine()`, which behaves largely like the method of the same name in the `BufferedReader` class used in the previous recipe.

The following code shows an example of prompting for a name and reading it from the console:

main/src/main/java/io/ConsoleRead.java

```
public class ConsoleRead {
    public static void main(String[] args) {
        String name = System.console().readLine("What is your name?");
        System.out.println("Hello, " + name.toUpperCase());
    }
}
```

One complication is that the `System.console()` method can return `null` if the console isn't connected. Annoyingly, some IDEs, including Eclipse, don't manage to set up a controlling terminal when you use the Run As→Java Application mechanism. So production-quality code should always check for `null` before trying to use the `Console`. If it fails, use a logger or just plain `System.out`.

One facility the `Console` class is quite useful for is reading a password without having it echo. This has been a standard facility of command-line applications for decades, as the most obvious way of preventing *shoulder surfing*—somebody looking over your shoulder to see your password. Nonecho password reading is now supported in Java: the `Console` class has a `readPassword()` method that takes a `prompt` argument, intended to be used like: `cons.readPassword("Password:")`. This method returns an array of bytes, which can be used directly in some encryption and security APIs, or can easily be converted into a `String`. It is generally advised to overwrite the byte array after use to prevent security leaks when other code can access the stack, although the benefits of this are probably reduced when you've constructed a `String`. There's an example of this in the online code in *io/ReadPassword.java*.

10.4 Printing with Formatter and printf

Problem

You want an easy way to use `java.util.Formatter` class's capability for simple print-ing tasks.

Solution

Use `Formatter` for printing values with fine-grained control over the formatting. Use `String.format()` or `PrintWriter.printf()` / `PrintStream.printf()`.

Discussion

The `Formatter` class is patterned after C's `printf` routines. In fact, `PrintStream` and `PrintWriter` have convenience routines named `printf()` that simply delegate to the stream or writer's `format()` method, which uses a default `Formatter` instance. Unlike in C, however, Java is a strongly typed language, so invalid arguments will throw an exception rather than generating gibberish. There are also convenience routines `static String.format()` and `printf()` in `PrintWRiter`/`PrintStream` for use when you want to format a `String` without the bother of creating the `Formatter` explicitly.

The underlying `Formatter` class in `java.util` works on a `String` containing format codes. For each item that you want to format, you put a format code. The format code consists of a percent sign, optionally an argument number followed by a dollar sign, optionally a field width or precision, and a format type (e.g., d for decimal integer, that is, an integer with no decimal point, and f for floating point). A simple use might look like the following:

```
System.out.printf("%1$04d - the year of %2$f%n", 1956, Math.PI);
System.out.printf("%04d - the year of %f%n", 1956, Math.PI);
```

As shown in Figure 10-2, the "%1$04d" controls formatting of the year, and the "%2$f" controls formatting of the value of PI.[6]

---

[6] The central character in Yann Martel's novel *Life of Pi* would have been born in 1956, according to informa-tion in Wikipedia (*http://en.wikipedia.org/wiki/Life_of_pi*).

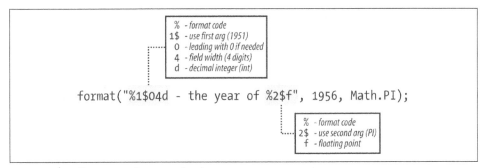

Figure 10-2. Format codes examined

Many format codes are available; Table 10-1 lists some of the more common ones. For a complete description, refer to the javadoc for `java.util.Formatter`.

Table 10-1. Formatter format codes

Code	Meaning
c	Character (argument must be `char` or integral type containing valid character value).
d	"decimal int"—integer to be printed as a decimal (radix 10) with no decimal point (argument must be integral type).
f	Floating-point value with decimal fraction (must be numeric); field width may be followed by decimal point and fractional digit field width; e.g., 7.2f.
e	Floating-point value in scientific notation.
g	Floating-point value, as per f or e, depending on magnitude.
s	Generic format; if value is null, prints "null"; else if arg implements `Formattable`, format as per `arg.for matTo()`; else format as per `arg.toString()`.
t	Date codes; follow with secondary code. Common date codes are shown in Table 10-2. Argument must be `long`, `Long`, `Calendar`, or `Date`.
n	Newline; insert the platform-dependent line ending character.
%	Insert a literal % character.

Note also that you may, but are not required to, put a *parameter order* number between the % and the format code. For example, in "%2$04d", the "2$" means to format the *second* parameter, regardless of the order of the parameters. This is primarily useful with dates (see the following example, where you need to format several different portions of the same `Date` or `Calendar`, or any time you want to format the same object more than once) and in internationalization, where different languages may require words to be in a different order within a sentence.

Some examples of using a `Formatter` are shown in Example 10-2.

Example 10-2. main/src/main/java/io/FormatterDemo.java

```
public class FormatterDemo {
    public static void main(String[] args) {

        // The arguments to all these format methods consist of
        // a format code String and 1 or more arguments.
        // Each format code consists of the following:
        // % - code lead-in
        // N$ - OPTIONAL parameter number (1-based) after the format code
        // N - field width
        // L - format letter (d: decimal(int); f: float; s: general; many more)
        // For the full(!) story, see javadoc for java.util.Formatter.

        // Most general (cumbersome) way of proceding.
        Formatter fmtr = new Formatter();
        Object result = fmtr.format("%1$04d - the year of %2$f", 1956, Math.PI);
        System.out.println(result);
        fmtr.close();

        // Shorter way using static String.format(), default parameter numbering.
        Object stringResult = String.format("%04d - the year of %f", 1956, Math.PI);
        System.out.println(stringResult);

        // A shorter way using PrintStream/PrintWriter.format, more in line with
        // other languages. But this way you should provide the newline delimiter
        // using %n (rather than \n as that is platform-dependent!).
        System.out.printf("%04d - the year of %f%n", 1956, Math.PI);

        // Format doubles with more control
        System.out.printf("PI is approximately %4.2f%n", Math.PI);
    }
}
```

Running FormatterDemo produces this:

```
C:> javac FormatterDates.java
C:> java io.FormatterDates
1956 - The year of 3.141593
1956 - The year of 3.141593
1956 - The year of 3.141593
PI is about 3.14
```

For formatting date and time objects, a large variety of format codes are available—about 40 in all. Date and time objects are discussed in Chapter 6. Table 10-3 shows the more common date/time format codes. Each must be preceded by a t, so to format the first argument as a year, you would use %1$tY.

Table 10-2. Formatting codes for dates and times

Format code	Meaning
Y	Year (at least four digits)
m	Month as two-digit (leading zeros) number
B	Locale-specific month name (b for abbreviated)
d	Day of month (two digits, leading zeros)
e	Day of month (one or two digits)
A	Locale-specific day of week (*a* for abbreviated)
H or I	Hour in 24-hour (H) or 12-hour (I) format (two digits, leading zeros)
M	Minute (two digits)
S	Second (two digits)
P/p	Locale-specific AM or PM in uppercase (if P) or lowercase (if p)
R or T	24-hour time combination: %tH:%tM (if R) or %tH:%tM:%tS (if T)
D	Date formatted as *%tm/%td/%ty*

In my opinion, embedding these codes directly in applications that you distribute or make available as web applications is often a bad idea, because any direct use of them assumes that you know the correct order to print these fields in all locales around the world. Trust me, you don't. Instead of these, I recommend the use of `Date` `TimeFormatter`, covered in Recipe 6.2, to control the order of arguments. However, for quick-and-dirty work, as well as for writing log or data files that must be in a given format because some other program reads them, these are OK.

Some date examples are shown in Example 10-3.

Example 10-3. main/src/main/java/io/FormatterDates.java

```java
public class FormatterDates {
    public static void main(String[] args) {

        // Format number as dates e.g., 2020-06-28
        System.out.printf("%4d-%02d-%2d%n", 2020, 6, 28);

        // Format fields directly from a Date object: multiple fields from "1$"
        // (hard-coded formatting for Date not advisable; see I/O chapter)
        LocalDate today = LocalDate.now();
        // Print in a form like e.g., "July 4, 2020"
        System.out.printf("Today is %1$tB %1$td, %1$tY%n", today);
    }
}
```

Running this `FormatterDates` class produces the following output:

```
C:> java io.FormatterDates
2020-06-28
Today is January 01, 2020
```

10.5 Scanning Input with StreamTokenizer

Problem

You need to scan a file with more fine-grained resolution than the `readLine()` method of the `BufferedReader` class and its subclasses.

Solution

Use a `StreamTokenizer`, `readLine()` and a `StringTokenizer`, the `Scanner` class (see Recipe 10.6), regular expressions (Chapter 4), or one of several third-party parser generators.

Discussion

Though you could, in theory, read a file one character at a time and analyze each character, that is a pretty low-level approach. The `read()` method in the `Reader` class is defined to return `int` so that it can use the time-honored value -1 (defined as EOF in Unix *<stdio.h>* for years) to indicate that you have read to the end of the file:

main/src/main/java/io/ReadCharsOneAtATime.java

```
public class ReadCharsOneAtATime {

    void doFile(Reader is) throws IOException {
        int c;
        while ((c=is.read( )) != -1) {
            System.out.print((char)c);
        }
    }
}
```

Notice the cast to `char`; the program compiles fine without it, but it does not print correctly because c is declared as `int`. Variable c must be declared `int` to be able to compare against the end-of-file value -1. For example, the integer value corresponding to capital A treated as an `int` prints as 65, whereas with `(char)` prints the character A.

We discussed the `StringTokenizer` class extensively in Recipe 3.1. The combination of `readLine()` and `StringTokenizer` provides a simple means of scanning a file. Suppose you need to read a file in which each line consists of a name like *user@host.domain*, and you want to split the lines into users and host addresses. You could use this:

```
public class ScanStringTok {

    public static void main(String[] av) throws IOException {
        if (av.length == 0)
            System.err.printf("Usage: %s filename [...]%n",
                ScanStringTok.class.getSimpleName());
        else
            for (int i=0; i<av.length; i++)
                process(av[i]);
    }

    static void process(String fileName) {
        String s = null;
        try (BufferedReader is =
                new BufferedReader(new FileReader(fileName));) {
            while ((s = is.readLine()) != null) {
                StringTokenizer st = new StringTokenizer(s, "@", true);
                String user = (String)st.nextElement();
                st.nextElement();
                String host = (String)st.nextElement();
                System.out.println("User name: " + user +
                    "; host part: " + host);

                // Do something useful with the user and host parts...
            }
        } catch (NoSuchElementException ix) {
            System.err.println("Malformed input " + s);
        } catch (IOException e) {
            System.err.println(e);
        }
    }
}
```

The StreamTokenizer class in java.util provides slightly more capabilities for scanning a file. It reads characters and assembles them into words, or tokens. It returns these tokens to you along with a type code describing the kind of token it found. This type code is one of four predefined types (StringTokenizer.TT_WORD, TT_NUMBER, TT_EOF, or TT_EOL for the end-of-line) or the char value of an ordinary character (such as 32 for the space character). Methods such as ordinaryCharacter() allow you to specify how to categorize characters, while others such as slashSlashComment() allow you to enable or disable features.

Example 10-4 shows a StreamTokenizer used to implement a simple immediate-mode stack-based calculator:

```
2 2 + =
4
22 7 / =
3.141592857
```

I read tokens as they arrive from the `StreamTokenizer`. Numbers are put on the stack. The four operators (+, -, *, and /) are immediately performed on the two elements at the top of the stack, and the result is put back on the top of the stack. The = operator causes the top element to be printed, but is left on the stack so that you can say this:

```
4 5 * = 2 / =
20.0
10.0
```

Example 10-4. main/src/main/java/io/SimpleCalcStreamTok.java (simple calculator using StreamTokenizer)

```java
public class SimpleCalcStreamTok {
    /** The StreamTokenizer input */
    protected  StreamTokenizer tf;
    /** The output file */
    protected PrintWriter out = new PrintWriter(System.out, true);
    /** The variable name (not used in this version) */
    protected String variable;
    /** The operand stack */
    protected Stack<Double> s = new Stack<>();

    /* Driver - main program */
    public static void main(String[] av) throws IOException {
        if (av.length == 0)
            new SimpleCalcStreamTok(
                new InputStreamReader(System.in)).doCalc();
        else
            for (int i=0; i<av.length; i++)
                new SimpleCalcStreamTok(av[i]).doCalc();
    }

    /** Construct by filename */
    public SimpleCalcStreamTok(String fileName) throws IOException {
        this(new FileReader(fileName));
    }

    /** Construct from an existing Reader */
    public SimpleCalcStreamTok(Reader rdr) throws IOException {
        tf = new StreamTokenizer(rdr);
        // Control the input character set:
        tf.slashSlashComments(true);    // treat "//" as comments
        tf.ordinaryChar('-');          // used for subtraction
        tf.ordinaryChar('/');      // used for division
    }

    /** Construct from a Reader and a PrintWriter
     */
    public SimpleCalcStreamTok(Reader in, PrintWriter out) throws IOException {
        this(in);
```

```
        setOutput(out);
}

/**
 * Change the output destination.
 */
public void setOutput(PrintWriter out) {
    this.out = out;
}

protected void doCalc() throws IOException {
    int iType;
    double tmp;

    while ((iType = tf.nextToken()) != StreamTokenizer.TT_EOF) {
        switch(iType) {
        case StreamTokenizer.TT_NUMBER: // Found a number, push value to stack
            push(tf.nval);
            break;
        case StreamTokenizer.TT_WORD:
            // Found a variable, save its name. Not used here.
            variable = tf.sval;
            break;
        case '+':
            // + operator is commutative.
            push(pop() + pop());
            break;
        case '-':
            // - operator: order matters.
            tmp = pop();
            push(pop() - tmp);
            break;
        case '*':
            // Multiply is commutative.
            push(pop() * pop());
            break;
        case '/':
            // Handle division carefully: order matters!
            tmp = pop();
            push(pop() / tmp);
            break;
        case '=':
            out.println(peek());
            break;
        default:
            out.println("What's this? iType = " + iType);
        }
    }
}
void push(double val) {
    s.push(Double.valueOf(val));
}
```

```
double pop() {
    return ((Double)s.pop()).doubleValue();
}
double peek() {
    return ((Double)s.peek()).doubleValue();
}
void clearStack() {
    s.removeAllElements();
}
}
```

10.6 Scanning Input with the Scanner Class

Problem

You want to scan a simple input file consisting of various numbers and strings in a known format.

Solution

Read with Scanner's next() methods.

Discussion

The Scanner class lets you read an input source by tokens, somewhat analogous to the StreamTokenizer described in Recipe 10.5. The Scanner is more flexible in some ways (it lets you break tokens based on spaces or regular expressions) but less in others (you need to know the kind of token you are reading). This class bears some resemblance to the C-language scanf() function, but in the Scanner you specify the input token types by calling methods like nextInt(), nextDouble(), and so on. Here is a simple example of scanning:

```
String sampleDate = "25 Dec 1988";

try (Scanner sDate = new Scanner(sampleDate)) {
    int dayOfMonth = sDate.nextInt();
    String month = sDate.next();
    int year = sDate.nextInt();
    System.out.printf("%d-%s-%02d%n", year, month, dayOfMonth);
}
```

The Scanner recognizes Java's eight built-in types, in addition to BigInteger and BigDecimal. It can also return input tokens as Strings or by matching regular expressions (see Chapter 4). Table 10-3 lists the "next" methods and corresponding "has" methods; the "has" method returns true if the corresponding "next" method would succeed. There is no nextString() method; just use next() to get the next token as a String.

Table 10-3. Scanner methods

Returned type	"has" method	"next" method	Comment
String	hasNext()	next()	The next complete token from this scanner
String	hasNext(Pattern)	next(Pattern)	The next string that matches the given regular expression (regex)
String	hasNext(String)	next(String)	The next token that matches the regex pattern constructed from the specified string
BigDeci mal	hasNextBigDeci mal()	nextBigDeci mal()	The next token of the input as a BigDecimal
BigIn teger	hasNextBigIn teger()	nextBigIn teger()	The next token of the input as a BigInteger
boolean	hasNextBoolean()	nextBoolean()	The next token of the input as a boolean
byte	hasNextByte()	nextByte()	The next token of the input as a byte
double	hasNextDouble()	nextDouble()	The next token of the input as a double
float	hasNextFloat()	nextFloat()	The next token of the input as a float
int	hasNextInt()	nextInt()	The next token of the input as an int
String	N/A	nextLine()	Reads up to the end-of-line, including the line ending
long	hasNextLong()	nextLong()	The next token of the input as a long
short	hasNextShort()	nextShort()	The next token of the input as a short

The Scanner class is constructed with an input source, which can be an InputStream, a String, or Readable (Readable is an interface that Reader and all its subclasses implement).

One way to use the Scanner class is based on the Iterator pattern, using while (scan ner.hasNext()) to control the iteration. Example 10-5 shows the simple calculator from Recipe 10.5 rewritten[6] to use the Scanner class.

Example 10-5. main/src/main/java/io/simpleCalcScanner.java (simple calculator using java.util.Scanner)

```
public class SimpleCalcScanner {
    /** The Scanner */
    protected Scanner scan;

    /** The output */
    protected PrintWriter out = new PrintWriter(System.out, true);
```

---

6 If this were code in a maintained project, I might factor out some of the common code among these two calculators, as well as the one in Recipe 5.12, and divide the code better using interfaces. However, this would
detract from the simplicity of self-contained examples.

```java
/** The variable name (not used in this version) */
protected String variable;

/** The operand stack; no operators are pushed,
 * so it can be a stack of Double
 */
protected Stack<Double> s = new Stack<>();

/* Driver - main program */
public static void main(String[] args) throws IOException {
    if (args.length == 0)
        new SimpleCalcScanner(
            new InputStreamReader(System.in)).doCalc();
    else
        for (String arg : args) {
            new SimpleCalcScanner(arg).doCalc();
        }
}

/** Construct a SimpleCalcScanner by name */
public SimpleCalcScanner(String fileName) throws IOException {
    this(new FileReader(fileName));
}

/** Construct a SimpleCalcScanner from an open Reader */
public SimpleCalcScanner(Reader rdr) throws IOException {
    scan = new Scanner(rdr);
}

/** Construct a SimpleCalcScanner from a Reader and a PrintWriter */
public SimpleCalcScanner(Reader rdr, PrintWriter pw) throws IOException {
    this(rdr);
    setWriter(pw);
}

/** Change the output to go to a new PrintWriter */
public void setWriter(PrintWriter pw) {
    out = pw;
}

protected void doCalc() throws IOException {
    double tmp;

    while (scan.hasNext()) {
        if (scan.hasNextDouble()) {
            push(scan.nextDouble());
        } else {
            String token;
            switch(token = scan.next()) {
            case "+":
                // Found + operator, perform it immediately.
```

```
                    push(pop() + pop());
                    break;
                case "-":
                    // Found - operator, perform it (order matters).
                    tmp = pop();
                    push(pop() - tmp);
                    break;
                case "*":
                    // Multiply is commutative.
                    push(pop() * pop());
                    break;
                case "/":
                    // Handle division carefully: order matters!
                    tmp = pop();
                    push(pop() / tmp);
                    break;
                case "=":
                    out.println(peek());
                    break;
                default:
                    out.println("What's this? " + token);
                    break;
            }
        }
    }
}

void push(double val) {
    s.push(Double.valueOf(val));
}

double pop() {
    return ((Double)s.pop()).doubleValue();
}

double peek() {
    return ((Double)s.peek()).doubleValue();
}

void clearStack() {
    s.removeAllElements();
}
}
```

10.7 Scanning Input with Grammatical Structure

Problem

You need to parse a file whose structure can be described as grammatical (in the sense of computer languages, not natural languages).

Solution

Use one of many parser generators.

Discussion

Although the `StreamTokenizer` class (see Recipe 10.5) and `Scanner` (see Recipe 10.6) are useful, they know only a limited number of tokens and have no way of specifying that the tokens must appear in a particular order. To do more advanced scanning, you need some special-purpose scanning tools. Parser generators have a long history in computer science. The best-known examples are the C-language `yacc` (Yet Another Compiler Compiler) and `lex`, released with Seventh Edition Unix in the 1970s and discussed in *lex & yacc* by Doug Brown et al. (O'Reilly), and their open source clones *bison* and *flex*. These tools let you specify the lexical structure of your input using some pattern language such as regular expressions (see Chapter 4). For example, you might say that an email address consists of a series of alphanumerics, followed by an at sign (@), followed by a series of alphanumerics with periods embedded, like this:

```
name:   [A-Za-z0-9]+@[A-Za-z0-0.]
or
name: \w+#[\w.]
```

The tool then writes code that recognizes the characters you have described. These tools also have a grammatical specification, which says, for example, that the keyword `EMAIL` must appear, followed by a colon, followed by a `name` token, as previously defined.

There are several good third-party parser generator tools for Java. They vary widely based on complexity, power, and ease of use:

- One of the best known and most elaborate is ANTLR (*http://www.antlr.org*).

- JavaCC is an open source project at *https://javacc.org*.

- JParsec lets you write the parser in straight Java, so it's all built at compile time (most of the others require a separate parse generation step, with the build and debugging issues that raises). JParsec is on GitHub (*https://github.com/abailly/jparsec*). * JFlex (*http://jflex.de*) and CUP (*http://www2.cs.tum.edu/projects/cup*) work together like the original *yacc* and *lex*, as grammar parser and lexical scanner, respectively.

- Parboiled uses *Parsing Expression Grammar* (PEG) to also build the parser at compile time. See GitHub (*https://github.com/sirthias/parboiled*) for more information. * The *Rats!* parser generator is part of the eXTensible Compiler Project (*http://cs.nyu.edu/rgrimm/xtc*) at New York University.

- There are others; a more complete list is maintained at Java Source (*http://java-source.net/open-source/parser-generators*).

These parser generators can be used to write grammars for a wide variety of programs, from simple calculators—such as the one in Recipe 10.6—through HTML and CORBA/IDL, up to full Java and C/C++ parsers. Examples of these are included with the downloads. Unfortunately, the learning curve for parsers in general precludes providing a simple and comprehensive example here, let alone comparing them intelligently. Refer to the documentation and the numerous examples provided with each distribution.

As an alternative to using one of these, you could simply roll your own recursive descent parser; and once you learn how to do so, you may find it's not really that difficult, quite possibly even less hassle than dealing with the extra parser generator software (depending on the complexity of the grammar involved, obviously).

Java developers have a range of choices, including simple line-at-a-time scanners using `StringTokenizer`, fancier token-based scanners using `StreamTokenizer`, a `Scanner` class to scan simple tokens (see Recipe 10.6), regular expressions (see Chapter 4), and third-party solutions including grammar-based scanners based on the parsing tools listed here.

Understanding I/O Options: StandardOpenOptions, FileAttribute, PosixFileAttribute, and More

There are several sets of options that can be applied when creating or opening a file. The main option sets that can be applied include those listed in Table 10-4:

Table 10-4. Sets of options

Name	Examples	Usage/notes
`CopyOption`	`StandardCopyOp tion.REPLACE_EXISTING`	`Files` methods that copy
`LinkOption`	`LinkOption.NOFOL LOW_LINKS`	`Files` methods that write data or read attributes
`FileAttribute`		Name-value pair, used in `Files.cre ate*()` methods
`OpenOption`	`StandardOpenOp tion.READ,APPEND`	`Files.new{In,Out}put Stream()`
`PosixFilePermis sion`	`OWNER_READ,OTHER_WRITE`	`FileAttribute`
`PosixFilePermis sions`	`Set<PosixFilePermission>`	Conversions to/from rwx strings

A list of the standard OpenOption values is in Table 10-5. These control how a file is to be accessed.

Table 10-5. OpenOption StandardOpenOption values

Name	Meaning
APPEND	Write at the end of an existing file instead of overwriting it.
CREATE	Create the file if it does not exist.
CREATE_NEW	Create the file only if it is new; fails with FileAlreadyExistsExcep tion if file already exists.
DELETE_ON_CLOSE	Delete the file when the stream is closed. Useful for temporary files.
DSYNC	Write data synchronously, i.e., every write is to be synchronized to disk immediately.
READ	Open the file for reading.
SPARSE	Create as a sparse file, e.g., for random-access writing.
SYNC	Write data and metadata synchronously, i.e., every write or attribute change is to be synchronized to disk immediately.
TRUNCATE_EXISTING	If the file exists, open for writing at the beginning, removing all contents at open time.
WRITE	Open for write access.

POSIX is the IEEE's Portable Operating System Specification for Unix-like operating systems. Java's PosixPermission and its wrapper PosixPermissions are used to control who can do what to a file on disk. These are based on the Unix/POSIX permissions laid down in early Unix systems in the early 1970s. There are three actors: owner (which Unix calls user), group, and other (everyone else). Groups is a Unix/POSIX mechanism: a user can be in one or many groups and has permissions based on all the groups they are in; this is an early form of privilege separation. There are three permissions: read, write, and execute. The latter grants permission to execute a file, but is also used to grant permission to search (list) a directory. For decades these have been expressed as a nine-character permissions string. For example, rwxr–r-- means the user has read, write, and execute permissions on a given file; other members of the file owner's group have read-only access, and everyone else also has read-only access. The PosixPermissions wrapper class has methods for converting between these concise strings and a Set of individual PosixPermission enum constants. The enum constants are the nine combinations of OWNER, GROUP, and OTHERS with READ, WRITE, and EXECUTE. Here is a JShell example showing these file permission conversion routines:

```
jshell> Set<PosixFilePermission> perms =
  PosixFilePermissions.fromString("rwxr-xr--");
perms ==> [OWNER_READ, OWNER_WRITE, OWNER_EXECUTE, GROUP_READ,
  GROUP_EXECUTE, OTHERS_READ]
```

```
jshell> Set<PosixFilePermission> nPerms =
  Set.of(PosixFilePermission.OWNER_READ, PosixFilePermission.GROUP_READ);
nPerms ==> [GROUP_READ, OWNER_READ]

jshell> PosixFilePermissions.toString(nPerms)
$7 ==> "r--r-----"
```

You can further convert the Set<PosixFilePermission> into a FileAttribute to be used with the Files class createFile() or createDirectory() operations:

```
jshell> PosixFilePermissions.asFileAttribute(nPerms)
$8 ==> java.nio.file.attribute.PosixFilePermissions$1@ed17bee

jshell> $8.name()
$9 ==> "posix:permissions"

jshell> $8.value()
$10 ==> [OWNER_READ, GROUP_READ]

jshell> Files.createFile(Path.of("/tmp/xx"), $8);
$41 ==> /tmp/xx

jshell> /exit

$ ls -l /tmp/xx
-r--r----- 1 ian  wheel  0 Dec 23 11:14 /tmp/xx
$
```

We see the file was created with only owner-read and group-read permissions, as requested. Note that on *nix systems there is a user setting umask that may remove or mask out permissions, so what you ask for may not be exactly what you get.

You can examine the attributes of a file using the FileAttribute interface or its filesystem-specific subtypes. Here we'll use the PosixFileAttributeView to show the owner and permissions of the file we created:

```
PosixFileAttributes attrs =
    Files.getFileAttributeView(filePath,
        PosixFileAttributeView.class)
    .readAttributes();
System.out.format("File %s Owned by %s has perms %s%n",
    filePath,
    attrs.owner().getName(),
    PosixFilePermissions.toString(attrs.permissions()));
```

There are other filesystem-specific views, such as DosFilewAttributeView for use on FAT filesystems. FAT was copied from CPM-86 into the earliest releases of MS-DOS, and expanded versions of it are still in use on USB memory cards and in consumer devices.

10.8 Copying a File

Problem

You need to copy a file in its entirety.

Solution

Use one of the Java 11 `Files.copy()` methods. If on an older release, use the explicit read and write methods in the `Readers`/`Writers` or `InputStream`/`OutputStreams`.

Discussion

The `Files` class has several overloads of a copy method that makes quick work of this requirement:

```
Path copy(Path, Path, CopyOption...) throws java.io.IOException;
long copy(InputStream, Path, CopyOption...) throws IOException;
long copy(Path, OutputStream) throws IOException;
```

For example:

```
Path p = Paths.get("my_new_file");
InputStream is = // open some file for reading
long newFileSize = Files.copy(is, p);
```

Long ago, Java's I/O facilities did not package a lot of the common operations like copying one file to another or reading a file into a `String`. So back then I wrote my own package of helper methods. Users of older JDK versions may want to use `FileIO` from my utilities package `com.darwinsys.util`. Here's a simple demo program that uses `FileIO` to copy a source file to a backup file:

main/src/demo/java/io/FileIoDemo.java

```
package com.darwinsys.io;

import java.io.IOException;

public class FileIoDemo {
    public static void main(String[] av) {
        try {
            FileIO.copyFile("FileIO.java", "FileIO.bak");
            FileIO.copyFile("FileIO.class", "FileIO-class.bak");
        } catch (IOException e) {
            System.err.println(e);
        }
    }
}
```

My `copyFile` method takes several forms, depending on whether you have two file-names, a filename and a `PrintWriter`, and so on. The code for `FileIO` itself is not shown here but is online, in the darwinsys API download.

10.9 Reassigning the Standard Streams

Problem

You need to reassign one or more of the standard streams `System.in`, `System.out`, or `System.err`.

Solution

Construct an `InputStream` or `PrintStream` as appropriate, and pass it to the appropriate set method in the `System` class.

Discussion

The ability to reassign these streams corresponds to what Unix (or DOS command line) users think of as *redirection*, or *piping*. This mechanism is commonly used to make a program read from or write to a file without having to explicitly open it and go through every line of code changing the read, write, print, etc. calls to refer to a different stream object. The open operation is performed by the command-line interpreter in Unix or DOS or by the calling class in Java.

Although you could just assign a new `PrintStream` to the variable `System.out`, best practice is to use the defined method to replace it:

```
String LOGFILENAME = "error.log";
System.setErr(new PrintStream(new FileOutputStream(LOGFILENAME)));
System.out.println("Please look for errors in " + LOGFILENAME);
// Now assume this is somebody else's code; you'll see it
//   writing to stderr...
int[] a = new int[5];
a[10] = 0;     // here comes an ArrayIndexOutOfBoundsException
```

The stream you use can be one that you've opened, as here, or one you inherited:

```
System.setErr(System.out);     // merge stderr and stdout to same output file.
```

It could also be a stream connected to or from another `Process` you've started (see Recipe 18.1), a network socket, or a URL. Anything that gives you a stream can be used.

10.10 Duplicating a Stream as It Is Written; Reassigning Standard Streams

Problem

You want anything written to a stream, such as the standard output System.out or the standard error System.err, to appear there but *also* be logged in to a file.

Solution

Subclass PrintStream and have its write() methods write to two streams. Then use system.setErr() or setOut() to replace the existing standard stream with a Print Stream subclass.

Discussion

Some classes are meant to be subclassed. Here we're just subclassing PrintStream and adding a bit of functionality: a second PrintStream! I wrote a class called TeePrint Stream, named after the ancient Unix command *tee*. That command allowed you to duplicate, or tee off (from plumber's pipe tee, not the game of golf or the local pest) a copy of the data being written on a pipeline between two programs.

The original Unix *tee* command is used like this: the | character creates a pipeline in which the standard output of one program becomes the standard input to the next. This often-used example of pipes shows how many users are logged into a Unix server:

```
who | wc -l
```

This runs the *who* program (which lists who is logged in to the system, one name per line, along with the terminal port and login time) and sends its output, not to the terminal, but rather into the standard input of the word count (*wc*) program. Here, *wc* is being asked to count lines, not words, hence the -l option. To *tee* a copy of the intermediate data into a file, you might say:

```
who | tee wholist | wc -l
```

which creates a file *wholist* containing the data. For the curious, the file *wholist* might look something like this:

```
ian      ttyC0    Mar 14 09:59
ben      ttyC3    Mar 14 10:23
ian      ttyp4    Mar 14 13:46  (laptop.darwinsys.com)
```

So both the previous command sequences would print 3 as their output.

`TeePrintStream` is an attempt to capture the spirit of the *tee* command. It can be used like this:

```
System.setErr(new TeePrintStream(System.err, "err.log"));
// ...lots of code that occasionally writes to System.err... Or might.
```

`System.setErr()` is a means of specifying the destination of text printed to `System.err` (there are also `System.setOut()` and `System.setIn()`). This code results in any messages that printed to `System.err` to print to wherever `System.err` was previously directed (normally the terminal, but possibly a text window in an IDE) and to the file *err.log*.

This technique is not limited to the three standard streams. A `TeePrintStream` can be passed to any method that wants a `PrintStream`. Or, for that matter, an `Output Stream`. And you can adapt the technique for `BufferedInputStreams`, `PrintWriters`, `BufferedReaders`, and so on.

Example 10-6 shows the source code for `TeePrintStream`.

Example 10-6. main/src/main/java/io/TeePrintStream.java

```java
public class TeePrintStream extends PrintStream {
    /** The original/direct print stream */
    protected PrintStream parent;

    /** The filename we are tee-ing too, if known;
     * intended for use in future error reporting.
     */
    protected String fileName;

    /** The name for when the input filename is not known */
    private static final String UNKNOWN_NAME = "(opened Stream)";

    /** Construct a TeePrintStream given an existing PrintStream,
     * an opened OutputStream, and a boolean to control auto-flush.
     * This is the main constructor, to which others delegate via "this".
     */
    public TeePrintStream(PrintStream orig, OutputStream os, boolean flush)
    throws IOException {
        super(os, true);
        fileName = UNKNOWN_NAME;
        parent = orig;
    }

    /** Construct a TeePrintStream given an existing PrintStream and
     * an opened OutputStream.
     */
    public TeePrintStream(PrintStream orig, OutputStream os)
    throws IOException {
        this(orig, os, true);
```

```
    }

    /* Construct a TeePrintStream given an existing Stream and a filename.
     */
    public TeePrintStream(PrintStream os, String fn) throws IOException {
        this(os, fn, true);
    }

    /* Construct a TeePrintStream given an existing Stream, a filename,
     * and a boolean to control the flush operation.
     */
    public TeePrintStream(PrintStream orig, String fn, boolean flush)
    throws IOException {
        this(orig, new FileOutputStream(fn), flush);
        fileName = fn;
    }

    /** Return true if either stream has an error. */
    public boolean checkError() {
        return parent.checkError() || super.checkError();
    }

    /** override write(). This is the actual "tee" operation. */
    public void write(int x) {
        parent.write(x);      // "write once;
        super.write(x);       // write somewhere else."
    }

    /** override write(). This is the actual "tee" operation. */
    public void write(byte[] x, int o, int l) {
        parent.write(x, o, l);    // "write once;
        super.write(x, o, l);     // write somewhere else."
    }

    /** Close both streams. */
    public void close() {
        parent.close();
        super.close();
    }

    /** Flush both streams. */
    public void flush() {
        parent.flush();
        super.flush();
    }
}
```

It's worth mentioning that I do *not* need to override all the polymorphic forms of
print() and println(). Because these all ultimately use one of the forms of write(),
if you override the print and println methods to do the *tee*-ing as well, you can get
several additional copies of the data written out.

10.11 Reading/Writing a Different Character Set

Problem

You need to read or write a text file using a particular encoding.

Solution

Convert the text to or from internal Unicode by specifying a converter when you construct an `InputStreamReader` or `PrintWriter`.

Discussion

Classes `InputStreamReader` and `OutputStreamWriter` are the bridge from byte-oriented `Streams` to character-based `Readers`. These classes read or write bytes and translate them to or from characters according to a specified character encoding. The UTF-16 character set used inside Java (`char` and `String` types) is a 16-bit character set. But most character sets—such as ASCII, Swedish, Spanish, Greek, Turkish, and many others—use only a small subset of that. In fact, many European language character sets fit nicely into 8-bit characters. Even the larger character sets (script-based and pictographic languages) don't all use the same bit values for each particular character. The encoding, then, is a mapping between Java characters and an external storage format for characters drawn from a particular national or linguistic character set.

To simplify matters, the `InputStreamReader` and `OutputStreamWriter` constructors are the only places where you can specify the name of an encoding to be used in this translation. If you do not specify an encoding, the platform's (or user's) default encoding is used. `PrintWriters`, `BufferedReaders`, and the like all use whatever encoding the `InputStreamReader` or `OutputStreamWriter` class uses. Because these bridge classes only accept `Stream` arguments in their constructors, the implication is that if you want to specify a nondefault converter to read or write a file on disk, you must start by constructing not a `FileReader` or `FileWriter`, but a `FileInputStream` or `FileOutputStream`!

```
// io/UseConverters.java
BufferedReader fromKanji = new BufferedReader(
    new InputStreamReader(new FileInputStream("kanji.txt"), "EUC_JP"));
PrintWriter toSwedish = new PrinterWriter(
    new OutputStreamWriter(new FileOutputStream("sverige.txt"), "Cp278"));
```

Not that it would necessarily make sense to read a single file from Kanji and output it in a Swedish encoding. For one thing, most fonts would not have all the characters of both character sets; and, at any rate, the Swedish encoding certainly has far fewer characters in it than the Kanji encoding. Besides, if that were all you wanted, you could use a JDK tool with the ill-fitting name *native2ascii* (see its documentation for details). A list of the supported encodings is also in the JDK documentation, in the file *docs/guide/internat/encoding.doc.html*. A more detailed description is found in Appendix B of *Java I/O*.

10.12 Those Pesky End-of-Line Characters

Problem

You really want to know about end-of-line characters.

Solution

Use \r and \n in whatever combination makes sense.

Discussion

If you are reading text (or bytes containing ASCII characters) in line mode using the readLine() method, you'll never see the end-of-line characters, and if you're using a PrintWriter with its println() method, the same applies. Thus you won't be cursed with having to figure out whether \n, \r, or \r\n appears at the end of each line.

If you want that level of detail, you have to read the characters or bytes one at a time, using the read() methods. The only time I've found this necessary is in networking code, where some of the line-mode protocols assume that the line ending is \r\n. Even here, though, you can still work in line mode. When writing, pass \r\n into the print() (not +deal with the characters:

```
outputSocket.print("HELO " + myName + "\r\n");
String response = inputSocket.readLine();
```

For the curious, the strange spelling of "hello" is used in SMTP, the mail sending protocol, where commands are four letters.

10.13 Beware Platform-Dependent File Code

Problem

Chastened by the previous recipe, you now wish to write only platform-independent code.

Solution

Use readLine() and println(). Avoid use of \n by itself; use File.separator if you must.

Discussion

As mentioned in Recipe 10.12, if you just use `readLine()` and `println()`, you won't have to think about the line endings. But a particular problem, especially for former programmers of C and related languages, is using the \n character in text strings to mean a newline. What is particularly distressing about this code is that it works—sometimes—usually on the developer's own platform. But it will probably fail someday, on some other system:

```
String myName;
public static void main(String[] argv) {
    BadNewline jack = new BadNewline("Jack Adolphus Schmidt, III");
    System.out.println(jack);
}
/**
 * DON'T DO THIS. THIS IS BAD CODE.
 */
public String toString() {
    return "BadNewlineDemo@" + hashCode() + "\n" + myName;
}

// The obvious Constructor is not shown for brevity; it's in the code
```

The real problem is not that it fails on some platforms, though. What's really wrong is that it mixes formatting and I/O, or tries to. Don't mix line-based display with `toString()`; avoid *multiline strings*—output from `toString()` or any other string-returning method. If you need to write multiple strings, then say what you mean:

```
String myName;
public static void main(String[] argv) {
    GoodNewline jack = new GoodNewline("Jack Adolphus Schmidt, III");
    jack.print(System.out);
}

protected void print(PrintStream out) {
    out.println(toString());   // classname and hashcode
    out.println(myName);       // print name  on next line
}
```

Alternatively, if you need multiple lines, you could return an array or `List` of strings.

10.14 Reading/Writing Binary Data

Problem

You need to read or write binary data, as opposed to text.

Solution

Use a `DataInputStream` or `DataOutputStream`.

Discussion

The `Stream` classes have been in Java since the beginning of time and are optimal for reading and writing bytes rather than characters. The data layer over them, comprising `DataInputStream` and `DataOutputStream`, is configured for reading and writing binary values, including all of Java's built-in types. Suppose that you want to write a binary integer plus a binary floating-point value into a file and read it back later. This code shows the writing part:

```
public class WriteBinary {
    public static void main(String[] argv) throws IOException {
        int i = 42;
        double d = Math.PI;
        String FILENAME = "binary.dat";
        DataOutputStream os = new DataOutputStream(
            new FileOutputStream(FILENAME));
        os.writeInt(i);
        os.writeDouble(d);
        os.close();
        System.out.println("Wrote " + i + ", " + d + " to file " + FILENAME);
    }
}
```

Should you need to write all the fields from an object, you should probably use one of the methods described in Recipe 12.6.

10.15 Reading and Writing JAR or ZIP Archives

Problem

You need to create and/or extract from a JAR archive or a file in the well-known ZIP archive format, as established by PkZip and used by Unix zip/unzip and WinZip.

Solution

You could use the *jar* program in the Java Development Kit because its file format is identical to the ZIP format with the addition of the *META-INF* directory to contain additional structural information. But because this is a book about programming, you are probably more interested in the `ZipFile` and `ZipEntry` classes and the stream classes to which they provide access.

Discussion

The class `java.util.zip.ZipFile` is not an I/O class *per se*, but a utility class that allows you to read or write the contents of a JAR or ZIP-format file.[6] When constructed, it creates a series of `ZipEntry` objects, one to represent each entry in the archive. In other words, the `ZipFile` represents the entire archive, and the `ZipEntry` represents one entry, or one file that has been stored (and compressed) in the archive. The `ZipEntry` has methods like `getName()`, which returns the name that the file had before it was put into the archive, and `getInputStream()`, which gives you an `Input Stream` that will transparently uncompress the archive entry by filtering it as you read it. To create a `ZipFile` object, you need either the name of the archive file or a `File` object representing it:

```
ZipFile zippy = new ZipFile(fileName);
```

To see whether a given file is present in the archive, you can call the `getEntry()` method with a filename. More commonly, you'll want to process all the entries; for this, use the `ZipFile` object to get a list of the entries in the archive, in the form of an `Enumeration` (see Recipe 7.6), as is done here:

```
Enumeration all = zippy.entries( );
while (all.hasMoreElements( )) {
    ZipEntry entry = (ZipEntry)all.nextElement( );
    ...
}
```

We can then process each entry as we wish. A simple listing program could be this:

```
if (entry.isDirectory( ))
    println("Directory: " + e.getName( ));
else
    println("File: " + e.getName( ));
```

A fancier version would extract the files. The program in Example 10-7 does both: it lists by default, but with the -x (extract) switch, it actually extracts the files from the archive.

Example 10-7. main/src/main/java/io/UnZip.java

```
public class UnZip {
    /** Constants for mode listing or mode extracting. */
    public static enum Mode {
        LIST,
        EXTRACT;
    }
```

---

6 There is no support for adding files to an existing archive, so make sure you put all the files in at once or be prepared to re-create the archive from scratch.

```java
/** Whether we are extracting or just printing TOC */
protected Mode mode = Mode.LIST;

/** The ZipFile that is used to read an archive */
protected ZipFile zippy;

/** The buffer for reading/writing the ZipFile data */
protected byte[] b = new byte[8092];

/** Simple main program, construct an UnZipper, process each
 * .ZIP file from argv[] through that object.
 */
public static void main(String[] argv) {
    UnZip u = new UnZip();

    for (int i=0; i<argv.length; i++) {
        if ("-x".equals(argv[i])) {
            u.setMode(Mode.EXTRACT);
            continue;
        }
        String candidate = argv[i];
        // System.err.println("Trying path " + candidate);
        if (candidate.endsWith(".zip") ||
            candidate.endsWith(".jar"))
                u.unZip(candidate);
        else System.err.println("Not a zip file? " + candidate);
    }
    System.err.println("All done!");
}

/** Set the Mode (list, extract). */
protected void setMode(Mode m) {
    mode = m;
}

/** Cache of paths we've mkdir()ed. */
protected SortedSet<String> dirsMade;

/** For a given Zip file, process each entry. */
public void unZip(String fileName) {
    dirsMade = new TreeSet<String>();
    try {
        zippy = new ZipFile(fileName);
        @SuppressWarnings("unchecked")
        Enumeration<ZipEntry> all = (Enumeration<ZipEntry>) zippy.entries();
        while (all.hasMoreElements()) {
            getFile((ZipEntry)all.nextElement());
        }
    } catch (IOException err) {
        System.err.println("IO Error: " + err);
        return;
    }
```

```
        }

        protected boolean warnedMkDir = false;

        /** Process one file from the zip, given its name.
         * Either print the name, or create the file on disk.
         */
        protected void getFile(ZipEntry e) throws IOException {
            String zipName = e.getName();
            switch (mode) {
            case EXTRACT:
                if (zipName.startsWith("/")) {
                    if (!warnedMkDir)
                        System.out.println("Ignoring absolute paths");
                    warnedMkDir = true;
                    zipName = zipName.substring(1);
                }
                // if a directory, just return. We mkdir for every file,
                // since some widely used Zip creators don't put out
                // any directory entries, or put them in the wrong place.
                if (zipName.endsWith("/")) {
                    return;
                }
                // Else must be a file; open the file for output
                // Get the directory part.
                int ix = zipName.lastIndexOf('/');
                if (ix > 0) {
                    String dirName = zipName.substring(0, ix);
                    if (!dirsMade.contains(dirName)) {
                        File d = new File(dirName);
                        // If it already exists as a dir, don't do anything
                        if (!(d.exists() && d.isDirectory())) {
                            // Try to create the directory, warn if it fails
                            System.out.println("Creating Directory: " + dirName);
                            if (!d.mkdirs()) {
                                System.err.println(
                                "Warning: unable to mkdir " + dirName);
                            }
                            dirsMade.add(dirName);
                        }
                    }
                }
                System.err.println("Creating " + zipName);
                FileOutputStream os = new FileOutputStream(zipName);
                InputStream  is = zippy.getInputStream(e);
                int n = 0;
                while ((n = is.read(b)) >0)
                    os.write(b, 0, n);
                is.close();
                os.close();
                break;
            case LIST:
```

```
        // Not extracting, just list
        if (e.isDirectory()) {
            System.out.println("Directory " + zipName);
        } else {
            System.out.println("File " + zipName);
        }
        break;
    default:
        throw new IllegalStateException("mode value (" + mode + ") bad");
    }
    }
}
```

See Also

People sometimes confuse the ZIP archive file format with the similarly named gzip compression format. Gzip-compressed files can be read or written with the GZipIn putStream and GZipOutputStream classes from java.io.

10.16 Finding Files in a Filesystem-Neutral Way with getResource() and getResourceAsStream()

Problem

You want to load objects or files without referring to their absolute location in the filesystem. You might want to do this for one of the following reasons:

- You are in a server (Java EE) environment.
- You want to be independent of file paths.
- You want to read a file in a unit test.
- You expect users to deploy the resource "somewhere" on the LASSPATH (possibly even inside a JAR file).

Solution

Use getClass() or getClassLoader() and either getResource() or getResourceAs Stream().

Discussion

There are three varieties of getResource() methods, some of which exist (with the exact same signature) both in the Class class (see Chapter 17) and in the Class

---

Loader class (see Recipe 17.5). The methods in `Class` delegate to the `ClassLoader`, so there is little difference between them. The methods are summarized in Table 10-6.

Table 10-6. The getResource methods*

Method signature	In Class	In ClassLoader
`public InputStream getResourceAsStream(String);`	Y	Y
`public URL getResource(String);`	Y	Y
`public Enumeration<URL> getResources(String) throws IOException;`	N	Y

The first method is designed to quickly and easily locate a resource, or file, on your CLASSPATH. Using the `Class` version, or the other one with a standard `ClassLoader` implementation, the resource can be a physical file or a file inside a JAR file. If you define your own classloader, your imagination is the limit, as long as it can be represented as an `InputStream`. This is commonly used as shown here:

```
InputStream is = getClass().getResourceAsStream("foo.properties");
// then do something with the InputStream...
```

The second form returns a URL, which can be interpreted in various ways (see the discussion of reading from a URL in Recipe 12.1).

The third form, only usable with a `ClassLoader` instance, returns an `Enumeration` of URL objects. This is intended to return all the resources that match a given string; remember that a CLASSPATH can consist of pretty much any number of directories and/or JAR files, so this will search all of them. This is useful for finding a series of configuration files and merging them, perhaps. Or for finding out whether there is more than one resource/file of a given name on your CLASSPATH.

Note that the resource name can be given as either a relative path or as an absolute path. Assuming you are using Maven (see Recipe 1.7), then for the absolute path, place the file relative to *src/main/resources/* directory. For the relative path, place the file in the same directory as your source code. The same rules apply in an IDE, assuming you have made *src/main/java* and *src/main/resources* be treated as source folders in your IDE configuration. The idea is that resource files get copied to your CLASSPATH folder. For example, if you have two resource files, *src/main/resources/one.txt* and *src/main/java/MyPackage/two.txt*, and your project is configured as described, these two lines would work, if accessed from a program in `MyPackage`:

```
Class<?> c = getClass();
InputStream isOne = getResourceAsStream("/one.txt");   // note leading slash
InputStream isTwo = getResourceAsStream("two.txt");    // without leading slash
```

In either case, getResource() and getResourceAsStream() will return null if they don't find the resource; you should always check for null to guard against faulty deployment. If it doesn't find anything matching, getResources() will return an empty Enumeration.

If the file path has slashes between components (as in *package/subpackage*), the name you path into any of the getResource methods should have a period in place of the slash.

10.17 Getting File Information: Files and Path

Problem

You need to know all you can about a given file on disk.

Solution

Use java.nio.file.Files methods.

Discussion

The java.nio.file.Files class has a plural name both to differentiate it from the legacy File class that it replaces and to remind us that it sometimes works on multiple files. There are two types of static methods in the Files class, information and operational. The informational ones (see Table 10-7) simply give you information about one file, such as boolean exists() or long size(). The operational ones (see Table 10-8) either make changes to the filesystem or open a file for reading or writing. Each of the operational ones can throw the checked exception IOException; only a few of the informational ones can.

The vast majority of these methods have argument(s) of type java.nio.file.Path. A Path represents a path into the filesystem, that is, a set of directories and possibly a file, like "C:\Users\user\Downloads" or "/home/ian/Downloads". The path may or may not exist as a file on disk at the time you create a Path representing it. The Files class can tell you whether the file represented by a given Path exists, can bring that Path into being as a file or as a directory, and can either change the corresponding file's attributes or even destroy it if it does exist. Path objects are easily created with Path.of(String name), which has several overloads.

Files in conjunction with Path offers pretty well everything you'd need to write a full-blown file manager application, let alone the needs of a more typical application needing file information and/or directory access. The `Files` class has a series of static `boolean` methods that give basic information.

Table 10-7. Public static informational methods in java.nio.file.Files

Return type	Method	Notes
boolean	exists(Path, LinkOption...);	
Object	getAttribute(Path, String, LinkOption...);	
<V extends FileAttributeView> V	getFileAttributeView(Path, Class<V>, LinkOption...);	
FileTime	getLastModifiedTime(Path, LinkOption...);	
UserPrincipal	getOwner(Path, LinkOption...);	
Set<PosixFilePermission>	getPosixFilePermissions(Path, LinkOption...);	
boolean	isDirectory(Path, LinkOption...);	
boolean	isExecutable(Path);	If Executable by current user
boolean	isHidden(Path);	If a "dot file" on Unix, or "hidden" attribute set on some OSes
boolean	isReadable(Path);	If Readable by current user
boolean	isRegularFile(Path, LinkOption...);	
boolean	isSameFile(Path, Path) throws IOException;	Has to unwind filesys complexities like "..", symlinks, ...
boolean	isSymbolicLink(Path);	
boolean	isWritable(Path);	If Writable by current user
long	mismatch(Path, Path);	
boolean	notExists(Path, LinkOption...);	
String	probeContentType(Path) throws IOException;	Tries to return MIME type of data
Path	readSymbolicLink(Path) throws IOException;	
long	size(Path);	

By "current user" we mean the account under which the current JVM instance is being run.

Most of these methods are demonstrated in Example 10-8.

Example 10-8. main/src/main/java/io/FilesInfos.java

```
println("exists", Files.exists(Path.of("/")));
println("isDirectory", Files.isDirectory(Path.of("/")));
println("isExecutable", Files.isExecutable(Path.of("/bin/cat")));
println("isHidden", Files.isHidden(Path.of("~/.profile")));
println("isReadable", Files.isReadable(Path.of("lines.txt")));
println("isRegularFile", Files.isRegularFile(Path.of("lines.txt")));
println("isSameFile", Files.isSameFile(Path.of("lines.txt"),
    Path.of("../main/lines.txt")));
```

```
println("isSymbolicLink", Files.isSymbolicLink(Path.of("/var")));
println("isWritable", Files.isWritable(Path.of("/tmp")));
println("isDirectory", Files.isDirectory(Path.of("/")));
println("notexists",
    Files.notExists(Path.of("no_such_file_as_skjfsjljwerjwj")));
println("probeContentType", Files.probeContentType(Path.of("lines.txt")));
println("readSymbolicLink", Files.readSymbolicLink(Path.of("/var")));
println("size", Files.size(Path.of("lines.txt")));
```

Obviously the paths chosen are somewhat system-specific, but when run on my Unix system, the `boolean` methods all returned `true`, and the last three returned this:

```
probeContentType returned text/plain
readSymbolicLink returned private/var
size returned 78
```

Table 10-8 shows the methods that make changes to filesystem entities.

Table 10-8. Public static operational methods in java.nio.file.Files

Return type	Method
long	copy(InputStream, Path, CopyOption...);
long	copy(Path, OutputStream);
Path	copy(Path, Path, CopyOption...);
Path	createDirectories(Path, FileAttribute<?>...);
Path	createDirectory(Path, FileAttribute<?>...);
Path	createFile(Path, FileAttribute<?>...);
Path	createLink(Path, Path);
Path	createSymbolicLink(Path, Path, FileAttribute<?>...);
Path	createTempDirectory(Path, String, FileAttribute<?>...);
Path	createTempDirectory(String, FileAttribute<?>...);
Path	createTempFile(Path, String, String, FileAttribute<?>...);
Path	createTempFile(String, String, FileAttribute<?>...);
void	delete(Path);
boolean	deleteIfExists(Path);
Stream<Path>	find(Path, int, BiPredicate<Path, BasicFileAttributes>, FileVisitOption...);
Stream<String>	lines(Path);
Stream<String>	lines(Path, Charset);
Stream<Path>	list(Path);
Path	move(Path, Path, CopyOption...);
BufferedReader	newBufferedReader(Path);
BufferedReader	newBufferedReader(Path, Charset);
BufferedWriter	newBufferedWriter(Path, Charset, OpenOption...);
BufferedWriter	newBufferedWriter(Path, OpenOption...);

Return type	Method
SeekableByteChannel	newByteChannel(Path, OpenOption...);
SeekableByteChannel	newByteChannel(Path, Set<? extends OpenOption>, FileAttribute<?>...);
DirectoryStream<Path>	newDirectoryStream(Path);
DirectoryStream<Path>	newDirectoryStream(Path, String);
InputStream	newInputStream(Path, OpenOption...);
OutputStream	newOutputStream(Path, OpenOption...);
byte[]	readAllBytes(Path);
List<String>	readAllLines(Path);
List<String>	readAllLines(Path, Charset);
<A extends BasicFileAttributes> A	readAttributes(Path, Class<A>, LinkOption...);
Map<String, Object>	readAttributes(Path, String, LinkOption...);
String	readString(Path);
String	readString(Path, Charset);
Path	setAttribute(Path, String, Object, LinkOption...);
Path	setLastModifiedTime(Path, FileTime);
Path	setOwner(Path, UserPrincipal);
Path	setPosixFilePermissions(Path, Set<PosixFilePermission>);
Path	write(Path, Iterable<? extends CharSequence>, Charset, OpenOption...);
Path	write(Path, Iterable<? extends CharSequence>, OpenOption...);
Path	write(Path, byte[], OpenOption...);
Path	writeString(Path, CharSequence, Charset, OpenOption...);
Path	writeString(Path, CharSequence, OpenOption...);

Path is an interface whose implementation is provided by a provider class called File system. Path has many methods, listed in Table 10-9.

Table 10-9. Public static operational methods in java.nio.file.Path

Access	Return type	Method
static	Path	of(String, String...);
static	Path	of(URI);
abstract	FileSystem	getFileSystem();
abstract	boolean	isAbsolute();
abstract	Path	getRoot();
abstract	Path	getFileName();
abstract	Path	getParent();
abstract	int	getNameCount();
abstract	Path	getName(int);
abstract	Path	subpath(int, int);

Access	Return type	Method
abstract	boolean	startsWith(Path);
default	boolean	startsWith(String);
abstract	boolean	endsWith(Path);
default	boolean	endsWith(String);
abstract	Path	normalize();
abstract	Path	resolve(Path);
default	Path	resolve(String);
default	Path	resolveSibling(Path);
default	Path	resolveSibling(String);
abstract	Path	relativize(Path);
abstract	URI	toUri();
abstract	Path	toAbsolutePath();
abstract	Path	toRealPath(LinkOption...) throws IOException;
default	File	toFile();
abstract	WatchKey	register(WatchService, WatchEvent$Kind<?>[], WatchEvent$Modifier...) throws IOException;
default	WatchKey	register(WatchService, WatchEvent$Kind<?>...) throws IOException;
default	Iterator<Path>	iterator();
abstract	int	compareTo(Path);
abstract	boolean	equals(Object);
abstract	int	hashCode();
abstract	String	toString();
default	int	compareTo(Object);

To find the information about one file, you can use the informational methods in Files and Path, as shown in Example 10-9.

Example 10-9. main/src/main/java/dir_file/FileStatus.java (getting file information)

```java
public class FileStatus {
    public static void main(String[] argv) throws IOException {

        // Ensure that a filename (or something) was given in argv[0]
        if (argv.length == 0) {
            System.err.println("Usage: FileStatus filename");
            System.exit(1);
        }
        for (String a : argv) {
            status(a);
        }
    }
```

```
public static void status(String fileName) throws IOException {
    System.out.println("---" + fileName + "---");

    // Construct a Path object for the given file.
    Path p = Path.of(fileName);

    // See if it actually exists
    if (!Files.exists(p)) {
        System.out.println("file not found");
        System.out.println();     // Blank line
        return;
    }
    // Print full name
    System.out.println("Canonical name " + p.normalize());
    // Print parent directory if possible
    Path parent = p.getParent();
    if (parent != null) {
        System.out.println("Parent directory: " + parent);
    }
    // Check if the file is readable
    if (Files.isReadable(p)) {
        System.out.println(fileName + " is readable.");
    }
    // Check if the file is writable
    if (Files.isWritable(p)) {
        System.out.println(fileName + " is writable.");
    }

    // See if file, directory, or other. If file, print size.
    if (Files.isRegularFile(p)) {
        // Report on the file's size and possibly its type
        System.out.printf("File size is %d bytes, content type %s\n",
                Files.size(p),
                Files.probeContentType(p));
    } else if (Files.isDirectory(p)) {
        System.out.println("It's a directory");
    } else {
        System.out.println("I dunno! Neither a file nor a directory!");
    }

    // Report on the modification time.
    final FileTime d = Files.getLastModifiedTime(p);
    System.out.println("Last modified " + d);

    System.out.println();     // blank line between entries
}
```

When run on MS Windows with the three arguments shown, it produces this output:

```
C:\javasrc\dir_file>java dir_file.FileStatus    / /tmp/id /autoexec.bat
---/---
Canonical name C:\
File is readable.
```

```
File is writable.
Last modified 1970-01-01T00:00:00.00000Z
It's a directory

---/tmp/id---
file not found

---/autoexec.bat---
Canonical name C:\AUTOEXEC.BAT
Parent directory: \
File is readable.
File is writable.
Last modified 2019-10-13T12:43:05.123918Z
File size is 308 bytes.
```

As you can see, the so-called *canonical name* not only includes a leading directory root of *C:*, but also has had the name converted to uppercase. You can tell I ran that on Windows. That version of Windows did not maintain timestamps on directories; the value 0L gets interpreted as January 1, 1970 (not accidentally the same time base as used on Unix since that time). On Unix, it behaves differently:

```
$ java dir_file.FileStatus / /tmp/id /autoexec.bat
---/---
Canonical name /
File is readable.
It's a directory
Last modified 2019-12-16T01:14:05.226108Z

---/tmp/id---
Canonical name /tmp/id
Parent directory: /tmp
File is readable.
File is writable.
File size is 36768 bytes, content type null
Last modified 2019-12-21T18:46:27.402108Z

---/autoexec.bat---
file not found

$
```

A typical Unix system has no *autoexec.bat* file. And Unix filenames (like those on a Mac) can consist of upper- and lowercase characters: what you type is what you get.

Legacy compatibility

To use a Path with legacy code that needs the older java.io.File, simply use File oldType = Path.toFile():

```
jshell> Path p = Path.of("/");
p ==> /
```

```
jshell> File f = p.toFile();
f ==> /
```

To go the other way, the File class has been retrofitted with a toPath() method:

```
jshell> File f = new File("/");
f ==> /

jshell> Path p = f.toPath();
p ==> /
```

10.18 Creating a New File or Directory

Problem

You need to create a new file on disk but not write any data into it; you need to create a directory before you can create files in it.

Solution

For an empty file, use a java.nio.file.Files object's createFile(Path) method. Use the Files class's createDirectory() or createDirectories() method to create a directory.

Discussion

Files

You could easily create a new file by constructing a FileOutputStream or FileWriter (see Recipe 12.6). But then you'd have to remember to close it as well. Sometimes you want a file to exist, but you don't want to bother putting anything into it. This might be used, for example, as a simple form of interprogram communication: one program could test for the presence of a file and interpret that to mean that the other program has reached a certain state. Example 10-10 is code that simply creates an empty file for each name you give.

Example 10-10. main/src/main/java/dir_file/Creat.java (creation of a file on disk)

```
/** Create file(s) by name. Final "e" omitted in homage to UNIX system call. */
public class Creat {
    public static void main(String[] argv) throws IOException {

        // Ensure that a filename (or something) was given in argv[0]
        if (argv.length == 0) {
            throw new IllegalArgumentException("Usage: Creat filename [...]");
        }
```

```
        for (String arg : argv) {
            // Constructing a Path object doesn't affect the disk, but
            // the Files.createFile() method does.
            final Path p = Path.of(arg);
            final Path created = Files.createFile(p);
            System.out.println(created);
        }
    }
}
```

`java.nio.file.createFile()` has an overload that takes a second argument of type `OpenOption`. This is an empty interface that is implemented by the `StandardOpenOp tion` enumeration. These options are listed in Table 10-5.

Directories

Of the two methods used for creating directories, `createDirectory()` creates just one directory, whereas `createDirectories()` creates any intermediate directories that are needed. For example, if */home/ian* exists and is a directory, the call

```
shell> Files.createDirectory(Path.of("/Users/ian/abc"))
$11 ==> /Users/ian/abc
```

will succeed (unless the directory is already there), but the call

```
jshell> Files.createDirectory(Path.of("/Users/ian/once/twice/again"))
```

will fail with a `java.nio.file.NoSuchFileException` because the directory named *once* does not exist. To create this path of directories, as you might expect by now, use `createDirectories()` (plural):

```
jshell> Files.createDirectories(Path.of("/Users/ian/once/twice/again"))
$14 ==> /Users/ian/once/twice/again
```

Both variants return a `Path` object referring to the new directory if they succeed and throw an exception if they fail. Notice that it is possible (but not likely) for `createDir ectories()` to create some of the directories and then fail; in this case, the newly created directories are left in the filesystem.

10.19 Changing a File's Name or Other Attributes

Problem

You need to change a file's name on disk or some of its other attributes, such as setting the file to read-only or changing its modification time.

Solution

To change the name (or location), use a `java.nio.file.Files` static `move()` method. For other attributes, use `setLastModifiedTime()` to change the timestamp, or one of several other setters for mode or permission attributes.

Discussion

Similar to the Unix command line, there is no separate rename operation; the move methods provide all functions for putting a file somewhere else, whether that is to the same name in a different directory, a different name in the same directory, or a different name on a different disk or filesystem. Accordingly, the `Files.move()` method requires two `Path` objects, one referring to the existing file and another referring to the new name. Then call the `Files.move()` method, passing both path objects, first the existing and then the desired name. This is easier to see than to explain, so here goes:

```java
public class Rename {
    public static void main(String[] argv) throws IOException {

        // Construct the Path object. Does NOT create a file on disk!
        final Path p = Path.of("MyCoolDocument"); // The file we will rename

        // Setup for the demo: create a new "old" file
        final Path oldName = Files.exists(p) ? p : Files.createFile(p);

        // Rename the backup file to "mydoc.bak"
        // Renaming requires a Path object for the target.
        final Path newName = Path.of("mydoc.bak");
        Files.deleteIfExists(newName); // In case previous run left it there
        Path p2 = Files.move(oldName, newName);
        System.out.println(p + " renamed to " + p2);
    }
}
```

For changing the attributes, there are several methods available, listed in Table 10-10. Each of these has a return value of type `boolean`, with `true` meaning success.

Table 10-10. Files attribute setters

Method signature	Description
`setExecutable(boolean executable)`	Convenience method to set owner's execute permission for this file
`setExecutable(boolean executable, boolean ownerOnly)`	Sets the owner's or everybody's execute permission for this file
`setLastModified(long time)`	Sets the last-modified time of the file or directory that this file names

Method signature	Description
setReadable(boolean readable)	Convenience method to set owner's read permission for this file
setReadable(boolean readable, boolean ownerOnly)	Sets the owner's or everybody's read permission for this file
setReadOnly()	Convenience for setReadable(false)
setWritable(boolean writable)	A convenience method to set the owner's write permission for this file
setWritable(boolean writable, boolean ownerOnly)	Set owner's or everybody's write permission for this file

For the methods that take two arguments, the first enables or disables the feature on the given file that matches the method name, and the second controls whether the operation applies to the owner only or to everyone. The second argument is ignored if the file lives on a filesystem that doesn't support multiuser permissions or if the operating system doesn't support that. All the methods described in this recipe return true if they succeed and false otherwise.

For example, boolean setReadable(boolean readable, boolean ownerOnly) lets you specify who can read the given file. The readable argument is true or false depending on whether you want it readable or not. The ownerOnly argument tries to extend the readability choice to all users on a multiuser operating system, and is ignored if not applicable.

setLastModified() allows you to play games with the modification time of a file. This is normally not a good game to play, but it is useful in some types of backup/restore programs. This method takes an argument that is the number of milliseconds (not seconds) since the beginning of Unix time (January 1, 1970). You can get the original value for the file by calling getLastModified() (see Recipe 10.17), or you can get the value for a given date by calling the ZonedDateTime's toInstant().getEpochSecond() method (see Recipe 6.3) and multiplying by 1,000 to convert seconds to milliseconds.

I encourage you to explore the operation of these methods using JShell (see Recipe 1.4). I'd suggest having a second window in which you can run ls -l or dir commands to see how the file is affected. Example 10-11 shows some of these methods being explored in JShell.

Example 10-11. Exploring Files

```
jshell> var f = File.createTempFile("foo", "bar");
f ==> /tmp/foo9391300789087780984bar

jshell> f.createNewFile();
$4 ==> false
```

```
jshell> f.setReadOnly();
$5 ==> true

jshell> f.canRead();
$6 ==> true

jshell> f.canWrite();
$7 ==> false

jshell> f.setReadable(true);
$8 ==> true

jshell> f.canWrite();
$9 ==> false

jshell> f.setReadable(false, false);
$10 ==> true

jshell> f.canWrite();
$11 ==> false
```

10.20 Deleting a File

Problem

You need to delete one or more files from the disk.

Solution

Use `java.nio.file.Files` object's `delete(Path)` or `deleteIfExists(Path)` method.
These delete the files referred to by the `Path` argument (subject of course to permissions) and directories (subject to permissions and to the directory being empty).

Discussion

This is not complicated. Simply construct a `Path` object for the file you wish to delete,
and call the static `Files.delete()` method:

```java
public class Delete {
    public static void main(String[] argv) throws IOException {

        // Construct a File object for the backup created by editing
        // this source file. The file probably already exists.
        // Some text editors create backups by putting ~ at end of filename.
        File bkup = new File("Delete.java~");
        // Now, delete it:
        bkup.delete();
```

```
        }
    }
```

Recall the caveat about permissions in the introduction to this chapter: if you don't have permission, you can get a return value of false or, possibly, a `SecurityExcep tion`. Note also that there are some differences between platforms. Some versions of Windows allow Java to remove a read-only file, but Unix does not allow you to remove a file unless you have write permission on the directory it's in. Nor does Unix allow you to remove a directory that isn't empty (there is even an exception, `Director yNotEmptyException`, for the latter case). Here is a version of `Delete` with reporting of success or failure:

```java
public class Delete2 {

    static boolean hard = false; // True for delete, false for deleteIfExists

    public static void main(String[] argv) {
        for (String arg : argv) {
            if ("-h".equals(arg)) {
                hard = true;
                continue;
            }
            delete(arg);
        }
    }

    public static void delete(String fileName) {
        // Construct a File object for the file to be deleted.
        final Path target = Path.of(fileName);

        // Now, delete it:
        if (hard) {
            try {
                System.out.print("Using Files.delete(): ");
                Files.delete(target);
                System.err.println("** Deleted " + fileName + " **");
            } catch (IOException e) {
                System.out.println("Deleting " + fileName + " threw " + e);
            }
        } else {
            try {
                System.out.print("Using deleteIfExists(): ");
                if (Files.deleteIfExists(target)) {
                    System.out.println("** Deleted " + fileName + " **");
                } else {
                    System.out.println(
                        "Deleting " + fileName + " returned false.");
                }
            } catch (IOException e) {
                System.out.println("Deleting " + fileName + " threw " + e);
            }
```

```
        }
    }
}
```

The -h option allows this program to switch between delete() and deleteIfEx
ists(); you can see the difference by running it on things that exist, don't exist, and
are not empty, using both methods. The output looks something like this on my Unix
box:

```
$ ls -ld ?
-rw-r--r--  1 ian  512   0 Dec 21 16:35 a
drwxr-xr-x  2 ian  512  64 Dec 21 16:35 b
drwxr-xr-x  3 ian  512  96 Dec 21 16:22 c
$ java -cp target/classes dir_file.Delete2 a b c d
Using deleteIfExists(): ** Deleted a **
Using deleteIfExists(): ** Deleted b **
Using deleteIfExists(): Deleting c threw
  java.nio.file.DirectoryNotEmptyException: c
Using deleteIfExists(): Deleting d returned false.
# Here I put the files back the way they were, then run again with -h
$ java -cp target/classes dir_file.Delete2 -h a b c d
Using Files.delete(): ** Deleted a **
Using Files.delete(): ** Deleted b **
Using Files.delete(): Deleting c threw
  java.nio.file.DirectoryNotEmptyException: c
Using Files.delete(): Deleting d threw java.nio.file.NoSuchFileException: d
$ ls -l c
total 2
drwxr-xr-x  2 ian  ian  512 Oct  8 16:50 d
$ java dir_file.Delete2 c/d c
Using deleteIfExists(): ** Deleted c/d **
Using deleteIfExists(): ** Deleted c **
$
```

10.21 Creating a Transient/Temporary File

Problem

You need to create a file with a unique temporary filename and/or or arrange for a file
to be deleted when your program is finished.

Solution

Use the java.nio.file.Files createTempFile() or createTempDirectory()
method. Use one of several methods to ensure your file is deleted on exit.

Discussion

The Files class has static methods for creating temporary files and directories. Note that a temporary file in this context is not deleted automatically; it is simply created in a directory that is set aside for temporary files on that operating system (e.g., /tmp on Unix). Here are the methods for creating tempory files and directories:

Path createTempFile(Path dir, String prefix, String suffix, FileAttribute<?>... attrs)
> Creates a new empty file in the specified directory, using the given prefix and suffix strings to generate its name

Path createTempFile(String prefix, String suffix, FileAttribute<?>... attrs)
> Creates an empty file in the default temporary-file directory, using the given prefix and suffix to generate its name

Path createTempDirectory(Path dir, String prefix, FileAttribute<?>... attrs)
> Creates a new directory in the specified directory, using the given prefix to generate its name

Path createTempDirectory(String prefix, FileAttribute<?>... attrs)
> Creates a new directory in the default temporary-file directory, using the given prefix to generate its name

The file attributes are discussed in the sidebar "Understanding I/O Options: StandardOpenOptions, FileAttribute, PosixFileAttribute, and More" on page 321.

There are various ways to arrange for a file to be deleted automatically. One is to use the legacy java.io.File class, which has a explicit deleteOnExit() method. This arranges for any file (no matter how it was created) to be deleted if it still exists when the program exits. Here we arrange for a backup copy of a program to be deleted on exit, and we also create a temporary file and arrange for it to be removed on exit. Both files are gone after the program runs:

```
public class TempFiles {
    public static void main(String[] argv) throws IOException {

        // 1. Making an existing file temporary
        // Construct a File object for the backup created by editing
        // this source file. The file probably already exists.
        // My editor creates backups by putting ~ at the end of the name.
        File bkup = new File("Rename.java~");
        // Arrange to have it deleted when the program ends.
        bkup.deleteOnExit();

        // 2. Create a new temporary file.

        // Make a file object for foo.tmp, in the default temp directory
        Path tmp = Files.createTempFile("foo", "tmp");
        // Report on the filename that it made up for us.
```

```
            System.out.println("Your temp file is " + tmp.normalize());
            // Arrange for it to be deleted at exit.
            tmp.toFile().deleteOnExit();
            // Now do something with the temporary file, without having to
            // worry about deleting it later.
            writeDataInTemp(tmp);
        }

        public static void writeDataInTemp(Path tempFile) throws IOException {
            // This version is dummy. Use your imagination.
            Files.writeString(tempFile, "This is a temp file");
        }
    }
```

When run on a Unix system, this program looked like this, proving that the file was created but removed when the JVM exited:

```
$ java TempFiles.java
Your temp file is /tmp/foo84233219102150546891tmp
$ ls -l /tmp/foo84233219102150546891tmp
ls: /tmp/foo84233219102150546891tmp: No such file or directory
$
```

The createTempFile() method is like createNewFile() (see Recipe 10.18) in that it does create the file. Also be aware that, should the Java Virtual Machine terminate abnormally, the deletion probably will not occur. There is no way to undo the setting of deleteOnExit() short of renaming the file or something drastic like powering off the computer before the program exits.

Another way to arrange for any file to be deleted when you are finished with it is to create it with the DELETE_ON_CLOSE option (see Table 10-5) so it will be deleted when you close the file.

A third, less likely method is to instead use a JVM shutdown hook (*https://darwin sys.com/java/shutdownhook.html*). DELETE_ON_CLOSE is probably the best option, particularly in a long-running application, like most server-side apps. In these situations, the server could be running for weeks, months, or even years. In the meantime all the temp files would accumulate and the JVM would accumulate a large list of deferred work that it needs to perform upon shutdown. You'd probably run out of disk space or server memory or some other resource. For most long-running apps of this kind, it's better to use DELETE_ON_CLOSE or even the explicit delete() operation. Another alternative is to use a scheduler service to periodically trigger removal of old temporary files.

10.22 Listing a Directory

Problem

You need to list the filesystem entries named in a directory.

Solution

Use the java.nio.file.Files static method Stream<Path> list(Path dir), pass-ing the Path representing the directory.

Discussion

The java.nio.file.Files class contains several methods for working with directo-ries. If you just want to list the contents of a directory, use its list(Path) method. For example, to list the filesystem entities named in the current directory, just write the following:

```
Files.list(Path.of(".")).forEach(System.out::println);
```

This can become a complete program with as little as the following code. Note that on many systems the Path objects are returned in the order they occur in the directory, which isn't sorted. In this simple example we use the Stream.sorted() method to order the entries alphabetically:

```
public class Ls {
    public static void main(String args[]) throws IOException {
        Files.list(Path.of("."))
            .sorted()
            .forEach(dir -> {
                System.out.println(dir);
            });
    }
}
```

Of course, there's lots of room for elaboration. You could print the names in multiple columns across the page. Or even down the page because you know the number of items in the list before you print. You could omit filenames with leading periods, as does the Unix *ls* program. Or print the directory names first; I once used a directory lister called *lc* that did this, and I found it quite useful.

If you want to process the directory recursively, you should *not* check each entry to see if it's a file or directory and recurse on directories. Instead, you should use one of the walk() or walkFileTree() methods discussed in Recipe 10.26; these handle recursion for you. There is also a set of Files.newDirectoryStream() methods, with and without filter callbacks and other arguments, that return a Directory Stream<Path>.

10.23 Getting the Directory Roots

Problem

You want to know about the top-level directories, such as *C:* and *D:* on Windows.

Solution

Use the static method `FileSystems.getDefault().getRootDirectories()`, which returns an `Iterable` of `Path` objects, one for each root directory. You can print them or do other operations on them.

Discussion

Operating systems differ in how they organize filesystems out of multiple disk drives or partitions. Microsoft Windows has a low-level device-oriented approach in which each disk drive has a root directory named *A:* for the first floppy (if you still have one!), *C:* for the first hard drive, and other letters for CD-ROM and network drives. This approach requires you to know the physical device that a file is on. Unix, Linux, and macOS have a high-level approach with a single root directory */*; and different disks or partitions are mounted, or connected, into a single unified tree. This approach sometimes requires you to figure out where a device file is mounted. Perhaps neither is easier, though the Unix approach is a bit more consistent. Either way, Java makes it easy for you to get a list of the roots.

The static method `FileSystems.getDefault().getRootDirectories()` returns an `Iterable<Path>` containing the available filesystem roots for whatever platform you are running on. Here is a short program to list these:

```
FileSystems.getDefault().getRootDirectories().forEach(System.out::println);

C:> java dir_file.DirRoots
A:\
C:\
D:\
C:>
```

As you can see, the program listed my floppy drive (even though the floppy drive was not only empty, but left at home while I wrote this recipe on my notebook computer in my car in a parking lot), the hard disk drive, and the CD-ROM drive.

On Unix there is only one root directory:

```
$ java dir_file.DirRoots
/
$
```

One thing that is left out of the list of roots is the so-called *UNC filename*. UNC file-names are used on some Microsoft platforms to refer to a network-available resource that hasn't been mounted locally on a particular drive letter. If your system still uses these, be aware they will not show up in the listDirectoryRoots() output.

10.24 Using the FileWatcher Service to Get Notified About File Changes

Problem

You want to be notified when some other application updates one or more of the files in which you are interested.

Solution

Use the java.nio.file.FileWatchService to get notified of changes to files auto-matically, instead of having to examine the files periodically.

Discussion

It is fairly common for a large application to want to be notified of changes to files, without having to go and look at them periodically. For example, a Java Enterprise web server wants to know when Servlets and other components get updated. An IDE wants to know when files were modified by an external editor or a build script. Many modern operating systems have had this capability for some time, and now it is avail-able in Java.

These are the basic steps to using the FileWatchService:

1. Create a Path object representing the directory you want to watch.

2. Get a WatchService by calling, for example, FileSystems.getDefault().new WatchService().

3. Create an array of Kind enumerations for the things you want to watch (in our example we watch for files being created or modified).

4. Register the WatchService and the Kind array onto the Path object.

5. From then on, you wait for the watcher to notify you. A typical implementation is to enter a while (true) loop calling the WatchService's take() method to get an event and interpret the events to figure out what just happened.

Example 10-12 is a program that does just that. In addition, it starts another thread to actually do some filesystem operations so that you can see the WatchService operating.

Example 10-12. main/src/main/java/nio/FileWatchServiceDemo.java

```java
public class FileWatchServiceDemo {

    final static String TEMP_DIR_PATH = "/tmp";
    static final String FILE_SEMA_FOR = "MyFileSema.for";
    final static Path SEMAPHORE_PATH = Path.of(TEMP_DIR_PATH ,FILE_SEMA_FOR);
    static volatile boolean done = false;
    final static ExecutorService threadPool = Executors.newSingleThreadExecutor();

    public static void main(String[] args) throws Throwable {
        String tempDirPath = "/tmp";
        System.out.println("Starting watcher for " + tempDirPath);
        System.out.println("Semaphore file is " + SEMAPHORE_PATH);
        Path p = Paths.get(tempDirPath);
        WatchService watcher =
            FileSystems.getDefault().newWatchService();
        Kind<?>[] watchKinds = { ENTRY_CREATE, ENTRY_MODIFY };
        p.register(watcher, watchKinds);
        threadPool.submit(new DemoService());
        while (!done) {
            WatchKey key = watcher.take();
            for (WatchEvent<?> e : key.pollEvents()) {
                System.out.println(
                    "Saw event " + e.kind() + " on " +
                    e.context());
                if (e.context().toString().equals(FILE_SEMA_FOR)) {
                    System.out.println("Semaphore found, shutting down watcher");
                    done = true;
                }
            }
            if (!key.reset()) {
                System.err.println("WatchKey failed to reset!");
            }
        }
    }

    /**
     * Nested class whose only job is to wait a while, create a file in
     * the monitored directory, and then go away.
     */
    private final static class DemoService implements Runnable {
        public void run() {
            try {
                Thread.sleep(1000);
                System.out.println("DemoService: Creating file");
                Files.deleteIfExists(SEMAPHORE_PATH); // clean up from previous run
                Files.createFile(SEMAPHORE_PATH);
                Thread.sleep(1000);
                System.out.println("DemoService: Shutting down");
            } catch (Exception e) {
                System.out.println("Caught UNEXPECTED " + e);
```

```
        }
      }
    }
  }
}
```

10.25 Program: Save User Data to Disk

Problem

You need to save user data to disk in a Java application. This may be in response to File→Save in a GUI application, saving the file in a text editor, or saving configuration data in a non-GUI application. You have heard (correctly) that a well-behaved application should never lose data.

Solution

Use this five-step plan, with appropriate variations:

1. Create a temporary file; arrange for it to be removed automatically with `deleteOnExit(true)`.

2. Write the user data to this file. Data format translation errors, if any, will be thrown during this process, leaving the previous version of the user's data file intact.

3. Delete the backup file if it exists.

4. Rename the user's previous file to *.bak*.

5. Rename the temporary file to the saved file.

Discussion

As developers, we have to deal with the fact that saving a file to disk is full of risk. There are many things that can go wrong in saving data, yet it is one of the most critical parts of most applications. If you lose data that a person has spent hours inputting, or even lose a setting that a user feels strongly about, she will despise your whole application. The disk might fill up while we're writing it, or it might be full before we start. This is a user's error, but we have to face it. So here's a more detailed discussion of the little five-step dance we should go through:

1. Create a temporary file that we will write to. Set this file to `deleteOnExit(true)` so that if we fail in a later step we don't clutter the disk. Because we are later going to rename this file to become the user's real file, and we don't want to run out of disk space during the rename, it is important that we create the file on the same disk drive partition (*drive letter* or *mount point*) as the user's real file; otherwise

the rename will silently morph into a copy-and-delete, which could fail due to lack of disk space. See Recipe 10.21 for methods of deleting a file on exit.

2. Write the user data to this new temporary file. If we are transforming data—say, getting it from a JDBC ResultSet or writing objects using a XML transformer—an exception could be thrown. If we're not careful, these exceptions can cause the user's data to be lost.

3. Delete the backup file if it exists. First time we do this it won't exist; after that it probably will. Be prepared either way.

4. Rename the user's previous file to *.bak_.

5. Rename the temporary file to the save file.

This may seem like overkill, but it prevents career kill. I've done pretty much this in numerous apps with various save file formats. This plan is the only really safe way around all the problems that can occur. For example, the final step has to be a rename not a copy, regardless of size considerations, to avoid the problem of the disk filling up. So, to be correct, you have to ensure that the temp file gets created on the same disk partition (drive letter or mount point) as the user's file.

This is the basic plan to use the FileSaver:

- Instantiate it by calling the constructor.
- Call the getWriter() or getOutputStream() method.
- Use the output file to write the data.
- Call finish() on the FileSaver object.

main/src/main/java/com/darwinsys/io/FileSaver.java

```java
// package com.darwinsys.io;
public class FileSaver {

    private enum State {
        /** The state before and after use */
        AVAILABLE,
        /** The state while in use */
        INUSE
    }
    private State state;
    private final Path inputFile;
    private final Path tmpFile;
    private final Path backupFile;

    private OutputStream mOutputStream;
    private Writer mWriter;

    public FileSaver(Path inputFile) throws IOException {
```

```
        // Step 1: Create temp file in right place; must be on same disk
        // as the original file, to avoid disk-full troubles later.
        this.inputFile = inputFile;
        tmpFile = Path.of(inputFile.normalize() + ".tmp");
        Files.createFile(tmpFile);
        tmpFile.toFile().deleteOnExit();
        backupFile = Path.of(inputFile.normalize() + ".bak");
        state = State.AVAILABLE;
    }

    /**
     * Return a reference to the contained File object, to
     * promote reuse (File objects are immutable so this
     * is at least moderately safe). Typical use would be:
     * <pre>
     * if (fileSaver == null ||
     *    !(fileSaver.getFile().equals(file))) {
     *          fileSaver = new FileSaver(file);
     * }
     * </pre>
     * @return the File object for the file to be saved
     */
    public Path getFile() {
        return inputFile;
    }

    /** Return an output file that the client should use to
     * write the client's data to.
     * @return An OutputStream, which should be wrapped in a
     *       buffered OutputStream to ensure reasonable performance.
     * @throws IOException if the temporary file cannot be written
     */
    public OutputStream getOutputStream() throws IOException {

        if (state != State.AVAILABLE) {
            throw new IllegalStateException("FileSaver not opened");
        }
        mOutputStream = Files.newOutputStream(tmpFile);
        state = State.INUSE;
        return mOutputStream;
    }

    /** Return an output file that the client should use to
     * write the client's data to.
     * @return A BufferedWriter to write on the new file.
     * @throws IOException if the temporary file cannot be written
     */
    public Writer getWriter() throws IOException {

        if (state != State.AVAILABLE) {
            throw new IllegalStateException("FileSaver not opened");
```

```
        }
        mWriter = Files.newBufferedWriter(tmpFile);
        state = State.INUSE;
        return mWriter;
    }

    /** Close the output file and rename the temp file to the original name.
     * @throws IOException If anything goes wrong
     */
    public void finish() throws IOException {

        if (state != State.INUSE) {
            throw new IllegalStateException("FileSaver not in use");
        }

        // Ensure both are closed before we try to rename.
        if (mOutputStream != null) {
            mOutputStream.close();
        }
        if (mWriter != null) {
            mWriter.close();
        }

        // Delete the previous backup file if it exists.
        Files.deleteIfExists(backupFile);

        // Rename the user's previous file to itsName.bak,
        // UNLESS this is a new file.
        if (Files.exists(inputFile) &&
            Files.move(inputFile, backupFile) == null) {
            throw new IOException(
                "Could not rename file to backup file " + backupFile);
        }

        // Rename the temporary file to the save file.
        if (Files.move(tmpFile, inputFile) == null) {
            throw new IOException("Could not rename temp file to save file");
        }
        state = State.AVAILABLE;
    }
}
```

Acknowledgments

The code in this program is my own, based on my experience in various applications. I was prompted to package it up this way, and write it up, by a post by Brendon McLean to the mailing list for the now-defunct Java Application Framework JSR-296 (*http://jcp.org/en/jsr/detail?id=296*).

10.26 Program: Find—Walking a File Tree

The program shown in Example 10-13 implements a subset of the Windows *Find Files* dialog or the Unix *find* command. It has most of the structure needed to build a more complete version of either of these. It accepts the following options from standard Unix find (with limits):

-n *name*
   Name to look for. Can include shell wildcards if quoted from the shell.

-s *size*
   Size of file to look for. Can prefix with a plus sign to indicate greater than or a minus sign to indicate less than.

-a, -o
   And or or, but only one of these, between a -n and a -s.

The Files class has four methods for walking a file tree. Two return a lazily populated Stream<Path>, and the other two invoke a callback FileVisitor for each file or directory found. My find implementation uses the first one; the four are summarized in Table 10-11.

Table 10-11. Files tree walk methods

Return	Signature
Stream<Path>	walk(Path start, FileVisitOption... options)
Stream<Path>	walk(Path start, int maxDepth, FileVisitOption... options)
Path	walkFileTree(Path start, FileVisitor<? super Path> visitor)
Path	walkFileTree(Path start, Set<FileVisitOption> options, int maxDepth, FileVisitor<? super Path> visitor)

Using the walk() methods is as simple as this:

```
Files.walk(startingPath).forEach(path -> {
        // Do something with Path path; might be file, directory or other...
}
```

That code is near the start of the startWalkingAt() method in Example 10-13.

Example 10-13. main/src/main/java/dir_file/Find.java

```
/**
 * Find - find files by name, size, or other criteria. Non-GUI version.
 */
public class Find {

    public enum Conjunction { AND, OR };
```

```java
    private static Logger logger = Logger.getLogger(Find.class.getSimpleName());
    static boolean started;

    /** Main program
     * @throws IOException If the Files.walkTree does so
     */
    public static void main(String[] args) throws IOException {
        Find finder = new Find();

        if (args.length == 0) {
            finder.startWalkingAt(".");
        } else {
            for (int i = 0; i < args.length; i++) {
                if (args[i].charAt(0) == '-') {
                    switch(args[i].substring(1)) {
                    case "name":
                        finder.filter.setNameFilter(args[++i]);
                        continue;
                    case "size":
                        finder.filter.setSizeFilter(args[++i]);
                        continue;
//                      Not implemented by back-end yet
//                      case "a":
//                          finder.filter.addConjunction(Conjunction.AND);
//                          continue;
//                      case "o":
//                          finder.filter.addConjunction(Conjunction.OR);
//                          continue;
                    default: throw new IllegalArgumentException(
                        "Unknown argument " + args[i]);
                    }
                }
                finder.startWalkingAt(args[i]);
            }
            if (!started) {
                finder.startWalkingAt(".");
            }
        }
    }

    protected FindFilter filter = new FindFilter();

    public static void usage() {
        System.err.println(
            "Usage: Find [-n namefilter][-s sizefilter][dir...]");
        System.exit(1);
    }

    /** doName - handle one filesystem object by name */
    private void startWalkingAt(String s) throws IOException {
        logger.info("doName(" + s + ")");
```

```
            started = true;
            Path f = Path.of(s);
            if (!Files.exists(f)) {
                System.out.println(s + " does not exist");
                return;
            }
            Files.walk(f).forEach(fp -> {
                try {
                    if (Files.isRegularFile(fp))
                        doFile(fp);
                    else if (Files.isDirectory(fp)) {
                        doDir(fp);
                    } else {
                        System.err.println("Unknown type: " + s);
                    }
                } catch (IOException e) {
                    throw new RuntimeException("IO Exception: " + e);
                }
            });
        }

    /** doFile - process one regular file.
     * @throws IOException */
    private void doFile(Path f) throws IOException {
        if (filter.accept(f)) {
            System.out.println("f " + f);
        }
    }

    /** doDir - process a directory */
    private void doDir(Path d) {
        System.out.println("d " + d.normalize());
    }
}
```

Example 10-14 shows a class called FindFilter, the backend implementation of Find.

Example 10-14. main/src/main/java/dir_file/FindFilter.java

```
/** Class to encapsulate the filtration for Find.
 * For now just set*Filter() methods. Really needs to be a real
 * data structure (maybe LinkedList<FilterOp> or a Tree) for complex
 * requests like:
 *    -n "*.html" -a \( -size < 0 -o mtime < 5 \).
 */
public class FindFilter {
    private enum SizeMode {GT, EQ, LT};
    SizeMode sizeMode;
    Find.Conjunction conj;
    long size;
    String name;
    Pattern nameRE;
```

```
boolean debug = false;

void setSizeFilter(String sizeFilter) {
    System.out.println("FindFilter.setSizeFilter()");
    sizeMode = SizeMode.EQ;
    char c = sizeFilter.charAt(0);
    if (c == '+') {
        sizeMode = SizeMode.GT;
        sizeFilter = sizeFilter.substring(1);
    } else {
        if (c == '-') {
            sizeMode = SizeMode.LT;
            sizeFilter = sizeFilter.substring(1);
        }
    }
    size = Long.parseLong(sizeFilter);
}

/** Add a conjunction */
public void addConjunction(Find.Conjunction conj) {
    System.out.println("FindFilter.addConjunction()");
    if (this.conj != null) {
        throw new IllegalArgumentException(
            "Only one conjucntion allowed in this version");
    }
    this.conj = conj;
}

/** Convert the given shell wildcard pattern into internal form (an RE) */
void setNameFilter(String nameToFilter) {
    nameRE = makeNameFilter(nameToFilter);
}

Pattern makeNameFilter(String name) {
    StringBuilder sb = new StringBuilder('^');
    for (char c : name.toCharArray()) {
        switch(c) {
            case '.':    sb.append("\\."); break;
            case '*':    sb.append(".*"); break;
            case '?':    sb.append('.'); break;
            // Some chars are special to RE and have to be escaped
            case '[':    sb.append("\\["); break;
            case ']':    sb.append("\\]"); break;
            case '(':    sb.append("\\("); break;
            case ')':    sb.append("\\)"); break;
            default:     sb.append(c); break;
        }
    }
    sb.append('$');
    if (debug) {
        System.out.println("RE=\"" + sb + "\".");
    }
```

```java
        // Should catch PatternException and rethrow for better diagnostics
        return Pattern.compile(sb.toString());
    }

    /** Do the filtering. For now, only filter on name, size or name+size */
    public boolean accept(Path p) throws IOException {
        if (debug) {
            System.out.println("FindFilter.accept(" + p + ")");
        }

        if (nameRE != null) {
            return nameRE.matcher(p.getFileName().toString()).matches();
        }

        // size handling
        if (sizeMode != null) {
            long sz = Files.size(p);
            switch (sizeMode) {
            case EQ:
                return (sz == size);
            case GT:
                return (sz > size);
            case LT:
                return (sz < size);
            }
        }

        // Catchall
        return false;
    }

    public String getName() {
        return name;
    }
}
```

## CHAPTER 11

Data Science and R

Data science is a relatively new discipline that first came to the attention of many with this article by O'Reilly's Mike Loukides (*https://www.oreilly.com/ideas/what-is-data-science*). While there are many definitions in the field, Loukides distills his detailed observation of and participation in the field into this definition:

> A data application acquires its value from the data itself, and creates more data as a result. It's not just an application with data; it's a data product. Data science enables the creation of data products.

One of the main open source ecosystems for data science software is at Apache and includes Hadoop (*https://hadoop.apache.org*) (which includes the HDFS distributed filesystem, Hadoop Map/Reduce,[6] Ozone object store, and Yarn scheduler), the Cassandra distributed database (*https://cassandra.apache.org*), and the Spark compute engine (*https://spark.apache.org*). Read the "Modules and Related Tools" section of the Hadoop page for a current list.

What's interesting here is that a great deal of this infrastructure, which is taken for granted by data scientists, is written in Java and Scala (a JVM language). Much of the rest is written in Python, a language that complements Java.

Data science problems may involve a lot of setup, so we'll only give one example from traditional DS, using the Spark framework. Spark is written in Scala so it can be used directly by Java code.

---

6 *Map/Reduce* is a famous algorithm pioneered by Google to handle large data problems. An unspecified number of generators process *map* data—such as words on a web page or the page's URL—and a single (usually) reduce process reduces the maps to a manageable form, such as a list of all the pages that contain the given words. Early on, data science went overboard on trying to do everything with Map/Reduce; now the pendulum has swung back to using compute engines like Spark.

In the rest of the chapter I'll focus on a language called R, which is widely used both in statistics and in data science (well, also in many other sciences; many of the graphs you see in refereed journal articles are prepared with R). R is widely used and is useful to know. Its primary implementation was not written in Java, but in a mixture of C, Fortran, and R itself. But R can be used within Java, and Java can be used within R. I'll talk about several implementations of R and how to select one, and then I'll show techniques for using Java from R and R from Java, as well as using R in a web application.

11.1 Machine Learning with Java

Problem

You want to use Java for machine learning and data science, but everyone tells you to use Python.

Solution

Use one of the many powerful Java toolkits available for free download.

Discussion

It's sometimes said that machine learning (ML) and deep learning have to be done in C++ for efficiency or in Python for the wide availability of software. While these languages have their advantages and their advocates, it is certainly possible to use Java for these purposes. However, setting up these packages and presenting a short demo tends to be longer than would fit in this book's typical recipe format.

With industry giant Amazon having released its Java-based Deep Java Learning (DJL) library as this book was going to press, and many other good libraries available (with quite a few supporting CUDA (*https://developer.nvidia.com/cuda-zone*) for faster GPU-based processing) (see Table 11-1), there is no reason to avoid using Java for ML. With the exception of DJL, I've tried to list packages that are still being maintained and have a decent reputation among users.

Table 11-1. Some Java machine learning packages

Library name	Description	Info URL	Source URL
ADAMS	Workflow engine for building/maintaining data-driven, reactive workflows; integration with business processes	*https://adams.cms.waikato.ac.nz/*	*https://github.com/waikato-datamining/adams-base*
Deep Java Library	Amazon's ML library	*https://djl.ai*	*https://github.com/awslabs/djl*

Library name	Description	Info URL	Source URL
Deeplearning4j	DL4J, Eclipse's distributed deep-learning library; integrates w/ Hadoop and Apache Spark	*https://deeplearning4j.org/*	*https://github.com/eclipse/deeplearning4j*
ELKI	Data mining toolkit	*https://elki-project.github.io/*	*https://github.com/elki-project/elki*
Mallet	ML for text processing	mallet.cs.umass.edu	*https://github.com/mimno/Mallet.git*
Weka	ML algorithms for data mining; tools for data preparation, classification, regression, clustering, association rules mining, and visualization	*https://www.cs.waikato.ac.nz/ml/weka/index.html*	*https://svn.cms.waikato.ac.nz/svn/weka/trunk/weka*

See Also

The book *Data Mining: Practical Machine Learning and Techniques* by Ian Witten et al. (Morgan Kaufmann) was written by the team behind Weka.

See also Eugen Parschiv's list of Java AI software packages (*https://www.baeldung.com/java-ai*).

11.2 Using Data In Apache Spark

Problem

You want to process data using Spark.

Solution

Create a `SparkSession`, use its `read()` function to read a `DataSet`, apply operations, and summarize results.

Discussion

Spark is a massive subject! Entire books have been written on using it. Quoting Data-bricks (*https://databricks.com*), home of much of the original Spark team:[6]

> Apache Spark™ has seen immense growth over the past several years, becoming the de-facto data processing and AI engine in enterprises today due to its speed, ease of use, and sophisticated analytics. Spark unifies data and AI by simplifying data preparation at massive scale across various sources, providing a consistent set of APIs for both data

---

6 DataBricks offers several free ebooks on Spark from their website; it also offers commercial Spark add-ons.

engineering and data science workloads, as well as seamless integration with popular AI frameworks and libraries such as TensorFlow, PyTorch, R and SciKit-Learn.

I cannot convey the whole subject matter in this book. However, one thing Spark is good for is dealing with lots of data. In Example 11-1, we read an Apache-format log-file and find (and count) the lines with 200, 404, and 500 responses.

Example 11-1. spark/src/main/java/sparkdemo/LogReader.java

```java
import org.apache.spark.sql.SparkSession;
import org.apache.spark.sql.Dataset;
import org.apache.spark.api.java.function.FilterFunction;

/**
 * Read an Apache Logfile and summarize it.
 */
public class LogReader {

    public static void main(String[] args) {

        final String logFile = "/var/wildfly/standalone/log/access_log.log";    ❶
        SparkSession spark =
            SparkSession.builder().appName("Log Analyzer").getOrCreate();       ❷
        Dataset<String> logData = spark.read().textFile(logFile).cache();        ❸

        long good = logData.filter(                                             ❹
        new FilterFunction<>() {public boolean call(String s) {
                    return s.contains("200");
                }
            }).count();

        long bad = logData.filter(new FilterFunction<>() {
                public boolean call(String s) {
                    return s.contains("404");
                }
            }).count();

        long ugly = logData.filter(new FilterFunction<>() {
                public boolean call(String s) {
                    return s.contains("500");
                }
            }).count();

        System.out.printf(                                                      ❺
            "Successful transfers %d, 404 tries %d, 500 errors %d\n",
            good, bad, ugly);

        spark.stop();
    }
}
```

❶ Set up the filename for the logfile. It probably should come from `args`.

❷ Start up the Spark `SparkSession` object—the runtime.

❸ Tell Spark to read the logfile and keep it in memory (cache).

❹ Define the filters for 200, 404, and 500 errors. They should be able to use lambdas to make the code shorter, but there's an ambiguity between the Java and Scala versions of `FilterFunction`.

❺ Print the results.

To make this *compile*, you need to add the following to a Maven POM file:

```
<dependency>
    <groupId>org.apache.spark</groupId>
    <artifactId>spark-sql_2.12</artifactId>
    <version>2.4.4</version>
    <scope>provided</scope>
</dependency>
```

Then you should be able to do `mvn package` to get a JAR file packaged.

The use of the `provided` scope is because we will also download the Apache Spark runtime package from the Spark Download page (*https://spark.apache.org/down loads.html*) in order to *run* the application. Unpack the distribution and set the `SPARK_HOME` environment to the root of it:

```
SPARK_HOME=~/spark-3.0.0-bin-hadoop3.2/
```

Then you can use the `run` script that I've provided in the source download (*javasrc/ spark*).

Spark is designed for larger-scale computing than what's in this simple example, so its voluminous output simply dwarfs the output from my simple sample program. Nonetheless, for an approximately 42,000-line file, I did get this result, buried among the logging:

```
Successful transfers 32555, 404 tries 6539, 500 errors 183
```

As mentioned, Spark is a massive subject but a necessary tool for most data scientists. You can program Spark in Java (obviously), or in Scala. Scala is a JVM language that promotes functional programming (see this Scala tutorial for Java devs (*https:// www.dhgarrette.com/nlpclass/scala/basics.html*)) in Python and probably other languages. You can learn more at *https://spark.apache.org* or from the many books, videos, and tutorials online.

11.3 Using R Interactively

Problem

You don't know the first thing about R, and you want to.

Solution

R has been around for ages, and its predecessor S for a decade before that. There are many books and online resources devoted to this language. The official home page is at *https://www.r-project.org*. There are many online tutorials; the R Project hosts one (*https://cran.r-project.org/doc/contrib/Paradis-rdebuts_en.pdf*). R itself is available in most systems' package managers, and it can be downloaded from the official download site (*https://cran.r-project.org/mirrors.html*). The name *CRAN* in these URLs stands for Comprehensive R Archive Network, named in a similar fashion to TeX's CTAN and the Perl language's CPAN.

In this example we'll write some data from a Java program and then analyze and graph it using R interactively.

Discussion

This is merely a brief intro to using R interactively. Suffice to say that R is a valuable interactive environment for exploring data. Here are some simple calculations to show the flavor of the language: a chatty startup (so long I had to cut part of it), simple arithmetic, automatic printing of results if not saved, half-decent errors when you make a mistake, and arithmetic on vectors. You may see some similarities to Java's JShell (see Recipe 1.4); both are REPL (Read-Evaluate-Print Loop) interfaces. R adds the ability to save your interactive session (*workspace*) when exiting the program, so all your data and function definitions are restored next time you start R. A simple interactive session showing a bit of the syntax of R might look like this:

```
$ R

R version 3.6.0 (2019-04-26) -- "Planting of a Tree"
Copyright (C) 2019 The R Foundation for Statistical Computing
Platform: x86_64-apple-darwin15.6.0 (64-bit)

R is free software and comes with ABSOLUTELY NO WARRANTY.
You are welcome to redistribute it under certain conditions.
Type 'license()' or 'licence()' for distribution details.

...

> 2 + 2
[1] 4
> x = 2 + 2
```

```
> x
[1] 4
> r = 10 20 30 40 50
Error: unexpected numeric constant in "r = 10 20"
> r = c(10,20,30,45,55,67)
> r
[1] 10 20 30 45 55 67
> r+3
[1] 13 23 33 48 58 70
> r / 3
[1]   3.333333  6.666667 10.000000 15.000000 18.333333 22.333333
>quit()
Save workspace image? [y/n/c]: n
$
```

R purists will usually use the *assignment arrow* ← in lieu of the = sign when assigning. If you like that, go for it.

This short session barely scratches the surface: R offers hundreds of built-in functions, sample datasets, over a thousand add-on packages, built-in help, and much more. For interactive exploration of data, R is really the one to beat.

Some people prefer a GUI frontend to R. RStudio (*https://rstudio.com*) is the most widely used GUI frontend.

Now we want to write some data from Java and process it in R (we'll use Java and R together in later recipes in this chapter). In Recipe 5.9 we discussed the `java.util.Random` class and its `nextDouble()` and `nextGaussian()` methods. The `nextDouble()` and related methods try to give a flat distribution between 0 and 1.0, in which each value has an equal chance of being selected. A Gaussian or normal distribution is a bell curve of values from negative infinity to positive infinity, with the majority of the values clustered around zero (0.0). We'll use R's histogramming and graphics functions to examine visually how well they do so:

```
Random r = new Random();
for (int i = 0; i < 10_000; i++) {
    System.out.println("A normal random double is " + r.nextDouble());
    System.out.println("A gaussian random double is " + r.nextGaussian());
```

To illustrate the different distributions, I generated 10,000 numbers each using nex tRandom() and nextGaussian(). The code for this is in *Random4.java* (not shown here) and is a combination of the preceding sample code with code to print just the numbers into two files. I then plotted histograms using R; the R script used to generate the graph is in *javasrc* under *src/main/resources*, but its core is shown in Example 11-2. The results are shown in Figure 11-1.

Example 11-2. R commands to generate histograms

```
png("randomness.png")
us <- read.table("normal.txt")[[1]]
ns <- read.table("gaussian.txt")[[1]]

layout(t(c(1,2)), respect=TRUE)

hist(us, main = "Using nextRandom()", nclass = 10,
     xlab = NULL, col = "lightgray", las = 1, font.lab = 3)

hist(ns, main = "Using nextGaussian()", nclass = 16,
     xlab = NULL, col = "lightgray", las = 1, font.lab = 3)
dev.off()
```

The png() call tells R which graphics device to use. Others include X11() and Post
script(). read.table() reads data from a text file into a table; the [1] gives us just
the data column, ignoring some metadata. The layout() call says we want two
graphics objects displayed side by side. Each hist() call draws one of the two histograms. And dev.off() closes the output and flushes any writing buffers to the PNG
file. The result is shown in Figure 11-1.

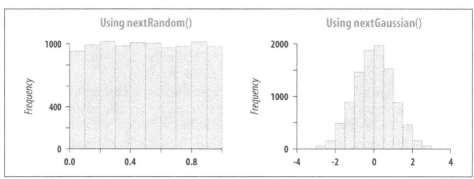

Figure 11-1. Flat (left) and Gaussian (right) distributions

11.4 Comparing/Choosing an R Implementation

Problem

You're not sure which implementation of R to use.

Solution

Look at original R, Renjin, and FastR.

Discussion

The original for R was S, an environment for interactive programming developed by John Chambers and others at AT&T Bell Labs starting in 1976. I ran into S when supporting the University of Toronto Statistics Department, and again when reviewing a commercial implementation of it, SPlus, for a long-ago glossy magazine called *Sun Expert*. AT&T was only making S source available to universities and to commercial licensees who could not further distribute the source. Two developers at the University of Auckland, Ross Ihaka and Robert Gentleman, developed a clone of S, starting in 1995. They named it R after their own first initials and as a play on the name S. (There is precedent for this: the *awk* language popular on Unix/Linux was named for the initials of its designers Aho, Weinberger, and Kernighan). R grew quickly because it was very largely compatible with S and was more readily available. This implementation of original R is actively managed by the R Foundation for Statistical Computing (*https://r-project.org*), which also manages the Comprehensive R Archive Network (*https://cran.r-project.org*).

Renjin (*http://renjin.org*) is a fairly complete implementation of R in Java. This project provides built JAR files via their own Maven repository.

FastR (*https://jaxenter.com/fastr-r-virtual-machine-java-140667.html*) is another implementation in Java, designed to run in the faster GraalVM and supporting direct invocation of JVM code from almost any other programming language. The technical lead of the FastR descibes the implementation in this blog post (*https://medium.com/graalvm/faster-r-with-fastr-4b8db0e0dceb*).

Besides these implementations, R's popularity has led to development of many access libraries for invoking R from many popular programming languages. Rserve (*https://www.rforge.net/Rserve*) is a TCP/IP networked access mode for R, for which Java wrappers exist.

11.5 Using R from Within a Java App: Renjin

Problem

You want to access R from within a Java application using Renjin.

Solution

Add Renjin to your Maven or Gradle build, and call it via the Script Engines mechanism described in Recipe 18.3.

Discussion

Renjin is a pure-Java, open source reimplementation of R and provides a script engines interface. Add the following dependency to your build tool:

```
org.renjin:renjin-script-engine:3.5-beta76
```

Of course there is probably a later version of Renjin than the one shown above by the time you read this; use the latest unless there's a reason not to.

Note that you will also need a `<repository>` entry since the maintainers put their artifacts in the repo at `nexus.betadriven.com` instead of the usual Maven Central. Here's what I used (obtained from *https://www.renjin.org/downloads.html*):

```
<repositories>
    <repository>
        <id>bedatadriven</id>
        <name>bedatadriven public repo</name>
        <url>https://nexus.bedatadriven.com/content/groups/public/</url>
    </repository>
</repositories>
```

Once that's done, you should be able to access Renjin via the Script Engines framework, as in Example 11-3.

Example 11-3. main/src/main/java/otherlang/RenjinScripting.java

```
/**
 * Demonstrate interacting with the "R" implementation called "Renjin"
 */
public static void main(String[] args) throws ScriptException {
    ScriptEngineManager manager = new ScriptEngineManager();
    ScriptEngine engine = manager.getEngineByName("Renjin");
    engine.put("a", 42);
    Object ret = engine.eval("b <- 2; a*b");
    System.out.println(ret);
}
```

Because R treats all numbers as floating point, like many interpreters, the value printed is `84.0`.

One can also get Renjin to invoke a script file; Example 11-4 invokes the same script used in Recipe 11.3 to generate and plot a batch of pseudorandom numbers.

Example 11-4. Renjin with a script file

```
private static final String R_SCRIPT_FILE = "/randomnesshistograms.r";
private static final int N = 10000;

public static void main(String[] argv) throws Exception {
    // java.util.Random methods are non-static, do need to construct
```

```
    Random r = new Random();
    double[] us = new double[N], ns = new double[N];
    for (int i=0; i<N; i++) {
        us[i] = r.nextDouble();
        ns[i] =r.nextGaussian();
    }
    try (InputStream is =
        Random5.class.getResourceAsStream(R_SCRIPT_FILE)) {
        if (is == null) {
            throw new IllegalStateException("Can't open R file ");
        }
        ScriptEngineManager manager = new ScriptEngineManager();
        ScriptEngine engine = manager.getEngineByName("Renjin");
        engine.put("us", us);
        engine.put("ns", ns);
        engine.eval(FileIO.readerToString(new InputStreamReader(is)));
    }
}
```

Renjin can also be used as a standalone R implementation if you download an all-dependencies JAR file from *https://renjin.org/downloads.html*.

11.6 Using Java from Within an R Session

Problem

You are partway through a computation in R and realize that there's a Java library to do the next step. Or for any other reason, you need to call Java code from within an R session.

Solution

Install rJava, call .jinit(), and use J() to load classes or invoke methods.

Discussion

Here is the part of an interactive R session in which we install rJava, initialize it by calling .jinit(), and invoke java.time.LocalDate.now() to get the current date:

```
> install.packages('rJava')                       ❶
trying URL 'http://.../rJava_0.9-11.tgz'
Content type 'application/x-gzip' length 745354 bytes (727 KB)
==================================================
downloaded 727 KB


The downloaded binary packages are in
    /tmp//Rtmp6XYZ9t/downloaded_packages
> library('rJava')                                 ❷
```

```
> .jinit()
> J('java.time.LocalDate', 'now')                    ❸
[1] "Java-Object{2019-11-22}"
> d=J('java.time.LocalDate', 'now')$toString()       ❹
> d
[1] "2019-11-22"
```

❶ Install the rJava package; only needs to be done once.

❷ load rJava, and initialize it with .jinit(); both needed in every R session.

❸ The J function takes one argument of a full class name. If only that argument is given, a class descriptor (like a java.lang.Class object) is returned. If more than one argument is given, the second is a static method name, and any subsequent arguments are passed to that method.

❹ Returned objects can have Java methods invoked with the standard R \$ notation; here the toString() method is invoked to return just a character string instead of a LocalDate object.

The .jcall function gives you more control over calling method and return types:

```
> d=J('java.time.LocalDate', 'now')                      ❶
> .jcall(d, "I", 'getYear')                              ❷
[1] 2019
>
> .jcall("java/lang/System","S","getProperty","user.dir") ❸
[1] "/home/ian"
> c=J('java/lang/System')                                ❹
> .jcall(c, "S", 'getProperty', 'user.dir')
[1] "/home/ian"
>
```

❶ Invoke Java LocalDate.now() method and save result in R variable *d*.

❷ Invoke Java getYear() method on the LocalDate object; the "I" tells jcall to expect an integer result.

❸ Call System.getProperty("user.dir") and print the result; the "S" tells .jcall to expect a string return.

❹ If you will be using a class several times, save the Class object, and pass it as the first argument of .jcall().

There are more capabilities here; consult the documentation (*https://cran.r-project.org/web/packages/rJava*) and a developer.com article (*https://www.developer.com/java/ent/getting-started-with-r-using-java.html*).

11.7 Using FastR, the GraalVM Implementation of R

Problem

You use the R language but feel a need for speed.

Solution

Use FastR, Oracle's GraalVM reimplementation of the R language.

Discussion

Assuming you have installed GraalVM as described in Recipe 1.2, you can just type the following command:

```
$ gu install R
Downloading: Component catalog from www.graalvm.org
Processing component archive: FastR
Downloading: Component R: FastR  from github.com
Installing new component: FastR (org.graalvm.R, version 19.2.0.1)
NOTES:
---------------
The user specific library directory was not created automatically.
You can either create the directory manually or edit file
/Library/Java/JavaVirtualMachines/graalvm-ce-19.2.0.1/Contents/
   Home/jre/languages/R/etc/Renviron
to change it to any desired location. Without user specific library
directory, users will need write permission for the GraalVM home
directory in order to install R packages.
...
[more install notes]
```

If you have set your PATH to have GraalVM before other directories, the command *R* will now give you the GraalVM version of R. To access the standard R, you will have to either set your PATH or give a full path to the R installation. On all Unix and Unix-like systems, the command *which R* will reveal all R commands on your PATH:

```
$ which R
/Library/Java/JavaVirtualMachines/graalvm-ce-19.2.0.1/Contents/Home/bin/R
/usr/local/bin/R
```

Let's just run it:

```
$ R
R version 3.5.1 (FastR)
Copyright (c) 2013-19, Oracle and/or its affiliates
Copyright (c) 1995-2018, The R Core Team
Copyright (c) 2018 The R Foundation for Statistical Computing
Copyright (c) 2012-4 Purdue University
Copyright (c) 1997-2002, Makoto Matsumoto and Takuji Nishimura
All rights reserved.
```

```
FastR is free software and comes with ABSOLUTELY NO WARRANTY.
You are welcome to redistribute it under certain conditions.
Type 'license()' or 'licence()' for distribution details.

R is a collaborative project with many contributors.
Type 'contributors()' for more information.

Type 'q()' to quit R.
[Previously saved workspace restored]

> 2 + 2
[1] 4
> ^D
Save workspace image? [y/n/c]: n
$
```

From that point on, you should be able to do practically anything that you would do in standard R, since this R's source code is largely derived from the R Foundation's source.

11.8 Using R in a Web App

Problem

You want to display R's data and graphics in a web page on a web server.

Solution

There are several approaches that would achieve this effect:

- Prepare the data, generate graphics as we did in Recipe 11.3, and then incorporate both into a static web page.
- Use one of several R add-on web frameworks (*https://cran.r-project.org/web/ views/WebTechnologies.html#web-and-server-frameworks*), such as shiny (*https:// cran.r-project.org/web/packages/shiny/index.html*) or Rook (*https://cran.r-project.org/web/packages/Rook/index.html*).
- Invoke a JVM implementation of R from within a Servlet, JSF, Spring Bean, or other web-tier component.

Discussion

The first approach is trivial, and doesn't need discussion here.

For the second, I'll actually use timevis, which in turn uses shiny. This isn't built in to the R library, so we first have to install it, using R's install.packages():

```
$ R
> install.packages('timevis')
> quit()
$
```

This may take a while as it downloads and builds multiple dependencies.

For this demo I have a small dataset with some basic information on medieval litera-
ture, which I load and display using shiny:

```
# Draw the timeline for the epics.

epics = read.table("epics.txt", header=TRUE, fill=TRUE)

# epics

library("timevis")

timevis(epics)
```

When run, this creates a temporary file containing HTML and JavaScript to allow
interactive exploration of the data. The library also opens this in a browser, shown in
Figure 11-2. One can explore the data by expanding or contracting the timeline and
scrolling sideways.

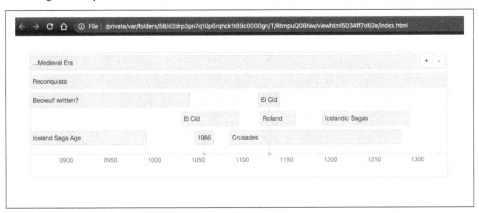

Figure 11-2. TimeVis (shiny) in action

Where there are two boxes (Cid, Sagas), the first is when the life or stories took place,
and the second is when they were written down.

To expose this on the public web, copy the file (whose full path is revealed in the
browser titlebar) and the *lib* folder in that same directory into a directory served by
the web server. Or just use File→Save As→Complete Web Page within the browser.
Either way, you must do this while the R session is running, as the temporary files are
deleted when the session ends. Or, if you are familiar with the shiny framework, you
can insert the timevis visualization into a shiny application.

## CHAPTER 12

Network Clients

12.0 Introduction

Java can be used to write many types of networked programs. In traditional socket-based code, the programmer is responsible for structuring the interaction between the client and server; the TCP *socket code* simply ensures that whatever data you send gets to the other end. In higher-level types, such as HTTP, RMI, CORBA, and EJB, the software takes over more control. Sockets are often used for connecting to legacy servers; if you were writing a new application from scratch, you'd be better off using a higher-level service.

It may be helpful to compare sockets with the telephone system. Telephones were originally used for analog voice traffic, which is pretty unstructured. Then it began to be used for some layered applications; the first widely popular one was facsimile transmission, or fax. Where would fax be without the widespread availability of voice telephony? The second wildly popular layered application historically was dial-up TCP/IP. This coexisted with the web to become popular as a mass-market service. Where would dial-up IP be without widely deployed voice lines? And where would the internet be without dial-up IP? Fax and dial-up are mostly gone now, but they paved the way for your smartphone's networked ability, which is what makes it useful (and even seductive as a time sink).

Sockets are layered like that too. The web, RMI, JDBC, CORBA, and EJB are all layered on top of sockets. HTTP is now the most common protocol and should generally be used for new applications when all you want is to get data from point b to point a.

Ever since the alpha release of Java (originally as a sideline to the HotJava browser) in May 1995, Java has been popular as a programming language for building network applications. It's easy to see why, particularly if you've ever built a networked application in C. First, C programmers have to worry about the platform they are on. Unix uses synchronous sockets, which work rather like normal disk files vis-à-vis reading and writing, whereas Microsoft OSes use asynchronous sockets, which use callbacks to notify when a read or write has completed. Java glosses over this distinction. Further, the amount of code needed to set up a socket in C is intimidating. Just for fun, Example 12-1 shows the typical C code for setting up a client socket. And remember, this is only the Unix part. And only the part that makes and closes the connection. To be portable to Windows, it would need some additional conditional code (using C's #ifdef mechanism). C's #include mechanism requires that exactly the right files be included, and some files have to be listed in particular orders (Java's import mechanism is much more flexible).

Example 12-1. main/src/main/java/network/Connect.c (C client setup)

```c
#include <sys/types.h>
#include <sys/socket.h>
#include <netinet/in.h>
#include <netdb.h>
#include <stdio.h>
#include <string.h>
#include <fcntl.h>

int
main(int argc, char *argv[])
{
    char* server_name = "localhost";
    struct hostent *host_info;
    int sock;
    struct sockaddr_in server;

    /* Look up the remote host's IP address */
    host_info = gethostbyname(server_name);
    if (host_info == NULL) {
        fprintf(stderr, "%s: unknown host: %s\n", argv[0], server_name);
        exit(1);
    }

    /* Create the socket */
    if ((sock = socket(AF_INET, SOCK_STREAM, 0)) < 0) {
        perror("creating client socket");
        exit(2);
    }

    /* Set up the server's socket address */
    server.sin_family = AF_INET;
    memcpy((char *)&server.sin_addr, host_info->h_addr,
                    host_info->h_length);
    server.sin_port = htons(80);
```

```
    /* Connect to the server */
    if (connect(sock,(struct sockaddr *)&server,sizeof server) < 0) {
        perror("connecting to server");
        exit(4);
    }

    /* Finally, we can read and write on the socket. */
    /* ... */

    (void) close(sock);
}
```

In the first recipe, we'll see how to do the connect in essentially one line of Java (plus a bit of error handling). We'll then cover error handling and transferring data over a socket. Next, we'll take a quick look at a `datagram` or UDP client that implements most of the TFTP (Trivial File Transfer Protocol) that has been used for two decades to boot diskless workstations. We'll end with a program that connects interactively to a chat server.

A common theme through most of these client examples is to use existing servers so that we don't have to generate both the client and the server at the same time. Most of these are services that exist on any standard Unix platform. If you can't find a Unix server near you to try them on, let me suggest that you take an old PC, maybe one that's underpowered for running the latest Microsoft software, and put up a free, open source Unix system on it. My personal favorite is OpenBSD (*https:// openbsd.org*), and the market's overall favorite is Linux. Both are readily available and can be installed for free over the internet, and they offer all the standard services used in the client examples, including the time servers and TFTP. Both have free Java implementations available.

I also provide basic coverage of web services clients. The term "web services" has come to mean program-to-program communication using HTTP. The two general categories are SOAP-based and REST-based. REST services are very simple—you send an HTTP request and get back a response in plain text, or JSON (Chapter 14) or XML. SOAP is more complicated and not covered in this book. There is more information on the client-side connections in *Java Network Programming (http:// shop.oreilly.com/product/0636920028420.do)* by Elliotte Harold (O'Reilly). I don't cover the server-side APIs for building web services—JAX-RS and JAX-WS—because these are covered in several O'Reilly books (*http://search.oreilly.com/?q=java+enter prise*).

12.1 HTTP/REST Web Client

Problem

You need to read from a URL, for example, to connect to a RESTful web service or to download a web page or other resource over HTTP/HTTPS.

Solution

Use the standard Java 11 HttpClient or the URLConnection class.

This technique applies anytime you need to read from a URL, not just a RESTful web service.

Discussion

Prior to Java 11, you had to either use the URLConnection class or download and use the older Apache HTTP Client Library. With Java 11, there is a fairly easy-to-use and flexible API in standard Java. It also supports HTTP/2.0; which the Apache HttpClient does not as of early 2020, and the legacy URLConnection, which is unlikely ever to support HTTP/2.0.

As our simple example, we'll use Google's Suggest service, that is, what you see when you type the first few characters of a search into the Google web search engine.

This Google service supports various output formats. The base URL is just the following:

```
https://suggestqueries.google.com/complete/search?client=firefox&q=
```

Append to it the word you want suggestions on. The client=firefox tells it we want a simple JSON format; with client=chrome it contains more fields.

To use the Java HTTP Client API, you need a HttpClient object, which you get using the Builder pattern, then create a Request object:

```java
// This object would be kept for the life of an application
HttpClient client = HttpClient.newBuilder()
    .followRedirects(Redirect.NORMAL)
    .version(Version.HTTP_1_1)
    .build();

// Build the HttpRequest object to "GET" the urlString
HttpRequest req =
    HttpRequest.newBuilder(URI.create(urlString +
        URLEncoder.encode(keyword)))
    .header("User-Agent", "Dept of Silly Walks")
    .GET()
    .build();
```

The `HttpRequest` object can be sent using the client to get a `HttpResponse` object, from which you can get the status and/or the body. Sending can be done either synchronously (if you need the results right away) or asynchronously (if you can usefully do something else in the meantime). This example shows sending it both synchronously and asynchronously:

```
// Send the request - synchronously
HttpResponse<String> resp =
    client.send(req, BodyHandlers.ofString());

// Collect the results
if (resp.statusCode() == 200) {
    String response = resp.body();
    System.out.println(response);
} else {
    System.out.printf("ERROR: Status %d on request %s\n",
        resp.statusCode(), urlString);
}

// Send the request - asynchronously
client.sendAsync(req, BodyHandlers.ofString())
    .thenApply(HttpResponse::body)
    .thenAccept(System.out::println)
    .join();
```

Here is the output; the line has been broken at commas to make it fit on the page:

```
$ java HttpClientDemo.java
["darwin",["darwin thompson","darwin","darwin awards","darwinism",
 "darwin australia","darwin thompson fantasy","darwin barney",
 "darwin theory","darwinai","darwin dormitorio"]]
```

Should you not wish to use the `HttpClient` library, you *could* use the legacy code in `java.net`, since all we usually need here is the ability to open and read from a URL. Here is the code using a `URLConnection`:

```
public class RestClientURLDemo {
    public static void main(String[] args) throws Exception {
        URLConnection conn = new URL(
            HttpClientDemo.urlString + HttpClientDemo.keyword)
            .openConnection();
        try (BufferedReader is =
            new BufferedReader(new InputStreamReader(conn.getInputStream()))) {

            String line;
            while ((line = is.readLine()) != null) {
                System.out.println(line);
            }
        }
    }
}
```

The output should be identical to what the `HttpClient` version produced.

See Also

Don't confuse this HttpClient with the older Apache HttpClient Library (*https://hc.apache.org/httpcomponents-client-ga/index.html*).

You can find more information on REST services (including implementing the server-side components for them) in Bill Burke's *RESTful Java with JAX-RS 2.0, 2nd Edition* (*http://shop.oreilly.com/product/0636920028925.do*) (O'Reilly).

12.2 Contacting a Socket Server

Problem

You need to contact a server using TCP/IP.

Solution

Just create a java.net.Socket, passing the hostname and port number into the constructor.

Discussion

There isn't much to this in Java. When creating a socket, you pass in the hostname and the port number. The java.net.Socket constructor does the gethostbyname() and the socket() system call, sets up the server's sockaddr_in structure, and executes the connect() call. All you have to do is catch the errors, which are subclassed from the familiar IOException. Example 12-2 sets up a Java network client but doesn't actually do any I/O yet. It uses try-with-resources to ensure that the socket is closed automatically when we are done with it.

Example 12-2. main/src/main/java/network/ConnectSimple.java (simple client connection)

```
import java.net.Socket;

/* Client with NO error handling */
public class ConnectSimple {

    public static void main(String[] argv) throws Exception {

        try (Socket sock = new Socket("localhost", 8080)) {

            /* If we get here, we can read and write on the socket "sock" */
            System.out.println(" *** Connected OK ***");

            /* Do some I/O here... */
```

```
            }
        }
}
```

This version does no real error reporting, but a version called *ConnectFriendly* does; we'll see this version in Recipe 12.4.

See Also

Java supports other ways of using network applications. You can also open a URL and read from it (see Recipe 12.8). You can write code so that it will run from a URL, when opened in a web browser, or from an application.

12.3 Finding and Reporting Network Addresses

Problem

You want to look up a host's address name or number or get the address at the other end of a network connection.

Solution

Get an InetAddress object.

Discussion

The InetAddress object represents the internet address of a given computer or host. It has no public constructors; you obtain an InetAddress by calling the static getBy Name() method, passing in either a hostname like *darwinsys.com* or a network address as a string, like 1.23.45.67. All the "lookup" methods in this class can throw the checked UnknownHostException (a subclass of java.io.IOException), which must be caught or declared on the calling method's header. None of these methods actually contact the remote host, so they do not throw the other exceptions related to network connections.

The method getHostAddress() gives you the numeric IP address (as a string) corresponding to the InetAddress. The inverse is getHostName(), which reports the name of the InetAddress. This can be used to print the address of a host given its name, or vice versa:

```
public class InetAddrDemo {
    public static void main(String[] args) throws IOException {
        String hostName = "darwinsys.com";
        String ipNumber = "8.8.8.8"; // currently a well-known Google DNS server

        // Show getting the InetAddress (looking up a host) by host name
```

```
        System.out.println(hostName + "'s address is " +
            InetAddress.getByName(hostName).getHostAddress());

        // Look up a host by address
        System.out.println(ipNumber + "'s name is " +
            InetAddress.getByName(ipNumber).getHostName());

        // Look up my localhost addresss
        final InetAddress localHost = InetAddress.getLocalHost();
        System.out.println("My localhost address is " + localHost);

        // Show getting the InetAddress from an open Socket
        String someServerName = "google.com";
        // assuming there's a web server on the named server:
        try (Socket theSocket = new Socket(someServerName, 80)) {
            InetAddress remote = theSocket.getInetAddress();
            System.out.printf("The InetAddress for %s is %s%n",
                someServerName, remote);
        }
    }
}
```

You can also get an InetAddress from a Socket by calling its getInetAddress()
method. You can construct a Socket using an InetAddress instead of a hostname
string. So, to connect to port number myPortNumber on the same host as an existing
socket, you'd use this:

```
InetAddress remote = theSocket.getInetAddress( );
Socket anotherSocket = new Socket(remote, myPortNumber);
```

Finally, to look up all the addresses associated with a host—a server may be on more
than one network—use the static method getAllByName(host), which returns an
array of InetAddress objects, one for each IP address associated with the given name.

A static method getLocalHost() returns an InetAddress equivalent to localhost or
127.0.0.1. This can be used to connect to a server program running on the same
machine as the client.

If you are using IPv6, you can use Inet6Address instead.

See Also

See NetworkInterface in Recipe 13.2, which lets you find out more about the net‐
working of the machine you are running on. There is no way to look up services in
the standard API yet—that is, to find out that the HTTP service is on port 80. Full
implementations of TCP/IP have always included an additional set of resolvers; in C,

the call getservbyname("http", "tcp"); would look up the given service[6] and return a servent (service entry) structure whose s_port member would contain the value 80. The numbers of established services do not change, but when services are new or installed in nonroutine ways, it is convenient to be able to change the service number for all programs on a machine or network (regardless of programming language) just by changing the services definitions. Java should provide this capability in a future release.

12.4 Handling Network Errors

Problem

You want more detailed reporting than just IOException if something goes wrong.

Solution

Catch a greater variety of exception classes. SocketException has several subclasses; the most notable are ConnectException and NoRouteToHostException. The names are self-explanatory: the first means that the connection was refused by the machine at the other end (the server machine), and the second completely explains the failure. Example 12-3 is an excerpt from the Connect program, enhanced to handle these conditions.

Example 12-3. ConnectFriendly.java

```
public class ConnectFriendly {
    public static void main(String[] argv) {
        String server_name = argv.length == 1 ? argv[0] : "localhost";
        int tcp_port = 80;
        try (Socket sock = new Socket(server_name, tcp_port)) {

            /* If we get here, we can read and write on the socket. */
            System.out.println(" *** Connected to " + server_name  + " ***");

            /* Do some I/O here... */

        } catch (UnknownHostException e) {
            System.err.println(server_name + " Unknown host");
            return;
        } catch (NoRouteToHostException e) {
            System.err.println(server_name + " Unreachable" );
```

---

6 The location where it is looked up varies. It might be in a file named */etc/services* on Unix; in the *services* file in a subdirectory of \ *or* _*winnt* in Windows; in a centralized registry such as Sun's Network Information Services (NIS, formerly YP); or in some other platform- or network-dependent location.

```
        return;
    } catch (ConnectException e) {
        System.err.println(server_name + " connect refused");
        return;
    } catch (java.io.IOException e) {
        System.err.println(server_name + ' ' + e.getMessage());
        return;
    }
    }
}
```

12.5 Reading and Writing Textual Data

Problem

Having connected, you wish to transfer textual data.

Solution

Construct a BufferedReader or PrintWriter from the socket's getInputStream() or getOutputStream().

Discussion

The Socket class has methods that allow you to get an InputStream or OutputStream to read from or write to the socket. It has no method to fetch a Reader or Writer, partly because some network services are limited to ASCII, but mainly because the Socket class was decided on before there were Reader and Writer classes. You can always create a Reader from an InputStream or a Writer from an OutputStream using the conversion classes. This is the paradigm for the two most common forms:

```
BufferedReader is = new BufferedReader(
    new InputStreamReader(sock.getInputStream( )));
PrintWriter os = new PrintWriter(sock.getOutputStream( ), true);
```

Example 12-4 reads a line of text from the daytime service, which is offered by full-fledged TCP/IP suites (such as those included with most Unixes). You don't have to send anything to the Daytime server; you simply connect and read one line. The server writes one line containing the date and time and then closes the connection.

Running it looks like the following code. I started by getting the current date and time on the local host, then ran the DaytimeText program to see the date and time on the server (machine *darian* is one of my Unix servers):

```
C:\javasrc\network>date
Current date is Sun 01-23-2000
Enter new date (mm-dd-yy):
C:\javasrc\network>time
```

```
Current time is  1:13:18.70p
Enter new time:
C:\javasrc\network>java network.DaytimeText darian
Time on darian is Sun Jan 23 13:14:34 2000
```

The code is in class DaytimeText, shown in Example 12-4.

Example 12-4. DaytimeText.java

```java
public class DaytimeText {
    public static final short TIME_PORT = 13;

    public static void main(String[] argv) {
        String server_name = argv.length == 1 ? argv[0] : "localhost";

        try (Socket sock = new Socket(server_name,TIME_PORT);
            BufferedReader is = new BufferedReader(new
                InputStreamReader(sock.getInputStream()));) {
            String remoteTime = is.readLine();
            System.out.println("Time on " + server_name + " is " + remoteTime);
        } catch (IOException e) {
            System.err.println(e);
        }
    }
}
```

The second example, shown in Example 12-5, shows both reading and writing on the same socket. The Echo server simply echoes back whatever lines of text you send it. It's not a very clever server, but it is a useful one. It helps in network testing and also in testing clients of this type!

The converse() method holds a short conversation with the Echo server on the named host; if no host is named, it tries to contact localhost, a universal alias[6] for the machine the program is running on.

Example 12-5. main/src/main/java/network/EchoClientOneLine.java

```java
public class EchoClientOneLine {
    /** What we send across the net */
    String mesg = "Hello across the net";

    public static void main(String[] argv) {
        if (argv.length == 0)
            new EchoClientOneLine().converse("localhost");
```

---

6 It used to be universal, when most networked systems were administered by full-time systems people who had been trained or served an apprenticeship. Today many machines on the internet don't have localhost configured properly.

```
        else
            new EchoClientOneLine().converse(argv[0]);
    }

    /** Hold one conversation across the net */
    protected void converse(String hostName) {
        try (Socket sock = new Socket(hostName, 7);) { // echo server.
            BufferedReader is = new BufferedReader(new
                InputStreamReader(sock.getInputStream()));
            PrintWriter os = new PrintWriter(sock.getOutputStream(), true);
            // Do the CRLF ourself since println appends only a \r on
            // platforms where that is the native line ending.
            os.print(mesg + "\r\n"); os.flush();
            String reply = is.readLine();
            System.out.println("Sent \"" + mesg  + "\"");
            System.out.println("Got  \"" + reply + "\"");
        } catch (IOException e) {
            System.err.println(e);
        }
    }
}
```

It might be a good exercise to isolate the reading and writing code from this method into a NetWriter class, possibly subclassing PrintWriter and adding the \r\n and the flushing.

12.6 Reading and Writing Binary or Serialized Data

Problem

Having connected, you wish to transfer binary data, either raw binary data or serialized Java objects.

Solution

For plain binary date, construct a DataInputStream or DataOutputStream from the socket's getInputStream() or getOutputStream(). For serialized Java object data, construct an ObjectInputStream or ObjectOutputStream.

Discussion

The simplest paradigm for reading/writing on a socket is this:

```
DataInputStream is = new DataInputStream(sock.getInputStream());
DataOutputStream is = new DataOutputStream(sock.getOutputStream( ));
```

If the volume of data might be large, insert a buffered stream for efficiency. The paradigm is this:

```
DataInputStream is = new DataInputStream(
    new BufferedInputStream(sock.getInputStream( )));
DataOutputStream is = new DataOutputStream(
    new BufferedOutputStream(sock.getOutputStream( )));
```

The program example in Example 12-6 uses another standard service that gives out the time as a binary integer representing the number of seconds since 1900. Because the Java Date class base is 1970, we convert the time base by subtracting the difference between 1970 and 1900. When I used this exercise in a course, most of the students wanted to *add* this time difference, reasoning that 1970 is later. But if you think clearly, you'll see that there are fewer seconds between 1999 and 1970 than there are between 1999 and 1900, so subtraction gives the correct number of seconds. And because the Date constructor needs milliseconds, we multiply the number of seconds by 1,000.

The time difference is the number of years multiplied by 365, plus the number of leap days between the two dates (in the years 1904, 1908, ..., 1968)—19 days.

The integer that we read from the server is a C-language unsigned int. But Java doesn't provide an unsigned integer type; normally when you need an unsigned number, you use the next-larger integer type, which would be long. But Java also doesn't give us a method to read an unsigned integer from a data stream. The DataInput Stream method readInt() reads Java-style signed integers. There are readUnsigned Byte() methods and readUnsignedShort() methods, but no readUnsignedInt() method. Accordingly, we synthesize the ability to read an unsigned int (which must be stored in a long, or else you'd lose the signed bit and be back where you started from) by reading unsigned bytes and reassembling them using Java's bit-shifting operators:

At the end of the code, we use the new date/time API (see Chapter 6) to construct and print a LocalDateTime object to show the current date and time on the local (client) machine:

```
$ date
Thu Dec 26 09:48:36 EST 2019
java network.RDateClient aragorn
Remote time is 3786360519
BASE_DIFF is 2208988800
Time diff == 1577371719
Time on aragorn is 2019-12-26T09:48:39
Local date/time = 2019-12-26T09:48:41.208180
$
```

The name *aragorn* is the hostname of one of my OpenBSD Unix computers. Looking at the output, you can see that the server agrees within a second or two. That confirms the date calculation code in Example 12-6. This protocol is commonly known as rdate, so the client code is called RDateClient.

Example 12-6. main/src/main/java/network/RDateClient.java

```java
public class RDateClient {
    /** The TCP port for the binary time service. */
    public static final short TIME_PORT = 37;
    /** Seconds between 1970, the time base for dates and times
     * Factors in leap years (up to 2100), hours, minutes, and seconds.
     * Subtract 1 day for 1900, add in 1/2 day for 1969/1970.
     */
    protected static final long BASE_DAYS =
        (long)((1970-1900)*365 + (1970-1900-1)/4);

    /* Seconds since 1970 */
    public static final long BASE_DIFF = (BASE_DAYS * 24 * 60 * 60);

    public static void main(String[] argv) {
        String hostName;
        if (argv.length == 0)
            hostName = "localhost";
        else
            hostName = argv[0];

        try (Socket sock = new Socket(hostName,TIME_PORT);) {
            DataInputStream is = new DataInputStream(new
                BufferedInputStream(sock.getInputStream()));
            // Read 4 bytes from the network, unsigned.
            // Do it yourself; there is no readUnsignedInt().
            // Long is 8 bytes on Java, but we are using the
            // existing time protocol, which uses 4-byte ints.
            long remoteTime = (
                ((long)(is.readUnsignedByte()) << 24) |
                ((long)(is.readUnsignedByte()) << 16) |
                ((long)(is.readUnsignedByte()) <<  8) |
                ((long)(is.readUnsignedByte()) <<  0));
            System.out.println("Remote time is " + remoteTime);
            System.out.println("BASE_DIFF is " + BASE_DIFF);
            System.out.println("Time diff == " + (remoteTime - BASE_DIFF));
            Instant time = Instant.ofEpochSecond(remoteTime - BASE_DIFF);
            LocalDateTime d = LocalDateTime.ofInstant(time, ZoneId.systemDefault());
            System.out.println("Time on " + hostName + " is " + d.toString());
            System.out.println("Local date/time = " + LocalDateTime.now());
        } catch (IOException e) {
            System.err.println(e);
        }
    }
}
```

Object serialization is the ability to convert in-memory objects to an external form that can be sent serially (a byte at a time). To read or write Java objects via serialization, you need only construct an ObjectInputStream or ObjectOutputStream from an `InputStream` or `OutputStream`; in this case, the socket's `getInputStream()` or `getOutputStream()`.

This program (and its server) provide a service that isn't a standard part of the TCP/IP stack; it's a service I made up as a demo. The server for this service is introduced in Recipe 13.3. The client code in Example 12-7 is quite similar to the `Daytime Binary` program in the previous recipe, but the server sends us a `LocalDateTime` object already constructed. Example 12-7 shows the portion of the client code that differs from Example 12-6.

Example 12-7. main/src/main/java/network/DaytimeObject.java

```java
try (Socket sock = new Socket(hostName, TIME_PORT);) {
    ObjectInputStream is = new ObjectInputStream(new
        BufferedInputStream(sock.getInputStream()));

    // Read and validate the Object
    Object o = is.readObject();
    if (o == null) {
        System.err.println("Read null from server!");
    } else if ((o instanceof LocalDateTime)) {

        // Valid, so cast to LocalDateTime, and print
        LocalDateTime d = (LocalDateTime) o;
        System.out.println("Time on " + hostName + " is " + d);
    } else {
        throw new IllegalArgumentException(
            String.format("Wanted LocalDateTime, got %s, a %s",
                o, o.getClass()));
    }
}
```

I ask the operating system for the date and time, and then I run the program, which prints the date and time on a remote machine:

```
$ date
Thu Dec 26 09:29:02 EST 2019
C:\javasrc\network>java network.DaytimeObject aragorn
Time on aragorn is 2019-12-26T09:29:05.227397
C:\javasrc\network>
```

Again, the results agree within a few seconds.

12.7 UDP Datagrams

Problem

You need to use a datagram connection (UDP) instead of a stream connection (TCP).

Solution

Use `DatagramSocket` and `DatagramPacket`.

Discussion

Datagram network traffic is a kindred spirit to the underlying packet-based Ethernet and IP (Internet Protocol) layers. Unlike a stream-based connection such as TCP, datagram transports like UDP transmit each *packet*, or chunk of data, as a single entity with no necessary relation to any other.[6] A common analogy is that TCP is like talking on the telephone, whereas UDP is like sending postcards or maybe fax messages.

The differences show up most in error handling. Packets can, like postcards, go astray. When was the last time the postman rang your bell to tell you that the post office had lost one of several postcards it was supposed to deliver to you? That's not going to happen, because the post office doesn't keep track of postcards. On the other hand, when you're talking on the phone and there's a noise burst—like somebody yelling in the room, or even a bad connection—you notice the failure in real time, and you can ask the person at the other end to repeat what they just said.

With a stream-based connection like a TCP socket, the network transport layer handles errors for you: it asks the other end to retransmit. With a datagram transport such as UDP, you have to handle retransmission yourself. It's kind of like numbering the postcards you send so that you can go back and resend any that don't arrive—a good excuse to return to your vacation spot, perhaps.

Another difference is that datagram transmission preserves message boundaries. That is, if you write 20 bytes and then write 10 bytes when using TCP, the program reading from the other end will not know if you wrote one chunk of 30 bytes, two chunks of 15, or even 30 individual characters. With a `DatagramSocket`, you construct a `Data gramPacket` object for each buffer, and its contents are sent as a *single* entity over the network; its contents will not be mixed together with the contents of any other buffer. The `DatagramPacket` object has methods like `getLength()` and `setPort()`.

Ian's Basic Steps: UDP Client

UDP is a bit more involved, so I'll list the basic steps for generating a UDP client:

1. Create a `DatagramSocket` with no arguments (the form that takes two arguments is used on the server).

---

6 The UDP packet may need to be fragmented by some networks, but this is not germane to us at the UDP level, because it will reassemble the network packets into our single-entity UDP packet at the other end.

2. Optionally `connect()` the socket to an `InetAddress` (see Recipe 12.3) and port number.

3. Create one or more `DatagramPacket` objects; these are wrappers around a byte array that contains data you want to send and is filled in with data you receive.

4. If you did not `connect()` the socket, provide the `InetAddress` and port when constructing the `DatagramPacket`.

5. Set the packet's length and use `sock.send(packet)` to send data to the server.

6. Use `sock.receive()` to retrieve data.

So why would we even use UDP? UDP has a lot less overhead than TCP, which can be particularly valuable when sending huge amounts of data over a reliable local network or a few hops on the internet. Over long-haul networks, TCP is probably preferred because TCP handles retransmission of lost packets for you. And obviously, if preserving record boundaries makes your life easier, that may be a reason for considering UDP. UDP is also the way to perform Multicast (broadcast to many receivers simultaneously), though Multicast is out of scope for this discussion.

Example 12-8 is a short program that connects via UDP to the `Daytime` date and time server used in Recipe 12.5. Because UDP has no real notion of connection, the client typically initiates the conversation, which sometimes means sending an empty packet; the UDP server uses the address information it gets from that to return its response.

Example 12-8. main/src/main/java/network/DaytimeUDP.java

```java
public class DaytimeUDP {
    /** The UDP port number */
    public final static int DAYTIME_PORT = 13;

    /** A buffer plenty big enough for the date string */
    protected final static int PACKET_SIZE = 100;

    /** The main program that drives this network client.
     * @param argv[0] hostname, running daytime/udp server
     */
    public static void main(String[] argv) throws IOException {
        if (argv.length < 1) {
            System.err.println("usage: java DayTimeUDP host");
            System.exit(1);
        }
        String host = argv[0];
        InetAddress servAddr = InetAddress.getByName(host);
        DatagramSocket sock = new DatagramSocket();
        //sock.connect(servAddr, DAYTIME_PORT);
        byte[] buffer = new byte[PACKET_SIZE];
```

```
        // The udp packet we will send and receive
        DatagramPacket packet = new DatagramPacket(
            buffer, PACKET_SIZE, servAddr, DAYTIME_PORT);

        /* Send empty max-length (-1 for null byte) packet to server */
        packet.setLength(PACKET_SIZE-1);
        sock.send(packet);
        System.out.println("Sent request");

        // Receive a packet and print it.
        sock.receive(packet);
        System.out.println("Got packet of size " + packet.getLength());
        System.out.print("Date on " + host + " is " +
            new String(buffer, 0, packet.getLength()));

        sock.close();
    }
}
```

I'll run it to my Unix box just to be sure that it works:

```
$
$ java network.DaytimeUDP aragorn
Sent request
Got packet of size 26
Date on aragorn is Sat Feb  8 20:22:12 2014
$
```

12.8 URI, URL, or URN?

Problem

Having heard these terms, you want to know the difference between a URI, URL, and URN.

Solution

Read on. Or see the javadoc for *java.net.uri*.

Discussion

A URL is the traditional name for a network address consisting of a scheme (like HTTP) and an address (site name) and resource or pathname. But there are three distinct terms in all:

- URI (Uniform Resource Identifier)
- URL (Uniform Resource Locator)

- URN (Uniform Resource Name)

A discussion near the end of the Java documentation for the new class explains the relationship among URI, URL, and URN. URIs form the set of all identifiers. URLs and URNs are subsets.

URIs are the most general; a URI is parsed for basic syntax without regard to the scheme, if any, that it specifies, and it need not refer to a particular server. A URL includes a hostname, scheme, and other components; the string is parsed according to rules for its scheme. When you construct a URL, an `InputStream` is created automatically. URNs name resources but do not explain how to locate them; typical examples of URNs that you will have seen include `mailto:` and `news:` references.

The main operations provided by the `URI` class are normalization (removing extraneous path segments including "..") and relativization (this should be called "making relative," but somebody wanted a single word to make a method name). A `URI` object does not have any methods for opening the URI; for that, you would normally use a string representation of the URI to construct a URL object, like so:

```
URL x = new URL(theURI.toString( ));
```

The program in Example 12-9 shows examples of normalizating, making relative, and constructing a URL from a URI.

Example 12-9. main/src/main/java/network/URIDemo.java

```
public class URIDemo {
    public static void main(String[] args)
    throws URISyntaxException, MalformedURLException {

        URI u = new URI("https://darwinsys.com/java/../openbsd/../index.jsp");
        System.out.println("Raw: " + u);
        URI normalized = u.normalize();
        System.out.println("Normalized: " + normalized);
        final URI BASE = new URI("https://darwinsys.com");
        System.out.println("Relativized to " + BASE + ": " + BASE.relativize(u));

        // A URL is a type of URI
        URL url = new URL(normalized.toString());
        System.out.println("URL: " + url);

        // Demo of non-URL but valid URI
        URI uri = new URI("bean:WonderBean");
        System.out.println(uri);
    }
}
```

12.9 Program: TFTP UDP Client

This program implements the client half of the TFTP application protocol, a once-well-known service that has been used in the Unix world for network booting of workstations since before Windows 3.1, now primarily used for network bootstrapping of computers. I chose this protocol because it's widely implemented on the server side, so it's easy to find a test server for it.

The TFTP protocol is a bit odd. The client contacts the server on the well-known UDP port number 69, from a generated port number,[6] and the server responds to the client from a generated port number. Further communication is on the two generated port numbers.

Getting into more detail, as shown in Figure 12-1, the client initially sends a read request with the filename and reads the first packet of data. The read request consists of two bytes (a short) with the read request code (short integer with a value of 1, defined as OP_RRQ), two bytes for the sequence number, then the ASCII filename, null terminated, and the mode string, also null terminated. The server reads the read request from the client, verifies that it can open the file and, if so, sends the first data packet (OP_DATA), and then reads again. The client reads from its end and, if the read is OK, turns the packet into an acknowledgement packet, and sends it. This read-acknowledge cycle is repeated until all the data is read. Note that each packet is 516 bytes (512 bytes of data, plus 2 bytes for the packet type and 2 more for the packet number) except the last, which can be any length from 4 (zero bytes of data) to 515 (511 bytes of data). If a network I/O error occurs, the packet is resent. If a given packet goes astray, both client and server are supposed to perform a timeout cycle. This client does not, but the server does. You could add timeouts either using a thread (see Recipe 16.4) or by invoking setSoTimeout() on the socket and, if packets do get lost, catching the SocketTimeoutException, retransmitting the ACK (or RRQ), perhaps up to some max number of attempts. This is left as an exercise for the reader. The current version of the client code is shown in Example 12-10.

---

6 When the application doesn't care, these port numbers are usually made up by the operating system. For example, when you call a company from a pay phone or cell phone, the company doesn't usually care what number you are calling from, and if it does, there are ways to find out. Generated port numbers generally range from 1024 (the first nonprivileged port; see Chapter 13) to 65535 (the largest value that can be held in a 16-bit port number).

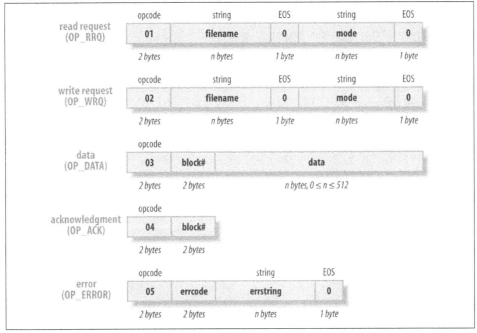

Figure 12-1. The TFTP protocol packet formats

Example 12-10. main/src/main/java/network/RemCat.java

```java
public class RemCat {
    /** The UDP port number */
    public final static int TFTP_PORT = 69;
    /** The mode we will use - octet for everything. */
    protected final String MODE = "octet";

    /** The offset for the code/response as a byte */
    protected final int OFFSET_REQUEST = 1;
    /** The offset for the packet number as a byte */
    protected final int OFFSET_PACKETNUM = 3;

    /** Debugging flag */
    protected static boolean debug = false;

    /** TFTP op-code for a read request */
    public final int OP_RRQ = 1;
    /** TFTP op-code for a read request */
    public final int OP_WRQ = 2;
    /** TFTP op-code for a read request */
    public final int OP_DATA = 3;
    /** TFTP op-code for a read request */
    public final int OP_ACK   = 4;
    /** TFTP op-code for a read request */
```

```java
    public final int OP_ERROR = 5;

    protected final static int PACKET_SIZE = 516;     // == 2 + 2 + 512
    protected String host;
    protected InetAddress servAddr;
    protected DatagramSocket sock;
    protected byte buffer[];
    protected DatagramPacket inp, outp;

    /** The main program that drives this network client.
     * @param argv[0] hostname, running TFTP server
     * @param argv[1..n] filename(s), must be at least one
     */
    public static void main(String[] argv) throws IOException {
        if (argv.length < 2) {
            System.err.println("usage: rcat host filename[...]");
            System.exit(1);
        }
        if (debug)
            System.err.println("Java RemCat starting");
        RemCat rc = new RemCat(argv[0]);
        for (int i = 1; i<argv.length; i++) {
            if (debug)
                System.err.println("-- Starting file " +
                    argv[0] + ":" + argv[i] + "---");
            rc.readFile(argv[i]);
        }
    }

    RemCat(String host) throws IOException {
        super();
        this.host = host;
        servAddr = InetAddress.getByName(host);
        sock = new DatagramSocket();
        buffer = new byte[PACKET_SIZE];
        outp = new DatagramPacket(buffer, PACKET_SIZE, servAddr, TFTP_PORT);
        inp = new DatagramPacket(buffer, PACKET_SIZE);
    }

    /* Build a TFTP Read Request packet. This is messy because the
     * fields have variable length. Numbers must be in
     * network order, too; fortunately Java just seems
     * naturally smart enough :-) to use network byte order.
     */
    void readFile(String path) throws IOException {
        buffer[0] = 0;
        buffer[OFFSET_REQUEST] = OP_RRQ;        // read request
        int p = 2;               // number of chars into buffer

        // Convert filename String to bytes in buffer , using "p" as an
        // offset indicator to get all the bits of this request
        // in exactly the right spot.
```

```
byte[] bTemp = path.getBytes();      // i.e., ASCII
System.arraycopy(bTemp, 0, buffer, p, path.length());
p += path.length();
buffer[p++] = 0;           // null byte terminates string

// Similarly, convert MODE ("stream" or "octet") to bytes in buffer
bTemp = MODE.getBytes();      // i.e., ASCII
System.arraycopy(bTemp, 0, buffer, p, MODE.length());
p += MODE.length();
buffer[p++] = 0;           // null terminate

/* Send Read Request to tftp server */
outp.setLength(p);
sock.send(outp);

/* Loop reading data packets from the server until a short
 * packet arrives; this indicates the end of the file.
 */
do {
    sock.receive(inp);
    if (debug)
        System.err.println(
            "Packet # " + Byte.toString(buffer[OFFSET_PACKETNUM])+
            "RESPONSE CODE " + Byte.toString(buffer[OFFSET_REQUEST]));
    if (buffer[OFFSET_REQUEST] == OP_ERROR) {
        System.err.println("rcat ERROR: " +
            new String(buffer, 4, inp.getLength()-4));
        return;
    }
    if (debug)
        System.err.println("Got packet of size " +
            inp.getLength());

    /* Print the data from the packet */
    System.out.write(buffer, 4, inp.getLength()-4);

    /* Ack the packet. The block number we
     * want to ack is already in buffer so
     * we just change the opcode. The ACK is
     * sent to the port number which the server
     * just sent the data from, NOT to port
     * TFTP_PORT.
     */
    buffer[OFFSET_REQUEST] = OP_ACK;
    outp.setLength(4);
    outp.setPort(inp.getPort());
    sock.send(outp);
} while (inp.getLength() == PACKET_SIZE);

if (debug)
    System.err.println("** ALL DONE** Leaving loop, last size " +
        inp.getLength());
```

```
        }
}
```

To test this client, you need a TFTP server. If you are on a Unix system that you administer, you can enable the TFTP server to test this client just by editing the file */etc/inetd.conf* and restarting or reloading the *inetd* server (Linux uses a different mechanism, which may vary depending on which distribution you are on). *inetd* is a program that listens for a wide range of connections and starts the servers only when a connection from a client comes along (a kind of lazy evaluation).[6] I set up the traditional */tftpboot* directory, put this line in my *inetd.conf*, and reloaded inetd:

```
tftp dgram udp wait root /usr/libexec/tftpd tftpd -s /tftpboot
```

Then I put a few test files, one named *foo*, into the */tftpboot* directory. Running

```
$ java network.RemCat localhost foo
```

produced what looked like the file. But just to be safe, I tested the output of RemCat against the original file, using the Unix *diff* comparison program. No news is good news:

```
$ java network.RemCat localhost foo | diff - /tftpboot/foo
```

So far so good. Let's not slip this program on an unsuspecting network without exercising the error handling at least briefly:

```
$ java network.RemCat localhost nosuchfile
remcat ERROR: File not found
$
```

12.10 Program: Sockets-Based Chat Client

This program is a simple chat program. You can't break in on ICQ or AIM with it, because they each use their own protocol.[7] Rather, this program simply writes to and reads from a server. The server for this will be presented in Chapter 13. How does it look when you run it? Figure 12-2 shows me chatting all by myself one day.

The code is reasonably self-explanatory. We read from the remote server in a thread to make the input and the output run without blocking each other; this is discussed in Chapter 16. The reading and writing are discussed in this chapter. The program is shown in Example 12-11.

---

6 Beware of security holes; don't turn a TFTP server loose on the internet without first reading a good security book, such as *Building Internet Firewalls* (*http://shop.oreilly.com/product/9781565928718.do*) by D. Chapman et al. (O'Reilly).

7 For an open source program that provides an IM service to let you talk to both from the same program, check out Jabber at *http://www.jabber.org*.

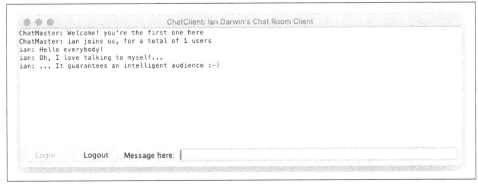

ChatMaster: Welcome! you're the first one here
ChatMaster: ian joins us, for a total of 1 users
ian: Hello everybody!
ian: Oh, I love talking to myself...
ian: ... It guarantees an intelligent audience :-)

Figure 12-2. Chat client in action

Example 12-11. main/src/main/java/chat/ChatClient.java

```java
public class ChatClient extends JFrame {

    private static final long serialVersionUID = -3686334002367908392L;
    private static final String userName =
        System.getProperty("user.name", "User With No Name");
    /** The state of logged-in-ness */
    protected boolean loggedIn;
    /* The main Frame. */
    protected JFrame cp;
    /** The default port number */
    protected static final int PORTNUM = ChatProtocol.PORTNUM;
    /** The actual port number */
    protected int port;
    /** The network socket */
    protected Socket sock;
    /** PrintWriter for sending lines on socket */
    protected PrintWriter pw;
    /** TextField for input */
    protected JTextField tf;
    /** TextArea to display conversations */
    protected JTextArea ta;
    /** The Login Button */
    protected JButton loginButton;
    /** The LogOUT button */
    protected JButton logoutButton;
    /** The TitleBar title */
    final static String TITLE = "ChatClient: Ian Darwin's Chat Room Client";

    final Executor threadPool = Executors.newSingleThreadExecutor();

    /** set up the GUI */
    public ChatClient() {
        cp = this;
        cp.setTitle(TITLE);
```

```java
        cp.setLayout(new BorderLayout());
        port = PORTNUM;

        // The GUI
        ta = new JTextArea(14, 80);
        ta.setEditable(false);          // readonly
        ta.setFont(new Font("Monospaced", Font.PLAIN, 11));
        cp.add(BorderLayout.NORTH, ta);

        JPanel p = new JPanel();

        // The login button
        p.add(loginButton = new JButton("Login"));
        loginButton.setEnabled(true);
        loginButton.requestFocus();
        loginButton.addActionListener(e -> {
                login();
                loginButton.setEnabled(false);
                logoutButton.setEnabled(true);
                tf.requestFocus();      // set keyboard focus in right place!
        });

        // The logout button
        p.add(logoutButton = new JButton("Logout"));
        logoutButton.setEnabled(false);
        logoutButton.addActionListener(e -> {
                logout();
                loginButton.setEnabled(true);
                logoutButton.setEnabled(false);
                loginButton.requestFocus();
        });

        p.add(new JLabel("Message here:"));
        tf = new JTextField(40);
        tf.addActionListener(e -> {
                if (loggedIn) {
                    pw.println(ChatProtocol.CMD_BCAST+tf.getText());
                    tf.setText("");
                }
        });
        p.add(tf);

        cp.add(BorderLayout.SOUTH, p);

        cp.setDefaultCloseOperation(JFrame.EXIT_ON_CLOSE);
        cp.pack();
    }

    protected String serverHost = "localhost";

    /** LOG ME IN TO THE CHAT */
    public void login() {
```

```java
    /** BufferedReader for reading from socket */
    BufferedReader is;

    showStatus("In login!");
    if (loggedIn)
        return;
    try {
        sock = new Socket(serverHost, port);
        is = new BufferedReader(new InputStreamReader(sock.getInputStream()));
        pw = new PrintWriter(sock.getOutputStream(), true);
        showStatus("Got socket");

        // FAKE LOGIN FOR NOW - no password needed
        pw.println(ChatProtocol.CMD_LOGIN + userName);

        loggedIn = true;

    } catch(IOException e) {
        warn("Can't get socket to " +
            serverHost + "/" + port + ": " + e);
        cp.add(new JLabel("Can't get socket: " + e));
        return;
    }

    // Construct and start the reader: from server to textarea.
    // Make a Thread to avoid lockups.
    Runnable readerThread = new Runnable() {
        public void run() {
            String line;
            try {
                while (loggedIn && ((line = is.readLine()) != null))
                    ta.append(line + "\n");
            } catch(IOException e) {
                showStatus("Lost another client!\n" + e);
                return;
            }
        }
    };
    threadPool.execute(readerThread);
}

/** Log me out, Scotty, there's no intelligent life here! */
public void logout() {
    if (!loggedIn)
        return;
    loggedIn = false;
    try {
        if (sock != null)
            sock.close();
    } catch (IOException ign) {
        // so what?
    }
```

```
    }

    public void showStatus(String message) {
        System.out.println(message);
    }

    private void warn(String message) {
        JOptionPane.showMessageDialog(this, message);
    }

    /** A main method to allow the client to be run as an Application */
    public static void main(String[] args) {
        ChatClient room101 = new ChatClient();
        room101.pack();
        room101.setVisible(true);
    }
}
```

See Also

There are many better-structured ways to write a chat client, including WebSockets, RMI, and JMS. RMI is Java's RPC interface and is included both in Java SE and Java EE; it is not described in this edition of this book, but you can find the RMI chapter from previous editions on the my website (*http://darwinsys.com/java/rmi*). The other technologies are part of the Java Enterprise so, again, I refer you to Arun Gupta's *Java EE 7 Essentials*.

If your communication goes over the public internet, you do need to encrypt your socket connection, so check out Sun's JSSE (Java Secure Socket Extension). If you took my earlier advice and used the standard HTTP protocol, you can encrypt the conversation just by changing the URL to https.

For a good overview of network programming from the C programmer's point of view, see the late W. Richard Stevens' *Unix Network Programming* (Prentice Hall). Despite the book's name, it's really about socket and TCP/IP/UDP programming and covers all parts of the (Unix) networking API and protocols such as TFTP in amazing detail.

12.11 Program: Simple HTTP Link Checker

Checking links is an ongoing problem for website owners as well as those who write technical documentation that links to external sources (e.g., people like the author of the book you are now reading). *Link checkers* are the tool they inevitably use to validate the links in their pages, be they web pages or book pages. Implementing a link checker is basically a matter of (a) extracting links and (b) opening them. Thus, we have the program in Example 12-12. I call it KwikLinkChecker as it is a bit on the quick-and-dirty side—it doesn't validate the content of the link to be sure it still contains what it once did; so if, say, an open source project forgets to renew its domain registration, and it gets taken over by a porn site, well, KwikLinkChecker will never know. But that said, it does its job reasonably well, and reasonably quickly.

Example 12-12. darwinsys-api/src/main/java/com/darwinsys/tools/
KwikLinkChecker.java

```java
/**
 * Check one HTTP link; not recursive. Returns a LinkStatus with
 * boolean success, and the filename or an error message in the
 * message part of the LinkStatus.  The end of this method is one of
 * the few places where a whole raft of different "catch" clauses is
 * actually needed for the intent of the program.
 * @param urlString the link to check
 * @return the link's status
 */
@SuppressWarnings("exports")
public LinkStatus check(String urlString) {
    try {
        HttpResponse<String> resp = client.send(
            HttpRequest.newBuilder(URI.create(urlString))
            .header("User-Agent", getClass().getName())
            .GET()
            .build(),
            BodyHandlers.ofString());

        // Collect the results
        if (resp.statusCode() == 200) {
            System.out.println(resp.body());
        } else {
            System.out.printf("ERROR: Status %d on request %s\n",
                resp.statusCode(), urlString);
        }

        switch (resp.statusCode()) {
        case 200:
            return new LinkStatus(true, urlString);
        case 403:
            return new LinkStatus(false,"403: " + urlString );
        case 404:
            return new LinkStatus(false,"404: " + urlString );
        }
        return new LinkStatus(true, urlString);
    } catch (IllegalArgumentException | MalformedURLException e) {
        // JDK throws IAE if host can't be determined from URL string
        return new LinkStatus(false, "Malformed URL: " + urlString);
    } catch (UnknownHostException e) {
        return new LinkStatus(false, "Host invalid/dead: " + urlString);
    } catch (FileNotFoundException e) {
        return new LinkStatus(false,"NOT FOUND (404) " + urlString);
    } catch (ConnectException e) {
```

```
          return new LinkStatus(false, "Server not listening: " + urlString);
      } catch (SocketException e) {
          return new LinkStatus(false, e + ": " + urlString);
      } catch (IOException e) {
          return new LinkStatus(false, e.toString()); // includes failing URL
      } catch (Exception e) {
          return new LinkStatus(false, urlString + ": " + e);
      }
  }
}
```

Fancier link checkers are surely available, but this one works for me.

## CHAPTER 13

Server-Side Java

13.0 Introduction

Sockets form the underpinnings of almost all networking protocols. JDBC, RMI, CORBA, EJB, and the non-Java RPC (Remote Procedure Call) and NFS (Network File System) are all implemented by connecting various types of sockets together. Socket connections can be implemented in most any language, not just Java: C, C++, Perl, and Python are also popular, and many others are possible. A client or server written in any one of these languages can communicate with its opposite written in any of the other languages. Therefore, it's worth taking a quick look at how the Serv erSocket behaves, even if you wind up utilizing the higher-level services such as RMI, JDBC, CORBA, or EJB.

The discussion looks first at the ServerSocket itself, then at writing data over a socket in various ways. Finally, I show a complete implementation of a usable network server written in Java: the chat server from the client in the previous chapter.

Most production work in server-side Java uses the Java Enterprise Edition (Java EE), recently transferred from Oracle to the Eclipse Software Foundation and renamed to Jakarta but widely referred to by the previous name (and occasionally by its very old name, "J2EE," which was retired in 2005). Java EE provides scalability and support for building well-structured, multitiered distributed applications. EE provides the servlet framework; a servlet is a strategy object that can be installed into any standard Java EE web server. EE also provides two web view technologies: the original JSP (Java-Server Pages) and the newer, component-based JSF (JavaServer Faces). Finally, EE provides a number of other network-based services, including EJB3 remote access and Java Messaging Service (JMS). These are outside the scope of this book; they are covered in other books, such as Arun Gupta's *Java EE 7 Essentials: Enterprise Developer Handbook*. This chapter is only for those who need or want to build their own server from the ground up.

13.1 Opening a Server Socket for Business

Problem

You need to write a socket-based server.

Solution

Create a ServerSocket for the given port number.

Discussion

The ServerSocket represents the other end of a connection, the server that waits patiently for clients to come along and connect to it. You construct a ServerSocket with just the port number.[6] Because it doesn't need to connect to another host, it doesn't need a particular host's address as the client socket constructor does.

Assuming the ServerSocket constructor doesn't throw an exception, you're in business. Your next step is to await client activity, which you do by calling accept(). This call blocks until a client connects to your server; at that point, the accept() returns to you a Socket object (not a ServerSocket) that is connected in both directions to the

---

6 You may not be able to pick just any port number for your own service, of course. Certain well-known port numbers are reserved for specific services and listed in your *services* file, such as 22 for Secure Shell and 25 for SMTP. Also, on server-based operating systems, ports below 1024 are considered privileged ports and require root or administrator privilege to create. This was an early security mechanism; today, with zillions of single-user desktops connected to the internet, it provides little real security, but the restriction remains.

ServerSocket object on the client (or its equivalent, if written in another language). Example 13-1 shows the code for a socket-based server.

Example 13-1. main/src/main/java/network/Listen.java

```java
public class Listen {
    /** The TCP port for the service. */
    public static final short PORT = 9999;

    public static void main(String[] argv) throws IOException {
        ServerSocket sock;
        Socket  clientSock;
        try {
            sock = new ServerSocket(PORT);
            while ((clientSock = sock.accept()) != null) {

                // Process it, usually on a separate thread
                // to avoid blocking the accept() call.
                process(clientSock);
            }

        } catch (IOException e) {
            System.err.println(e);
        }
    }

    /** This would do something with one client. */
    static void process(Socket s) throws IOException {
        System.out.println("Accept from client " + s.getInetAddress());
        // The conversation would be here.
        s.close();
    }
}
```

You would normally use the same socket for both reading and writing, as shown in the next few recipes.

You may want to listen only on a particular network interface. Though we tend to think of network addresses as computer addresses, the two are not the same. A network address is actually the address of a particular network card, or network interface connection, on a given computing device. A desktop computer, laptop, tablet, or mobile phone might have only a single interface, hence a single network address. But a large server machine might have two or more interfaces, usually when it is connected to several networks. A network router is a box, either special purpose (e.g., a Cisco router), or general purpose (e.g., a Unix host), that has interfaces on multiple networks *and* has both the capability and the administrative permission to forward packets from one network to another. A program running on such a server machine might want to provide services only to its inside network or its outside network. One way to accomplish this is by specifying the network interface to be listened on. Suppose you want to provide a different view of web pages for your intranet than you provide to outside customers. For security reasons, you probably wouldn't run both these services on the same machine. But if you wanted to, you could do this by providing the network interface addresses as arguments to the ServerSocket constructor.

However, to use this form of the constructor, you don't have the option of using a string for the network address's name, as you did with the client socket; you must convert it to an InetAddress object. You also have to provide a backlog argument, which is the number of connections that can queue up to be accepted before clients are told that your server is too busy. The complete setup is shown in Example 13-2.

Example 13-2. main/src/main/java/network/ListenInside.java

```java
public class ListenInside {
    /** The TCP port for the service. */
    public static final short PORT = 9999;
    /** The name of the network interface. */
    public static final String INSIDE_HOST = "acmewidgets-inside";
    /** The number of clients allowed to queue */
    public static final int BACKLOG = 10;

    public static void main(String[] argv) throws IOException {
        ServerSocket sock;
        Socket  clientSock;
        try {
            sock = new ServerSocket(PORT, BACKLOG,
                InetAddress.getByName(INSIDE_HOST));
            while ((clientSock = sock.accept()) != null) {

                // Process it.
                process(clientSock);
            }

        } catch (IOException e) {
            System.err.println(e);
        }
    }

    /** Hold server's conversation with one client. */
    static void process(Socket s) throws IOException {
        System.out.println("Connected from  " + INSIDE_HOST +
            ": " + s.getInetAddress(  ));
        // The conversation would be here.
        s.close();
    }
}
```

`InetAddress.getByName()` looks up the given hostname in a system-dependent way, referring to a configuration file in the */etc* or *\windows* directory, or to some kind of resolver such as the Domain Name System. Consult a good book on networking and system administration if you need to modify this data.

13.2 Finding Network Interfaces

Problem

You wish to find out about the computer's networking arrangements.

Solution

Use the `NetworkInterface` class.

Discussion

Every computer on a network has one or more "network interfaces." On typical desktop machines, a network interface represents a network card or network port or some software network interface, such as the loopback interface. Each interface has an operating system–defined name. On most versions of Unix, these devices have a two- or three-character device driver name plus a digit (starting from 0), for example, `eth0` or `en0` for the first Ethernet on systems that hide the details of the card manufacturer, or `de0` and `de1` for the first and second Digital Equipment[6] DC21x4x-based Ethernet card, `xl0` for a 3Com EtherLink XL, and so on. The loopback interface is almost invariably `lo0` on all Unix-like platforms.

So what? Most of the time this is of no consequence to you. If you have only one network connection, like a cable link to your ISP, you really don't care. Where this matters is on a server, where you might need to find the address for a given network, for example. The `NetworkInterface` class lets you find out. It has static methods for listing the interfaces and other methods for finding the addresses associated with a given interface. The program in Example 13-3 shows some examples of using this class. Running it prints the names of all the local interfaces. If you happen to be on a computer named *laptop*, it prints the machine's network address; if not, you probably want to change it to accept the local computer's name from the command line; this is left as an exercise for the reader.

---

6 Digital Equipment was absorbed by Compaq, which was then absorbed by HP, but the name remains de because the engineers who name such things don't care for corporate mergers anyway.

Example 13-3. main/src/main/java/network/NetworkInterfaceDemo.java

```
public class NetworkInterfaceDemo {
    public static void main(String[] a) throws IOException {
        Enumeration<NetworkInterface> list =
            NetworkInterface.getNetworkInterfaces();
        while (list.hasMoreElements()) {
            // Get one NetworkInterface
            NetworkInterface iface = list.nextElement();
            // Print its name
            System.out.println(iface.getDisplayName());
            Enumeration<InetAddress> addrs = iface.getInetAddresses();
            // And its address(es)
            while (addrs.hasMoreElements()) {
                InetAddress addr = addrs.nextElement();
                System.out.println(addr);
            }

        }
        // Try to get the Interface for a given local (this machine's) address
        InetAddress destAddr = InetAddress.getByName("laptop");
        try {
            NetworkInterface dest = NetworkInterface.getByInetAddress(destAddr);
            System.out.println("Address for " + destAddr + " is " + dest);
        } catch (SocketException ex) {
            System.err.println("Couldn't get address for " + destAddr);
        }
    }
}
```

13.3 Returning a Response (String or Binary)

Problem

You need to write a string or binary data to the client.

Solution

The socket gives you an InputStream and an OutputStream. Use them.

Discussion

The client socket examples in the previous chapter called the getInputStream() and getOutputStream() methods. These examples do the same. The main difference is that these ones get the socket from a ServerSocket's accept() method. Another distinction is, by definition, that normally the server creates or modifies the data and sends it to the client. Example 13-4 is a simple Echo server, which the Echo client of

Recipe 12.5 can connect to. This server handles one complete connection with a client, then goes back and does the accept() to wait for the next client.

Example 13-4. main/src/main/java/network/EchoServer.java

```java
public class EchoServer {
    /** Our server-side rendezvous socket */
    protected ServerSocket sock;
    /** The port number to use by default */
    public final static int ECHOPORT = 7;
    /** Flag to control debugging */
    protected boolean debug = true;

    /** main: construct and run */
    public static void main(String[] args) {
        int p = ECHOPORT;
        if (args.length == 1) {
            try {
                p = Integer.parseInt(args[0]);
            } catch (NumberFormatException e) {
                System.err.println("Usage: EchoServer [port#]");
                System.exit(1);
            }
        }
        new EchoServer(p).handle();
    }

    /** Construct an EchoServer on the given port number */
    public EchoServer(int port) {
        try {
            sock = new ServerSocket(port);
        } catch (IOException e) {
            System.err.println("I/O error in setup");
            System.err.println(e);
            System.exit(1);
        }
    }

    /** This handles the connections */
    protected void handle() {
        Socket ios = null;
        while (true) {
            try {
                System.out.println("Waiting for client...");
                ios = sock.accept();
                System.err.println("Accepted from " +
                    ios.getInetAddress().getHostName());
                try (BufferedReader is = new BufferedReader(
                            new InputStreamReader(ios.getInputStream(), "8859_1"));
                        PrintWriter os = new PrintWriter(
                            new OutputStreamWriter(ios.getOutputStream(), "8859_1"),
```

```
                        true);) {
                String echoLine;
                while ((echoLine = is.readLine()) != null) {
                    System.err.println("Read " + echoLine);
                    os.print(echoLine + "\r\n");
                    os.flush();
                    System.err.println("Wrote " + echoLine);
                }
                System.err.println("All done!");
            }
        } catch (IOException e) {
            System.err.println(e);
        }
    }
    /* NOTREACHED */
    }
}
```

To send a string across an arbitrary network connection, some authorities recommend sending both the carriage return and the newline character; many protocol specifications require that you do so. This explains the \r\n in the code. If the other end is a DOS program or a Telnet-like program, it may be expecting both characters. On the other hand, if you are writing both ends, you can simply use println()—followed always by an explicit flush() before you read—to prevent the deadlock of having both ends trying to read with one end's data still in the PrintWriter's buffer!

If you need to process binary data, use the data streams from java.io instead of the readers/writers. I need a server for the DaytimeBinary program of Recipe 12.6. In operation, it should look like the following:

```
C:\javasrc\network>java network.DaytimeBinary
Remote time is 3161316799
BASE_DIFF is 2208988800
Time diff == 952284799
Time on localhost is Sun Mar 08 19:33:19 GMT 2014

C:\javasrc\network>time/t
Current time is  7:33:23.84p

C:\javasrc\network>date/t
Current date is Sun 03-08-2014

C:\javasrc\network>
```

Well, it happens that I have such a program in my arsenal, so I present it in Example 13-5. Note that it directly uses certain public constants defined in the client class. Normally these are defined in the server class and used by the client, but I wanted to present the client code first.

Example 13-5. main/src/main/java/network/DaytimeServer.java

```java
public class DaytimeServer {
    /** Our server-side rendezvous socket */
    ServerSocket sock;
    /** The port number to use by default */
    public final static int PORT = 37;

    /** main: construct and run */
    public static void main(String[] argv) {
        new DaytimeServer(PORT).runService();
    }

    /** Construct a DaytimeServer on the given port number */
    public DaytimeServer(int port) {
        try {
            sock = new ServerSocket(port);
        } catch (IOException e) {
            System.err.println("I/O error in setup\n" + e);
            System.exit(1);
        }
    }

    /** This handles the connections */
    protected void runService() {
        Socket ios = null;
        DataOutputStream os = null;
        while (true) {
            try {
                System.out.println("Waiting for connection on port " + PORT);
                ios = sock.accept();
                System.err.println("Accepted from " +
                    ios.getInetAddress().getHostName());
                os = new DataOutputStream(ios.getOutputStream());
                long time = System.currentTimeMillis();

                time /= 1000;    // Daytime Protocol is in seconds

                // Convert to Java time base.
                time += RDateClient.BASE_DIFF;

                // Write it, truncating cast to int since it is using
                // the Internet Daytime protocol which uses 4 bytes.
                // This will fail in the year 2038, along with all
                // 32-bit timekeeping systems based from 1970.
                // Remember, you read about the Y2038 crisis here first!
                os.writeInt((int)time);
                os.close();
            } catch (IOException e) {
                System.err.println(e);
            }
        }
    }
```

```
        }
}
```

13.4 Returning Object Information Across a Network Connection

Problem

You need to return an object across a network connection.

Solution

Create the object you need, and write it using an `ObjectOutputStream` created on top of the socket's output stream.

Discussion

The program in Example 12-7 in the previous chapter reads a `Date` object over an `ObjectInputStream`. Example 13-6, the `DaytimeObjectServer` (the other end of that process), is a program that constructs a `Date` object each time it's connected to and returns it to the client.

Example 13-6. main/src/main/java/network/DaytimeObjectServer.java

```java
public class DaytimeObjectServer {
    /** The TCP port for the object time service. */
    public static final short TIME_PORT = 1951;

    public static void main(String[] argv) {
        ServerSocket sock;
        Socket    clientSock;
        try {
            sock = new ServerSocket(TIME_PORT);
            while ((clientSock = sock.accept()) != null) {
                System.out.println("Accept from " +
                    clientSock.getInetAddress());
                ObjectOutputStream os = new ObjectOutputStream(
                    clientSock.getOutputStream());

                // Construct and write the Object
                os.writeObject(LocalDateTime.now());

                os.close();
            }

        } catch (IOException e) {
            System.err.println(e);
        }
    }
```

```
        }
}
```

13.5 Handling Multiple Clients

Problem

Your server needs to handle multiple clients.

Solution

Use a thread for each.

Discussion

In the C world, several mechanisms allow a server to handle multiple clients. One is to use a special system call `select()` or `poll()`, which notifies the server when any of a set of file/socket descriptors is ready to read, ready to write, or has an error. By including its rendezvous socket (equivalent to our `ServerSocket`) in this list, the C-based server can read from any of a number of clients in any order. Java does not provide this call, because it is not readily implementable on some Java platforms. Instead, Java uses the general-purpose `Thread` mechanism, as described in Chapter 16 (threads are now commonplace in many programming languages, though not always under that name). Each time the code accepts a new connection from the `Server` `Socket`, it immediately constructs and starts a new thread object to process that client.[6]

The Java code to implement accepting on a socket is pretty simple, apart from having to catch `IOExceptions`:

```
/** Run the main loop of the Server. */
void runServer( ) {
    while (true) {
        try {
            Socket clntSock = sock.accept( );
            new Handler(clntSock).start( );
        } catch(IOException e) {
            System.err.println(e);
        }
    }
}
```

---

6 There are some limits to how many threads you can have, which affect only very large, enterprise-scale servers. You can't expect to have thousands of threads running in the standard Java runtime. For large, high-performance servers, you may wish to resort to native code (see Recipe 18.6) using `select()` or `poll()`.

To use a thread, you must either subclass `Thread` or implement `Runnable`. The `Han`
`dler` class must be a subclass of `Thread` for this code to work as written; if `Handler`
instead implemented the `Runnable` interface, the code would pass an instance of the
`Runnable` into the constructor for `Thread`, as in:

```
Thread t = new Thread(new Handler(clntSock));
t.start( );
```

But as written, `Handler` is constructed using the normal socket returned by `accept()`
and normally calls the socket's `getInputStream()` and `getOutputStream()` methods
and holds its conversation in the usual way. I'll present a full implementation, a threaded echo client. First, a session showing it in use:

```
$ java network.EchoServerThreaded
EchoServerThreaded ready for connections.
Socket starting: Socket[addr=localhost/127.0.0.1,port=2117,localport=7]
Socket starting: Socket[addr=darian/192.168.1.50,port=13386,localport=7]
Socket starting: Socket[addr=darian/192.168.1.50,port=22162,localport=7]
Socket ENDED: Socket[addr=darian/192.168.1.50,port=22162,localport=7]
Socket ENDED: Socket[addr=darian/192.168.1.50,port=13386,localport=7]
Socket ENDED: Socket[addr=localhost/127.0.0.1,port=2117,localport=7]
```

Here I connected to the server once with my `EchoClient` program and, while still
connected, called it up again (and again) with an operating system–provided Telnet
client. The server communicated with all the clients concurrently, sending the
answers from the first client back to the first client, and the data from the second client back to the second client. In short, it works. I ended the sessions with the end-of-
file character in the program and used the normal disconnect mechanism from the
Telnet client. Example 13-7 is the code for the server.

Example 13-7. main/src/main/java/network/EchoServerThreaded.java

```java
public class EchoServerThreaded {

    public static final int ECHOPORT = 7;

    public static void main(String[] av) {
        new EchoServerThreaded().runServer();
    }

    public void runServer() {
        ServerSocket sock;
        Socket clientSocket;

        try {
            sock = new ServerSocket(ECHOPORT);

            System.out.println("EchoServerThreaded ready for connections.");

            /* Wait for a connection */
```

```
            while (true) {
                clientSocket = sock.accept();
                /* Create a thread to do the communication, and start it */
                new Handler(clientSocket).start();
            }
        } catch (IOException e) {
            /* Crash the server if IO fails. Something bad has happened */
            System.err.println("Could not accept " + e);
            System.exit(1);
        }
    }

    /** A Thread subclass to handle one client conversation. */
    class Handler extends Thread {
        Socket sock;

        Handler(Socket s) {
            sock = s;
        }

        public void run() {
            System.out.println("Socket starting: " + sock);
            try (BufferedReader is = new BufferedReader(
                        new InputStreamReader(sock.getInputStream())));
                    PrintStream os = new PrintStream(
                        sock.getOutputStream(), true);) {
                String line;
                while ((line = is.readLine()) != null) {
                    os.print(line + "\r\n");
                    os.flush();
                }
                sock.close();
            } catch (IOException e) {
                System.out.println("IO Error on socket " + e);
                return;
            }
            System.out.println("Socket ENDED: " + sock);
        }
    }
}
```

A lot of short transactions can degrade performance, because each client causes the creation of a new threaded object. If you know or can reliably predict the degree of concurrency that is needed, an alternative paradigm involves the precreation of a fixed number of threads. But then how do you control their access to the Server Socket? A look at the ServerSocket class documentation reveals that the accept() method is not synchronized, meaning that any number of threads can call the method concurrently. This could cause bad things to happen. So I use the synchron ized keyword around this call to ensure that only one client runs in it at a time, because it updates global data. When no clients are connected, you will have one (randomly selected) thread running in the `ServerSocket` object's `accept()` method, waiting for a connection, plus *n-1* threads waiting for the first thread to return from the method. As soon as the first thread manages to accept a connection, it goes off and holds its conversation, releasing its lock in the process so that another randomly chosen thread is allowed into the `accept()` method. Each thread's `run()` method has an infinite loop beginning with an `accept()` and then holding the conversation. The result is that client connections can get started more quickly, at a cost of slightly greater server startup time. Doing it this way also avoids the overhead of constructing a new `Handler` or `Thread` object each time a request comes along. This general approach is similar to what the popular Apache web server does, although it normally creates a number or pool of identical processes (instead of threads) to handle client connections. Accordingly, I have modified the `EchoServerThreaded` class shown in Example 13-7 to work this way, as you can see in Example 13-8.

Example 13-8. main/src/main/java/network/EchoServerThreaded2.java

```java
public class EchoServerThreaded2 {

    public static final int ECHOPORT = 7;

    public static final int NUM_THREADS = 4;

    /** Main method, to start the servers. */
    public static void main(String[] av) {
        new EchoServerThreaded2(ECHOPORT, NUM_THREADS);
    }

    /** Constructor */
    public EchoServerThreaded2(int port, int numThreads) {
        ServerSocket servSock;

        try {
            servSock = new ServerSocket(port);

        } catch (IOException e) {
            /* Crash the server if IO fails. Something bad has happened */
            throw new RuntimeException("Could not create ServerSocket ", e);
        }

        // Create a series of threads and start them.
        for (int i = 0; i < numThreads; i++) {
            new Handler(servSock, i).start();
        }
    }

    /** A Thread subclass to handle one client conversation. */
    class Handler extends Thread {
        ServerSocket servSock;
```

```
    int threadNumber;

    /** Construct a Handler. */
    Handler(ServerSocket s, int i) {
        servSock = s;
        threadNumber = i;
        setName("Thread " + threadNumber);
    }

    public void run() {
        /*
         * Wait for a connection. Synchronized on the ServerSocket while
         * calling its accept() method.
         */
        while (true) {
            try {
                System.out.println(getName() + " waiting");

                Socket clientSocket;
                // Wait here for the next connection.
                synchronized (servSock) {
                    clientSocket = servSock.accept();
                }
                System.out.println(
                    getName() + " starting, IP=" +
                    clientSocket.getInetAddress());
                try (BufferedReader is = new BufferedReader(
                        new InputStreamReader(clientSocket.getInputStream()));
                        PrintStream os = new PrintStream(
                            clientSocket.getOutputStream(), true);) {
                    String line;
                    while ((line = is.readLine()) != null) {
                        os.print(line + "\r\n");
                        os.flush();
                    }
                    System.out.println(getName() + " ENDED ");
                    clientSocket.close();
                }
            } catch (IOException ex) {
                System.out.println(getName() + ": IO Error on socket " + ex);
                return;
            }
        }
    }
}
```

It is quite possible to implement a server of this sort with NIO, the "new" (back in J2SE 1.4) I/O package. However, the code to do so outweighs anything in this chapter, and it is fraught with issues. There are several good tutorials on the internet for the person who truly needs the performance gain of using NIO to manage server connections.

13.6 Serving the HTTP Protocol

Problem

You want to serve up a protocol such as HTTP.

Solution

Create a `ServerSocket` and write some code that speaks the particular protocol. Or, better, use a Java-powered web server such as Apache Tomcat or a Java Enterprise Edition (Java EE) server such as JBoss WildFly.

Discussion

You can implement your own HTTP protocol server for very simple applications, which we'll do here. For any serious development, you want to use the Java Enterprise Edition; see the note at the beginning of this chapter.

This example just constructs a `ServerSocket` and listens on it. When connections come in, they are replied to using the HTTP protocol. So it is somewhat more involved than the simple `Echo` server presented in Recipe 13.3. However, it's not a complete web server; the filename in the request is ignored, and a standard message is always returned. This is thus a *very* simple web server; it follows only the bare minimum of the HTTP protocol needed to send its response back. For a real web server written in Java, get Tomcat from the Apache Tomcat website (*http://tomcat.apache.org*) or any of the Jakarta/JavaEE Application Servers. The code shown in Example 13-9, however, is enough to understand how to build a simple server that responds to requests using a protocol.

Example 13-9. main/src/main/java/network/WebServer0.java

```
public class WebServer0 {
    public static final int HTTP = 80;
    public static final String CRLF = "\r\n";
    ServerSocket s;
    /** A link to the source of this program, used in error message */
    static final String VIEW_SOURCE_URL =
    "https://github.com/IanDarwin/javasrc/tree/master/main/src/main/
      java/network";

    /**
     * Main method, just creates a server and call its runServer().
     */
```

```
public static void main(String[] args) throws Exception {
    System.out.println("DarwinSys JavaWeb Server 0.0 starting...");
    WebServer0 w = new WebServer0();
    int port = HTTP;
    if (args.length == 1) {
        port = Integer.parseInt(args[0]);
    }
    w.runServer(port);        // never returns!!
}

/** Get the actual ServerSocket; deferred until after Constructor
 * so subclass can mess with ServerSocketFactory (e.g., to do SSL).
 * @param port The port number to listen on
 */
protected ServerSocket getServerSocket(int port) throws Exception {
    return new ServerSocket(port);
}

/** RunServer accepts connections and passes each one to handler. */
public void runServer(int port) throws Exception {
    s = getServerSocket(port);
    while (true) {
        try {
            Socket us = s.accept();
            Handler(us);
        } catch(IOException e) {
            System.err.println(e);
            return;
        }

    }
}

/** Handler() handles one conversation with a Web client.
 * This is the only part of the program that "knows" HTTP.
 */
public void Handler(Socket s) {
    BufferedReader is;    // inputStream, from Viewer
    PrintWriter os;       // outputStream, to Viewer
    String request;       // what Viewer sends us.
    try {
        String from = s.getInetAddress().toString();
        System.out.println("Accepted connection from " + from);
        is = new BufferedReader(new InputStreamReader(s.getInputStream()));
        request = is.readLine();
        System.out.println("Request: " + request);

        os = new PrintWriter(s.getOutputStream(), true);
        os.print("HTTP/1.0 200 Here is your data" + CRLF);
        os.print("Content-type: text/html" + CRLF);
        os.print("Server-name: DarwinSys NULL Java WebServer 0" + CRLF);
        String reply1 = "<html><head>" +
```

```
                "<title>Wrong System Reached</title></head>\n" +
                "<h1>Welcome, ";
        String reply2 = ", but...</h1>\n" +
                "<p>You have reached a desktop machine " +
                "that does not run a real Web service.\n" +
                "<p>Please pick another system!</p>\n" +
                "<p>Or view <a href=\"" + VIEW_SOURCE_URL + "\">" +
                "the WebServer0 source on github</a>.</p>\n" +
                "<hr/><em>Java-based WebServer0</em><hr/>\n" +
                "</html>\n";
        os.print("Content-length: " +
                (reply1.length() + from.length() + reply2.length()) + CRLF);
        os.print(CRLF);
        os.print(reply1 + from + reply2 + CRLF);
        os.flush();
        s.close();
    } catch (IOException e) {
        System.out.println("IOException " + e);
    }
    return;
    }
}
```

13.7 Securing a Web Server with SSL and JSSE

Problem

You want to protect your network traffic from prying eyes or malicious modification while the data is in transit.

Solution

Use the Java Secure Socket Extension, JSSE, to encrypt your traffic.

Discussion

JSSE provides services at a number of levels, but the simplest way to use it is simply to get your ServerSocket from an SSLServerSocketFactory instead of using the ServerSocket constructor directly. SSL is the Secure Sockets Layer; a revised version is known as TLS. It is specifically for use on the web. To secure other protocols, you'd have to use a different form of the SocketFactory.

The SSLServerSocketFactory returns a ServerSocket that is set up to do SSL encryption. Example 13-10 uses this technique to override the getServerSocket() method in Recipe 13.6. If you're thinking this is too easy, you're wrong!

Example 13-10. main/src/main/java/network/JSSEWebServer0

```
/**
 * JSSEWebServer - subclass trivial WebServer0 to make it use SSL.
 * N.B. You MUST have set up a server certificate (see the
 * accompanying book text), or you will get the dreaded
 * javax.net.ssl.SSLHandshakeException: no cipher suites in common
 * (because without it JSSE can't use any of its built-in ciphers!).
 */
public class JSSEWebServer0 extends WebServer0 {

    public static final int HTTPS = 8443;

    public static void main(String[] args) throws Exception {
        if (System.getProperty("javax.net.ssl.keyStore") == null) {
            System.err.println(
                "You must pass in a keystore via -D; see the documentation!");
            System.exit(1);
        }
        System.out.println("DarwinSys JSSE Server 0.0 starting...");
        JSSEWebServer0 w = new JSSEWebServer0();
        w.runServer(HTTPS);          // never returns!!
    }

    /** Get an HTTPS ServerSocket using JSSE.
     * @see WebServer0#getServerSocket(int)
     * @throws ClassNotFoundException the SecurityProvider can't be instantiated.
     */
    protected ServerSocket getServerSocket(int port) throws Exception {

        SSLServerSocketFactory ssf =
            (SSLServerSocketFactory)SSLServerSocketFactory.getDefault();

        return ssf.createServerSocket(port);
    }

}
```

That is, indeed, all the Java code one needs to write. You do have to set up an SSL Certificate. For demonstration purposes, this can be a self-signed certificate; the steps in *https://darwinsys.com/java/selfsigncert.html* (steps 1–4) will suffice. You have to tell the JSSE layer where to find your keystore:

```
java -Djavax.net.ssl.keyStore=/home/ian/.keystore -Djavax.net.ssl.
keyStorePassword=secrit JSSEWebServer0
```

The typical client browser raises its eyebrows at a self-signed certificate (see Figure 13-1), but, if the user okays it, will accept the certificate.

Figure 13-2 shows the output of the simple WebServer0 being displayed over the HTTPS protocol (notice the padlock in the lower-right corner).

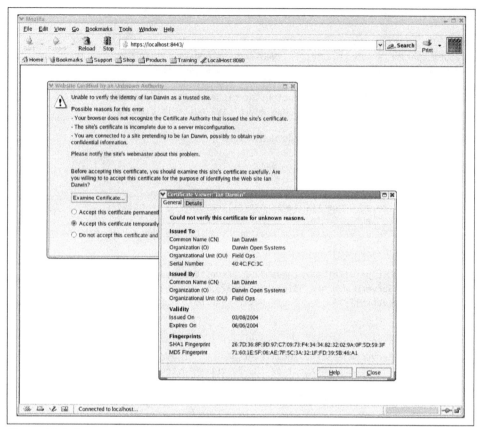

Figure 13-1. Browser caution

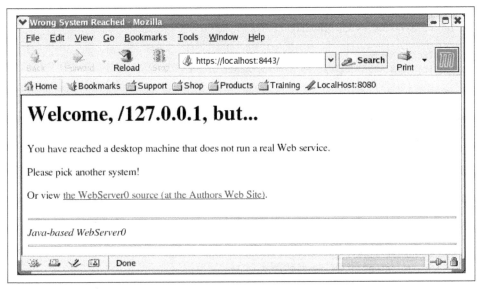

Figure 13-2. With encryption

See Also

JSSE can do much more than encrypt web server traffic; this is, however, sometimes seen as its most exciting application. For more information on JSSE, see the Sun website (*http://java.sun.com/products/jsse*) or *Java Security* by Scott Oaks (O'Reilly).

13.8 Creating a REST Service with JAX-RS

Problem

You want to implement a RESTful server by using the provided Java EE/Jakarta EE APIs.

Solution

Use JAX-RS annotations on a class that provides a service; install it in an enterprise application server.

Discussion

This operation consists of both coding and configuration.

The coding steps consist of creating a class that extends the JAX-RS `Application` class and adding annotations to a class that provides a service.

Here is a minimal `Application` class:

```
import javax.ws.rs.ApplicationPath;
import javax.ws.rs.core.Application;

@ApplicationPath("")
public class RestApplication extends Application {
        // Empty
}
```

Example 13-11 is a "Hello, World"–type service class with the annotations needed to make it a service class and to have three sample methods.

Example 13-11. restdemo/src/main/java/rest/RestService.java

```
@Path("")
@ApplicationScoped
public class RestService {

    public RestService() {
        System.out.println("RestService.init()");
    }

    @GET @Path("/timestamp")
    @Produces(MediaType.TEXT_PLAIN)
    public String getDate() {
        return LocalDateTime.now().toString();
    }

    /** A Hello message method
     */
    @GET @Path("/greeting/{userName}")
    @Produces("text/html")
    public String doGreeting(@PathParam("userName")String userName) {
        System.out.println("RestService.greeting()");
        if (userName == null || userName.trim().length() <= 3) {
            return "Missing or too-short username";
        }
        return String.format(
            "<h1>Welcome %s</h1><p>%s, We are glad to see you back!",
            userName, userName);
    }

    /** Used to download all items */
    @GET @Path("/names")
    @Produces(MediaType.APPLICATION_JSON)
    public List<String> findTasksForUser() {
        return List.of("Robin", "Jedunkat", "Lyn", "Glen");
    }
}
```

Now the class must be deployed. If we have created a proper Maven project structure (see Recipe 1.7) and have provided an application-server-specific Maven plug-in, and our development server is running, we can use some variation on mvn deploy. In the present case I have set this up, in the *rest* subdirectory, for deployment to WildFly, a Java Enterprise server from the JBoss open source community (though somewhat dated), funded by RedHat Inc. I need only say mvn wildfly:deploy to have the application compiled, packaged, and deployed to my server.

For deploying REST services as a microservice based on Eclipse MicroProfile, you may wish to investigate the Quarkus Framework (*https://quarkus.io*).

Once the service is deployed, you can explore it interactively with a browser or, for simple GET requests, a Telnet client:

```
$ telnet localhost 8080 # output cleaned up
Escape character is '^]'.
GET /rest/timestamp HTTP/1.0
Connection: keep-alive

HTTP/1.1 200 OK
Content-Type: text/plain;charset=UTF-8

2019-10-16T19:54:31.42

GET /rest/greeting/Ian%20Darwin HTTP/1.0

HTTP/1.1 200 OK
Content-Type: text/html;charset=UTF-8

<h1>Welcome Ian Darwin</h1><p>Ian Darwin, We are glad to see you back!

get /rest/names HTTP/1.0
Accept: Application/JSON

HTTP/1.1 200 OK
Content-Type: application/json

["Robin","Jedunkat","Lyn","Glen"]
^] (CTRL/C)
$
```

An issue with REST is that there is not an official standard for documenting the API or protocol offered by a server (there are several competing specifications). So people writing clients must either rely on plain documentation offered by the server's developers, or use trial and error to discover the protocol. Our example here is simple enough that we don't have this problem, but imagine a class with 20 or 30 methods in it.

The Spring Framework offers an API that is very similar to the JAX-RS API used here; if you are already using Spring, it may be simpler to use their annotations.

13.9 Network Logging

Problem

Your class is running inside a server container, and its debugging output is hard to obtain.

Solution

Use a network-based logger like the Java Logging API (JUL), the Apache Logging Services Project's Log4j, or the simple one shown here.

Discussion

Getting the debug output from a desktop client is fairly easy on most operating systems. But if the program you want to debug is running in a container like a servlet engine or an EJB server, it can be difficult to obtain debugging output, particularly if the container is running on a remote computer. It would be convenient if you could have your program send messages back to a program on your desktop machine for immediate display. Needless to say, it's not that hard to do this with Java's socket mechanism.

Many logging APIs can handle this:

- Java has had for years a standard logging API JUL (discussed in Recipe 13.12) that talks to various logging mechanisms, including Unix syslog.
- The Apache Logging Services Project produces Log4j, which is used in many open source projects that require logging (see Recipe 13.11).
- The Apache Jakart Commons Logging (JCL) (*http://commons.apache.org/proper/commons-logging*). Not discussed here; similar to the others.
- SLF4J (Simple Logging Facade For Java, see Recipe 13.10) is the newest and, as the name implies, a facade that can use the others.
- And, before these became widely used, I wrote a small, simple API to handle this type of logging function. My netlog is not discussed here because it is preferable to use one of the standard logging mechanisms; its code is in the *logging* subdirectory of the *javasrc* repo if you want to exhume it.

The JDK logging API, Log4j, and SFL4J are more fully fleshed out and can write to such destinations as a file; an OutputStream or Writer; or a remote Log4j, Unix syslog, or Windows Event Log server.

The program being debugged is the client from the logging API's point of view—even though it may be running in a server-side container such as a web server or application server—because the network client is the program that initiates the connection. The program that runs on your desktop machine is the "server" program for sockets because it waits for a connection to come along.

If you want to run any network-based logger reachable from any public network, you need to be more aware of security issues. One common form of attack is a simple denial-of-service (DoS), during which the attacker makes a lot of connections to your server in order to slow it down. If you are writing the log to disk, for example, the attacker could fill up your disk by sending lots of garbage. In common use, your log listener would be behind a firewall and not reachable from outside; but if this is not the case, beware of the DoS attack.

13.10 Setting Up SLF4J

Problem

You want to use a logging API that lets you use any of the other logging APIs, for example, so that your code can be used in other projects without requiring them to switch logging APIs.

Solution

Use SLF4J: get a `Logger` from the `LoggerFactory`, and use its various methods for logging.

Discussion

Using SLF4J requires only one JAR file to compile, *slf4j-api-1.x.y.jar* (where *x* and *y* will change over time). To actually get logging output, you need to add one of several implementation JARs to your runtime CLASSPATH, the simplest of which is *slf4j-simple-1.x.y.jar* (where *x* and *y* should match between the two files).

Once you've added those JAR files to your build script or on your CLASSPATH, you can get a `Logger` by calling `LoggerFactory.getLogger()`, passing either the string name of a class or package or just the current `Class` reference. Then call the logger's logging methods. A simple example is in Example 13-12.

Example 13-12. main/src/main/java/logging/Slf4jDemo.java

```
public class Slf4jDemo {

    final static Logger theLogger =
            LoggerFactory.getLogger(Slf4jDemo.class);

    public static void main(String[] args) {
```

```
        Object o = new Object();
        theLogger.info("I created this object: " + o);

    }
}
```

There are various methods used to log information at different levels of severity, which are shown in Table 13-1.

Table 13-1. SLF4j logging methods

Name	Meaning
trace	Verbose debugging (disabled by default)
debug	Verbose debugging
info	Low-level informational message
warn	Possible error
error	Serious error

One of the advantages of SLF4j over most of the other logging APIs is the avoidance of the dead string anti-pattern. In the use of many other logger APIs you may find code like the following:

```
logger.log("The value is " + object + "; this is not good");
```

This can lead to a performance problem, in that the object's `toString()` is implicitly called, and two string concatenations are performed, before we even know if the logger is going to use them! If this is in code that is called repeatedly, a lot of overhead can be wasted.

This led the other logging packages to offer code guards, based on logger methods that can find out very quickly if a logger is enabled, leading to code like the following:

```
if (logger.isEnabled()) {
        logger.log("The value is " + object + "; this is not good");
}
```

This solves the performance problem but clutters the code! SLF4J's solution is to use a mechanism similar to (but not quite compatible with) Java's `MessageFormat` mechanism, as shown in Example 13-13.

Example 13-13. main/src/main/java/logging/Slf4jDemo2.java

```
public class Slf4jDemo2 {

    final static Logger theLogger = LoggerFactory.getLogger(Slf4jDemo2.class);

    public static void main(String[] args) {
```

```
    try {
        Person p = new Person();
        // populate person's fields here...
        theLogger.info("I created an object {}", p);

        if (p != null) {    // bogus, just to show logging
            throw new IllegalArgumentException("Just testing");
        }
    } catch (Exception ex) {
        theLogger.error("Caught Exception: " + ex, ex);
    }
  }
}
```

Although this doesn't demonstrate network logging, it is easy to accomplish that in conjunction with a logging implementation like Log4j or JUL (Java Util Logging, a standard part of the JDK), which allow you to provide configurable logging. Log4j is described in the next recipe.

See Also

The SLF4J website contains a manual (*http://www.slf4j.org/manual.html*) that discusses the various CLASSPATH options. There are also some Maven artifacts (*http://mvnrepository.com/artifact/org.slf4j*) for the various options.

13.11 Network Logging with Log4j

Problem

You wish to write log file messages using Log4j.

Solution

Get a Logger and use its log() method or the convenience methods. Control logging by changing a properties file. Use the org.apache.logging.log4j.net package to make it network based.

Discussion

 This recipe describes Version 2 of the Log4j API. Between Version 1 and Version 2, there are changes to the package names, filenames, and the method used to obtain a logger. If you see code using, for example, Logger.getLogger("class name"), that code is written to the older API, which is no longer maintained (the Log4j website refers to Log4j 1.2, and versions up to 2.12, as "legacy"; we are using 2.13 in this recipe). A good degree of compatibility is offered for code written to the 1.x API; see *https://logging.apache.org/log4j/2.x/manual/compatibility.html*.

Logging using Log4j is simple, convenient, and flexible. You need to get a Logger object from the static method LogManager.getLogger(), The Logger has public void methods (debug(), info(), warn(), error(), and fatal()), each of which takes one Object to be logged (and an optional Throwable). As with System.out.println(), if you pass in anything that is not a String, its toString() method is called. A generic logging method is also included:

```
public void log(Level level, Object message);
```

The Level class is defined in the Log4j 2 API. The standard levels are, in order, DEBUG < INFO < WARN < ERROR < FATAL. That is, debug messages are considered the least important, and fatal the most important. Each Logger has a level associated with it; messages whose level is less than the Logger's level are silently discarded.

A simple application can log messages using these few statements:

```
public class Log4JDemo {

    private static Logger myLogger = LogManager.getLogger();

    public static void main(String[] args) {

        Object o = new Object();
        myLogger.info("I created an object: " + o);

    }
}
```

If you compile and run this program with no *log4j2.properties* file, it does not produce any logging output (see the *log4j2demos* script in the source folder). We need to create a configuration file whose default name is *log4j2.properties*. You can also provide the logfile name via System Properties: -Dlog4j.configurationFile=URL.

Log4j configuration is very flexible, and therefore very complex. Even their own documentation admits that "Trying to configure Log4j without understanding [the logging architecture] will lead to frustration." See this Apache website for full details on the logging configuration file location and format (*https://logging.apache.org/ log4j/2.x/manual/configuration.html*).

Every `Logger` has a `Level` to specify what level of messages to write. It will also have an `Appender`, which is the code that writes the messages out. A `ConsoleAppender` writes to `System.out`, of course; other loggers write to files, operating system–level loggers, and so on. A simple configuration file looks something like this:

```
# Log4J2 properties file for the logger demo programs.
# tag::generic[] # Ensure file gets copied for Java Cookbook

# WARNING - log4j2.properties must be on your CLASSPATH,
# not necessarily in your source directory.

# The configuration file for Version 2 is different from V1!

rootLogger.level = info
rootLogger.appenderRef.stdout.ref = STDOUT

appender.console.type = Console
appender.console.name = STDOUT
appender.console.layout.type = PatternLayout
appender.console.layout.pattern = %m%n
appender.console.filter.threshold.type = ThresholdFilter
appender.console.filter.threshold.level = debug
```

This file gives the root logger a level of `DEBUG`, which causes it to write all messages. The config file also sets up an appender of `APPENDER1`, which is configured on the next few lines. Note that I didn't have to refer to the `com.darwinsys Logger`. Because every `Logger` inherits from the root logger, a simple application needs to configure only the root logger. The properties file can also be an XML document, or you can write your own configuration parser (almost nobody does this).

 If the logging configuration file is not found, the default root logger defaults the root logger to `Level.ERROR`, so you will not see any output below the `ERROR` level.

With the configuration file in place, the demonstration works better. Running this program (with the appropriate `CLASSPATH` as done in the scripts) produces this output:

```
$ java Log4j2Demo
I created an object: java.lang.Object@477b4cdf
$
```

A common use of logging is to log a caught `Exception`, as shown in Example 13-14.

Example 13-14. main/src/main/java/Log4JDemo2.java (Log4j—catching and logging)

```
public class Log4JDemo2 {

    private static Logger myLogger = LogManager.getLogger();

    public static void main(String[] args) {

        try {
            Object o = new Object();
            myLogger.info("I created an object: " + o);
            if (o != null) {     // bogus, just to show logging
                throw new IllegalArgumentException("Just testing");
            }
        } catch (Exception ex) {
            myLogger.error("Caught Exception: " + ex, ex);
        }
    }
}
```

When run, `Log4JDemo2` produces the expected output:

```
$ java Log4JDemo2
I created an object: java.lang.Object@477b4cdf
Caught Exception: java.lang.IllegalArgumentException: Just testing
java.lang.IllegalArgumentException: Just testing
        at logging.Log4JDemo2.main(Log4JDemo2.java:17) [classes/:?]
$
```

Much of the flexibility of Log4j 2 stems from its use of external configuration files; you can enable or disable logging without recompiling the application. A properties file that eliminates most logging might have this entry:

```
rootLogger.level = fatal
```

Only fatal error messages print; all levels less than that are ignored.

To log from a client to a server on a remote machine, the `SocketAppender` can be used. There is also an `SmtpAppender` to send urgent notices via email. See *https://logging.apache.org/log4j/2.x/manual/appenders.html* for details on all the supported Appenders. Here is *log4j2-network.properties*, the socket-based networking version of the configuration file:

```
# Log4J2 properties file for the NETWORKED logger demo programs.
# tag::generic[] # Ensure file gets copied for Java Cookbook
```

```
# WARNING - log4j2.properties must be on your CLASSPATH,
# not necessarily in your source directory.

# The configuration file for Version 2 is different from V1!

rootLogger.level = info
rootLogger.appenderRef.stdout.ref = STDOUT

appender.console.type = Socket
appender.console.name = STDOUT
appender.console.host = localhost
appender.console.port = 6666
appender.console.layout.type = PatternLayout
appender.console.layout.pattern = %m%n
appender.console.filter.threshold.type = ThresholdFilter
appender.console.filter.threshold.level = debug
```

This file gets passed to the demo programs via a Java System Property in the netde
mos script:

```
build=../../../../target/classes
log4j2_jar=\
${HOME}/.m2/repository/org/apache/logging/log4j/log4j-api/2.13.0/log4j-
api-2.13.0.jar:\
${HOME}/.m2/repository/org/apache/logging/log4j/log4j-core/2.13.0/log4j-
core-2.13.0.jar

echo "==> Log4JDemo"
java -Dlog4j.configurationFile=log4j2-network.properties \
        -classpath ".:${build}:${log4j2_jar}" logging.Log4JDemo

echo "==> Log4JDemo2"
java -Dlog4j.configurationFile=log4j2-network.properties \
        -classpath ".:${build}:${log4j2_jar}" logging.Log4JDemo2
```

When run with the *log4j2-network.properties* file, you have to arrange for a listener on
the other end. On Unix systems the nc (or netcat) program will work fine:

```
$ nc -kl 6666
I created an object: java.lang.Object@37ceb1df
I created an object: java.lang.Object@37ceb1df
Caught Exception: java.lang.IllegalArgumentException: Just testing
java.lang.IllegalArgumentException: Just testing
        at logging.Log4JDemo2.main(Log4JDemo2.java:17) [classes/:?]
^C
$
```

Netcat option -l says to listen on the numbered port; -k tells it to keep listening, that
is, to reopen the connection when the client closes it, as happens when each demo
program exits.

There is a performance issue with some logging calls. Consider some expensive operation, like a toString() or two along with several string concatenations passed to a Log.info() call in an often-used piece of code. If this is placed into production with a higher logging level, all the work will be done but the resultant string will never be used. In older APIs we used to use "code guards," methods like "isLoggerEnabled(Level)," to determine whether to bother creating the string. Nowadays, the preferred method is to create the string inside a lambda expression (see Chapter 9). All the log methods have an overload that accepts a Supplier argument (Example 13-15).

Example 13-15. main/src/main/java/logging/Log4J2Lambda.java

```
public class Log4JLambda {

    private static Logger myLogger = LogManager.getLogger();

    public static void main(String[] args) {

        Person customer = getPerson();
        myLogger.info( () -> String.format(
            "Value %d from Customer %s", customer.value, customer) );

    }
```

This way the string operations will only be performed if needed: if the logger is operating at the INFO level it will call the Supplier and if not, it won't do the expensive operation.

When run as part of the *log4j2demos* script, this prints:

```
Value 42 from Customer Customer[Robin]
```

For more information on Log4j, visit its main website (*http://logging.apache.org/log4j*). Log4j 2 is free software, distributed under the Apache Software Foundation license.

13.12 Network Logging with java.util.logging

Problem

You wish to write logging messages using the Java logging mechanism.

Solution

Get a Logger, and use it to log your messages and/or exceptions.

Discussion

The Java Logging API (package `java.util.logging`) is similar to, and was obviously inspired by, the Log4j package. You acquire a `Logger` object by calling the static `Logger.getLogger()` with a descriptive `String`. You then use instance methods to write to the log; these methods include the following:

```
public void log(java.util.logging.LogRecord);
public void log(java.util.logging.Level,String);
// and a variety of overloaded log( ) methods
public void logp(java.util.logging.Level,String,String,String);
public void logrb(java.util.logging.Level,String,String,String,String);

// Convenience routines for tracing program flow
public void entering(String,String);
public void entering(String,String,Object);
public void entering(String,String,Object[]);
public void exiting(String,String);
public void exiting(String,String,Object);
public void throwing(String,String,Throwable);

// Convenience routines for log( ) with a given level
public void severe(String);
public void warning(String);
public void info(String);
public void config(String);
public void fine(String);
public void finer(String);
public void finest(String);
```

As with Log4j, every `Logger` object has a given logging level, and messages below that level are silently discarded:

```
public void setLevel(java.util.logging.Level);
public java.util.logging.Level getLevel( );
public boolean isLoggable(java.util.logging.Level);
```

As with Log4j, objects handle the writing of the log. Each logger has a `Handler`:

```
public synchronized void addHandler(java.util.logging.Handler);
public synchronized void removeHandler(java.util.logging.Handler);
public synchronized java.util.logging.Handler[] getHandlers( );
```

Each `Handler` has a `Formatter`, which formats a `LogRecord` for display. By providing your own `Formatter`, you have more control over how the information being passed into the log gets formatted.

Unlike Log4j, the Java SE logging mechanism has a default configuration, so Example 13-16 is a minimal logging example program.

Example 13-16. main/src/main/java/logging/JulLogDemo.java

```
public class JulLogDemo {
    public static void main(String[] args) {

        Logger myLogger = Logger.getLogger("com.darwinsys");

        Object o = new Object();
        myLogger.info("I created an object: " + o);
    }
}
```

Running it prints the following:

```
$ juldemos
Jan 31, 2020 1:03:27 PM logging.JulLogDemo main
INFO: I created an object: java.lang.Object@5ca881b5
$
```

As with Log4j, one common use is in logging caught exceptions; the code for this is in Example 13-17.

Example 13-17. main/src/main/java/logging/JulLogDemo2.java (catching and logging an exception)

```
public class JulLogDemo2 {
    public static void main(String[] args) {

        System.setProperty("java.util.logging.config.file",
            "logging/logging.properties");

        Logger logger = Logger.getLogger("com.darwinsys");

        try {
            Object o = new Object();
            logger.info("I created an object: " + o);
            if (o != null) {    // bogus, just to show logging
                throw new IllegalArgumentException("Just testing");
            }
        } catch (Exception t) {
            // All-in-one call:
            logger.log(Level.SEVERE, "Caught Exception", t);
            // Alternate: Long form, more control.
            // LogRecord msg = new LogRecord(Level.SEVERE, "Caught exception");
            // msg.setThrown(t);
            // logger.log(msg);
        }
    }
}
```

As with Log4j, `java.util.logging` accepts a lambda expression (and has since Java 8); see Example 13-18.

Example 13-18. main/src/main/java/logging/JulLambdaDemo.java

```java
/** Demonstrate how Java 8 Lambdas avoid extraneous object creation
 * @author Ian Darwin
 */
public class JulLambdaDemo {
    public static void main(String[] args) {

        Logger myLogger = Logger.getLogger("com.darwinsys.jullambda");

        Object o = new Helper();

        // If you change the log call from finest to info,
        // you see both the systrace from the toString,
        // and the logging output. As it is here,
        // you don't see either, so the toString() is not called!
        myLogger.finest(() -> "I created this object: " + o);
    }

    static class Helper {
        public String toString() {
            System.out.println("JulLambdaDemo.Helper.toString()");
            return "failure!";
        }
    }
}
```

See Also

A good general reference on this chapter's topic is *Java Network Programming* by Elliotte Harold.

The server side of any network mechanism is extremely sensitive to security issues. It is easy for one misconfigured or poorly written server program to compromise the security of an entire network! Of the many books on network security, two stand out: *Firewalls and Internet Security* by William R. Cheswick et al. (Addison-Wesley) and a series of books with *Hacking Exposed* in the title, the first in the series by Stuart McClure et al. (McGraw-Hill).

This completes my discussion of server-side Java using sockets. A chat server could be implemented using several technologies, such as RMI (Remote Methods Invocation), an HTTP web service, JMS (Java Message Service), and a Java Enterprise API that handles store-and-forward message processing. This is beyond the scope of this book, but there's an example of an RMI chat server in the *chat* folder of the source distribution, and there's an example of a JMS chat server in *Java Message Service* by Mark Richards et al. (O'Reilly).

## CHAPTER 14

Processing JSON Data

14.0 Introduction

JSON, or JavaScript Object Notation, is all of the following:

- A simple, lightweight data interchange format.
- A simpler, lighter alternative to XML.
- Easy to generate with `println()` or with one of several APIs.
- Recognized directly by the JavaScript parser in all web browsers.
- Supported with add-on frameworks for all common languages (Java, C/C++, Perl, Ruby, Python, Lua, Erlang, Haskell, to name a few); a ridiculously long list of supported languages (including two dozen parsers for Java alone) is right on the home page (*http://json.org*).

A simple JSON message might look like this:

json/src/main/resources/json/softwareinfo.json/

```
{
    "name": "robinparse",
    "version": "1.2.3",
    "description": "Another Parser for JSON",
    "className": "RobinParse",
    "contributors": [
        "Robin Smythe",
        "Jon Jenz",
        "Jan Ardann"
    ]
}
```

As you can see, the syntax is simple, nestable, and amenable to human inspection.

The JSON home page (*http://json.org*) provides a concise summary of JSON syntax. There are two kinds of structure: JSON objects (maps) and JSON arrays (lists). JSON objects are sets of name and value pairs, which can be represented either as a `java.util.Map` *or* as the properties of a Java object. For example, the fields of a `Local Date` (see Recipe 6.1) object for April 1, 2019, might be represented like this:

```
{
        "year": 2019,
        "month": 4,
        "day" : 1
}
```

JSON arrays are ordered lists, represented in Java either as arrays or as `java.util.Lists`. A list of two dates might look like this:

```
{
        [{
                "year": 2019,
                "month": 4,
                "day" : 1
        },{
                "year": 2019,
                "month": 5,
                "day" : 15
        }]
}
```

JSON is free-format, so the preceding could also be written, with some loss of human readability but no loss of information or functionality, as this:

```
{[{"year":2019,"month":4,"day":1},{"year":2019,"month":5,"day":15}]}
```

Hundreds of parsers have, I'm sure, been written for JSON. A few that come to mind in the Java world include the following:

`stringtree.org`
    Very small and lightweight

`json.org parser`
    Widely used because it's free and has a good domain name

`jackson.org parser`
    Widely used because it's very powerful and used with Spring Framework and with JBoss RESTEasy and Wildfly

`javax.json`
    Oracle's official but currently EE-only standard

This chapter shows several ways of processing JSON data using some of the various APIs just listed. The official `javax.json` API is only included in the Java EE, not the Java SE, so it is unlikely to see very much use on the client side. This API uses some names in common with the `org.json` API, but not enough to be considered compatible.

Because this is a book for client-side Java developers, nothing will be made of the ability to process JSON directly in server-generated, browser-based JavaScript, though this can be very useful in building enterprise applications.

14.1 Generating JSON Directly

Problem

You want to generate JSON without bothering to use an API.

Solution

Get the data you want, and use `println()` or `String.format()` as appropriate.

Discussion

If you are careful, you can generate JSON data yourself. For the utterly trivial cases, you can just use `PrintWriter.println()` or `String.format()`. For significant volumes, however, it's usually better to use one of the APIs.

This code prints the year, month, and date from a `LocalTime` object (see Recipe 6.1). Some of the JSON formatting is delegated to the `toJson()` method:

```
/**
 * Convert an object to JSON, not using any JSON API.
 * BAD IDEA - should use an API!
 */
public class LocalDateToJsonManually {

    private static final String OPEN = "{";
    private static final String CLOSE = "}";

    public static void main(String[] args) {
        LocalDate dNow = LocalDate.now();
        System.out.println(toJson(dNow));
    }

    public static String toJson(LocalDate dNow) {
        StringBuilder sb = new StringBuilder();
        sb.append(OPEN).append("\n");
        sb.append(jsonize("year", dNow.getYear()));
        sb.append(jsonize("month", dNow.getMonth()));
        sb.append(jsonize("day", dNow.getDayOfMonth()));
        sb.append(CLOSE).append("\n");
        return sb.toString();
    }
```

```
        public static String jsonize(String key, Object value) {
            return String.format("\"%s\": \"%s\",\n", key, value);
        }
    }
```

Of course, this is an extremely trivial example. For anything more involved, or for the common case of having to parse JSON objects, using one of the frameworks will be easier on your nerves.

14.2 Parsing and Writing JSON with Jackson

Problem

You want to read and/or write JSON using a full-function JSON API.

Solution

Use Jackson, the full-blown JSON API.

Discussion

Jackson provides many ways of working. For simple cases, you can have POJO (Plain Old Java Objects) converted to/from JSON more or less automatically, as is illustrated in Example 14-1.

Example 14-1. json/src/main/java/json/ReadWriteJackson.java (reading and writing POJOs with Jackson)

```
public class ReadWriteJackson {

    public static void main(String[] args) throws IOException {
        ObjectMapper mapper = new ObjectMapper();                    ❶

        String jsonInput =                                          ❷
                "{\"id\":0,\"firstName\":\"Robin\",\"lastName\":\"Wilson\"}";
        Person q = mapper.readValue(jsonInput, Person.class);
        System.out.println("Read and parsed Person from JSON: " + q);

        Person p = new Person("Roger", "Rabbit");                   ❸
        System.out.print("Person object " + p +" as JSON = ");
        mapper.writeValue(System.out, p);
    }
}
```

❶ Create a Jackson `ObjectMapper` that can map POJOs to/from JSON.

❷ Map the string `jsonInput` into a `Person` object with one call to `readValue()`.

---

❸ Convert the `Person` object p into JSON with one call to `writeValue()`.

Running this example produces the following output:

```
Read and parsed Person from JSON: Robin Wilson
Person object Roger Rabbit as JSON = {"id":0,"firstName":"Roger",
        "lastName":"Rabbit","name":"Roger Rabbit"}
```

As another example, this code reads the example file that opened this chapter (which happens to have been a description of a JSON parser). Notice the declaration `List<String>` for the array of contributors:

```java
public class SoftwareParseJackson {
    final static String FILE_NAME = "/json/softwareinfo.json";

    public static void main(String[] args) throws Exception {
        ObjectMapper mapper = new ObjectMapper(); ❶

        InputStream jsonInput =
            SoftwareParseJackson.class.getResourceAsStream(FILE_NAME);
        if (jsonInput == null) {
            throw new NullPointerException("can't find " + FILE_NAME);
        }
        SoftwareInfo sware = mapper.readValue(jsonInput, SoftwareInfo.class);
        System.out.println(sware);
    }

}
```

❶ The `ObjectMapper` does the actual parsing of the JSON input.

Running this example produces the following output:

```
Software: robinparse (1.2.3) by [Robin Smythe, Jon Jenz, Jan Ardann]
```

Of course there are cases where the mapping gets more involved; for this purpose, Jackson provides a set of annotations to control the mapping. But the default mapping is pretty good!

There is also a streaming API for Jackson; refer to the website for details.

14.3 Parsing and Writing JSON with org.json

Problem

You want to read/write JSON using a midsized, widely used JSON API.

Solution

Consider using the org.json API , also known as JSON-Java; it's widely used and is also used in Android.

Discussion

The *org.json* package is not as advanced as Jackson, nor as high level; it makes you think and work in terms of the underlying JSON abstractions instead of at the Java code level. For example, here is the *org.json* version of reading the software description from the opening of this chapter:

```java
public class SoftwareParseOrgJson {
    final static String FILE_NAME = "/json/softwareinfo.json";

    public static void main(String[] args) throws Exception {

        InputStream jsonInput =
            SoftwareParseOrgJson.class.getResourceAsStream(FILE_NAME);
        if (jsonInput == null) {
            throw new NullPointerException("can't find" + FILE_NAME);
        }
        JSONObject obj = new JSONObject(new JSONTokener(jsonInput));          ❶
        System.out.println("Software Name: " + obj.getString("name"));       ❷
        System.out.println("Version: " + obj.getString("version"));
        System.out.println("Description: " + obj.getString("description"));
        System.out.println("Class: " + obj.getString("className"));
        JSONArray contribs = obj.getJSONArray("contributors");               ❸
        for (int i = 0; i < contribs.length(); i++) {                        ❹
            System.out.println("Contributor Name: " + contribs.get(i));
        }
    }

}
```

❶ Create the JSONObject from the input.

❷ Retrieve individual String fields.

❸ Retrieve the JSONArray of contributor names.

❹ org.json.JSONArray doesn't implement Iterable, so you can't use a forEach loop.

Running it produces the expected output:

```
Software Name: robinparse
Version: 1.2.3
Description: Another Parser for JSON
Class: RobinParse
```

```
Contributor Name: Robin Smythe
Contributor Name: Jon Jenz
Contributor Name: Jan Ardann
```

JSONObject and JSONArray use their toString() method to produce (correctly formatted) JSON strings, like this:

```
public class WriteOrgJson {
    public static void main(String[] args) {
        JSONObject jsonObject = new JSONObject();
        jsonObject.put("Name", "robinParse").          ❶
            put("Version", "1.2.3").
            put("Class", "RobinParse");
        String printable = jsonObject.toString();      ❷
        System.out.println(printable);
    }
}
```

❶ Nice that it offers a fluent API to allow chaining of method calls.

❷ toString() converts to textual JSON representation.

Running this produces the following:

```
{"Name":"robinParse","Class":"RobinParse","Version":"1.2.3"}
```

See Also

The org.json library code including its javadoc documentation is online at *https://github.com/stleary/JSON-java*. (under the name JSON-java to differentiate it from the other packages).

14.4 Parsing and Writing JSON with JSON-B

Problem

You want to read/write JSON using a midsized, standards-conforming JSON API.

Solution

Consider using JSON-B, the new Java standard (JSR-367).

Discussion

The JSON-B (JSON Binding) API is designed to make it simple to read/write Java POJOs. This is neatly illustrated by the code in Example 14-2.

Example 14-2. json/src/main/java/json/ReadWriteJsonB.java (reading/writing JSON with JSON-B)

```java
public class ReadWriteJsonB {

    public static void main(String[] args) throws IOException {

        Jsonb jsonb = JsonbBuilder.create();              ❶

        // Read
        String jsonInput =                                ❷
                "{\"id\":0,\"firstName\":\"Robin\",\"lastName\":\"Williams\"}";
        Person rw = jsonb.fromJson(jsonInput, Person.class);
        System.out.println(rw);

        String result = jsonb.toJson(rw);                 ❸
        System.out.println(result);
    }
}
```

❶ Create a `Jsonb` object, your gateway to JSON-B services.

❷ Obtain a JSON string, and convert it to a Java object using `jsonb.fromJson()`.

❸ Convert a `Person` object back to a JSON string using the inverse `jsonb.toJson()`.

Note that the methods are sensibly named and that no annotations are needed on the Java entity class to make this work. However, there is an API that allows us to customize it. For example, the `fullName` property is really just a convenience for concatenating the first name and last name with a space between. As such, it's completely redundant and does not need to be transmitted over a JSON network stream. However, running the program produces this output:

```
{"firstName":"Robin","fullName":"Robin Williams","id":0,"lastName":"Williams"}
```

We need only add the `@JsonbTransient` annotation to the `getFullName()` accessor in the `Person` class to eliminate the redundancy; running the program now produces this smaller output:

```
{"firstName":"Robin","id":0,"lastName":"Williams"}
```

See Also

As with most other JSON APIs, there is full support for customization, ranging from the simple annotation shown here up to writing complete custom serializer/deserializer helpers. See the JSON-B spec page (*https://javaee.github.io/jsonb-spec*), the JSON-B home page (*http://json-b.net*), and this longer tutorial online (*https://www.baeldung.com/java-json-binding-api*).

14.5 Finding JSON Elements with JSON Pointer

Problem

You have a JSON document and want to extract only selected values from it.

Solution

Use `javax.json`'s implementation of *JSON Pointer*, the standard API for extracting selected elements from JSON.

Discussion

The Internet Standard RFC 6901 (*https://tools.ietf.org/html/rfc6901*) spells out in detail the syntax for JSON Pointer, a language-independent syntax for matching elements in JSON documents. Obviously inspired by the XML syntax XPath, JSON Pointer is a bit simpler than XPath because of JSON's inherent simpllicity. Basically a JSON Pointer is a string that identifies an element (either simple or array) within a JSON document. The `javax.json` package provides an object model API somewhat similar to the XML DOM API for Java, letting you create immutable objects to represent objects (via `JsonObjectBuilder` and `JsonArrayBuilder`) or to read them from JSON string format via a `Reader` or `InputStream`.

JSON Pointers begin with a "/" (inherited from XPath), followed by the name of the element or subelement we want to look for. Suppose we extend our `Person` example from Example 14-2 to add an array of roles the comedian played, looking like this:

```
{"firstName":"Robin","lastName":"Williams",
        "age": 63,"id":0,
        "roles":["Mork", "Mrs. Doubtfire", "Patch Adams"]}
```

Then the following JSON Pointers should generate the given matches:

```
/firstName => Robin
/age => 63
/roles => ["Mork","Mrs. Doubtfire","Patch Adams"]
/roles/1 => "Mrs. Doubtfire"
```

The program in Example 14-3 demonstrates this.

Example 14-3. json/src/main/java/json/JsonPointerDemo.java

```java
public class JsonPointerDemo {

    public static void main(String[] args) {
        String jsonPerson =
            "{\"firstName\":\"Robin\",\"lastName\":\"Williams\"," +
                "\"age\": 63," +
```

```
                "\"id\":0," +
                "\"roles\":[\"Mork\", \"Mrs. Doubtfire\", \"Patch Adams\"]}";

        System.out.println("Input: " + jsonPerson);

        JsonReader rdr =
                Json.createReader(new StringReader(jsonPerson));      ❶
        JsonStructure jsonStr = rdr.read();
        rdr.close();

        JsonPointer jsonPointer;
        JsonString jsonString;

        jsonPointer = Json.createPointer("/firstName");              ❷
        jsonString = (JsonString)jsonPointer.getValue(jsonStr);
        String firstName = jsonString.getString();
        System.out.println("/firstName => " + firstName);

        JsonNumber num =                                             ❸
                (JsonNumber) Json.createPointer("/age").getValue(jsonStr);
        System.out.println("/age => " + num + "; a " + num.getClass().getName());

        jsonPointer = Json.createPointer("/roles");                  ❹
        JsonArray roles = (JsonArray) jsonPointer.getValue(jsonStr);
        System.out.println("/roles => " + roles);
        System.out.println("JsonArray roles.get(1) => " + roles.get(1));

        jsonPointer = Json.createPointer("/roles/1");                ❺
        jsonString = (JsonString)jsonPointer.getValue(jsonStr);
        System.out.println("/roles/1 => " + jsonString);
    }
}
```

❶ Create the `JsonStructure`, the gateway into this API, from a `JsonReader`, using a
   `StringReader`.

❷ Create a JSON Pointer for the `firstName` element, and get the `JsonString` from
   the element's value. Since `getValue()` will throw an exception if the element is
   not found, use `jsonPointer.containsValue(jsonStr)` to check first, if not sure
   if the element will be found.

❸ Same for `age`, but using more fluent syntax. If you print the class name for the
   match in `/age`, it will report an implementation-specific implementation class,
   such as `org.glassfish.json.JsonNumberImpl$JsonIntNumber`. Change the age
   in the XML from 63 to 63.5 and it will print a class with `BigDecimal` in its name.
   Either way, `toString()` on this object will return just the numeric value.

❹ In the JSON file, `roles` is an array. Thus, getting it using a JSON Pointer should return a `JsonArray` object, so we cast it to a reference of that type. This behaves somewhat like an immutable `List` implementation, so we call `get()`. JSON array indices start at zero, as in Java.

❺ Retrieve the same array element directly, using a pattern with "/1" to mean the numbered element in the array.

It is possible (but fortunately not common) for a JSON element name to contain special characters such as a slash. Most characters are not special to JSON Pointer, but to match a name containing a slash (/), the slash must be entered as ~1, and since that makes the tilde (~) special, tilde characters must be entered as ~0. Thus if the Person JSON file had an element like `"ft/pt/~"`, you would look for it with `Json.create Pointer("/ft~1pt~1~0");`.

See Also

The JSON Pointer API has additional methods that let you modify values and add/ remove elements. The offical home page for `javax.json`, which includes JSON Pointer, is at *jakarta.ee* (*https://jakarta.ee/specifications/jsonp/1.1*). The javadoc for `javax.json` is linked to from that page.

Summary

Many APIs exist for Java. Jackson is the biggest and most powerful; org.json, javax.json, and JSON-B are in the middle and StringTree (which I didn't give an example of because it doesn't have a Maven Artifact available) is the smallest. For a list of these and other JSON APIs, consult *https://www.json.org/json-en.html* and scroll past the syntax summary.

## CHAPTER 15

Packages and Packaging

15.0 Introduction

One of the better aspects of the Java language is that it has defined a very clear packaging mechanism for categorizing and managing its large API. Contrast this with most other languages, where symbols may be found in the C library itself or in any of dozens of other libraries, with no clearly defined naming conventions.[6] APIs consist of one or more package, packages consist of classes, and classes consist of methods and fields. Anybody can create a package, with one important restriction: you or I cannot create a package whose name begins with the four letters java. Packages named java. or javax. are reserved for use by Oracle's Java developers, under the management of the Java Community Process (JCP). When Java was new, there were about a dozen packages in a structure that is very much still with us, though it has quadrupled in size; some of these packages are shown in Table 15-1.

Table 15-1. Java packages basic structure

Name	Function
java.awt	Graphical user interface
java.io	Reading and writing
java.lang	Intrinsic classes (String, etc.)
java.lang.annotation	Library support for annotation processing
java.math	Math library

---

6 This is not strictly true. On Unix in C, at least, there is a distinction between normal include files and those in the *sys* subdirectory, and many structures have names beginning with one or two letters and an underscore in the password structure, like pw_name, pw_passwd, and pw_home. But this is nowhere near as consistent as Java's java.* naming conventions.

Name	Function
`java.net`	Networking (sockets)
`java.nio`	"New" I/O (not new anymore): channel-based I/O
`java.sql`	Java database connectivity
`java.text`	Handling and formatting/parsing dates, numbers, messages
`java.time`	Java 8: modern date/time API (JSR-311)
`java.util`	Utilities (collections, date)
`java.util.regex`	Regular expressions
`javax.naming`	JNDI
`javax.print`	Support for printing
`javax.script`	Java 6: scripting engines support
`javax.swing`	Modern graphical user interface

Many packages have been added over the years, but the initial structure has stood the test of time fairly well. In this chapter, I'll show you how to create and document your own packages, and then I'll discuss a number of issues related to deploying your package in various ways on various platforms.

This chapter also covers the more traditional meaning of packaging, as in, creating a package of your program for others to use. This covers the Java Platform Modules System (JPMS) introduced in Java 9. We also cover `jlink`, a tool for creating a mini-Java distribution containing your application and only the parts of the JDK that you actually use. We do not yet cover the `jpackage` tool for packaging applications, because it's not yet in the JDK; it may arrive with Java 14 or 15.

15.1 Creating a Package

Problem

You want to be able to import classes and/or organize your classes, so you want to create your own package.

Solution

Put a `package` statement at the front of each file, and recompile with `-d` or a build tool or IDE.

Discussion

The `package` statement must be the very first noncomment statement in your Java source file—preceding even `import` statements—and it must give the full name of the package. Package names are expected to start with your domain name backward; for

---

example, my internet domain is *darwinsys.com*, so most of my packages begin with `com.darwinsys` and a project name. The utility classes used in this book and meant for reuse are in one of the `com.darwinsys` packages listed in Recipe 1.6, and each source file begins with a statement, such as this:

```
package com.darwinsys.util;
```

The demonstration classes in the *JavaSrc* repository do not follow this pattern; they are in packages with names related to the chapter they are in or the `java.*` package they relate to; for example, `lang` for basic Java stuff, `structure` for examples from the data structuring chapter (Chapter 7), `threads` for the threading chapter (Chapter 16), and so on. It is hoped that you will put them in a "real" package if you reuse them in your application!

Once you have package statements in place, be aware that the Java runtime, and even the compiler, will expect the compiled *.class* files to be found in their rightful place (i.e., in the subdirectory corresponding to the full name somewhere in your CLASS PATH settings). For example, the class file for `com.darwinsys.util.FileIO` must *not* be in the file *FileIO.class* in my CLASSPATH but must be in *com/darwinsys/util/ FileIO.class* relative to one of the directories or archives in my CLASSPATH. Accordingly, if you are compiling with the command-line compiler, it is customary (almost mandatory) to use the `-d` command-line argument when compiling. This argument must be followed by the name of an existing directory (often . is used to signify the current directory) to specify where to build the directory tree. For example, to compile all the *.java* files in the current directory, and create the directory path under it (e.g., create *./com/darwinsys/util* in the example), use this:

```
javac -d . *.java
```

This creates the path (e.g., *com/darwinsys/util/*) relative to the current directory and puts the class files into that subdirectory. This makes life easy for subsequent compilations and also for creating archives, which is covered in Recipe 15.5.

Of course, if you use a build tool such as Maven (see Recipe 1.7), this will be done correctly by default (Maven), so you won't have to remember to keep doing it!

Note that in all modern Java environments, classes that do not belong to a package (the *anonymous package*) cannot be listed in an `import` statement, although they can be referred to by other classes in that package. They also cannot become part of a JPMS module.

15.2 Documenting Classes with Javadoc

Problem

You have heard about this thing called *code reuse* and would like to promote it by allowing other developers to use your classes.

Solution

Use javadoc. Write the comments when you write the code.

Discussion

Javadoc is one of the great inventions of the early Java years. Like so many good things, it was not wholly invented by the Java folks; earlier projects such as Knuth's Literate Programming had combined source code and documentation in a single source file. But the Java folks did a good job on it and came along at the right time. Javadoc is to Java classes what *man pages* are to Unix, or what Windows Help is to Windows applications: it is a standard format that everybody expects to find and knows how to use. Learn it. Use it. Write it. Live long and prosper (well, perhaps that's not guaranteed). But all that HTML documentation that you learned from writing Java code, the complete reference for the JDK—did you think they hired dozens of tech writers to produce it? Nay, that's not the Java way. Java's developers wrote the documentation comments as they went along, and when the release was made, they ran javadoc on all the zillions of public classes and generated the documentation bundle at the same time as the JDK. You can, should, and really must do the same when you are preparing classes for other developers to use.

All you have to do to use javadoc is to put special *javadoc comments* into your Java source files. These are similar to multiline Java comments, but they begin with a slash and *two* stars and end with the normal star-slash. Javadoc comments must appear immediately before the definition of the class, method, or field that they document; if placed elsewhere, they are ignored.

A series of keywords, prefixed by the at sign, can appear inside doc comments in certain contexts. Some are contained in braces. The keywords as of Java 8 are listed in Table 15-2.

Table 15-2. Javadoc keywords

Keyword	Use
@author	Author name(s)
{@code *text*}	Displays text in code font without HTML interpretation
@deprecated	Causes deprecation warning
{@docroot}	Refers to the root of the generated documentation tree
@exception	Alias for @throws
{@inheritDoc}	Inherits documentation from nearest superclass/superinterface
@link	Generates inline link to another class or member
@linkplain	As @link but displays in plain text
{@literal *text*}	Displays text without interpretation
@param *name description*	Argument name and meaning (methods only)
@return	Return value
@see	Generate cross-reference link to another class or member
@serial	Describes serializable field
@serialData	Describes order and types of data in serialized form
@serialField	Describes serializable field
@since	JDK version in which introduced (primarily for Sun use)
@throws	Exception class and conditions under which thrown
{@value [*ref*]}	Displays values of this or another constant field
@version	Version identifier

Example 15-1 is a somewhat contrived example that shows some common javadoc keywords in use. The output of running this through javadoc is shown in a browser in Figure 15-1.

Example 15-1. main/src/main/java/javadoc/JavadocDemo.java

```
public class JavadocDemo extends JPanel {

    private static final long serialVersionUID = 1L;

    /**
     * Construct the GUI
     * @throws java.lang.IllegalArgumentException if constructed on a Sunday.
     */
    public JavadocDemo() {
        // We create and add a pushbutton here,
        // but it doesn't do anything yet.
        Button b = new Button("Hello");
        add(b);                        // connect Button into component
        // Totally capricious example of what you should not do
```

```
        if (Calendar.getInstance().get(Calendar.DAY_OF_WEEK) == Calendar.SUNDAY) {
            throw new IllegalArgumentException("Never On A Sunday");
        }
    }

    /** paint() is an AWT Component method, called when the
     * component needs to be painted. This one just draws colored
     * boxes in the window.
     *
     * @param g A java.awt.Graphics that we use for all our
     * drawing methods.
     */
    public void paint(Graphics g) {
        int w = getSize().width, h = getSize().height;
        g.setColor(Color.YELLOW);
        g.fillRect(0, 0, w/2, h);
        g.setColor(Color.GREEN);
        g.fillRect(w/2, 0, w, h);
        g.setColor(Color.BLACK);
        g.drawString("Welcome to Java", 50, 50);
    }
}
```

The javadoc tool works fine for one class but really comes into its own when dealing with a package or collection of packages. You can provide a package summary file for each package, which will be incorporated into the generated files. Javadoc generates thoroughly interlinked and crosslinked documentation, just like that which accompanies the standard JDK. There are several command-line options; I normally use -author and -version to get it to include these items, and often -link to tell it where to find the standard JDK to link to.

Run javadoc -help for a complete list of options, or see the full documentation online at Oracle's website (*https://docs.oracle.com/en/java/javase/13/docs/specs/man/ javadoc.html*). Figure 15-1 shows one view of the documentation that the class shown in Example 15-1 generates when run as the following:

```
$ javadoc -author -version JavadocDemo.java
```

If you run this with Java 9+, it will also include a fully functional search box, shown in the upper right of Figure 15-1. This is implemented in JavaScript, so it should work in any modern browser.

Be aware that quite a few files are generated, and one of the generated files will have the same name as each class, with the extension *.html*. If you happened to have an HTML file documenting the class, and you generate javadoc in the source directory, the *.html* file is silently overwritten with the javadoc output. If you wish to avoid cluttering up your source directories with the generated files, the -d __directorypath option to javadoc allows you to place the generated files into the specified directory.

Figure 15-1. Javadoc opened in a browser

See Also

Javadoc has numerous other command-line arguments. If documentation is for your own use only and will not be distributed, you can use the -link option to tell it where your standard JDK documentation is installed so that links can be generated to standard Java classes (like String, Object, and so on). If documentation is to be distributed, you can omit -link or use -link with a URL to the appropriate Java API page on Oracle's website. See the online tools documentation for all the command-line options.

The output that javadoc generates is fine for most purposes. It is possible to write your own Doclet class to make the javadoc program into a class documentation verifier, a Java-to-other-format (such as Java-to-RTF) documentation generator, or whatever you like. Those are actual examples; see the javadoc tools documentation that comes with the JDK for documents and examples, or go to Oracle's website (*https:// docs.oracle.com/en/java/javase/13/docs/specs/man/javadoc.html*). Visit Doclet (*http:// www.doclet.com*) for a somewhat dated but useful collection of Doclets and other javadoc-based tools.

Javadoc Versus JavaHelp

Javadoc is for programmers using your classes; for a GUI application, end users will probably appreciate standard online help. This is the role of the JavaHelp API, which is not covered in this book but is fully explained in *Creating Effective JavaHelp* by Kevin Lewis (O'Reilly), which every GUI application developer should read. JavaHelp is another useful specification that was somewhat left to coast during the Sun sellout to Oracle; it is now hosted on *java.net* at javahelp (*https://javaee.github.io/javahelp*).

15.3 Beyond Javadoc: Annotations/Metadata

Problem

You want to generate not just documentation from your source code, but also other code artifacts. You want to mark code for additional compiler verification.

Solution

Use the Java Annotations, or Metadata, facility.

Discussion

The continuing success of the open source tool XDoclet (*http://xdoclet.source forge.net*)—originally used to generate the tedious auxiliary classes and deployment descriptor files for the widely criticized EJB2 framework—led to a demand for a similar mechanism in standard Java. Java *Annotations* were the result. The *annotation* mechanism uses an interface-like syntax, in which both declaration and use of annotations use the name preceded by an at character (@). This was chosen, according to the designers, to be reminiscent of "Javadoc tags, a preexisting ad hoc annotation facility in the Java programming language." Javadoc is ad hoc only in the sense that its @ tags were never fully integrated into the language; most were ignored by the compiler, but @deprecated was always understood by the compiler (see Recipe 1.9).

Annotations can be read at runtime by use of the Reflection API; this is discussed in Recipe 17.10, where I also show you how to define your own annotations. Annotations can also be read post–compile time by tools such as code generators (and others to be invented, perhaps by you, gentle reader!).

Annotations are also read by *javac* at compile time to provide extra information to the compiler.

For example, a common coding error is overloading a method when you mean to override it, by mistakenly using the wrong argument type. Consider overriding the equals method in Object. If you mistakenly write

```
public boolean equals(MyClass obj) {
    ...
}
```

then you have created a new overload that will likely never be called, and the default version in Object will be called. To prevent this, an annotation included in java.lang

---

is the `Override` annotation. This has no parameters but simply is placed before the method call, like this:

```
/**
 * AnnotationOverrideDemo - Simple demonstation of Metadata being used to
 * verify that a method does in fact override (not overload) a method
 * from the parent class. This class provides the method.
 */
abstract class Top {
    public abstract void myMethod(Object o);
}

/** Simple demonstation of Metadata being used to verify
 * that a method does in fact override (not overload) a method
 * from the parent class. This class is supposed to do the overriding,
 * but deliberately introduces an error to show how the modern compiler
 * behaves
 */
class Bottom {

    @Override
    public void myMethod(String s) {     // EXPECT COMPILE ERROR
        // Do something here...
    }
}
```

Attempting to compile this results in a compiler error that the method in question does not override a method, even though the annotation says it does; this is a fatal compile-time error:

```
C:> javac AnnotationOverrideDemo.java
AnnotationOverrideDemo.java:16: method does not override a method
        from its superclass
        @Override public void myMethod(String s) {     // EXPECT COMPILE ERROR
          ^
1 error
C:>
```

15.4 Preparing a Class as a JavaBean

Problem

You have a class that you would like to use as a JavaBean.

Solution

Make sure the class meets the JavaBeans requirements. Optionally, create a JAR file containing the class, a manifest, and any ancillary entries.

Discussion

Several kinds of Java components are called either Beans or JavaBeans:

- Visual components for use in GUI builders, as discussed in this recipe.
- Plain Old Java Objects (POJOs), or components meant for reuse.
- Java Enterprise has Enterprise JavaBeans (EJBs), JSP JavaBeans, JSF Managed Beans, and CDI Beans, containing features for building enterprise-scale applications. Creating and using Java EE components is more involved than regular JavaBeans and would take us very far afield, so they are not covered in this book. When you need to learn about enterprise functionality, turn to *Java EE 7 Essentials* by Arun Gupta.
- The Spring Framework (*http://springframework.org*) also uses the term "Beans" (or "Spring Beans") for the objects it manages.

What all these types of beans have in common are certain naming paradigms. All public properties should be accessible by get/set accessor methods. For a given property Prop of type Type, the following two methods should exist (note the capitalization):

```
public Type getProp( );
public void setProp(Type)
```

For example, the various AWT and Swing components that have textual labels all have the following pair of methods:

```
public String getText( );
public void setText(String newText);
```

One commonly permitted variance to this pattern is that, for boolean or Boolean arguments, the getter method is usually called isProp() rather than getProp().

You should use this set/get design pattern (set/get methods) for methods that control a bean. Indeed, this technique is useful even in nonbean classes for regularity. The bean containers for the APIs listed at the start of this section generally use Java introspection (see Chapter 17) to find the set/get method pairs, and some use these to construct properties editors for your bean. Bean-aware IDEs, for example, provide editors for all standard types (colors, fonts, labels, etc.). You can supplement this with a BeanInfo class to provide or override information.

The bare minimum a class requires to be usable as a JavaBean is the following:

- The class must have a no-argument constructor.
- The class should use the set/get paradigm.

- The class must implement `java.io.Serializable`, although many containers don't enforce this.

- Depending on the intended use, the class file might need to be packaged into a JAR file (see Recipe 15.5).

Note that a JavaBean with no *required* inheritance or `implements` is also called a POJO. Most new Java frameworks accept POJO components, instead of (as in days of yore) requiring inheritance (e.g., Struts 1 `org.struts.Action` class) or implementation of interfaces (e.g., EJB2 `javax.ejb.SessionBean` interface).

Here is a sample JavaBean that might have been a useful addition to one's Java GUI toolbox, the `LabelText` widget. It combines a label and a one-line text field into a single unit, making it easier to compose GUI applications. A demo program in the online source directory sets up three `LabelText` widgets, as shown in Figure 15-2.

Figure 15-2. LabelText bean

The code for `LabelText` is shown in Example 15-2. Notice that it is serializable and uses the set/get paradigm for most of its public methods. Most of the public set/get methods simply delegate to the corresponding methods in the label or the text field. There isn't really a lot to this bean, but it's a good example of aggregation, in addition to being a good example of a bean.

Example 15-2. darwinsys-api/src/main/java/com/darwinsys/swingui/LabelText.java

```
// package com.darwinsys.swingui;
public class LabelText extends JPanel implements java.io.Serializable {

    private static final long serialVersionUID = -8343040707105763298L;
    /** The label component */
    protected JLabel theLabel;
    /** The text field component */
    protected JTextField theTextField;
    /** The font to use */
    protected Font myFont;

    /** Construct the object with no initial values.
     * To be usable as a JavaBean there must be a no-argument constructor.
     */
    public LabelText() {
        this("(LabelText)", 12);
    }
```

```
/** Construct the object with the label and a default textfield size */
public LabelText(String label) {
    this(label, 12);
}

/** Construct the object with given label and textfield size */
public LabelText(String label, int numChars) {
    this(label, numChars, null);
}

/** Construct the object with given label, textfield size,
 * and "Extra" component
 * @param label The text to display
 * @param numChars The size of the text area
 * @param extra A third component such as a cancel button
 * may be null, in which case only the label and textfield exist.
 */
public LabelText(String label, int numChars, JComponent extra) {
    super();
    setLayout(new BoxLayout(this, BoxLayout.X_AXIS));
    theLabel = new JLabel(label);
    add(theLabel);
    theTextField = new JTextField(numChars);
    add(theTextField);
    if (extra != null) {
        add(extra);
    }
}

/** Get the label's horizontal alignment */
public int getLabelAlignment() {
    return theLabel.getHorizontalAlignment();
}

/** Set the label's horizontal alignment */
public void setLabelAlignment(int align) {
    theLabel.setHorizontalAlignment(align);
}

/** Get the text displayed in the text field */
public String getText() {
    return theTextField.getText();
}

/** Set the text displayed in the text field */
public void setText(String text) {
    theTextField.setText(text);
}

/** Get the text displayed in the label */
public String getLabel() {
```

```
        return theLabel.getText();
    }

    /** Set the text displayed in the label */
    public void setLabel(String text) {
        theLabel.setText(text);
    }

    /** Set the font used in both subcomponents. */
    public void setFont(Font f) {
        // This class' constructors call to super() can trigger
        // calls to setFont() (from Swing.LookAndFeel.installColorsAndFont),
        // before we create our components, so work around this.
        if (theLabel != null)
            theLabel.setFont(f);
        if (theTextField != null)
            theTextField.setFont(f);
    }

    /** Adds the ActionListener to receive action events from the textfield */
    public void addActionListener(ActionListener l) {
        theTextField.addActionListener(l);
    }

    /** Remove an ActionListener from the textfield. */
    public void removeActionListener(ActionListener l) {
        theTextField.removeActionListener(l);
    }
}
```

Once it's compiled, it's ready to be packaged into a JAR. Most build tools such as Maven will do this work for you.

15.5 Archiving with JAR

Problem

You want to create a Java archive (JAR) file from your package (or any other collection of files).

Solution

Use *jar*.

Discussion

The *jar* archiver is Java's standard tool for building archives. Archives serve the same purpose as the program libraries that some other programming languages use. Java normally loads its standard classes from archives, a fact you can verify by running a simple "Hello, World" program with the -verbose option:

```
java -verbose HelloWorld
```

Creating an archive is a simple process. The *jar* tool takes several command-line arguments: the most common are c for create, t for table of contents, and x for extract. The archive name is specified with -f and a filename. The options are followed by the files and directories to be archived, like this:

```
jar cvf /tmp/MyClasses.jar .
```

The dot at the end is important; it means the current directory. This command creates an archive of all files in the current directory and its subdirectories into the file */tmp/MyClasses.jar*.

Most applications of JAR files depend on an extra file that is always present in a true JAR file, called a *manifest*. This file always lists the contents of the JAR and their attributes; you can add extra information into it. The attributes are in the form name: value, as used in email headers, properties files (see Recipe 7.10), and elsewhere. Some attributes are required by the application, whereas others are optional. For example, Recipe 15.6 discusses running a main program directly from a JAR; this requires a Main-Program header. You can even invent your own attributes, such as the following:

```
MySillyAttribute: true
MySillynessLevel: high (5'11")
```

You store this in a file called, say, *manifest.stub*,[6] and pass it to *jar* with the -m switch. *jar* includes your attributes in the manifest file it creates:

```
jar -cv -m manifest.stub -f /tmp/com.darwinsys.util.jar .
```

The *jar* program and related tools add additional information to the manifest, including a listing of all the other files included in the archive.

If you use a tool like Maven (see Recipe 1.7), it automatically creates a JAR file from your source project just by saying mvn package.

---

6 Some people like to use names like *MyPackage.mf* so that it's clear which package it is for; the extension *.mf* is arbitrary, but it's a good convention for identifying manifest files.

15.6 Running a Program from a JAR

Problem

You want to distribute a single large file containing all the classes of your application and run the main program from within the JAR.

Solution

Create a JAR file with a `Main-Class:` line in the manifest; run the program with the `java -jar` option.

Discussion

The *java* command has a `-jar` option that tells it to run the main program found within a JAR file. In this case, it will also find classes it needs to load from within the same JAR file. How does it know which class to run? You must tell it. Create a one-line entry like this, noting that the attribute fields are case-sensitive and that the colon must be followed by a space:

```
Main-Class: com.somedomainhere.HelloWorld
```

Place that in a file called, say, *manifest.stub*, and assuming that you want to run the program `HelloWorld` from the given package. You can then use the following commands to package your app and run it from the JAR file:

```
C:> javac HelloWorld.java
C:> jar cvmf manifest.stub hello.jar HelloWorld.class
C:> java -jar hello.jar
Hello, World of Java
C:>
```

You can now copy the JAR file anywhere and run it the same way. You do not need to add it to your `CLASSPATH` or list the name of the main class.

On GUI platforms that support it, you can also launch this application by double-clicking the JAR file. This works on macOS, Microsoft Windows, and many X Windows desktops.

In real life you would probably automate this with Maven, where your POM file would contain, among other things, the following:

```
<project ...>
    ...
    <packaging>jar</packaging>
    ...
    <build>
        <plugins>
            <plugin>
```

```
            <groupId>org.apache.maven.plugins</groupId>
            <artifactId>maven-jar-plugin</artifactId>
            <version>2.4</version>
            <configuration>
                <archive>
                    <manifest>
                        <addclasspath>true</addclasspath>
                        <mainClass>${main.class}</mainClass>
                    </manifest>
                </archive>
            </configuration>
        </plugin>
    </plugins>
</build>
</project>
```

With this in place, mvn package will build a runnable JAR file. However, if your class has external dependencies, the preceding steps will not package them, and you will get a missing class exception when you run it. For this, you need to use the Maven assembly plug-in:

```
<plugin>
    <groupId>org.apache.maven.plugins</groupId>
    <artifactId>maven-assembly-plugin</artifactId>
    <version>2.6</version>
    <configuration>
        <descriptorRefs>
            <descriptorRef>jar-with-dependencies</descriptorRef>
        </descriptorRefs>
        <archive>
            <manifest>
                <addDefaultImplementationEntries>true
                </addDefaultImplementationEntries>
                <mainClass>${main.class}</mainClass>
                <!-- <manifestFile>manifest.stub</manifestFile> -->
            </manifest>
            <manifestEntries>
                <Vendor-URL>http://YOURDOMAIN.com/SOME_PATH/</Vendor-URL>
            </manifestEntries>
        </archive>
    </configuration>
</plugin>
```

Now, the invocation mvn package assembly:single will produce a runnable JAR with all dependencies. Note that your *target* folder will contain both *foo-0.0.1-SNAPSHOT.jar* and *foo-0.0.1-SNAPSHOT-jar-with-dependencies.jar*; the latter is the one you need.

The *jpackage* tool (mentioned in this chapter's introduction) will do much the same job as *assembly:single*, and is expected to ship with Java 14.

15.7 Packaging Web Tier Components into a WAR File

Problem

You have some web-tier resources and want to package them into a single file for deploying to the server.

Solution

Use *jar* to make a web archive (WAR) file. Or, as mentioned earlier, use Maven with packaging=*war*.

Discussion

Servlets are server-side components for use in web servers. They can be packaged for easy installation into a web server. A *web application* in the Servlet API specification is a collection of HTML and/or JSP pages, servlets, and other resources. A typical directory structure might include the following:

```
Project Root Directory
├── README.asciidoc
├── index.html - typical web pages
|── signup.jsp - ditto
├── WEB-INF Server directory
       ├── classes - Directory for individual .class files
       ├── lib    - Directory for Jar files needed by app
       └── web.xml - web app Descriptor ("Configuration file")
```

Once you have prepared the files in this way, you just package them up with a build tool. Using Maven, with <packaging>war</packaging>, your tree might look like this:

```
Project Root Directory
├── README.asciidoc
├── pom.xml
└── src
    └── main
        ├── java
        │   └── foo
        │       └── WebTierClass.java
        └── webapp
            ├── WEB-INF
            │   ├── classes
            │   ├── lib
            │   └── web.xml
            ├── index.html
            └── signup.jsp
```

Then mvn package will compile things, put them in place, and create the WAR file for you, leaving it under *target*. Gradle users would use a similar directory structure.

You could also invoke *jar* manually, though this has little to recommend it. You then deploy the resulting WAR file into your web server. For details on the deployment step, consult the documentation on the particular server you're using.

See Also

For more information on signing and permissions, see *Java Security* by Scott Oaks. For more information on the JDK tools mentioned here, see the documentation that accompanies the JDK you are using.

15.8 Creating a Smaller Distribution with jlink

Problem

You are distributing your application to end users, and you want to minimize the size of your download.

Solution

Modularize your application (see Recipe 15.9), use jdeps to get a complete list of the modules it uses, then use jlink to create the mini-Java, and distribute that to your users.

Discussion

jlink is a command-line tool introduced in Java 9 that can make up a mini-Java distribution containing only your application and the JDK classes it uses. That is, it omits any of the thousands of JDK classes that your app will never use.

First, you need to compile and package your module-info and your application code. You can use Maven or Gradle, or just use the JDK tools directly:

```
$ javac -d . src/*.java
$ jar cvf demo.jar module-info.class  demo
```

If you wish to see the list of modules that will be included, you can optionally run the jdeps tool to get this list:

```
$ jdeps --module-path . demo.jar
demo
 [file:///Users/ian/workspace/javasrc/jlink/./]
   requires mandated java.base (@11.0.2)
demo -> java.base
```

```
demo          -> java.io      java.base
demo          -> java.lang    java.base
```

Once the classes have been compiled, you can run the jlink tool to build a mini-java distribution with your demo app imbedded:

```
jlink --module-path . --no-header-files \
    --no-man-pages --compress=2 --strip-debug \
    --launcher rundemo=demo/demo.Hello \
    --add-modules demo --output mini-java
```

The --launcher *name=module/main* argument asks jlink to create a script file named *name* to run the application.

If you got no errors, you should be able to run it either with the *java* command or with the generated shell script:

```
$ mini-java/bin/java demo.Hello
Hello, world.
$ mini-java/bin/rundemo
Hello, world.
$
```

You might want to copy the entire mini-Java folder to a machine that doesn't have a regular Java installation and run it there in order to be sure you don't have any missing dependencies.

The concept of a mini-distribution is appealing, but you must consider these issues:

- There is no upgrade mechanism for such mini-Javas. These are quite suitable for microservice deployments where you rebuild often. For applications shipped to customers, though, you'd have to regenerate them and get your customers to download and reinstall (on short notice whenever there's a security update).

- Disk space is generally no longer expensive relative to the cost of your time in maintaining such a distribution.

Thus, you have to decide if this is worthwhile for your application.

15.9 Using JPMS to Create a Module

Problem

You want your packaged archive to work smoothly with the Java Modules System (JPMS).

Solution

Create a *module-info.java* file in the root of the source directory.

Discussion

The file *module-info.java* was introduced in Java 9 to provide the compiler and tools with information about your library's needs and what it provides. Note that this is not even a valid Java class filename because it contains a minus sign. The module also has a group of pseudokeywords, which only have their special meaning inside a module file. The simplest *module-info* is the following:

```
module foo {
    // Empty
}
```

But just as a Java class with no members won't get you very far in the real world, neither will this empty module file. We need to provide some additional information. For this example, I will modularize my `darwinsys-api`, a collection of 40 or so randomly accumulated classes that I reuse sometimes. Remember that Jigsaw (the module system's early name) was initially proposed as a way of modularizing the overgrown JDK itself. Most applications will need the module `java.base` (which is always included). If they need AWT, Swing, or certain other desktop-application-related classes, they also need `java.desktop`. Thus I add the following line into the module definition:

```
require java.desktop
```

This code also has some JUnit-annotated classes and makes use of JavaMail API, so we need those as well. JUnit, however, is only needed at test time. While Maven offers `scopes` for compile, test, and runtime, the modules system does not. Thus we could omit JUnit from the POM file and add it to Eclipse. But then `maven test` will not work.

And unfortunately, as of this writing, there does not appear to be modularized version of JavaMail either. Fortunately, there is a feature known as *automatic modules*, by which if you place a JAR file on the module path that doesn't declare a module, its JAR filename will be used as the basis of an automatically generated module. So we'll also add the following:

```
requires mail;
```

Unfortunately, when we compile, Maven's Java Compiler module spits out this scary-looking warning:

```
[WARNING] ********************************************************************
[WARNING] * Required filename-based automodules detected. Please don't publish
            this project to a public artifact repository! *
[WARNING] ********************************************************************
```

Given that there are so many public Java API libraries out there, and that most of them depend on other libraries in turn, I wonder: how is that state supposed to end? Nonetheless, I have heeded that warning, and so people will continue to use the auto-module version of com.darwinsys.api until I stumble across modularized JavaMail and JUnit4 APIs.

The *module-info* also lists any packages that your module desires to make available, that is, its public API. So we need a series of export commands:

```
exports com.darwinsys.calendar;
exports com.darwinsys.csv;
exports com.darwinsys.database;
...
```

By default, packages that are exported can not be examined using the Reflection API. To allow a module to introspect (use the Reflection API) on another, say, a domain model used with JPA, use opens.

One of the points of Java interfaces is to allow multiple implementations of a service. This is supported in JPMS by the service feature. Where an API is defined as one or more interfaces in one module, and multiple implementations are provided, each in its own module, the implementation module(s) can define an implementation using provides ... with, as in the following:

```
requires com.foo.interfacemodule;
provides com.foo.interfacemodule.Interface with com.foo.implmodule.ImplClass;
```

The completed *module-info* for the darwinsys-api module is shown in Example 15-3.

Example 15-3. DarwinSys-API module-info

```
module com.darwinsys.api {

    requires java.desktop;
    requires java.persistence;
    requires java.prefs;
    requires java.sql;
    requires java.sql.rowset;
    requires javax.servlet.api;
    requires mail;
    requires junit;

    exports com.darwinsys.calendar;
    exports com.darwinsys.csv;
    exports com.darwinsys.database;
    exports com.darwinsys.diff;
    exports com.darwinsys.formatting;
    exports com.darwinsys.locks;
    provides com.darwinsys.locks.LockManager
```

```
        with com.darwinsys.locks.LockManagerImpl;
    exports com.darwinsys.model;
    opens com.darwinsys.model;
    // another dozen and a half packages...
}
```

A module wanting to use the lock interface feature would need a `requires com.dar winsys` and might do something like this in code:

```
import java.util.ServiceLoader;
import java.util.Optional;

Optional<LockManager> opt = ServiceLoader.load(LockManager.class).findFirst();
if (!opt.isPresent()) {
    throw new RuntimeException("Could not find implementation of LockManager");
}
LockManager mgr = opt.get();
```

The `Optional` interface is described in Recipe 8.6.

See Also

JPMS is relatively new, and library providers are still learning to use it properly. An early posting was *https://openjdk.java.net/projects/jigsaw/quick-start*. A plan for migrating to modules can be found at *http://tutorials.jenkov.com/java/ modules.html#migrating-to-java-9*. A discussion about preparing a multi-module Maven application is at *https://www.baeldung.com/maven-multi-module-project-java- jpms*. The book *Java 9 Modularity: Patterns and Practices for Developing Maintainable Applications* (*http://shop.oreilly.com/product/0636920049494.do*) by Sander Mak and Paul Bakker is probably the most comprehensive treatment of JPMS.

## CHAPTER 16

Threaded Java

16.0 Introduction

We live in a world of multiple activities. A person may be talking on the phone while doodling or reading a memo. A multifunction office machine may scan one fax while receiving another and printing a document from somebody's computer. We expect the GUI programs we use to be able to respond to a menu while updating the screen. But ordinary computer programs can do only one thing at a time. The conventional computer programming model—that of writing one statement after another, punctuated by repetitive loops and binary decision making—is sequential at heart.

Sequential processing is straightforward but not as efficient as it could be. To enhance performance, Java offers *threading*, the capability to handle multiple flows of control within a single application or process. Java provides thread support and, in fact, requires threads: the Java runtime itself is inherently multithreaded. For example, window system action handling and Java's garbage collection—that miracle that lets us avoid having to free everything we allocate, as others must do when working in languages at or below C level—run in separate threads.

Just as multitasking allows a single operating system to give the appearance of running more than one program at the same time on a single-processor computer, multi-threading can allow a single program or process to give the appearance of working on more than one thing at the same time. Multithreading leads to more interactive graphics and more responsive GUI applications (the program can draw in a window while responding to a menu, with both activities occurring more or less independently), more reliable network servers (if one client does something wrong, the server continues communicating with the others), and so on.

Note that I did not say "multiprocessing" in the previous paragraph. The term multitasking is sometimes erroneously called multiprocessing, but that term in fact refers to different issue: it's the case of two or more CPUs running under a single operating system. Multiprocessing per se is nothing new: IBM mainframes did it in the 1970s, Sun SPARCstations did it in the 1980s, and Intel PCs did it in the 1990s. Since the mid-2010s, it has become increasingly hard to buy a single-processor computer packaged inside anything larger than a wristwatch. True multiprocessing allows you to have more than one process running concurrently on more than one CPU. Java's support for threading includes multiprocessing, as long as the operating system supports it. Consult your system documentation for details.

Though most modern operating systems provide threads, Java was the first mainstream programming language to have intrinsic support for threaded operations built right into the language. The semantics of `java.lang.Object`, of which all objects are instances, includes the notion of monitor locking of objects, and some methods (`notify`, `notifyAll`, `wait`) are meaningful only in the context of a multithreaded application. Java also has language keywords such as `synchronized` to control the behavior of threaded applications.

Now that the world has had years of experience with threaded Java, experts have started building better ways of writing threaded applications. The Concurrency Utilities, specified in JSR 166[6] and included in all modern Java releases, are heavily based on the `util.concurrent` package by Professor Doug Lea of the Computer Science Department at the State University of New York at Oswego. This package aims to do for the difficulties of threading what the Collections classes (see Chapter 7) did for structuring data. This is no small undertaking, but they pulled it off.

The `java.util.concurrent` package includes several main sections:

- Executors, thread pools (`ExecutorServices`), and `Futures`/`CompletableFutures`
- Queues and `BlockingQueues`
- Locks and conditions, with JVM support for faster locking and unlocking
- Synchronizers, including `Semaphores` and `Barriers`
- Atomic variables

In this chapter I will focus on the first set of these, thread pools and `Futures`.

An implementation of the `Executor` interface is, as the name implies, a class that can execute code for you. The code to be executed can be the familiar `Runnable` or a new interface `Callable`. One common kind of `Executor` is a *thread pool*. The `Future` interface represents the future state of something that has been started; it has

---

6 JSR stands for Java Specification Request. The Java Community Process calls standards, both proposed and adopted, JSRs. See *http://www.jcp.org* for details.

---

methods to wait until the result is ready. A CompletableFuture is an implementation of Future that adds many additional methods for chaining CompletableFutures and post-applied methods.

These brief definitions are oversimplifications. Addressing all the issues is beyond the scope of this chapter, but I do provide several examples.

16.1 Running Code in a Different Thread

Problem

You need to write a threaded application.

Solution

Write code that implements Runnable; pass it to an Executor, or instantiate a Thread and start it.

Discussion

There are several ways to implement threading, and they all require you to implement the Runnable or Callable interface. Runnable has only one method, and it returns no value; this is its signature:

```
public interface java.lang.Runnable {
  public abstract void run();
}
```

Callable has similarly only one method, but the call() method returns a specific type so the interface has a type parameter (V here, for "value"):

```
public interface java.util.concurrent.Callable<V> {
  public abstract V call() throws Exception;
}
```

You must provide an implementation of the run() or call() method. There is nothing special to this method; it's an ordinary method and you could call it yourself. But if you did, what then? There wouldn't be the special magic that launches it as an independent flow of control, so it wouldn't run concurrently with your main program or flow of control. For this, you need to invoke the magic of thread creation.

The original way of using threads, no longer generally recommended, is to create Thread objects directly and call their start() method, which would cause the thread to call the run() method after the new thread had been initialized. There was no support for the Callable interface in the original threads model. You create threads by doing one of the following things:

- Subclass `java.lang.Thread` (which implements `Runnable`) and override the `run()` method.

- Create your `Runnable` and pass it into the `Thread` constructor.

- With Java 8+, as shown in Recipe 9.0, you can use a lambda expression to implement `Runnable`.

This approach is no longer recommended because of issues such as performance (`Thread` objects are expensive to create and tear down, and a thread is unusable once its `run()` method returns). Because it is no longer recommended to invoke threading in this fashion, I no longer show examples of doing so. There are some examples in the online source, in the *threads* directory; see especially *ThreadsDemo4*.

Instead, the recommended way to perform threaded operations is to use the `java.util.concurrent` package's `ExecutorService`. An `ExecutorService` is, as its name implies, a service class that can execute code for you. The code to be executed can be in a `Runnable` or a `Callable`. You obtain an `ExecutorService` by invoking a factory method on the `Executors` class. The code in Example 16-1 shows a simple example of a thread pool.

Example 16-1. main/src/main/java/threads/ThreadPoolDemo.java

```
final ExecutorService pool = Executors.newFixedThreadPool(HOWMANY);
List<Future<Integer>> futures = new ArrayList<>(HOWMANY);
for (int i = 0; i < HOWMANY; i++) {
    Future<Integer> f = pool.submit(new DemoRunnable(i));
    System.out.println("Got 'Future' of type " + f.getClass());
    futures.add(f);
}
Thread.sleep(3 * 1000);
done = true;
for (Future<Integer> f : futures) {
    System.out.println("Result " + f.get());
}
pool.shutdown();
```

This will print a series of lines like the following, showing the threads running interspersed:

```
Running Thread[pool-1-thread-3,5,main]
Running Thread[pool-1-thread-3,5,main]
Running Thread[pool-1-thread-1,5,main]
Running Thread[pool-1-thread-1,5,main]
```

Note that there are several submission methods, the first in the parent interface `Execu tor` and two more in `ExecutorService`:

```
public void execute(Runnable);
public Future<T> submit(Callable<T>);
public Future<T> submit(Runnable);
```

That is, execute() takes a Runnable and returns nothing, whilst the submit() methods both return a Future<T> (for the method submit(Runnable), the type parameter x is always java.lang.Void).

When you are finished with the thread pool, you should call its shutDown() method.

Understanding Future and CompletableFuture

Future is an interface representing a claim ticket on some deliverable that may or may not be ready. It's a software analogue of the claim ticket you are given when you take laundry in to a dry cleaning service or take some item in to be repaired. The following describes the important methods of the Future interface:

```
public interface java.util.concurrent.Future<V> {
    public abstract boolean isDone();
    public abstract V get() throws InterruptedException,
        java.util.concurrent.ExecutionException;
    public abstract V get(long, java.util.concurrent.TimeUnit)
        throws InterruptedException,
        java.util.concurrent.ExecutionException,
        java.util.concurrent.TimeoutException;
    public abstract boolean cancel(boolean);
    public abstract boolean isCancelled();
}
```

The purpose of each method in this interface is shown here:

isDone()
> Returns true if the operation that will deliver the result has completed

get()
> Will return the deliverable immediately if isDone() is true; else will block indefinitely until it becomes true

get(long, TimeUnit)
> Will return the deliverable immediately if isDone() is true, blocking until it becomes true, or until the specified time has elapsed, in which case it will throw a TimeoutException

cancel(boolean)
> Will cancel the operation if it hasn't started (if the boolean is false) or even if it is in process (if the boolean is true)

isCancelled()
> Returns true if the operation has been canceled

Future is commonly returned from a thread pool execute() operation, as shown in Example 16-2.

Example 16-2. main/src/main/java/threads/FutureFromThreadpool.java

```
double d = 2;
Callable<Double> computeTotal = () -> d + d;
Future<Double> future = threadPool.submit(computeTotal);
while (!future.isDone()) {
    Thread.sleep(100);
}
double value = future.get();
process(value);
threadPool.shutdown();
```

There are many classes implementing Future in various parts of Java SE and Jakarta. The most general and powerful is CompletableFuture<V>, so called because you can control it by calling a complete(V) method at any time. This has far too many public methods (120) for a complete treatment here. In fairness, the number of methods is high because many methods can accept either a Runnable or a Callable, and many have multiple overloads (a plain one, one with Async appended to the name, and one with Async that lets you provide the Executor). I'll show examples of these shortly.

You can create an empty CompletableFuture by calling a no-argument constructor, making this available to some calling code, and calling its complete() method when you have a result:

```
CompletableFuture<Integer> cf = new CompletableFuture<>();
// Do some work
cf.complete();
```

Many of the more interesting methods in CompletableFuture have to do with chaining operations. First, you can specify a function to be invoked automatically when the result is ready:

```
public CompletableFuture<Void> thenRun(java.lang.Runnable);
public CompletableFuture<Void> thenRunAsync(java.lang.Runnable);
public CompletableFuture<Void> thenRunAsync(java.lang.Runnable, Executor);
public <U> CompletableFuture<U> thenApply(
    Function<? super T,
        ? extends U>);
public <U> CompletableFuture<U> thenApplyAsync(
    Function<? super T,
        ? extends U>);
public <U> CompletableFuture<U> thenApplyAsync(
    Function<? super T,
        ? extends U>, Executor);
public CompletableFuture<Void> thenAccept(Consumer<? super T>);
public CompletableFuture<Void> thenAcceptAsync(Consumer<? super T>);
public CompletableFuture<Void> thenAcceptAsync(
    Consumer<? super T>, Executor);
```

These methods will invoke the given Runnable, Consumer, or Function after the Future is completed. Each of these exists in the three forms as mentioned above. The first will run it on the same thread as the main task. The second method will run it in a default executor. The third allows you to provide your own executor. Example 16-3 is a simple demo of creating a CompletableFuture, giving it a thenApply method call and a final run method, both of which don't fire until the Future is completed.

Example 16-3. main/src/main/java/threads/CompletableFutureSimple.java

```java
class CompletableFutureSimple {
    static String twice(String x) { return x + ' ' + x; }

    public static void main(String[] args) {
        CompletableFuture<String> cf = new CompletableFuture<>();
        cf.thenApply(x -> twice(x))
          .thenAccept(x -> System.out.println(x));
        // Possibly some computation going on here... Then:
        cf.complete("Hello");
    }
}
```

The online source includes *CompletableFutureDemo.java*, which offers some more sophisticated examples.

16.2 Displaying a Moving Image with Animation

Problem

You need to update a graphical display while other parts of the program are running.

Solution

Use a background thread to drive the animation.

Discussion

One common use of threads is an animator, a class that displays a moving image. This animator program does just that. It draws a graphical image at locations around the screen; the location is updated and redrawn from a different Thread for each such image so that all the animations run in parallel. You can see the program running in Figure 16-1.

Figure 16-1. Animator

The code for the animator program consists of two classes, Sprite (see Example 16-4) and Bounce[6] (see Example 16-5). A Sprite is one image that moves around; Bounce is the main program.

Example 16-4. main/src/main/java/threads/Sprite.java (part of animator program)

```java
/** A Sprite is one Image that moves around the screen on its own */
public class Sprite extends Component implements Runnable {
    private static final long serialVersionUID = 1L;
    protected static int spriteNumber = 0;
    protected int number;
    protected int x, y;
    protected Component parent;
    protected Image image;
    protected volatile boolean done = false;
    /** The time in mSec to pause between each move. */
    protected volatile int sleepTime = 250;
```

---

6 The title belies some unfulfilled ambitions to make the animations follow the bouncing curves seen in some flashier animation demonstrations.

```java
/** The direction for this particular sprite. */
protected Direction direction;
enum Direction {
    VERTICAL, HORIZONTAL, DIAGONAL
}
/** Construct a Sprite with a Component parent, image and direction.
 * Construct and start a Thread to drive this Sprite.
 */
public Sprite(Component parent, Image image, Direction direction) {
    this.parent = parent;
    this.image = image;
    this.direction = direction;
    this.number = Sprite.spriteNumber++;
    setSize(image.getWidth(this), image.getHeight(this));
}

/** Construct a Sprite with the default direction */
public Sprite(Component parent, Image image) {
    this(parent, image, Direction.DIAGONAL);
}

/** Stop this Sprite. */
public void stop() {
    System.out.println("Stopping " + number);
    done = true;
}

/** Adjust the motion rate */
protected void setSleepTime(int n) {
    sleepTime = n;
}

/**
 * Run one Sprite around the screen.
 * This version just moves them around either across, down, or
 * at some 45-degree angle.
 */
public void run() {
    int width = parent.getSize().width;
    int height = parent.getSize().height;
    // Set initial location
    x = (int)(Math.random() * width);
    y = (int)(Math.random() * height);
    // Flip coin for x & y directions
    int xincr = Math.random()>0.5?1:-1;
    int yincr = Math.random()>0.5?1:-1;
    while (!done) {
        width = parent.getSize().width;
        height = parent.getSize().height;
        if ((x+=xincr) >= width)
            x=0;
        if ((y+=yincr) >= height)
```

```
                y=0;
            if (x<0)
                x = width;
            if (y<0)
                y = height;
            switch(direction) {
                case VERTICAL:
                    x = 0;
                    break;
                case HORIZONTAL:
                    y = 0;
                    break;
                case DIAGONAL:
                    // Let it wrap around
                    break;
            }
            //System.out.println("from " + getLocation() + "->" + x + "," + y);
            setLocation(x, y);
            repaint();
            try {
                Thread.sleep(sleepTime);
            } catch (InterruptedException e) {
                return;
            }
        }
    }

    /** paint -- just draw our image at its current location */
    public void paint(Graphics g) {
        g.drawImage(image, 0, 0, this);
    }
}
```

This example features several uses of the `volatile` keyword. The `volatile` keyword is used to inform Java that a variable is subject to change by more than one thread, so that its current value must always be fetched when it is used. Absent this keyword, it is legal for Java to use a cached version of the given variable. That increases performance when a variable is only used in one thread, but (without `volatile`) can give incorrect results when the variable is modified in one thread and observed in another.

Example 16-5. main/src/main/java/threads/Bounce.java (part of animator program)

```
public class Bounce extends JPanel {

    private static final long serialVersionUID = -53591626217195202l3L;
    /** The main Panel */
    protected JPanel p;
    /** The image, shared by all the Sprite objects */
    protected Image img;
    /** A Thread Pool */
```

```
protected ExecutorService tp = Executors.newCachedThreadPool();
/** A Vector of Sprite objects. */
protected List<Sprite> v = new Vector<Sprite>(); // multithreaded, use Vector;

public static void main(String[] args) {
    JFrame jf = new JFrame("Bounce Demo");
    jf.add(new Bounce(args.length > 0 ? args[0] : null));
    jf.setSize(300, 300);
    jf.setVisible(true);
    jf.setDefaultCloseOperation(JFrame.EXIT_ON_CLOSE);
}

public Bounce(String imgName) {
    setLayout(new BorderLayout());
    JButton b = new JButton("Add a Sprite");
    b.addActionListener(e -> {
        System.out.println("Creating another one!");
        Sprite s = new Sprite(this, img);
        tp.execute(s);
        p.add(s);
        v.add(s);
    });
    add(b, BorderLayout.NORTH);
    add(p = new JPanel(), BorderLayout.CENTER);
    p.setLayout(null);
    if (imgName == null) imgName = "duke.gif";
    final URL resource = getClass().getResource("/" + imgName);
    if (resource == null) {
        throw new IllegalStateException("Could not load image " + imgName);
    }
    img = Toolkit.getDefaultToolkit().getImage(resource);
    MediaTracker mt = new MediaTracker(this);
    mt.addImage(img, 0);
    try {
        mt.waitForID(0);
    } catch(InterruptedException e) {
        throw new IllegalArgumentException(
            "InterruptedException while loading image " + imgName);
    }
    if (mt.isErrorID(0)) {
        throw new IllegalArgumentException(
            "Couldn't load image " + imgName);
    }
    JButton stopper = new JButton("Shut down");
    stopper.addActionListener(e -> {
        stop();
        tp.shutdown();
    });
    add(stopper, BorderLayout.SOUTH);
}

public void stop() {
```

```
        for (Sprite s : v) {
            s.stop();
        }
        v.clear();
        try {
            tp.awaitTermination(5, TimeUnit.SECONDS);
            System.out.println("ThreadPool is shut down, ending program");
            System.exit(0);
        } catch (InterruptedException e) {
            // Empty
        }
    }
}
```

16.3 Stopping a Thread

Problem

You need to stop a thread.

Solution

Don't use the Thread.stop() method; instead, use a boolean tested at the top of the main loop in the run() method.

Discussion

Though you can use the thread's stop() method, it is not recommended. That's because the method is so drastic that it can never be made to behave reliably in a program with multiple active threads. That is why, when you try to use it, the compiler will generate deprecation warnings. The recommended method is to use a boolean variable in the main loop of the run() method. The program in Example 16-6 prints a message endlessly until its shutDown() method is called; it then sets the controlling variable done to false, which terminates the loop. This causes the run() method to return, ending its processing.

Example 16-6. main/src/main/java/threads/StopBoolean.java

```
public class StopBoolean {

    // Must be volatile to ensure changes visible to other threads.
    protected volatile boolean done = false;

    Runnable r = () -> {
        while (!done) {
            System.out.println("StopBoolean running");
            try {
```

```
            Thread.sleep(720);
        } catch (InterruptedException ex) {
            // nothing to do
        }
    }
    System.out.println("StopBoolean finished.");
};

public void shutDown() {
    System.out.println("Shutting down...");
    done = true;
}

public void doDemo() throws InterruptedException {
    ExecutorService pool = Executors.newSingleThreadExecutor();
    pool.submit(r);
    Thread.sleep(1000*5);
    shutDown();
    pool.shutdown();
    pool.awaitTermination(2, TimeUnit.SECONDS);
}

public static void main(String[] args) throws InterruptedException {
    new StopBoolean().doDemo();
}
}
```

Running it looks like this:

```
StopBoolean running
StopBoolean running
StopBoolean running
StopBoolean running
StopBoolean running
StopBoolean running
StopBoolean running
StopBoolean finished.
```

But what if your thread is blocked reading from a network connection? You then cannot check a boolean, because the thread that is reading is asleep. This is what the stop method was designed for, but, as we've seen, it is now deprecated. Instead, you can simply close the socket. The program shown in Example 16-7 intentionally deadlocks itself by reading from a socket that you are supposed to write to, simply to demonstrate that closing the socket does in fact terminate the loop.

Example 16-7. main/src/main/java/threads/StopClose.java

```
public class StopClose extends Thread {
    protected Socket io;

    public void run() {
```

```
        try {
            io = new Socket("java.sun.com", 80);     // HTTP
            BufferedReader is = new BufferedReader(
                new InputStreamReader(io.getInputStream()));
            System.out.println("StopClose reading");

            // The following line will deadlock (intentionally), since HTTP
            // enjoins the client to send a request (like "GET / HTTP/1.0")
            // and a null line, before reading the response.

            String line = is.readLine();     // DEADLOCK

            // Should only get out of the readLine if an interrupt
            // is thrown, as a result of closing the socket.

            // So we shouldn't get here, ever:
            System.out.printf("StopClose FINISHED after reading %s!?", line);
        } catch (IOException ex) {
            System.out.println("StopClose terminating: " + ex);
        }
    }

    public void shutDown() throws IOException {
        if (io != null) {
            // This is supposed to interrupt the waiting read.
            synchronized(io) {
                io.close();
            }
        }
        System.out.println("StopClose.shutDown() completed");
    }

    public static void main(String[] args)
    throws InterruptedException, IOException {
        StopClose t = new StopClose();
        t.start();
        Thread.sleep(1000*5);
        t.shutDown();
    }
}
```

When run, it prints a message that the close is happening:

```
StopClose reading
StopClose terminating: java.net.SocketException: Resource temporarily unavail-
able
```

"But wait," you say. "What if I want to break the wait, but not really terminate the socket?" A good question, indeed, and there is no perfect answer. But you can *interrupt* the thread that is reading; the read is interrupted by a java.io.Interrupte dIOException, and you can retry the read. The file *Intr.java* in this chapter's source code shows this.

16.4 Rendezvous and Timeouts

Problem

You need to know whether something finished or whether it finished in a certain length of time.

Solution

Start that something in its own thread and call its `join()` method with or without a timeout value.

Discussion

The `join()` method of the target thread is used to suspend the current thread until the target thread is finished (returns from its `run()` method). This method is overloaded; a version with no arguments waits forever for the thread to terminate, whereas a version with arguments waits up to the specified time. For a simple example, I create (and start!) a simple thread that just reads from the console terminal, and the main thread simply waits for it. When I run the program, it looks like this:

```
darwinsys.com$ java threads.Join
Starting
Joining
Reading
hello from standard input # waits indefinitely for me to type this line
Thread Finished.
Main Finished.
darwinsys.com$
```

Example 16-8 lists the code for the `join()` demo.

Example 16-8. main/src/main/java/threads/Join.java

```java
public class Join {
    public static void main(String[] args) {
        Thread t = new Thread() {
            public void run() {
                System.out.println("Reading");
                try {
                    System.in.read();
                } catch (java.io.IOException ex) {
                    System.err.println(ex);
                }
                System.out.println("Thread Finished.");
            }
        };
        System.out.println("Starting");
```

```
        t.start();
        System.out.println("Joining");
        try {
            t.join();
        } catch (InterruptedException ex) {
            // should not happen:
            System.out.println("Who dares interrupt my sleep?");
        }
        System.out.println("Main Finished.");
    }
}
```

As you can see, it uses an inner class Runnable (see Recipe 16.1) in Thread t to be runnable.

16.5 Synchronizing Threads with the synchronized Keyword

Problem

You need to protect certain data from access by multiple threads.

Solution

Use the synchronized keyword on the method or code you wish to protect.

Discussion

I discussed the synchronized keyword briefly in Recipe 13.5. This keyword specifies that only one thread at a time is allowed to run the given method (or any other synchronized method in the same class) in a given object instance (for static methods, only one thread is allowed to run the method at a time). You can synchronize methods or smaller blocks of code. It is easier and safer to synchronize entire methods, but this can be more costly in terms of blocking threads that could run. You can simply add the synchronized keyword on the method. For example, many of the methods of Vector (see Recipe 7.4) are synchronized in order to ensure that the vector does not become corrupted or give incorrect results when two threads update or retrieve from it at the same time.

Bear in mind that threads can be interrupted at almost any time, in which case control is given to another thread. Consider the case of two threads appending to a data structure at the same time. Let's suppose we have the same methods as Vector, but we're operating on a simple array. The add() method simply uses the current number of objects as an array index, then increments it:

```
public void add(Object obj) {
    data[max] = obj;   ❶
    max = max + 1;     ❷
}
```

Threads A and B both wish to call this method. Suppose that Thread A gets interrupted after ❶ but before ❷, and then Thread B gets to run.

❶   Thread B does ❶, overwriting the contents of data[max]; we've now lost all reference to the object that Thread A passed in!

❷   Thread B then increments max at ❷ and returns. Later, Thread A gets to run again; it resumes at ❷ and increments max past the last valid object. So not only have we lost an object, but we have an uninitialized reference in the array. This state of affairs is shown in Figure 16-2.

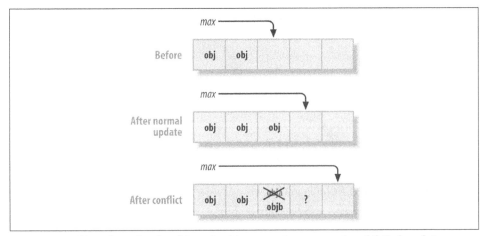

Figure 16-2. Non-thread-safe add method in operation: normal and failed updates

Now you might think, "No problem, I'll just combine the two lines of code!":

```
data[max++] = obj;
```

As the game show host sometimes says, "Bzzzzt! Thanks for playing!" This change makes the code a bit shorter but has absolutely no effect on reliability. Interrupts don't happen conveniently on Java statement boundaries; they can happen between any of the many JVM machine instructions that correspond to your program. The code can still be interrupted after the store and before the increment. The only good solution is to use proper synchronization.

Making the method synchronized means that any invocations of it will wait if one thread has already started running the method:

```
public synchronized void add(Object obj) {
    ...
}
```

Any time you wish to synchronize some code, but not an entire method, use the synchronized keyword on an unnamed code block within a method, like this:

```
public void add(Object obj) {
    synchronized (someObject) {
        // this code will execute in one thread at a time
    }
}
```

The choice of object to synchronize on is up to you. Sometimes it makes sense to synchronize on the object containing the code, as in Example 16-9. For synchronizing access to an ArrayList, it would make sense to use the ArrayList instance, like this:

```
synchronized(myArrayList) {
    if (myArrayList.indexOf(someObject) != -1) {
        // do something with it.
    } else {
        create an object and add it...
    }
}
```

Example 16-9 is a web servlet that I wrote for use in the classroom, following a suggestion from fellow Learning Tree instructor Scott Weingust.[6] It lets you play a quiz show game of the style where the host asks a question and the first person to press their buzzer (buzz in) gets to try to answer the question correctly. To ensure against having two people buzz in simultaneously, the code uses a synchronized block around the code that updates the Boolean buzzed variable. And for reliability, any code that accesses this Boolean is also synchronized.

Example 16-9. main/src/main/java/threads/BuzzInServlet.java

```
public class BuzzInServlet extends HttpServlet {

    /** The attribute name used throughout. */
    protected final static String WINNER = "buzzin.winner";

    /** doGet is called from the contestants web page.
     * Uses a synchronized code block to ensure that
     * only one contestant can change the state of "buzzed".
     */
    public void doGet(HttpServletRequest request, HttpServletResponse response)
    throws ServletException, IOException {
```

---

6 A *servlet* is a low-level server-side API for interacting with remote clients; today it would probably be written in the form of a JavaServer Faces (JSF) handler.

```java
        ServletContext application = getServletContext();

        boolean iWon = false;
        String user = request.getRemoteHost() + '@' + request.getRemoteAddr();

        // Do the synchronized stuff first, and all in one place.
        synchronized(application) {
            if (application.getAttribute(WINNER) == null) {
                application.setAttribute(WINNER, user);
                application.log("BuzzInServlet: WINNER " + user);
                iWon = true;
            }
        }

        response.setContentType("text/html");
        PrintWriter out = response.getWriter();

        out.println("<html><head><title>Thanks for playing</title></head>");
        out.println("<body bgcolor=\"white\">");

        if (iWon) {
            out.println("<b>YOU GOT IT</b>");
            // TODO - output HTML to play a sound file :-)
        } else {
                out.println("Thanks for playing, " + request.getRemoteAddr());
                out.println(", but " + application.getAttribute(WINNER) +
                    " buzzed in first");
        }
        out.println("</body></html>");
}

/** The Post method is used from an Administrator page (which should
 * only be installed in the instructor/host's localweb directory).
 * Post is used for administrative functions:
 * 1) to display the winner;
 * 2) to reset the buzzer for the next question.
 */
public void doPost(HttpServletRequest request, HttpServletResponse response)
throws ServletException, IOException {
    ServletContext application = getServletContext();

    response.setContentType("text/html");
    HttpSession session = request.getSession();

    PrintWriter out = response.getWriter();

    if (request.isUserInRole("host")) {
        out.println("<html><head><title>Welcome back, " +
            request.getUserPrincipal().getName() + "</title><head>");
        out.println("<body bgcolor=\"white\">");
        String command = request.getParameter("command");
        if (command.equals("reset")) {
```

```
                    // Synchronize what you need, no more, no less.
                    synchronized(application) {
                        application.setAttribute(WINNER, null);
                    }
                    session.setAttribute("buzzin.message", "RESET");
                } else if (command.equals("show")) {
                    String winner = null;
                    synchronized(application) {
                        winner = (String)application.getAttribute(WINNER);
                    }
                    if (winner == null) {
                        session.setAttribute("buzzin.message",
                            "<b>No winner yet!</b>");
                    } else {
                        session.setAttribute("buzzin.message",
                            "<b>Winner is: </b>" + winner);
                    }
                }
                else {
                    session.setAttribute("buzzin.message",
                        "ERROR: Command " + command + " invalid.");
                }
                RequestDispatcher rd = application.getRequestDispatcher(
                    "/hosts/index.jsp");
                rd.forward(request, response);
            } else {
                out.println("<html><head><title>Nice try, but... </title><head>");
                out.println("<body bgcolor=\"white\">");
                out.println(
                    "I'm sorry, Dave, but you know I can't allow you to do that.");
                out.println("Even if you are " + request.getUserPrincipal());
            }
            out.println("</body></html>");
        }
}
```

Two HTML pages lead to the servlet. The contestant's page simply has a large link (<a href=/servlet/BuzzInServlet>). Anchor links generate an HTML GET, so the servlet engine calls doGet():

```
<html><head><title>Buzz In!</title></head>
<body>
<h1>Buzz In!</h1>
<p>
<font size=+6>
<a href="servlet/BuzzInServlet">
Press here to buzz in!
</a>
</font>
```

The HTML is pretty plain, but it does the job. Figure 16-3 shows the look and feel.

Figure 16-3. BuzzInServlet in action

The game show host has access to an HTML form with a POST method, which calls the doPost() method. This displays the winner to the game show host and resets the buzzer for the next question.

```
<html><head><title>Reset Buzzer</title></head>
<body>
<h1>Display Winner</h1>
<p>
<b>The winner is:</b>
<form method="post" action="servlet/BuzzInServlet">
    <input type="hidden" name="command" value="show">
    <input type="hidden" name="password" value="syzzy">
    <input type="submit" name="Show" value="Show">
</form>
<h1>Reset Buzzer</h1>
<p>
<b>Remember to RESET before you ask the contestants each question!</b>
<form method="post" action="servlet/BuzzInServlet">
    <input type="hidden" name="command" value="reset">
    <input type="hidden" name="password" value="syzzy">
    <input type="submit" name="Reset" value="RESET!">
</form>
```

A password is provided; it's hardcoded here, but in reality the password would come from a properties file (Recipe 7.10) or a servlet initialization parameter (as described in *Java Servlet Programming* [O'Reilly]):

The game show host functionality is shown in Figure 16-4.

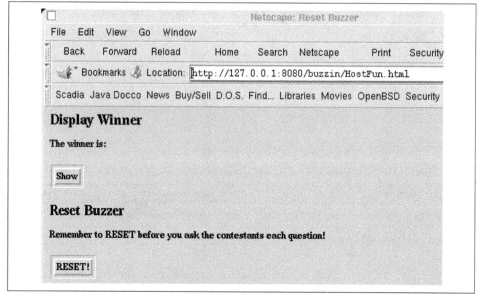

Figure 16-4. BuzzInServlet game show host function

For a more complete game, of course, the servlet would keep a Stack (see Recipe 7.16) of people in the order they buzzed in, in case the first person doesn't answer the question correctly. Access to this would have to be synchronized, too.

16.6 Simplifying Synchronization with Locks

Problem

You want an easier means of synchronizing threads.

Solution

Use the Lock mechanism in `java.util.concurrent.locks`.

Discussion

Use the `java.util.concurrent.locks` package; its major interface is Lock. This interface has several methods for locking and one for unlocking. Here is the general pattern for using it:

```
Lock thelock = ....
try {
        lock.lock( );
        // do the work that is protected by the lock
} finally {
        lock.unlock( );
}
```

The point of putting the `unlock()` call in the `finally` block is, of course, to ensure that it is not bypassed if an exception occurs (the code may also include one or more `catch` blocks, as required by the work being performed).

The improvement here, compared with the traditional synchronized methods and blocks, is that using a Lock actually looks like a locking operation! And, as I mentioned, several means of locking are available, shown in Table 16-1.

Table 16-1. Locking methods of the Lock class

Return type	Method	Meaning
void	`lock( )`	Get the lock, even if you have to wait until another thread frees it first
boolean	`tryLock( )`	Get the lock only if it is free right now
boolean	`tryLock(long time, TimeUnit units) throws InterruptedException`	Try to get the lock, but only wait for the length of time indicated
void	`lockInterruptibly( ) throws InterruptedException`	Get the lock, waiting unless interrupted
void	`unlock( )`	Release the lock

The `TimeUnit` class lets you specify the units for the amount of time specified, including `TimeUnit.SECONDS`, `TimeUnit.MILLISECONDS`, `TimeUnit.MICROSECONDS`, and `TimeUnit.NANOSECONDS`.

In all cases, the lock must be released with `unlock()` before it can be locked again.

The standard Lock is useful in many applications, but depending on the application's requirements, other types of locks may be more appropriate. Applications with asymmetric load patterns may benefit from a common pattern called the *reader-writer lock*; I call this one a readers-writer lock to emphasize that there can be many readers but only one writer. It's actually a pair of interconnected locks; any number of readers can hold the read lock and read the data, as long as it's not being written (shared read access). A thread trying to lock the write lock, however, waits until all the readers are finished and then locks them out until the writer is finished (exclusive write access). To support this pattern, both the ReadWriteLock interface and the implementing class ReentrantReadWriteLock are available. The interface has only two methods, readLock() and writeLock(), which provide a reference to the appropriate Lock implementation. *These methods do not, in themselves, lock or unlock the locks*; they only provide access to them, so it is common to see code like this:

```
rwlock.readLock( ).lock( );
...
rwlock.readLock( ).unlock( );
```

To demonstrate ReadWriteLock in action, I wrote the business logic portion of a web-based voting application. It could be used in voting for candidates or for the more common web poll. Presuming that you display the results on the home page and change the data only when somebody takes the time to click a response to vote, this application fits one of the intended criteria for ReadWriteLock—that is, that you have more readers than writers. The main class, ReadersWritersDemo, is shown in Example 16-10. The helper class BallotBox is online; it simply keeps track of the votes and returns a read-only Iterator upon request. Note that in the run() method of the reading threads, you could obtain the iterator while holding the lock but release the lock before printing it; this allows greater concurrency and better performance, but it could (depending on your application) require additional locking against concurrent update.

Example 16-10. main/src/main/java/threads/ReadersWriterDemo.java

```java
public class ReadersWriterDemo {
    private static final int NUM_READER_THREADS = 3;

    public static void main(String[] args) {
        new ReadersWriterDemo().demo();
    }

    /** Set this to true to end the program */
    private volatile boolean done = false;

    /** The data being protected. */
    private BallotBox theData;

    /** The read lock / write lock combination */
    private ReadWriteLock lock = new ReentrantReadWriteLock();

    /**
     * Constructor: set up some quasi-random initial data
     */
```

```java
public ReadersWriterDemo() {
    List<String> questionsList = new ArrayList<>();
    questionsList.add("Agree");
    questionsList.add("Disagree");
    questionsList.add("No opinion");
    theData = new BallotBox(questionsList);
}

/**
 * Run a demo with more readers than writers
 */
private void demo() {

    // Start two reader threads
    for (int i = 0; i < NUM_READER_THREADS; i++) {
        new Thread() {
            public void run() {
                while (!done) {
                    lock.readLock().lock();
                    try {
                        theData.forEach(p ->
                            System.out.printf("%s: votes %d%n",
                                p.getName(),
                                p.getVotes()));
                    } finally {
                        // Unlock in "finally" to be sure it gets done.
                        lock.readLock().unlock();
                    }

                    try {
                        Thread.sleep(((long)(Math.random()* 1000)));
                    } catch (InterruptedException ex) {
                        // nothing to do
                    }
                }
            }
        }.start();
    }

    // Start one writer thread to simulate occasional voting
    new Thread() {
        public void run() {
            while (!done) {
                lock.writeLock().lock();
                try {
                    theData.voteFor(
                        // Vote for random candidate :-)
                        // Performance: should have one PRNG per thread.
                        (((int)(Math.random()*
                        theData.getCandidateCount())))));
                } finally {
                    lock.writeLock().unlock();
```

```
        }
        try {
            Thread.sleep(((long)(Math.random()*1000)));
        } catch (InterruptedException ex) {
            // nothing to do
        }
    }
}
}.start();

// In the main thread, wait a while then terminate the run.
try {
    Thread.sleep(10 * 1000);
} catch (InterruptedException ex) {
    // nothing to do
} finally {
    done = true;
}
}
}
```

Because this is a simulation and the voting is random, it does not always come out 50/50. In two consecutive runs, the following were the last line of each run:

```
Agree(6), Disagree(6)
Agree(9), Disagree(4)
```

See Also

The Lock interface also makes available Condition objects, which provide even more flexibility. Consult the online documentation for more information.

16.7 Simplifying Producer/Consumer with the Queue Interface

Problem

You need to control producer/consumer implementations involving multiple threads.

Solution

Use the Queue interface or the BlockingQueue subinterface.

Discussion

As an example of the simplifications possible with the java.util.Concurrent package, consider the standard producer/consumer program. An implementation synchronized using traditional Thread code (wait() and notifyAll()) is in the

online source as ProdCons2. Example 16-11, *ProdCons15.java*, uses the java
.util.BlockingQueue (a subinterface of java.util.Queue) to reimplement Prod
Cons2 in about two-thirds the number of lines of code, and it's simpler. The application simply puts items into a queue and takes them from it. In the example, I have
four producers and only three consumers, so the producers eventually wait. Running
the application on one of my older notebooks, the producers' lead over the consumers increases to about 350 over the 10 seconds or so of running it.

Example 16-11. main/src/main/java/threads/ProdCons15.java

```java
public class ProdCons15 {

    protected volatile boolean done = false;

    /** Inner class representing the Producer side */
    class Producer implements Runnable {

        protected BlockingQueue<Object> queue;

        Producer(BlockingQueue<Object> theQueue) { this.queue = theQueue; }

        public void run() {
            try {
                while (!done) {
                    Object justProduced = getRequestFromNetwork();
                    queue.put(justProduced);
                    System.out.println(
                        "Produced 1 object; List size now " + queue.size());
                }
            } catch (InterruptedException ex) {
                System.out.println("Producer INTERRUPTED");
            }
        }

        Object getRequestFromNetwork() {    // Simulation of reading from client
            try {
                    Thread.sleep(10); // simulate time passing during read
            } catch (InterruptedException ex) {
                System.out.println("Producer Read INTERRUPTED");
            }
            return new Object();
        }
    }

    /** Inner class representing the Consumer side */
    class Consumer implements Runnable {
        protected BlockingQueue<Object> queue;

        Consumer(BlockingQueue<Object> theQueue) { this.queue = theQueue; }
```

```
        public void run() {
            try {
                while (true) {
                    Object obj = queue.take();
                    int len = queue.size();
                    System.out.println("List size now " + len);
                    process(obj);
                    if (done) {
                        return;
                    }
                }
            } catch (InterruptedException ex) {
                    System.out.println("CONSUMER INTERRUPTED");
            }
        }

        void process(Object obj) {
            // Thread.sleep(123) // Simulate time passing
            System.out.println("Consuming object " + obj);
        }
    }

    ProdCons15(int nP, int nC) {
        BlockingQueue<Object> myQueue = new LinkedBlockingQueue<>();
        for (int i=0; i<nP; i++)
            new Thread(new Producer(myQueue)).start();
        for (int i=0; i<nC; i++)
            new Thread(new Consumer(myQueue)).start();
    }

    public static void main(String[] args)
    throws IOException, InterruptedException {

        // Start producers and consumers
        int numProducers = 4;
        int numConsumers = 3;
        ProdCons15 pc = new ProdCons15(numProducers, numConsumers);

        // Let the simulation run for, say, 10 seconds
        Thread.sleep(10*1000);

        // End of simulation - shut down gracefully
        pc.done = true;
    }
}
```

ProdCons15 is superior to ProdCons2 in almost all aspects. However, the queue sizes
that are output no longer necessarily exactly reflect the size of the queue after the
object is inserted or removed. Because there's no longer any locking ensuring atomic-
ity here, any number of queue operations could occur on other threads between the
Producer thread's queue.put() and the Consumer thread's queue size query.

16.8 Optimizing Parallel Processing with Fork/Join

Problem

You want to optimize use of multiple processors and/or large problem spaces.

Solution

Use the Fork/Join framework.

Discussion

Fork/Join is an ExecutorService intended mainly for reasonably large tasks that can naturally be divided recursively, where you don't have to ensure equal timing for each division. It uses work-stealing to keep threads busy.

The basic means of using Fork/Join is to extend RecursiveTask or RecursiveAction and override its compute() method along these lines:

```
if (assigned portion of work is "small enough") {
        perform the work myself
} else {
        split my work into two pieces
        invoke the two pieces and await the results
}
```

There are two classes: RecursiveTask and RecursiveAction. The main difference is that RecursiveTask has each step of the work returning a value, whereas RecursiveAction does not. In other words, the RecursiveAction method compute() has a return type of void, whereas the RecursiveAction method of the same name has a return type of T, some type parameter. You might use RecursiveTask when each call returns a value that represents the computation for its subset of the overall task, in other words, to divide a problem like summarizing data—each task would summarize one part and return that. You might use RecursiveAction to operate over a large data structure performing some transform of the data in place.

There are two demos of the Fork/Join framework here, named after the ForkJoin Task that each subclasses:

- RecursiveTaskDemo uses fork() and join() directly.

- RecursiveActionDemo uses invokeAll() to invoke the two subtasks. invoke() is just a fork() and a join(); and invokeAll() just does this repeatedly until done. Compare the versions of compute() in Examples 16-12 and 16-13 and this will make sense.

Example 16-12. main/src/main/java/threads/RecursiveActionDemo.java

```java
/** A trivial demonstration of the "Fork-Join" framework:
 * square a bunch of numbers using RecursiveAction.
 * We use RecursiveAction here b/c we don't need each
 * compute() call to return its result; the work is
 * accumulated in the "dest" array.
 * @see RecursiveTaskDemo when each computation has to return a value.
 * @author Ian Darwin
 */
public class RecursiveActionDemo extends RecursiveAction {

    private static final long serialVersionUID = 3742774374013520116L;

    static int[] raw = {
        19, 3, 0, -1, 57, 24, 65, Integer.MAX_VALUE, 42, 0, 3, 5
    };
    static int[] sorted = null;

    int[] source;
    int[] dest;
    int length;
    int start;
    final static int THRESHOLD = 4;

    public static void main(String[] args) {
        sorted = new int[raw.length];
        RecursiveActionDemo fb =
            new RecursiveActionDemo(raw, 0, raw.length, sorted);
        ForkJoinPool pool = new ForkJoinPool();
        pool.invoke(fb);
        System.out.print('[');
        for (int i : sorted) {
            System.out.print(i + ",");
        }
        System.out.println(']');
    }

    public RecursiveActionDemo(int[] src, int start, int length, int[] dest) {
        this.source = src;
        this.start = start;
        this.length = length;
        this.dest = dest;
    }

    @Override
    protected void compute() {
        System.out.println("RecursiveActionDemo.compute()");
        if (length <= THRESHOLD) { // Compute Directly
            for (int i = start; i < start + length; i++) {
                dest[i] = source[i] * source[i];
            }
```

```
        } else {                          // Divide and Conquer
            int split = length / 2;
            invokeAll(
              new RecursiveActionDemo(source, start,         split,         dest),
              new RecursiveActionDemo(source, start + split, length - split, dest));
        }
    }
}
```

Example 16-13. main/src/main/java/threads/RecursiveTaskDemo.java

```
/**
 * Demonstrate the Fork-Join Framework to average a large array.
 * Running this on a multi-core machine as e.g.,
 * $ time java threads.RecursiveTaskDemo
 * shows that the CPU time is always greater than the elapsed time,
 * indicating that we are making use of multiple cores.
 * That said, it is a somewhat contrived demo.
 *
 * Use RecursiveTask<T> where, as in this example, each call returns
 * a value that represents the computation for its subset of the overall task.
 * @see RecursiveActionDemo when each computation does not return a value,
 * e.g., when each is just working on some section of a large array.
 * @author Ian Darwin
 */
public class RecursiveTaskDemo extends RecursiveTask<Long> {

    private static final long serialVersionUID = 3742774374013520116L;

    static final int N = 10000000;
    final static int THRESHOLD = 500;

    int[] data;
    int start, length;

    public static void main(String[] args) {
        int[] source = new int[N];
        loadData(source);
        RecursiveTaskDemo fb = new RecursiveTaskDemo(source, 0, source.length);
        ForkJoinPool pool = new ForkJoinPool();
        long before = System.currentTimeMillis();
        pool.invoke(fb);
        long after = System.currentTimeMillis();
        long total = fb.getRawResult();
        long avg = total / N;
        System.out.println("Average: " + avg);
        System.out.println("Time :" + (after - before) + " mSec");
    }

    static void loadData(int[] data) {
        Random r = new Random();
        for (int i = 0; i < data.length; i++) {
```

```
            data[i] = r.nextInt();
        }
    }

    public RecursiveTaskDemo(int[] data, int start, int length) {
        this.data = data;
        this.start = start;
        this.length = length;
    }

    @Override
    protected Long compute() {
        if (length <= THRESHOLD) { // Compute Directly
            long total = 0;
            for (int i = start; i < start + length; i++) {
                total += data[i];
            }
            return total;
        } else {                        // Divide and Conquer
            int split = length / 2;
            RecursiveTaskDemo t1 =
                new RecursiveTaskDemo(data, start,        split);
            t1.fork();
            RecursiveTaskDemo t2 =
                new RecursiveTaskDemo(data, start + split, length - split);
            return t2.compute() + t1.join();
        }
    }
}
```

The biggest undefined part there is "small enough"; you may have to do some experimentation to see what works well as a chunk size. Or, better yet, write more code using a feedback control system, measuring the system throughput as the parameter is dynamically tweaked up and down, and have the system automatically arrive at the optimal value for that particular computer system and runtime. This is left as an extended exercise for the reader.

16.9 Scheduling Tasks: Future Times, Background Saving in an Editor

Problem

You need to schedule something for a fixed time in the future. You need to save the user's work periodically in an interactive program.

Solution

For one-shot future tasks, use the Timer service with a TimerTask object. For recurring tasks, either use a background thread, or use the Timer service and recompute the next time. For more complex tasks, such as running something at high noon every second Thursday, consider using a third-party scheduling library such as Quartz (*http://www.quartz-scheduler.org*) or, in JavaEE/Jakarta, the EJB Timer Service (*https://eclipse-ee4j.github.io/jakartaee-tutorial/ejb-basicexamples005.html*).

Discussion

There are several ways of scheduling things in the future. For one-shot scheduling, you can use the Timer service from java.util. For recurring tasks, you can use a Runnable, which sleeps in a loop.

Here is an example of the Timer service in java.util. These are the basics of using this API:

1. Create a Timer service object.

2. Use it to schedule instances of TimerTask with a legacy Date object indicating the date and time.

The example code in Example 16-14 uses Item as a subclass of TimerTask to perform a simple notification action in the future, based on reading lines with year-month-day-hour-minute Task, such as the following:

```
2020 12 25 10 30 Get some sleep.
2020 12 26 01 27 Finish this program
2020 12 25 01 29 Document this program
```

Example 16-14. main/src/main/java/threads/ReminderService.java

```java
public class ReminderService {

    /** The Timer object */
    Timer timer = new Timer();

    class Item extends TimerTask {
        String message;
        Item(String m) {
            message = m;
        }
        public void run() {
            message(message);
        }
    }
}
```

```
    public static void main(String[] argv) throws Exception {
        new ReminderService().loadReminders();
    }

    private String dfPattern = "yyyy MM dd hh mm ss";
    private SimpleDateFormat formatter = new SimpleDateFormat(dfPattern);

    protected void loadReminders() throws Exception {

        Files.lines(Path.of("ReminderService.txt")).forEach(aLine -> {

            ParsePosition pp = new ParsePosition(0);
            Date date = formatter.parse(aLine, pp);
            String task = aLine.substring(pp.getIndex());
            if (date == null) {
                System.out.println("Invalid date in " + aLine);
                return;
            }
            System.out.println("Date = " + date + "; task = " + task);
            timer.schedule(new Item(task), date);
        });
    }
```

In real life the program would need to run for long periods of time and use some more sophisticated messaging pattern; here we only show the timing scheduling portion.

The code fragment in Example 16-15 creates a background thread to handle background saves, as in most word processors.

Example 16-15. main/src/main/java/threads/ReminderService.java

```
public class AutoSave extends Thread {
    /** The FileSave interface is implemented by the main class. */
    protected FileSaver model;
    /** How long to sleep between tries */
    public static final int MINUTES = 5;
    private static final int SECONDS = MINUTES * 60;

    public AutoSave(FileSaver m) {
        super("AutoSave Thread");
        setDaemon(true);        // so we don't keep the main app alive
        model = m;
    }

    public void run() {
        while (true) {          // entire run method runs forever.
            try {
                sleep(SECONDS*1000);
            } catch (InterruptedException e) {
                // do nothing with it
```

```
            }
            if (model.wantAutoSave() && model.hasUnsavedChanges())
                model.saveFile(null);
        }
    }

    // Not shown:
    // 1) saveFile() must now be synchronized.
    // 2) method that shuts down main program be synchronized on *SAME* object
}

/** Local copy of FileSaver interface, for compiling AutoSave demo. */
interface FileSaver {
    /** Load new model from fn; if null, prompt for new fname */
    public void loadFile(String fn);

    /** Ask the model if it wants AutoSave done for it */
    public boolean wantAutoSave();

    /** Ask the model if it has any unsaved changes, don't save otherwise */
    public boolean hasUnsavedChanges();

    /** Save the current model's data in fn.
     * If fn == null, use current fname or prompt for a filename if null.
     */
    public void saveFile(String fn);
}
```

As you can see in the run() method, this code sleeps for five minutes (300 seconds), then checks whether it should do anything. If the user has turned autosave off, or hasn't made any changes since the last save, nothing needs to be done. Otherwise, we call the saveFile() method in the main program, which saves the data to the current file. It would be smarter to save it to a recovery file of some name, as the better word processors do.

What's not shown is that now all the methods must be synchronized. It's easy to see why if you think about how the save method would work if the user clicked the Save button at the same time that the autosave method called it, or if the user clicked Exit while the file save method had just opened the file for writing. The strategy of saving to a recovery file gets around some of this, but it still needs a great deal of care.

See Also

For details on java.util.concurrent, see the documentation accompanying the JDK. For background on JSR 166, see Doug Lea's home page (*http://gee.cs.oswego.edu*) and his JSR 166 page (*http://gee.cs.oswego.edu/dl/concurrency-interest/index.html*).

A great reference on Java threading is *Java Concurrency in Practice* by Brian Goetz et al. (Addison-Wesley).

Project Loom: Fibers and Continuations (*https://wiki.openjdk.java.net/display/loom/Main*) aims to promote easier-to-use, lighter-weight concurrency mechanisms.

## CHAPTER 17

Reflection, or "A Class Named Class"

17.0 Introduction

The class `java.lang.Class` and the reflection package `java.lang.reflect` provide a number of mechanisms for gathering information from the Java Virtual Machine. Known collectively as *reflection*, these facilities allow you to load classes on the fly, to find methods and fields in classes, to generate listings of them, and to invoke methods on dynamically loaded classes. There is even a mechanism to let you construct a class from scratch (well, actually, from an array of bytes) while your program is running. This is about as close as Java lets you get to the magic, secret internals of the Java machine.

The JVM itself is a large program, normally written in C and/or C++, that implements the Java Virtual Machine abstraction. You can get the source for OpenJDK and other JVMs via the internet, which you could study for months. Here we concentrate on just a few aspects, and only from the point of view of a programmer using the JVM's facilities, not how it works internally; that is an implementation detail that could vary from one vendor's JVM to another.

I'll start with loading an existing class dynamically, move on to listing the fields and methods of a class and invoking methods, and end by creating a class on the fly using a `ClassLoader`. One of the more interesting aspects of Java, and one that accounts for its flexibility (applets in days of yore, servlets, web services, and other dynamic APIs) while also once being part of its perceived speed problem, is the notion of *dynamic loading*. For example, even the simplest "Hello, Java" program has to load the class file for your `HelloJava` class, the class file for its parent (usually `java.lang.Object`), the class for `PrintStream` (because you used `System.out`), the class for `PrintStream`'s parent, and `IOException`, and its parent, and so on. To see this in action, try something like this:

```
java -verbose HelloJava | more
```

To take another example, when applets were popular, a browser would download an applet's bytecode file over the internet and run it on your desktop. How does it load the class file into the running JVM? We discuss this little bit of Java magic in Recipe 17.4. The chapter ends with replacement versions of the JDK tools *javap* and a cross-reference tool that you can use to become a famous Java author by publishing your very own reference to the complete Java API.

17.1 Getting a Class Descriptor

Problem

You want to get a Class object from a class name or instance.

Solution

If the type name is known at compile time, you can get the class instance using the compiler keyword .class, which works on any type that is known at compile time, even the eight primitive types.

Otherwise, if you have an object (an instance of a class), you can call the java.lang.Object method getClass(), which returns the Class object for the object's class (now that was a mouthful!):

```
System.out.println("Trying the ClassName.class keyword:");
System.out.println("Object class: " + Object.class);
System.out.println("String class: " + String.class);
System.out.println("String[] class: " + String[].class);
System.out.println("Calendar class: " + Calendar.class);
System.out.println("Current class: " + ClassKeyword.class);
System.out.println("Class for int: " + int.class);
System.out.println();

System.out.println("Trying the instance.getClass() method:");
System.out.println("Sir Robin the Brave".getClass());
System.out.println(Calendar.getInstance().getClass());
```

When we run it, we see this:

```
C:\javasrc\reflect>java ClassKeyword
Trying the ClassName.class keyword:
Object class: class java.lang.Object
String class: class java.lang.String
String[] class: class [Ljava.lang.String;
Calendar class: class java.util.Calendar
Current class: class ClassKeyword
Class for int: int
```

```
Trying the instance.getClass( ) method:
class java.lang.String
class java.util.GregorianCalendar

C:\javasrc\reflect>
```

Nothing fancy, but as you can see, you can get the Class object for almost anything known at compile time, whether it's part of a package or not.

17.2 Finding and Using Methods and Fields

Problem

You need to find arbitrary method or field names in arbitrary classes.

Solution

Use the reflection package `java.lang.reflect`.

Discussion

If you just wanted to find fields and methods in one particular class, you wouldn't need this recipe; you could simply create an instance of the class using new and refer to its fields and methods directly. But this allows you to find methods and fields in any class, even classes that have not yet been written! Given a class object created as in Recipe 17.1, you can obtain a list of constructors, a list of methods, or a list of fields. The method `getMethods()` lists the methods available for a given class as an array of Method objects. Similarly, `getFields()` returns a list of Field objects. Because constructor methods are treated specially by Java, there is also a `getConstructors()` method, which returns an array of Constructor objects. Even though Class is in the package `java.lang`, the Constructor, Method, and Field objects it returns are in `java.lang.reflect`, so you need an import of this package. The ListMethods class (see Example 17-1) shows how get a list of methods in a class whose name is known at runtime.

Example 17-1. main/src/main/java/reflection/ListMethods.java

```java
public class ListMethods {
    public static void main(String[] argv) throws ClassNotFoundException {
        if (argv.length == 0) {
            System.err.println("Usage: ListMethods className");
            return;
        }
        Class<?> c = Class.forName(argv[0]);
        Constructor<?>[] cons = c.getConstructors();
        printList("Constructors", cons);
```

```
        Method[] meths = c.getMethods();
        printList("Methods", meths);
    }
    static void printList(String s, Object[] o) {
        System.out.println("*** " + s + " ***");
        for (int i=0; i<o.length; i++)
            System.out.println(o[i].toString());
    }
}
```

For example, you could run Example 17-1 on a class like java.lang.String and get a
fairly lengthy list of methods; I'll only show part of the output so you can see what it
looks like:

```
> java reflection.ListMethods java.lang.String
*** Constructors ***
public java.lang.String( )
public java.lang.String(java.lang.String)
public java.lang.String(java.lang.StringBuffer)
public java.lang.String(byte[])
// and many more...
*** Methods ***
public static java.lang.String java.lang.String.copyValueOf(char[])
public static java.lang.String java.lang.String.copyValueOf(char[],int,int)
public static java.lang.String java.lang.String.valueOf(char)
// and more valueOf( ) forms...
public boolean java.lang.String.equals(java.lang.Object)
public final native java.lang.Class java.lang.Object.getClass( )
// and more java.lang.Object methods...
public char java.lang.String.charAt(int)
public int java.lang.String.compareTo(java.lang.Object)
public int java.lang.String.compareTo(java.lang.String)
```

You can see that this could be extended (almost literally) to write a BeanMethods class
that would list only the set/get methods defined in a JavaBean (see Recipe 15.4).

Alternatively, you can find a particular method and invoke it, or find a particular field
and refer to its value. Let's start by finding a given field, because that's the easiest.
Example 17-2 is code that, given an Object and the name of a field, finds the field
(gets a Field object) and then retrieves and prints the value of that Field as an int.

Example 17-2. main/src/main/java/reflection/FindField.java

```
public class FindField {

    public static void main(String[] unused)
    throws NoSuchFieldException, IllegalAccessException {

        // Create instance of FindField
        FindField gf = new FindField();
```

```
        // Create instance of target class (YearHolder defined below).
        Object o = new YearHolder();

        // Use gf to extract a field from o.
        System.out.println("The value of 'currentYear' is: " +
            gf.intFieldValue(o, "currentYear"));
    }

    int intFieldValue(Object o, String name)
    throws NoSuchFieldException, IllegalAccessException {
        Class<?> c = o.getClass();
        Field fld = c.getField(name);
        int value = fld.getInt(o);
        return value;
    }
}

/** This is just a class that we want to get a field from */
class YearHolder {
    /** Just a field that is used to show getting a field's value. */
    public int currentYear = Calendar.getInstance().get(Calendar.YEAR);
}
```

What if we need to find a method? The simplest way is to use the methods
getMethod() and invoke(). But this is not altogether trivial. Suppose that somebody
gives us a reference to an object. We don't know its class but have been told that it
should have this method:

```
public void work(String s) { }
```

We wish to invoke work(). To find the method, we must make an array of Class
objects, one per item in the parameter list. So, in this case, we make an array containing only a reference to the class object for String. Because we know the name of the
class at compile time, we'll use the shorter invocation String.class instead of
Class.forName(). This, plus the name of the method as a string, gets us entry into
the getMethod() method of the Class object. If this succeeds, we have a Method
object. But guess what? In order to invoke the method, we have to construct yet
another array, this time an array of Object references actually containing the data to
be passed to the invocation. We also, of course, need an instance of the class in whose
context the method is to be run. For this demonstration class, we need to pass only a
single string, because our array consists only of the string. Example 17-3 is the code
that finds the method and invokes it.

Example 17-3. main/src/main/java/reflection/GetAndInvokeMethod.java

```
/**
 * Get a given method, and invoke it.
 * @author Ian F. Darwin, http://www.darwinsys.com/
```

```
*/
public class GetAndInvokeMethod {

    /** This class is just here to give us something to work on,
     * with a println() call that will prove we got into it.
     */
    static class X {
        public void work(int i, String s) {
            System.out.printf("Called: i=%d, s=%s%n", i, s);
        }
        // The main code does not use this overload.
        public void work(int i) {
            System.out.println("Unexpected call!");
        }
    }
    public static void main(String[] argv) {
        try {
            Class<?> clX = X.class; // or Class.forName("X");

            // To find a method we need the array of matching Class types.
            Class<?>[] argTypes = {
                int.class,
                String.class
            };

            // Now find a Method object for the given method.
            Method worker = clX.getMethod("work", argTypes);

            // To INVOKE the method, we need the invocation
            // arguments, as an Object array.
            Object[] theData = {
                42,
                "Chocolate Chips"
            };

            // The obvious last step: invoke the method.
            // First arg is an instance, null if static method
            worker.invoke(new X(), theData);

        } catch (Exception e) {
            System.err.println("Invoke() failed: " + e);
        }
    }
}
```

Not tiny, but it's still not bad. In most programming languages, you couldn't do that in the 40 lines it took us here.

A word of caution: when the arguments to a method are of a primitive type, such as int, you do not pass Integer.class into getMethod(). Instead, you must use the class object representing the primitive type int. The easiest way to find this class is in

---

the Integer class, as a public constant named TYPE, so you'd pass Integer.TYPE. The same is true for all the primitive types; for each, the corresponding wrapper class has the primitive class referred to as TYPE.

Java also includes a mechanism called a MethodHandle that was intended both to simplify and to generalize use of Reflection to invoke methods; we do not cover it here because in practice it has not shown to be a significant improvement over using the Reflection API.

17.3 Accessing Private Methods and Fields via Reflection

Problem

You want to access private fields and have heard you can do so using the Reflection API.

Solution

It's generally a bad idea to access private fields. But if you have to, and the Security Manager allows you to use Reflection, you can.

Discussion

There is occasionally a need to access private fields in other classes. For example, I did so recently in writing a JUnit test case that needed to see all the fields of a target class. The secret is to call the Field or Method descriptor's setAccessible() method passing the value true before trying to get the value or invoke the method. It really is that easy, as shown in Example 17-4.

Example 17-4. main/src/main/java/reflection/DefeatPrivacy.java

```
class X {
    @SuppressWarnings("unused") // Used surreptitiously below.
    private int p = 42;
    int q = 3;
}

/**
 * Demonstrate that it is, in fact, all too easy to access private members
 * of an object using Reflection, using the default SecurityManager
 */
public class DefeatPrivacy {

    public static void main(String[] args) throws Exception {
        new DefeatPrivacy().process();
    }
```

```
private void process() throws Exception {
    X x = new X();
    System.out.println(x);
    // System.out.println(x.p); // Won't compile
    System.out.println(x.q);
    Class<? extends X> class1 = x.getClass();
    Field[] flds = class1.getDeclaredFields();
    for (Field f : flds) {
        f.setAccessible(true);      // bye-bye "private"
        System.out.println(f + "==" + f.get(x));
        f.setAccessible(false);     // reset to "correct" state
    }
  }
}
```

 Use this with *extreme care*, because it can defeat some of the most cherished principles of Java programming.

17.4 Loading and Instantiating a Class Dynamically

Problem

You want to load classes dynamically, just like web servers load your servlets.

Solution

Use `class.forName("ClassName");` and the class's `newInstance( )` method.

Discussion

Suppose you are writing a Java application and want other developers to be able to extend your application by writing Java classes that run in the context of your application. In other words, these developers are, in essence, using Java as an extension language, in the same way that applets are an extension of a web browser. You would probably want to define a small set of methods that these extension programs would have and that you could call for such purposes as initialization, operation, and termination. The best way to do this is, of course, to publish a given, possibly abstract, class that provides those methods and get the developers to subclass from it. Sound familiar? It should. This is just how web browsers such as Netscape allow the deployment of applets.

We'll leave the thornier issues of security and of loading a class file over a network socket for now and assume that the user can install the classes into the application directory or into a directory that appears in the CLASSPATH at the time the program is run. First, let's define our class. We'll call it Cooklet (see Example 17-5) to avoid infringing on the overused word *applet*. Pretend each subclass will represent the code to drive some elaborate kind of food-preparing-and-cooking appliance through the steps of one traditional recipe. And we'll initially take the easiest path from ingredients to cookies before we complicate it.

Example 17-5. Cooklet.java

```java
/** A simple class, just to provide the list of methods that
 * users need to provide to be usable in our application.
 * Note that the class is abstract so you must subclass it,
 * but the methods are non-abstract so you don't have to provide
 * dummy versions if you don't need a particular functionality.
 */
public abstract class Cooklet {

    /** The initialization method. The Cookie application will
     * call you here (AFTER calling your no-argument constructor)
     * to allow you to initialize your code
     */
    public void initialize( ) {
    }

    /** The work method. The cookie application will call you
     * here when it is time for you to start cooking.
     */
    public void work( ) {
    }

    /** The termination method. The cookie application will call you
     * here when it is time for you to stop cooking and shut down
     * in an orderly fashion.
     */
    public void terminate( ) {
    }
}
```

Now, because we'll be baking, er, making this available to other people, we'll probably want to cook up a demonstration version too; see Example 17-6.

Example 17-6. main/src/main/java/reflection/DemoCooklet.java

```java
public class DemoCooklet extends Cooklet {
    public void work() {
        System.out.println("I am busy baking cookies.");
    }
    public void terminate() {
        System.out.println("I am shutting down my ovens now.");
```

```
        }
}
```

But how does our application use it? Once we have the name of the user's class, we need to create a Class object for that class. This can be done easily using the static method `Class.forName()`. Then we can create an instance of it using the Class object's `newInstance()` method; this calls the class's no-argument constructor. Then we simply cast the newly constructed object to our `Cooklet` class, and we can call its methods! It actually takes longer to describe this code than to look at the code, so let's do that now; see Example 17-7.

Example 17-7. main/src/main/java/reflection/Cookies.java

```
public class Cookies {
    public static void main(String[] argv) {
        System.out.println("Cookies Application Version 0.0");
        Cooklet cooklet = null;
        String cookletClassName = argv[0];
        try {
            Class<Cooklet> cookletClass =
                (Class<Cooklet>) Class.forName(cookletClassName);
            cooklet = cookletClass.newInstance();
        } catch (Exception e) {
            System.err.println("Error " + cookletClassName + e);
        }
        cooklet.initialize();
        cooklet.work();
        cooklet.terminate();
    }
}
```

And if we run it?

```
$ java Cookies DemoCooklet
Cookies Application Version 0.0
I am busy baking cookies.
I am shutting down my ovens now.
$
```

Of course, this version has rather limited error handling. But you already know how to fix that. Your ClassLoader can also place classes into a package by constructing a Package object; you should do this if loading any medium-sized set of application classes.

17.5 Constructing a Class from Scratch with a ClassLoader

Problem

You need to load a class from a nonstandard location and run its methods.

Solution

Examine the existing loaders such as `java.net.URLClassLoader`. If none is suitable, write and use your own `ClassLoader`.

Discussion

A `ClassLoader`, of course, is a program that loads classes. One `ClassLoader` is built into the Java Virtual Machine, but your application can create others as needed. Learning to write and run a working `ClassLoader` and using it to load a class and run its methods is a nontrivial exercise. In fact, you rarely need to write a `ClassLoader`, but knowing how is helpful in understanding how the JVM finds classes, creates objects, and calls methods.

`ClassLoader` itself is abstract; you must subclass it, presumably providing a `load Class()` method that loads classes as you wish. It can load the bytes from a network connection, a local disk, RAM, a serial port, or anywhere else. Or you can construct the class file in memory yourself, if you have access to a compiler.

There is a general-purpose loader called `java.net.URLClassLoader` that can be used if all you need is to load classes via the web protocol (or, more generally, from one or more URLs).

You must call the `ClassLoader loadClass()` method for any classes you wish to explicitly load from it. Note that this method is called to load all classes required for classes you load (superclasses that aren't already loaded, for example). However, the JVM still loads classes that you instantiate with the `new` operator normally via classpath.

When writing a `ClassLoader`, your `loadClass()` method needs to get the class file into a byte array (typically by reading it), convert the array into a `Class` object, and return the result.

What? That sounds a bit like "And Then a Miracle Occurs..." And it is. The miracle of class creation, however, happens down inside the JVM, where you don't have access to it. Instead, your `ClassLoader` has to call the `protected defineClass()` method in your superclass (which is `java.lang.ClassLoader`). This is illustrated in Figure 17-1, where a stream of bytes containing a hypothetical `Chicken` class is converted into a ready-to-run `Chicken` class in the JVM by calling the `defineClass()` method.

Figure 17-1. ClassLoader in action

What next?

To use your ClassLoader subclass, you need to instantiate it and call its loadClass() method with the name of the class you want to load. This gives you a Class object for the named class; the Class object in turn lets you construct instances, find and call methods, etc. Refer back to Recipe 17.2.

17.6 Constructing a Class from Scratch with JavaCompiler

Problem

You'd rather construct a class dynamically by generating source code and compiling it.

Solution

Use the JavaCompiler from javax.tools.

Discussion

There are many cases where you might need to generate code on the fly. If you're writing a framework, you might want to introspect on a model class to find its fields, and generate accessors for them on the fly. As we've seen in Recipe 17.2, you can do this with the Field class. However, for a high-volume operation it may well be more efficient to generate direct access code.

The Java Compiler API has been around since Java 1.6 and is fairly easy to use for simple cases. Here are the basic steps:

- Get the JavaCompiler object for your current Java Runtime. If it's not available, either give up altogether, or fall back to using reflection.

- Get a `CompilerTask` (which is also a `Callable`) to run the compilation, passing input and outputs.
- Invoke the `Callable`, either directly or by using an `ExecutorService`.
- Check the results. If true, invoke the class.

This is demonstrated in Example 17-8.

Example 17-8. main/src/main/java/reflection/JavaCompilerDemo.java

```
package reflection;

import java.lang.reflect.Method;
import java.net.URI;
import java.util.List;
import java.util.concurrent.Callable;

// tag::main[]
import javax.tools.JavaCompiler;
import javax.tools.SimpleJavaFileObject;
import javax.tools.ToolProvider;

/** Demo the Java Compiler API: Create a class, compile, load, and run it.
 * N.B. Will not run under Eclipse due to classpath settings;
 * best run it standalone using "java JavaCompiler.java"
 * @author Ian Darwin
 */
public class JavaCompilerDemo {
    private final static String PACKAGE = "reflection";
    private final static String CLASS = "AnotherDemo";
    private static boolean verbose;
    public static void main(String[] args) throws Exception {
        String source = "package " + PACKAGE + ";\n" +             ❶
            "public class " + CLASS + " {\n" +
            "\tpublic static void main(String[] args) {\n" +
            "\t\tString message = (args.length > 0 ? args[0] : \"Hi\")" + ";\n" +
            "\t\tSystem.out.println(message + \" from AnotherDemo\");\n" +
            "\t}\n}\n";
        if (verbose)
            System.out.print("Source to be compiled:\n" + source);

        JavaCompiler compiler = ToolProvider.getSystemJavaCompiler();  ❷
        if (compiler == null) {
            throw new IllegalStateException("No default compiler, giving up.");
        }
        Callable<Boolean> compilation =
            compiler.getTask(null, null, null, List.of("-d","."), null, ❸
            List.of(new MySource(CLASS, source)));
        boolean result = compilation.call();                           ❹
        if (result) {
            System.out.println("Compiled OK");
```

```
            Class<?> c = Class.forName(PACKAGE + "." + CLASS);        ❺
            System.out.println("Class = " + c);
            Method m = c.getMethod("main", args.getClass());          ❻
            System.out.println("Method descriptor = " + m);
            Object[] passedArgs = { args };
            m.invoke(null, passedArgs);                               ❼
        } else {
            System.out.println("Compilation failed");
        }
    }
}
// end::main[]

class MySource extends SimpleJavaFileObject {
    final String source;
    MySource(String fileName, String source) {
        super(URI.create("string:///" + fileName.replace('.', '/') +
                Kind.SOURCE.extension), Kind.SOURCE);
        this.source = source;
    }
    @Override
    public CharSequence getCharContent(boolean ignoreEncodingErrors) {
        return source;
    }
}
```

❶ The source code that we want to compile. In real life it would probably be dynamically generated, maybe using a `StringBuffer`.

❷ Get a reference to the default `JavaCompiler` object.

❸ Ask the compiler to create a `CompilerTask` to do the compilation. `CompilerTask` is also `Callable` and we save it under that type. The `-d` and `.` are standard *javac* arguments. `MySource` extends the compiler-provided API class `SimpleJavaFileObject` to give access to a file by creating a *file://* URL.

❹ A `Callable` can be put into a thread pool (`ExecutorService`) (see Recipe 16.1); we don't need this capability but the Compiler API returns it. We invoke the `Callable` directly.

❺ Assuming the `result` was `true` indicating success, we load the class with `Class.forName()`.

❻ We have to find the `main()` method in the generated class. We reuse the `String[].class` type from args, since all `main` methods have the same argument.

❼ Finally, we can invoke the main method, reusing the incoming args array to pass any *welcome* message along.

Running this program with and without an argument shows that the argument passed to the JavaCompilerDemo is being passed correctly to the generated Another Demo class:

```
$ java src/main/java/reflection/JavaCompilerDemo.java
Compiled OK
Class = class reflection.AnotherDemo
Method descriptor = public static void
  reflection.AnotherDemo.main(java.lang.String[])
Hi from AnotherDemo
$ java src/main/java/reflection/JavaCompilerDemo.java Welcome
Compiled OK
Class = class reflection.AnotherDemo
Method descriptor = public static void
  reflection.AnotherDemo.main(java.lang.String[])
Welcome from AnotherDemo
$
```

There is a lot to explore in the Compiler API, including the JavaFileManager that lets you control the placement of class files (other than by using -d as we did here), listeners to monitor compilation, and control of output and error streams. Consult the javax.tools.JavaCompiler documentation (*https://docs.oracle.com/javase/8/docs/api/javax/tools/JavaCompiler.html*) for details.

17.7 Performance Timing

Problem

Slow performance?

Solution

Use a *profiler*, or time individual methods using System.currentTimeMillis() before and after invoking the target method; the difference is the time that method took.

Discussion

Profilers

Profiling tools—profilers—have a long history as one of the important tools in a programmer's toolkit. A commercial profiling tool will help find bottlenecks in your program by showing both the number of times each method was called and the amount of time in each.

Quite a bit of useful information can be obtained from a Java application by use of the `VisualVM` tool, which was part of the Oracle JDK up until Java 8. With Java 9 this tool was open-sourced, and it's now available from the VisualVM project (*https://visu alvm.github.io/index.html*).

Another tool that is part of the JDK is Java Flight Recorder (*https://en.wikipedia.org/wiki/JDK_Flight_Recorder*), which is now open-sourced and built into the JDK. Its data is meant to be analyzed by Java Mission Control (*https://en.wikipedia.org/wiki/JDK_Mission_Control*). There are also third-party profilers that will give more detailed information; a web search will find current commercial offerings.

Measuring a single method

The simplest technique is to save the JVM's accumulated time before and after dynamically loading a main program and then calculate the difference between those times. Code to do just this is presented in Example 17-11; for now, just remember that we have a way of timing a given Java class.

One way of measuring the efficiency of a particular operation is to run it many times in isolation. The overall time the program takes to run thus approximates the total time of many invocations of the same operation. Gross numbers like this can be compared if you want to know which of two ways of doing something is more efficient. Consider the case of string concatenation versus `println()`. The code

```
println("Time is " + n.toString( ) + " seconds");
```

will probably work by creating a `StringBuilder`; appending the string `"Time is"`, the value of `n` as a string, and `"seconds"`; and finally converting the finished `StringBuilder` to a `String` and passing that to `println()`. Suppose you have a program that does a lot of this, such as a Java servlet that creates a lot of HTML this way, and you expect (or at least hope) your website to be sufficiently busy so that doing this efficiently will make a difference. There are two ways of thinking about this:

- Theory A: this string concatenation is inefficient.
- Theory B: string concatenation doesn't matter; `println()` is inefficient, too.

A proponent of Theory A might say that because `println()` just puts stuff into a buffer, it is very fast and that string concatenation is the expensive part.

How to decide between Theory A and Theory B? Assume you are willing to write a simple test program that tests both theories. Let's just write a simple program both ways and time it. Example 17-9 is the timing program for Theory A.

Example 17-9. main/src/main/java/performance/StringPrintA.java

```java
public class StringPrintA {
    public static void main(String[] argv) {
        Object o = "Hello World";
        for (int i=0; i<100000; i++) {
            System.out.println("<p><b>" + o.toString() + "</b></p>");
        }
    }
}
```

StringPrintAA (in the *javasrc* repo but not printed here) is the same but explicitly uses a StringBuilder for the string concatenation. Example 17-10 is the tester for Theory B.

Example 17-10. main/src/main/java/performance/StringPrintB.java

```java
public class StringPrintB {
    public static void main(String[] argv) {
        Object o = "Hello World";
        for (int i=0; i<100000; i++) {
            System.out.print("<p><b>");
            System.out.print(o.toString());
            System.out.print("</b></p>");
            System.out.println();
        }
    }
}
```

Timing results

I ran StringPrintA, StringPrintAA, and StringPrintB twice each on the same computer. To eliminate JVM startup times, I ran them from a program called TimeNoArgs, which takes a class name and invokes its main() method, using the Reflection API. TimeNoArgs and a shell script to run it, *stringprinttimer.sh*, are in the *performance* folder of the *javasrc* source repository. Here are the results:

2004 program	Seconds
StringPrintA	17.23, 17.20 seconds
StringPrintAA	17.23, 17.23 seconds
StringPrintB	27.59, 27.60 seconds

2014 program	Seconds
StringPrintA	0.714, 0.525 seconds
StringPrintAA	0.616, 0.561 seconds
StringPrintB	1.091, 1.039 seconds

Although the times went down by a factor of roughly 20 over a decade due to both JVM improvements and faster hardware, the ratios remain remarkably consistent: StringPrintB, which calls print() and println() multiple times, takes roughly twice as long.

Moral: don't guess. If it matters, time it.

Another moral: multiple calls to System.out.print() cost more than the same number of calls to a StringBuilder's append() method, by a factor of roughly 1.5 (or 150%). Theory B wins; the extra println calls appear to save a string concatenation but make the program take substantially longer.

Other aspects of performance: GC

There are many other aspects of software performance. One that is fundamental to Java is garbage collection behavior. Sun/Oracle usually discusses this at JavaOne. For example, see the 2003 JavaOne presentation "Garbage Collection in the Java Hot-Spot Virtual Machine" (*http://www.oracle.com/technetwork/java/javase/tech/ts-3153-coomes-19899-dsf-150093.pdf*). See also the 2007 JavaOne talk by the same GC development team, "Garbage Collection-Friendly Programming," TS-2906 (*https://docs.huihoo.com/javaone/2007/java-se/TS-2906.pdf*). JavaOne 2010 featured an updated presentation entitled "The Garbage Collection MythBusters" (*https://oreil.ly/java-world-the-garbage-collection-mythbusters*).

A timing program

It's pretty easy to build a simplified time command in Java, given that you have System.currentTimeMillis() to start with. Run my Time program, and, on the command line, specify the name of the class to be timed, followed by the arguments (if any) that class needs for running. The program is shown in Example 17-11. The time that the class took is displayed. But remember that System.currentTimeMillis() returns clock time, not necessarily CPU time. So you must run it on a machine that isn't running a lot of background processes. And note also that I use dynamic loading (see Recipe 17.4) to let you put the Java class name on the command line.

Example 17-11. main/src/main/java/performance/Time.java

```
public class Time {
    public static void main(String[] argv) throws Exception {
        // Instantiate target class, from argv[0]
        Class<?> c = Class.forName(argv[0]);

        // Find its static main method (use our own argv as the signature).
        Class<?>[] classes = { argv.getClass() };
        Method main = c.getMethod("main", classes);
```

```
// Make new argv array, dropping class name from front.
// Normally Java doesn't get the class name, but in
// this case the user puts the name of the class to time
// as well as all its arguments...
String nargv[] = new String[argv.length - 1];
System.arraycopy(argv, 1, nargv, 0, nargv.length);

Object[] nargs = { nargv };

System.err.println("Starting class " + c);

// About to start timing run. Important to not do anything
// (even a println) that would be attributed to the program
// being timed, from here until we've gotten ending time.

// Get current (i.e., starting) time
long t0 = System.currentTimeMillis();

// Run the main program
main.invoke(null, nargs);

// Get ending time, and compute usage
long t1 = System.currentTimeMillis();

long runTime = t1 - t0;

System.err.println(
        "runTime="  + Double.toString(runTime/1000D));
    }
}
```

Of course, you can't directly compare the results from the operating system time command with results from running this program. There is a rather large, but fairly constant, initialization overhead—the JVM startup and the initialization of Object and System.out, for example—that is included in the former and excluded from the latter. One could even argue that my Time program is more accurate because it excludes this constant overhead. But, as noted, it must be run on a single-user machine to yield repeatable results. And no fair running an editor in another window while waiting for your timed program to complete!

See Also

Java Performance by Scott Oaks (O'Reilly) provides information on tuning Java performance.

17.8 Printing Class Information

Problem

You want to print all the information about a class, similar to the way *javap* does.

Solution

Get a `Class` object, call its `getFields()` and `getMethods()`, and print the results.

Discussion

The JDK includes a program called *javap*, the Java Printer. Sun's JDK version normally prints the outline of a class file—a list of its methods and fields—but can also print out the Java bytecodes or machine instructions. The Kaffe package did not include a version of *javap*, so I wrote one and contributed it (see Example 17-12). The Kaffe folks have expanded it somewhat, but it still works basically the same. My version doesn't print the bytecodes; it behaves rather like Sun's behaves when you don't give its version any command-line options.

The `getFields()` and `getMethods()` methods return arrays of `Field` and `Method`, respectively; these are both in package `java.lang.reflect`. I use a `Modifiers` object to get details on the permissions and storage attributes of the fields and methods. In many Java implementations, you can bypass this and simply call `toString()` in each `Field` and `Method` object (as I do here for `Constructors`). Doing it this way gives me a bit more control over the formatting.

Example 17-12. main/src/main/java/reflection/MyJavaP.java

```
public class MyJavaP {

    /** Simple main program, construct self, process each class name
     * found in argv.
     */
    public static void main(String[] argv) {
        MyJavaP pp = new MyJavaP();

        if (argv.length == 0) {
            System.err.println("Usage: MyJavaP className [...]");
            System.exit(1);
        } else for (int i=0; i<argv.length; i++)
            pp.doClass(argv[i]);
    }

    /** Format the fields and methods of one class, given its name.
     */
    protected void doClass(String className) {
```

```
try {
    Class<? extends Object> c = Class.forName(className);

    final Annotation[] annotations = c.getAnnotations();
    for (Annotation a : annotations) {
        System.out.println(a);
    }

    System.out.println(c + " {");

    Field fields[] = c.getDeclaredFields();
    for (Field f : fields) {
        final Annotation[] fldAnnotations = f.getAnnotations();
        for (Annotation a : fldAnnotations) {
            System.out.println(a);
        }
        if (!Modifier.isPrivate(f.getModifiers()))
            System.out.println("\t" + f + ";");
    }

    Constructor<? extends Object>[] constructors = c.getConstructors();
    for (Constructor<? extends Object> con : constructors) {
        System.out.println("\t" + con + ";");
    }

    Method methods[] = c.getDeclaredMethods();
    for (Method m : methods) {
        final Annotation[] methodAnnotations = m.getAnnotations();
        for (Annotation a : methodAnnotations) {
            System.out.println(a);
        }
        if (!Modifier.isPrivate(m.getModifiers())) {
            System.out.println("\t" + m + ";");
        }
    }
    System.out.println("}");
} catch (ClassNotFoundException e) {
    System.err.println("Error: Class " +
        className + " not found!");
} catch (Exception e) {
    System.err.println("JavaP Error: " + e);
}
        }
    }
}
```

17.9 Listing Classes in a Package

Problem

You want to get a list of all the classes in a package.

Solution

You can't, in the general case. There are some limited approaches, most involving CLASSPATH scanning.

Discussion

There is no way to find out all the classes in a package, in part because, as we just saw in Recipe 17.5, you can add classes to a package at any time! And, for better or for worse, the JVM and standard classes such as java.lang.Package do not even allow you to enumerate the classes currently in a given package.

The nearest you can come is to look through the CLASSPATH. And this will surely work only for local directories and JAR files; if you have locally defined or network-loaded classes, this is not going to help. In other words, it will find compiled classes, but not dynamically loaded ones. There are several libraries that can automate this for you, and you're welcome to use them. The code to scan the CLASSPATH is fairly simple at heart, though, so classy developers with heart will want to examine it. Example 17-13 shows my ClassesInPackage class with its one static method. The code works but is rather short on error handling, and it will crash on nonexistent packages and other failures.

The code goes through a few gyrations to get the CLASSPATH as an enumeration of URLs, then looks at each element.

file

URLs will contain the pathname of the file containing the *.class* file, so we can just list it.

jar

URLs contain the filename as "file:/path_to_jar_file!package/name," so we have to pull this apart; the "package name" suffix is slightly redundant in this case because it's the package we asked the ClassLoader to give us.

Example 17-13. main/src/main/java/reflection/ClassesInPackage.java

```
public class ClassesInPackage {

    /** This approach began as a contribution by Paul Kuit at
     * http://stackoverflow.com/questions/1456930/, but his only
     * handled single files in a directory in classpath, not in Jar files.
     * N.B. Does NOT handle system classes!
     * @param packageName
     * @return
     * @throws IOException
     */
    public static String[] getPackageContent(String packageName)
```

```
        throws IOException {

    final String packageAsDirName = packageName.replace(".", "/");
    final List<String> list = new ArrayList<>();
    final Enumeration<URL> urls =
            Thread.currentThread().
            getContextClassLoader().
            getResources(packageAsDirName);
    while (urls.hasMoreElements()) {
        URL url = urls.nextElement();
        // System.out.println("URL = " + url);
        String file = url.getFile();
        switch (url.getProtocol()) {
        case "file":
            // This is the easy case: "file" is
            // the full path to the classpath directory
            File dir = new File(file);
            for (File f : dir.listFiles()) {
                list.add(packageAsDirName + "/" + f.getName());
            }
            break;
        case "jar":
            // This is the harder case; "file" is of the form
            // "jar:/home/ian/bleah/darwinsys.jar!com/darwinsys/io"
            // for some jar file that contains at least one class from
            // the given package.
            int colon = file.indexOf(':');
            int bang = file.indexOf('!');
            String jarFileName = file.substring(colon + 1, bang);
            JarFile jarFile = new JarFile(jarFileName);
            Enumeration<JarEntry> entries = jarFile.entries();
            while (entries.hasMoreElements()) {
                JarEntry e = entries.nextElement();
                String jarEntryName = e.getName();
                if (!jarEntryName.endsWith("/") &&
                    jarEntryName.startsWith(packageAsDirName)) {
                    list.add(jarEntryName);
                }
            }
            break;
        default:
            throw new IllegalStateException(
            "Dunno what to do with URL " + url);
        }
    }
    return list.toArray(new String[] {});
}

public static void main(String[] args) throws IOException {
    String[] names = getPackageContent("com.darwinsys.io");
    for (String name : names) {
        System.out.println(name);
```

```
        }
        System.out.println("Done");
    }
}
```

Note that if you run this application in the *javasrc* project, it will list the members of the demonstration package (`com.darwinsys.io`) twice, because it will find them both in the build directory and in the JAR file. If this is an issue, change the `List` to a `Set` (see Recipe 7.3).

17.10 Using and Defining Annotations

Problem

You need to know how to use annotations in code or to define your own annotations.

Solution

Apply annotations in your code using `@AnnotationName` before a class, method, field, etc. Define annotations with `@interface` at the same level as `class`, `interface`, etc.

Discussion

Annotations are a way of adding additional information beyond what the source code conveys. Annotations may be directed at the compiler or at runtime examination. Their syntax was somewhat patterned after javadoc annotations (such as `@author`, `@version` inside doc comments). Annotations are what I call *class-like things* (so they have initial-cap names) but are prefixed by `@` sign where used (e.g., `@Override`). You can place them on classes, methods, fields, and a few other places; they must appear immediately before what they annotate (ignoring space and comments). A given annotation may only appear once in a given position (this is relaxed in Java 8 or 9).

As an example of the benefits of a compile-time annotation, consider the common error made when overriding: as shown in Example 17-14, a small error in the method signature can result it an overload when an override was intended.

Example 17-14. MyClass.java (an example of why we need annotations)

```
public class MyClass {

    public boolean equals(MyClass object2) {
        // compare, return boolean
    }
}
```

The code will compile just fine on any release of Java, but it is incorrect. The standard contract of the equals() method (see Recipe 8.1) requires a method whose solitary argument is of type java.lang.Object. The preceding version creates an accidental overload. Because the main use of equals() (and its buddy method hashCode(); see Recipe 8.1) is in the Collections classes (see Chapter 7), this overloaded method will never get called, resulting both in dead code and in incorrect operation of your class within Sets and Maps.

The solution is very simple: using the annotation java.lang.Override, as in Example 17-15, informs the compiler that the annotated method is required to override a method inherited from a supertype (such as a superclass or an interface). If not, the code will not compile.

Example 17-15. MyClass.java with @Override annotation

```
public class MyClass {

    @Override
    public boolean equals(MyClass object2) {
        // compare, return boolean
    }
}
```

This version of equals(), while still incorrect, will be flagged as erroneous at compile time, potentially avoiding a lot of debugging time. This annotation, on your own classes, will help both at the time you write new code and as you maintain your codebase; if a method is removed from a superclass, all the subclasses that still attempt to override it *and* have the @Override annotation will cause an error message, allowing you to remove a bunch of dead code.

The second major use of annotations is to provide metadata at runtime. For example, the Java Persistence API (JPA, see *https://darwinsys.com/db_in_java*) uses its own set of annotations from the package javax.persistence to mark up entity classes to be loaded and/or persisted. A JPA entity class might look like Example 17-16.

Example 17-16. main/src/main/java/domain/Person.java (JPA annotations)

```
@Entity
public class Person {

    int id;
    protected String firstName;
    protected String lastName;

    public Person() {
        // required by JPA; must code it since we need 2-arg form.
    }
```

```java
    public Person(String firstName, String lastName) {
        this.firstName = firstName;
        this.lastName = lastName;
    }

    @Id @GeneratedValue(strategy=GenerationType.AUTO, generator="my_poid_gen")
    public int getId() {
        return id;
    }

    public void setId(int id) {
        this.id = id;
    }

    public String getFirstName() {
        return firstName;
    }

    public void setFirstName(String firstName) {
        this.firstName = firstName;
    }

    @Column(name="surname")
    public String getLastName() {
        return lastName;
    }

    public void setLastName(String lastName) {
        this.lastName = lastName;
    }

    @Override
    public String toString() {
        return getFullName();
    }

    @Transient /* synthetic: cannot be used in JPA queries. */
    public String getFullName() {
        StringBuilder sb = new StringBuilder();
        if (firstName != null)
            sb.append(firstName).append(' ');
        if (lastName != null)
            sb.append(lastName);
        if (sb.length() == 0)
            sb.append("NO NAME");
        return sb.toString();
    }
}
```

The @Entity annotation at class level directs JPA to treat this as a data object to be mapped into the database. The @Id informs JPA that this id is the primary key property, and the @GeneratedValue tells it how to assign the primary key values for newly created objects. The @Column annotation is only needed when the column name in the relational database differs from the expected name based on the property; in this case, the SQL database designer has used surname, whereas the Java developer wants to use lastName.

I said that annotations are class-like things, and therefore, you can define your own. The syntax here is a bit funky; you use @interface. It is rumored that the team developing this feature was either told not to, or was afraid to, introduce a new keyword into the language, due to the trouble that doing so had caused when the enum keyword was introduced in Java SE 1.4. Or, maybe they just wanted to use a syntax that was more reminiscent of the annotation's usage. At any rate, Example 17-17 is a trivial example of a custom annotation.

Example 17-17. Trivial annotation defined

```
package lang;

public @interface MyToyAnnotation {
}
```

Annotations are class-like things, so they should be named the same way—that is, names that begin with a capital letter and, if public, are stored in a source file of the same name (e.g, *MyToyAnnotation.java*).

Compile the Example 17-17 with *javac* and you'll see there's a new *MyToyAnnotation.class* file. In Example 17-18, we examine this with *javap*, the standard JDK class inspection tool.

Example 17-18. Running javap on trivial annotation

```
$ javap lang.MyToyAnnotation
Compiled from "MyToyAnnotation.java"
public interface lang.MyToyAnnotation extends java.lang.annotation.Annotation {
}
$
```

As it says, an Annotation is represented in the class file format as just an interface that extends Annotation (to answer the obvious question, you could write simple interfaces this way, but it would be a truly terrible idea). In Example 17-19, we take a quick look at Annotation itself.

Example 17-19. The Annotation Interface in Detail

```
$ javap java.lang.annotation.Annotation
Compiled from "Annotation.java"
```

```
public interface java.lang.annotation.Annotation {
  public abstract boolean equals(java.lang.Object);
  public abstract int hashCode();
  public abstract java.lang.String toString();
  public abstract java.lang.Class<? extends java.lang.annotation.Annotation>
    annotationType();
}
$
```

Annotations can be made such that the compiler will only allow them in certain points in your code. Example 17-20 is one that can only go on classes or interfaces.

Example 17-20. Sample Annotation for Classes, Interfaces, etc.

```
@Target(ElementType.TYPE)
@Retention(RetentionPolicy.RUNTIME)
public @interface MyAnnotation {
}
```

The `@Target` specifies where the annotation can be used: `ElementType.TYPE` makes it usable on classes, interfaces, class-like things such as enums, even annotations! To restrict it to use just on annotations, there is `ElementType.ANNOTATION_TYPE`. Other types include `METHOD`, `FIELD`, `CONSTRUCTOR`, `LOCAL_VARIABLE`, `PACKAGE`, and `PARAMETER`. So, this annotation is itself annotated with two `@ANNOTATION_TYPE`-targeted annotations.

Usage of annotations with an existing framework requires consulting their documentation. Using annotations for your own purpose at runtime requires use of the Reflection API, as shown in Example 17-21.

One more thing to note about annotations is that they may have attributes. These are defined as methods in the annotation source code but used as attributes where the annotation is used. Example 17-21 is an annotated annotation with one such attribute.

Example 17-21. main/src/main/java/lang/AnnotationDemo.java

```
/**
 * A sample annotation for types (classes, interfaces);
 * it will be available at run time.
 */
@Target(ElementType.TYPE)
@Retention(RetentionPolicy.RUNTIME)
public @interface AnnotationDemo {
    public boolean fancy() default false;
    public int order() default 42;
}
```

```
/** A simple example of using the annotation */
@AnnotationDemo(fancy=true)
@Resource(name="Dumbledore")
class FancyClassJustToShowAnnotation {

    /** Print out the annotations attached to this class */
    public static void main(String[] args) {
        Class<?> c = FancyClassJustToShowAnnotation.class;
        System.out.println("Class " + c.getName() + " has these annotations:");
        for (Annotation a : c.getAnnotations()) {
            if (a instanceof AnnotationDemo) {
                AnnotationDemo ad = (AnnotationDemo)a;
                System.out.println("\t" +a +
                    " with fancy=" + ad.fancy() +
                    " and order " + ad.order());
            } else {
                System.out.println("\tSomebody else's annotation: " + a);
            }
        }
    }
}
```

AnnotationDemo has the meta-annotation @Target(ElementType.TYPE) to indicate
that it can annotate user-defined types (such as classes). Other ElementType choices
include METHOD, FIELD, and PARAMETER. If more than one is needed, use array initializer syntax.

AnnotationDemo also has the @Retention(RetentionPolicy.RUNTIME) annotation to
request that it be preserved until runtime. This is obviously required for any annotation that will be examined by a framework at runtime.

These two meta-annotations are common on user-defined annotations that will be
examined at runtime.

The class FancyClassJustToShowAnnotation shows using the AnnotationDemo annotation, along with a standard Java one (the @Resource annotation).

Refer to Recipe 17.11 for a full example of using this mechanism.

17.11 Finding Plug-In-Like Classes via Annotations

Problem

You want to do plug-in-like things without using an explicit plug-in API.

Solution

Define an annotation for the purpose, and use it to mark the plug-in classes.

Discussion

Suppose we want to model how the Java EE standard `javax.annotations.Named` or `javax.faces.ManagedBean` annotations work; for each class that is so annotated, convert the class name to an instance-like name (e.g, lowercase the first letter), and do something special with it. You'd want to do something like the following:

1. Get the list of classes in the given package(s) (see Recipe 17.9).

2. Check if the class is annotated.

3. If so, save the name and `Class` descriptor for later use.

This is implemented in Example 17-22.

Example 17-22. main/src/main/java/reflection/PluginsViaAnnotations

```
/** Discover "plugins" or other add-in classes via Reflection using Annotations */
public class PluginsViaAnnotations {

    /**
     * Find all classes in the given package which have the given
     * class-level annotation class.
     */
    public static List<Class<?>> findAnnotatedClasses(String packageName,
        Class<? extends Annotation> annotationClass) throws Exception {

        List<Class<?>> ret = new ArrayList<>();
        String[] clazzNames = ClassesInPackage.getPackageContent(packageName);
        for (String clazzName : clazzNames) {
            if (!clazzName.endsWith(".class")) {
                continue;
            }
            clazzName = clazzName.replace('/', '.').replace(".class", "");
            Class<?> c = null;
            try {
                c = Class.forName(clazzName);
            } catch (ClassNotFoundException ex) {
                System.err.println("Weird: class " + clazzName +
                    " reported in package but gave CNFE: " + ex);
                continue;
            }
            if (c.isAnnotationPresent(annotationClass) &&
                    !ret.contains(c))
                    ret.add(c);

        }
        return ret;
    }
```

We can take this one step further and support particular method annotations, similar to javax.annotations.PostCreate, which is meant to decorate a method that is to be called after an instance of the bean has been instantiated by the framework. Our flow is now something like this, and the code is shown in Example 17-23:

1. Get the list of classes in the given package(s) (again, see Recipe 17.9).

2. If you are using a class-level annotation, check if the class is annotated.

3. If this class is still of interest, get a list of its methods.

4. For each method, see if it contains a given method-specific annotation.

5. If so, add the class and method to a list of invocable methods.

Example 17-23. main/src/main/java/reflection/PluginsViaAnnotations (find annotated methods)

```java
/**
 * Find all classes in the given package which have the given
 * method-level annotation class on at least one method.
 */
public static List<Class<?>> findClassesWithAnnotatedMethods(String packageName,
        Class<? extends Annotation> methodAnnotationClass) throws Exception {
    List<Class<?>> ret = new ArrayList<>();
    String[] clazzNames = ClassesInPackage.getPackageContent(packageName);
    for (String clazzName : clazzNames) {
        if (!clazzName.endsWith(".class")) {
            continue;
        }
        clazzName = clazzName.replace('/', '.').replace(".class", "");
        Class<?> c = null;
        try {
            c = Class.forName(clazzName);
            // System.out.println("Loaded " + c);
        } catch (ClassNotFoundException ex) {
            System.err.println("Weird: class " + clazzName +
                " reported in package but gave CNFE: " + ex);
            continue;
        }
        for (Method m : c.getDeclaredMethods()) {
            // System.out.printf("Class %s Method: %s\n",
            //     c.getSimpleName(), m.getName());
            if (m.isAnnotationPresent(methodAnnotationClass) &&
                    !ret.contains(c)) {
                ret.add(c);
            }
        }
    }
    return ret;
}
```

See Also

Recipe 17.10 and the rest of this chapter.

17.12 Program: CrossRef

You've probably seen those other Java books that consist entirely of listings of the Java API for version thus-and-such of the JDK. I don't suppose you thought the authors of these works sat down and typed the entire contents from scratch. As a programmer, you would have realized, I hope, that there must be a way to obtain that information from Java. But you might not have realized how easy it is! If you've read this chapter faithfully, you now know that there is one true way: make the computer do the walking. Example 17-24 is a program that puts most of the techniques together. This version generates a cross-reference listing, but by overriding the last few methods, you could easily convert it to print the information in any format you like, including an API reference book. You'd need to deal with the details of this or that publishing software—FrameMaker, troff, T$_E$X, or whatever—but that's the easy part.

This program makes fuller use of the Reflection API than did MyJavaP in Recipe 17.8. It also uses the java.util.zip classes (see Recipe 10.15) to crack the JAR archive containing the class files of the API. Each class file found in the archive is loaded and listed; the listing part is similar to MyJavaP.

Example 17-24. main/src/main/java/reflection/CrossRef.java

```java
public class CrossRef extends APIFormatter {

    /** Simple main program, construct self, process each .ZIP file
     * found in CLASSPATH or in argv.
     */
    public static void main(String[] argv) throws IOException {
        CrossRef xref = new CrossRef();
        xref.doArgs(argv);
    }

    /**
     * Print the fields and methods of one class.
     */
    protected void doClass(Class<?> c) {
        startClass(c);
        try {
            Field[] fields = c.getDeclaredFields();
            Arrays.sort(fields, new Comparator<Field>() {
                public int compare(Field o1, Field o2) {
                    return o1.getName().compareTo(o2.getName());
                }
            });
            for (int i = 0; i < fields.length; i++) {
```

```
                Field field = (Field)fields[i];
                if (!Modifier.isPrivate(field.getModifiers()))
                    putField(field, c);
                // else System.err.println("private field ignored: " + field);
            }

            Method methods[] = c.getDeclaredMethods();
            Arrays.sort(methods, new Comparator<Method>() {
                public int compare(Method o1, Method o2) {
                    return o1.getName().compareTo(o2.getName());
                }
            });
            for (int i = 0; i < methods.length; i++) {
                if (!Modifier.isPrivate(methods[i].getModifiers()))
                    putMethod(methods[i], c);
                // else System.err.println("pvt: " + methods[i]);
            }
        } catch (Exception e) {
            e.printStackTrace();
        }
        endClass();
    }

    /** put a Field's information to the standard output.  */
    protected void putField(Field fld, Class<?> c) {
        println(fld.getName() + " field " + c.getName() + " ");
    }

    /** put a Method's information to the standard output.  */
    protected void putMethod(Method method, Class<?> c) {
        String methName = method.getName();
        println(methName + " method " + c.getName() + " ");
    }

    /** Print the start of a class. Unused in this version,
     * designed to be overridden */
    protected void startClass(Class<?> c) {
    }

    /** Print the end of a class. Unused in this version,
     * designed to be overridden */
    protected void endClass() {
    }

    /** Convenience routine, short for System.out.println */
    protected final void println(String s) {
        System.out.println(s);
    }
}
```

You probably noticed the methods startClass() and endClass(), which are null.
These methods are placeholders designed to make subclassing easy for when you

need to write something at the start and end of each class. One example might be a fancy text formatting application in which you need to output a bold header at the beginning of each class. Another would be XML, where you'd want to write a tag like `<class>` at the front of each class and `</class>` at the end. Example 17-25 is an XML-specific subclass that generates (limited) XML for each field and method.

Example 17-25. main/src/main/java/reflection/CrossRefXML.java

```java
public class CrossRefXML extends CrossRef {

    public static void main(String[] argv) throws IOException {
        CrossRef xref = new CrossRefXML();
        xref.doArgs(argv);
    }

    /** Print the start of a class.
     */
    protected void startClass(Class<?> c) {
        println("<class><classname>" + c.getName() + "</classname>");
    }

    protected void putField(Field fld, Class<?> c) {
        println("<field>" + fld + "</field>");
    }

    /** put a Method's information to the standard output.
     * Marked protected so you can override it (hint, hint).
     */
    protected void putMethod(Method method, Class<?> c) {
        println("<method>" + method + "</method>");
    }

    /** Print the end of a class.
     */
    protected void endClass() {
        println("</class>");
    }
}
```

By the way, if you publish a book using either of these and get rich, "Remember, remember me!"

See Also

We have not investigated all the ins and outs of reflection or the ClassLoader mechanism, but by now you should have a basic idea of how it works.

Perhaps the most important omissions are SecurityManager and ProtectionDomain. Only one SecurityManager can be installed in a given instance of the JVM (e.g., to prevent malicious code from providing its own!). A browser running the old Java Applet API, for example, provides a `SecurityManager` that is far more restrictive than the standard one. Writing such a `SecurityManager` is left as an exercise for the reader —an important exercise for anyone planning to load classes over the internet! (For more information about security managers and the Java Security APIs, see *Java Security* by Scott Oaks (O'Reilly). A `ProtectionDomain` can be provided with a `Class Loader` to specify all the permissions needed for the class to run.

I've also left unexplored many topics in the JVM; see the (somewhat dated) O'Reilly books *Java Virtual Machine* by Troy Downing and Jon Meyer, and *Java Language Reference* by Mark Grand. You can also read the Sun/Oracle *Java Language Specification* and *JVM Specification* documents (both updated with new releases, available online (*https://docs.oracle.com/en/java/javase/13/docs*)), for a lifetime of reading enjoyment and edification!

The Apache Software Foundation maintains a vast array of useful software packages that are free to get and use. Source code is always available without charge from its website. Two packages you might want to investigate include the Commons BeanUtils and the Byte Code Engineering Library (BCEL). The Commons BeanUtils (*http://commons.apache.org/beanutils*) claims to provide easier-to-use wrappers around some of the Reflection API. BCEL is a third-party toolkit for building and manipulating bytecode class files. Written by Markus Dahm, BCEL has become part of the Apache Commons Project (*http://commons.apache.org/bcel*).

## CHAPTER 18

Using Java with Other Languages

18.0 Introduction

Java has several methods of running programs written in other languages. You can invoke a compiled program or executable script using `Runtime.exec()`, as I'll describe in Recipe 18.1. There is an element of system dependency here, because you can only run external applications under the operating system they are compiled for. Alternatively, you can invoke one of a number of scripting languages (or *dynamic languages*)—running the gamut: awk, bsh, Clojure, Ruby, Perl, Python, Scala—using `javax.script`, as illustrated in Recipe 18.3. Or you can drop down to C level with Java's *native code* mechanism and call compiled functions written in C/C++; see Recipe 18.6. From native code, you can call to functions written in just about any language. Not to mention that you can contact programs written in any language over a socket (see Chapter 13), with HTTP services (see Chapter 13), or with Java clients in RMI or CORBA clients in a variety of languages.

There is a wide range of other JVM languages, including these:

- BeanShell, a general scripting language for Java.

- Groovy (*https://groovy-lang.org*) is a Java-based scripting language that pioneered the use of closures in the Java language ecosystem. It also has a rapid-development web package called Grails (*http://grails.org*) and a build tool called Gradle (see Recipe 1.8). Gradle is also used as the build tool in modern Android development.

- Jython (*http://jython.org*), a full Java implementation of Python.

- JRuby (*http://jruby.org*), a full Java implementation of the Ruby language.

- Scala (*http://scala-lang.org*), a JVM language that claims to offer the "best of functional and OO" languages.

- Clojure (*http://clojure.org*), a predominantly functional Lisp-1 (*https://en.wikipe dia.org/wiki/Common_Lisp#The_function_namespace*) dialect for the JVM.
- Renjin (*http://renjin.org*) (pronounced "R engine"), a fairly complete open source clone of the R statistics package with the ability to scale to the cloud. See Recipe 11.5 for an example using Renjin.

These are JVM-centric, and some can be called directly from Java to script, or vice versa, without using `javax.script`. A list of these languages can be found on Wikipedia (*http://en.wikipedia.org/wiki/List_of_JVM_languages*).

18.1 Running an External Program from Java

Problem

You want to run an external program from within a Java program.

Solution

Use one of the `exec()` methods in the `java.lang.Runtime` class. Or set up a `Process Builder` and call its `start()` method.

Discussion

The `exec()` method in the `Runtime` class lets you run an external program. The command line you give is broken into strings by a simple `StringTokenizer` (see Recipe 3.1) and passed on to the operating system's "execute a program" system call. As an example, here is a simple program that uses `exec()` to run *kwrite*, a windowed text editor program.[6] On Windows, you'd have to change the name to `notepad` or `word pad`, possibly including the full pathname, for example, *c:/windows/notepad.exe* (you can also use backslashes, but be careful to double them because the backslash is special in Java strings):

```
public class ExecDemoSimple {
    public static void main(String av[]) throws Exception {

        // Run the "notepad" program or a similar editor
        Process p = Runtime.getRuntime().exec("kwrite");

        p.waitFor();
    }
}
```

---

6 *kwrite* is Unix-specific; it's a part of the K Desktop Environment (KDE) (*http://www.kde.org*).

When you compile and run it, the appropriate editor window appears:

```
$ javac -d . ExecDemoSimple.java
$ java otherlang.ExecDemoSimple # causes a KWrite window to appear.
$
```

This version of exec() assumes that the pathname contains no blanks because these break proper operation of the StringTokenizer. To overcome this potential problem, use an overloaded form of exec(), taking an array of strings as arguments. Example 18-1 runs the Windows or Unix version of the Firefox web browser, assuming that Firefox was installed in the default directory (or another directory that is on your PATH). It passes the name of a help file as an argument, offering a kind of primitive help mechanism, as displayed in Figure 18-1.

Example 18-1. main/src/main/java/otherlang/ExecDemoNS.java

```
public class ExecDemoNS extends JFrame {
    private static final String BROWSER = "firefox";

    Logger logger = Logger.getLogger(ExecDemoNS.class.getSimpleName());

    /** The name of the help file. */
    protected final static String HELPFILE = "./help/index.html";

    /** A stack of process objects; each entry tracks one running process */
    Stack<Process> pStack = new Stack<>();

    /** main - instantiate and run */
    public static void main(String av[]) throws Exception {
        String program = av.length == 0 ? BROWSER : av[0];
        new ExecDemoNS(program).setVisible(true);
    }

    /** The path to the binary executable that we will run */
    protected static String program;

    /** Constructor - set up strings and things. */
    public ExecDemoNS(String program) {
        super("ExecDemo: " + program);
        this.program = program;

        Container cp = getContentPane();
        cp.setLayout(new FlowLayout());
        JButton b;
        cp.add(b=new JButton("Exec"));
        b.addActionListener(e -> runProgram());
        cp.add(b=new JButton("Wait"));
        b.addActionListener(e -> doWait());
        cp.add(b=new JButton("Exit"));
        b.addActionListener(e -> System.exit(0));
        pack();
```

```
    }

    /** Start the help, in its own Thread. */
    public void runProgram() {

        new Thread() {
            public void run() {

                try {
                    // Get a "file:" URL for the Help File
                    URL helpURL = this.getClass().getClassLoader().
                        getResource(HELPFILE);

                    // Start the external browser from the Java Application.

                    String osname = System.getProperty("os.name");
                    String run;
                    if ("Mac OS X".equals(osname)) {
                        run = "open -a " + program;
                        // "if" allows for other OSes needing special handling
                    } else {
                        run = program;
                    }

                    pStack.push(Runtime.getRuntime().exec(run + " " + helpURL));

                    logger.info("In main after exec " + pStack.size());

                } catch (Exception ex) {
                    JOptionPane.showMessageDialog(ExecDemoNS.this,
                        "Error" + ex, "Error",
                        JOptionPane.ERROR_MESSAGE);
                }
            }
        }.start();

    }

    public void doWait() {
        if (pStack.size() == 0) {
            logger.info("Nothing to wait for.");
            return;
        }
        logger.info("Waiting for process " + pStack.size());
        try {
            Process p = pStack.pop();
            p.waitFor();
            // wait for process to complete
            // (may not work as expected for some old Windows programs)
            logger.info("Process " + p + " is done.");
        } catch (Exception ex) {
            JOptionPane.showMessageDialog(this,
```

```
                    "Error" + ex, "Error",
                    JOptionPane.ERROR_MESSAGE);
        }
    }

}
```

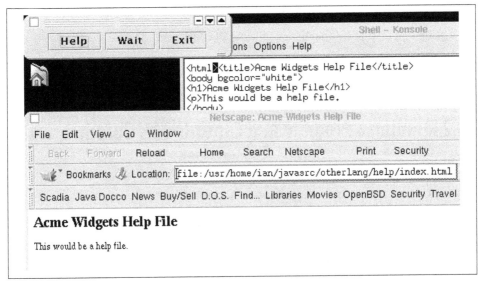

Figure 18-1. ExecDemoNS in action

A newer class, `ProcessBuilder`, replaces most nontrivial uses of `Runtime.exec()`. This `ProcessBuilder` uses generic collections to let you modify or replace the environment, as shown in Example 18-2.

Example 18-2. main/src/main/java/otherlang/ProcessBuilderDemo.java

```
    List<String> command = new ArrayList<>();            ❶
    command.add("notepad");
    command.add("foo.txt");
    ProcessBuilder builder = new ProcessBuilder(command);❷
    builder.environment().put("PATH",
            "/windows;/windows/system32;/winnt");        ❸
    final Process godot = builder.directory(
        new File(System.getProperty("user.home"))).      ❹
        start();
    System.err.println("Waiting for Godot");             ❺
    godot.waitFor();                                     ❻
```

❶   Set up the command-line argument list: editor program name and filename.

❷ Use that to start configuring the `ProcessBuilder`.

❸ Configure the builder's environment to a list of common MS Windows directories.

❹ Set the initial directory to the user's home, and start the process!

❺ I always wanted to be able to use this line in code.

❻ Wait for the end of our little play.

For more on `ProcessBuilder`, see the javadoc for `java.lang.ProcessBuilder`.

18.2 Running a Program and Capturing Its Output

Problem

You want to run a program but also capture its output.

Solution

Use the `Process` object's `getInputStream()`; read and copy the contents to `System.out` or wherever you want them.

Discussion

The original notion of standard output and standard error was that they would always be connected to the terminal; this notion dates from an earlier time when almost all computer users worked at the command line. Today, a program's standard output and error output do not always automatically appear anywhere. Arguably there should be an automatic way to make this happen. But for now, you need to add a few lines of code to grab the program's output and print it:

```
public class ExecDemoLs {

    private static Logger logger =
        Logger.getLogger(ExecDemoLs.class.getSimpleName());

    /** The program to run */
    public static final String PROGRAM = "ls"; // "dir" for Windows
    /** Set to true to end the loop */
    static volatile boolean done = false;

    public static void main(String argv[]) throws IOException {

        final Process p;          // Process tracks one external native process
        BufferedReader is;    // reader for output of process
```

```
    String line;

    p = Runtime.getRuntime().exec(PROGRAM);

    logger.info("In Main after exec");

    // Optional: start a thread to wait for the process to terminate.
    // Don't just wait in main line, but here set a "done" flag and
    // use that to control the main reading loop below.
    Thread waiter = new Thread() {
        public void run() {
            try {
                p.waitFor();
            } catch (InterruptedException ex) {
                // OK, just quit.
                return;
            }
            System.out.println("Program terminated!");
            done = true;
        }
    };
    waiter.start();

    // getInputStream gives an Input stream connected to
    // the process p's standard output (and vice versa). We use
    // that to construct a BufferedReader so we can readLine() it.
    is = new BufferedReader(new InputStreamReader(p.getInputStream()));

    while (!done && ((line = is.readLine()) != null))
        System.out.println(line);

    logger.info("In Main after EOF");

    return;
    }
}
```

This is such a common occurrence that I've packaged it up into a class called ExecAnd
Print, which is part of my com.darwinsys.lang package. ExecAndPrint has several
overloaded forms of its run() method (see the documentation for details), but they
all take at least a command and optionally an output file to which the command's
output is written. Example 18-3 shows the code for some of these methods.

Example 18-3. darwinsys-api/src/main/java/com/darwinsys/lang/ExecAndPrint.java

```
/** Need a Runtime object for any of these methods */
protected final static Runtime r = Runtime.getRuntime();

/** Run the command given as a String, output to System.out
 * @param cmd The command
 * @return The command's exit status
```

```
 * @throws IOException if the command isn't found
 */
public static int run(String cmd) throws IOException {
    return run(cmd, new OutputStreamWriter(System.out));
}

/** Run the command given as a String, output to "out"
 * @param cmd The command and list of arguments
 * @param out The output file
 * @return The command's exit status
 * @throws IOException if the command isn't found
 */
public static int run(String cmd, Writer out) throws IOException {

    Process p = r.exec(cmd);

    FileIO.copyFile(new InputStreamReader(p.getInputStream()), out, true);
    try {
        p.waitFor();    // wait for process to complete
    } catch (InterruptedException e) {
        return -1;
    }
    return p.exitValue();
}
```

As a simple example of using `exec()` directly along with `ExecAndPrint`, I'll create three temporary files, list them (directory listing), and then delete them. When I run the `ExecDemoFiles` program, it lists the three files it has created:

```
-rw-------  1 ian  wheel  0 Jan 29 14:29 file1
-rw-------  1 ian  wheel  0 Jan 29 14:29 file2
-rw-------  1 ian  wheel  0 Jan 29 14:29 file3
```

Its source code is in Example 18-4.

Example 18-4. main/src/main/java/otherlang/ExecDemoFiles.java

```
// Get and save the Runtime object.
Runtime rt = Runtime.getRuntime();

// Create three temporary files (the slow way!)
rt.exec("mktemp file1");
rt.exec("mktemp file2");
rt.exec("mktemp file3");

// Run the "ls" (directory lister) program
// with its output sent into a file
String[] args = { "ls", "-l", "file1", "file2", "file3" };
ExecAndPrint.run(args);

rt.exec("rm file1 file2 file3");
```

A process isn't necessarily destroyed when the Java program that created it exits or bombs out. Simple text-based programs will be, but window-based programs like *kwrite* Netscape, or even a Java-based JFrame application, will not. For example, our ExecDemoNS program started Netscape, and when ExecDemoNS's Exit button is clicked, ExecDemoNS exits but Netscape stays running. What if you want to be sure a process has completed? The Process object has a waitFor() method that lets you do so, and an exitValue() method that tells you the return code from the process. Finally, should you wish to forcibly terminate the other process, you can do so with the Process object's destroy() method, which takes no argument and returns no value. Example 18-5 is ExecDemoWait, a program that runs whatever program you name on the command line (along with arguments), captures the program's standard output, and waits for the program to terminate.

Example 18-5. main/src/main/java/otherlang/ExecDemoWait.java

```java
// A Runtime object has methods for dealing with the OS
Runtime r = Runtime.getRuntime();
Process p;          // Process tracks one external native process
BufferedReader is;  // reader for output of process
String line;

// Our argv[0] contains the program to run; remaining elements
// of argv contain args for the target program. This is just
// what is needed for the String[] form of exec.
p = r.exec(argv);

System.out.println("In Main after exec");

// getInputStream gives an Input stream connected to
// the process p's standard output. Just use it to make
// a BufferedReader to readLine() what the program writes out.
is = new BufferedReader(new InputStreamReader(p.getInputStream()));

while ((line = is.readLine()) != null)
    System.out.println(line);

System.out.println("In Main after EOF");
System.out.flush();
try {
    p.waitFor();     // wait for process to complete
} catch (InterruptedException e) {
    System.err.println(e);      // "Can't Happen"
    return;
}
System.err.println("Process done, exit status was " + p.exitValue());
```

See Also

You wouldn't normally use any form of `exec()` to run one Java program from another in this way; instead, you'd probably create it as a thread within the same process, because this is generally quite a bit faster (the Java interpreter is already up and running, so why wait for another copy of it to start up?). See Chapter 16.

When building industrial-strength applications, note the cautionary remarks in the Java API docs for the `Process` class concerning the danger of losing some of the I/O due to insufficient buffering by the operating system.

18.3 Calling Other Languages via javax.script

Problem

You want to invoke a script written in some other language from within your Java program, running in the JVM, with the ability to pass variables directly to/from the other language.

Solution

If the script you want is written in any of the two-dozen-plus supported languages, use `javax.script`. Those languages include awk, Perl, Python, Ruby, BeanShell, PNuts, Ksh/Bash, R (Renjin), and several implementations of JavaScript.

Discussion

One of the first tasks when using this API is to find out the installed scripting engines, and then pick one that is available. The `ScriptEnginesDemo` program in Example 18-6 lists the installed engines and runs a simple script in the default language, ECMAScript (aka JavaScript).

Example 18-6. main/src/main/java/otherlang/ScriptEnginesDemo.java

```
public class ScriptEnginesDemo {

    public static void main(String[] args) throws ScriptException {
        ScriptEngineManager scriptEngineManager = new ScriptEngineManager();

        // Print list of supported languages
        scriptEngineManager.getEngineFactories().forEach(factory ->
            System.out.println(factory.getLanguageName()));

        // Run a script in the JavaScript language
        String lang = "JavaScript";
        ScriptEngine engine =
```

```
            scriptEngineManager.getEngineByName(lang);
        if (engine == null) {
            System.err.println("Could not find engine");
            return;
        }
        engine.eval("print(\"Hello from " + lang + "\");");
    }
}
```

Example 18-7 is a very simple demo of calling Python from Java using `javax.script`
`ing`. We know the name of the scripting engine we want to use: Python. We'll use the
in-vm implementation known as `jython`, which was originally called JPython but was
changed due to a trademark issue. Once we put the *jython-standalone-2.nnn.jar* onto
our CLASSPATH, the script engine is automatically detected. Just in case it fails, we
print a verbose message including a list of the engines that are available.

Example 18-7. main/src/main/java/otherlang/PythonFromJava.java

```
/**
 * demo using Python (jython) to get a Java variable, print, and change it.
 * @author Ian Darwin
 */
public class PythonFromJava {
    private static final String PY_SCRIPTNAME = "pythonfromjava.py";

    public static void main(String[] args) throws Exception {
        ScriptEngineManager scriptEngineManager = new ScriptEngineManager();

        ScriptEngine engine = scriptEngineManager.getEngineByName("python");
        if (engine == null) {
            final String message =
                "Could not find 'python' engine; add its jar to CLASSPATH";
            System.out.println(message);
            System.out.println("Available script engines are: ");
            scriptEngineManager.getEngineFactories().forEach(factory ->
                System.out.println(factory.getLanguageName()));
            throw new IllegalStateException(message);
        }

        final Bindings bindings = engine.getBindings(ScriptContext.ENGINE_SCOPE);
        bindings.put("meaning", 42);

        // Let's run a python script stored on disk (well, on classpath):
        InputStream is =
            PythonFromJava.class.getResourceAsStream("/" + PY_SCRIPTNAME);
        if (is == null) {
            throw new IOException("Could not find file " + PY_SCRIPTNAME);
        }
        engine.eval(new InputStreamReader(is));
        System.out.println("Java: Meaning is now " + bindings.get("meaning"));
```

```
        }
}
```

See Also

Before Oracle dismantled java.net, there used to be a list of many languages (see this archived list (*https://web.archive.org/web/20140909141915/https://java.net/projects/scripting/sources/svn/show/trunk/engines*); the links don't work, but it shows the extent of the languages that were available). Back then, you could download the script engines from that site. I am not aware of a current official list of engines, unfortunately. However, the list maintained as part of the scripting project per se can be found in an unofficial source code repository, by viewing *https://github.com/scijava/javax-scripting*, from which it should in theory be possible to build the one you want. A dozen or so other engines are maintained by others outside this project; for example, there is a `Perl5` script engine from Google Code (*https://code.google.com/archive/p/javaperlscripting*).

There is a also a list of Java-compatible scripting languages (*http://java-source.net/open-source/scripting-languages*) (not necessarily all using `javax.script`).

It is possible to roll your own scripting engine; see my write-up at *https://darwinsys.com/java/scriptengines.html*.

18.4 Mixing Languages with GraalVM

Problem

GraalVM aims to be multilanguage, and you'd like to use different languages in the VM.

Solution

Use *gu* (graal utility) to install additional language packs and call other languages.

Discussion

While GraalVM positions itself as able to support a wide variety of programming languages, the number currently supported is small but growing. Let's try invoking Python code from within Java. Assuming you've installed Graal itself as per Recipe 1.2, you should have *gu* on your executable path, so try the following:

```
$ gu install python
Downloading: Component catalog from www.graalvm.org
Processing component archive: Graal.Python
Downloading: Component python: Graal.Python  from github.com
Installing new component: Graal.Python (org.graalvm.python, version 19.2.0.1)
```

```
IMPORTANT NOTE:
- - - - - - - - - - - - - - - -
Set of GraalVM components that provide language implementations have changed.
  The Polyglot native image and polyglot native C library may be out of sync:
- new languages may not be accessible
- removed languages may cause the native binary to fail on missing resources
  or libraries.
To rebuild and refresh the native binaries, use the following command:
        Library/Java/JavaVirtualMachines/graalvm-ce-19.2.0.1/Contents/Home/bin/gu
        rebuild-images

You may need to install "native-image" component which provide the rebuild
tools.
```

Then the code in Example 18-8 can be used.

Example 18-8. graal/src/JavaCallPython.java

```java
import java.io.*;
import java.util.stream.*;
import org.graalvm.polyglot.*;

/**
 * GraalVM polyglot: calling Python from Java/
 */
// tag::main[]
public class JavaCallPython {

    public static void main(String[] args) throws java.io.IOException {

        try (Context context = Context.create("jython")) {
            Value result = context.execute("2 + 2");
            System.out.println(result.asString());
        }
    }
}
// end::main[]
```

18.5 Marrying Java and Perl

Problem

You want to call Java from Perl, or vice versa.

Solution

To call Java from Perl, use the Perl Inline::Java module. To go the other way—calling Perl from Java—use javax.script, as in Recipe 18.3.

Discussion

Perl is often called a glue language that can be used to bring together diverse parts of the software world. But, in addition, it is a full-blown language for creating software. A wealth of extension modules provide ready-to-run solutions for quite diverse problems, and most of these modules are available free from CPAN, the Comprehensive Perl Archive Network (*http://www.cpan.org*). Also, as a scripting language, it is ideally suited for rapid prototyping. On the other hand, although building graphical user interfaces is definitely possible in Perl, it is not exactly one of the language's strengths. So you might want to construct your GUI using Java Swing, and, at the same time, reuse business logic implemented in Perl.

Fortunately, among the many CPAN modules, Inline::Java makes the integration of Perl and Java a breeze. Let's assume first that you want to call into Java from Perl. For business logic, I have picked a CPAN module that measures the similarity of two strings (the so-called *Levenshtein edit distance*). Example 18-9 shows the complete source. You need at least version 0.44 of the module Inline::Java; previous versions did not support threaded applications properly, so use of Swing wasn't possible.

Using the module this way requires that the Java source be included in the Perl script with special delimiters, as shown in Example 18-9.

Example 18-9. Swinging.pl

```
#! /usr/bin/perl
# Calling Java from Perl

use strict;
use warnings;

use Text::Levenshtein qw( );
  # Perl module from CPAN to measure string similarity

use Inline 0.44 "JAVA" =&gt; "DATA";  # pointer to the Inline java source
use Inline::Java qw(caught);   # helper function to determine exception type

my $show = new Showit;      # construct Java object using Perl syntax
$show-&gt;show("Just another Perl hacker");             # call method on that object

eval {
  # Call a method that will call back to Perl;
  # catch exceptions, if any.
  print "matcher: ", $show-&gt;match("Japh", shift||"Java"),
  " (displayed from Perl)\n";
};
if ($@) {
  print STDERR "Caught:", caught($@), "\n";
  die $@ unless caught("java.lang.Exception");
```

```
    print STDERR $@->getMessage( ), "\n";
}

__END__

__JAVA__
// Java starts here
import javax.swing.*;
import org.perl.inline.java.*;

class Showit extends InlineJavaPerlCaller {
  // extension only neeeded if calling back into Perl

  /** Simple Java class to be called from Perl, and to call back to Perl
   */
  public Showit( ) throws InlineJavaException { }

  /** Simple method */
  public void show(String str) {
    System.out.println(str + " inside Java");
  }

  /** Method calling back into Perl */
  public int match(String target, String pattern)
      throws InlineJavaException, InlineJavaPerlException {

    // Calling a function residing in a Perl Module
    String str = (String)CallPerl("Text::Levenshtein", "distance",
        new Object [] {target, pattern});

    // Show result
    JOptionPane.showMessageDialog(null, "Edit distance between '" + target +
        "' and '" + pattern + "' is " + str,
        "Swinging Perl", JOptionPane.INFORMATION_MESSAGE);
    return Integer.parseInt(str);
  }

}
```

Since this uses the Text::Levenshtein and the Inline::Java modules, you will have to install that. Here's the standard way:

```
$ perl -MCPAN -e shell
> install Text::Levenshtein
> install Inline::Java
> quit
```

On some systems there may be an OS-specific module; for example, on OpenBSD Unix, it's this:

```
$ doas pkg_add p5-Text-LevenshteinXS
```

In a simple Perl+Java program like this, you don't even need to write a separate Java source file: you combine all the code, Perl and Java alike, in one single file. You do not need to compile anything, either; just execute it by typing:

```
perl Swinging.pl
```

(You can also add a string argument.) After a little churning, a Java message box pops up, telling you that the distance between Japh and Java is 2. At the same time, your console shows the string "Just another Perl hacker inside Java." When you close the message box, you get the final result "matcher: 2 (displayed from Perl)."

In between, your Perl program has created an instance of the Java class Showit by calling its constructor. It then called that object's show() method to display a string from within Java. It then proceeded to call the match() method, but this time, something more complicated happens: the Java code calls back into Perl, accessing method distance of module Text::Levenshtein and passing it two strings as arguments. It receives the result, displays it in a message box, and finally, for good measure, returns it to the Perl main program that it had been called from.

Incidentally, the eval { } block around the method call is the Perlish way of catching exceptions. In this case, the exception is thrown from within Java.

If you restart the program, you will notice that startup time is much shorter, which is always good news. Why is that so? On the first call, Inline::Java took the input apart, precompiled the Java part, and saved it to disk (usually, in a subdirectory called _Inline_). On subsequent calls, it just makes sure that the Java source has not changed and then calls the class file that is already on disk. (Of course, if you surreptitiously changed the Java code, it is recompiled just as automagically.) Behind the scenes, even stranger things are going on, however. When the Perl script is executed, a Java server is constructed and started unbeknownst to the user, and the Perl part and the Java bits communicate through a TCP socket (see Chapter 13).

Marrying two platform-independent languages, like Perl and Java, in a portable way skirts many portability problems. When distributing inlined applications, be sure to supply not just the source files but also the contents of the _Inline_ directory. (It is advisable to purge that directory and to rebuild everything just before distribution time; otherwise, old compiled versions left lying around might make it into the distribution.) Each target machine needs to repeat the magic steps of Inline::Java, which requires a Java compiler. In any case, the Inline::Java module must be installed.

Because Perl has Inline modules for a number of other languages (ordinary languages like C, but others as exotic as Befunge), one might even consider using Perl as glue for interoperation between those other languages, jointly or separately, and Java. I am sure many happy hours can be spent working out the intricacies of such interactions.

See Also

You can find full information on `Inline::Java` on CPAN (*http://search.cpan.org*) or in the POD (Plain Old Documentation) that is installed along with the module itself.

18.6 Calling Other Languages via Native Code

Problem

You wish to call native C/C++ functions from Java, either for efficiency or to access hardware- or system-specific features.

Solution

Use JNI, the Java Native Interface. Or, use GraalVM.

Discussion

Java lets you load native or compiled code into your Java program. Why would you want to do such a thing? The best reason would probably be to access OS-dependent functionality, or existing code written in another language. A less good reason would be speed: native code can sometimes run faster than Java, though this is becoming less important as computers get faster and more multicore. Like everything else in Java, the native code mechanism is subject to security restrictions; for example, applets were not allowed to access native code.

The native code language bindings are defined for code written in C or C++. If you need to access a language other than C/C++, write a bit of C/C++ and have it pass control to other functions or applications, using any mechanism defined by your operating system.

Due to such system-dependent features as the interpretation of header files and the allocation of the processor's general-purpose registers, your native code may need to be compiled by the same C compiler used to compile the Java runtime for your platform. For example, on Solaris you can use SunPro C or maybe gcc. On Win32 platforms, use Microsoft visual C++ Version 4.x or higher (32 bit). For Linux and macOS, you should be able to use the provided gcc-based compiler. For other platforms, see your Java vendor's documentation.

Also note that the details in this section are for the Java Native Interface (JNI) of Java 1.1 and later, which differs in some details from 1.0 and from Microsoft's native interface.

Ian's Basic Steps: Java Calling Native Code

To call native code from Java, follow these steps:

1. Write Java code that calls a native method.
2. Compile this Java code.
3. Create an *.h* file using *javah*.
4. Write a C function that does the work.
5. Compile the C code into a loadable object.
6. Try it!

The first step is to write Java code that calls a native method. To do this, use the keyword `native` to indicate that the method is native, and provide a static code block that loads your native method using `System.loadLibrary()`. (The dynamically loadable module is created in step 5.) Static blocks are executed when the class containing them is loaded; loading the native code here ensures it is in memory when needed!

Object variables that your native code may modify should carry the `volatile` modifier. The file *HelloJni.java*, shown in Example 18-10, is a good starting point.

Example 18-10. main/src/main/java/jni/HelloJni.java

```
/**
 * A trivial class to show Java Native Interface 1.1 usage from Java.
 */
public class HelloJni {
  int myNumber = 42; // used to show argument passing

  // declare native class
  public native void displayHelloJni();

  // Application main, call its display method
  public static void main(String[] args) {
    System.out.println("HelloJni starting; args.length="+
                args.length+"...");
    for (int i=0; i<args.length; i++)
                System.out.println("args["+i+"]="+args[i]);
    HelloJni hw = new HelloJni();
    hw.displayHelloJni();// call the native function
    System.out.println("Back in Java, \"myNumber\" now " + hw.myNumber);
  }

  // Static code blocks are executed once, when class file is loaded
  static {
    System.loadLibrary("hello");
```

```
    }
}
```

The second step is simple; just use *javac HelloJni.java* as you normally would. You probably won't get any compilation errors on a simple program like this; if you do, correct them and try the compilation again.

Next, you need to create an *.h* file. Use *javah* to produce this file:

javah jni.HelloJni   // produces HelloJni.h

The *.h* file produced is a glue file, not really meant for human consumption and particularly not for editing. But by inspecting the resulting *.h* file, you'll see that the C method's name is composed of the name Java, the package name (if any), the class name, and the method name:

```
JNIEXPORT void JNICALL Java_HelloJni_displayHelloWorld(JNIEnv *env,
    jobject this);
```

Then create a C function that does the work. You must use the same function signature as is used in the *.h* file.

This function can do whatever it wants. Note that it is passed two arguments: a JVM environment variable and a handle for the this object. Table 18-1 shows the correspondence between Java types and the C types (JNI types) used in the C code.

Table 18-1. Java and JNI types

Java type	JNI	Java array type	JNI
byte	jbyte	byte[]	jbyteArray
short	jshort	short[]	jshortArray
int	jint	int[]	jintArray
long	jlong	long[]	jlongArray
float	jfloat	float[]	jfloatArray
double	jdouble	double[]	jdoubleArray
char	jchar	char[]	jcharArray
boolean	jboolean	boolean[]	jbooleanArray
void	jvoid		
Object	jobject	Object[]	jobjectArray
Class	jclass		
String	jstring		
array	jarray		
Throwable	jthrowable		

Example 18-11 is a complete C native implementation. Passed an object of type HelloJni.java, it increments the integer myNumber contained in the object.

Example 18-11. main/src/main/java/jni/HelloJni.c

```c
#include <jni.h>
#include "HelloJni.h"
#include <stdio.h>
/*
 * This is the Java Native implementation of displayHelloJni.
 */
JNIEXPORT void JNICALL Java_HelloJni_displayHelloJni(JNIEnv *env, jobject this) {
  jfieldID fldid;
  jint n, nn;

  (void)printf("Hello from a Native Method\n");

  if (this == NULL) {
    fprintf(stderr, "'this.' pointer is null!\n");
    return;
  }
  if ((fldid = (*env)->GetFieldID(env,
        (*env)->GetObjectClass(env, this), "myNumber", "I")) == NULL) {
    fprintf(stderr, "GetFieldID failed");
    return;
  }

  n = (*env)->GetIntField(env, this, fldid);/* retrieve myNumber */
  printf("\"myNumber\" value is %d\n", n);

  (*env)->SetIntField(env, this, fldid, ++n);/* increment it! */
  nn = (*env)->GetIntField(env, this, fldid);

  printf("\"myNumber\" value now %d\n", nn); /* make sure */
  return;
}
```

Finally, you compile the C code into a loadable object. Naturally, the details depend on platform, compiler, etc. For example, on Windows, you could use this:

```
> set JAVA_HOME=C:\java          # or wherever
> set INCLUDE=%JAVA_HOME%\include;%JAVA_HOME%\include\Win32;%INCLUDE%
> set LIB=%JAVA_HOME%\lib;%LIB%
> cl HelloJni.c -Fehello.dll -MD -LD
```

And on Unix, you could use this:

```
$ export JAVAHOME=/local/java    # or wherever
$ cc -I$JAVAHOME/include -I$JAVAHOME/include/solaris \
      -G HelloJni.c -o libhello.so
```

Example 18-12 is a makefile for Unix.

Example 18-12. main/src/main/java/jni/Makefile (Unix version)

```
# Configuration Section

CFLAGS_FOR_SO = -G # Solaris
CFLAGS_FOR_SO = -shared
CSRCS         = HelloJni.c
# JAVA_HOME should be been set in the environment
#INCLUDES     = -I$(JAVA_HOME)/include -I$(JAVAHOME)/include/solaris
#INCLUDES     = -I$(JAVA_HOME)/include -I$(JAVAHOME)/include/openbsd
INCLUDES      = -I$(JAVA_HOME)/include

all:       testhello testjavafromc

# This part of the Makefile is for C called from Java, in HelloJni
testhello:        hello.all
        @echo
        @echo "Here we test the Java code \"HelloJni\" that calls C code."
        @echo
        LD_LIBRARY_PATH=`pwd`:. java HelloJni

hello.all:        HelloJni.class libhello.so

HelloJni.class: HelloJni.java
        javac HelloJni.java

HelloJni.h:       HelloJni.class
        javah -jni HelloJni

HelloJni.o::      HelloJni.h

libhello.so:      $(CSRCS) HelloJni.h
    $(CC) $(INCLUDES) $(CFLAGS_FOR_SO) $(CSRCS) -o libhello.so

# This part of the Makefile is for Java called from C, in javafromc
testjavafromc:    javafromc.all hello.all
    @echo
    @echo "Now we test HelloJni using javafromc instead of java"
    @echo
    ./javafromc HelloJni
    @echo
    @echo "That was, in case you didn't notice, C->Java->C. And,"
    @echo "incidentally, a replacement for JDK program \"java\" itself!"
    @echo


javafromc.all:    javafromc

javafromc:    javafromc.o
    $(CC) -L$(LIBDIR) javafromc.o -ljava -o $@

javafromc.o:      javafromc.c
```

```
    $(CC) -c $(INCLUDES) javafromc.c

clean:
    rm -f core *.class *.o *.so HelloJni.h
clobber: clean
    rm -f javafromc
```

And you're done! Just run the Java interpreter on the class file containing the main program. Assuming that you've set whatever system-dependent settings are necessary (possibly including both CLASSPATH and LD_LIBRARY_PATH or its equivalent), the program should run as follows:

```
C> java jni.HelloJni
Hello from a Native Method    // from C
"myNumber" value is 42        // from C
"myNumber" value now 43       // from C
Value of myNumber now 43      // from Java
```

Congratulations! You've called a native method. However, you've given up portability; the Java class file now requires you to build a loadable object for each operating system and hardware platform. Multiply {Windows, Mac OS X, Sun Solaris, HP/UX, Linux, OpenBSD, NetBSD, FreeBSD} times {Intel-32, Intel-64/AMD64, Arm, Arm-64, and maybe SPARC64, PowerPC, and HP-PA}, and you begin to see the portability issues.

Beware that problems with your native code can and will crash the runtime process right out from underneath the Java Virtual Machine. The JVM can do nothing to protect itself from poorly written C/C++ code. Memory must be managed by the programmer; there is no automatic garbage collection of memory obtained by the system runtime allocator. You're dealing directly with the operating system and sometimes even the hardware, so, be careful. Be very careful.

See Also

If you need more information on Java native methods, you might be interested in the comprehensive treatment found in *Essential JNI: Java Native Interface* by Rob Gordon (Prentice Hall).

18.7 Calling Java from Native Code

Problem

You need to go the other way, calling Java from C/C++ code.

Solution

Use JNI again.

Discussion

JNI (Java Native Interface) provides an interface for calling Java from C, with calls to:

1. Create a JVM.
2. Load a class.
3. Find and call a method from that class (e.g., main).

JNI lets you add Java to legacy code. That can be useful for a variety of purposes and lets you treat Java code as an extension language.

The code in Example 18-13 takes a class name from the command line, starts up the JVM, and calls the main() method in the class.

Example 18-13. main/src/main/java/jni/javafromc.c (Calling Java from C)

```c
/*
 * This is a C program that calls Java code.
 * This could be used as a model for building Java into an
 * existing application as an extention language, for example.
 */

#include <stdio.h>
#include <jni.h>

int
main(int argc, char *argv[]) {
    int i;
    JavaVM *jvm;         /* The Java VM we will use */
    JNIEnv *myEnv;          /* pointer to native environment */
    JDK1_1InitArgs jvmArgs; /* JNI initialization arguments */
    jclass myClass, stringClass;    /* pointer to the class type */
    jmethodID myMethod;      /* pointer to the main() method */
    jarray args;         /* becomes an array of Strings */
    jthrowable tossed;     /* Exception object, if we get one. */

    JNI_GetDefaultJavaVMInitArgs(&jvmArgs);     /* set up the argument pointer */
    /* Could change values now, like: jvmArgs.classpath = ...; */

    /* initialize the JVM! */
    if (JNI_CreateJavaVM(&jvm, &myEnv, &jvmArgs) < 0) {
        fprintf(stderr, "CreateJVM failed\n");
        exit(1);
    }

    /* find the class named in argv[1] */
    if ((myClass = (*myEnv)->FindClass(myEnv, argv[1])) == NULL) {
        fprintf(stderr, "FindClass %s failed\n", argv[1]);
        exit(1);
```

```
    }

    /* find the static void main(String[]) method of that class */
    myMethod = (*myEnv)->GetStaticMethodID(
        myEnv, myClass, "main", "([Ljava/lang/String;)V");
    /* myMethod = (*myEnv)->GetMethodID(myEnv, myClass, "test", "(I)I"); */
    if (myMethod == NULL) {
        fprintf(stderr, "GetStaticMethodID failed\n");
        exit(1);
    }

    /* Since we're calling main, must pass along the command line arguments,
     * in the form of Java String array
     */
    if ((stringClass = (*myEnv)->FindClass(myEnv, "java/lang/String")) == NULL){
        fprintf(stderr, "get of String class failed!!\n");
        exit(1);
    }

    /* make an array of Strings, subtracting 1 for progname & 1 for the
     * java class name */
    if ((args = (*myEnv)->NewObjectArray(myEnv, argc-2, stringClass, NULL))==NULL) {
        fprintf(stderr, "Create array failed!\n");
        exit(1);
    }

    /* fill the array */
    for (i=2; i<argc; i++)
        (*myEnv)->SetObjectArrayElement(myEnv,
            args, i-2, (*myEnv)->NewStringUTF(myEnv, argv[i]));

    /* finally, call the method. */
    (*myEnv)->CallStaticVoidMethodA(myEnv, myClass, myMethod, &args);

    /* And check for exceptions */
    if ((tossed = (*myEnv)->ExceptionOccurred(myEnv)) != NULL) {
        fprintf(stderr, "%s: Exception detected:\n", argv[0]);
        (*myEnv)->ExceptionDescribe(myEnv);    /* writes on stderr */
        (*myEnv)->ExceptionClear(myEnv);       /* OK, we're done with it. */
    }

    (*jvm)->DestroyJavaVM(jvm);    /* no error checking as we're done anyhow */
    return 0;
}

====
```

Afterword

Writing this book—and keeping it up to date—has been a humbling experience. It has taken far longer than I had predicted or than I would like to admit. And, of course, it's not finished yet. Despite my best efforts and those of the technical reviewers, editors, and many other talented folks, a book this size is bound to contain errors, omissions, and passages that are less clear than they might be. Do let us know if you happen across any of these things; you can view and submit errata through them the book's catalog page (*https://shop.oreilly.com/product/0636920304371.do*). Subsequent editions will incorporate changes sent in by readers just like you!

It has been said that you don't really know something until you've taught it. I have found this true of lecturing, and I find it equally true of writing.

I tell my students that when Java was very young, it was possible for one person to study hard and know almost everything about it. After a release or two, this was no longer true. Today, nobody in his or her right mind would seriously claim to "know all about Java"—if they do, it should cause your bogosity detector to go off at full volume. And the amount you need to know keeps growing. How can you keep up? Java books? Java magazines? Java courses? Conferences? There is no single answer; all of these are useful to some people. Oracle and others have programs that you should be aware of:

- For many years, JavaOne was the dominant conference on Java, put on by Sun Microsystems and briefly by Oracle. Recently, Oracle has folded this into Code One (*https://oracle.com/code-one*), the annual Oracle conference.

- Marcus Biel has a pretty complete list of worldwide Java conferences (*https://marcus-biel.com/java-conferences-2019*).

- The Oracle Java Technology Network (*https://www.oracle.com/technetwork/java*), a free web-based service for getting the latest APIs, news, and views.

- Over Java's lifetime, the publishing industry has changed a lot. There used to be several Java-related magazines published in print, some of whose articles would appear on the web. Today there are, so far as I know, no print magazines dedicated to Java. Oracle currently (2020) publishes the online-only *Java Magazine* every month with technical articles on many aspects of Java (including some by yours truly); see the magazine's website (*https://blogs.oracle.com/javamagazine*) to view the latest issue and back issues.

- The Java Community Process (*https://jcp.org*), the home of Java standardization and enhancement.

- The OpenJDK community (*https://openjdk.java.net*) maintains and builds the open source version of the "official" JDK.

- O'Reilly books (*https://java.oreilly.com*) and conferences (*https://conferences.oreilly.com*) are among the very best available!

- I keep my own list of Java resources that I update sporadically, on my Java site (*https://darwinsys.com/java*); follow the link to Java Resources.

- The most interesting advanced topic discussions show up in Heinz Kabutz's Java Specialists Newsletter (*https://www.javaspecialists.eu*).

There is no end of Java APIs to learn about. And there are still more books to be written . . . and read.

Java Then and Now

Introduction: Always in Motion the Java Is

Java has always been a moving target for developers and writers. I meet developers in my commercial training programs who are still not aware of some of the features added to ancient Java releases, let alone current ones. This appendix looks at each of the major releases of Java. See Jon Byous's Sun Microsystems article "Java Technology: The Early Years" for a review of Java's early history. You can also find a copy at the Paderborn University website.[6]

Details on releases prior to Java 8 are considered ancient history and have been moved to my website, *https://darwinsys.com/java/ancientHistory.html*.

What Was New in Java 8

Java 8 Language Changes

The biggest new feature in the Java 8 language is lambda expressions. After a decade of debate on how to implement them, closures, or lambda expressions, finally arrived with Java 8. This is such a vast topic that it gets an entire chapter in this edition; see Chapter 9.

Annotations can now be placed on structured types.

---

6 Sun Microsystems, "Java Technology: The Early Years" article can be found at *https://web.archive.org/web/20090311011509/http://java.sun.com/features/1998/05/birthday.html* and on the Paderborn University website at *http://gcc.upb.de/www/WI/WI2/wi2_lit.nsf/7544f3043ee53927c12573e70058bbb6/abf8d70f07c12eb3c1256de900638899/$FILE/Java%20Technology%20-%20An%20early%20history.pdf*.

Java 8 API Changes

Java 8 brings in the new date/time API from JSR-310. This provides a more consistent and sensible set of classes and routines for dealing with time. Chapter 6 has been completely rewritten to use the new API, ending with a recipe showing various conversions between the old and new APIs.

Java 8 introduced functional programming techniques such as closures, Streams, and parallel collections, which we discuss in Chapter 9. In support of Streams, there are new methods in interfaces such as List, Map, and Set, which had until now been largely unchanged since the long-gone days of Java 1.1. Fortunately the Java 8 language support adds a default method type in interfaces, so your custom implementations of these interfaces are not required to change (as long as you make sure you change your IDE settings to an up-to-date compiler level).

As one example of default methods in action, Iterable gets a new default method called forEach(), which lets you write code like this:

```
myList.forEach(e -> /* do something with e here... */);
```

This is discussed further in "Iterable.forEach method (Java 8)" on page 198.

A new JavaScript implementation codenamed *Nashorn* is available via javax.script (see Recipe 18.3) and can also be run from the command line.

Javadoc (see Recipe 15.2) was extended to the javax.tools API.

Annotations can be repeated, obviating the need to manually code wrapper annotations, for example, javax.persistence.NamedQueries (plural), which is just a container for a list of javax.persistence.NamedQuery (singular) annotations.

Finally, Java provides support for Base 64 encoding/decoding in the form of java.util.Base64 with two nested classes for encoding and decoding.

There were also dozens of other small changes, such as those covered by OpenJDK (*http://openjdk.java.net/projects/jdk8/features*).

What Was New in Java 9

Java 9 is best known for introducing the Java Platform Module System, JPMS.

Since the JDK itself is modularized (the original intention of JPMS!), the new jlink tool lets you build a minimal JDK with only the parts needed for your modularized application.

Another new tool is JShell, a REPL (Read-Evaluate-Print-Loop) expression evaluator for Java. Also known as an interactive Java, JShell is useful for prototyping, trying out new ideas, and so on. JShell is covered in Recipe 1.4.

This release also marked the beginning of the six-month major release cadence, in which a new major release (Java 10, Java 11, etc) would be made available every six months. At the same time, Java 8 and Java 11 were declared to be LTS (Long-Term Support) releases.

Java 9 Language Changes

The new *module-info* file introduces several pseudokeywords, words which have reserved meaning only in a *module-info* file, but can still be used as user-defined names in Java classes. These include module, requires, exports, provides, with, and a few others. This also impacts the meaning of the visibility modifiers when used within a module.

Interfaces (which added default methods in Java 8) now allow private methods as well, for use by default methods.

Java 9 API Changes

Improvements to the Streams API, with several new methods in the Stream interface.

Improvements to the Collections API, including the of() factory method to quickly create a List or Set from several values.

What Was New in Java 10 (March 2018)

Java 10 is famous for the var keyword and the first actual release on the six-month cadence.

Java 10 introduces GraalVM, a just-in-time compiler (like HotSpot) but written in Java.

In Java 10, the OpenJDK version of the *cacerts* file is fully populated, making it far more likely that connecting via https will work out of the box.

The javah tool for native code headers is removed, replaced by equivalent-or-better functionality in javac itself.

Java 10 Language Changes

The var keyword, for local variables only, allows you to not fuss over the actual type of a variable. Of course the compiler must be able to infer the type of the variable. Let's explore some options in jshell:

```
jshell> var x = 10;
x ==> 10

jshell> var y = 123.4d;
```

```
y ==> 123.4

jshell> var z = java.time.LocalDateTime.now();
z ==> 2019-08-31T20:47:36.440491

jshell> var map = new HashMap<String,Integer>();
map ==> {}

jshell> map.put("Meh", 123);
$4 ==> null

jshell> var huh;
|  Error:
|  cannot infer type for local variable huh
|    (cannot use 'var' on variable without initializer)
|  var huh;
|  ^......^

jshell>
```

Somewhat surprisingly, var is not actually a language keyword, so this word can still be used as a user-defined name:

```
jshell> var var = 123;
var ==> 123

jshell> var
var ==> 123
```

See *https://developer.oracle.com/java/jdk-10-local-variable-type-inference.html* for explanation and more details on var.

Java 10 API Changes

List and Set add the new copyOf() method to make a truly unmodifiable copy; the previous List.unmodifiableList() made an *unmodifiable view*, which would appear to change if the underlying List were changed.

See Also

Quite a few old features were removed or deprecated; see this list on DZone (*https://dzone.com/articles/java-10-new-features-and-enhancements*).

Simon Ritter has an article titled "Java 10 Pitfalls for the Unwary" (*https://www.azul.com/jdk-10-pitfalls-for-the-unwary*).

What Was New in Java 11 (September 2018)

Java 11 introduced what I call "single-file run-from-source" (JEP 330); you can now type the following:

```
java HelloWorld.java
```

and the Java command will both compile and run the named program. This makes it *much* easier to work with single files, which is the primary thing it works with. If you have two or more files, the second through *n*th must be compiled and on your CLASS PATH; the source file you specify on the command line must be the one with main() and must not be compiled on your CLASSPATH. So it's good for simple things, but not for complex applications.

See also this list on DZone (*https://dzone.com/articles/90-new-features-and-apis-in-jdk-11*).

Java 11 API Changes

For a more complete list of Java 11 changes, see this DZone list (*https://dzone.com/articles/90-new-features-and-apis-in-jdk-11*).

What Was New in Java 12 (March 2019)

Java 12 introduced the notion of *Preview Changes*, features added to the JDK but not yet made part of the official specification. This is basically what others might have called beta mode; if enough users indicate that they have serious issues with a Preview Mode feature, the JDK team can fix it or even kill it off before declaring it part of the JDK specification (or declaring it dead).

Java 12 Language Changes

- switch statements that can yield a value (Preview)

Java 12 API Changes

Some of the more visible changes:

- A Tee Collector for Streams (copies input to multiple output Streams).
- A CompactNumberFormat, replacing my ScaledNumberFormat (prints the number 2,048 as 2K, for example).
- String.indent(n) returns a copy of the String with *n* spaces prepended.

- GC improvements (JEP 189: Shenandoah: Low-Pause-Time GC); pause-time improvements to G1 GC.

There are numerous other minor changes; see *https://www.azul.com/39-new-features-and-apis-in-jdk-12* and *https://openjdk.java.net/projects/jdk/12*.

What Is New in Java 13 (September 2019)

Java 13 was the latest official release as of this writing. It includes the following features:

- Improved garbage collection (again)
- Improved application class-data sharing (AppCDS) to allow writing an archive of all classes used in an app
- Text blocks (*http://cr.openjdk.java.net/~jlaskey/Strings/TextBlocksGuide_v9.html*) to replace and simplify multiline `String` literals (Preview)
- Improvements to `switch` statements that can yield a value
- Rewrite of the `Socket` and `ServerSocket` implementation (not changing the API)

See also this JavaWorld article (*https://www.javaworld.com/article/3341388/jdk-13-the-new-features-coming-to-java-13.html*).

Looking Ahead

There will be a Java 14 in 2020, around the time that this book goes to press.

These are some of the features that are in the works:

- Record types (in Preview; see Recipe 7.18).
- Sealed types, which permit a class designer to control subclassing by enumerating all the allowed subclasses. The syntax at present looks like this:
  ```
  public abstract sealed class Person permits Customer, SalesRep {
      ...
  }
  class Customer extends Person {
      ...
  }
  ```
- Text blocks, a.k.a. multiline text strings, delimited with a triplet of double quotes:
  ```
  String long = """
  This is a long
  text String."""
  ```

- A new packaging tool, `jpackage`, which will generate a complete self-installing application on the main supported operating systems.

There are several other interesting JEPs for Java 14. A complete list can be found at OpenJDK (*https://openjdk.java.net/projects/jdk/14*). The JEPs linked from that page are interesting reading for those interested in the rationale for (and the amount of work that goes into) each of these new features.

There will also be a Java 15 in 2020, but it entered Early Access just as this book was going to print, so we don't have coverage of it in this edition. "Always in motion Java's future is," Yoda says.

The Evolution of Client-Side Java: Applets, Browser Wars, Swing, JavaFX

While you can infer some of this from the per-JDK revision notes given in the rest of this appendix, it seems fitting to provide a unified narrative on the role of Java in the desktop.

Java began its public life as a vehicle for embedding flashy dynamic content in web pages via Java applets. Applets got off to a flying start with their incorporation in the Netscape line of browsers in 1995–96. Incidentally, part of the cross-licensing agreement between Sun and Netscape was that Netscape could use the term "JavaScript" for what was then its "LiveScript" web scripting language.

Applets never took over the world for a variety of reasons, including the fact that Microsoft never allowed Java applets to become a full player in Internet Explorer (at that time one of the most widely used browsers), users' fear of security issues (some of which surfaced from time to time), difficulties of installing and updating, and the increasing capabilities of CSS and JavaScript, and later HTML5.

There were some large users—for example, the Blackboard product (*http://black board.com*) used for student–instructor communication in hundreds of colleges and universities. However, even these have had issues of compatibility, sometimes requiring students to load a particular update like JDK 1.6 Update 42 in order to be supported on a given release of Blackboard.

Along the way, the original AWT GUI package was supplanted by Swing, a newer and better GUI package. Around this time, the `Applet` class was supplemented with the `JApplet` class to allow `Applet`s to be full users of Swing GUI classes.

Yet Java was never without competition on the desktop. Adobe Flash came along soon after Java. It was single-sourced and came from the home of Illustrator and Photoshop, which the web's graphic designers loved, and therefore Flash prospered.

More recently, the browsers themselves have become competitors to both Java and Flash. The HTML5 standard introduces a large number of technologies such as increased JavaScript, the `Canvas` object for graphics, and access to some local devices.

Many new projects today are starting with HTML5. Though JavaScript is not as nice a programming environment as Java, its familiarity to the large number of web developers in circulation has helped it dominate large areas of desktop development. So both Java applets and Adobe Flash are dead or dying, replaced by browser-native capabilities.

One of Sun's responses was to target a new technology that is now called JavaFX to the desktop. JavaFX can be used in browsers or in desktop applications. It does provide considerable benefits to GUI and graphics developers. There is information on JavaFX at *https://openjfx.io*.

Also in the area of client-side technologies, Sun insisted from the beginning that mobile phone developers use the Java Micro Edition (ME), based on a severely cutdown JVM and a totally different user interface package. Fortunately for Sun, BlackBerry (then called Research In Motion, or RIM), agreed to this. At the time, it made sense—when the early versions of BlackBerry OS came out, mobile CPUs were slow, and memory was limited, so a tiny LCDUI made sense.

When Google wanted to expand into the mobile space to expand the reach of its advertising business, it soon found—and bought—a company called Android that had a Linux-based OS with a rewritten Java implementation. Android's developers had tried to reason with Sun about using more complete Java on mobile, given how mobile device CPU and memory were growing, but the negotiations were not successful. So Android went off and built its own user interface, which has since become the most widely used Java platform. But during this time, Sun was acquired by Oracle.

Live on stage at the first JavaOne conference after the acquisition, Larry Ellison welcomed Android as part of the Java ecosystem. But when Android continued its meteoric rise, Oracle's lawyers thought they could muscle in on this, and Oracle sued Google for a billion dollars, alleging copyright, trademark, and trade secret violations. The suit was very complex, but one of the most important aspects was Oracle's claim that it could copyright the API separately from the code. Thus, anybody ever wanting to write a class called String with the methods described in the String class's javadoc page would—in Oracle's theory—have to apply for permission from Oracle. Needless to say, several old-line software companies like Microsoft lined up with Oracle, while the entire open source world lined up with Google, fearing the "chilling effects" this would have on the entire open source world. And, fortunately for Android and for the open source world, so did the judge. This suit was won by Google, but Oracle launched an appeal, which unfortunately for the open source world, was successful.

Oh, and back to BlackBerry. Unfortunately for BlackBerry, as time and Moore's law marched on in tandem, Java ME did not keep in step and was left behind. BlackBerry, obligated to stay on the ME platform, and unable to modify the Java ME classes, had to spend billions of dollars in R&D through the late 1990s and the 2000s building a parallel package structure to provide modern GUI and device capabilities, which it did all through OS versions 5, 6, and 7. When it finally dawned on RIM management that the JVM+OS combination itself was the bottleneck, they first tried to make their current JVM run on QNX, a Unix-based operating system from a company of the same name, which RIM acquired. This was doomed to failure, but a skunkworks project within the company took the open source Android and made that run in a matter of weeks. Management decided to abandon Java ME and Java as its main development language but allow Java-based Android apps to run as almost-first-class citizens in the BB10 environment. Alas, it took them a year and a half to get QNX working well enough on its new BlackBerry 10 devices that they could release it. During this time of uncertainty its sales tanked. BB10 was available for a while and worked well enough (and ran most Android apps). But unfortunately, the delay in getting to market was fatal, and BlackBerry devices now run Android. BlackBerry is repositioning QNX as an automotive platform and is selling security software. BlackBerry as a mobile platform is thus dead.

Java continues to be used on the desktop (although the market for desktop apps is steadily losing ground to mobile devices and increasingly capable native applications) and in mobile (particularly on Android devices). Java also continues to be heavily used in enterprise environments using packages like Java EE servers, JSP/JSF pages, Spring Framework, and Hibernate.

Index

for loop, 68, 198, 200, 208
Ford, Neal
    Functional Thinking, 276
forEach() method, 192, 199, 208, 249, 582
fork() method, 511
fork/join framework, 511-514
format() method, 70, 92, 308
formatting
    dates/times, 172-173
    numbers, 142-146
    with correct plurals, 149
Fowler, Martin
    on Continuous Integration (CI), 34
    Refactoring, xxi
    UML Distilled, xxi
Friedl, Jeffrey
    Mastering Regular Expressions, 99
functional interface, 198, 274, 276
functional programming, 273-295
    about, 273-276
    closures, 276-279
    custom interfaces, 281-283
    lambdas, 276-279
    method references, 289-293
    mixins, 293-295
    parallel streams, 288-289
    streams and, 283-287
Functional Thinking (Ford), 276
Future interface, 487

G

Gafter, Neal
    Java Puzzlers books, xiii
Gamma, Erich
    Design Patterns, xx, 31
Gang of Four (GoF), xx, 239
Garbage Collection in the Java HotSpot Virtual
    Machine paper, 536
The Garbage Collection MythBusters presenta-
    tion, 536
Garbage-Collection-Friendly Programming,
    TS-2906, 536
general programming books, xx
generic types, 191, 194-197
Gentleman, Robert, 375
get() method, 193, 194, 201, 487
getByName() method, 389
getCharAt() method, 59
getClass() method, 336, 520

getClassLoader() method, 336
getConstructors() method, 521
getenv() method, 44
getFields() method, 521, 538
getHostAddress() method, 389
getInetAddress() method, 390
getInputStream() method, 333, 392, 394, 397,
    418, 424, 560
getInstance() method, 262
getLastModified() method, 348
getLength() method, 398
getLocalHost() methd, 390
GetMark program, xiv
getMethod() method, 521, 523, 538
getName() method, 333
getNextMeeting() method, 180
getopt library, 126
getOutputStream() method, 359, 392, 394, 397,
    418, 424
getProp() method, 470
getResource() method, 336-338, 336
getResourceAsStream() method, 336-338, 336
getWriter() method, 359
getYear() method, 378
Git, 20
git clone command, 16, 19
git pull command, 16, 19
GitHub (website), 20, 41
GitLab, 41
GNU make, 21
GnuWin32, 98
Goetz, Brian
    Java Concurrency in Practice, 517
GoF (Gang of Four), xx, 239
Google Code, 566
Google Guice, 265
Gordon, Rob
    Essential JNI: Java Native Interface, 576
graal module (Maven), 16
GraalVM
    about, 3-5, 583
    FastR, 379-380
    mixing languages with, 566
    website, 4
Gradle
    about, 15, 21, 22, 555
    automating with, 27-29
    dependency management and, 22
    website, 22, 28

About the Author

Ian F. Darwin has worked in the computer industry for several decades. He wrote the freeware file(1) command used on Linux and BSD, and is the author of *Checking C Programs with Lint, Android Cookbook*, and more than a hundred articles and several courses on C, Unix, and Java. In addition to programming and consulting, Ian teaches Unix and Java courses for Learning Tree International, one of the world's largest technical training companies. He has a M.Sc. in Computing from Staffordshire University and several technical certifications. His eclectic website can be found at *https://darwinsys.com*. Along with his wife and children, Ian used to raise chickens on a rural property.

Colophon

The animal on the cover of *Java Cookbook*, Fourth Edition, is a domestic chicken (*Gallus domesticus*). Domestic chickens are descended from the wild red jungle fowl of India. Domesticated over 8,000 years ago in the area that is now Vietnam and Thailand, chickens are raised for meat and eggs, and the males for sport as well (although cockfighting is currently illegal in many places).

With their big, heavy bodies and small wings, these birds are well suited to living on the ground, and they can fly only short distances. Their four-toed feet are designed for scratching in the dirt, where they find the elements of their usual diet: worms, bugs, seeds, and various plant matter.

A male chicken is called a rooster and a female is known as a hen. The incubation period for a chicken egg is about three weeks; newly hatched chickens are precocial, meaning they have downy feathers and can walk around on their own right after emerging from the egg. They're also not dependent on their mothers for food; not only can they procure their own, but they also can live for up to a week after hatching on egg yolk that remains in their abdomen after birth.

The topic of chickens comes up frequently in ancient writings. Chinese documents date their introduction to China to 1400 BC, Babylonian carvings mention them in 600 BC, and Aristophanes wrote about them in 400 BC. The rooster has long symbolized courage: the Romans thought chickens were sacred to Mars, god of war, and the first French Republic chose the rooster as its emblem.

The cover illustration is by Karen Montgomery, based on a black and white engraving from Dover. The cover fonts are Gilroy Semibold and Guardian Sans. The text font is Adobe Minion Pro; the heading font is Adobe Myriad Condensed; and the code font is Dalton Maag's Ubuntu Mono.

O'REILLY®

There's much more where this came from.

Experience books, videos, live online training courses, and more from O'Reilly and our 200+ partners—all in one place.

Learn more at oreilly.com/online-learning

CPSIA information can be obtained
at www.ICGtesting.com
Printed in the USA
BVHW071414200320
575546BV00007B/103